LIFE AND LETTERS

OF

MANDELL CREIGHTON, D.D.

VOL. I.

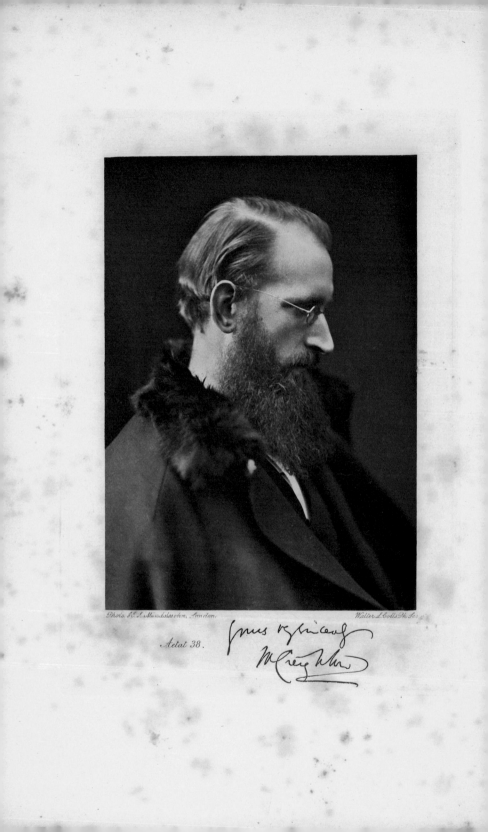

Photo G. J. Mendelssohn, London.   Walter L. Colls. Ph. Sc.

Aetat 38.

LIFE AND LETTERS

OF

MANDELL CREIGHTON

D.D. Oxon. AND Cam.

SOMETIME BISHOP OF LONDON

HON. FELLOW OF MERTON COLLEGE OXFORD AND EMMANUEL COLLEGE CAMBRIDGE :
D.C.L. OXFORD AND DURHAM : LL.D. GLASGOW AND HARVARD : LITT.D. OF DUBLIN :
FELLOW OF THE SOCIETÀ ROMANA DI STORIA PATRIA :
MEMBER OF THE MASSACHUSETTS HISTORICAL SOCIETY AND OF THE
AMERICAN CHURCH HISTORY SOCIETY :
PROFESSOR OF ANCIENT LITERATURE AT THE ROYAL ACADEMY :
MEMBER OF HER MAJESTY'S MOST HONOURABLE PRIVY COUNCIL

BY HIS WIFE

'I determined to know nothing among you save Jesus Christ '

IN TWO VOLUMES –VOL. I.

WITH PORTRAITS AND OTHER ILLUSTRATIONS

FOURTH IMPRESSION

LONGMANS, GREEN, AND CO.

39 PATERNOSTER ROW, LONDON
NEW YORK AND BOMBAY

1904

TO HIS CHILDREN

AND

TO ALL WHO LOVED HIM

I DEDICATE

THE STORY OF THE LIFE OF ONE

TO WHOM LOVE WAS THE SUPREME REVEALER

AND LIFE BUT AN OPPORTUNITY

FOR LOVING

———

'LOVE IS ALL AND DEATH IS NOUGHT'

PREFACE

IT was only the encouragement of those who loved him best that emboldened me to undertake the task of writing my husband's life. There are many who think that a man's life should never be written by one very near to him, and least of all by his wife; and I am fully conscious of the difficulties which have lain in my way. On the other hand, there were reasons which would have made it specially difficult to find anyone else fitted to do the work. My husband never kept a diary, he had no regular correspondents to whom he told his daily doings, so that there is little available material for drawing up a record of the more intimate side of his life. Moreover, the nature of his activities up to the time of his appointment as bishop, enabled me in an exceptional manner to share his interests and his occupations. We were almost constantly together; the longest separation of our married life was when he went for three weeks to Moscow for the coronation of the Emperor. I have, therefore, at any rate the requisite knowledge. One of the obvious dangers in my way I have consistently and steadily tried to avoid. I have wished always to tell the whole truth, to remember that I am the wife of one who said that he would like his epitaph to be 'He tried to write true history.' I have hidden nothing, my one desire has been to show him as he really was, to keep back nothing. To those who love a man everything about him is interesting, but I have tried to discriminate between what is merely of personal and what is of real interest as throwing light upon his character. In writing this book I have ever had before my mind the great company of those who loved him. Many of these knew but little of him, for many loved him who saw him very seldom. I have felt that they will be eager to know more about the man they loved. Many who knew him well in one sphere of his activities, in Oxford, in Embleton, in London, know little about the other portions of his life. It will interest them to see how he bore himself under very varying circumstances. Yet no doubt I shall be told that this, like all other biographies, is too long. It is an easy criticism. But will those of my critics who appreciated my husband for his literary gifts remember that there are others to whom he was primarily a shepherd of souls, and will those who are curious to discover his ecclesiastical policy remember that to others his activity as an historian seemed of even greater importance?

When our dear friend of many long years' standing, Dr. Copleston, now Bishop of Calcutta, heard that I had undertaken to write this book he wrote to me ' In this case the man is far more interesting than the movements and controversies in which he was engaged, and the portrait of the man will be of permanent value after the events are forgotten.' It is this portrait which I have tried to give. My object has been to tell what he did and was. I have not aimed at writing a history of the events in which he took part. The ritual difficulties which troubled his last years are not yet definitely settled, and it would have been undesirable to have tried to give a full account of them. For my purpose they have only been of importance in so far as they called out his opinions, and showed his ways of dealing with men.

I have wished that his own words should explain what manner of man he was, and tell of the interests which absorbed him ; but this has not always been possible. Every biographer knows what disappointing work collecting a man's letters is. Some have been destroyed. Others, though care-fully kept somewhere, cannot be found. The letters that have been kept can seldom give a just idea of the relative strength of a man's friendships, since their preservation de-pends more upon the habits of his correspondents than upon the nature of the tie which bound him to them. For many periods of my husband's life I have been left without much help from letters. None of those written to his family before our marriage have been preserved. Several of his closest early friends have kept none of theirs. But though I have many lost letters to regret, I have to thank very many for the kindness with which they have put all theirs at my dis-posal. Whenever possible I have allowed letters to tell the story of his life and thought.

I have designated some of his more intimate correspon-dents by initials, so that, when it has not been desirable to give names, it may still be possible to know which letters were addressed to the same persons. The portions omitted from the various letters are either repetitions or details of no gene-ral interest ; there were no sharp sayings or ill-natured criti-cisms to be left out.

In appreciating his qualities I have always tried to use the words of others rather than my own, and I have to thank many who gladly, for the love they bore him, have helped me by writing appreciations of his work and character.

Of himself, of the freshness and vigour of his personality, of his talk, brilliant, sympathetic, paradoxical, humorous in turn, no written word can give an adequate idea. I can only hope that through these pages there may breathe something of his spirit, and that the temper of his mind may reveal itself to the sympathetic reader.

In conclusion I would thank all those who have helped me. They are too numerous to name. But I should like to thank especially the Archbishop of Canterbury, the Bishop of Calcutta, the Bishop of Rochester, Mrs. Benson and

Dr. Prothero for their constant sympathy and readiness to advise me on difficult points, and my husband's old friend Mr. J. R. Thursfield for his kindness in looking through all the proofs. Perhaps I may be allowed to add a word of thanks to my publisher, Mr. C. J. Longman, my husband's friend as well as publisher ; his sympathetic co-operation has been a constant support and encouragement.

I feel convinced that no one with a difficult and yet precious task to perform could have been more generously helped than I have been by the encouragement, the constant interest, the tender sympathy of the many friends who gathered round my husband in every sphere of his varied life. I thank them all, and can but hope that the record of the life of the man they loved may bring him close to them as a constant source of joy and comfort.

LOUISE CREIGHTON.

HAMPTON COURT PALACE :
June 1, 1904.

CONTENTS

OF

THE FIRST VOLUME

CHRONOLOGICAL TABLE

Birth 1843

Goes to Durham School 1857

Goes to Oxford 1862

First Class Moderations 1864

First Class Litteræ Humaniores 1866

Second Class Law and Modern History 1866

Fellow and Tutor of Merton 1866

Marriage 1872

Vicar of Embleton 1875

Rural Dean of Alnwick 1880

Publication of first vols. of the ' History of the Papacy ' . . 1882

Elected Dixie Professor 1884

Appointed Canon of Worcester 1885

Editor of the ' English Historical Review ' 1885

Journey to America 1886

Publication of Vols. III. and IV. of the ' History of the Papacy . 1887

Appointed Canon of Windsor 1890

Consecrated Bishop of Peterborough 1890

Publication of Vol. V. of the ' History of the Papacy ' . . . 1894

Journey to Moscow 1896

Appointed Bishop of London 1897

Death 1901

LIST OF ILLUSTRATIONS

PHOTOGRAVURE PLATES

OTHER ILLUSTRATIONS

LIFE

OF

MANDELL CREIGHTON

CHAPTER I

EARLY DAYS

MANDELL CREIGHTON was born at Carlisle on July 5, 1843.
His grandfather, James Creighton, had come from the Scottish Lowlands to Carlisle as a young joiner. There he
became a partner in his employer's business, which he developed and ultimately made his own. He is described as a
silent man with a sound judgment, upright and honourable,
and much respected ; and it is recorded that his funeral was
more largely attended than any other before that time in
Carlisle.

His son Robert still further extended his father's business.
He moved to larger premises in Castle Street, opposite the
Cathedral, where he had a furnishing and decorating establishment, described as of high reputation throughout the
North of England. Robert Creighton was a man of much
natural shrewdness and business capacity, and of an active and
enterprising mind. He went largely into the timber trade,
and was also much occupied with municipal business, taking
a prominent part in the affairs of the city. He was long a
member of the Council of the Corporation, and held the office
of Mayor in 1866.

Robert Creighton married in 1842 Sarah Mandell, the
tenth child of Thomas Mandell, a yeoman farmer living on a

farm called Carlisle Gate near Bolton in Cumberland. Among the Mandells there were several, both of Sarah's generation and of her father's, who went to Cambridge, and distinguished themselves. An uncle of Sarah's was Fellow and Tutor of Queens' College, Cambridge, and a very able man. One of her brothers was ninth Wrangler and Fellow of St. John's. Sarah was living with one of her brothers at Wetheral, near Carlisle, when she came to know Robert Creighton. Brother and sister were devotedly attached, and he must have been a man of jealously strong affections, for it was assumed that he would never consent to his sister's marriage. The young couple accordingly took what was no uncommon step in those days, and eloped to Gretna Green. They were afterwards married by special licence at Carlisle in St. Mary's Church, then the nave of the Cathedral. Sarah was not forgiven by her brother, who never spoke to her again. She is described as a tall woman, with a fine figure, good-looking and kind-hearted, but very quick with her tongue. She seems to have been capable of inspiring great devotion. To her children she could be but the dimmest of memories, for she died in 1850, but she left her husband broken-hearted, and he never married again.

Four children, two sons and two daughters, of whom one died in infancy, were born to her. Mandell was the eldest, and seems to have been the most like his mother in appearance. No good portrait of her exists, but he was so unlike his father and brother and sister as not to seem to belong to the same family. He had little recollection of his mother. His father was very reserved, and never spoke of her to his children; his daughter can only remember his once mentioning her. A sister of Robert Creighton's came to take care of the desolate home. Her nephews and niece were much attached to her, and she was devoted to them; but Aunt Jane must have found her position one of anxious responsibility, for when I came to know her in later years, she was fond of saying that she could never recommend any one to undertake to bring up their brother's children.

It was over the shop in Castle Street that Mandell's childhood was passed. The windows of the living rooms looked on the Cathedral, and maimed fragment though it is, no doubt it exercised its influence on the boy's mind and laid the foundation for that strong love of architecture and antiquity which characterised him in after life. To live in the border city was an education in itself. There is a strong local feeling in Carlisle, and Cumbrians always stand closely by one another. Carlisle has been a city of steady rather than of rapid growth. Its citizens have not, as a rule, been men who made large fortunes, or indulged in luxurious ways of living. The city has a somewhat grim aspect, befitting a border town. The object of its inhabitants is clearly work not pleasure, and the pleasure most easily accessible to those who seek for change is escape to the purple hills whose outline can be seen on the horizon.

Mandell Creighton grew up in a simple hardworking atmosphere, where strong Liberal principles prevailed. The work that came to hand had to be done as a matter of course. There was not much outward show of affection in the home life. The father was very undemonstrative, and drew out no signs of affection from his children. He made them feel that he expected them to do their duty, and impressed them with the idea that he had a quiet ingrained contempt for those without force of character or capacity : those who, to use a favourite expression of his, had not 'their head screwed on the right way.' There is no record of his having had any special tastes or amusements of his own, except that he played whist and taught his children to play, treating their mistakes with remorseless severity. There were few books and pictures in the house, nothing to stimulate a love for literature or art. There was no spoiling or indulgence in the family. The younger son as a very small boy when overheard grumbling against one of his masters was at once silenced by his father's remark : ' If I hear any more such grumbling, I shall write a note for you to take to him to ask him to cane you.' But if his children were compelled to respect authority, there was no undue interference with their liberty, and provided they did what was demanded of them, they were allowed to follow their own tastes and inclinations. He believed that a boy must be allowed to follow his own bent, so long as he worked, and worked hard.

A nephew of Mrs. Creighton's, William Mandell Gunson,

was a frequent visitor at the house. He was a distinguished member of the University of Cambridge, who graduated with high honours in the Classical and Mathematical Triposes in 1847, and was shortly afterwards elected to a fellowship at Christ's College, where he served his University with unfailing devotion for thirty years. Mr. Gunson on the way to and from his mother's house, Baggrow, near Carlisle, used to stop at Castle Street. He was not much younger than his aunt, as his mother had been her eldest sister, and a strong friendship united the two families. There was an academic flavour about Mr. Gunson's visits, and they formed a link between the tradesman's family and the learned world outside. The shrewd capable man of business knew how to admire the scholarship of the University don, and to see in his success too the result of hard work. Mr. Gunson took much interest in his bright little cousin, and amused himself with teaching him his alphabet.

But few anecdotes of Mandell's childhood are preserved. From a baby he was a remarkably active, restless child, always apt to get into mischief, unless kept harmlessly employed. He was sent at an early age to a dame's school kept by a Miss Ford, who tied him to the leg of the table in order to keep him quiet. As soon as he learnt how to read, an unfailing occupation for his energies was found, and from that moment he was constantly absorbed in books. In 1852 he went on from the dame's school to the Cathedral School. A new scheme has turned the Cathedral School into a Grammar School with a fine building. In those days it consisted of two spacious rooms grafted on to some old ecclesiastical building, just within the Close and perched on the old city wall. When Creighton first went to it, the head master was the Rev. C. H. Lowry, a man whose fine looks must have impressed even the small boy, for in years long after he used to speak of him as one of the best-looking men he had ever known. Mr. Lowry went to a country living less than a year after Creighton joined the school but he remembers the high opinion held by Creighton's form master of his ability, industry, and good conduct.

The next head master was the Rev. William Bell, of Brasenose College, Oxford, of whom one of his former pupils writes : ' He was short, broad-shouldered, scholar, oar, boxer, and bubbling over with energy. It was his active eager vitality that stirred ambitious longings within us, and his unselfishness that encouraged us to go further afield.'

A party of six boys hung together in specially close companionship in work and play during the early Carlisle school days : T. W. Cartmell, now Tutor of Christ's College, Cambridge, and his brother, now a Carlisle solicitor ; the two Hetheringtons, one of whom was afterwards Fellow of Trinity College, Cambridge ; and the two Creighton brothers. It was then that Creighton received from his brother his first nickname, 'Homer,' which clung to him amongst old schoolfellows for many years. It was given because of the rapidity and ease with which he construed. One schoolfellow says that his most distinct recollection of Creighton was the way in which all the small boys went to ' Homer ' ' for help with their lessons.'

None of the six were great at athletics in the usual sense ; but even then Creighton's taste for walking and his love for the country had begun to show themselves. His mother had been a good rider and driver, and had been fond of taking her boys long drives, thus sowing the seed of that love for nature which only strengthened with every year of Creighton's life. After her death the boys had a pony, but they had so many accidents that at last the pony was sent away ; and though later on he made several trials, Creighton never cared for riding. Walking was the only exercise and amusement he desired. Even as a boy he led his companions for long rambles into the country, when tongues and legs vied with one another as to which could move faster. A younger companion who frequently accompanied him on these walks recalls ' the talk and chaff and jokes, which though sometimes above his head were delightful to listen to, and stimulating even to a little boy's intelligence.'

In November 1857 Creighton was sent to Durham to try for a King's Scholarship at the Grammar School. The examination was conducted by the Canons Residentiary of the Cathedral and the Head Master of the School. In that year for the first time Latin verse was required, a fact of which the Carlisle masters must have been ignorant, and Creighton, who as yet had done no Latin verse, was orced to leave the paper blank.　But when one examiner urged this against him, Archdeacon Thorp rejoined, ' Ah, but what good answers he gave to the questions ! '　He was elected in spite of his lack of Latin versification, a want which he soon supplied.　On going to Durham in the beginning of 1858, he was placed in the fourth form, and he went rapidly up the school.　In June 1859 he was in the head master's class, and in June 1861 he was head boy.　A frequent prize winner throughout his school career, in his last term he carried off, besides his form prize, prizes for Classics, Hellenistic Greek (the language of the New Testament), Greek Iambics, English verse, Greek prose, and English essay ; besides being honourably mentioned for French, and Latin hexameters.　In mathematics, he always did well, being second in his last term.　But in after years he used to say that though he could do them all right, he never understood what they were about.　His own later judgment on his school career was that he never worked steadily enough, but trusted too much to his natural cleverness, which always enabled him by putting on a spurt at the last to come out top.

He gained the school prize for English poetry, but his long poem on Sicily has nothing to distinguish it from other exercises of the kind.　He did not become a scribbler of verse, and only very few poems of his remain, written at long intervals through his life.

His head master, speaking of the general character of his work, says that ' the great distinction which marked his early days at school was his proficiency—I may say his superiority—in all kinds of composition, English, Latin, and Greek. . . . This is saying a great deal when I remember who were then his associates in the sixth form.'　A schoolfellow writes :

' IIis scholarship was strong rather than neat ; and he was never content until he had thoroughly mastered any difficulty in his work.　In getting up our classical work for our head master, it was our custom for four or five of us to take it in turns to construe, whilst the others listened and criticised ; Creighton's habit at such time was to lie flat on his back on the table and to translate any classic we had to get up for the next morning ; he always too made it a point of honour that the Livy lesson which we had every Monday morning should

Walter L. Colls. Ph.Sc.

Mandell Creighton,
Aetat 15.

not be looked at beforehand; we were to translate it as an
unseen, and I am not sure that this plan did not later stand
us in good stead.'

He is said to have already shown a liking for history, and
on one occasion he created some indignation by carefully
preparing the history paper for an examination when the
form generally had conspired to neglect it.

At school he made many friends. Some of their letters
to him which remain, testify to the most devoted and romantic
affection. He made no mark in games; already so short-
sighted as to be obliged to wear spectacles, he could not see
to play cricket, but his unbounded energy made him enjoy
football. He did not in any way separate himself from the
athletic interests of the school; he always scored at the
cricket matches, and accompanied the eleven when they went
to play elsewhere. Except for the ordinary childish ailments,
he did not know what illness was, and used in later life to
speak scornfully of these degenerate days, when schoolboys
are so often in the sanatorium.

Long walks remained his favourite recreation. He
explored every corner of the country round Durham, and
began to take an interest in botany, making a collection of
dried flowers which won the school prize. Though never in
any sense a scientific botanist, this taste remained with him
through life; he always noticed the flowers on his walks, and
could unfailingly be appealed to for their names. The Creighton family spent their holidays sometimes at Allonby or Silloth
by the sea, or at Moffat among the moors. Wherever they
were, Creighton would lead his brother and sister off to explore
the country. Sometimes the tramps were too long for the
others, and Creighton would go alone. He collected wild
flowers, moths, and ferns, and always knew how to find his
way across country.

As he grew older he would go for walking excursions of
several days together with his friends, and the lake country
was naturally their favourite resort. On one occasion four of
them started together from Penrith, each with five pounds in
his pocket, and in ten days saw all the lakes and climbed
many of the hills, walking often further than was good for them.
Shortly after he left school, Creighton with three com-

panions went for a walking tour in Scotland, of which one
of the party writes :

'One day we walked from Braemar over the top of Ben
Macdui, a walk of forty miles with no house of call. We got
entangled in the pine woods of Rothiemurchus, and blundered
along interlacing cart tracks till we finally reached Loch
Morlich dead beaten. There we were seized with the desperate
idea that a bathe would revive us, for our crusts of bread and
cheese had disappeared long before. This was the last straw,
and even dressing became a serious difficulty. However, we
fortunately stumbled across a lodge of the Duke of Richmond's, and the keeper gave us oatcake and milk. After this,
though some of us had dropt to sleep over the table, oatcake
in hand, we reached Aviemore.'

He describes the same tour to an old schoolfellow.

To W. A. Nixon   'Aug. 16.

'We had amazing fun certainly. Whenever Legard was
getting tired, I used to enter into an argument with him about
anything that came first, which he used to carry on so fiercely
that he quite forgot his fatigues. You should have seen the
way we bathed ! One day we bathed four times and walked
thirty-two miles, which was pretty well for a day's work. The
weather was dreadfully hot, and we could not possibly have
lived even, without bathing. Another day we were among
the mountains from 7.30 in the morning till 10.30 at night ;
and were pretty considerably hungry at the end of it. Besides
that, I have been loafing about Northumberland a good deal
and seeing all the old ruins with which it abounds.'

Among other incidents of Creighton's school days, it is
recorded that he accidentally discovered that he had considerable powers as a mesmerist. For a time he used to practise
these for the amusement of the boys ; but the authorities
naturally interfered, and he himself felt it to be a dangerous
gift and entirely discontinued its practice. In after life he
would refer to his schoolboy performances as a mesmerist,
but he never again tried to exert his powers. A schoolfellow
writes :

'In character he was a boy with a determined will of his
own, and moreover he had the courage of his opinions, never
flinching, after he became a school monitor, from doing his
duty however disagreeable it might be. Another side of his

character was shown in his unvaried kindness towards younger boys, ever ready to sympathise with them and help them in their work.'

Mrs. Holden, the wife of his head master, says that her clearest remembrance of him is seeing him in his latter years at school, morning after morning, pacing the yards of the school playground, each arm stretched out over the shoulders of as many boys as could get near him, all turning round together like a wheel at the end of the walk. The small boys used to watch for his appearance, and would rush to take up their positions under his outstretched arms, each eager to be nearest to him. In just such a way up to the last months of his life did he pace his garden with arms resting on the shoulders of his children and their friends.

His own judgment, when in after life he looked back on his years at school as monitor, was that he was a terrible prig. If so, he got through the period of priggishness once and for all, for it used to be said of him as a man that, if such a thing were possible, he was too little of a prig.

No specially strong religious influence seems to have been brought to bear upon him either at home or at school. It was the Cathedral at Durham, with its beautiful services under the direction of Dr. Dykes as precentor, which not only cultivated his musical and artistic tastes, but was the strongest religious influence of his boyhood. The best music of the English school, the music of Purcell and Gibbons and others, was frequently heard at Durham in those days. Creighton loved it, and never lost his preference for it. When in after life he was closely connected with other cathedrals, he used to deplore the way in which the modern sentimentalists had banished the school of music which seemed to him so typical of what was best in the English Church.

The deeper influence of the Durham Cathedral services was equally great. He said that to him it had been of permanent value that the school possessed no chapel, and that therefore on Sundays and Saints' days they attended service in the Cathedral, the King's Scholars in surplices as members of the foundation. This connexion with the Cathedral also led the Canons, who as professors at the University were men of intellectual distinction, to take a personal interest in the King's Scholars, which no doubt had a stimulating influence, and was the beginning of friendships which Creighton was glad to renew when circumstances brought him back to the North.

But though the Cathedral services undoubtedly nourished the religious life of the boy, there is no clue as to what led him first to decide to take Holy Orders. He told me that this had always been his intention from boyhood, and his schoolfellows record the fact that the resolution was already taken when he was at school. Home influence was not in its favour. His father, though himself a regular attendant at church, had a strong contempt for the clergy, founded partly on what he considered their unbusinesslike habits ; and it must be owned that strange tales are told of the lives and characters of some of the Cumbrian clergy before the days of Bishop Harvey Goodwin. Anyhow, Robert Creighton was disappointed at his son's decision to take Orders, though, true to his principles, he made no objection, and continued to give him every help and encouragement to make his life his own way. The decision appears to have been entirely the boy's own, uninfluenced by anyone from without. Mrs. Holden remembers prophesying his future, and assuring him that he would some day be a bishop.

Probably the best insight into Creighton's mind as a schoolboy is obtained from what he called his pastoral, a long letter written a year or more after he left school to a friend who had succeeded him as head of the school. Both from the light it throws on the mind of the writer, and on the character of the school of that day, it is sufficiently interesting to be given in full.

(1864)

' Carlisle : St. Bartholomew's Day.

' My dear Sherlock,—I am going to take the liberty of writing a few observations on the duties of the monitors, and the best way of fulfilling them. They are such as my own experience as monitor taught me, and such as I have found out by thought since then. It is a subject on which I thought a great deal while I was at school, and have also compared notes with others since then ; if, therefore, my experience can be of any use to you, here it is. I wish you would also give my letter to the other monitors, House and School, to read, and if any one of you finds an answer in it to any doubts he has had in his own mind, my purpose in writing it will have been fully answered. I know that I am laying myself open to the charge of presumption in thus volunteering my advice, but I am sure you will all of you forgive me, and take what I say in the spirit in which it is written. You will excuse me if I say that I think you need it : you are all of you still young to be monitors : you have all come to office rather suddenly : you have no monitor of long standing left among you whose advice you would all agree to take ; and, lastly, you have peculiar difficulties to contend with owing to the size of the school and the ill feeling which, more or less, I was very sorry to see, prevailed in the school against the monitors.

' I will, however, speak first about the duties of monitors in general ; and then will give you in particular a few hints.

' A monitor's duty, then, is, to try and benefit the school in every way he can, especially morally : a schoolboy can do nothing, of course, for the teaching of his fellows, but he *can* do everything for their moral good : you monitors have now before you a chance which you never can have again, of benefiting or injuring (for if you do not do one, you *must* do the other) very many of your fellows. Boys are very easily turned and guided : a kind look, a kind word, a piece of advice from one of you may, humanly speaking, be the means of determining for good the course of many a boy's life : a few words of advice may often be the turning point to a boy hard pressed by temptations. One never feels this enough at the time : one never knows, or, at any rate, never recognises enough, that every glance of our eye is either a blessing or a curse to everyone on whom it falls. It is a very serious responsibility which you have taken upon yourselves : if any of you has not as yet regarded it in any more serious light than a matter of course, which happens to any fellow who gets near the head of the school, let me beg of him to think some more this very night. You will see then, at once, that the *chief* influence of a monitor lies in *his example*; but this is a point on which I have seen many people deceive themselves—they trust to what they call "the force of *silent* example." That is most pernicious : if you content yourselves with merely keeping school rules and doing what is right yourselves and keeping out of the way of any fellows who you know are doing wrong, or if you stand by and listen to them saying what they ought not,

without reproof, *you are doing wrong* : fellows will only say,
" Oh ! he's a monitor, and has to look rather solemn, but he
doesn't mind." No, that won't do : it is part of the essence
of good to fight against evil. I need not remind you of how
little use Eli found " silent example," aye, and mild reproof
as well : you must set your faces strongly against all that
is bad, and must put down not only all that you find in the
course of your walk, but also you must go out of it to find
it. Never let a single thing go unreproved that your conscience disagrees with. Never be led away by pity of the
offender, but regard rather the immense amount of harm
he may do to others if you let him go on as he is.

'This that I have said applies to everything you do. To
be more particular : you will find it necessary to be very
consistent : fellows won't stand being pulled up for breaking
one school rule, when they know you break another. If
you go out smoking, you cannot, without causing great ill
feeling, pull a fellow up for going to publics, though the one
thing is infinitely more important than the other. Again,
you must not be led away from your duty by seeing that the
under-masters do not act nearly so strictly as you : you
stand or fall by yourselves, and have nothing to do with
them : you will find your power, if you only use it rightly,
greater than anyone's except the head master's. The
principal things you have to guard against are, first of all :
talking filth, or any kind of indecency : that is the worst evil,
by very far the worst that can befall a school. I am glad to
say I don't think that prevails, to any very great extent, at
Durham ; but if you find it, crush it with all your might.
Again, going to publics is the greatest evil you have to
contend with, especially in this football half-year. It seems
a very natural thing to do, and I have no doubt you have
many of you gone yourselves before now ; however, you
must see its evil results : drunkenness has very small beginnings, but nothing is more essentially degrading : you must
guard against the smallest attempts at it. It is specially
harmful because it is so naturally regarded as a joke, and any
fellow drunk must of course be seen by a lot of little
fellows. Discourage going to publics : let no one, on any
pretext whatever, say he has seen any of you monitors there ;
and show no mercy to any fellow whom you find drunk.
Bullying, I think, you will not have much to do with, nor
with dishonesty ; but both of these your own instincts, and
popular feeling in general, would teach you how to deal with.
The only other particular I need mention is : irreverence at
prayers in the morning or in the Cathedral. It is a very bad

sign if fellows talk, or learn rep. (as I have often known them to do) during prayers. Be careful to attend to Holden's rules of being in school early in the mornings, and so on : *reverence* is a very useful habit for all to cultivate : do not neglect to speak quietly to those whom you see misbehaving in those points.

'And now I have told you all I think is particularly important as regards your duties. The next question is : how are you to fulfil them all, how impress these lessons on others ? Of course it is impossible to teach anybody unless you are first convinced of the truth of what you are trying to teach. Look at these things I have mentioned : consider them well : see what harm a breach of any of these rules is likely to do to the boys themselves and to others with whom they have to do : do not think how *natural* it is for fellows to do these things, how you did them yourselves ; or if you do so, let the thought only redouble your vigilance. Never think how little good all your endeavours are doing ; how you are only getting hated, and not doing a bit of good ; how things like this cannot be helped, and it is no good making a noise about them ; how perhaps after all you are too strict, and things are not so bad as you think. Such are the thoughts, I well know, which will often occur to every one of you : do you put them aside, they are temptations to neglect your duty. It is not a question of private feeling : if you see any one doing wrong, and do not try to set him right, part of the blame of his wrong-doing lies at your door. Such is the view you ought to take of your monitorship altogether, and you ought to care nothing for being evil spoken of : if you only have confidence in yourselves, you will outlive that soon enough. However as regards influencing boys, a kind word, or a warning word, is the best way : be kind but firm : always be gentle as long as you can, and speak kindly to fellows, however much you may think or know they are trying to insult you. Do not be overbearing : *ask* them to do a thing rather than *command* them : do not stand too much on your dignity—a thing to which new monitors are rather prone. Do not be above talking to the little fellows and trying to help them : you may often be able to give them good advice by the way, and you will also accustom them—a great thing—to come to you for advice when they really want it. Be sociable with all : do not brand a fellow as " bad " and so shun him, but rather let such shun you ; you will find they will do so, if you are doing as you ought ; but while associating with all, be firm, yet gentle, in putting down by word anything

you think wrong.   As regards punishment, I strongly
recommend giving a fellow a thrashing, the fellows like it
best themselves—better than setting impositions or reporting.   Setting impositions is essentially weak, and shams
master too much : I should only recommend it in the case
of fellows so little, or so weak, you did not like to thrash
them, or as an addition to a thrashing when you felt the
latter was not enough.   For drunkenness and beastliness (also
for bullying and stealing, of course) thrash a fellow at once,
as hard as ever you like—you cannot give him too much;
but let me recommend that no fellow be thrashed by any of
you hastily or in a passion, but that before thrashing a fellow
you consult some of your brother monitors.   Remember,
never thrash a fellow a *little*, always *hard* : and it is always
well that he be thrashed by more than one of the monitors.
Again, as regards disobedience to monitorial authority, that
is a thing which you ought all deeply to resent : disobedience
to *one* you ought to regard as affecting all : never say, " Oh,
so-and-so is a fool : if he can't make fellows obey, I can't help
him."   You ought to help him most decidedly.   I particularly
urge this upon you : you *must* be united, or you *must* fall.
Disobedience, therefore, to a monitor's command ought to be
taken in hand by you all, and I should recommend you to
have the disobedient fellow into the study, and all of you
thrash him well.   You must have seen yourselves what a
fatal error was lately made in this respect : you must act in
concert, and with resolution, and I can promise you that after
you all have thrashed three fellows, at the most, for disobedience to any of you, you will not, except it be through
your own fault, have to complain of it again.   Try, all of
you, to be cordial towards your brother monitors : often talk
to each other and consult each other about things in
general.   As regards reporting to " Bung," [1] there are only two
cases in which I should think it at all allowable : in cases of
continued disobedience; e.g. if the monitors all together
thrashed a fellow twice for disobedience, and he still was
stubborn, then report him ; or if you saw a fellow hopelessly
bad, and doing mischief which you had no power to stop,
warn him that you will report him, and if you nail him again
do so.   I should not recommend this, however, unless you
had a strong enough case to get him sent away.   And now,
if you ask me *how* you are to do all this, I am sure you will
all feel where the best help is to be found ; also you will find
a frequent attendance at the Holy Communion a very great
assistance to you indeed.   It is no easy task you have to do,

[1] The school nickname for Dr. Holden, the Head Master.

or, at least, it ought not to be; but that is all the more reason why you should be careful. I have in this letter just jotted down such things as came into my head: they will, at any rate, supply you with food for thought and discussion; and if there is anything else on which I have not given you my opinion, and any of you would like to have it, I shall be most truly happy to give them it. You will pardon me, all of you, for having arrogated to myself the right of sermonising.'

To W. A. Nixon   'Sept. 5, 1864.

'My dear Nixon,— . . . When I got your letter I was engaged in meditating over topics for the pastoral epistle which I sent to Sherlock, and the next day I sat down to write that: it took me three hours hard work to think it out carefully and write it; and as it contained an answer to your question, I thought that would obviate the necessity for my writing at once. I hope my few hints proved useful to you. Remember, I am very far from presuming that my opinions are right: I simply wrote what seemed to me best, and my only design was that you should each of you consider it, and come to what conclusion on the subjects I mentioned, you thought fit. I am quite convinced that the method I there recommended for putting down insubordination is the best one for you: I hope it will be followed; but I must tell you, by the way, that among all sets of monitors there will be most probably a majority of feeble and useless ones, and the work—the real work, I mean—will in all cases be done by one or two: therefore you must not feel discouraged if you see fellows above you in the school neglecting their plain duty: it is no reason you should not do yours because others don't do theirs.' . . .

His interest in his old school remained very keen, and he often revisited it, once walking there all the way from Oxford in three days, in order to be present at the School Speeches. He writes about a visit there in 1866:

'I finished my walk to Durham most successfully, and stayed there about ten days, which I enjoyed very much, making new friends among the boys, and prying curiously into the state of things in general in the school. I regret to say I did not find them altogether such as I should like: the old monitors had not been firm enough, and had considerably diminished their influence: so I, as the best thing I could do, chummed violently with the fellows who will be monitors, and tried to impress upon them some notion of their duties; but that is all twaddle, and not at all interesting to the general public.'

CHAPTER II

UNDERGRADUATE DAYS : 1862–1866

CREIGHTON decided to try for a scholarship at Oxford, a decision which greatly vexed his cousin, Mr. Gunson, who wished him to go to Cambridge. It is clear that he was right in choosing Oxford as his university, for nothing could have suited the particular character of his mind better than the reading required for the School of Litteræ Humaniores. Mr. Gunson expressed his irritation strongly in a letter which Creighton, after reading, quietly put into the fire, saying simply that it was an angry letter. Mr. Gunson took some little time to get over his disappointment, but their relations became in time again quite cordial.

Creighton tried first for a classical scholarship at Balliol, when Mr. Paravicini was elected, and then at Merton, where he was elected to a classical postmastership in June 1862. He went into residence in the following October. His postmastership was worth 70l. a year: his father gave him no regular allowance, but he was free to ask for such money as he needed on the understanding that his Oxford course once ended, he was to look for no more help from home. He never got into debt, nor spent more than his father approved, and he had no remembrance of ever having felt stinted ; but the impression produced, at least upon his richer companions, was that his means were narrow. He had no extravagant tastes, his home training led him to live simply, and he would not have considered himself justified in gratifying his love for beautiful things with his father's money. His rooms, which were attics on the top floor in Mob Quad, were plainly furnished, and destitute of the usual adornments dear to the hearts of undergraduates.

There were only about forty men at Merton when

Creighton went up; but in 1864 the Merton New Building was opened, and the number of undergraduates increased to fifty-six. The majority were Eton men, brought there through the influence of the Warden, Dr. Marsham, men who loved hunting and other sports, had plenty of money to spend, and no particular intention of doing any work. Speaking at a Merton Gaudy some twenty years later, Creighton described the College in his undergraduate days as 'an ideal educational establishment, because everyone went his own way : there were those who gambled or hunted or worked, and no man interfered with them. The man who loafed in the High, loafed because that was what he wanted to do, and that was much better for him than being forced into doing something which he did not want to do.' The postmasters, as the scholars at Merton are called, formed of course a nucleus of reading men; but Creighton's tastes were never exclusive, and then, as always, he liked, and knew how to get on with, all manner of men. Neither was there any tendency at Merton to break up into sets. The whole College formed one single wine club, meeting in turn in the rooms of the different men every night after dinner, which then took place at six. Dessert and wine were provided by the host, but not much wine was drunk : there was an immense deal of talk : most of the men stayed only from forty to fifty minutes, but a few would stay all the evening.

Creighton had a strong feeling for the common life of the College, and insisted that it was the duty of each individual member to contribute what he could to raise it morally and intellectually. His views on the subject are developed in his sermons in the College Chapel, preached as a young Fellow in the light of his own experience. As at school he had been interested in the younger boys, so at college he took every opportunity of getting to know the freshmen. Mr. G. Saintsbury, who was a year junior to him, remembers how they first made acquaintance because Creighton brought him his testamur for Smalls, 'a friendly act, at least in the case of a freshman he hardly knew.' Dr. Copleston (now Bishop of Calcutta), who was two years his junior, tells how they made friends because he was drawn to row in one of the scratch fours got together in the October term to try the new arrivals, of which Creighton happened to be captain. Creighton at once asked him to walk down to the river with him, and this was constantly repeated. The opening of the New Building when he was entering his third year, gave Creighton a great opportunity for what Mr. Saintsbury calls 'his innocently Socratic habit of taking up ingenuous freshmen, whom, unlike most takers-up, he never put down again.' It was his custom to call on all freshmen, and he would take pains to be of use to them if possible. Mr. Saintsbury says that in the discussions which they used to have 'on all things in heaven and earth, at all hours of the day and night, nothing came up so often as a pet idea of Creighton's about influence. He thought that everybody ought to try and influence others as much as he could.' His ideas as to the way in which influence should be exerted probably changed very much with wider experience. In after life he certainly considered strong personal influence a thing to be avoided, as decidedly weakening to character. He wrote in 1871 to one who was very ready to be guided by him :

'I think you want me to do too much for you in separate actions and decisions. . . . Draw as largely as you like on my experience, but come to your conclusions, because your trust in me makes my experience yours, and so enables you to see your way more clearly, but let it be always your way, not my way ; don't take my advice unless it convinces you, get to the bottom of it . . . and if you do accept it, let it be because you quite agree with it, not because it is mine.'

All through his life he increasingly felt his responsibility to others. He wished to teach, to guide, to develop their character by affection and sympathy, to get them to think for themselves ; but he always wished them to be themselves, and never tried to impress himself on them, or get them to take his views. Probably it was this same sense of responsibility, this same desire to help, which was expressed in his less mature days as a desire for influence.

Merton owned in those days three University oars, and the College eight, in which Creighton rowed seven, was one of the best boats on the river. This helped him to get to know men who were more given to athletics than to reading.

'There was,' writes Dr. Copleston, 'a good deal of very foolish but not very harmful rowdyism in Merton then ;

bear-fighting at the wine club, breaking of furniture and windows, and kindling of bonfires. Creighton was never to be found where these were going on; and yet he was not felt to be uncomfortably strict or at all censorious. I admire now what did not strike me then—the quiet tact with which he kept clear of these follies, without making himself unpleasant to those who enjoyed them, among whom were some of his dearest friends, notably William Foster.'

This harmless rowdyism reached its height with a famous bonfire in Mob Quad on November 5, 1865, a dangerous proceeding in so confined a space, among some of the oldest buildings in Oxford. Creighton was then in lodgings, and he took no part in the bonfire, of which his friend Foster was the hero.

The College authorities considered the bonfire too serious a breach of discipline to be passed over, and next day all the men in College were gated. I think it was on this occasion that the old Warden, Dr. Marsham, was asked by the tutors to speak seriously to the men about their unruly conduct. Thus urged, he addressed the assembled College, and rebuked them for behaving in such an ungentlemanly manner, concluding with these words: 'And all I can say, gentlemen, is, that if you want to behave like barbarian savages, why,—ahem—ahem—you should come and ask leave first.'

The undergraduates determined to show their indignation at what they considered unjustifiable conduct on the part of the dons, and organised nightly during the following week solemn processions round the Fellows' Quad. Creighton, who, being in lodgings, had not been gated, was employed to fetch in after dinner a supply of penny whistles and other musical instruments, armed with which, with tea-trays as drums, making the most horrible din, and letting off squibs and crackers as they went, the undergraduates marched round and round the Fellows' Quad. The dons had the good sense to remain quietly in the Common Room; they likened the performance to the procession round the walls of Jericho, and Professor Esson was fond of chaffing Creighton on the subject, and saying: 'You expected the walls of the College to fall down, but they stood firm.' On one occasion, however, the procession was stopped in a moment by a message brought by the porter from the Warden to say, that he would be obliged if the gentlemen would not make quite so much noise, as he had a party.

William Foster, the hero of the bonfire, was a tall broad-shouldered man, with a fair beard, and blue eyes which looked out upon the world with the frank joy of a bright pure nature. He was the centre of a little group of specially close friends, consisting of himself, Creighton, R. T. Raikes, and C. Boyd (afterwards Archdeacon of Ceylon), the quadri-lateral, as they called themselves ; Boyd belonged to University, the rest were all Merton men. Foster seems to have possessed all those qualities which call forth the special admiration and affection of young men. It is told of him that when the undergraduates played a game, popular at that time, in which marks were given for the various qualities of the players, Foster always came out with head marks. Within the quadrilateral of friends, he inspired specially strong feelings of attachment. The four were never happier than when together, whether in vacation or in term time. There was no lack of sentimentality in their friendship. They exchanged rings as marks of devotion, each of the four wearing a gold band set with three turquoises to symbolise the others.

Writing in January 1866 to R. T. Raikes, Creighton says :

' However much I may like other people, my feelings towards them are entirely different in kind to those I feel to the three within the mystic circle.'

At Christmas, 1864, just as this close bond of friendship was forming, Creighton writes to R. T. Raikes :

' Do you know I always look upon vac.'s with a sort of melancholy satisfaction, as in them in my solitary hours, when I have nothing to think about, I am driven to review my conduct during the last term, and consider how very feeble it has been : in reviewing last term I have to observe with a sigh that it has been very pleasant but . . . very, very idle. I have learnt an immense amount morally, I believe, and have had my views of human nature considerably expanded, and I shall always remember last term with the most intense pleasure, for in it I got to *know* you, my dear Robert, and Boyd : therefore a very memorable term will it ever be to me. I do so well remember now the exact moment when

Photo. Hills & Saunders.

THE QUADRILATERAL, 1864.

R. T. RAIKES.   C. T. BOYD.

M. CREIGHTON.   W. H. FOSTER.

you were sitting in my arm-chair, talking about friendship, and my better nature rose up within me and said, " You thought him weak, did you ?　Oh, you fool ! he is a hundred times better than you : down and grovel at once." You don't mind me talking in this way, do you, old fellow ? I really can't help it, and am just going ahead without the least thought of what will come next.　However, all this is a digression : my conscience tells me I must work a great deal harder next term, and I am hanged if I see how I can do it. I must see and talk to you and Foster and Eudo and Frank and Saintsbury, and ever so many more, and how I am to do all that and read hard, I don't see, and would be glad of any hint you could give me for that purpose.　The only scheme I can devise is to convert you all into hard-reading men, though that I confess seems somewhat desperate.　However, I shall have all the rest of the vac. to perpend and meditate on that point.　I am trying to read hard now, though without very much effect.'

Attachment to the members of the quadrilateral did not prevent the constant formation of new friendships.　In the Lent Term, 1865, Creighton writes to Raikes, who was at Putney, coaching :

'I have begun to like rather three people (don't be alarmed at the large number, please) ; the first because he is likely to have some influence in the College, which he will use for good, also because he likes Frank ; the second because he is a good fellow (I mean *morally* not *socially* good), and is very jolly ; the third because he is not altogether on the spot, and I want to try if he cannot get a little nearer : in this last operation I shall want you to help me ; also in the two first if you like.'

One of Creighton's closest friends was George Saintsbury, now Professor of English Literature at the University of Edinburgh, known to all his undergraduate friends as ' The Saint.'　Creighton's own nickname was ' The Professor,' which was soon shortened to ' The P.' or ' P.' alone, and was used among old friends during his whole life.　Saintsbury and Creighton happened to be the only men in Merton at that time reading for honours in Greats.　They together took essays to Jowett, and went to W. W. Shirley's[1] and Jowett's lectures.　It was a chance attendance at a course of Shirley's

---

[1] Regius Professor of Ecclesiastical History and Canon of Christ Church, 1863–1866.

lectures which first roused Creighton's interest in Ecclesiastical History, as he recorded many years afterwards in his inaugural lecture as Dixie Professor at Cambridge. Saintsbury and Creighton were fond of reading in one another's rooms, as well as of sitting up talking till the small hours of the morning. In Creighton's last year they shared for a term a lodging in the High.

It would be impossible to enumerate Creighton's undergraduate friends. Dr. Copleston writes :

' He was loved by many and liked by all. . . . He especially loved men who were boyish, frank, pure, and overflowing with high spirits. His range of friends was large, but those who were nearest to him might have been divided into two classes : those whom he valued for originality of temper, and those whom I have attempted to describe. . . . The second group included some who could hardly be called reading men at all. Towards these Creighton considered himself more or less seriously to be playing the part of a Socratic Mentor ; and his affection for them was a marked feature of his character.'

He already felt in some degree what was so characteristic of his later life, that all have claims on our affection, and writes thus to a friend in 1866 :

' Affections for particular persons ought to increase one's universal charity ; one ought to extend to all, the attributes which excited our love for some particular object. I tell you this because, you know, I have always regarded you as a little deficient in general appreciation of persons, never feeling sufficiently that all are good, or else they would not be, and that it is possible by regarding the good in all to do much to obliterate the bad which one is compelled to see. . . . You have power enough to evangelise greatly. Who knows but that your next triumph may be the conversion of a mathematician ? I am, however, bound to confess that this is a feat before which the boldest heart might quail.'

Dr. Copleston describes him at this time as ' not very different from what he was in later life, though both his face and his bearing increased in refinement as he grew older. He had at the age of twenty a strong and active figure, and a hearty laugh ; but though he was not in any sense awkward, I do not think he gave any promise either of the grace of attitude and movement, or of the charm of manner, which

afterwards belonged to him.' He was always extremely lithe
and active, fond of twisting himself into all sorts of contor-
tions, and of taking up impossible positions. W. Foster
describes him as ' howling with laughter, and flinging his legs
wildly round his venerable head.' He was obliged always to
wear spectacles, as he was very shortsighted. In 1866 he
began to grow his beard, which was pale auburn in colour.
His hair was fair and thick and wavy, with no suggestion of
possible baldness.

In the Long Vacation of 1864, when Creighton was staying
at W. Foster's home, Foxearth Vicarage, the two friends
decided to form a college whist club.

To R. T. Raikes

' You and Foster and I should proceed calmly to choose
out nine other fellows, whom we should like to have : each of
us make out a list of nine separately, and then compare and
see who have the most votes, then quietly ask each of these
fellows if they would join. . . . We can settle on our lists the
first night of next term, and get into swing as soon as
possible.'

The whist club was formed as suggested. It included
besides the quadrilateral, amongst others, Copleston, Saintsbury, Sir Stafford Northcote, Foster Alleyne, &c., all Merton
men, and its exclusiveness was somewhat resented in the
College. Oxford was just then taking up the modern
scientific game, and Creighton was a keen player : whist was
the only game he ever cared for, until like so many others he
gave it up for bridge, but in after years he seldom played
except when with some old College friend or with his
children. Rowing was his only form of athletics : he considered that it interfered less with reading than any other
sport. He never fired a gun nor visited a racecourse in his
life. Walking remained his chief recreation, and all his friends
tell of the long walks they took together.

' He had,' says Mr. Saintsbury, ' an amiable knack of
organising expeditions. I remember one Trinity Sunday,
1865, when he and I and two men drove to Witney, went to
church there, then walked for twenty miles or so through
Wychwood, dined late at the Marlborough Arms, and drove
back to Oxford just in time for twelve o'clock, on one of the
most glorious summer nights I ever remember.'

Creighton to R. T. Raikes   'Fifth Sunday in Lent, 1865.

'My dear Robert,— . . . Let me tell you first how I have been spending my day. I got up at 8.30 and breakfasted with Saintsbury, and afterwards he and I went off to the Church of SS. Philip and James. I had never been to service there before, and I liked it immensely. I never saw an altar I liked so much, or where the effect was so good. Afterwards we discovered Potter and Everest among the congregation, so we joined them unto us and went all in a body for a walk to Wolvercot and Wytham, and lunched at Godstow; and it was such a jolly morning, and we had old Saintsbury on the fuss about things in general. One of his observations was very great: he said that when he was a parson he would strictly adhere to the Canon, and report to the Bishop all his parishioners who did not fast on Fridays, and would prosecute his village butcher in the Court of Arches for selling meat on that day. We then went to Evensong at St. Thomas's at three o'clock, and were the entire congregation except Prothero and the Sunday school girls, who were catechised by Mr. Chamberlain in a lugubrious manner, during which time I refreshed my memory on points of doctrine by perusing the XXXIX Articles, Everest went to sleep, Saintsbury contemplated a picture of the Virgin which he carries about in his Prayer Book, and Potter blinked dismally and thoughtfully through his eye-glass. . . .'

As an undergraduate Creighton was a decided High Churchman. When he went up to Oxford frequent Communions were not yet usual in college chapels: Mr. Burgon had instituted an eight o'clock Communion at St. Mary's, which Creighton attended, otherwise he seldom left his College chapel for a more elaborate service. Merton Chapel served as the church of St. John's for a small parish of some 120 souls. In Creighton's days the Rev. H. W. Sargent had charge of this parish, and spared no trouble to make his choir and service worthy of the building in which it was held. The service is said to have realised very nearly the highest type of parish worship, at a time when such services were comparatively rare, and in after years Creighton often spoke of the pleasure it had given him. The College services were simple enough, but the mere fact of worshipping in so noble a building was sufficient to stimulate devotion in one with a keen appreciation of architecture. Creighton was particular in his religious observances, and with a few other kindred spirits joined in observing the fasts of the Church. They absented themselves on Fridays and other fast days from dinner in hall, and had tea in turn in one another's rooms, during which they read aloud St. Augustine's 'Confessions.' This proceeding was not altogether popular in College : they were sometimes called 'the Saints,' and once an attempt was made to screw them up. But the machinations of the enemy were heard, the 'Saints' sallied forth : their assailants fled before them, and locked themselves for safety into a neighbouring room.

Creighton was at all times reserved about his deeper religious feelings. 'He took,' says Dr. Copleston, 'Church principles for granted, and did not talk much about them : if he did, it was to assert rather than to argue.' He was interested in matters of ritual and religious observance, and was a severe critic of slovenliness in the performance of Church services.

To R. T. Raikes   'Carlisle : Jan. 10, 1865.

'Oh, do you know how dreadfully I have been sickened with Protestants in this vac.? . . . I grieve to say I cannot speak of my Christmas services as you can : the only daily service here is at the Cathedral, and that is quite in the humdrum respectable line, so much a matter of course that they never take the brown holland off the altar for it—"it is too much trouble, and gives the dust more time to settle," was the reason the old verger gave me for not doing so, and he moreover added that he always used to take it off till forbidden by the Dean, I think it was, or else a canon, from motives of additional carefulness for the Church property ! The small boy choristers amuse themselves all the time by squabbling and pinching each other in the middle of a chant, the men are perpetually turning over their music and restoring large folios to their place with a horrid bang in the middle of the lessons, while the precentor sits blinking above, looking down on all this irreverence, which he plainly sees, with an air of abject helplessness. I am sorry to say, since Christmas I have not gone nearly so often as I ought, but the service is at a most unpleasant hour, viz. ten, which spoils your morning entirely.'

He became a very strong advocate of the duty of attending daily service.

'August 23, 1866.

'I have made out lately several opinions which do not
agree well with Cis Hook or Will, and they become occasionally scandalised : my last has been adverse to family prayers,
on the ground that you ought to send all your servants to
daily service ; and adverse to grace, on the ground that it is
low to fix on the filling of your belly as the highest action of
your daily life, and solemnly thank God for that.'

'The Knowe, Aspatria : September 18, 1866.

'You understand that in all the violent sentiments I give
vent to, I do not at all mean that I would act up to them ; e.g.
in the case of family prayers, I always read them at home,
because, though theoretically they are untenable and do a
great deal of harm by reconciling people's consciences to not
attending daily service, still in practice the advantages in
individual cases are so great as to counterbalance the
general wrongfulness of the proceeding; and moreover,
though I do read them myself at home because I don't
attend daily service, still if I was head of a household I
would not allow my family or those of my servants who did
go to daily service to attend them, and so would keep clearly
before the eyes of the rest the purely provisional nature of
the proceeding, and so to some extent remind them of the
existence of a church.   And so all my "fusses" may be said
by those who understand not, to mean nothing, because their
practical results are not evident in my actions, but they
prevent one losing oneself in a general maze, and con-
founding as undisputed truths mere foolish practices which
have grown up from the conditions in which the soul is
placed.'

Occasional remarks in his letters show that his intention
to take Orders remained unchanged.   He did not talk about
it, but his most intimate friends always regarded it as a
settled fact.   He never spoke in after life of any preacher or
religious teacher as having exercised a special influence over
him, and he was not a reader of sermons.   Among his
teachers he always said that the one to whom he owed far the
most was Dr. Edward Caird, now Master of Balliol, then
Fellow and Tutor of Merton, his tutor when he was reading
for his final Schools.   The other tutor in Merton with whom
he had most to do was Mr. William Sidgwick.   Dr. Caird
writes :

'He was undoubtedly the ablest man in the College at the time. His philosophical work with me was always done carefully and thoroughly, and in it he gave proof of a well-balanced judgment and considerable critical power; but he was not specially attracted towards philosophical studies. He already gave evidence of practical sagacity, and had much influence with the other undergraduates, of which he made a good use. He was very independent and not easily influenced by others, and had a tendency to strike out a new line for himself on any subject that interested him. Generally his tutors felt that he was a man of thoroughly healthy mind, who could be trusted to take a reasonable view of any question, and to help to keep up the moral and intellectual tone of the College.'

A friend recalls that Dr. Caird said of him : 'Creighton possesses common sense in a degree which amounts to genius.'

John Stuart Mill was then a predominant influence in Oxford, an influence against which both Creighton and Saintsbury rebelled. Under Dr. Caird's guidance he imbibed Kant's philosophy with much satisfaction, and also learnt something of Hegel. He developed what he called a theory of the unity of contradictories, about which his friends used to chaff him, but which he asserted helped to explain many difficulties.

His views about philosophy may be illustrated by some extracts from a letter written in 1868 to Miss Alleyne, the sister of one of his friends, who had asked his advice about her reading.

'As to the general good of teaching after a certain period of the mind's growth, I quite agree with you that its direct influence ceases ; but it is useful to prevent intellectual narrowness—it forces upon us the prominence of things we have rather slurred over as uninteresting, and also it is often a strong stimulus, accidentally opening up a striking line of thought. Its use to the individual must depend on his feelings on those points : if you have a great stock of things on hand, don't plunge into another ; but if you have none of pre-eminent interest, then I think it is worth while doing so.

'As to philosophy, you have asked a very difficult question. . . . You must not either regard philosophy as anything definite which can be mastered or learned : various systems of philosophy are merely the historical expressions in a regulated system of the vague views, the mere strivings after the incomprehensible, which men always must feel. You will say this is what you have always regarded religion. So it is : religion and philosophy differ little : they deal with the same problems ; but the essence of religion is that it deals with the heart, with the feelings, the imagination : the essence of philosophy is that it deals with the reason, with the head only. Hence they seem to differ and to be in mortal con- flict ; yet it is obviously impossible they really can be. But this is a digression to a very large and dangerous question. Philosophical systems, then, are merely representations of the vague aspirations of the time, and must be read as such. . . . As to reading, I think you will not find the technicalities so perplexing if you consider what the systems mean. The problems treated of are so great that language cannot be found for their expression, hence the technicalities, which differ in every system. . . . Of course the materialists, who explain man's mind by reference to the world, are much more lucid than the idealists, who explain the world by the mind : this, as being an invisible process, requires harder words to express it.

'You see, then, that philosophy is a large subject, requiring much reading. I forgot to call your attention to the differ- ence between metaphysical and moral philosophy : most of my remarks have been about metaphysics.' After advising a number of books to be read, he concludes : ' You will think I have prescribed largely ; but I mean you to read any of those you may most readily come across : if you find them dull, leave off soon, and try another. . . . Excuse the inordinate length of my lecture. . . . On gazing at these sheets I find it difficult to acquit myself of something resembling pedantry : you asked for a drink of water ; I have sent you a shower bath. Forgive me.'

There are constant complaints in his undergraduate letters that he has not been able to read as much as he wished. He always tried to get through a great deal of reading at home in vacation.

To C. A. Potter   'Christmas, 1864.

' I have been striving hard to read, and seem to myself to be doing so ; but I resolved not to humbug myself, and think I was reading hard because I did so whenever nothing else came in the way, which is generally the theory of reading in the vac. ; and it is astonishing, admitting that, how very often things come in the way ; but I carefully time myself every day and enter the result in a pocket-book, and I can assure you it does not nearly look so much on paper, and takes the conceit out of one considerably when put in that bare and naked form.'

Several times he spent portions of the vacation at Oxford in order to read in peace. He went up in January 1865, a week before term, to have 'a private read with Sidg., which will be more or less entertaining.' His friends could not understand how he got through all the reading that he did, but all his life he possessed an uncommon power of concentrated and rapid work. He read quickly, absorbed what he wished to retain, and left the rest. He would assert that he had not a good memory, and he did not consider an exceptional memory a valuable gift. But if his memory was not of exceptional quality it was a most useful one, for he always remembered all that he wished, or that it was useful for him to remember. He had the capacity, which he retained through life, of working at all times and amidst the most disturbing circumstances. He liked to read in his friends' rooms, and on summer days carried his books out in a punt and read moored under the trees that overhang the Cherwell. He read from a genuine desire for knowledge, and with a strong feeling of the duty incumbent on every man to make the most of his capacities. Speaking of a man who took a lower view of the subject, he wrote : ' I have never got over the feelings of horror with which I heard him tell me that he regarded his class merely as a means for procuring pecuniary emoluments in after life.' Books of many and varied kinds besides those needed for the Schools were read and discussed with his friends. In 1865 he writes :

' I have been reading Carlyle's " Latter Day Pamphlets," which are simply scrumptious, and which I believe in to a great extent, though they are utterly radical and entirely subversive of everything as at present established.'

' He was full of Carlyle,' writes Dr. Copleston ; ' he and Saintsbury talked about the "immensities" and the "everlasting no," and divided us all into those who were " in contact " and those who were not " in contact " with the great Heart of the Universe. A little later, but still as an undergraduate, he talked more of Browning than of Carlyle and often read pieces to me. He was especially fond of puzzling me with

those which suggest some paradox in casuistry.   The first
piece he ever read to me, I think, was " A Light Woman."
Somewhat later he read me the whole of " Bishop Blougram,"
and pretended to defend him.   He read admirably, and I
was a good listener, but not an apt scholar in Browning.   I
stumbled at his rough passages, and Creighton delighted in
scandalising me.'

He was a great lover of Tennyson as well as of Browning,
and made early acquaintance with the poems of Morris and
Swinburne.   Mr. Saintsbury recalls bringing down to Oxford
three copies of Swinburne's ' Poems and Ballads ' as soon as
they appeared, and giving one to Creighton, who proceeded
at once to read them aloud lying in a hammock in a friend's
room from lunch to chapel, and went on again after dinner,
till some one pulled away the book and took his turn at
reading.

He read novels, of course.   In 1864 he wrote :

' I have been reading " Jane Eyre " very hard, and meditating thereon, and find my old impression strengthened that it
is the best novel ever written, containing the greatest knowledge and keenest power of analysing character.'

And in 1865 :

' I have been reading lately " The Mill on the Floss."
I like it more than any novel I have ever read.'

Creighton's vacations as an undergraduate were always
spent in England.   He visited his friends, chiefly W. Foster
and R. T. Raikes, in their homes, and indulged his love for
walking by going on foot all across England from one place
where he was visiting to another.   He also went for many
walking tours.

To C. A. Potter, after a walking tour in the Highlands, 1864

' I am sorry to say that I have already acquired a most
inveterate taste for roaming.   I feel like Tennyson's " Ulysses,"
who finds that after his wanderings he cannot possibly sit
quiet in Ithaca.   I am always desirous of walking to all sorts
of places and doing all sorts of things, and am the most restless being imaginable.'

To R. T. Raikes, 1865

' I wish some kindly deity or philanthropic old gentleman

would say to me, " I pray thee read no more; go, here is 100*l*., walk with the help of that and a stick." '

His friends laughed at him for what they considered an exaggerated enthusiasm. W. Foster wrote (1864): ' The Professor raves about walking. He will go on all the vac. I expect. I don't envy him, as it is decidedly a case in which " there is limits." ' Another friend wrote to him : ' I hope your career will never be temporarily cut short by your arrest as a tramp without visible means of subsistence.' When once he proposed to walk, I know not from where, to pay a promised visit at Foxearth, W. Foster wrote in serious remonstrance :

' Beloved P. F.,—You are a Hass ! a Hidiot ! a Howl. You are ruining your constitution. You will be seriously ill ! You will hinder your reading. You are tempting Providence, you old oaf ! Don't be such a fool as to walk, but come in the train like a Christian. . . . The guv. thinks you very foolish, if not wicked, to attempt it. You are really very silly, dear P., to do such a wild thing.'

Portions of each vacation were spent at his home in Carlisle. There, as a rule, he managed to get through a great deal of reading. He did not get from the members of his family any sympathy in his special studies : he wrote, ' Everybody at home knows that my point of view is absolutely different, so we don't mind one another.' He said of his father a few years later : ' He never refused me anything in my life, though his manner made it difficult to ask for anything I did not decidedly want.' His sister, who was seven years younger than himself, was at school and much away from home, to his great regret. He interested himself in her studies and liked to direct her reading, and whenever she could she accompanied him on his long walks. His brother was in his father's business, and had little understanding of academic pursuits. Creighton wrote of him, August 16, 1865 : ' He regards me as an impracticable dreamer—good enough at grubbing in books, but with theories utterly useless on every material point, and his only hope for me is that experience may put me right.' Ordinary society possessed no attraction for Creighton.

To R. T. Raikes   'Carlisle : January 10, 1865.

'I live very quietly here, and know only few people, as we see very little society. The other day I went to a ball (night I should have said), and, oh, gracious, I was driven quite misanthropical for some time afterwards. I knew very few people, and never had such toil in my life in manufacturing conversation. I talked the very smallest talk I ever was compelled to do, and felt more or less like a squeezed orange for some days. It was my first go this winter, and I never felt it such a bore before ; and I have long been meditating whether it is one's duty to undergo operations of that nature quietly, or steadfastly refuse to have anything to do with them at all. I cannot quite decide at present which is the righter course.'

The society of his chosen friends was all he needed, and he had not yet felt the call to enlarge his sympathies, though his utterances about society showed much more violent feelings than anyone would have gathered from his conduct, for he was never a recluse, and was always lively and talkative when with others.

To R. T. Raikes   'The Knowe, Aspatria : September 18, 1866.

'I must confess that " society," as generally understood, I detest and abhor : that you should talk to a man because you like and understand him is not only pleasant, but useful and right ; but that you should entertain and be entertained by a series of people whose moral sentiments you disapprove of, whose pursuits you take no interest in, and whose intellectual capacities you are unable after some search to discover, and the sight of whom induces a fit of bad humour, during which you abuse them soundly and expose their feebleness so disgustingly forced upon your notice, and all this solely because they happen to live in the neighbourhood, seems to me to be an unparalleled monstrosity.'

'Carlisle : December 31, 1867.

'The sole thing to be said for " society " seems to me to be that it fills you with temporary vanity ; vanity inspires you to effort of some sort ; and effort is the sole source of pleasure. Pleasure, however, so obtained, stands to rational pleasure in the same relation that the pleasures of dram drinking do to those of a temperate life. Family enjoyments have not even that stimulus : everybody knows you too well to think you better-looking or cleverer or a better dancer than you are: and so you have no inducement to the requisite effort.'

Creighton as an undergraduate felt no desire for any but male friends. The 'grave tenderness' of which his friends speak was shown to them only. It happened that his most intimate friends had no sisters, his own sister was considerably younger than himself, and he had no experience of friendship with women of any age, and did not amuse himself by falling in love. To his friends he showed almost passionate love and tenderness, but women had no interest for him. He writes to R. T. Raikes:

'Lynton: August 8, 1866.

' I don't know what you think, but I find ladies in general are very unsatisfactory mental food : they seem to have no particular thoughts or ideas, and though for a time it is flattering to one's vanity to think one may teach them some, it palls after a while. Of course at a certain age, when you have a house and so on, you get a wife as part of its furniture, and find her a very comfortable institution; but I doubt greatly whether there were ever many men who had thoughts worth recounting, who told those thoughts to their wives at first, or who expected them to appreciate them. I should like to hear from Tennyson a comparison of his feelings towards Arthur Hallam and towards his wife. I believe men are driven into matrimony by the necessities of life, which tend to make friendship impossible by engrossing all a man's thoughts.'

His friends' love affairs he watched with anxious interest and treated with a wisdom almost beyond his years and experience. He writes:

'Lynton: August 23, 1866.

' The sight of them [a young couple on their wedding tour] made Will quite maudlin; but I try my best to repress him, and he has not said anything about himself for some time. I don't think anything will ever come of his attachment: in fact I don't mind whispering to you that I think his governor is quite right. She is older than he is, and by the time Will is old enough to think of marrying he will begin to see it : it is therefore very advisable to prevent him talking about it, partly because talking on the subject tends to make the matter traditional, and fasten the external forms on a man's mind after the spirit has gone (a thing much to be feared in

Will's case, as he is too honest to see the difference), partly
too because a man feels ashamed of unsaying a thing he has
said to many. I tell you this as a reason for not encouraging
him more than necessary next term to talk on the subject :
I should be glad to hear if you agree with me.'

'February 19, 1867.

'Will is very sad and solemn this term : he is still in love,
I am afraid, and thinks about it more than the ideal wise man
ought to : I mean that I am rather unable to appreciate the
point of view of grieving because your gov. objects to
an engagement until you are in something resembling a position to marry ; but I suppose it is necessary to keep a pet
skeleton, and if Will chooses that one, why, I have no doubt
it will answer admirably.'

Of the nature of Creighton's intercourse with his friends
and of his talk, perhaps the best idea can be gathered from
the words of Dr. Copleston, who writes :

'This is what I now consider the most remarkable feature
in the Creighton of Merton as I remember him—his pleasure
in discussing moral problems, or rather in announcing his
verdicts on questions of conduct. His favourite beginning
was, " You know, Cop., I'm quite clear that "—here followed
some decision which he knew would surprise me.
'These verdicts were by no means always such as a riper
judgment would ratify, but they were always suggestive.
Their shrewdness was only surpassed by their vigour. I
remember the great severity of his manner, though his
language was not violent, in denouncing the conduct of some
men who had used the Ash Wednesday holiday—this must
have been early in 1865—for vicious indulgence. What
moved his indignation was that they should have gone
straight from the Commination Service to bring down a curse
upon themselves. He once came into my room after a long
Sunday walk with E. G. W., in the course of which they had
lunched at an inn. W. had said during luncheon, " Do you
think this is right that we are doing ? " and Creighton had
replied, " If it were not right, we should not be doing it." He
found great interest in reporting this decision and challenging
criticism. I owe him a great debt for the following, for it
embodies a moral maxim of which the importance can hardly
be overrated. I believe it to be only a specimen among
many—though a conspicuously good one—of the wise sayings
which he would blurt out, to the surprise of companions who

expected nothing so serious. I had said in regard to some action—I forget what—which I knew, I suppose, in my heart was better left undone : " Do you think there is any harm in doing so-and-so ? " He replied, " No, there's no harm in it ; but you'll go to the devil if you do it."

' I am afraid that what I have written might give the impression that Creighton at this time was a " prig." Nothing could be farther from the fact if by " prig " is meant one who obtrudes his moral judgment pretentiously. In the region of " the immensities " he was no doubt priggish, like any other clever young man steeped in " Sartor Resartus," but on the moral side he was neither obtrusive nor pretentious. His dogmatic manner, then as in after life, did not imply pretension : it was rather the εἰρωνεία of humility, it was never intended to be taken quite seriously. And εἰρωνεία in every form was too dear to him, for him ever to obtrude advice : even in face of actual evil, a contemptuous silence or sarcastic expression of indifference was more common with him than the utterance of indignation. I think he scarcely ever as an undergraduate gave offence by his plain speaking. His sharp repartee would often hurt a friend for a moment, but then he was quick and tender to make amends ; and when his paradoxes scandalised a weak brother, he would instantly assert that the contrary was equally true or more so.

' The tenderness which lay beneath what was abrupt or severe in him, may be illustrated by a little story which shows him as a shrewd observer of human nature at a stage in which it does not always command the sympathy of an undergraduate. In one of our walks a long way out of Oxford, we passed a mother or nurse who was trying in vain to quiet a crying baby. Creighton turned back after we had passed them, and clapped his hands loudly close to the face of the crying child, and rejoined me without a word. I was astonished both at the procedure and at its success ; but he explained it as if he had done it before : " Anything that startles them will do : it changes the current of their thoughts."

' The favourite subject of his talk on these walks was, as I have implied, people and their conduct. He was fond of analysing the conduct of his friends, and estimating their ability. He would apply the like analysis to himself. Saintsbury told me one day that Creighton had said to him that morning : ' Do you know, Saint, I have come to the conclusion that you are an abler man than I am ?' According to the measures by which we undergraduates estimated ability, literary facility, and aptitude for philosophical discussion, he was right: we had not taken into account that predominant interest in moral issues and that insight into conduct and character which I now see to have been Creighton's chief distinction.

'So much stronger was this interest in conduct than any literary interest, that history was the only form of literature possible to him. But even so, I have always maintained that he was only accidentally a man of letters.

'Those who knew him only in later life may think, when I describe his conversation as an undergraduate, that I am unconsciously drawing my description from what he afterwards became, so early marked and so little afterwards altered were some of the characteristics by which he was popularly known. But I draw direct from a vivid recollection of the early days in which I saw far more of him than I ever afterwards did. On the surface, and perhaps a little below it, he was a rash speaker: he leapt before he looked, though his leap was often in the right direction. But a little below the surface he was a shrewd and steady thinker, and from time to time he brought up from that lower level, not without feeling, a serious thought. These accumulated, as years went on, with a store of wisdom; but I am speaking of the beginnings. He was often sarcastic; sharp, but not bitter; severe, but not sneering.

'He was already fond of paradox, and would introduce his most adventurous creations with the phrase, "I am perfectly clear," or "I have come to the conclusion." When he was tired or annoyed his paradoxes were more glaring, and if their inconsistency aroused a protest, as they often did, from dear simple-hearted Foster—"Come, I say, P., you said before," &c.—he would at once withdraw his "conclusion" and assert the contrary, perhaps winding up with, "What does it matter? What matters? Nothing matters." He had already matured the two sister propositions, that a fool is worse than a criminal, and that all the worst deeds have been done conscientiously. But what he really hated was wickedness, and if he had been taxed with his love for good simple souls, he would not have hesitated to reply that the wicked man is the only real fool. He was profoundly convinced that unintelligent acquiescence in opinions, though these might be true, was immoral and dangerous; that it was good for people to be shocked and to have their beliefs shaken up.'

Though Creighton never obtruded advice on his friends, when asked for it he gave it with absolute directness, as is shown in the two following letters. They were written to an intimate undergraduate friend who had just left Oxford, and belong to the year after he got his Fellowship; but I insert them here, as they help to illustrate his relations with his friends.

'Oxford: April 5, 1867.

'The question on which you ask my advice is a very difficult one, and is one on which your views and mine differ so widely that I don't think my opinion likely to be of much use. You start from the conviction that living beyond one's income is a necessity, and that it is absurd to expect anyone not to do it—the notion of self-denial in the least respect is inconceivable: for a tradesman to imagine that the pleasure he affords you by letting you have what you want is not a sufficient recompense to him, seems to you monstrous. If your debts were paid to-morrow they would be just as large in three years more, and so on to the end of the chapter. A good lesson of stern reality might perhaps change your views: you are a person who will never learn without being taught—and that too in the same way as the men of Succoth. The small amount of trouble requisite in asking for the money in the way you propose will not be of any warning to you whatever. Moreover, on general grounds, straightforwardness is the best way, and obviously the only right course for you is to tell your father, accept as your due the sorrow of seeing the sorrow you have caused to others, and learn, in a way never to be forgotten, not to do the like again. Such is my earnest advice to you—advice which I have often thought over (you don't suppose I did not foresee that I should some day have to answer some such question as you have now put?)—advice, however, which I don't for a moment suppose you will follow. I give it, not forgetting the circumstances of the case—the inconvenience as well as grief it would cause your father, your general loss of self-respect in the eyes of all at home, and so on. But still you have sown the wind, and you consequently will have to reap the whirlwind. Better get in your crop and have done with it, than have a lifelong harvest going on. The course I have told you is the only possible one of solving your difficulties at all rightly in my opinion.

'As to the more immediate question, I should regard the course you propose as distinctly wrong. To put yourself under obligations to a man, simply because he is willing to allow you to do so; to treat him as a most intimate friend when you in no sense feel towards him as such, is not, I think, justifiable.

'Moreover, the calmness with which you propose to go on without any prospect of recognition, or the least intention of taking any trouble to save money, or even of trying to make any by industry of any sort, is wonderful and sublime.

'And now you have my opinions ; they are not mild, but I know you will not be angry with me. You won't, I am quite aware, make any use of what I have written ; you will be at first indignant, and then think I have been harsh ; but I wish you to consider your general views on pecuniary matters, and see if you could not be to some degree economical. How this is possible you can only tell yourself. Your conduct and views on such matters have always been to me inexplicable and utterly incomprehensible.

'Farewell : don't write any more on the subject, but tell me what you have done when you have done it.

'Ever your loving
'P.'

'October 4, 1867.

'I am really very glad to hear that your father knows about your pecuniary difficulties. Sad as the revelation might be, it was obviously inevitable, as of course you would have found yourself unable to carry out your arrangement for paying 100*l.* a year ; and there comes a limit to the patience even of Oxford tradesmen. So, my dear ——, it was better your father should know at once than have to do so later ; every year would have made difficulties greater, and to get rid of the responsibility will be a great relief to you. I have seen, and you no doubt are conscious, that the knowledge of those debts has had a distinctly bad moral effect on your character, as all concealment from one to whom one feels trust is due, necessarily disturbs the equal tenor of one's life. Poor old ——, I am very sorry for you ; it is a sad thing to tell a father like yours, and I can only say I am glad you have managed to do it so easily.'

Any account of Creighton's undergraduate friends would be incomplete without mentioning H. J. Hood, of Brasenose (now Mr. Registrar Hood), one of the very dearest of them all. As a Brasenose man he was naturally not much mixed up with the special little band of Merton friends, though intimate with many of them. Writing of him a few years later, Creighton says : 'His affection to me has been enormous and always will be, also mine to him. . . . He was more worshipped up here than anyone I ever saw, so that I felt still more his voluntary attachment to me, and the extreme wrath which he incurred from others for his preference for me.' It was a friendship based on the most absolute mutual understanding and confidence, which needed no words or outward tokens, and as it began so it remained till death parted the friends. I do not think that Creighton ever spoke much at the Union, but he was its President in 1867, and Librarian in 1868.

In 1864 he took a first-class in Moderations, and in the summer of 1866 a first-class in Litteræ Humaniores. A friend wrote to him :

'Of course you were the best first. I am very glad at your success only as a step to the Rev. Mandell Creighton, Senior Tutor and Principal of Postmasters, when Merton will indeed be a paradise.'

After a very brief interval he set to work to read for the then undivided School of Law and Modern History. As soon as term was over he visited his old school.

'Durham : June 25.

'I have been engaged in walking here from Derby during the late wet weather. You may imagine the delights I experienced in the process. I am staying with my old head master at present, and was engaged all this morning in lecturing to his Vth and VIth forms ; an exertion which I felt almost too much for this very hot weather. I enjoy being back again at my old school immensely. I must go home soon and commence the Great Law and History trick, though I feel very disinclined to begin, and regard the amount of work I have to do as to some extent hopeless.'

'July 11.

'I want to do my best for Law and History, and I foresee that I need more reading than I can by any means get.'

The actual books to be got through before the examination in the autumn, were more than could possibly be managed in so short a time, but he much enjoyed the work, and wrote :

'I like the history business much ; it is amusing and at the same time instructive. . . . I shall not be able to get up my work sufficiently well; but hang the expense! what's the odds of a class?'

At the end of July, Creighton allowed himself a few days' holiday, when the Quadrilateral stayed together at Treberfydd, the home of R. T. Raikes. He then went on with W. Foster to join a number of friends in a reading party which he had organised under the direction of Mr. Thomas Arnold at Lynton. Mrs. Arnold and her family were there as well, but the young men lived by themselves in a house called Summit Castle, where Creighton did the housekeeping. They saw nothing of Mrs. Arnold and her family, and it was not till some years later in Oxford that his lifelong friendship with her eldest daughter, now Mrs. Humphry Ward, began. This reading party was always remembered with much pleasure by all concerned. On August 8, Creighton writes to R. T. Raikes, who was on another reading party, preparing for the Mathematical Schools :

'We are all very comfortable and jolly, and spend our days in reading very fairly hard, . . . and in much walking and also much eating; the entire operation being interspersed with much laughter on every occasion. . . . We are quite apart from the rest of mankind, and have no connexion with them nor any desire for it : quieter days could not be passed by anyone . . . there is much to see and to admire, and the walks seem inexhaustible.'

He spent the last part of the vacation at home.

To C. A. Potter   'Carlisle : October 1.

'About this period a vac. begins to pall, and I get into a state of morbid contemplation, having no continual intellectual friction to take off the edges of one's rapidly forming theories. And here let me tell you that . . . I am determined, in case I get a fellowship, to give myself up to study and literary labour in general, and seek to do nought else. I think your observations on the subject are not free from fallacy; you seem to think that such a life is useless. Let me ask, who do you think does more good and has more influence, Jowett and Liddon, or let us say Archdeacon Denison? . . . I could do much more positive good at present as a don at Oxford than in any other capacity I am aware of, and could besides have plenty of time for study and no social duties or troubles: if I have this I may possibly (whether or no I can only discover by time, patience, study, and self-knowledge) add something to the knowledge of mankind—add one little stone to the temple which it is raising; or if I can only supply a little more mortar for the good of others, I will not have lived altogether in vain. To give you some small idea of what has dawned upon me lately in the way of duty, I may mention a study of German, Italian, and Spanish, together with an acquaintance with their literature and travels in the countries; a study of the entire history of Europe; of Hebrew, and the theology of the Early Church. When some such little things as these have been gone through, I may then be sufficiently conscious of my own ignorance to commence with fear and trembling to say my little say. Such a life is far from being one of idleness or necessary selfishness. I can take no steps nor think of them which may interfere with it: I shall resign myself to a bookworm's fate. Why I have conceived this I can only say is owing to the flood of new subjects which my history reading has opened up to me, and the consciousness of my duty has only slowly dawned upon me.'

After less than six months' preparation Creighton went up for the examination in the Law and Modern History School. He had not had time even to open some of the books required. His examiners were Professor Stubbs, Mr. Boase, and Mr. James Bryce, all afterwards close friends and colleagues. A friend, Mr. Foster Alleyne, writes: 'I was present at his *viva voce* examination, which lasted for an hour and a half, and he stood it well.' The ability of some of his papers struck Mr. Bryce so much that he has preserved them. But his knowledge was not sufficient for a distinguished place in the class list, and he only obtained a second class. Writing to Mr. Bryce shortly afterwards on some other matter, he said, 'I am very glad that I only got a second class, for I should have thought very poorly of the school if I had got a first.'

To C. A. Potter

'I may observe by the way that my second in Law and History was to me no disappointment. I clearly knew when I went in that I should get no more, and so did not expect it. I have not read a bit this term, partly from general feebleness of body, and partly that I found I could not really

trouble to cram facts which were of no importance in my
eyes except as illustrating theories, and which I consequently
could not remember except in such connexions as they first
struck me—connexions which it by no means followed that
the examiners should appreciate with equal clearness. A
very little extra trouble would have got me a first : if I had
to do it over again I should no doubt take that additional
trouble : as it is, my only regret is at not having pleased the
governor more.'

Though reading for the Law and Modern History
School had filled him with new interests, to which he was to
remain faithful through life, he was always glad that his
intellectual training had been gained by reading for the
School of Litteræ Humaniores ; nothing, he thought, could
fit a man better for any form of intellectual work afterwards.

Mr. Jowett asked him to stand for a Fellowship at Balliol,
but he preferred to remain faithful to his own College if they
would have him, and stood for a Fellowship at Merton at the
end of 1866. The open Fellowship was given to a Christ
Church man, and Creighton was offered a clerical Fellowship with immediate prospect of tutorial work. He did not
hesitate to accept this, as his intention had always been to
take Orders ; indeed, he did not even feel it worth while to
mention the fact that his was a clerical Fellowship when
writing immediately after the election.

To R. T. Raikes   'Oxford : December 22, 1866.

'My dear Robin,—I just scribble you a line because I
think it may interest you generally to know that I have got
a Fellowship. . . . It is now five, and the election took
place at two. I passed a morning of anxious expectation
in about as much misery as possible. . . . Do you know
already I feel an old, old man ? I have been selecting rooms
in College . . . also I have been settling lectures for next
term, and generally looking profound on all sorts of subjects,
together with paying all manner of bell-ringing people.'

There was then no History Tutor in Merton, and Creighton
was at once asked to undertake the historical teaching, as well
as some work for the Great Schools and the Pass Schools.
He gave his first lectures in the following term still wearing
his scholar's gown, as there had not been an opportunity

for him to take his degree. Among his first pupils were Copleston, and another man of the same standing, who also became an intimate and lifelong friend, Robert Bridges of Corpus, the poet.

Of his most intimate undergraduate friends none but Copleston remained up in Oxford; but he never forgot a friend, and kept up close relations with many of them. In 1867 one of the great sorrows of his life came upon him in the sudden death of W. Foster, who died alone at Rome of cholera. I record this here because it seemed to him to be the close of his undergraduate life.

To R. T. Raikes

'If there was anyone about whose future career I seemed to myself certain, it was Will. I thought I should in after days so often see him, and looked forward to many a meeting with him. I feel quite as you do that his loss puts a gulf between me and the past : in all my undergraduate recollections he cannot but form a central figure. Oh, Robin, it seems very hard, and very hard to understand.'

In 1866 Will Foster had written of himself, 'Humblest and least worthy of the society [the Quadrilateral] as I am, I have at least the glory of being the string on which the three pearls hang, the link which first cemented it together.' And so he remained a link to bind many besides the special four together ; ever rousing bright and loving memories in the hearts of all who knew him.

CHAPTER III

FELLOW AND TUTOR

THE Oxford of 1867, when Creighton first became Fellow and
Tutor, was in many respects very different from the Oxford of
1900. The days of married Fellows had not begun ; and
the advantages of Oxford as a residential place had not been
discovered. The Parks were only just being laid out, and
very few villas were to be seen on the roads which stretched
out into the country. Young Oxford was then, as perhaps
it still is, clever, omniscient, literary ; but the keen interest in
social questions which stirred Oxford some fifteen years later,
had not yet shown itself.

The University took little or no part in civic matters.
T. H. Green, who about this time was becoming prominent
as a Tutor of Balliol, was one of the first among University
men to realise his responsibility as a citizen of Oxford and
take part in the affairs of the city, an example which has
since been largely followed. In theological quarters the
storms raised by the appearance of 'Essays and Reviews' in
1861, by the disputes over Jowett's salary as Greek Professor
(1860–1865), and by the Bishop Colenso controversy in 1862,
had passed away. They had left a feeling of uneasiness and
suspicion. Dr. Pusey was looked upon as a mysterious
power; it was known that he was privately consulted by
many, and wielded in consequence a far-reaching authority,
and he and his followers were apt to be suspected of having
some ulterior object in whatever policy they pursued. Ritual
controversies continued to disturb the country, but there was
no special trouble at Oxford, and purely academic questions
were not again mixed up with theological disputes, but were
fought out on their own merits. The prevailing intellectual
atmosphere of Oxford was distinctly non-theological rather

than anti-theological. Probably one of the chief causes of intellectual agitation was the supposed opposition between science and religion. The old views as to the creation and the position of man in the animal world, had been rudely shaken by the revelations of the comparatively new science of geology, and by the publication of Darwin's great work on 'The Origin of Species.' So unsettled were men's minds that Dr. Pusey wrote in 1871 : 'The fight is . . . as to the existence of a Personal God, the living of the soul after death, or whether we have any souls at all.' It is perhaps hard to realise now how great was the unrest, how deeply shaken the very foundations of religion seemed to be.

Creighton, though a true lover and careful observer of nature, was never much attracted by scientific studies ; and he was not seriously affected by these controversies. His was not a mind to be troubled because at the onset it might seem difficult, or even impossible, to harmonise seemingly conflicting truths. He saw that, wonderful though the revelations of natural science might be, it could not, as he said many years later, 'prescribe limits to all other investigations and admit of no methods save its own. . . . Man has further questions to ask, to which no answer can be given by the methods known to natural science.'[1] He held then, what is now much more generally recognised, that there is no real antagonism between science and religion, so long as each remains within its proper sphere. His views on the question are further illustrated by the following extracts from letters.

'Merton : November 17, 1871.

' It seems to me, even if science proved ever so clearly that there was no force without matter, still the extension of that from things that can be observed to things which cannot be observed, e.g. the soul and God, would seem to me to be a step to which my reason would by no means compel me. Science always seems to me to forget that it is concerned only with things observed, and however much it may play upon men's minds to get them to extend principles from the natural world to the spiritual, it only does so by appealing to one of the lowest of man's intellectual qualities, viz. his desire for simplicity rather than for truth. Science is now in exactly the same position as metaphysics was in the Middle Ages—

[1] Address at the Birmingham Church Congress, 1893.

then men were content to speculate, and never took the trouble
to observe the simplest things : now science is content to observe things outside man, and is angrily intolerant of any yearn-
ing attempt man makes to get inside himself. " You fool, what
are you doing there ? Shut the door, and go back to your
retort and microscope." . . . I shall go on falling more and
more behind the age till the day comes when Bastian is
made dictator and orders me to be burnt for views pernicious
to the well-being of society.'

'November 20, 1871.

' Our position towards science is to accept its truths and
disregard its hypotheses. In morals or in the mental sciences
it is not so : there all is relative, and every scrap of knowledge
helps the individual who possesses it, but scraps of science
only mislead, and the untrained mind confuses hypotheses
with law. . . . I quoted A——'s two positions to Esson on
Saturday : he was quite angry : he said, " What is force—what
is matter ? Science does not know, perhaps never will know :
they are mere names to cover certain things : we call certain
effects *force* ; but how are we to know that we ever get to all
effects ? How can we be sure we have exhausted all causes
in nature ? The man of real knowledge would never argue
from small hypotheses." He was far from thinking that science
could be a gospel ; and on sounding him I gathered he
thought that science tended to make those who studied it
profoundly indifferent to the question of God, and the soul,
and so on : not that it gave them any ground to affirm or
deny them, but it tended to show them enough to make life
tolerable without them.'

Side by side with the tendency towards materialism produced by the wonders of modern scientific discovery, went
the æsthetic movement which aimed at making this life at
least a thing of beauty. Æstheticism was strong in Oxford
owing to the presence of Walter Pater, one of its most gifted
exponents. Pater was thoroughly consistent in his love of
beauty, and in his earliest writings maintained that the poetic
passion, the desire for beauty, the love of art for art's sake,
will enable a man to gain the greatest number of pulsations
of pleasure in the little interval before death takes him.
Creighton had considerable sympathy with the æsthetic
movement. He wore neck-ties made of Helbronner's beautiful silks, and began to collect objects of art. But æstheticism
was to him neither a gospel nor a fashion. He had a genuine

delight in beautiful things, and liked to surround himself with them. But his taste was always both catholic and individual, not limited by the traditions or fancies of any particular school, and he indulged it solely for his own delight.

In politics young Oxford was in those days chiefly Liberal. It had been a great shock when, at the general election of 1865, Mr. Gladstone, who had represented the University since 1847, was thrown out by a Tory candidate. His defeat was mainly owing to the new regulation according to which voting papers could be sent by post. This gave a preponderance to the votes of the non-residents; the majority of the residents, including Pusey and Liddon as well as Jowett and Pattison, were in favour of Gladstone.

It was an age of reform, and reform in Oxford meant the emancipation of the University from the control of the Church. It followed that the Tory party and the Church were allied in resisting reforms in this direction. The Liberal party in the University was held together by the movement for the abolition of religious tests. The Act of 1854, which followed on the University Commission of 1850, had abolished religious tests on matriculation and on taking the B.A. degree; but the Liberals in both Universities wished to proceed further and abolish all theological restrictions on degrees. Petitions to this effect were sent up from Oxford in 1863 and 1868; and after a contest which lasted nine years, the Government in 1871 passed a measure through Parliament abolishing all University tests. The measure was viewed with much alarm by Dr. Pusey and others of his party, as likely to lead to the entire secularisation of the University, and its destruction as a place suited for the education and training of the clergy of the Church of England. Creighton, never a lover of restrictions, and at all times profoundly convinced of the paramount importance of liberty, was in favour of the abolition of tests. To him a University was primarily a place dedicated to the pursuit of knowledge; and the plea that nothing should be done to make Oxford less specially adapted to be a training place for the clergy in particular would have had little weight with him. But he took no active part in promoting the measure, beyond a sympathetic interest.

Not only with regard to the abolition of tests, but in all directions there was at this time an anxious desire for reform within the University. The Act of 1854 had done much to sweep away abuses ; it had converted the University into a place of education, and had devoted its revenues partly to subsidise teachers and partly to scholarships and prizes to incite young men to be taught. The influence of these changes had done much to heighten the standard of education in England in general. But the results of the altered system did not give entire contentment to those who worked it. There were great activity and zeal among the teachers, and these very qualities helped to make them find their work unsatisfying. During the years which followed Creighton's election to a Fellowship, a feverish desire for change seemed to possess the University, and the most varied opinions prevailed among the reformers. Creighton described life in Oxford as like 'life in a house which always has the workmen about it.' Another, who had left Oxford for a most laborious post in practical life, said : 'I can never come to Oxford for a holiday ; it is far too busy a place for that. It seems to me to be perpetual motion and no progress.'

Among the leading men in Oxford were Benjamin Jowett (elected Master of Balliol in 1870) and Mark Pattison (elected Rector of Lincoln in 1861). Jowett's aim was to make the University more fitted to train those who were to play a part in the world afterwards, and with this view he tried to bring Oxford more into touch with the outer world. The attention which his Sunday parties excited shows that at that time the intercourse between Oxford and the great world of society was not so frequent as he and others helped it to become. Pattison, on the other hand, looked upon the University as primarily a place of learning. He put forward his views in 1868 in a 'Memoir on Academical Reorganisation.' At first they met with but little favour ; but the principles which he there laid down germinated slowly, and an increasing number of persons in the University became ready to recognise the claims of research and to urge its endowment.

The teachers of Natural Science were also anxiously bringing forward their demands for more consideration in a university which till then had done but little to include in its organisation the necessary machinery for their studies. The New Museum and the Physical Laboratories in the Parks were the visible fruits of their exertions.

Dr. Pusey and his friends by the foundation of Keble College in 1868, laboured to counteract in some measure what they considered the general secularisation of Oxford, and to insure the existence of at least one decidedly Church of England college. The activity of the University in these years was also shown by the new buildings of more or less pretension, by which many colleges increased their accommodation for students. At the same time a class of unattached students was created, with the view of extending the advantages of university teaching to those who could not afford the expense of college life.

The Oxford Local Examinations had been started in 1857, and the germ of the University Extension movement could be seen in the formation in various towns of Associations for Promoting Higher Education, to which university men gave courses of lectures. In these ways Oxford was exercising an increasing influence on education in the country at large.

Within the University itself, the predominant influence of John Stuart Mill in matters of thought was slowly passing away, to be superseded by that of Herbert Spencer. At the same time the philosophy of Comte, which was brought forward by Richard Congreve and his pupils at Wadham, had attracted considerable attention. This was counteracted by the growing influence of the teaching of T. H. Green, who began to lecture at Balliol in 1866. He was a disciple of Hegel, and though his power was of slow growth, probably no teacher of his time made a deeper impression on the thought of the most serious among the undergraduates. A decided Liberal in politics and in secular matters generally, his influence made for a less negative attitude in theology than the influence of Mill or Herbert Spencer.

It was thus at a time of great intellectual activity within the University that Creighton began his career as Fellow and Tutor. There may have been too much restlessness and desire for change, there certainly was a tendency to treat everything as an open question, which led to a general sense of insecurity in matters of opinion, but the intellectual atmosphere was free from the bitter party strife which had distracted the University some few years before.

Creighton did not take much part in university politics. 'He always had,' says a contemporary, 'rather a contempt for the business side of Oxford life, for the meetings and committees, and for the type of man that was wrapped up in them.' He groaned over the long College meetings, and used to spend the weary hours they occupied in writing letters, while managing at the same time to attend sufficiently to what he called 'the flow of the Warden's dulcet eloquence.' His energies were mainly given to the improvement of the history teaching and to the work of his own College. The year that he became Fellow, Merton lost its most distinguished member by Mr. Caird's acceptance of a Glasgow Professorship. The health of Mr. William Sidgwick, the brilliant Senior Tutor, was not good, and before long it became necessary for him to give up much of his work. The Warden was growing very old; he was a survival of a former state of things, in temper and tastes an old-fashioned country gentleman, whose main ambition for the College was that it should be filled with young men of good county families. Among the Fellows the two most prominent perhaps were Mr. George Brodrick (afterwards Warden of the College), and Mr. C. S. Roundell, both non-residents, though they often visited Oxford and took a real share in College affairs. As they were men of decided intellectual and political interests, their visits did much to keep the Common Room talk from becoming absorbed by subjects of merely local importance. In 1860 there had been hardly any Common Room life at Merton. Perhaps some three of the junior Fellows dined in Hall, but the rest dined alone in their own rooms. By degrees the College had grown more sociable, and the Common Room became famous for its brilliant talk. Oxford contained few better talkers than Mr. W. Sidgwick, and a contemporary says that Creighton soon challenged his hitherto unquestioned conversational primacy in the Common Room. Mr. C. L. Shadwell (Fellow of Oriel) writes:

'I remember the rapidity with which he rose to be the dominant spirit in his own College. Merton was already a brilliant, active, lively, sociable College; but when he came to join the Common Room, he seemed to step easily into the first place.'

The College was for those days decidedly secular in character. Dr. Talbot (Bishop of Rochester) remembers that when he dined there he felt the tone very uncongenial. The Warden was then the only lay head in Oxford, and there were many laymen among the Fellows; Mr. W. Sidgwick laid aside his Orders about this time; the most prominent member of the teaching staff, Mr. Esson (now Savilian Professor of Geometry), was a layman; and some of the older Fellows, though in Orders, belonged to the old-fashioned type of clerical Fellows. The most noteworthy among them was Mr. H. M. Wilkins, a first-rate scholar, and the author of many very successful school books. He was almost absolutely deaf, and in consequence lived the life of a recluse. But he liked to entertain his friends at sumptuous lunches and dinners, when he gave them rare and precious wines to drink, and indulged in witty and often cynical comments on his fellow-creatures. He took great interest in the College kitchen and wine cellar, and agitated for reforms in their management with the same seriousness and zeal as others gave to reforms in the Schools or the Church.

Among the clerical Fellows the most prominent was Mr. N. Freeling, an Oxford parish priest, whose saintly life and character won him universal respect and made him a man of weight in College councils. Mr. T. L. Papillon, a scholar of Balliol, had been elected Fellow of Merton the year before Creighton, and with many common opinions as to the needs of the College, they worked together most harmoniously as colleagues till Papillon left in 1868 for a Rugby mastership.

Creighton was called upon to take up full tutorial work after only the brief pause of the Christmas vacation. He had had less than six months in which to study modern history, before he was called upon to teach it; so that he had to continue his studies and carry on his teaching side by side. The Christmas vacation was spent in preparing lectures for the coming term.

To R. T. Raikes   'Merton: February 19, 1867.

'As for myself, I am pretty hard worked, and find it hard to succeed in seeing all the people I should like to see. . . . I am now simply scribbling in a hurry, and with a distinct consciousness that I ought to be reading some Roman History with a view to lecturing thereon. I find myself very comfortable in my new capacity, and am treated with all possible kindness and forbearance both by my colleagues and by the undergraduates.'

'March 17, 1867.

'I am looking forward with feelings of some pleasure to the end of term, which desirable consummation comes off in a week, and when I shall rest from my labours and take to my reading. I feel rather like an old pump at present— somewhat tired of perpetually spouting, and rather conscious that I have poured out much more than will ever be used for any good purposes.'

Many of his special friends were still up as undergraduates, and he did not change the nature of his relations with them. 'The P., though the best of dons,' writes W. Foster, 'is yet very much occupied, and has to divide his attentions when at leisure among many friends.' He continued to interest himself in the College boat, and in the summer of 1867 he and Papillon rowed in the Merton eight to fill up the crew. After that they confined themselves to coaching the boat, and joined the crew known as the Ancient Mariners, which consisted of a number of graduates from different colleges who rowed together for exercise.

Though all his friends agree in describing Creighton as a man who changed extraordinarily little throughout his life, this was a period of great moral and intellectual development for him. He was for the first time independent, and possessed of what for a man with his habits were ample means. He was beginning to grow conscious of his powers, and was coming out from the narrow circle of undergraduate life into a larger sphere. It seems as if at first he was inclined to indulge too much his tendency to sarcastic criticism, and to an intellectual contempt which later on he condemned with perhaps all the greater severity, because he knew from personal experience its temptations. The following letters from an intimate friend throw some light on the phase through which he was passing.

'August 8, 1867.

'My dear P.,—I will not have you speak disparagingly of everybody, notably of everybody whom you think a "fool." I shall probably have that cognomen tacked instantly on your regard of me, but I cannot help it. I will enter a solemn protest for once. Now you do not really mean it; if you did, it would be more pardonable. We are told that all men are liars, we are nowhere told that all men are fools. . . . Well, whether you mean it or not, you certainly do not act up to it Do you not verily take to your all-containing heart divers whom I should distinctly dignify with the obnoxious title? . . . What does this imply? Either that you treat your fellow beings as playthings . . . or that the actions of your heart are far kinder than the words of your mouth. . . . I think, P., that you are the strangest compound of grimness and tenderness that I ever saw or conceived. . . .'

'September 8, 1867.

'I think, my dear Mentor, that the reason why people give you the impression that they do not take so much interest in you as they ought, is just because you are my dear Mentor. You seem to stand on a sort of pinnacle raised above the ordinary British mortal (which, thank God, is true enough), in such a self-contained manner as to make no demand upon people's sympathies. You, who seem so much older than your years, seem so strong and bold and great, that men pay you an unconscious compliment when they avoid speaking to you about yourself. You do not seem to need it. Mortals would come to you to give you their confidence, but would scarcely ask for yours in return, simply because they would be almost afraid.'

Unfortunately his answers to these letters have not been preserved; but the following letter to another friend shows what he felt.

'October 4, 1867.

'I have come back from my travels in many respects a wiser man; but I am at present much perplexed and troubled in my mind. It has just begun to dawn upon me now that my actions and sayings are of any consequence: before, I used to think they mattered to no one outside the walls of Merton and to few inside, but now I see that I cannot hold that theory any more—that I am seriously responsible for all I do, and so I feel a need of broader sympathies. You know that up to this time I have been careless on this point—that I have liked a few, have looked on the majority of men with indifference and on some with contempt. Is this right?

How far is one answerable to oneself alone for one's actions?
How far is one answerable to every one whom those actions
may even remotely concern? How far is one's own conscience to be identified with ideal truth? How far with
narrow prejudices gathered in one's past life, and still
narrower traditions thrust upon one without thought at all,
and the entire mixture well seasoned with selfishness? I think
this last is no unfair analysis of what many people call their
" conscience." Whether it be mine or not, I dare scarcely ask
myself. Please tell me your views on the subject : tell me if
you think me liable to be narrow and prejudiced and selfish,
and tell me on what subjects, that so I may strive to amend.'

Though his intention to be ordained was unchanged, he
no longer retained the extreme High Church views which he
had held as an undergraduate. This made some of those
who had sympathised with him before, and regarded him as
one of themselves, feel anxious lest he was drifting away
altogether, whilst those who only knew him slightly did not
realise that he cared much about religion at all. His social
gifts made him a welcome guest in many common rooms, and
his circle of friends and acquaintances constantly increased.
He was at no time cautious as to what he said.

'Fascinating as he was in his talk,' says Canon Scott
Holland, ' he always in those days, and, I fancy, to the last,
treated conversation as a glorious game, an intellectual frolic,
into the fictions and conventions of which he would fling himself without any after-thoughts as to consequences, playing
the game with gusto, for the joy of liberating his faculties in
the keen amusement of a gymnastic exercise. As a game it
was delightful. It allowed him to throw off the burden of
responsibility. But it was only a game that he was playing,
like a conjuror tossing magic balls.' [1]

A contemporary and friend writes :

' We all talked freely and often flippantly in those days.
We were not irreligious, still less libertine in thought or
action, but intellectual moods and phases interested us more
than religious experiences. We assumed perhaps that all
sensible men were of the same religion, and that all sensible
men kept their religion to themselves, and we persuaded
ourselves that a hazy and rather nonchalant agnosticism
was the mental attitude of all. If a man showed a marked

[1] Memorial sermon preached in St. Paul's Cathedral, January 20, 1901.

inclination to orthodoxy, we regarded it as a sign of intellectual inferiority, and being young we assumed of course that no other point of view was possible than that which we occupied ourselves. I think Creighton never yielded to this dominant mood of negative dogmatism. His mind moved in an orbit of its own, a much wider orbit than that in which we moved under a prevalent attraction which affected him very little Essentially historical rather than speculative, he saw sooner and more clearly than we did, how much there was of transient in a theory of life and thought which we regarded as final. I am sure that in his innermost thought he must have laid more stress on the spiritual side of human nature than we did ; but we did not talk much about such things in those days, and as he had little sympathy with mere external and mechanical orthodoxy, I think he often reverted to paradox in order to conceal differences on which he did not care to insist. He never wore his spiritual heart on his sleeve, and for this reason many thought he had none to wear.'

This reserve as regards his real opinions, combined with his enjoyment of paradox and an inclination to what seemed to many flippancy in speech, led to his being much misunderstood at this time. Some of those who in earlier intimacy had seen something of his deeper self, felt anxious and puzzled. Others who only knew him superficially, and who had listened to his conversational extravagances, had no suspicion of the real seriousness beneath. Few recognised that, a true Cumbrian at bottom, he was fundamentally then, as always, a man of profound and proud reserve. His easy sympathetic sociability, his humour and his ready powers of expression, absolutely disguised this fundamental reserve.

Dr. Copleston says ' he allowed himself at this time to be seriously misunderstood ; ' people spoke of ' the outer veil of paradox ' which had to be pierced before one got to the real man. Some words he wrote in 1871 help to explain what he was striving after.

' I am weak if you like, but always sincere : I talk to a man as I feel inclined, which pleases me, or as I think he would like, which pleases him : the process is purely emotional. A little while after, some one talks to me on the same subject, a different train of thought comes into my mind, I form rational and clear views where all was hazy : I say something quite opposite to what I assented to half an hour

ago. Am I a humbug? I only know I mean to be sincere—
I am honest in both utterances. All that can be laid to my
charge is, that I am not consistent : i.e. that I did not grasp
the sum total of knowledge in my cradle, and exhaust all
mental processes in my infancy.'

I think that one reason why he was often misunderstood,
both then and in after life, was that he never troubled about
what people thought of him. He was absolutely unself-
conscious, and had that kind of simplicity, produced by a want
of self-consciousness, with which no one ever credits a clever
man, and which sometimes leads to his being called egotistical.
He was too much interested or amused by the subject he was
discussing, by the ideas he was playing with, to consider
whether he was shocking his hearers or not. If anything
humorous occurred to him, it had to come out; he did not
stop to ask himself whether it might be misunderstood. But
it is certain that he puzzled people.

'Dull and solemn people,' writes Mr. J. R. Thursfield,
'thought him flippant : shallow people thought him insincere.
No man of his time was so constantly, so freely, and so
variously canvassed, not always favourably but invariably as
a rare and strange portent, not to be readily classified in any
familiar category of human nature. I remember that once,
on a tour in Holland with two friends, we talked of him daily
and never exhausted the subject ; and years afterwards I was
told that it had become so much the custom to discuss him
at the shooting lodge of one of his friends in Scotland, that
some one proposed in fun to levy a fine on any one who mentioned his name.'

Merton was not in a very satisfactory condition when
Creighton became tutor. A spirit of insubordination had
prevailed since the disturbance over the great bonfire in
1865, and the dons hoped that Creighton would be able to
help to bring about a better state of things. His position
was not altogether easy, for he had still many intimate friends
among the undergraduates whom he was called upon to
reduce to greater order. He had no intention of giving up
his friendships, and was in and out of the undergraduates'
rooms as much as possible. This led to some misunderstanding. The undergraduate mind could not understand a don
who would walk or talk with him in the afternoon, sometimes

with his arm on his shoulder as his custom was, and yet
punish him for some misdemeanour at night. Even one of
his most intimate friends remembers being 'silly enough to
be rather angry with him, because he did not get off some
youngsters who were gated for an assault on some one's windows.' This mixture of friendliness and sternness continued
to puzzle some of the undergraduates during the whole of
Creighton's career as a don. When he remonstrated, he
appealed to reason and good feeling rather than to authority.
'Do you not think you are a great fool?' he said to a conceited youth, and then left him to answer the question for
himself. Whether they understood him or not, the undergraduates could not help seeing that he understood them.

His own feelings on the subject are shown in the following
extracts from letters written some years later.

'Merton College, Oxford: May 3, 1871.

'. . . I am at present in the state of a man much bored, as
I shall have to execute to-morrow summary justice on some
young men, who, beguiled by the clearness of the nights, and
the general delights of a summer term, exceeded proper limits
in the making of noise last night. It is a nuisance being in
the position of trying to raise a standard and elevate a society;
it cannot be done without acts of harshness to individuals
which cost me much effort; nothing is more awful than the
application of a rigid system of law. My spirits have been
depressed in consequence.'

'May 4.

'I have had to say very unpleasing things to-day; to wit,
to send a young man down for making a noise: he has just
parted from me in by no means a Christian state of mind
after denouncing violently my policy and conduct. You had
better not inquire about my character from any of the undergraduates of my College while you are here, or you will find
me denounced in most glowing terms as a tyrant of the blackest
dye. To establish law and order in a college is by no means
an easy matter; but you know I rather enjoy fighting a battle
of that kind, and am absolutely impervious to any displays
of temper or indignation; still, it is a bore. Why can't people
behave as they ought to?'

'Merton College: November 17, 1871.

'You don't remember, don't you, how, when you were in
Oxford in May, I was bored by having a fearful quarrel with
all my undergraduates? Yet I don't think I let it prey

much on my spirits, undesirable from every point of view as it was ; and if it had gone a little farther it would have made an end of my Oxford career.   At the time I knew quite clearly it would blow over, and so did not very much care, though I knew that for some time by forty men and all their friends my name would be greeted with execrations.   What makes me think of this is, that this afternoon I was having a walk with one of my bitterest foes then, who tends to think now apparently that I am a well-meaning but misguided person.   I let him think as he likes : I only know I won.'

One of his former undergraduate pupils writes : ' His power of understanding young people was a great source of strength to him, and enabled him to preserve perfect authority.   I believe that he read us undergraduates like open books.   He was not always complimentary, but I am sure that he understood us.'

An undergraduate who came up to Merton shortly after Creighton took his degree writes :

' He always interested himself in the rowing and other amusements of the College, and thus gained a real influence among the more or less idle men.   His influence in the College was very great.   He never forgot that he was a don, and yet he always treated us as his personal friends, and I remember many occasions when a few quiet merrily sarcastic words from him stopped things which we at the time thought amusing, but which we afterwards knew did neither us nor the College any good.   The wildest men of our set would bow to a word from him, when if any other don had interfered it would certainly have increased the trouble.   His idea of discipline was not to be a schoolmaster, but to make it more a matter of gentlemanly behaviour and " common sense " (a favourite expression of his which often made us feel very foolish), and I think this was one of the causes of his great success, and of the sincere affection and admiration we all had for him.'

Creighton's intimate knowledge of the life of the under-graduates made him keen about a number of reforms which he was soon in a position to carry out.   Mr. Robert Wilson had been elected Fellow of Merton at Christmas, 1867, and was appointed Junior Bursar.   Creighton, who had been elected Junior Dean in 1868, was made Principal of the Postmasters

in 1869, an office which corresponds to that of Senior Tutor in
other colleges.   In Mr. Robert Wilson he found a colleague
with whom he was entirely in sympathy, and during all his
years in Oxford they worked together in pursuit of the same
aims for the good of the College.   One of their desires was to
diminish the expenses of the undergraduates, and improve the
domestic organisation of the College.   For the first time the
dons recognised their responsibility for the expenditure of
the men, and a number of sumptuary bye-laws were passed in
1869 by a committee appointed for the purpose.   Private
dinners in men's rooms were forbidden, and a limit fixed to
the expenditure on breakfasts and lunches.

The laborious and lengthy business of reforming the
kitchen was next undertaken.   Creighton and Wilson undertook it mainly for economic reasons, and were warmly supported by Mr. Wilkins on culinary grounds.   Mr. Wilkins
took the matter very seriously.   Creighton writes on the
subject :

' Since dinner I have been having a conversation with
Wilkins, the deaf man : the process is rather severe, as all
one's remarks have to be written on a slate.   He expatiated
on the need of reform in the College kitchen, and we shed
common tears over the fact that our cook could not make a
bisque d'écrevisses or a *suprême de volaille* : that he had not a
truffle on the premises, and other interesting topics. I sketched
a gigantic scheme of reform to be inaugurated some day, and
he seemed happier in contemplating it.   I felt myself a fearful hypocrite, as I did not care two straws about the matter.'

In the end Mr. Wilkins composed a lengthy and eloquent
statement on the defects of the kitchen and the cellar, which
he entrusted to Creighton to read at the College meeting, while
he sat by, following the reading which he could not hear, and
chuckling when his favourite points were made.   The kitchen
reforms were not completed till 1872, when the system which
still prevails was inaugurated.

Before his day, each tutor had done as seemed good in
his own eyes, but Creighton now tried in every possible way to
bring them together.   He instituted a common breakfast and
lunch, intended at first for the tutors only, but the other resident
Fellows soon took to coming also.   He arranged weekly

tutors' meetings to discuss the work and conduct of the undergraduates. At the beginning of term the tutors divided the freshmen among them. Each undertook the men reading for honours in his own subject, as well as a certain number of passmen. Creighton took the history men, and lectured on the history required for Litteræ Humaniores, and to passmen generally.

Experience soon led him to see how much the history teaching would gain if there could be co-operation between the teachers in the various colleges. The first experiment of this kind had been tried by Mr. Esson in connexion with the teaching of mathematics, just about the time when Creighton became Fellow ; but he acted without authorisation from the College, and met with some disapproval in consequence. According to existing arrangements, a student could only attend the lectures of the history tutor in his own college, or of a University professor ; if he needed teaching in historical subjects which they could not give, he had to engage a private coach. Creighton and Esson now joined in obtaining authorisation for a system of intercollegiate lectures from a College meeting held in February 1868. In consequence, the history tutors of Merton, Oriel, and Corpus threw open their lectures to the undergraduates of these three colleges. Other colleges soon joined, and in 1869 an Association of Tutors was formed, which, beginning with the tutors of six colleges, included before long all the history teachers in the University. They met together once a term to arrange lectures for the following term, so as to cover all the teaching required for the History Schools. In 1874 it was agreed that the members of the Association should periodically dine together, and Dr. Bright (now Master of University) gave the first, and Creighton the second, dinner.

A great stimulus had been given to historical studies in Oxford by the appointment in 1866 of Dr. Stubbs as Regius Professor of Modern History. Creighton was glad to work under his leadership, and to aid, both by example and guidance, in giving the Oxford Historical School that turn in the direction of solid research which is still its leading characteristic. Writing in 1892 a retrospect of these years, he said :

'With Stubbs began the scientific pursuit of modern history, as he impressed his views upon us younger men. We worked out among us a scheme of lectures covering the whole field, and were the pioneers of the " Intercollegiate Lectures" which now prevail at both Universities. The needs of this scheme threw upon me the ecclesiastical, and especially the papal history, which no one else took.'

Before the Act of 1854, the academical reformers, who laboured to improve the teaching at the University, had aimed primarily at increasing the number of professors. This had led to a general extension of the professorial method of teaching, and in Creighton's teaching days the leading tutors became, to all intents and purposes, professors, and lectured to large classes in their college halls. The development of the intercollegiate system increased this tendency, and led, in consequence, to considerable discussion as to the part left to professors in the educational work of the University. Writing on the subject, shortly after leaving Oxford,[1] Creighton said :

'It is difficult at present to know what a professor ought to do. On all sides complaints are heard that the professors' lectures are unattended. This has become more and more the case lately, owing partly to the fact of greater energy among tutors, and partly to the greater organisation of college lectures. Knots of colleges combine for lecturing purposes, and so every undergraduate has a large choice of lectures which he may attend. The object of college lectures is to prepare men for the University examinations. College tutors are engaged in this as their chief object, and are therefore more likely to be adepts at the tricks and knacks requisite for that purpose than is the professor of maturer years and larger knowledge. As examinations have increased in intensity, the art of preparing men for them has become more and more of a trade. In earlier days, when colleges were more negligent, many professors, such as Mr. Jowett and Mr. Goldwin Smith, gave a most valuable stimulus to teaching, and stirred up college tutors to greater activity. But now the tutors are alive and alert, . . . the professors, even if they wished to do so, would hardly succeed in competing with them in the art of preparing for the Schools. . . . The professors rarely attempt to teach solely

---

[1] Paper on 'The Endowment of Research' (*Macmillan's Magazine*, 1876).

with reference to the examinations, and if they attempt to do so they fail, because, with much greater knowledge and far wider experience, they still cannot do it so well as those whose trade it is. The professors, on the other hand, try to lecture on subjects, or parts of subjects, which have no direct bearing on the examinations : they have a very small audience. Nor is this surprising ; tutors and undergraduates alike are too busy to attend to anything except their own work. Such is the tyranny of the system of examinations that it often happens that professors, whose name alone would command a crowded audience if they were lecturing in any other town in England, lecture in Oxford to well-nigh empty benches.'

Having stated the problem, he proceeds to show how 'the only real function which remains for professors to accomplish is that of research,' and that, in consequence, 'the increase of the professoriate is to be looked upon as a desirable step only because it is another name for the endowment of research.' To recognise this as the primary object of the professoriate would, in his opinion, clear away many difficulties, and provide for that endowment of research for which Pattison and others were so urgently pleading. 'The duties of the professor must be primarily duties of research, not educational work. If this were clearly recognised, they would be saved from vain competition with college tutors,[1] and 'might be trusted to be willing and anxious to lecture whenever they could obtain a sympathetic audience.'

To Creighton himself, the necessity of teaching with reference to examinations was increasingly trying. On the one hand he was interested in research, in the pursuit of knowledge for its own sake ; on the other hand he was keenly interested in his pupils, and eager to kindle in them a thirst for knowledge. The examination system, he felt, could not do that, and was at best a means 'of stimulating young men

[1] He makes an exception in the case of the professors of the physical sciences, because the laboratories and museums which their studies require must be University buildings, and the University teachers must therefore have in their hands the chief part of the education in these subjects. Also, since bishops require the attendance of all ordination candidates at the lectures of the divinity professors, the latter must give the chief part of the education needed by theological students.

to acquire a great mass of varied information, and to develop readiness of thought and expression.' He always attempted, as far as possible in his own lectures, to lead men on to study for themselves. He used to tell his hearers that they must not rely on him for correct facts and dates, those they could find in any text-book, but he wished to give them what they could not find for themselves. His lectures were never the mere contents of his note-books, read out slowly that his hearers might take them down easily. Neither were they carefully written out and polished. His plan was to have rather full notes, and then lecture extempore, with a quick delivery, but such perfectly clear enunciation that he was always easy to follow, though taking notes—and especially taking notes of his most striking and original utterances— was not so easy.

In those days there was not much attention given in Oxford to the style and manner of lecturing. Creighton happened to be once taken by his friend Robert Bridges, who was then studying medicine in London, to hear Sir William Savory lecture on Systematic Surgery at St. Bartholomew's Hospital. Savory's lucid style, his crisp sentences, his avoidance of everything slipshod, impressed him much, especially in comparison with the careless style of lecturing prevalent in Oxford. This led him to give much more attention to his own method. He always rather despised eloquence, and avoided carefully anything like wordiness or flowery speech. His aim was to be lucid, incisive, not so much to give information as to arouse interest, to make his hearers think, to show them the ideas which lie behind the facts of history, to get at the truth. He never used history as a vehicle for opinion. ' How fascinating it all was,' writes an old pupil ; 'how vivid and sparkling ! He never sacrificed truth to effect, but he never suffered even truth to be dull.' Dr. Knox (now Bishop of Manchester) writes :

' My own recollection of his lectures is that of the hall full of men from all colleges, listening with real attention to lectures which were quite unlike the typical Oxford lecture of the day. He made the old days live again : we saw and knew the actors in the scenes ; we understood the connexion

of events. Yet all was done with such ease and simplicity that it seemed as though any one might have delivered
the lectures.'

He soon began to attract large audiences, even on
subjects which were not of first importance in the Schools.
He writes, April 19, 1871 :

' To-day I began my lectures, and was at first frightened,
though afterwards gratified, to find my class for Italian
history numbered the huge amount of sixty-three. I began
originally by lecturing to four or five, they have gradually
increased to twenty, thirty, and forty, but sixty-three surpassed my wildest expectations.'

Always interested in women's education, he was one of
the first to admit women to his lectures : at first they had to
sit in the gallery of the hall, quite apart from the undergraduates. About 1870 he accepted invitations to give
courses of lectures to some of the newly formed Ladies'
Associations, and lectured on Dante and the Italian
Renaissance, in Clifton, Birmingham, and Falmouth.

His more individual work with his pupils was as
stimulating as his lectures. A fellow lecturer writes :

' I remember the quickness with which he discovered in
his pupils their possibilities of success, and the wisdom with
which he guided them into the lines which best fitted them.'

Among his pupils was Lord Randolph Churchill, who
came to Merton in 1867. Creighton early discerned his
ability, and was much interested in him. Churchill did not
forget his tutor, and wrote to him in 1883 :

' You are quite wrong to say that in my mind " you are only
a vague memory." Among several letters I have received,
yours has given me the greatest pleasure. It has always
been pleasant to me to think that the historical studies which
I too lightly carried on under your guidance have been of
increasing value to me in calculating and carrying out actions
which to many appear erratic, and if they ever lead to any
substantial result it will be owing to those years at Merton
when you alone so kindly and continually endeavoured to
keep me up to the mark. It is indeed a pleasure to me to
know that you have not forgotten your former rather unsatisfactory pupil, and that you follow, not without interest and

perhaps with some hope, a course of which fate has not yet determined the form or the end.'

The Rev. J. W. Diggle, a contemporary of Lord Randolph, writes:

' I shall never forget taking him my first essay. He read it in absolute silence, then he said: " This essay might easily have been worse : there are some good things in it, but good things in an essay don't make an essay good. A good essay ought to have a beginning and a middle and an end. This has a beginning and an end, but no middle. You must do better next time. You must learn to put a middle in, and you'll do all right." After that it was my weekly delight, at times mingled with a little trembling, to take my essay to him. When he " sat on " me, I liked it. Even his fault-finding was always so radiant, so light-bringing, so cynical and sardonic at times, yet always so absolutely true. And when you did even decently he praised quite generously ; though not forgetting, for the sake of sharpening your wits, to mix a little pepper with his praise.'

Another pupil writes :

' It was always a pleasure to work for and with him, and he had a most delightful way of correcting our mistakes, and in a half-joking manner making us see how simple were points which we could not understand. Instead of the usual dry lectures of other tutors, his were always bright, and we looked forward to them as a pleasure instead of trying to cut them. I have never forgotten how when I was in for Mods., and he saw I was treating it very casually, and was more interested in athletics, he asked me to his room one night, put me in an armchair with a pipe, and began to talk about athletics ; and then I suddenly found that I was having a most interesting talk on the athletic pursuits of the old Greek heroes, and so we passed to my Greek books, and I saw for the first time their great interest, and from that day I always loved my Homer. He often repeated his invitation, and, fond as I was of evening amusements, I always gave them up willingly for my talks with him. He generally had a kitten on his lap, and if I ever got sleepy or inattentive he used to throw it on to my knees.'

To a pupil, obliged to leave Oxford on account of ill health

' October 27, 1871.

' My dear Jebb,—Don't be discouraged, and don't expect your work to produce an immediate effect. First you have in reading history a number of detached facts, then you will find you long for principles to connect them, and your principles will seem to drive out the facts, and finally you will find the facts will begin to cluster round the principles, and you will have a knowledge both general and particular; on many points, however, you will necessarily know nothing, they are chinks which will have to be left for future filling in.

'Don't make abstracts of your books, but try to make a scheme of your subject and fill it in gradually.' He proceeds to give careful directions as to the books to be read, and ends, 'Let me hear again towards the end of term how you get on.'

Mr. Jebb writes, 1901:

'I have felt throughout my life since that I owed more to him in the way of intellectual help and stimulus than to any other person in the world. Not that I ever knew him intimately. My intercourse with him was simply that which all his other pupils enjoyed.

'No recollection of my life is stronger than that of sitting in his rooms at Merton while I read my essays to him. He was very fond of cats, and generally kept one on his knee, which he stroked while I read my essay to him. Then when I had finished came the clear and trenchant criticism, which never failed to throw a flood of new light on the subject of one's efforts.'

Creighton and Wilson were both anxious to enliven the Chapel services, and in 1869 they persuaded the more musical undergraduates to form a choir for the Sunday evening service. The men were willing enough to sing, but they hesitated at the idea of putting on surplices and entering chapel in a procession, for fear of the possible ridicule of their friends.

'But,' writes one of them, 'Creighton instantly saw the reason of our hesitation, and in his cheeriest and most helpful way brushed away our shyness; and after the first Sunday everyone was much pleased, and the service became a bright and cheerful one instead of a most dull routine.'

Up till 1864 the Holy Communion had only been celebrated twice a term in Chapel; in 1864 it was ordered to be celebrated four times, and in 1870 on every Sunday in term. Attendance at Chapel was compulsory during the whole of Creighton's time as Tutor, except for Nonconformists. In 1869 fines for non-attendance were abolished, and instead it was ordered that undergraduates guilty of non-attendance should be admonished by the Principal of the Postmasters. After persistent non-attendance they might be reported to the Warden for censure ; his habit under such circumstances was to exhort them to behave like gentlemen.

Early in 1868 Creighton moved into the rooms which he describes as ' very jolly, and to me probably a permanent residence for many years to come.' They were in the beautiful grey building which looks over Christ Church meadow, and consisted of a large room below, which he used as library, lecture-room, and dining-room, connected by a small private staircase with a sitting-room and bedroom above ; vines climbed the grey walls, and festooned his windows, which looked out over the meadows. In these rooms he had space to gratify his taste for beautiful things. He began to frequent old curiosity shops and to buy blue china and old oak. He bought with much care and deliberation, and was very proud of his purchases. The oak bookcases which he designed himself were added to year after year as his library grew, and he remained always faithful to his first pattern. His own views on the subject are expressed in a letter written in 1871.

'Merton College.

'I think it is quite as difficult to furnish a room as to form a character. A room ought to be an indication of the character of its inhabitants. All people err who fall into rules on the subject. I think, for instance, Lady B.'s drawing-room errs as being too colourless in that point : she has sought out abstract rules of combination of colours which are too subtle for the uneducated eye without an explanation, and has paid too little attention to the personal opinions of those who were to inhabit it : we come round again to the old view about the primal necessity of self-development. I was pleased to-day with Mrs. P., who was in my room, and said she approved of it very much because . . . it gave the effect of a thoroughly individual and masculine taste throughout. If my view is right, all that can be urged on the individual is the necessity, firstly, of thinking that a room is a matter of personal thought, not to be left to an upholsterer ; secondly, that a room ought to make for the good of those who habitually reside in it, and ought to accord with their tastes and interests.'

F 2

He was genuinely attached to his possessions, and perhaps partial in his liking for anything which belonged to him. But most of his early treasures were of real artistic merit and beauty, and remained with him to form at last the chief ornaments of his home at Fulham. This delight in furnishing was a new thing in those days ; even his college servants were interested in his rooms ; one of them once attended a sale in the vacation, and bought a number of fine blue china plates which he thought Creighton would like, and let him have them for the moderate price which he had given for them.

Creighton's were considered show rooms, and his friends brought their visitors to see them. He was always delighted to show hospitality, and many were the entertainments he gave. He invited the relations of his pupils when they were up, as well as the relations of his friends, and gave dinner parties to the increasing number of his acquaintances in Oxford. He was very particular about the arrangement of his flowers and his table, and attended to every detail himself. But his love for society in general did not increase. He writes :

'December 1868.

' I conclude that dining out is a weariness to the flesh, and also takes up a good deal of time.'

And to R. T. Raikes, just before paying him a visit :

' Please don't get me an invitation to a dance. I am, as you know, not fond of my fellow creatures in the abstract ; so please leave me at home to read a book in peace : I know you won't mind my perversities, I am a confirmed old fogey.'

He felt the rush of Oxford life a good deal. His strong personal interest in his pupils was in collision with his constant desire to study for himself. College affairs did not always go quite smoothly, and he speaks of himself at times as ' terribly bored and very busy.'

To R. T. Raikes 'Carlisle : April 3, 1868.

' As you observe in your last letter, the change from Oxford to Carlisle is considerable : the luxury of going to bed regularly at 10.30, and feeling you can lie in bed as long as you like—of living in a household of five persons, and knowing you need not talk to them unless you like, and would certainly be an arrant fool if you troubled to talk to anyone else—all this is indeed delightful to the wearied and wounded soul. I am getting surfeited of seeing so many people and talking so much, and with such sham profundity as I have to do at Oxford. I spend my days in reading English history, in taking a mild ride by myself, occasionally in playing whist.'

'Oxford : May 30, 1869.

' I am looking forward with exceeding great joy to the end of term, having a hunger for a little reading for myself, and a great desire to be able to peruse a book in the evening without feeling the necessity of lecturing on it the next morning.'

Part of his vacations he spent at Carlisle reading, or when possible quietly in Oxford. But he was now in a position to travel, and from 1867 onwards his favourite holiday was a ramble on the Continent. He began, like everyone else, with Switzerland ; and the descent of a few days into North Italy revealed to him the country which was to give him the keenest joys and deepest intellectual interests of his life.

To R. T. Raikes   'Pontresina : July 22, 1867.

' I took my first expedition among the ice in the shape of the ascent of Monte Rosa. About Alpine mountaineering the most enormous twaddle is talked : it is really very easy with a good guide, but without a guide of course it is impossible, or at least extremely dangerous. The real truth is, that the guide pulls you through all inevitable difficulties, and avoids all that can possibly be avoided. It also sounds very awful to be told that we were $13\frac{1}{2}$ hours in the ascent of Monte Rosa; but this includes halts every three hours for food, and also the pace is very slow, never more than $3\frac{1}{2}$ an hour over level, and in the steepest ascents it is very slow indeed, as the guide has to cut steps for you in the ice ; consequently the real fatigue is not so very enormous. . . . Switzerland is very stupendous, but I own that a week of mountains at a time is enough for me . . . the uniform white colour of the mountains palls upon one. Shape alone without colour will not make a landscape that can satisfy one for ever, I find. To descend into Italy was lovely. In a few hours we passed from extreme cold to extreme heat ; from the barren fir trees of the Alp to the lovely chestnuts, vines, olives, and acacias of an Italian valley ; from the chilling tints of the snow to the brilliant colours of an Italian climate : also from the ugly stupid faces of the Swiss to the finely moulded faces and quiet expressions of the Italians.   I liked Italy immensely, though the heat was so intense I was not sorry to get to more Alpine regions again.'

He used to tell an amusing incident in connexion with this journey.   One of his companions was Mr. W. Sidgwick, a member of the Alpine Club.   One morning they went out for a stroll together on a glacier with their ice axes, but without a guide.   They came to a difficult place, where it was necessary to cut every step in the ice, and deep crevasses opened on either side.   Sidgwick led the way, and Creighton had to follow ; it seemed to him extremely perilous, and as he put it, ' I had to screw my head on tight and grind my teeth, but I was not going to give in.'   They got over the dangerous part, and walked back to their hotel without a word on the subject.   Some time afterwards, in an Oxford common room men were talking over Alpine experiences, when Sidgwick said, ' I was never in real danger but once, and that was when I was with you, Creighton, on that glacier.' Creighton exclaimed in surprise that he had thought from Sidgwick's behaviour that he considered it quite an easy place, and so had not liked to show his own alarm.   ' By no means,' was the answer ; ' but when you, a mere novice, said nothing, and took it as something quite simple, I was not going to show that I was in a funk.'

This was the only time Creighton attempted high Alpine climbing.   He had found that he could do it, but it did not appeal to him.   He always said that above the line where the chestnuts grew, the mountains began to lose their charm for him.

After three weeks in Switzerland he went through South Germany to Dresden, where he settled down for a while with some men who had come there to read with him.   He writes :

'Dresden : September 20, 1867.

' I have been leading a happy life enough since last I wrote to you, and my studies of art and music have been progressing under the influence of a German climate.   Augsburg, Munich, Salzburg, the Salzkammergut, Vienna, and Prague have seen my face oft in their galleries and streets, and now Berlin alone awaits me ere I return to the land of my fathers.

We enjoy ourselves here greatly : we have a magnificent picture gallery for daily inspection, a very good opera for the rare occasions on which we take holidays. . . . I had a vain hope of learning German here, but find so little inducement, as everyone talks English quite well, that I have made little or no progress. I have succeeded in utterly ruining myself in purchases of photographs on my travels.'

In Dresden he heard some of Wagner's operas, then unknown in England, and he was the first to introduce Wagner to his musical friends in Carlisle, for whom he brought back some pianoforte arrangements of the operas. He took much pleasure in music, and attended concerts whenever he could. In the Long Vacation of 1868, after hearing 'Israel in Egypt' at the Crystal Palace Handel Festival, he rambled through the old towns in Belgium with a friend, and then up the Rhine to Heidelberg, where he waited for another friend.

To R. T. Raikes   'Heidelberg : July 10, 1868.

' You have no notion how nice it is travelling by oneself, instead of being always talking and generally excited. I now peruse my guide book calmly about far distant places till I almost begin to imagine myself there. I also occasionally wade through a page of German exercises. I smoke a good many pipes, and consume a good deal of the wine which this country produces, and which seems to me to be the most perfect wine made anywhere. In such occupations who would not be more than content?'

In 1869 he travelled in North Germany with H. J. Hood.

To Robert Bridges   ' Berlin : August 18, 1869.

' We have both of us gone a mucker in a copy of Mendel's lovely engraving of " La Bella " by Titian. This morning we went over the porcelain manufactory, and I need scarcely say that has hurried me to my ruin. . . . The only two things which have surprised me are the exceeding grandeur of the band in Hanover, and the exquisite beauty of a picture of " Adam and Eve " in Brunswick, about which critics squabble whether it is Giorgione or Palma : I am full of favour of the former.'

To R. T. Raikes   'September 14, 1869.

'Hood and I wandered in peace through Holland and North Germany, staying a fortnight in Dresden. We saw many pictures, heard much music, talked a certain amount of bad German to the natives, and of profound rubbish to one another. It was amusing : I should like to do it again.'

His great object on these journeys was to study art, and wherever he went he collected photographs and engravings. He now felt that for the present he had got all he wanted out of Northern Europe, and turned his thoughts to Italy. In the summer of 1870 Mr. Hood married, and asked Creighton to join him on his honeymoon in North Italy. The outbreak of the war between France and Germany made travelling uncertain. Creighton went slowly, as he did not wish 'to precipitate his meeting with Hood, for fear it should bore Mrs. Hood.'

To R. T. Raikes   'Aix-les-Bains: August 26, 1870.

' I want as much time as possible in Italy, and trust to see a good deal of Turin and Milan before I join Hood at Bellagio. . . . I am travelling at present *bona fide* for education in Italian language and art. . . . This is a most lovely place, and I have promptly added Piedmont and Savoy to my other prospective tours. . . . France is perfectly peaceful to pass through. I have met with no sign of animosity or of suspicion of any sort ; on the contrary, with the extremest courtesy from all the officials, even down to my cab driver in Paris. The people are, however, terribly depressed. Paris was fearfully listless, and here the people are very wrathful.'

Writing to a friend seventeen years afterwards, he recalls this time.

' I think I told you of that journey, which was to me most delightful. We all did as we liked. When they did not want me, they said so. When Hood did not want to go out, Mrs. Hood and I went our own way ; and at Venice we used to spend the evenings in playing whist with a dummy, and owing to our efforts Mrs. Hood is now a skilful player.'

This journey did much to fix the direction of his future tastes and studies. Books about art and the Italian Renaissance were then far from being so common as they have now become. Photographs were comparatively dear, and not as yet very good. Italy, except for the larger towns, was but little visited. Only the few in England read Dante. To Creighton a boundless field of study was opened out, which

exactly suited his natural tastes and inclinations. He had
found his subject, though it was some time before he defined
it.   At first the art of Italy attracted him almost more than
the history.   In March 1869, before a proposed visit to Mr.
Raikes, who was then married and settled in London, he had
written :

'I dimly purpose to spend much of my time in studying
(a) the National Gallery, (β) the sculptures and engravings
in the British Museum, and (γ) the pottery in the South
Kensington.   You see I have got a hobby ; it is what we all
come to.'

His tastes in art and literature were absolutely catholic.
He admired anything that was good of its kind, and objected
strongly to such criticism as savoured of narrowness and
exclusiveness.   He had a keen eye for seeing what were the
points of a picture, a statue, or a building.   'He of all men
whom I have known,' writes his friend the Rev. H. G. Woods,[1]
'took most to Italy, and therefore got most from it.'

He continued, as at all times in his life, to make new
friends.   He visited Mr. Alleyne at his home, and there made
acquaintance with his sisters, and at once, with his constant
educational tendency, began to direct their studies.   His
ways with the few young girls he knew in Carlisle, as elsewhere, were, according to his own confession, always didactic.
The youngest Miss Alleyne (now Mrs. Andrew Lang) recalls
his first visit when she was sixteen.

'We had never before had a young man to stay with us,
though somehow I never thought of Mr. Creighton as a
young man. . . . With his unfailing tact he adapted himself
to everybody's hobbies.   Mine were history and literature,
and he was always ready to discuss either, and give me what
he called "lectures" upon ancient history.'

In Oxford itself his circle of friends was constantly increasing.   He became intimate with Mr. J. R. Thursfield (then
Fellow of Jesus College), and Mr. H. G. Woods (then Fellow
of Trinity College), shortly after he took his degree, and with
Mr. Andrew Lang, who was elected a Fellow of Merton in
1868.   There were not many resident ladies in Oxford in those

---

[1] Formerly President of Trinity College, Oxford ; now Rector of Little
Gaddesden, Herts.

days, and Creighton knew few at all intimately, but he began
to see a good deal of Miss Arnold (now Mrs. Humphry
Ward), and of the sisters of Mr. Walter Pater.

Whilst during these years it is clear that he puzzled
many by his love of paradox, by his occasionally rash and
flippant speech, by the fact, as Dr. Copleston puts it, ' that
he did not give enough weight to the duty of showing on
which side he was,' the opinion in which he was held by
those who really knew him may be illustrated by the following quotation from a letter, written in 1868, from one
whose after career has shown that he possesses no common
power of judging men.

' Do you know, I think that some day, if you do not work
yourself to death in the interval, you will be very great. You
are, in my eyes already, and very dear too. But some day
you will have a great deal of influence, which will reach
very far.'

CHAPTER IV

ORDINATION AND ENGAGEMENT

CREIGHTON was ordained Deacon by the Bishop of Oxford in 1870. He doubtless waited so long because he felt that, in the rush of new work and responsibilities, he could not find sufficient time for preparation. Dr. Mackarness, who was then Bishop, does not seem to have given much consideration to the Fellows of Colleges whom he ordained. Creighton saw nothing of him personally, and was not invited to spend any days at Cuddesdon either then or when he was ordained Priest.

'He took his stand for God,' says Canon Scott Holland, 'and made his great decision at the extreme hour of intellectual tension, when the panic roused by the new criticism was at its height, and when the victorious efficacy of the scientific and critical methods appeared to have swept the field. It is difficult for us now to gauge the dismay of that bad hour. At the close of the sixties it seemed to us at Oxford almost incredible that a young don of any intellectual reputation for modernity should be on the Christian side. And Creighton by temperament lay open to the full force of the prevailing movement. No one could be more acutely sensitive to all that the critical spirit had to say. No one lent himself more freely to the æsthetic and other non-Christian influences of that distracted time. Yet, in spite of the swirling flood in which he found himself plunged, his inner steadiness of thought and will kept the balance.' [1]

His ordination was much commented on. He said to me in the following year that it was the habit in Oxford to assume that a man who took Orders must be either a fool or a knave, and that as people could not call him a fool, they had con-

[1] Memorial sermon preached in St. Paul's Cathedral on January 20, 1901.

cluded that he must be a knave. But he never then or at any subsequent time troubled to explain himself; he simply went his way and lived his life, and left that to speak for him.

His friends were not surprised, as they had always known what he intended ; but as he talked little of his opinions and his plans, his ordination came as a shock to those who judged him by the extravagance of some of his talk. Dr. Copleston says of the previous years: ' I was almost known in the openly churchmanlike set as Creighton's apologist. I never said, " He will come to us," but always, ' He is really with us." '

He preached his first sermon in the spring of 1871 at Wolvercot, a village near Oxford, where Mr. Freeling, his brother Fellow, was Vicar.

To L. von G.   'April 14, 1871.

' I have been writing my sermon for Sunday. I find I am getting lost in an attempt to write simple metaphysics in explaining what is meant by " the world " in opposition to man's spirit, to a rustic audience. I am afraid the entire conception will be impossible for them.'

At first he always wrote his sermons, and his great difficulty was to be sufficiently simple.

To L. von G.   'April 30, 1871.

' I feel that my literary style is always in the way in my sermons : it is very difficult to be plain to plain persons when one has undergone an elaborate training, but I hope to get on. Do you agree with me about the object of a sermon— that it should first give people a more accurate knowledge of the facts and statements of Scripture from an historical side, and should then pass on to impress a practical lesson ? If you only do the first you are merely antiquarian, if you only do the second you are adding to popular superstition by not treating the text of Scripture fairly : so it always seems to me. Moral lessons should be drawn from a careful and accurate statement of the facts : if the lesson you want to draw differs from the facts, say plainly why—don't distort your facts to suit your lesson : a good deal of sensible knowledge of the Bible might, I think, be disseminated by its teachers if they would take the trouble. I shall always try to do so.'

It was in February 1871 that Creighton first met his future wife.[1] His attention was attracted to her in a characteristic way. Yellow was a favourite colour of his, and was at that time little worn. At one of Ruskin's lectures, his quick eye noticed a girl wearing a yellow scarf, and seeing Mr. T. H. Ward speaking to her, he rushed up after the lecture to ask him, ' Who is that girl who has the courage to wear yellow ? ' I was staying with Sir Benjamin and Lady Brodie, in the house which has now become St. Hilda's College, and a few days after Mr. T. H. Ward, an old friend, invited me to lunch to meet Mr. Creighton. The easy hospitality of Oxford, the sight-seeing, the river—it was the time of the torpid races—provided us with opportunities of meeting. We at once found that we had many tastes in common. I had paid my first visit to Italy a year before, and was deep in the study of Italian art, so that at our first meetings we discussed Tintoretto and Titian; his store of photographs and his beautiful rooms were a great delight to me. In three weeks, the day before I left Oxford, we became engaged. He, however, refused to consider it an engagement till he had seen my father. He decided that it would not be right for us even to correspond before he had my father's permission, and he thought it best to wait till he could come and see him in person. So for a fortnight after I left Oxford there was no communication between us, till he was able at the end of term to come to my home at Sydenham. Many of the early days of our engagement were spent looking at pictures in the National Gallery and the Kensington Museum, or studying early Italian engravings in the Print Room at the British Museum.

Creighton, as he wrote in 1868, had imagined himself

---

[1] I was born at Peak Hill Lodge, Sydenham, in 1850. My father, Robert von Glehn, was a merchant, a native of Revel in Esthonia, one of the Russian Baltic provinces. His family originally belonged to the Rhine provinces, but had migrated to Hamburg and taken to trade, and then about the year 1600 had joined the German colony which settled in the Baltic provinces, and was granted special privileges with regard to religion and self-government by the Russian Emperors. My father's mother was a Scotchwoman, and he had been brought up with a strong admiration for everything English. He settled in England at the age of thirty, became a naturalised British subject, and married a Scotch lady, Agnes Duncan, by whom he had twelve children, of whom I was the tenth.

settled for many years to come in his Merton rooms : now he was forced to consider what he could do to enable him to marry. His first idea was to get a mastership, and he wrote to a friend about a possible vacancy at Harrow ; but his Oxford friends were anxious not to lose him.

To L. von G.   'Merton College : April 19, 1871.

'I am distracted by advice from every side what to do : several of the Fellows beseech me not to leave the College ; they are good enough to say that my continuance here is important to the Society ; they beseech me at all events to do nothing hastily, to wait till June, when we have our next College meeting, when they will reopen the question of allowing marriage to tutors. Others of my friends advise me at all events to keep my Tutorship, even if I vacate my Fellow-ship by marriage, and stay at Oxford taking pupils. I listen patiently and meditate : if Butler makes me a good offer, I still think I should go to Harrow, it opens out a career which residence here does not ; on the other hand, schoolmaster's work gives no time for self-culture, while work here does. . . . I should very much like to be a married Fellow here, but I see difficulties in the way of a society doing to meet the needs of one of its members what it deliberately refused to do in the abstract. . . .'

'April 25, 1871.

'I am really touched by the anxiety of people here to do all they can for me. . . . My fellow tutors are prepared to do anything they can to help me, although by so doing they lose promotion and consequent income.'

The College had already considered the question of married fellowships, and a statute had been drawn up which authorised the retention of a fellowship after marriage by a certain number of those holding college offices ; but owing to the strong opposition of the older Fellows, the college meeting of March 1871 had decided that action should be postponed till their objections had been further considered.

Creighton was a born teacher ; he used to say, 'I am nothing if I am not educational ;' but he had no special desire for a schoolmaster's life. After meeting a successful schoolmaster, he wrote : 'I infer that it requires more energy than thought or profundity to make a schoolmaster.' He never had any ambition either for place or wealth ; all he desired was enough to live upon quietly, so that he might

ÆTAT. 27.

carry on his studies and make use of those powers which he knew he possessed.

To L. von G.   'Merton College : May 17, 1871.

' I feel—you shall tell me if I am wrong—that we have a life before us of much good and use to others as well as ourselves. I see about me instances of men who are throwing themselves away on uncongenial work; not, I mean, doing things which are temporarily unpleasant to themselves, but things tending to make their future life much less useful to mankind than it might be. I do so wish we were settled in life, with our duties clearly put before us, our life to run. I am not, as you know, ambitious, but I know I can do some things fairly well, and it is hard to find a chance of doing them. . . . I want very much to find a sphere for both you and me. . . . Am I wrong? Do tell me. . . . I know we neither of us care for society in its technical sense, for grandeur or for luxury. . . .'

He was a good deal worried by the uncertainty, but by the end of May the matter was so far settled as to make it at least probable that he would be able to stay in Oxford.

To L. von G.   'Oxford : May 30, 1871.

'To-day I spent almost entirely in a College meeting, which lasted from ten till four. I never told you before how anxious I was about that College meeting : its chief object was to discuss married Fellows again, as Wilson had raised the point afresh for my benefit. It was carried almost unanimously, fourteen voting for it and only two against ; the two being the Warden, who always votes against all change, and an old Fellow of the age of seventy-five who always votes with him. I felt the compliment exceedingly, that persons who objected on principle should drop their objections on my account. . . . Our statute has now to receive the consent of the Archbishop of Canterbury and the Privy Council before any action can be taken. . . . If it passes, I shall have to apply, giving notice of three months, and then a majority of two-thirds is requisite to enable me to marry. So don't count upon anything with certainty yet, but I think the prospect looks cheering, at all events good enough to wait a little while for. . . . I think people have behaved most nicely to us, don't you think so ? '

Early in May I went with Mr. and Mrs. Hood and one of my sisters to visit him in Oxford. We stayed in lodgings, but spent our days and had our meals in his rooms, and met most of his friends. In June he spent some days at Marlborough examining the school, and in July I went with him to visit his family. His father had been left a complete invalid after a severe paralytic seizure in the previous winter, and had been forced to retire from business. He had settled in a small house in the tiny village of Kirkandrews near Carlisle. There we spent some very quiet weeks. Creighton was working hard at Dante and the history of his times, in preparation for a course of lectures which he was to deliver at Falmouth and Plymouth in September. He began to teach me Italian, and I was able to help him with German. He was very quick at learning both to read and speak a new language. He did not trouble himself about grammar, and had no sensitiveness as to his accent or frequent mistakes, but was content so long as he could say what he wanted and make himself understood. He used to say that it was absurd to wish to speak a foreign language like a native, when one was an Englishman ; and that as all English accents were bad, it was needless to trouble if one's own was a little worse than other people's.

He read at this time much of Goethe's poetry ; he never cared for his prose works, and in after years even lost much of his admiration for his poetry. But during these months he interested himself in working out a theory of life which he called *Entsagung* (renunciation), and which he found indicated in some lines by Goethe and in Lewes's Life of Goethe, and dwelt much upon it, as will be seen in subsequent letters. It meant to him the liberty which comes through the recognition of limits, as opposed to the view of life which consists in regarding duty as involving a constant call to self-sacrifice.

For relaxation he read the novels of George Sand, for whom he had a great admiration. Always a great novel reader, for many years he confined himself to French fiction. For German literature he never cared much ; he considered the language ugly, and thought that the German poets only excelled in their songs, and the novelists in their short stories. Of course he valued and admired the work of German students in every science, and probably read more German than any other language for his historical studies.

During these quiet weeks at Kirkandrews, his recreation as usual was walking. We explored every footpath and lane in the neighbourhood, and made excursions to some of the more beautiful spots in Cumberland.

At the end of August he settled in lodgings at Falmouth, and went each week to lecture at Plymouth. He had hoped to be able to get through a great deal of work in preparation for his lectures for the coming term, but the friendliness and hospitality of Falmouth made work difficult. He found in the various members of the Fox family a sympathetic and cultivated circle, anxious to see as much as possible of their lecturer. One of his first visits was to the beautiful garden of Mr. Robert Fox.[1]

To L. von G.   'Falmouth : September 2, 1871.

'Immediately after my lecture on Thursday, I was laid hold of by an elderly lady, carried off to her carriage, and driven away four miles to tea. Her name was Miss Fox. Her father, aged eighty-four, is more young and flourishing than anyone I ever saw. . . . There are many Quakers about here, which is nice. Mr. Fox has made acclimatisation the chief object of his life : acclimatisation of plants. The climate of Cornwall is particularly good for flowers. . . . Mr. Fox's garden was like fairyland : in front of his house a stream runs down a lovely valley for about three miles into the sea, which you see gleaming bright blue in the distance : the valley is filled with every kind of strange flower and tree arranged in wild luxuriance and profusion. You wander through tropical palms, through groves of magnolias, huge tree ferns, bamboos, Chinese shrubs, and every kind of wonder; meanwhile the little stream occasionally makes a rapid passage, at times is gathered into a quiet pool, where every rarest kind of water-plant is floating on the surface. I never was more completely taken by surprise in my life : I had never thought of seeing such a thing as the produce of the richest hothouses of Kew strewn in wild confusion down a lovely glade. . . . Another person who is very good to me, and has already given me a general invitation to come to

---

[1] Father of Caroline Fox, whose Journals give such a charming picture of the society in Falmouth for 1835–68. Caroline had died early this year, but her sister Miss Anna Maria Fox remained, a delightful and original woman. She used to come to the Dante lectures with a marmoset nestling inside the wide sleeve of her cloth jacket.

any meal I like in his house, is Dr. Tuke, a retired physician, also a Quaker. I find I am not likely to die here of the effects of solitude.'

Picnics and excursions were arranged for him, and his hopes of steady work disappeared.

'Under such circumstances what is to be done? I see Cornwall; I see men and manners; but how about reading? Everywhere the same difficulties come upon one; everywhere the conflict of the practical and the speculative life—of one's duties towards men in doing what one can to those one meets, and one's duties in improving oneself, for the ultimate good of oneself and others. It is hard to keep up the balance, to know what to do, how to restore equilibrium. Well, I give it up.'

On my asking whether it would not be wiser to decline some of the proffered hospitalities, he answered :

'September 11, 1871.

'I quite agree with you in your remarks to me about my manner of life here; but you never sufficiently allow for my view of *Entsagung*. My position is, I came here thinking I would be in a position to lead a quiet life of reading. I thought I should see few people and have much time to myself. I have not; I find people with intellectual interests who live in a narrow circle and see few strangers and hear few new things : am I justified in saying, "I am here to read, therefore I have no duties towards you"? Is the cause of education, of culture, in England at present to be forwarded by erudition, or by trying to work in every sphere you can, to kindle such enthusiasms as you can, to throw down such barriers as you can? If I were to say, "My duty is to read, and that only," I should not feel quite content. Here are clear duties, which I see definitely before me : would it or would it not be selfish to disregard them on the ground that there is a higher duty in preparing for Oxford lectures? I feel that the last course would save me trouble hereafter. Would it be right at present? Such is my question in trying to restore the equilibrium. The question is, what is one's highest duty? I think nothing is more untrue than to value lowly social influences; the work of culture is to be done as much by private as by public talk, as much by unauthoritative utterances at a dinner table, as by solemn ones in the pulpit or the newspaper. I don't agree with you about "squandering one's days at picnics and dinners." It is so when one lives in a place and knows one's neighbours intimately, and has said all one's say to them and lives one's life among them ; then dinners are merely a waste of time and an outcome of luxury. But here am I with five weeks of my entire lifetime to deliver my message, such as it is, to a few people who want to hear it. I have an authoritative position among them, such as I shall seldom have anywhere again. They summoned me to teach them by their own free will on some points, and they are willing to listen on more. Dare I refuse ? . . . I expected something quite else : I thought I should have been regarded with decent civility and left alone : on the other hand, I have the extremest cordiality.'

The Falmouth ladies admitted men to their course of lectures, and Mr. Howard Fox recalls being struck with his extraordinary command of language, and the fascinating way in which he treated the relations of Beatrice and Dante, so that he inspired his audience with his own enthusiasm for his subject, while he tried to lead them to seek with him for the moving motives in the history of the past. ' In society,' says Mr. Fox, 'he bore the burden of learning so lightly as to make us forget he had any. He would ask questions, suggest paradoxes, and listen most attentively to anything that was said in reply. He certainly succeeded in making us think, and had a most companionable way with young men ; his power to revel in pure nonsense was a striking character-istic.'

He seems to have taken Falmouth by storm. Among other memories, he is spoken of as being the first to call attention to artistic furnishing, and to introduce the inhabit-ants of Falmouth to Morris's wall-papers. He found the audiences at his lectures most appreciative, and some of his class did excellent work for him.

To L. von G.   ' August 30, 1871.

' My class at Plymouth is about fifty. I was not quite con-tent with my first lecture ; I felt it was pitched rather too high for the intelligence of those I saw around me, and then don't you know how one becomes dogmatic, the less one sees criticism. I shall be better in my next, I apprehend ; they must have more detail and fewer general principles.'

'Falmouth : September 1, 1871.

'My lecture here was a great success yesterday.   I was in good form, and said everything in good taste.   It is curious how one's audience affects one.   I felt at once here that I was addressing a much more cultivated set of people than at Plymouth, and the difference on my mind was enormous.   You see how wicked I am, what many people would call conceited ; but if one is placed in a position of authority by people, I humbly submit the only thing to do is to use that authority.'

'September 7, 1871.

'Plymouth being a much more decidedly business place than Falmouth, depresses the mind more.   However it may be, I feel that at Plymouth I am fighting uphill rather, and so tend to be more trenchant in my sayings.   I hear that many who generally come to lectures there did not, as they disapproved of the subject, and thought "Dante" not a fit book for a Protestant lady to read.   One forgets that there are such people in the world, and is quite taken aback at first by finding them in existence.   I notice one old lady at Plymouth who shakes her head and exchanges dissentient glances at my political opinions whenever they show themselves, and at my estimates of the Pope and Popery, consequently I go on to hit her harder ; if she won't take mustard as an article of diet, she shall have it in the shape of a blister.'

'September 12, 1871.

The Plymouth girls are certainly very good ; I see I marked six of their answers as first class.   Moreover, I find they have improved wonderfully in writing, and have paid attention to my remarks ; the way in which rhetoric and fine writing have disappeared is quite surprising. . . . It is quite nonsense to think that power of definition and precision of logical statement necessarily belong to a man more than to a woman.   These girls certainly show they are capable of dealing with an abstract subject in a most abstract way.'

He helped the Rector of Falmouth on most Sundays either by reading the service or preaching.   He even went to spend Sunday and preach twice at a country village, St. Wendron's, the Vicar of which was an Oxford man.   'I have views about the duties of clerical Fellows,' he wrote, 'and almost regard it as a duty at present to help any one who asks me.'   He walked a great deal about the neighbourhood with Mr. Howard Fox, and made expeditions with him to Tintagel, the Lizard, and other interesting parts of Cornwall. Picnics by land and sea were organised for him both at Falmouth and Plymouth. After describing the beauties of Mount Edgcumbe, he adds:

'I was amused at the way in which I went. One of my class asked me to go—a very nice-looking girl to whom I had been introduced. I assented, expecting a great assemblage: she appeared, accompanied by two others of my class. There was no chaperone: the eldest of the ladies was, however, some thirty-five, and might claim the privilege. I thought, however, the arrangement was nice, human, and intelligible; I liked it.'

Meanwhile, there was no certainty with regard to Creighton's future prospects. Before the end of the May Term, Mr. Edwards, the Senior Bursar of Merton, had also become engaged, and hoped to marry under the new statute. Creighton passed through Oxford on his way to Falmouth, and wrote from there.

'Merton: August 27, 1871.

'I received this morning a letter from the Warden saying that the Privy Council had given their assent to our statute. Let me talk to you on that point. At present our statute is merely a general one—at Christmas I can apply for it to be definite, and help you and me; but I cannot at once count upon it as certainly being done. Many private feelings of members may come in, and it is perfectly possible I may not reap the fruits of it. I speak in all seriousness. . . . The voting on such a point is secret, and you cannot overestimate the amount of private feeling in such things. However, I shall take the vote as final for myself, and if it goes against me I must look elsewhere. . . . I think it is quite probable I may get what I want, but not more than probable. But if it were carried we might be married before term begins, i.e. towards the end of January. Our meeting is on December 23. I could look after a house after that. Could you so think of the matter, without having any certainty before you, as to be prepared to be married at a month's notice without either giving your people too great certainty beforehand or coming on them too unexpectedly at last? In that case we would put off our honeymoon journey till the summer, when we would try to save money to ramble abroad.'

Some weeks later he heard that two more of the Fellows of Merton had become engaged.

'Falmouth: September 19, 1871.

'A letter I got last night has proved to me, in a way which cannot fail to give you a most melancholy satisfaction, my justification in beseeching you not to count upon my position at Oxford as even approximately settled. The letter is from Wallace, and tells me that the demon of matrimony has also seized Esson, and that there are at present four Fellows of Merton applying to the College for leave to marry and retain their fellowships. Now, four is the entire number which our new statute allows of; and to fill them all up at once would be reckless in the extreme, and would demand a superhuman amount of disinterestedness for the present Fellows to suppose that they would voluntarily and at once cut themselves off from a chance of succession for some time to any of these places. Now, regarding the matter dispassionately, and weighing the claims of the four applicants, which are all very great, if I was not one of the applicants myself, I would meet the difficulty by proposing that for the present it is inexpedient for the College to proceed under the recent statute, and so not do anything at all. That may be done ; or if not, it will be a struggle between rival candidates, and then all the older Fellows, who are very little interested in the educational aspect of the place, and know very little about its real working, will cut the knot by voting for Edwards and Esson on the ground that they are much older and have served the College much longer than Wallace and myself; that is the sort of argument that always weighs most with an old man. I don't feel particularly merry about the matter. I must candidly own that it appears before me in the light of a sell ; so much so, that it seems to me the sooner I look about me for a schoolmastership the better. I still have a sentimental desire to stay at Oxford : I still feel that the work there would be most congenial to me : but I feel too that I am young enough and have sufficient self-mastery to turn my mind to other work as well, and very possibly I may really get to like it better. Tell me, do you think I ought to wait till Christmas, for the votes of the College, or ought I to turn away my mind at once elsewhere ? I incline rather to wait and see, but our prospect of being married at Christmas becomes more and more shadowy. . . . I keep up my spirits : why repine ? I know everything will turn out well ultimately. Perhaps I am foolishly mistaking my vocation, and Oxford is not the place for me at all.'

'Plymouth: September 20, 1871.

'I had really, just as you had, quite counted on the consent of the College, and now everything is uncertain. The whole question has become now so complicated to the unhappy body of Fellows, that my one source of contentment is that I am not called upon to vote in the matter. It really is ludicrous. I feel quite angry with Esson and Wallace, and am inclined to ask them why in the world they could not have restrained themselves for a while. The whole matter is so comic, and the dilemma for the poor voters so truly terrible, that I feel quite conscience-stricken, when I think that I first involved them in it. Merton always has been regarded as the most advanced and maddest College in Oxford; but the spectacle of all its Fellows rushing headlong into matrimony at once will make everyone in Oxford die with laughter. I have at all events a dignified position: I was the first, and was not guilty of plagiarism; but it is too bad having the bread taken out of one's mouth in this way when the matter was for my benefit at first. Well, I think I shall play the farce out, and see the end of it: my position is at least a decent one. . . . To-day I have recovered rather from my depression: the humorous side of the whole matter now predominates in my mind. After all, it is only a bore at first going to be a schoolmaster. If Providence decides that I leave Oxford, I have no doubt it is better for us. He may have greater work for us to do elsewhere: let us go and do it without repining. Look at it in that way: after the first disappointment is over, which one can't help feeling, a deep-seated belief in the goodness of the new course ought to take possession of us. Let us be prepared for all emergencies.'

On returning to Oxford for the October Term, he apparently found that people in general assumed that his election was fairly certain. On October 27 he looked at a possible house.

'Merton: October 31, 1871.

'You see I am quite commencing to make plans and schemes, horrid as it is and objectionable as I have proved it to you so often. Tell me what you really think, if you would really mind going into lodgings until vaguely a house that suited us near the College turned up: that seems to me to be so generally vague, and Oxford lodgings are dear. But this is premature. . . .'

Houses in Oxford were then not easy to get, and when at last he found one of suitable size, a commonplace semi-

detached villa just finished on the Banbury Road, he decided
with many misgivings to take it, in the hope of being able
to sublet it if, after all, he was not able to remain in Oxford.
The house was taken on November 20, and it became an
almost daily occupation to visit it and superintend the details
of painting and papering, in which he took great interest.
He had no desire to conform to any rules of taste such as
were in those days being laid down with much dogmatism by
the leaders of the æsthetic movement. He writes :

' Happy thought! our rooms shall be what we want, not
what the faculty would prescribe for us. I would much
rather have something that we agreed upon, though it might
be all wrong, than be ever so right by taking other people's
advice . . . .'

There were moments when he was still troubled with
anxiety about the future.

' November 14.

' I sometimes feel quite terrified to think what would
occur if I did not get leave from the College. I should be
fearfully disappointed ; but I can scarcely conceive such a
contingency as very probable. Let us hope not.'

' November 19.

' If you inquire about my general state of mind, it is that
of a man who struggles to remain cheerful, and knows that
unless he keeps his wall a very solid one he will be absolutely
lost. If ever I were to begin and speculate on the possibilities of
not getting leave to stay here, and sometimes one feels tempted
to do so, I should simply collapse altogether under my work.'

' November 26.

' I have been haunted to-day by a notion how horrid it
would be if all our schemes came to nothing : there is yet a
month to wait before we know, and here we go on arranging
as if all were right : I shall never forgive myself if I cause
you a disappointment.'

It was an exceptionally busy term for him in many ways,
and he speaks repeatedly of his longing for the peace and
quiet of married life. On October 21 he did what he called ' a
very hard thing,' preached in College Chapel for the first time.

' October 18.

' It is most extremely hard to preach to men here : either
they slumber or they scoff. It is almost impossible to treat of

their real difficulties and dangers, because a young man never believes in them, and a number of young men together have no principles, and would scout the idea of having any if it were suggested. This will sound to you very horrid, but I am afraid you don't know the problems involved in managing or dealing with a lot of boys or young men.'

'October 21.

'I rather liked my sermon. . . . It was a very rational sermon. . . . Its point was that men here ought to remember that their common life was the great means of the education of one another, and ought consequently to regulate most rigidly their life, so as to not only work out their own culture, but also contribute to the general culture of the whole society, and help everyone else in so doing.'

'October 22.

'By the way, Freeling and Wilson told me this morning they liked my sermon, at which I was pleased. It is a great thing, in so critical a society as Oxford, to find that anybody ever likes anything.'

Creighton was nominated examiner in the Law and Modern History School, and this entailed much extra work, so that he was obliged to engage Mr. J. W. Diggle, an old pupil, to take some of his regular teaching. He made at this time his first small beginning in literary work, by reviewing some historical and other books sent him by an old College friend, Mr. C. P. Scott, editor of the 'Manchester Guardian.' He managed to pay two short visits to Sydenham, but otherwise was kept in Oxford by the Law and Modern History Examination till the College meeting on December 23, when his fate was decided. Mr. Wilkins liked to describe the result of that meeting by saying, 'My dear fellow, there were four seats in the matrimonial coach, and they were all immediately taken.'

During these years he wrote very little to friends. In December 1870 he had written to R. T. Raikes, 'I have lost my belief in the utility of letters at all.' I have, therefore, after much consideration decided to add a number of extracts from his letters to me. Those who read them will remember the circumstances under which they were written, for the eyes of one person only, and at a time when a man is likely to reveal himself with absolute frankness, because he is sure

of understanding sympathy. But though meant for one
person only, these letters throw so much light on what he
was and what he thought, that they are given for the sake of
those who want to know the real man as he then was.

' Merton College : April 15, 1871.

' Tell —— I am not blind to what the world might call your
faults, but I feel and know they are a thousand times fewer
than my own, and the question is, I trust, to us, and ought
to be to every thinking person, not " How much chaff ? "
but " Is there any wheat ? " (Forgive my repetition of a
quotation, I am fond of it.) If we each feel the other's heart is
right, thoroughly right, the faults are of little consequence.
The man of knowledge buys a picture for a few shillings, he
sees beneath the dirt of years strokes of a brush he cannot
mistake ; he cleans it carefully day by day, till forms of
beauty, passing all he expected or hoped, slowly reveal themselves ; he never doubted he had found a treasure, but such
a treasure he never dreamed to find. May it not be so with
both of us ? We never mistook each other, I hope, for more
than we were worth. . . .

' Don't expect that the reading of history will leave
definite knowledge of names and dates on your mind ;
nobody knows names and dates except very advanced
students and young men crammed for the Indian exam.
What is valuable in history is a general idea of the progress
of society and intelligence. Don't try and get more from
Gibbon.'

' Merton College : April 18, 1871.

' I don't approve of ——'s views about engagements ; in
one sense it is quite true that we are like everybody else in love.
Our feelings are those common to all human nature ; their external exhibitions, even the attempts at their internal analysis,
are common to much of the human race ; but because every
man has a face, every man has not the same face—rather the
reverse ; but everybody sees all about faces, and the differences are strongly impressed on the most casual spectator :
feelings of love cannot be expressed except by the two
persons concerned to one another : to the looker-on one
couple must resemble another. Moreover, the difference in
kinds of love must be a moral and intellectual difference,
and those are always the hardest to grasp clearly. Also I
don't agree (not merely on the principle of necessity, but of
rational choice) that it is undesirable to be engaged unless
you can marry at once. That is very good in the case of

two people who have known one another from childhood, and
go on increasing in knowledge, till one day it strikes them to
marry : they had better do so at once ; but it seems to me
the case is not the same for two persons who have met
casually, whose mutual admiration is sudden, and founded on
common principles.   That brings me to the consideration
of the difference between various kinds of love : perhaps
all kinds, at all events all we need think of, are much the
same at first: the shallowest natures feel the same noble
sentiments for a week or so as do the deepest : it is so with
all things that move the souls of men : a mob may be all
of it inspired with an equally genuine enthusiasm for a few
hours ; but how about all of them devoting their lives equally
to the object they screamed about yesterday ?   You and I,
I take it, don't want to scream with the rabble, to feel the
pleasure of a gush for the moment, and then sink back again to
the commonplace level : we want to devote our whole lives
to one another, and not to one another irrationally, but to
one another glorified and beatified, yet still real : to weave
the gossamer of sentiment into the web of common stuff,
and make the coarsest threads glitter with its brilliance.   Is
it an easy task ?   Is it one which the coarse mechanical
appliance of getting married to-morrow, and settling it somehow, will help us to do best ?   I should strongly doubt it :
our characters are, both of them, many-sided and not simple :
the position of marriage involves necessarily a loss of independence of judgment : you cannot estimate a thing so well
when it is fixed permanently at a given distance from you :
to see it at various distances, in various lights, to weigh
your treasure well, which you know you are going to sell all
you have and buy, but have not bought yet, will not this
help you to value to the full its preciousness, will not the
longings you have gone through make you esteem the
possession more ?   I don't want us to depend too much on
one another.   I want you to be you, and me to be me, and
yet both of us absolutely one ; and to do so we must each of
us fuse together the ideal and the real, not rush too soon to
grasp the real, and so sink the ideal.'

'Merton College : April 22, 1871.

'I have a horrid habit of taking up a subject and worry-
ing it, quite the reverse of what a letter ought to be artist-
cally considered ; but you know my great delight is the
consideration and discussion of minor psychological questions.
I like puzzling out a question, and finding something to say
about a given situation. . . . I was amused by being told

to-day that I was perfectly awful, through the wild exuber-
ance of my spirits : that it was expected I would soon be
going about with a red-hot poker, like a clown in a panto-
mime, and play pranks on old gentlemen. . . . I don't
think you appreciate my objection to Stanley's sermon : the
wording was all that could be wished : my objection was to
the contents, viz. that there were not any.   There was a
certain amount of general moral enthusiasm, to the intent that
it was desirable to be good rather than bad ; but I had
previously gathered that from other sources.   Seriously, I
mean that the University pulpit is meant for the production
of thought, not for the airing of rhetoric.   I have, however,
observed very much that people, in London especially,
admire rhetoric : now, on us Northerners it produces no
result : we look for the arguments.   I don't find it diminishes
my pleasure in hearing Stanley—rather increases it, as I
need not be distracted from the roll of the sentence by any
thought of its meaning.'

'Merton College : April 27, 1871.

'I think —— is nice up to a certain point, but without
any of the subtler shades of character in which genuine
delight consists.   You and I agree—do we not ?—in admiring
Leonardo's expression of the human soul, a vague shadowing
forth of infinite depths, a calmness suggesting unutterable
passion, a being with certain surroundings, but still no part
of those surroundings, dwarfing everything around by perpetually recalling the superiority of the self-summed human
soul.   I think people affect me in proportion as they do this.'

'April 28, 1871.

'You know I am not a tortuous person, but rather otherwise under all circumstances. . . . I am not, as you know,
and never was, conventional ; my friends have always been
the result of personal preference, and our friendship has
mostly been of their choosing.   I want no society in the
technical sense of the word, I loathe and abominate it : if
anyone cares for me, I am glad ; if anyone cares for my
dinners or my wine, that is a matter for his own taste and its
gratification.   If he cares for me, he must take me as I am.
I feel and know that you agree with me in this, and if I had
not I would never have proposed to live with you.   I might
have loved you, worshipped you, built you a temple in my
heart, and gone about my life the better for seeing you whenever I could : my ideal might have been heightened, but I
should have felt so strongly that it could never have been for

your happiness to ask you to live with me, that I would have considered it wrong to have done so.'

'April 29, 1871.

'Copleston made a profound remark the other day, that everyone thought their own love story exceedingly romantic. I think it is a true statement, but I never thought that of ours ; its genuineness and sincerity struck me more : two human souls absolutely rushed together because they saw there was nothing else to do consistently with continuing to exist. That was something better than romantic, was it not ? '

'Oxford: May 1, 1871.

'You have the advantage of me in reading Darwin : I am afraid I don't take sufficient interest in the subject of his speculations. I gather from scientific men that his view cannot ever claim to be more than a hypothesis, and they all estimate differently the amount of probability they attach to it ; and no one has yet told me of any course of inquiry which could be adopted to convert the hypothesis into an ascertained fact. Consequently the whole matter seems to me to be very ingenious and amusing, but I have not time for it, and would rather read some Italian history. You shall read all these books for me, and tell me all about them.

'As to your ponderings about love in a future state, either we do love those whom we loved on earth, or we sink all individual love in the general—a feeling of which we can have such scanty experience here that we cannot realise its completeness. Do you remember the lines :

> God gives us love—something to love
> He lends us ; but when love is grown
> To ripeness, that on which it fed
> Drops off, and love is left alone.

'I am afraid, however, I am a believer in the individualistic feeling, which must always leave its mark so strongly as to be associated with what one calls oneself in any condition whatever.

'I lunched to-day in the company of William Morris, the poet : he is a black-haired, bluff, healthy creature, miles removed from the artistic paganism of which he is the prophet. Surely the Greeks loved beauty in their persons, their dress, their manner, everything about them. Why cannot the modern pagan try to reproduce what was valuable in the Greeks, that would make any man a social missionary at all events ? Why cannot they construct a gospel of taste and show some slight self-sacrifice in carrying it out ? To

convert mankind by clean linen, to rebuke vice by a graceful
wave of the hand, and rise to power over men's hearts by the
exquisite refinement of a smile—these are the fruits one
expects from them and never gathers. They are but half-
hearted pedants after all. Pater is the only man who carries
out his views in the least. In him you feel the idea of beauty
absolutely dominates, and all that does not come under its
influence is to him external. You will find him worth a
study in that matter.'

'Merton College : May 19, 1871.

'Yes, I think lovers are selfish : I think married people
are selfish : the monkish doctrine of celibacy has truth in
it at the bottom of a sort : but it disregards the fact that few
people do actually lead lives for the good of others solely :
and it is no use legislating to get everybody to do so at
once. I don't think love makes us more selfish, only more
conscious of our selfishness : I don't do less, I do more for
those around me, but I know how little it is, much more
clearly than I used to do. . . . I agree with you most entirely
in reposing ourselves and all our hopes in God, and feeling
confident that He who has already brought us to such
wondrous great joys will never leave us or forsake us, and
that if any evil befall us we shall only have ourselves to blame.'

'Merton College: May 21, 1871.

'Let me try and explain what I think about religion as a
standard of practical life. What people exactly mean by
making religion a guide in life seems to me referable to two
heads : (1) being animated in one's general life by a love of
God, as a ruling motive; (2) taking as a practical example
for life the life of Christ. Some people mean by religion one
of these things, some the other, some both ; but the point at
which difficulties intellectual and otherwise arise to the
individual is the relation of these standards to his ordinary
practice. Some people seize hold of the love of God and
exalt this to a spasmodic passion, having impressionable
natures capable of momentary intensity, not of the continued
strain required for a moral life : such natures tend to monasticism, to religiosity, to formalism, or other things according
to their surroundings. Others, taking the love of God for
their standard, translate their main principle into a number
of practical axioms, and refer their separate acts to these
axioms as rules : their danger is to forget their main principle,
or rather put it into the background, and so gradually tend
to lower the strictness of the rules by submitting them too

much to the considerations of expediency which necessarily
follow upon practice, and which always require to be guarded
against by a continual screwing up one's axioms and keeping
them in tune by referring to the main principle. It is so in
any system of morals : utilitarian morals pure and simple
would always tend to degenerate unless perpetual reference
were kept up to their main principle, and it is because
that principle is so abstract that the process of rectifi-
cation is difficult to carry on at the same time as action. It
seems to me that every Comtist ought for his own sake
to take a week's absolute solitude every six months, and go
through a severe mental process to bring up his axioms to
his first principle : the wear and tear of life always tends to
drag them down. But the advantage of the religious
standard is, that not being purely intellectual, but largely
emotional, it can continually be repaired and heightened
unconsciously and without effort ; moreover, it can always
go on assimilating to itself new conditions and relationships of life, as the emotions act so much quicker than the
reason. Hence too arise the doubts which it begets : on the
one hand, intellectual processes seem from time to time to
clash with what one's emotions are engaged in preserving
and we all of us have struggles to co-ordinate our intellectual
results with our emotional standard : hence the cry that
thought and science make men godless. They may do so,
but they still oftener seem only to do so, or do so only
for a while. A sincere Christian, whose notion of God or
of Providence was founded largely on the idea of God's
creation of himself, with all the faculties he has, would be
shocked if his reason accepted the Darwinian hypothesis :
it might in some destroy the religious idea altogether ; others
might after a struggle see that the idea of God's love and
providence was not really affected by the fact of their
ancestors being tadpoles. Similarly, from the side of the
emotions, a new and strong feeling introduced into life at
first takes possession of it, seems to be a motive strong
enough in itself for everything : presently in practice it is not
found to be so, and then disappointment ensues, and the
feeling of disappointment is construed as being a just judgment for the abandonment of the calmness and repose which
a belief in God alone can give—hence the gloomy views of
life which some religionists continue to hold. Here, again,
the duty of a true man is, I think, to try and co-ordinate the
two emotions—to see in the one a reflex of the other, to
borrow for the human love that permanence which can only
properly belong to the divine, by merging unconsciously the

two—to add to the divine that intensity which can only come
from definiteness of view : so an entire knowledge of any
human soul can add to one's clearness of the abstract yet
concrete perfection of humanity exhibited in Christ; and
through that, to see more clearly the Godlike embodied in
every man, which can only be seen and grasped through
reading every man in the light of Christ. I never tried to
put my views on the point clearly before myself before : I
never thought them out clearly : I wrote them just as they
arose at your bidding : you have done much in making
me do so.'

'May 24, 1871.

'Yesterday you referred me to an article in the "Saturday,"
"The Profession of an English Matron." As far as I understand the article, it was the very essence of British clever
Philistinism. It made a smart summary of the intellectual
arguments of Mrs. Anderson : it then took the view of
cultivated respectability as embodied by the Bishop of
Peterborough, and gushed over it; and it flavoured its
remarks on these points by pandering to the very worst side
of the British character, its suspicion of ideas, its dislike to
the results of pure thought : it said Mrs. Anderson spoke
entirely to the head, the Bishop went straight to the heart
of the English people : a very nasty place to go to, the last
resting-place I should wish to be found in—a sloppy sort of
place, I take it. Surely the matter is simple : either a woman
equally with a man has a certain number of duties to those
immediately around her, which have to be done first and
always, and then outside that has also equally with the man
an unlimited sphere of usefulness for all her feelings and
talents—a sphere great in proportion solely to the amount
of power she has of working in it ; or, on the other hand, man
has duties generally, and woman has only duties specially,
and the duties of the two differ in kind. I must confess
(without any desire to prejudice your judgment) that I hold
with Mrs. Anderson ; and if I were to find you became in
any one line more useful than I was in any one line, I would
find it a plain duty for me to arrange my life so as to be
subordinate to yours. I hold most decidedly that the purpose
of the world is to get the greatest wisdom brought to bear
upon every subject, and that the duty of each person is to
rule those more foolish than himself, and obey those who are
more wise : the worst of it is, that it is so difficult to get many
people educated up to the point of having any standard of
wisdom and folly.'

' May 25, 1871.

'There can be no personal feeling in a matter where truth is concerned. Some one feels you to be selfish and thoughtless where you have not meant to be : you must have been so to some degree for the feeling to have arisen : say you have been so at once and offer to amend. You will then next time be able to see whether the first impression was true or not : you can test the subjectivity or objectivity of it by having taken all possible steps to destroy the first element. . . . The only way I can explain my terribleness on that point is that I try more habitually perhaps than most people to apply an intellectual standard to most things —not more so, however, on the whole than you do; but I hold most strongly and feel most strongly that every idea one has ought to be not so much useless mental furniture, but rather the very rod and staff of one's life and conversation. Let us have ideas, whether they are right or wrong—let us say what we think—toss out our crude opinions for criticism and destruction—refrain from nothing for fear of being thought foolish or extravagant or disreputable ; if it is genuine thought, it is worth uttering, not dogmatically, but through a desire to give it form and to have it criticised, examined, tested. I think that is as near an explanation of my point of view as I can give. Tell —— that my bark is worse than my bite ; that I don't really know anything, but am struggling to discover ; that there is nothing I court more than difference and discussion ; that I am most desirous of learning, and that I am perfectly conscious my experience has been very small, and so am most desirous to hear always the results of others.'

' Merton College : May 25, 1871.

' I tried, if you remember, once before to put clearly the only way by which it seemed to me such a position (the discharging of domestic duties) in some degree was to be reconciled to real high culture on the woman's part—viz. to regard all duties and responsibilities, high and low alike, as to be jointly shared by both ; by that means fewer difficulties are likely to arise,—In my experience I have seen more disturbances caused in households by sheer carelessness and thoughtlessness on the part of the males than by anything else ; while a woman, by being encouraged to brood over little cares, tends to forget the weightier matters of the law, and to disregard the precept that these ought she to have done, and not have left the others undone. . . . I must get *Rio* when Paris becomes peaceful again ; but the mention of that is too awful

just at present. If I were not supported by a very strong
historical conviction that the lines of progress of the future
were to proceed by means of the Teutonic race, and had I not
thought for some time that the mission of France to the
world had been discharged, I should have been quite broken
down by the present state of things : to see a nation
deliberately commit suicide is an unexpected phenomenon.
It seems to me scarcely to be hoped that any regeneration
will come out of all this ; but the whole question is beyond
discussion, especially in a letter. . . .

'To tell the truth is the chief duty of man—a very
difficult one, not to be done by the rules of the ordinary
blundering Briton : if one has conveyed a false impression,
one must apologise not from one's own point of view, but
from that of the person to whom one has unconsciously lied.'

'Merton College : May 26, 1871.

'I am glad you are pleased with Curtius : I think he gives
you a very good view of the development of the Hellenic
spirit ; he is not so sound or so accurate as other more
voluminous historians, but he tries to get hold of the feelings
of the people. Not all history is the same history, though all
are treated in the same way : some people's history is a
history of their wars, others of their constitution, others of
their society. Greek history is essentially a history of
thought : nothing is grander than the spectacle of a small
people in the infancy of the world boldly grappling with all
possible problems in society, in politics, in art, in literature.
Of course they narrowed the field to bring the problems
within compass : they had no notion of liberty as we understand it, as Christianity has made mankind understand it, an
inalienable heritage of all human beings : their life was
founded upon slavery—the cultivated few, the oppressed
many : hence the completeness and the incompleteness of all
their results ; they obtained results of the grandest kind, but
always limited in extent. Their culture was only for the few,
not for all. It is quite necessary not to be led away on that
point in studying Greek history : it gives no real analogies
for modern times ; its democracy is often quoted most
imbecilely ; we should call it an aristocracy of the most
oppressive kind.

'To-day, by the way, I attended a lecture of Taine's, who
is lecturing in French on the dramatists of the seventeenth
century, Racine and Molière, I presume : to-day he was purely
general, about the connexion of the drama with the life of the

times. *L'homme, c'est son milieu,* is his great principle for the explanation of all things. Do you remember a very clever article in the " Saturday " on one of his books by W. G. Clarke, ending with a statement that H. Taine ought to promulgate a new beatitude, " Blessed are the cocksure " ? Certainly a Frenchman's power of unlimited generalisation on no grounds is quite wonderful. . . . Pray understand I don't say women are the same as men, but I refuse to assume that they are different : it seems to me a theory either way is unnecessary, and, more than that, that we have not at present anything like materials for a universal solution of the question. Obviously there are some things which in society as at present arranged women must do ; but remember there are some savage tribes in which the relations are entirely reversed. There are many things which are the accidents of life : we try too much to make them laws of nature. I might find all women in my experience possessing certain qualities, marking them off to do certain things and excluding them from others, but that does not justify me in assuming a general law, still less in crying down women who want to do the things ordinarily prohibited. Experiment must solve the question, and experiments on a large scale never have been made : let them be made, by all means ; nothing but good can come of them. The question has quite recently been removed from the essentials of life to the accidents : no one now argues that women are necessarily inferior intellectually to men, they only argue that they are unfit to do such and such things ; possibly it may be so : I don't care one way or the other, but don't let us call anyone wicked for wishing to try. Will that do ? '

'Merton College : June 1, 1871.

'I think you had better not give X. any advice on the matter of his love affairs : they are always serious matters to interfere in. . . . Moreover, the responsibility of meddling in the inmost secrets of two human souls is much too serious a thing to be undertaken.

> It's a difficult thing to play with souls,
> And matter enough to save one's own,

is a good broad principle never to be lost sight of. One has such a natural desire to make things pleasant for the time, to accept present conditions as ultimate, to try and spare transitory heart-burnings to reduce the whole matter to calculation, and import one's own ideas and point of view. The really valuable thing in all such matters is the involuntary flare of the two souls concerned—a blaze never to be kindled, and if sincere never to be extinguished, artificially : if it is real, it will prevail ; if not, why should we care? It is merely a step in the progress of the individual.'

'Merton College : June 2, 1871.

'Your remarks about our manner to one another are quite true : I feel I cannot hope to conceal from myself that I am very much in love indeed ; and that being the case, why should I try and conceal it from others as if I were ashamed of it ? to say nothing of the fact that the process of concealment would be very painful, both in the moral degradation it would involve, and also in the intense disagreeableness of the actual process. I prefer to try and show people that I don't care less for them, or can be less useful to them, because I love you more, but rather that I can be in every way better to them, if they will only accept the facts of my life ; and if they won't accept them, then their interest in me must be very small, in fact scarcely appreciable. Let us be as happy as we can, however foolishly in the eyes of others ; they will soon come round to our point of view. I believe tremendously in my power of converting people, when I am persuaded of the truth of my own position. . . .

'Experience must be idealised as well as everything else to establish an ideal, and then all practical objections fall off harmlessly ; the theory must be judged by its internal consistency. . . . Please don't fight against the epithet "grim :" it is quite appropriate, I can assure you. I have long since applied it to myself, though most people don't. I mean by it an absence of *abandon*, an incapacity for living for the moment, a perpetual presence of law in one's daily life. You have that as much as I have. I don't think it is a bad thing to have : it is necessary if one's life is to move all in one piece, if it is not to be merely a mass of fragments. I had rather produce a deep impression on one person in my life, than please or amuse five thousand. It is ideas that make up the world : to have advanced, or made possible the advance of a great idea requires fixity, requires self-negation, requires a permanent self, requires reflection in all one does, requires— if so it must be called—"grimness."'

'Merton College : June 7, 1871.

'I think I see in your remarks about M. traces of a tendency which I used to have till experience crushed it, a tendency to too great analysis, a desire to grasp all at once the fruits of one's labours, to realise instantly one's ideal, to demand of all that they should instantly meet one on the broadest basis of human character and human life. It is natural, quite natural, only impossible ; one's exactingness wears off in time. It is impossible to get thorough sympathy except from those under exactly similar circumstances to oneself; a few years' difference in age, a little difference of past experience, raises a barrier not to be suddenly broken down—not to be overleapt. More and more one learns that it is useless to demand of people that they should rise to one's ideal, more and more one learns that it is necessary to adapt one's ideal to them : that is the real use of a high standard, that it should be something which enables one to help others from their own point of view, not to change all at once that point of view to one's own : to tolerate others, to feel their difficulties, to differ without disagreeing, to strive by greater knowledge to do here and there a kind action, to get above the turmoil of ordinary life, and have a clear definite point of view above it, from whence one can recognise the ordinary laws of life, and can occasionally give a prosperous turn to the fortunes of others—this is what we must aim at. To obtain first a secure mooring for oneself among the tempestuous sea of doubts and passions and difficulties, and then to be ready to warn others from shipwreck, or to save them when they are shipwrecked—this is all we can do. We cannot get others to steer by our own charts, or follow our course. Is that right ? It is a humble task, but of practical use : people trust one in proportion as they confide in one, and they give confidence according as they trust in our wisdom and in our capacity of understanding and appreciating and helping them. Many people can sympathise without understanding, many can understand without being able to help : no one can bare his soul to another unless he is sure of getting help and is convinced of his own unaided helplessness ; and unless all these convictions are present in anyone's mind, it is impossible they should confide, and so it is hopeless to ask for utter confidence, nor would it be desirable unless one's own help were to follow upon it. I had rather not have anyone's confidence unless it called for my help and I could give that help. Once I thought differently, once I grudged any corner that was not made manifest to me : now I see that too great self-revelation is a thing to be dreaded : self-analysis is impossible in any one of worth unless wrung from him in full accuracy by overpowering need : the mere feeling that some one is ready to give sympathy is not enough to force the effort to analysis : nor is it good for anyone to feel a desire for self-revelation merely for the purpose of revealing. Have you ever read Rousseau's " Confessions " ? It is the most loathsome book I ever read, simply for the reason that it insists upon the analysis of self for no sufficient object. It does not do to have the human soul upon the dissecting board always, or even often.'

'Marlborough College: June 21, 1871.

'You ask me about reading " Malgré tout." I feel now more clearly your difficulties on such points. I have been in the habit of judging too much everyone by myself. To me criticism has become so natural, I am so little likely to be carried away by anything. I stand so absolutely outside what I read that I really don't care what I do in that way. I see, however, that by no means all people are of that sort : that it is possible to be haunted by a horrid idea, never thought of before, to have unimagined terrors brought before one's mind. I don't think you will find any of that in "Malgré tout." . . . I think there is an elevated tone about G. Sand : she is never conventional, never commonplace, she is always within the limits, even in her wildest productions, of what is possible for a high ideal of human nature : she has no delight in villany for itself : the worst to say of her is that she glorifies the weaknesses of a strong character. She does not, as a second-rate person would do, justify them merely, and so be disgusting : she says "great souls have great weaknesses, and show them especially in the way which the world condemns." She fails of course to see that the test of great souls is to transform the world, not to rebel against it : she fails to see that weaknesses are not a necessary part of the greatness, and that her characters would be greater if they had no such weaknesses. Still, her exquisite feeling for nature, and her consummate artistic power, together with her psychological subtilty, always make her interesting to me. . . .'

'Marlborough College: June 24, 1871.

'I don't know what you would call a regular life, but I mean by it a life in which one habitually breakfasts at eight : try as you will to escape, that one fact pins you down to hopeless regularity : the whole day must centre round that. Now, an irregular life is one in which one breakfasts when one gets up, and gets up when one likes, occasionally choosing to sit up late and meditate lazily, occasionally choosing to do so when about three-quarters awake in the morning. It is a pleasant but mischievous life, provocative of much sweetness of character, but absolutely destructive of energy. By an energetic man I mean always a man who gets up the moment he is awake. It costs me a severe struggle every morning to get up at all. I commence my day with a serious moral conflict, which acts as a tonic to my whole nature. If I did not undergo that battle, I should be unnerved for the day. I am glad you did see my view that the object of life after all is to live—conscious energising in the world comes to nothing. St. Francis certainly was not guilty of it: he wished to lead the life to which his natural sympathies attracted him. His "marriage with poverty" is no mere allegorical expression. The life he led was the only one he wanted to lead : there is no conscious struggle to adapt his life to the purpose of teaching others. I don't find any self-conscious effort about St. Paul : do you think he thought that the simple record of his life would be read by all civilised men for all time ? Do you think his letters would be what they are if he had thought that out of his stray admonitions to struggling erring Christian communities millions of men would form their views of life and its duties ? What a mess he would have made if he had thought it his duty to sit down and write a philosophical and moral treatise setting forth Christianity in a plain and clear form so as to commend it to everybody ! We can never do anything except by the fact of our lives : and to lead a good life is quite enough to do. The only class of people I know who go in for consciously doing good and producing great things in the world are the Jesuits : their reputation answers for the effect upon themselves, the results they have wrought for the desirability of their method. . . . If you are doing any work it will be recognisable enough ; if you are not, begin contentedly in a little way at first. Such is my theory of life : it took me a long while to learn ; but since I have given up regenerating mankind by the million, I find it very hard to satisfy myself about my own wisdom in the smallest duties of life, still more about the goodness of my intentions and the singleness of heart in the process. It is very hard to get rid of one's lower self—to be utterly unpretentious, truthful, and charitable all at once.'

'Marlborough : Sunday, June 25, 1871.

'. . . Decidedly happiness consists in loving, not in being loved ; being loved can only make one conceited and selfish. Love is the true Jacob's ladder that reaches from earth to heaven, is the one rope extended to us poor creatures, to draw us from the pit in which we are struggling, to raise us above the perpetual changes and miseries of life to a knowledge of Beauty and Truth and Purity and Peace. The real use of being loved is that you can love more intensely one who

loves you ; but to love and labour for that love, to feel its
infinite value, and to struggle with the energy of despair
never to lessen or to lose it—such is the way to make life
the most perfect. I always thought so, and would have
expressed myself so long before I met you ; but my point of
view then was that love, as I meant it, was infinitely too
precious a thing to throw away on the sort of things I
imagined girls to be. I wished to give it all to men, to those
around me each in their degree ; but I found I was waxing
cold and cynical, till I met you and my life began afresh.'

'Falmouth : September 1, 1871.

'Trust that if your views are right, they will rightly
influence your conduct, and those who see you will be converted in time. I believe that I really like stating my views
to the utmost in contradiction to those I am among, on
account of the moral advantage of the process : you feel a
practical consistency forced upon you by the fact that you
are perpetually exposed to critical eyes. I feel a dogged
determination to show people who differ from me that
liberalism does not lead to irreligion, or Sabbath-breaking
to open immorality, or self-development to selfishness, or
liberty to lawlessness : all these points I find require practical
proof to many people, which can only be given by a decisive
statement of opinion accompanied by rigid rectitude of action.
. . . All systems opposed to the conventional ones have won
their way at first by the purity of life of their professors.

'I don't think you ought necessarily to seek a meaning
in Goethe's poems, or in any work of art. I always maintain
that if the art is good the moral does not matter ; not that
the moral is in such a case of no importance, but that if the
art is good there the moral necessarily exists exactly in proportion to the goodness of the art. . . . I used to disagree
most decidedly from your sweeping views about Dutch
pictures ; they seemed to me intolerant—much the same as
if a High Churchman refused to admit the nobility of an
action performed by a Quaker. Isn't the story told of
Northcote, who remarked to a critic of one of Reynolds's
pictures who said superciliously, " I don't see much in it,"
" Sir, if there wasn't more in it than you can see, there would
be very little indeed " ? The question about a work of art is :
Is the picture true, real, living ? Does it stand out distinctly?
Does it leave a clear impression on your mind ? If so, never
mind the meaning. The meaning will flash across you whenever the experience befalls you, that requires such an expres-

sion ; if it never befalls you, it may still befall thousands of
your fellow creatures. Nothing seems to me a more terrible
requirement than that of the present day that everybody
should paint, write, or speak moral platitudes. I am afraid
Carlyle and Ruskin are somewhat responsible for the idea.
But don't you think there is a profound meaning in " Der
Gott und die Bajadere " ? The notion of a sinful woman
raising herself to an equality with the Godhead by one
supreme act of self-sacrifice, is that an idea so commonplace
as not to be worth writing a poem about ? '

'Plymouth : September 5, 1871.

' I should have said your letter delighted me, but for the
news you gave me of D——'s death. My dear, it is awful ;
not that death is awful or even to be regretted, but I could
have borne with more composure the news of the death of
my most intimate friend. Learn from me what I never so
fully realised before, the self-reproach that follows upon the
omission of duty. I am most deeply grieved when I think
that D——'s appearance, manners, peculiarities stood in my
way of doing what I might have done : time after time I
have thought of his real merits, of his honesty, integrity, zeal,
conscientiousness, and I have thought, " Some day, when I have
more time, when I am less worried, I will try and see if I
cannot make his solitary life happier, make him less eccentric."
I have felt that it was hard for him to be condemned to
loneliness, to be cheered by scanty sympathy on his course,
which was an honest hard-fought one, because his voice was
loud, and other little matters. I feel that I have weakly
disregarded a noble human soul because it had an unsightly
body ; and now he has gone, and I cannot ask his pardon or
make amends. I tell you this that you may be spared a
similar thought ; it is well to feel in presence of the great
issues of life how mean, how ignoble, how thoroughly unworthy is any social standard—how goodness of soul is the
only thing one ought to care about, and that up to the fullest
of one's conviction on that point, ought one's acts to be. I
hope, I will pray that I may never again give way to such an
unworthy temptation. Oh, let us lay firm hold of life's
realities, for every deviation from these brings its own
remorse. . . .

' If you think somewhat, you will find that the past only
gives experience, the future holds out a goal before us, but
past and future alike are useful only as a means to make us
work better in the present : any thought of our past joys or our

future happiness which does not make the present brighter, easier, and more earnest, cannot be right. I cannot say where the error lies, but an error there must be somewhere, and any longing for the future which does not make the present happier, can, when realised, only end in disappointment of one sort or another. . . . If our thoughts of what we will some day have, cannot overpower our present desire to have it, believe me the transient is prevailing over the permanent part of our feelings.'

'Falmouth: September 5, 1871.

' I have never yet answered your question about Renan's "Vie de Jésus," because I did not know what to say. I never read it myself, so I don't know anything about it. I am opposed to protection, as you know; but, on the other hand, I am opposed to reading a book because it is naughty or unorthodox. Read it if you have any reason to believe it contains anything you want to know, but don't ever read a book because it made a sensation and obtained a notoriety by being naughty or unorthodox. I don't know that Renan's "Vie de Jésus" has anything to add to one's conception of Christ; I don't at all like that style of book: the Gospels are the best life of Christ, and historically the only authentic ones, and all such lives as Renan's are merely sensational ways of putting popularly results of criticism, which persons had much better take as results of criticism, not in the shape of a sentimental novel. I have looked into and admired as most profound Renan's "Averroès et l'Averroïsme:" read that if you can struggle with it. Also, as he is a splendid Semitic scholar, his translation of the Book of Job is, I believe, excellent; but unless you have some reason for believing that the "Vie de Jésus" contains some information you want, I would not read it. . . . I merely recommend as you asked me.'

'September 8, 1871.

' I wish you would study Goethe more, and grasp his doctrine of *Entsagung*, the doctrine that morality consists in the consciousness of self, and freedom and content are to be obtained only by the recognition of one's limits, and by self-identification with them ; so that what first appears as an iron barrier set before us by remorseless destiny, is by the mere process of its moral recognition transformed into an internal precept for our moral guidance, becomes a help rather than a hindrance, for it makes life more definite and its problem more soluble. . . . Meditate on the saying of Paul the prisoner, " Where the Spirit of the Lord is, there is liberty," and reflect how much it would seem to have to commend itself to the poor creatures to whom it was first addressed.'

'September 11, 1871.

'Goethe did not come to it till late, not till he was nearly forty years old; before that he had dashed himself with the full blaze of a strongly emotional nature all alight from one place to another: what happened was, that he was a candle for moths to burn their wings at, for he was a very strong man; but what would happen to a weak man under such circumstances is either that his light is extinguished, or reduced to such miserable dimensions that he has to crawl slowly about shading it with his hat. It is quite true that barriers may be overthrown, but never to any good purpose by merely emotional working. To Goethe I apprehend *Entsagung* meant to do honestly what was immediately before him, and then see if he was strengthened to do anything more.'

'September 12, 1871.

'*Entsagung* is a moral principle of absolutely universal application: you do not understand it if you regard it only as a doctrine for some people. Of course all moral truths both can be and are continually wrested by the unwary to their own damnation, so are all other truths without any hindrance to their absolute universality. *Entsagung* is merely the application of the doctrine of law to morals: the laws of nature carry their own penalties at once if infringed; the laws of society bring their penalties in the shape of gaols, and imprisonments, and hanging, the moral law does not bring its penalties at once. The individual finds temptations to disregard it; but just as one's liberty is not infringed by the fact that the fire burns, or that if detected in committing murder one will be hanged, so also is it not by obedience to the moral law. A man obeys the laws of nature instinctively, and the laws of society without effort, except against very violent passions. *Entsagung* is merely the name for the process by which he realises with equal vividness and obeys with equally little effort the law of his own nature, which he can only discover for himself. Many people don't discover it; but surely if morality is to be possible it must be grasped and obeyed, and one's impulses for the moment subordinated to the higher law of one's whole nature: in separate things one is impelled by one part of one's nature: morality enforces the subjection of that part to the whole, and *Entsagung* merely points out that obedience ought not to take the form of submission to an abstract external criterion of duty, as something apart from us and outside us, but rather ought to be a joyful resignation of one's partial self to one's universal self; the limit is that set by calm knowledge to momentary caprice. According to that notion self-sacrifice vanishes, all limits are recognised as self-imposed, are merely the utterances of one's entire self against one's partial self—hence there is pleasure in the most disagreeable duty, for the action performed is not regarded from its accidental accompaniments, but from its real bearing on one's permanent self. Meditate, and you will see my exposition is sound : it is the only basis of rational as opposed to emotional morality ; it involves the difference between content and discontent ; it makes man absolute master of circumstances, for they cannot affect his moral being in itself, but merely its momentary form to others.' [1]

'Falmouth: September 9, 1871.

' It always seems to me that one's opinion about anyone's character in the way of its goodness is a revelation, and to be regarded as such, and is to draw its own duties with it ; given, i.e. that you are strengthened to see clearly a struggling human soul, you are bound to do all you can to help it. . . .

' I should hate to be rich, because being rich is a profession, and as such it would bore me and give me a lot of work which I did not want, and would much rather not [have].'

'Falmouth : September 11, 1871.

' Let us get rid of that part of misery which comes from thinking about it : let me say I am out in the rain walking, I register a solemn protest in my own mind that it is beastly, I then walk on cheerfully and make the best of it. The good of the protest so registered is to be a rational principle to prevent me for the future from ever going out under such circumstances if I can help it : the cheerfulness for the present being an attempt to grapple with the difficulty.'

'Falmouth : September 15, 1871.

' I am amused at the conclusion we have come to in our argument about *Entsagung*. It is a word which I dare say Goethe uses only casually if at all, and which Lewes uses to denote briefly a general point of view. The word merely means, I apprehend, " renunciation," and is merely a right way

---

[1] On July 4, 1899, he wrote to a young friend : ' It is always hard to curb oneself within the limits of the possibilities of one's own particular life. How happiness consists in recognising limits, and how hard it is to do so ! '

of regarding that which everybody has practically to regard, phrase it as he will, the fact that we cannot in life get everything we want, that our ideal is considerably higher than what we really attain. Now the ordinary way in which the individual applies this is in the way of "self-sacrifice." Look at ——, for instance : everything she does which is contrary to her inclination is regarded as self-sacrifice. Well, another step is to do what one has to do doggedly, unresignedly, with ill-restrained fury, yet hopeful that a day will come when the bondage will be over, when one won't have to do anything one does not like, when the desires that are within will meet with gratification. . . . What I maintain is, that if one has not got what one wants, it is either because one ought not to have it, and cannot have it, or else because one is trying for it in the wrong way. In either case, observe, there is no room for repining or discontent ; if one ought not to have it, rejoice because one cannot get it, that ought to be a matter of the deepest gratitude. Shall we be miserable because a physician refuses to prescribe for us a poison for which we have an unhealthy appetite ? If, on the other hand, we are trying in the wrong way, then for Heaven's sake don't let us abuse Providence for our own imbecility, but let us learn the right way, or find it out by experience and value the experience as teaching it to us. But under no circumstances let us grumble or be wretched. You will say the process of trying after a thing which one will never get is painful during the time in which one has not found out that one will never get it. I answer, no, if the principle I advocate be grasped, because one is founded upon the rock of knowing that if it is good one can get it. Luckily, to a moral nature all experience tells, and limits naturally apply themselves. . . . All moral doctrine lies in the *recognition* of the rules or principles, not in the carrying them out : everybody obeys the doctrine of limits, not everyone recognises the fact and owns it ; the last persons in the world to be lazy, to be indolent, or to be cowardly are those who can recognise limits as self-imposed ; they are decidedly not under the power of circumstances, but rather are entire masters of them ; they are the more likely to be decided in their actions, to have a plan, to have an object. . . . You take an instance, and say you dislike anyone saying that their field of doing good is limited. Why should they not ? If they have not strength of character enough to make such a field as will content them, it certainly is limited by their own imbecility ; let them recognise that, and then they must cease to grumble about it, which is always something. Everybody can do a great deal, I grant you ; but he will do it the better for thinking beforehand how much he can do.'

'Falmouth : September 20, 1871.

'Ought love for you to make me discontented—to make me think less of my fellow creatures—less attentive to their good? On the contrary, ought not my love to you to make my fellow creatures more precious, because I know how good human nature can be? Ought it not to make me stronger in my own power of dealing with them, through the knowledge of myself you have given me? Ought I not to be more capable of helping them because you have destroyed all small feelings of vanity, have removed all trace of purely personal motive that I could have had in my intercourse with them? I think we would differ if we were to search in our estimate of the good to be done by means of what is technically called " society : " if you feel you can do missionary work in it, do it decidedly ; if not, cut the whole matter. . . .

'You know I believe in a period in the development of character when the mind turns from unrest to rest. I am becoming dimly conscious of the immense influence you have had upon me in that way. I was struggling blindly in that direction, striving to attain an absolute self, instead of a phenomenal one—quite conscious of the necessity of doing so, and trying to bridge over my conscious defect by cultivating a habit of self-assertion, which you recognised in me when you first saw me, and so I was an enigma to those around me, and was regarded as a " talker of paradoxes." In you all things have become new. I have emerged out of that. In all chief matters I more clearly see what I am, what I can do. You are to me everything ; but you are no source of unrest to me, or of weakness.'

'Falmouth : September 23, 1871.

'You say you cannot see how one can reasonably believe in God's personal interference in the concerns of this life. What do you mean by " personal " applied to God at all ? Still more, why " interference "? Either the world moves according to certain laws or it moves by chance. Mankind on gazing round the world has always observed certain great laws regulating great phenomena ; these he has called laws of nature in the present day, and the question between different kinds of thinkers at the present day is whether by " Nature " we mean a hard, stern, inexorable fate, or a wise and bountiful Providence. I don't see how one is to split the difference ; one or other must be the case : I happen to prefer the latter hypothesis, perhaps from cowardice, perhaps from conviction that it is most rational, but mainly I think because it is the only thing that makes life at all possible to me. . . . Having got one's Providence, I see clearly in history how mankind has worked under its direction always in the way of progress; I see that progress has always been that of the universal humanity, not of the individual man; consequently I don't object from this point of view to anything that befalls me; if man's progress demands or is furthered by my dying in a workhouse, I should be very glad; under any circumstances I should at least feel the consolations of martyrdom. The laws that regulate the moral world exist as much as those of the physical. Let us try to reduce to a rational basis the meaning of my saying that the event of next Christmas will be a clear direction from God of the sphere of our duty; if I am not kept on, it will be for some reason or another influencing the voters : either they don't want married Fellows, or they don't want me, or they think somebody else better, or they look at the whole question of College tuition in a different way to me, or some ten thousand other causes, now dormant, which still would some day have come out and crippled me when I was doing my best. Why, even on the very face of the matter, if I am not wanted it were well I should go; the election is only made for five years, it would be ghastly to be elected now and turned out in five years; I am now young and versatile, and could easily take to something else; any views that existed against me now would do so and more in five years' time. Hundreds of reasons crop up and suggest themselves. . . . Your difficulties are merely those of reading flimsy articles or milk-and-water philosophy : the Divine government of the world no more requires "personal interference" than it does perpetual miracles. The laws of nature are standing miracles, the laws of human conduct may be equally gathered and obeyed, and when perceived are just as much regulated by God, and calling for our trust in Him, as anything can be. Remember in this case I can analyse a little way, and could do so still further, but one cannot in all cases, and then it is well to apply one's general principle of confidence and trust in God, knowing that the principle is true, knowing that attention and submission will enable us to hear God's voice everywhere, will prevent us from fighting foolishly against the regulations He has made for the moral world. Discontent, soreness, grumbling, weakness—these are the results of not listening to God's voice, of not seeing His laws. There is to me no halfway house—either God rules the world, in which case He rules you and me, not directly by

special revelations, but indirectly by His mighty laws, which
we can obey if we will ; or He does not, in which case let us
get married to-morrow, draw out of my banker's all the money
I can find, go abroad, live happily till the money is spent, and
then choke ourselves with charcoal. . . . I am not in favour
of milk-and-water heresies, let us have strong ones if any ; I
hate feebleness.'

'Falmouth : September 24, 1871.

'You know that my other great moral doctrine, beside
that of moral limits, is that of freedom.   Freedom in its most
absolute sense is what the individual must have ; he must be
self-determined : all that is external must become internal if
it is to guide him well ; and so I preferred that your influence
should affect my whole being rather than my casual actions ;
that you should make me what you wanted by your own
power rather than by my submission. . . .

'Remember, according to my theory, contentment admits
of no degrees, depends on no circumstances.   One sees that
life depends on the perfection of character by effort, and so
looks about to find the sort of effort these circumstances
call for.   Then pleasure consists solely in the sense of power,
i.e. in successful effort.   It is hard to gauge success at once,
but one can easily have an internal standard in the testimony
of conscience that one has done all that one could in the way
towards the goal.   In that way contentment, pleasure, and
satisfaction may everywhere be had.   Man is entirely above
the power of circumstances ; but as a foundation for that
point of view, one must have the recognition of limits to get
a man to accept his circumstances ; in fact, the doctrine of a
providential government of the world is only another way of
putting the purely moral doctrine of limits.'

'Falmouth : September 27, 1871.

'I think pottering little unbeliefs are a disease of youth,
like the measles ; I like to see a young man take them well :
they'll perhaps do him no harm ultimately.   But I do feel about
him that he is very often spreading a contagion unwisely
among girls, who have not the same means of being cured.
The transition from traditional to rational beliefs is always
dangerous. . . .   I notice that many young men who have
got to rational beliefs (I must plead guilty to this crime
myself sometimes) very often dwell more in conversation on
the traditions they have abandoned, than on the truths they
have attained : that is natural, because the traditions stand
out clear, they have rationally abolished them, and they

think them noxious; but the truths they have got they hold in an individual form : it is hard to give them a general expression ; to put them before another without giving a false impression, or else becoming more personally serious than ordinary society admits of : moreover, their system has been built up upon their own moral nature, and to explain it requires immense confessions. Hence, for all these causes, a girl, in anything like intellectual society, tends either to be made very miserable by having her beliefs shaken, or, on the other hand, to be driven to bigotry by having her traditions intensified.'

'October 4.

'No conceivable arrangement of external circumstances will give anyone peace : it can only come from within. . . . Unless you learn peace for yourself, you will only get it by the hard lessons of experience, after much wear and tear.'

' Merton College : October 17, 1871.

' Plato's fifth book of the " Republic " is, as you say, unsatisfactory ; it is so because it is far too ascetic and far too impersonal : it credits man with an amount of disinterestedness and self-sacrifice which must be the end rather than the beginning of the individual's life. Observe how all partial theories end in the same, whatever they start from ; that is a most profound truth : be the basis what it may, be the aim good or bad, selfish or unselfish, partial views of human nature come to the same. Plato's highest ideal of unselfishness comes, as you say, to a degradation of human nature—monasticism ended in practical profligacy of the most degraded condition. You cannot say to man, " Be this or that," and make him become so. Let all schemes be as ideal as they choose in the end they have before them ; but the danger of such schemes is that to get to the end they assume the means : because man has a soul, they assume he has no body ; and lives founded on such assumptions, so far from making those who lead them happier and nobler, ultimately degrade them, because they are founded on lies. We must take ourselves as we are : such is my most decided view. And does not this help you to see how it comes about that I am no help, but rather seem strange and unsympathetic, to many ? . . . I quite sympathise with your wish to extend my usefulness ; I quite see your impatient desire that everyone should think of me as you think ; but then everyone is not like you. Human nature cannot be dealt with wholesale. Do all go for consolation to the same books? . . . I perfectly agree with ———'s criticism, it is most just; but I cannot at present from my circumstances, from the narrow limits of my practical experiences, pretend to that broad knowledge of the details of the ordinary life on which alone a broad sympathy can be founded. I am intolerant of weakness because I rarely see it; wrong doing I see enough, wrong thinking, carelessness, thoughtlessness, arrogance, to all these I am sufficiently liable; but the sense of being baffled by the world, of shrinking before its complications, I never see, and have no experience of. . . . I am merely the common practitioner. . . . I perfectly grant you that one ought to be "all things to all men;" but I must confess I am sufficiently humble to see that my present state of mind does not enable me to be so all at once. I find great difficulty about sermons. Ought one to listen to criticism or not? About manner, about literary points, it is of course most valuable; but about general scope and subject, is it of any good? Either one has a message— in which case, for Heaven's sake, out with it, even if those who hear it will tear you in pieces for it; or one has not, in which case don't bore anyone by your drivel any more. More than that, criticisms one is likely to hear are those of one's friends or acquaintances, which are always worthless, because they are founded upon a general view of one's character, not upon what is then heard. The last is all that ought to be criticised. I want to know what some one thought who heard me speak for twenty minutes, who never saw me before, who does not know that he will ever see me again. Of course one always likes to hear what people say; but is it right? Would it not be better to go straight on? The practical sympathies of daily life would prevent one from being hardened: one's utterances ought to be the outcome of one's life, and the life must be changed, not the words. . . .

'Thackeray deals only with the outside of life, with life as a social matter. The life of soul does not come within his scope; many people socially vulgar, and pretentious, or pushing, or mean, have yet depths of spiritual life. A girl whose conversation at dinner strikes me as being animated by vanity, may yet have mental struggles full of nobility: we ought to remember both sides. . . .'

'Merton College: October 18, 1871.

'I have perfectly forgotten my conversation with F———. I always forget everything I disagree with: either it immediately affects me and makes me alter my conduct, or else it goes. Remind me of what F—— thinks : I imagine his views of college life are founded on —— College, in which case I profoundly dissent.   I cannot think that the noblest function those in authority here can perform is to fold their hands and see their pupils go quietly or noisily, as the case may be, to the devil. Either I must struggle, with many failures I grant, to make the organisation of the whole society more perfect, its morals more pure, its habits more frugal and more industrious, or I must go away at once.   No doubt F—— will say my rules and regulations and attempts don't make it so : I answer that I am not such a fool as to think that societies are made good by rules any more than nations by Acts of Parliament, but that is no reason for getting your Acts all into a muddle.   But you know sufficiently the nature of my reforming views : you know that I hold that if they are right, and are honestly enforced, they will in the end prevail ; if they are wrong, they will fail, as they deserve, and I will be more glad than anyone else at their failure, when I see they were unwise. . . .

'I am amused at ——'s remark about the easy life I have led : if I were to write an autobiography, the reader would hardly say so.   My life seems easy now because my main lines are clear, because I know what I mean.   There is a magnificent passage in Dante, in canto xxvii. of the " Purgatorio," at the end, where Virgil bids adieu to Dante and gives his final charges.   Virgil (symbolising man's reason), sent by Beatrice (i.e. enlightened by God's grace), has led Dante through the Inferno (has shown him the exceeding sinfulness of sin), through the Purgatorio (has shown him the way of repentance and self-purification), and now at the entrance of the Earthly Paradise bids him go on his way in all peace and confidence. Read and meditate over the whole passage : it is not an instruction to Dante for his behaviour in the Heavenly Paradise, but the Earthly, it is the rule of the good man's happiness here.   I ponder over its grandeur and sublimity, and wonder if it can be true.

> Thy will henceforth is upright, free, and sound ;
> To slight its impulse were a sin—then be
> Lord of thyself, be mitred and be crowned.

Truly if Dante had not loved intensely and suffered intensely, he could not have written his great poem.   From canto xxvii. of the " Purgatorio " to the end is most profoundly interesting to me, and exceedingly grand : I should like to talk it all over with you some day : meanwhile read and ponder it.'

'Merton College : October 19, 1871.

'Is not your whole view about the position of sympathy rather excessive? Sympathy must flow out of one's character, I am afraid one cannot learn to be sympathetic in itself : i.e. if from your point of view of life, the difficulties of others seem foolish, or exaggerated, or what you will, is it otherwise than imposture to profess to think those difficulties natural? My notion is the greatest sympathy with genuine illness or genuine sorrow ; but I don't consider it a great virtue, or a type of a high character, to endure and encourage the complaints of an invalid who pours out his laments that the weakness of his frame does not allow him to drink port wine perpetually, though he is excessively fond of it. . . .

'You wonder at my calmness in supposing I may be quite wrong : you don't remember that I begin from within : I lead my own life. Do you remember the lines in "By the Fireside" on that subject? We cannot any of us who are honest be wrong : each of us picks up a little bit of right and makes the best of it. A person doing and saying quite the opposite to me may be quite as right as I am ; only I object to anyone going and shrieking against me because the little bit of right he has picked up is not the same as the little bit I have. My confidence in my own rightness would not be shaken by seeing that what I had thought wrong was probably right : it would only be a slight modification of my views.'

'Merton College : October 20, 1871.

'I have seen that one can really do no good by interference, that everybody must fight out his own battles. All one can do is to watch the conflict, and be ready to cheer the combatant when weary ; but, remember, this cheering must not be cowardly. It's no good saying to the panting, struggling creature, 'How hard it is for you to have to fight the battle' —it is no good encouraging him in the short intervals of the fight to look at his bruises and mourn over them : get liniments ready if you like, have all appliances at hand, but it is no good moaning over wounds, for wounds there must and will be. Each person's character must be formed by his conflict, and by that only. I twaddle on, for I feel my conflict in its main battle is over : my character is made, such as it is : I have not now the daily hand-to-hand fight, merely the skirmishing on the outposts : a reinforcement from you enabled me to win a decisive victory. If I am harsh and unsympathetic, remember it is your fault : you have brought me out of my last difficulties : I seem to know what the whole thing means.

I don't want now to help the soldiers to groan, I want to get them to win.   Learn, then—I am sure I am right—to see that wounds and destruction are necessary. . . . On family life falls the burden of making character in its small details : we all think how well we get on away from home, how much more we are understood, &c. (you know the sort of remark): quite true, but it is a different sort of thing : home is engaged with details, strangers with the broad lines of our character. . . .'

'Merton College : October 21, 1871.

'If such affection as one has to bestow does not come spontaneously, it will assuredly come no other way. . . . People never seem to see that affection cannot be reasoned about, or measured out by inches; you cannot count it up at the end of the week like clothes coming home from the wash. To object because one does not get enough or what one wants, is much the same as crying because the sun does not set at night with equal beauty.   Is it not the height of vanity, the height of selfishness, to demand affection ?   How can anyone say, " I am a great and noble creature; come and worship me, pour yourself out before me : I deserve it all." Surely, looked at in that way, it seems the height of blasphemy to demand it.   And is it not the highest pitch of selfishness to require that a perpetual stream of the same intensity should be continued whatever occupations may distract you, whatever new interests may fill your mind—still the most subtle, the most evanescent, the most inscrutable outcome of the human soul is to be exacted from you as by a rigorous taskmaster : you must make your tale of bricks with or without straw, it matters little.   I wish I could put the question equally clearly to ——— : all demands of that kind seem to me to be most ungenerous, to proceed utterly from selfishness. Again, at the risk of seeming egotistical, I must say, I have gone through it all : I have made such demands myself on others, I have found them failures, and that the article dribbled out at my request was not worth having ; but it took me a long while to learn it, and it is very useful when learned. . . . Do you know when I look at ———, the things they say remind me exactly of the little jealousies I used to feel at school, when I was always being hurt by my friends, and being wounded, and so on ; but I have never felt so since I came to Oxford : I have always felt that if I got any affection—well, put that down to the good ; if not, I must get on without it. . . .

'*Sunday.*—This morning I went to the University Sermon preached by the Rector of Lincoln.   It was very good : he took a survey of the phases of religious thought in England in the last century, and remarked that the old school of Anglican divines had been destroyed by Evangelicalism, which had given way to High Church.   The old Anglican had been rational, had been engaged with the proofs of Christianity, had had an intellectual platform : the Evangelicals had complained of them as being unedifying, had substituted private judgment, and made religion a matter of the emotions. As a reaction against this came the High Church, who opposed private judgment by authority, and made religion a matter of corporate membership.   He then proceeded to discuss the widening breach between Science and Theology, and argued in favour of the establishment of a rational school of theology.   It was very good, though it did not come to much as a solution of anything.'

' Merton College : October 23, 1871.

' Your remarks about family life are quite true ; but they are not confined to family life, they apply equally to life in any particular sphere : one wants to live the ideal life, the life of the soul, and tends to be disgusted with the real life, the life of the body.   There are always three solutions : that of the ascetic, who finds the ideal life in the destruction of the real ; that of the sensualist, who finds the real life so nice that he drops the ideal ; and the remaining plan of trying to find a synthesis of the two, of bringing them together, by self-consciousness, by knowledge, by self-renunciation, by all the means one can.   But the difficulty is that you cannot prescribe for anyone in the last course : he must find out the synthesis for himself, you cannot say in what way he will solve the problem.   To asceticism or sensuality the motives are simple, the path straight and forward, everyone sees how to begin ; but the other is the difficulty.   Don't imagine, therefore, that family difficulties are peculiar to families.'

' Merton College : October 24, 1871.

' Nobody can understand anyone else's love. . . . Love is a perpetual miracle : if one could understand it, what would be the good ? . . . Don't expect too much from anyone, don't ask for sympathy. It is like champagne : if it is handed round, well and good ; if not, don't try and prevail on the waiter to bring you a private bottle.   Let us see how everything ends in selfishness more or less profound, and how all unhappiness comes from making quite ludicrous demands and wanting what one cannot get. .
' Surely the truth at the bottom of your remarks is this :

poetry, painting, and music all ought to be founded on an idea of some sort: poetry most directly stimulates you to grasp the idea, and allures you least to linger on the form : music allures you most to linger on the form, and stimulates you least to grasp the idea. Hence, on the one hand it can deal with vaguer ideas, which is an advantage ; on the other it is more easy to get mere pleasure and no profit out of it. Surely the vast majority of the people who listen to music get nothing beyond pleasure out of it ; and that music is most generally popular which deals with sensual ideas, in proportion as it tries to embody intellectual ideas, it appeals to a smaller and more cultivated audience.'

'Merton College : October 25, 1871.

' You observe that you argued against Goethe's many-sidedness on the ground that he was only great as a poet. Is that fair? Poetry is only the form, many-sidedness consists in the idea. Did Goethe take a large and at the same time subtle view of the universe and of man? Surely he did in a wonderful degree : science, reason, passion—morality, immorality—the struggles of the soul, the indulgence of the body—these are only slight headings of the things he touched. I don't think Leonardo was many-sided in the same way : his character is too pronouncedly intellectual only, the faces in his pictures show exclusively refinement, tenderness, and subtle thought. It seems to me that Goethe as an artist approaches Titian, but with many a dash of Leonardo. It is true Leonardo knew many subjects—engineering, mathematics, the art of painting and that he was a polished man of society as well ; but Goethe was equally so, and I dare say a good many writers to the " Encyclopædia Britannica" could beat them both. No, I think Goethe would have a greater claim than Leonardo, though infinitely less than Shakespeare, whose *abandon* is perfectly marvellous. . . . If each of us could mould the world as suited him individually best, what would become of the common world of us all ? We ought to do whatever we like and get whatever we want—only we should be careful never to like or want what everybody cannot get ; aye, and get better and more from our having had.'

'Merton : October 29.

' We have long ago agreed that neither of us cares about the opinion of others about each other. . . . Such as I am, such must I be : people must take me or leave me. If ever I make myself agreeable, it is because people draw me to them,

I can't do things for the sake of effect . . . when you are conscious of criticism you cease to be spontaneous.

'To want sympathy, and not to find it, is a sure mark of either feebleness or selfishness ; you may either set to work to strengthen your character, so as to stand alone and work in your own might, or, on the other hand, by genuine tenderness, by genuine unselfishness, by real love for others, you must always command as much sympathy as you like : it is a commodity to be bought, if it is regarded as a necessary of life, at its proper price ; or it is, on the other hand, a luxury, and one may simplify one's life so far as to do without it.'

'Merton College : November 1, 1871.

'Your remarks about G. Sand and Thackeray are true : she is much greater than he is ; but is either of them first-rate ? I wonder. A true work of art ought to have a union of the internal and external : perfect artistic beauty should not be sacrificed to the idea to be expressed. Herein is the great beauty of the Leonardo face : it is quite beautiful in form, yet carries the intellectual expression to its highest point : the earthly and the unearthly, the bodily and the spiritual, the fleshly and the mental, are summed up in one representation. His women are women beyond all doubt; they have also immortal destinies written in their face, and have minds of surpassing depth and keenness. One could love them for ever. Don't you think so ? Now, applying that notion of artistic perfection to novels, they ought on the one hand to be a clear picture of life, omitting nothing of its elaboration, of its littleness, or of its grandeur, and on this background carefully and minutely finished in every detail there ought to stand out flashing forth more clearly in its intensity and singleness some human soul at some period of its development. Thackeray loses the soul in the elaboration of its surroundings : G. Sand neglects the surroundings, deliberately falsifies them, or invents a mere sketchy background. Much as I admire " La Petite Fadette," I cannot accept it as a genuine representation of Breton peasant life in the same way as "Adam Bede" is of the Lincolnshire peasant life, or " The Mill on the Floss " of a provincial town. . . . The grandeur of Shakespeare's Historical Plays is due to the fact that he does not shrink from taking actual facts of the most complicated and it would seem uninteresting and unattractive kind, quite unfit for artistic purposes, and on them as a background, which he paints in with the most careful and conscientious hand, he dashes out the struggles of a few human souls. He could not have enforced the same lessons, he could not have made his analysis so profound, if he had not been so true in his conditions. Now, the defect I feel in G. Sand is, her want of truth in these details makes her whole picture somewhat unreal : as fancy sketches of character her books are marvellous, as real lessons for practical guidance they fail ; and this is a want surely.'

'Merton College : November 4, 1871.

'Remember we fulfil our place in the general plan of the world by each living his own life : if that is so, there is an ideal life for you and me—meaning by "ideal" the highest life we are capable of : but it by no means follows that that would be the highest another couple were capable of. In a novel what is necessary is to get hold of the character truly, i.e. to regard the character as formed by its surroundings, as developing naturally and being what it is in virtue of what it was. Each man is the sum of his previous life and experience, he is the accretion of years of thought and years of external circumstance, and if you suddenly dash off with an ideal character and stick it down haphazard somewhere, you will produce the impression of unreality. It is not difficult to deal with ideals, with abstractions, with vacuities—every sermon I hear seems to be so engaged, and that is why it is so dull and useless. . . .'

'November 19.

'In social matters especially the conscious missionary is a bore ; let us live our own lives content whether people like us or not. . . . You and I may, if we try very hard, manage to lead a sincere, honest, simple life together. I believe that firmly, and I hope rationally—for I never mind telling you little things I observe about you, and you don't mind hearing them—but if we try to take any third person into our partnership we shall fail. I don't believe in the possibility of doing so.'

'Merton College : December 11, 1871.

'I like Jowett's sermon as much as you do, only my point of view is necessarily different from yours. It did me good to hear it. I think it is very noble ; but the question is, can such a view of Christianity as is there set forth make a practical system to set before the heathendom of England, and be a moral engine to elevate society ? Cultivated society, I grant you, will benefit from it greatly, it may be the universal system some day ; but will that touch the heart of the sinner, will men brought up on that go forth in a self-denying way to do battle with the more open forms of vice ? Again, are you right in saying that it shows how we should judge our present difficulties in the light of Christ's life? Is it not rather a delicate and artistic selection of such utterances of Christ as fit in with the opinions of Jowett? Is it exhaustive? How about the saying, " I came not to send peace, but the sword "? How about the innumerable dark sayings of Christ? It is of course easy to say people had better leave them alone, but they quite obviously won't. The more diligently a man studies a book, the more he imbibes its manifest lessons, surely the more he meditates over passages he cannot understand. I admire Jowett's sermons, I admire Liddon's, but I cannot say of either of them, as their admirers do, " Lo, here is the whole truth, there is nothing else." Both of them embody part of the truth : neither of them is universal. You know my bane is hankering after a universal system : I cannot be content speculatively, though I am practically quite easily, with the best that I can see : hence my constant inconsistencies. I take what I can get, but I cannot lose myself in that and say, " That is all." You know how I carry that everywhere. . . .

'You have a great capacity for losing your hold of moral principle at times : it is so hard a thing to hold it fast always, that no one could say he always had it; but it is a great help to firmness of hold to try and weave it into all one's actions, to make all one does seem great by keeping the great issues of every little act to one's moral self, clearly before one. . . .

'Is it not true that the affection that can be hurt by slight things is somewhat selfish? Does not the hurt arise from the feeling of loss of self-gratification? One has gone to the cupboard for jam, and it is all mouldy and bad, and one is terribly disappointed. Quite right if one's grief is for the poor jam and the sad change it has undergone; but if it is simply greediness—The wise person, it seems to me, is he who gets over his disappointment at once, then gets a knife and begins to scrape off the mildew, and is pleased at his dexterity in deftly removing it, and then finally sits down and has a good meal after all.'

'Merton College: December 12, 1871.

'I don't think you need fear we shall be too idle when we are married. I shall always have enough to do. That always strikes me as the nuisance of married life—strive as I may or as you may, still the practical side of life must be much more prominent to me than to you. I shall have a number of things to do, whereas your sphere will be all within my reach and knowledge, mine on the other hand will not be in your reach entirely. Will you mind? will you make allowances for that? will you not feel hurt when you think I am doing a number of things for other people that I had much better not do, but spend the time with you? I hope you will not do so, I hope you will trust me enough : it does not do to say that I might explain to you all that I am doing, as in practical life one's ultimate end is not manifest in the beginning—a number of small things are to be done unconsciously, because one dimly thinks they are better done than undone, while the ulterior good only slowly appears. You will try and keep that before you, won't you? You must not ever think that I want to keep anything from you ; but self-consciousness comes only after groping, and no articulate utterance can come forth till self-consciousness is attained. Please make up your mind to take on trust many things I do : if I am wrong, you can slowly convince me; but it will not be wise of you to lay orders on me to desist. . . . I quite agree with you about your views on visiting the poor : I always regret that I don't see my way to doing it: I feel hopelessly incompetent, and also I feel that my interests are sufficiently varied as it is, and would get hopelessly muddled if I were to try and indulge more of them ; but I should like you to do it, and when I can I will go with you, and you shall gradually teach me.

'If you get a " Manchester Guardian " to-morrow, you will find some remarks of mine in it : they are awfully dull. I was quite appalled when I saw them in print : I can only say that they took me some two hours altogether, and were a hurried production. I am always disgusted with everything I write. Do you know that Gibbon wrote his first volume eight times over before he was satisfied with it—that Balzac wrote multitudes of novels which an intelligent sister persuaded him to burn, before he broke out into one fit to publish and be the precursor of his mighty works? We have much to learn and go through before we are any good. Modern literature seems to me to ruin a man : the moment he can write anything, off he goes to a newspaper and drivels for the rest of his life : there is no effort, no self-restraint in his work. As Bridges remarked to-day, " All newspaper articles give you the notion of an able man spoilt." These again are general remarks : I seem to be in a platitudinarian spirit.'

'Merton College : December 14, 1871.

'I certainly think much of Tennyson's poem (" The Last Tournament "): it seems to me to bring out the effects of sins of incontinence in destroying any high ideal of society—surely a lesson which is necessary in the present day : it read to me like a protest wrung from him against the prevailing school of feebly passionate poetry.   Self-development must go together with self-restraint : the individual self and its desires must be perpetually conditioned by the universal self : one's desires should be such that they can be gratified without injury to anyone else.   I think the modern revival of taste and art tends to forget that. . . . In all things we must get to a universal element.   It is no good saying that love is peremptory, and will take no refusal.   No one ought to love where he may not or in a way that he may not : a feeling of admiration everyone may have.'

'Merton College : December 15, 1871.

' I never saw a family in which affection was outwardly displayed that did not suffer for it. . . . The affectionate side of life is opposed to the moral side.   It is only between two persons of great similarity of thought and of formed minds that affection can exist as interwoven with their moral life. . . . In a home life and its conduct quite naturally, and I think rightly, the critical and moral side prevails over the emotional.   If all the members were of the same age and had the same interests, it would be different. . . . I may like one of my undergraduates immensely, but if we became affectionate towards one another, we should cease to be useful to one another : my sense of moral responsibility towards him would be changed for one of mere pleasure in his presence ; his feeling of respect for my opinion, of identification of my orders with those of absolute law, would be entirely lost. . . . The parable . . . might be applied generally to any member of a family. It is difficult to realise that spontaneous affection is rare and demands special circumstances : only to people such as we are, or to very intimate friends, is it possible that the moral judgment should not interfere with spontaneous emotion, that no check from within comes upon the mere attraction from without, that feelings can be indulged without weakness. Of course it is hard for people to see that : I only learned it slowly : since then I have never expected too much, and have always got more than I expected.'

'December 17, 1871.

' To me the first month of our engagement was more completely a remaking of all things than the first month of marriage can be to you.   I have got over my alterations, and have even burned the rubbish. . . .

' I had a walk with Esson and Wallace, in which we discussed large questions of married life and Oxford society and all kinds of things, and all determined to be very economical, and quite wise in all sorts of ways, and we all railed at the foolish luxury of Oxford, and said we would away with it.

'Hard work is the cure for feeble thinkings. . . .'

'Examination Schools : December 18, 1871.

' I had rather a pleasant evening, and spent the greater part of dinner-time in an argument as to which was the greatest poet, Shakespeare or Dante : I am afraid my audience, not having read Dante, was unconvinced. Shakespeare was the greater man as being more universal, but Dante has more charm for me as being more intense. Shakespeare as a pure artist was engaged with the diversities of human character as they were ; Dante as the thoughtful and reflective genius was engaged rather with human life than with human character—was engaged with the general problem of life, not with its details : life never could be to him a number of detached observations or detached experiences—it was one great scheme : just as Leonardo differs from Titian. I see the points of both : I see the one is more truly an artist, will command a larger audience, but the other where he gets a hearing will stamp his mark deeper.'

'Kirkandrews : December 28, 1871.

' I wonder why you, who at all events ought to know me, join with the rabble about whom I don't care in accusing me of talking paradoxes, and of uttering misleading statements. If the object of discussion is to get to the truth, and if the object of talking about oneself is to try and say as near the truth as is possible, then I don't see how you can talk to please or instruct people : as you know and see, so must you speak, or not at all. Probably not to discuss at all is wise : but still, to discover even a glimpse of the truth to or from any one is worth the whole of the rest of life put together. Did Christ speak His parables with a view to indicate His character as a man of consistency, or a man of strong common sense, or a man to get on in the world ? We are told often enough what were the remarks made by those who heard Him. I apprehend that as it befell Him, so must it befall all who would be teachers. Meditate, and tell me if my view is tenable : it is not a view, but it is a necessity to me. . . . I cannot be content to say, "Peace, peace," where there is no peace, or to agree with what I feel to be thin and untrue. . . .

' Criticism to be real must not be dogmatic, but explanatory : it must say what the thing it is busy with means, and then it must leave mankind, with all its variety of thought and all its many-sided cravings, to say what is the worth of such a production. We may say to ourselves, " This we admire, and that not ; " we cannot say to mankind, " This you must admire, that you must hate." We can only show the folly of an idol and its futility ; if men still worship it, we cannot help them. I am sufficiently imbued with the Hellenic spirit to think that a sense of completeness, of flawlessness about anything, is a very great element. It seems to me that the artistic side of novel writing is shockingly disregarded : there is very little striving after good taste and artistic completeness and unity. " Romola " is the only English novel I remember which aims at it, and there one is conscious of excessive elaboration in every page. The only perfectly satisfactory novel, regarding it as a work of art, that I ever read is George Sand's " La Petite Fadette." '

'September 1874.

'I say what I think openly, and if anyone chooses to misrepresent me, well and good.... ——'s faults are just of the kind that are to me most open, and that I never lose sight of. I see in them—in society—the workings of a calculating self-consciousness, it is the very thing I see most keenly as it happens. I feel the loss of any spontaneity, and that always tells upon me, and prevents me from becoming quite natural and entirely throwing away reserve. If I am of any good, it is by virtue of the honesty with which I express my individual convictions. I want always to express them all, right or wrong, good or bad, nice or not, and their value solely lies in the fact that they are home-made and not imported. Now, that is just the sort of thing they don't care about : they think that opinions ought to be wise—but for wise opinions I go to the " Times " newspaper. What I want is something to lift one above one's daily surroundings. One has to live among them, therefore let me act sensibly ; but I don't care about taking a holiday in the shape of a walk along my own cart-road. I want to get away for a rapid trip, though I know all the while that I have to come back to the cart-road.'

' Kirkandrews : December 29.

'Up to the present time I have found life tolerably cheerful. I have learnt that when one can't get what one wants, one can at least leave off wanting it—I have learnt that what is, is best, that regrets are quite useless, that life in the present and future alone is useful for man : that no one need ever be disappointed or even seriously annoyed unless he chooses : cares may come and knock at the door, but the fault lies with him who is fool enough to open it.'

CHAPTER V

MARRIAGE AND LAST YEARS AT OXFORD

OUR wedding took place on January 8, 1872, at St. Bartholomew's Church, Sydenham. We were married by Creighton's brother Fellow, Robert Wilson.

'December 8, 1871.

' I asked Wilson to perform the service, and he said he would be delighted, about which I am glad, as I am fond of my College, and like in all things to identify myself with it as much as possible.'

Mr. Wilson was assisted by the Vicar of Sydenham, the Hon. and Rev. A. Legge, now Bishop of Lichfield. In accordance with our wishes it was a quiet wedding; there were no bridesmaids and no wedding breakfast, and the marriage service was followed by a celebration of Holy Communion. There was not much time left before the beginning of term, but we had a week in Paris, which we spent chiefly in seeing pictures, and on our way back we stopped at Amiens to visit the cathedral. Meanwhile Creighton's College servants, who were devoted to him,[1] had superintended the moving of his possessions, and arranged them as they thought he would like in the new house, and his white Persian cat was comfortably established on the hearthrug to welcome us. A few days were spent in hanging pictures, arranging his books and china, and then the work of the term began.

St. Giles's Road East was not numbered, and we had to choose a name for our house : we called it ' Middlemarch,' in re-

---

[1] He was an excellent master, though never familiar with his servants; he always knew how to get himself well served, and never had a servant who did not wish above all things to please him. ' Experience at Oxford,' he wrote, ' has taught me how to treat male servants : it is by being fearfully strict with them, though never losing your temper or being put out. I always treat waiters now as if they belonged to me alone. . . .'

membrance of George Eliot's novel, which was then coming out, a name which had the advantage of being easily remembered. The house was a mile from Merton. Creighton always went to college for early morning chapel and stayed on for the Fellows' breakfast, where he could see his colleagues and talk over college affairs with them. He lectured the whole morning, and then came home for lunch. In the afternoon, unless there were any meetings to attend, we walked together. We also frequently attended the lectures of the different professors given at the inconvenient hour of two o'clock. The professors he liked to hear were Dr. Stubbs, Sir Henry Maine, and sometimes Mr. Ruskin. He also attended with much pleasure and interest Dr. Mozley's lectures to graduates. He often had pupils again in the late afternoon ; the evenings, when there were no dinner engagements, were devoted to work. He used to dictate the notes of his lectures to me, gaining in this way greater freedom as he prepared them to roam among his books. Oxford was, as always, very hospitable. We dined out a good deal in colleges, where I was sometimes the only lady, for ladies were still rare in Oxford. The married tutors also entertained a great deal. If the college dinners were sometimes luxurious, the dinners given by the young married people were very simple. We were all comparatively poor, we were acquainted with one another's pecuniary position, and there was no desire for pretence ; to do everything as prettily and simply as possible, and at the most moderate cost, was our common ambition. The friends of whom we saw most were Mr. and Mrs. T. H. Green, Mr. and Mrs. T. H. Ward (who were married at Easter, 1872), Mr. Pater and his sisters, Mr. J. R. Thursfield and his mother, and somewhat later Mr. and Mrs. A. Johnson ; and among the residents in College, Andrew Lang, Robert Wilson, H. G. Woods, R. Copleston, Robert Laing, J. F. Bright (now Master of University College), and many others. We knew hardly any of the heads of colleges. Among the older and more distinguished members of the University, those who took most interest in the younger people were Professor and Mrs. Max Müller, Professor and Mrs. Bonamy Price, Mr. Jowett, Dr. Bradley, and Professor Henry Smith and his sister. Dinners were then as a rule at seven o'clock, only the great people dined at 7.30. My husband made a point of leaving at ten so as to have time to prepare his lectures for the next day. We always walked out to dinner, and the weather had to be very bad to make a cab necessary.

Creighton was very anxious that his marriage should in no way interfere with the closeness of his relations with his college. Besides breakfasting there daily, he dined in college at least once a week. On Sundays we always went to the three services at Merton Chapel, and often to the University Sermon; spending the morning after the Sermon in a long country walk.

All through his life he loved to show hospitality, and we entertained many guests in our small Oxford house. Among those who visited us I remember the Frederic Harrisons, G. Pembers, G. Saintsbury, Dr. Caird, Basil Champneys, Dr. Appleton (editor of ' The Academy '), the Henry Cromptons, C. P. Scott, and Robert Bridges, men of all kinds of opinions and pursuits. J. R. Green, the historian, an old friend of mine, who in these years was examining for the History Schools, frequently stayed with us when he came to Oxford. He and Creighton had so many interests in common that they enjoyed one another's society immensely, and discussed historical problems with unfailing zest.

Creighton had often felt fussed and worried by the small cares of college life, and had longed for peace and quietness in which he might be free to lead his own life. He had frequently asserted that his engagement had helped him much in this way. He would speak of love as the supreme revealer, as the way by which a man found himself. Before marriage he had written :

' November 15.

' Being with you makes me feel so much better afterwards : it is quite odd : I feel physically stronger and more self-contained and capable of work.'

' May.

' People's lives are dreary, as you say : rather, they have no lives at all. The majority of people seem to me to be so absolutely under the sway of their conditions as to find it impossible to do anything at all, or make anything out of them. Our lives will never be dreary, will they? We will always have in ourselves infinite stores of refreshment for one another.'

VOL. I.   K

'December 15, 1871.

'The object of affection, it seems to me, ought to be eminently real : people fail because they try by their love to build themselves a fool's paradise to dwell in ; surely what we want is more strength to live in the real world.'

'I have no picture of what kind of happiness we shall have . . . only I will have passed into a more advanced stage as a human being, and will be much better for it. I shall have more pleasure in life because I shall have broader views of life and a broader nature, but I don't know that I shall have more happiness ; I am not unhappy at present ; I don't think many people have much more happiness except those strong healthy creatures who sail through life with a grin on their face—and I don't envy them, but would rather be as I am. I admire Titian, but I had much rather be Leonardo. Well, then, I am happy at present, and intend to go on being happy : do you mind ? '

After marriage he wrote to his mother-in-law :

'January 28, 1872.

'My dear Mamma,—I am not a good letter writer ; that is to say, it requires a serious pressure to extract many letters out of me ; so you won't ever think me neglectful if my communications are scanty. It always seems to me that unless letters are written very often and very intimately they are only useful for very definite purposes when one has something definite to say, otherwise one can only look forward to a time of meeting when a little talk is more effectual than much ink shed. But I wanted to write to you, now that we are getting definitely settled into our house, and my work has well begun, and I see the sort of life we are likely to go on leading in all its little details, that I might tell you, when I looked at it calmly and quietly, how delighted I am with it, and how much better in every way I find it to be in reality than in my anticipations I had ever hoped for. I find everything much nicer than I expected : the troubles are fewer, in fact almost none. Louise is so admirable at managing everything, that I find I have less worry than I used to have among my multitude of servants at College. Again, the house is more comfortable than I had thought ; I like the effect of the furniture better : there are fewer things to regret than I had expected. I find also my work more easily arranged in accordance with my change of life than I had thought possible. By managing to go to chapel every morning and breakfasting in College I get to work quite early and get through it all by 1.30; also, as the Fellows all breakfast in common, I continue in that way to keep up my connexion with them, which is of considerable importance in every way. Of course breakfasting alone is a little dreary for Louise; but she sees the usefulness of the arrangement, and does not mind. As to Louise, I find that she is a hundred times better on closer acquaintance than even I had thought beforehand. I keep on seeing new reasons for adding more and more respect, and moral and intellectual approbation, to my feelings towards her. Do I draw a picture of a contented man? I think so. I should like you to come and judge of our contentment as soon as may be. . . . My satisfaction will soon become offensive if I pour forth so much.'

He was very particular about all the arrangements of his domestic life; his habits were simple, and he never expected personal attendance, but he liked what was done in the house to be well done, he accepted no excuses and overlooked no shortcomings. From everybody he asked the best they could give. Like all men of highly strung natures, he had a somewhat impatient and irritable temper. This was, as a rule, absolutely under control. I do not think he ever showed temper or irritability at meetings or with his pupils, or on any public occasions. But in private life he would sometimes express displeasure or vexation in sharp and cutting words; those who were nearest and dearest to him alone seemed able to arouse his irritation, partly, I think, because his very love for them made him expect so much from them, partly because he so absolutely identified himself with them that he felt their shortcomings as his own. But once the sharp word spoken, the temper was gone. Nothing was so obnoxious to him as to go back over any dispute, to demand any explanation; he called that 'to live in a sewer.' If he or any one else was guilty of temper, his only desire was to forget it as soon as possible. To an apology for a hasty word, or any act which might have displeased him, his invariable answer was, 'I have nothing to forgive.' I never knew him bear a grudge or cherish ill-will to any one even for the briefest space of time. I never heard him lose his temper with a servant; he would say that he was going to give a servant a most tremendous blowing up, and then,

K 2

when the servant arrived, speak in the kindest and gentlest way. His college servants liked to go on working for him after his marriage ; they would come and help him to bottle a cask of claret, and often brought us flowers from their gardens.

His strong respect for individual liberty showed itself in his attitude towards the opinions of others. He always wished to leave me absolute independence. He wrote, May 1871 :

'Remember, I will never give way to you in my views, but will teach you tolerance first, and then we will convert one another gradually.

'I don't want ever to make any demands from you, or to require you to do serious things for me, or to make any sacrifices of yourself. I want you as you are, or rather as you may be if perfectly free . . . to be all you ever could be.'

He maintained that each member of a family should be free to go his own way so long as it did not interfere with others, but that they had no right to demand not only that they should be allowed to go their own way, but that others should approve of that way.

In 1871 the Law and Modern History School was divided, and Creighton was appointed examiner for the new Modern History School.

He went every week in the Lent Term of 1872 to lecture to the Ladies' Association at Clifton, and in October he lectured at Birmingham. He also examined at Clifton College. The attendance at his lectures in Merton Hall steadily increased. He lectured among other things on the Ris of European Nationalities, and on Hildebrand and the Struggle about Investitures. Life was very busy and an increasing strain during term time. In the long vacation we spent some quiet weeks at Oxford to give him time for study, and then carried our books to his father's house at Kirkandrews, where he prepared a course of lectures to be given at Falmouth in August and September. While at Kirkandrews he preached every Sunday in a primitive little church like a barn in the neighbouring village of Beaumont. The Vicar was old and in bad health, and was glad of his help. It was here that, during this and later visits, he taught himself to preach extempore, then not so common a practice as it has since become. He used to prepare his early extempore sermons most carefully, and write very full notes for them.

At Falmouth we were warmly welcomed by the friends he had made the year before. Though I had heard a great deal about their kindness, it was a surprise to find how much they made of him, and the trouble they took to help us to enjoy our time in Falmouth. His lectures were on the Age of Charles V. He also preached every Sunday in the parish church, and his sermons attracted much attention. We discussed together the subjects of those early sermons, and one to which he gave much thought was on Elisha's demand for a double portion of Elijah's spirit. This he took as an illustration of the relations to be desired between old and young. A worthy spinster in the town was shocked at his treatment of the subject, and said she wondered what these young Oxford men were coming to; she had been brought up to consider the duties of children to their parents, but now it seemed that parents were to be taught their duties to their children. In later years he further developed this sermon and preached it when first asked to preach in St. Paul's Cathedral, where it called forth the warm admiration of Dean Church.[1]

On October 31 our first child was born at Oxford, and called Beatrice, in remembrance of her father's Dante studies. Creighton had hardly yet discovered how strong was his inborn sympathy and love for children. In 1871 he had written to me :

' Don't say you will take me to romp with ——'s children ; it would be a ghastly piece of hypocrisy on my part to do so. Let us tell the truth and shame the devil ; I will learn all those things in good time.'

Those who have seen him with children in later years will hardly believe that he could ever have written such words. His tender care of his wife is best shown by words written many years afterwards, to a young friend during the enforced absence of her husband before the birth of their first child.

[1] It now gives the title to a volume of his sermons called *The Heritage of the Spirit.*

'In a way it is a loss that X—— is not here, because he cannot cheer you up in those little things which you do not care to talk about to any one else. But the process makes a man feel rather mean : he learns how much a woman has to do for the human race, in which he can take no part. It teaches him infinite tenderness and gratitude.

'I am trying to explain a man's point of view. He is at best a stupid creature, isn't he? When he thinks about his wife and about the child that is to be, he always feels a ruffian somewhat, as if he ought to explain that he would take his share if he could, and is sorry that he can't.'

The following letter belongs to this period :

'Examination Schools, Oxford : December 14, 1872.

'My dear Thursfield,—You will with justice think me a beast for never having written to you ; but . . . partly my ordinary work was hard, partly an invalid wife consumes spare time, but chiefly the labour of making papers for the new Modern History School has almost brought my grey hairs to my waistcoat pocket : we had to make thirty papers in all kinds of unwonted subjects, and my heart sank within me, my head also was sorely wrought. Now, however, that is over, and my labours have sunk to the dreary monotony of the Pass Examination. . . . Well was it for thee, O Thursfield ! that by thy absence in a foreign land thou hast escaped the ghastly sight of Montagu Burrows lifting up his horn against Stanley and having it snipped off. I am convinced— and I commend this to the serious consideration of all practical politicians, of whom I regard you as the chief— that every time the moral and cultivated man exercises his right to vote, he seriously impairs both his morality and culture. The wrath one feels against opponents, the contempt for their intelligence, and the doubt about their honesty, this destroys that charity which is the highest aim of morality ; while, on the other hand, the necessity of stating your views broadly, of making up your mind decidedly, of urging all kinds of arguments on others which you only half believe, intellectually speaking, yourself—this destroys true culture and rubs off its bloom. My philosophy is becoming profound : I wish to chronicle my impressions of the events which I have seen. Woods showed me a letter from you in which you expressed your general views about German Universities and English University reform. The difference is clear : the German Universities depend upon their intellectual prestige for their existence and consequently are most anxious to secure the best possible professors : English Universities are, we are perpetually told, " National Institutions," and their permanence as such—also the fulfilment of their functions in accordance with the wishes of the vast majority of those who send their sons here—is much better promoted by having men like Rawlinson, Michell, and Wall professors, than men like Pattison or Henry Sidgwick. No German parent objects to a " dangerous " professor existing in a University to which his son goes ; but although we seem to ourselves in Oxford hide-bound enough, to the ordinary parent we are a very dangerous class, and I think we cannot hope to advance more rapidly than the bulk of the people. That is the price we have to pay in England for our solidity : we must move altogether; and I fear me our present University reforms in the interest of research don't make out a very good case in the eyes of the ordinary Briton in favour of that research. Mark Pattison is undoubtedly a researcher, so are we all ; but one Essay and Review and one edition of Pope's " Essay on Man " scarcely justify to the Philistine a large endowment ; nor can it be urged that abject poverty and hard work have prevented production. We live in days when we have to prove to our countrymen the value of knowledge, and we won't do it. The scientific men are always justifying their existence ; but Jowett's Crib to Plato and Fowler's Deductive Logic don't move the human heart very deeply. I could wish the academic cause were maintained by some men who had borne more of the burden and heat of the day. However, we must make the best of it, and protest as loudly as we can for the interests of learning. . ,. May you flourish and write to me again.

'Yours ever,
'M. CREIGHTON.'

From the first Creighton paid considerable attention to his daughter. He never went out to his work in the morning without going up to visit her, and when she was a few months old would play with her a great deal, and liked to have her on the floor by his side when at work. On Sundays, when her nurse was at church, he would take her out with me in her perambulator ; every stage in her development was followed with interest.

In the summer of 1873 we spent five weeks together in Italy. His studies were always more and more turning to Italian subjects. At first he had thought of possibly writing a history of Italian Art, but though his interest in art did not diminish, his interest in the history of Italy grew to be more absorbing, and his subject slowly began to shape itself. For the moment his desire was to get to know Italy. In those days, the smaller Italian towns were little visited, and the accommodation was somewhat rough. But to this he was indifferent. He was an admirable traveller, very simple in his demands, satisfied with everything that turned up, never tired, able to go a long while without food. What he disliked was a smart big hotel full of tourists. We reached Milan on August 20, and wandered on through Piacenza, Modena, Pistoja, Lucca, Pisa, and Siena to Florence. All these places were new to him, but he was so well prepared by previous reading, that he knew everywhere what he wanted to see. He seemed to have an instinct for finding out the special points of a place ; his quick observation showed him what the natives themselves had never noticed ; he liked to find out everything for himself, and never used a guide nor asked his way. He knew how to use a guide-book, and get from it all that it could give him, without being its slave. In Italian towns he always used the admirable German guide-book by Gsell-Fels, but he was a severe critic of guide-books, and would often talk of how he would like to write one himself, which should give just the right kind of information.

At that time of year there were no tourists in the towns, and we seemed to have Italy to ourselves. The heat was excessive. We used to get up between five and six, and, after breakfast outside a café, wander about seeing churches till lunch at ten o'clock, after which we took refuge from the heat in picture galleries or museums. The afternoon had to be spent resting with closed shutters till, after dinner at five o'clock, the cool of the evening tempted us out again. Creighton could enjoy a holiday thoroughly ; he loved to sit outside a café in the evenings, smoking and watching the people. At Florence we stayed nearly a fortnight, visiting Prato from there. Then we went on to Cortona, Arezzo, Perugia, Assisi, Ancona, Loreto, Rimini, Ravenna, and Bologna.

He was much impressed by Loreto. The superstition of the peasants, who crept on their knees round the sacred house, and polished with their kisses the marble griffins with which Sansovino had adorned its sumptuous covering, did not weigh with him so much as the poetry and pathos of the scene.   He dwelt on the contrast between the harsh unadorned walls of the sacred house within, venerated by so many simple souls as the home of the Blessed Virgin, and the luxury of the ornamentation which had been heaped on it from without.   He was charmed by the straightforward, practical devotion of the peasant women, who wished to show the Virgin the utmost possible reverence, but were not going to spoil their best petticoats, which they pinned up round them in the most businesslike way before they began to make their circuit, and by the dignified figure of the old soldier who with drawn sword kept guard within the entrance of the tiny house.   Assisi also impressed him much, and intensified his love for Francis, whom he called the poet among saints, whose life was his poem.

Creighton was reading at this time for Priest's Orders, and at Christmas, 1873, he was ordained Priest in Christ Church Cathedral.   He was very nervous over his examination, and so convinced that he had done disgracefully, that he went to Archdeacon Palmer, one of the examining chaplains, to say that he was sure he ought to withdraw his name; but the Archdeacon reassured him.

During these years he preached frequently in College Chapel.   There were four sermons in the term, and he preached several courses in different terms.   These sermons show how thoroughly he understood the dangers and oppor-tunities of undergraduate life.   The predominant note in them all is the call to effort, to rise from what he described as 'the languid indolence which only feebly hopes to fill up somehow the hours spent out of bed.'   They are full of shrewd bits of practical advice.

'Let not unprofitable talking on abstruse matters of speculation or small practical points of controversy be to you an excuse for indolence, a salve to your conscience when it pricks you with being idle, a cheap source of conviction to you that you are not as other men are, and that ordinary duties are not so binding upon you.'

'Never exercise your body without feeling it to be an addi-tional duty to exercise also your mind: never indulge your feelings without being conscious of an additional motive to train both mind and body, that so you may be better able to regulate your emotions and escape from their absorbing influence.'

'You cannot sever religion from the rest of your life, or tell off a certain province within which it may work : it must transform the whole of life . . . it must be at the bottom of your ordinary acts ; or it is of no avail to hand over to its keeping your extraordinary ones.'

'Strength of character cannot be developed in seclusion, however admirable the motive of that seclusion may be. You must live in the world, and live its evils down, and by your presence diminish their force for others.'

'Use rightly the hours which you spend in social converse. See that they are not too numerous, not stolen from your first and chiefest duties, or they will degenerate into mere idle, profitless talk : the length of time that anyone can talk during the day, with any reality in his words, can never be very large.'

'All men cannot be wise, labour as they will ; but every man can easily become foolish.'

'If the Christian let go the virtues of the natural man, he must suffer in consequence.'

'These two things must always go together and keep pace with one another—liberty and an increased sense of responsibility : otherwise liberty assuredly degenerates into licence.'

'The advice of prudence, of experience, applies, remember, to the means rather than to the end. Others who have tried before you can tell you where they failed, but their failure does not prove the end to be undesirable.'

He preached occasionally in different Oxford churches, and in 1874 began to help Mr. Deane, then Vicar of St. Giles's, by preaching for him regularly on Sundays.

In the beginning of 1873 Prince Leopold came to Oxford, and settled in a house just opposite to ours. He attended Creighton's lectures on the history of the Renaissance in Italy, and later had some private teaching from him. They saw a great deal of one another, and became real friends, and Creighton visited the Duke several times after he left Oxford. He formed a high opinion of his character and abilities. After his death he wrote :

'He was endowed with quick perceptions, and possessed great delicacy and refinement. He was full of interest and curiosity, and was singularly receptive of new ideas. But he always thought out questions seriously for himself. He had a large knowledge of literature and a great taste for the fine arts.' And again : ' No young man that I had ever come across attracted me so much. There was a fineness of mental and moral fibre which made him quite unlike anyone else. Circumstances and conditions might change from time to time, but the real man in him held a quite peculiar charm and grace and winningness. I genuinely loved him very much, and followed his doings with the keenest interest.'

The distance of his house from College added much to the fatigue of Creighton's work, and he gladly availed himself of the opportunity of renting a house in Merton Street which fell vacant in 1874. Beam Hall, as it was called, is an interesting old house belonging to Corpus Christi College, with some fine panelled rooms ; its windows look across the quiet seclusion of Merton Street to the grey buildings of the College and the lovely tower of the Chapel. We moved thither in August 1874, after the old house had been thoroughly done up, and found, as we hoped, that being so near was a great help to his work. He could be in and out of College constantly, and keep a watchful eye over the conduct of the undergraduates. Even in bed at night he would listen with anxious ears for possible fireworks or other unlawful noise. We had always tried to see as much as possible of the men, and now it was easier for them to come in on Sunday evenings or at other times.

Our second daughter was born in July 1874. She was named Lucia in remembrance of the lady who comforted Dante in the Earthly Paradise. That year we could take no long holiday, but my husband spent ten days alone in Normandy, and cultivated his taste for architecture by visiting Caen, Bayeux, Coutances, and Mont St. Michel. Just as we were settling into the house which we expected would be our home for a long time, he heard that Embleton, the best Merton living, had fallen vacant. Mr. Freeling and Mr. Edwards, the senior clerical Fellows, were pretty certain to refuse it, and it would then come to Creighton if he cared to take it. It was an agitating question, and he felt it difficult to see his way clear. During a short visit to his father in September he wrote to me :

'Kirkandrews: September 23, 1874.

'Your remarks about Embleton and the necessity for meditation are just: we cannot exaggerate the importance of the determination taken in the matter; it will decide our future. Your immediate remarks do not seem to me, however, to be of any great value. You give me two reasons against Embleton, which, you will permit me to say, are futile. When you ask who will take my place in Oxford, I am inclined to smile: never was a place where men are so easily replaced and so soon forgotten. . . .

'You next ask, what is the best thing for me to do? Where would I be most useful? I answer, a man is equally useful everywhere if he is doing his best. In talking about what is best for me there is a certain ambiguity. Do you mean best for my fame or for my happiness? About it being best for my fame, so far as that is concerned with being talked about by the set of people who do the most talking, that is best consulted by staying at Oxford; as to my abiding fame, if I ever had ever so little, I am not sure; as to my happiness, again, I am not sure. If you helped me on these points with your views, you would be doing more that was definitely useful.

'Your considerations, however, omit the most essential point. By going to Embleton I get quietness and security. . . . What is it that makes an Oxford life seem agreeable? You will answer, quiet, pleasant occupation, congenial society. I answer, at present I have no quiet. . . . A Cabinet minister has not to be more careful of his proceedings, or feel that he holds office on a less secure tenure. . . . I am, though nominally a Fellow of the College, really a subordinate official in the employment of the unmarried Fellows, of whom certainly a strong minority have expressed their opinion that they may treat a tutor as a governing body does a head master. . . . A change of Warden might render the College intolerable to me at any moment. . . . If I were unmarried I could hold my Fellowship and do work for other colleges, which would be pleasant enough; it is impossible to do enough teaching in Oxford without a Fellowship. I have no chance of any University office at present, or I would not dream of going. An Oxford life is delightful, if one has it properly; but in seven years more I have to sue for re-election. . . . Really, the state of things is this: I want to lead a literary, not an active life. Which helps me most, Embleton or Oxford?'

'Kirkandrews : September 24, 1874.

'My letter yesterday consisted of matter for your reflection. Don't suppose that the arguments there put forward are considered by me as conclusive of the matter. I only feel them to be very strong.

'Looking at the matter from my own point of view only, it seems to me things stand as follows :

ADVANTAGES OF OXFORD	ADVANTAGES OF EMBLETON
1. Stimulus of intellectual society.	1. Quiet and energy undisturbed by struggles concerning your work.
2. Facilities of consulting libraries.	2. Opportunity of uninterrupted work all the year round, and concentration of intellectual energy on one subject.

'Again, we cannot look to Oxford as our abiding resting-place. Shall we let ourselves grow old in its allurements before we quit it? We cannot secure a College living just when necessary. . . . That is the worst of it; literary application and tutoring don't run side by side. They may at a swell college. . . . The tendency of Oxford is to make me a teaching drudge, and prevent me from being a literary student.'

'Kirkandrews : September 26, 1874.

'. . . You say you like Oxford society more than I do: I grant it : you are younger, and have not had so much of it. I have long felt how trumpery it is; . . . an interchange of things meant to be clever, but not containing much that is real or true. It is more pleasant to talk over schemes of education in a drawing-room than to work them out in a poor parish; and "society" gives you all the advantage of looking very wise and very good without much cost of actual effort. I only make these remarks to clear up another point. I think on this matter our being separated for a week has done us much good. We have had to think and write away from one another, and perhaps have thereby learned to see the question more clearly.

'I submitted the question to Mr. Gunson yesterday, as an impartial person, knowing me and knowing colleges, and being worldly wise. I feel much strengthened by the fact that he, after carefully inquiring into the facts of the case, concluded that I would not be justified in letting Embleton pass. He concluded by saying, "You will miss books, but you must just economise and buy them. . . . My general view is certainly to take it if it comes, unless ocular inspection discloses some horrors." '

Before leaving the North he paid a flying visit to Embleton, and saw nothing to prejudice him against it; but no decision could be made immediately. The living had first to be offered to the senior Fellows, and time given to them to consider their decision. This was never doubtful; still it gave him an unnecessary amount of time to consider the question, and he was beset with conflicting advice.

The desire expressed both by his own College and by the University in general that he should stay in Oxford, was much stronger than he had anticipated. It was intimated to him, that if he decided to remain at Merton, he would in all probability be chosen as the next Warden. He did not pay much heed to this, particularly as he did not think that Merton would be likely to forgo what was then its unique privilege of having a lay head. But he was considerably shaken by the opinions expressed, and though there was much that was trying in his life, and he had had many worries of late, he was too fond of Oxford easily to decide to leave it. The subject was discussed till we wearied of it, and longed to submit it to some one who could settle it for us. But on the whole the older and more experienced among our friends were in favour of our going.

'You would not be so overworked,' wrote H. J. Hood, 'and your work would perhaps be more uniform and less anxious. . . . If it is really a good thing, and not a desolate waste, I think I should feel glad to think that you had settled into what would probably be a healthier sort of life, though it would be so much farther off.'

Just before his final decision was announced, Creighton was much pleased at receiving the following letter, signed by the thirty-six senior men among the Merton undergraduates:

'November 11, 1874.

'Dear Mr. Creighton,—As we hear that you have not yet decided whether to accept the vacant living or not, and think that perhaps our wishes may have some weight with you, we venture to express a fervent hope that you will remain among us, for we think that your departure would cause us an irreparable loss both in the lecture-room and in the management of the College.'

He referred to this in a letter written Sept. 8, 1891 :

'When I left Oxford for parochial work, I received a petition signed by all the undergraduates of Merton asking me to stay. It was a sore thing to turn away from such an expression of goodwill, but I have not regretted that more and more arduous work has followed on my decision.'

In 1892, when reviewing the reasons which led to his acceptance of Embleton, he says :

'I had felt that the manifold activities required of me— I was the Senior Tutor, and taught both ancient and modern history for honour men, besides taking a share in pass work— were an obstacle to gaining any thorough knowledge. I thought that the period of papal history between the Great Schism and the Reformation had never been adequately considered. In England, Gibbon skipped it, and Milman was tired out before he reached it. In German there was no connected book. So a desire for less mental dissipation led me into the country.'

When Mr. Esson heard of his decision, he said, 'Then you will end by being Archbishop of Canterbury.' Mark Pattison criticised it with his customary pessimism. 'What are you going into the country for?' 'To study history.' 'You can't study history without a library, and you can't get an adequate historical library unless you spend at least 1,000*l.* a year on books.'

The College asked him to retain his tutorship till the following Easter, and he determined therefore to spend a week or two of the Christmas vacation at Embleton, and then put in a *locum tenens* till Easter. His predecessor had held the living for about forty years, and there was much to be done to make the house ready for us. I was unable to go North with him in the Christmas vacation, when he went to Bishop Auckland on the way to Embleton in order to be instituted by Bishop Baring. The North gave him a characteristic welcome.

'Auckland Castle : December 31, 1874.

'There had been a thick fall of snow last night, and there was a good fog when I arrived. . . . The Bishop is a kindly old gentleman. . . . I was glad to find that I shall not quarrel with my Bishop. He objects to Ritualists on principle, but is pacific and kindly, and will not be hard to get on with. He is a regular old gossip, and knows all about everybody in his diocese. . . . The Bishop never said a word to me about my work, or what my views were, or what my intentions, or anything. I suppose bishops get so bullied that they don't like to interfere. He seemed to think that as I was not quite of his way of thinking, the less he meddled the better.'

'Embleton Vicarage : January 2, 1875.

'Romantic adventures befell me on entering my parish which at the time I reached it was something like the North Pole. When my train had got a little way from Newcastle, a great wind began to arise from the sea. When I landed at Christon Bank Station the snow was drifting fast before the wind, and the sky was black with clouds. No one was there to meet me, as I had said that I did not expect to be there before eight, whereas I got there at four. I started, however, to walk, as I thought the way was straight, and I could not miss it. But the sky grew blacker and the wind fiercer, and the drifting snow dimmed my spectacles so that I saw not, and I often sank up to my middle in a great bank of snow blown across the road. After an hour of simply struggling blindly onwards I saw a house, to which I made my way. I found I had come a wrong road, and on being directed rightly retraced my steps, though with some doubts, since the wind was rising more and more, whether I should ever find my way after all, since it was now five o'clock and getting dark. However, the lady of the house had seen me and despatched her household to bring me back, which with great difficulty they did. As luck would have it, this was the house of one of my churchwardens : his wife had guessed who I was when she heard a stranger had been inquiring the way, and her heart had warmed towards me. I asked for a man-servant to show me the way. Meanwhile we had some tea. The wind waxed higher ; at six o'clock, when I rose to go, the drift against the front gate prevented it from being opened. I had to stay all night, the roads being impassable. It was a fearful night ; the house shook before the blast, and the fine snow was blown in at every window. . . . This morning is a fine bright sunny morning, and the snow-drifts being somewhat hardened on the top, I made a kind of Alpine expedition hither : my great doubt now is whether it will be possible by any means the art of man can devise to get my luggage hither.'

'Embleton : January 3, 1875.

'The thaw set in here yesterday afternoon, and now with all the snow-drifts has reduced the roads to a state of slush perfectly awful to behold, and almost impossible to walk in. . . . I did my first Sunday school this morning, and found it not so bad ; but all the arrangements of every sort have fallen into waste during this interim, and I shall have to devote some energy to working them up. . . . I like the house at Embleton more and more ; it has great capabilities, but will want heaps of money to furnish : I quite shudder at the thought. . . . At present I go on slowly trying to find out things gradually, as there is so much quite new to me, and I have not yet got my views together. The village and the people are very much as I expected, and will require much labour to make an impression on. They will find our quiet ways a great change from the Rookes with their large family.'

‘ Embleton : January 5, 1875.

‘ The thaw goes on, but only makes the roads more impassable. I am regularly weather-bound, and see no chance of getting to see my parish in its length and breadth. The thaw turns the roads into deep mud, alternating with partially thawed snow-drifts, on which when you tread you stick up to your middle in slush. Yesterday afternoon I staggered over to Fallodon to see the Greys. Lady Grey is a brisk, talkative, active old lady, very Low Church, with a great interest in the souls of old women.'

‘ Embleton : January 8, 1875.

‘ To-day, as I told you, I went into Alnwick, which is a nice old place, not much of a town, but the castle is splendid, and the church very fine. . . . The people are very friendly, and generally well-disposed. I find the villagers very kindly, and a general desire to be hospitable : they are quite prepared to take me on trial, but they will not accept one without fair criticism, and their approval will never be without reserve. Blind enthusiasm is not to be expected ; but they are not the least cantankerous, and will give everyone a fair chance. Drunkenness is their great weakness ; otherwise they are just the good sturdy people I expected. . . . Embleton as a village is not much ; it is scattered about and huddled together along the ridge of rock between us and the sea. I have been down to the sea, which has the loveliest coloured sand I ever saw. I never saw sand so yellow. . . . I have not done a word of work except my review for the “ Academy ” and correct proofs of my “ Macmillan ” article.'

He made all necessary arrangements for the care of the parish and the preparation of the vicarage for our reception in March, and returned to Oxford for his last term. He was much gratified at the general expression of regret at his departure, and at the many signs of affection he received from his friends.

The last years in Oxford witnessed the beginning of his literary activity. He continued to review books on his own subjects for the 'Manchester Guardian.' He was also interested in 'The Academy' almost from its beginning in 1869 through his acquaintance with Dr. Appleton, its founder and editor. The distinctive feature of 'The Academy' was that its reviews were signed by the writers' names in full, and that every effort was therefore made to get men of eminence to review books on their own subject. Creighton was a frequent contributor during its early years.

These years saw the first issue of some of the series of historical, literary, and scientific text-books which have since become so common. J. R. Green originated the idea of a series of shilling primers which were published by Messrs. Macmillan, and he asked Creighton to undertake the one on Roman History. As he had long been engaged in teaching Roman History, Creighton found this an easy task, which he executed with prompt rapidity. He had the whole subject so clearly mapped out in his mind, and possessed such a true sense of proportion in dealing with any subject, however large, that he wrote the primer straight off, in the midst of all his other work, in just three weeks. It turned out to be a few hundred words more than the prescribed length, and he handed it over to me to cut out the requisite number of words. The primer appeared early in 1875, and has since sold steadily at the rate of several thousands a year. He used to say that one reason of the success of this series of primers was that they were just a convenient size and shape to be used by schoolboys as missiles to hurl at one another, and their consequent speedy destruction served to promote a rapid sale.

In this primer he showed that he could write history in an easy and simple style, and make it attractive to children. In its own way it is one of the best things he ever did. Lord Acton said of it to a common friend that he considered it the most masterly thing he had read for a long time.

In 1874 also he entered into an agreement with Messrs. Rivington to edit a series of Historical Biographies, of which he himself undertook one on Simon de Montfort, and he agreed to write a little book on the Age of Elizabeth for a series which Messrs. Longman were bringing out, and thus began the connexion with that great publishing firm which lasted his whole life and led in time to ties of real friendship. He began his work for the Age of Elizabeth in the autumn of 1874, but the book was not finished for some little time.

In 1873 he wrote for our friend Mr. George Grove, then editor of ' Macmillan's Magazine,' two articles on Æneas Silvius, Pope Pius II. He was much absorbed during that summer in the study of Æneas's letters, and it is one of the few occasions when I can recall that his literary work interfered with his sleep, till he was forced for a few days to put Æneas aside and go through a course of French novels to rest his brain. He subsequently contributed, at Mr. Grove's request, articles on Dante and other Italian subjects to ' Macmillan's Magazine.' [1]

The Merton undergraduates showed their appreciation of his work for them by a handsome present of books, and all came in a body to bid us farewell one evening at the end of term. It was impossible to leave Oxford without real sorrow, but we never once regretted the decision to go to Embleton. The importance of the years spent there for his intellectual, moral, and spiritual growth cannot be over-estimated. The change came just at the right time, when he had got out of Oxford the best that it could give, when had he stayed in Oxford he could not fail to have become absorbed in the details of University business, and to have felt increasingly the strain and anxiety of his College work. He went to the seclusion of a remote country parish with a rich store of friends, an inexhaustible supply of interests, and a love for his fellow creatures which till now had only been developed within somewhat narrow limits, but which, in a new and different sphere, was to develop hitherto little dreamt-of possibilities of sympathy and service.

[1] These articles and other historical essays were published in 1902, under the title, *Historical Essays and Reviews*. (Longmans & Co.)

CHAPTER VI

PAROCHIAL LIFE

THE connexion between the parish of Embleton and Merton College is almost as old as the College itself. Walter de Merton founded his College, the first in Oxford, in 1264. Ten years afterwards Edmund, Earl of Lancaster, son of Henry III., to whom the barony of Embleton had passed from Simon de Montfort, gave the advowson of Embleton Church to Merton College. In the same year Walter de Merton put forth the final statutes for the regulation of his new foundation. For more than a hundred years the successors of Edmund in the barony disputed the right of Merton to the advowson. The course of these disputes, and the frequent journeys of the Warden and Fellows of Merton to the North, of which full details are preserved in the College archives, throw much light upon the social customs of the times. Merton converted the living to a vicarage in 1332, and used the great tithes, in accordance with Edmund's directions, for the support of scholars and the increase of their number. Most of the Vicars of Embleton have been Fellows of Merton.

The parish of Embleton lies along the sea coast, forty miles to the north of Newcastle. It is seven miles long, and about five and a half miles broad. The North-Eastern Railway runs through it and connects it with the outer world. At first sight the district seems bleak and inhospitable. The fields are large, the hedges low, the lanes few and muddy. For six miles inland the country looks flat and uninteresting, till it rises towards the moors of Charlton and Chillingham, and on the north-west to the blue undulating heights of Cheviot. Neither do the villages add any charm. The cottages, built mostly of stone, many of the gloomy whin or basalt of the district, are meant strictly for use. They possess potato plots, but gardens are rare, and flower borders seldom to be seen. The external appearance of the houses is uncared for, though for the most part they are solid and well built. There seems little to attract the eye in the landscape, but the line of sea, bright blue under the north-east wind, with the great headland of Bamborough to the north, and, to the south, the serried basalt pillars of the cliff on which Dunstanborough rests dropping straight into the sea. But it is a country that takes hold of the heart. To those who can penetrate it, its charm is inexhaustible, and no other part of the world can rival its hold on the affections.

The wonderful air, bright and keen, stimulates the senses. The world seems a big place under the vast stretches of sky over undulating fields and sea, where the clouds mass in forms of rare dignity. The landscape painter, William Hunt, once said that nowhere else had he seen such statuesque clouds, clouds that waited to give the artist's pencil time to draw them. A closer inspection shows that the country is not so desolate as at first seemed. Every little hollow is wooded—long narrow belts of trees shelter the fields from the sweep of the sea winds. The soil is rich, and trees thrive wherever they are allowed to grow or can find any shelter. The basalt scattered over the whole district shows itself in strange cliffs, called 'heughs,' with perpendicular precipices facing inland, which are covered with rich vegetation and carpeted with flowers. Only those who have watched it at every season can tell the full beauty of the coast. Low sandhills fringe the land, covered with coarse grey-green grass and bracken, which turns into sheets of burnished gold in the autumn. Among the grass grow many flowers : in the spring sheets of cowslips, later on pale yellow roses, harebells, the purple red *geranium sanguineum*, and gay masses of ragwort. The sandhills take many shapes, giving shelter from every wind, and sunny nooks to bask in at all seasons of the year. Even in January we have picnicked on them. Here and there the purple brown almost black basalt crops out ; at Beadnell it makes a long point like a pier, at Dunstanborough a great cliff rising sheer from the sea, at Embleton a rugged rock island, reached at low tide

by a slippery causeway. Here and there the sands are strewn
with huge masses of black rock that form clear pools for the
anemones and crabs.   Nowhere else is the sand so yellow as
in the Embleton bay ; even a few miles south, at Alnmouth, it
is white in comparison.   The Embleton sand is made up of
fragments of yellow shells, churned fine by the storms of the
North Sea ; it is firm to the feet, perfect to walk on, marked with
the delicate footprints of birds, and alive with their presence.
The wild seashore, the great stretches of field and moor,
offer a free home to the birds who give life and variety
to every walk.   Sometimes the plaintive cry of a solitary
mother bird, as it wheels round one's head, adds to the
desolation of a grey day.   At another time the quivering
light of the silver wings of a great company of plovers, as
they rise from field or shore disturbed by one's approach,
gives a sense of joyous life.   Sometimes we would pass a
vast brown field white with the gulls which had flown in to
follow the ploughs, drawn perhaps by six or eight teams of
magnificent horses.

     The clear bright air gives a peculiar charm to the
colouring, sometimes luminous, grey and soft, at other
times radiant with the brilliance of blue sea and yellow
sands.   A friend who had lived much on the Riviera said
that the colours of our sea and beach rivalled even the
Mediterranean shore.   The Italian painter, Signor Costa,
remarked that the country reminded him of the Roman
Campagna, it was so *intime*.   It could be wild enough at
times.   The wind was seldom still, and in winter would
sweep over from the snow-covered Cheviots with biting force.
Sometimes, fortunately not often, we were wrapt for three
days at a time in a clinging mist driven in from the sea,
called a 'sea fret.'   A violent snow storm would make the
lanes impassable on account of the deep drifts gathered by the
wind.   But the neighbourhood of the sea tempered the cold
in winter, and most houses and gardens were placed so as to
be sheltered from the severity of the winds.   A low ridge of
basalt cliff lay between the vicarage at Embleton and the
sea, distant about a mile.   The garden was well sheltered
with trees ; visitors often recommended us to cut down some
of them to get a view, but we knew too well their value

EMBLETON VICARAGE.

as shelter, and besides there was no view to be got except
a rising slope of grass field. Its sheltered situation and rich
soil made the garden a delight. Everything was happy
there. Peaches, even figs, ripened on the red brick wall,
flowers grew with rich profusion. A friend who had travelled
much, visiting us one October, when the flowers, not yet
touched by frost, and luxuriant in their growth from the
frequent rains and heavy dews of the North, were still in their
full beauty, ran about in excitement exclaiming, ' Where am I ?
Am I in Italy or the South of France ? ' In such favourable circumstances we were encouraged to do much to
improve the garden. We filled up a ditch to make a tennis
lawn, and turned a field into a new kitchen garden with wide
rose borders.

The vicarage was a large and convenient house : the greater
part of it was modern, built of black basalt, which we covered
as far as possible with creepers, but the modern house was
built on to an old red sandstone tower. This tower was one
of those fortified peel towers which are found in the North.
The name ' peel ' is of uncertain derivation, but probably means
a pile. These towers were built as protection against the
raids of the Scots. A vaulted chamber on the ground
floor received the cattle, and a couple of rooms above
sheltered their owners with their families. Most of the older
farms and manor houses in Northumberland were built round
peels. They were not strong enough to stand a siege, but
could afford sufficient protection for men and cattle during a
Scottish raid. Embleton is one of the three fortified vicar-
ages in Northumberland ; probably the priest in old times
gave shelter in his peel to as many of his parishioners and
their beasts as he could accommodate.

The church surrounded with sycamores immediately ad-
joins the vicarage. There are traces of stonework that show
the existence of a church there early in the twelfth century.
The actual nave and tower of pleasant grey sandstone
were built between 1330 and 1340. The chancel is modern,
built some few years before Creighton went to the parish.
Northumbrian churches as a rule are plain and stern, and have
suffered much from the constant disturbances of a border district. Embleton church, with its grey tower rising among

the trees, is one of the best that remain, and has many points of interest. It is situated as conveniently as possible for a large and scattered parish, consisting of many different villages.

The parish has a population of about 1,700. It includes some five different villages, besides many large farms which with their surrounding cottages form almost villages by themselves. Embleton itself is a forlorn-looking place. It has grown up from a number of squatters' cottages scattered with no fixed plan on a long basalt ridge; few have any gardens adjoining them, and rough rock obtrudes through the scanty grass which covers the hill. It contains a population of about 600, and in that thinly populated district is a sort of metropolis. There are a couple of general shops where everything can be bought, a butcher or two, tailors, shoe-makers, and five public-houses.

The inhabitants of Embleton find occupation chiefly in the whinstone quarry which occupies one end of the ridge on which the village is built; the square blocks of basalt cut there go to pave Leeds and other northern towns, and are in such demand that the quarry always encroaches further upon the village. In our day the school stood in a most exposed position on the ridge near the quarry, on a site given by a former vicar, and the blasts that swept the hill used often to make it difficult to get to the school. But the encroachment of the quarry has since made it possible to dispose of the site, and build a school in a better situation. The 'blockers,' as the skilled labourers in the quarry were called, made high wages, and ordinary stone-breaking gave plenty of work for unskilled labourers, while the boys were employed in driving the stone carts to the station. Creighton often regretted the ease with which the boys could earn money, since it made it impossible for him to persuade fathers to try to give a likely lad a start in some skilled industry.

In many ways the moral standard of the village was very low, and it was a difficult place to improve. There was no resident squire, the chief employers of labour were on much the same level of cultivation as those they employed, and in some cases owned the public-houses and paid the wages there. Writing two years after he had left Embleton, Creighton said : ' I always felt myself engaged there (at Embleton) in downright warfare, and strove to get hold of the young . . . working through the school, the choir, the G.F.S., any possible organisation of the young, that here and there one or two might be got hold of who would make a testimony. The unchastity of Embleton was terrible—low, animal.'

The two villages in the parish next in importance to Embleton are Newton-by-the-Sea, two miles to the north, and Craster, a fishing village three miles to the south. The village and the squire of Craster alike take their name from a camp situated on a neighbouring heugh. The Crasters, one of the oldest families in Northumberland, have exercised a beneficent influence upon the inhabitants of their village, a sturdy, high-minded race of fisherfolk, many of whom have built their own cottages on land obtained from the squire. Like other fishermen, they had a strong tendency to Methodism, and used to hold open-air services on the beach and even in the neighbouring villages. But just about the time when we went to Embleton, they concentrated their energies on building a chapel for themselves, and with time their Methodism grew less militant. The fisherfolk kept much to themselves, and seldom married outside the village of some two hundred inhabitants ; there were old women there who had never been in a train, and knew and cared nothing about the outer world. There was hardly a soul in the village who was not called either Archbold or Simpson, so that it was difficult to distinguish between them.

Newton-by-the-Sea consisted of two villages, Upper Newton, and the Sea Houses, a small fishing village rather rougher than Craster, built round a central square which was filled up with pigstyes and middens.

The herring fishery was the harvest of the fisherfolk ; on summer evenings it was a joy to watch the fleets of herring boats putting out to sea with their great brown sails. Some of the men would follow the shoals of herrings with their boats to other parts of the coast, and be away for weeks at a time. During the herring fishery those who wished to see the people had to pursue them to the curing yards, where the heaps of silvery fish brought in carts from the boats were quickly cleaned, salted, and packed in barrels to be sent off to Italy and Spain for the consumption of the peasants in Lent. The cleaning and packing were done by the women, dressed for the purpose in oilskin jackets and petticoats. If herrings were sufficiently plentiful, a clever worker could earn as much as ten shillings in the day, and women collected from the country round to help in the curing. To the remark that it was dirty work, the ready rejoinder came at once, ' Aye, but the money's clean.'

In the winter came the haddock fishery, and for this long lines, some with three hundred, some with six hundred hooks, had to be baited by the women, who often had first to seek their bait on the rocks. To bait a line took three to four hours' work. Then perhaps the weather would be too stormy for the men to go out, and after waiting three days, the stale bait had to be pulled off and the work begun again. A fisherman's wife had a hard life, and it was seldom that love led a man so far to forget prudence as to choose a wife who had not been brought up to it. Parochial visits in the winter were paid as a rule to the family as they sat baiting the line, mother and daughters hard at work; often, in the middle of a visit, one would be startled by a gruff voice joining in from a box bed in the corner. A pair of legs would appear, and the head of the house would slowly climb out and join the party. He had been out most of the night fishing, and had to sleep in the day. In the spring, crab and lobster pots were set, and some sea trout were caught. The winter fishing of course was the most dangerous, and as father and sons almost invariably shared a boat, it sometimes happened that a family lost in one night all its male supports.[1]

Both Craster and Newton possessed coastguard stations, and Creighton valued much the introduction into his parish of men of such superior stamp and intelligence. Lifeboats were useless on that coast, but each station possessed a rocket apparatus, which, several times while we were at Embleton, was instrumental in saving crews from vessels driven on to that inhospitable shore.

---

[1] I believe that of late years the nature of the fishing industry has been much changed owing to the introduction of steam trawlers.

Christon Bank, a small village close to the station on the North-Eastern Railway, was inhabited chiefly by railway men and by the dependents of Sir George Grey, who lived close by at Fallodon. The other inhabitants of the parish were almost all agricultural. There were two farms of about 1,300 acres, and the rest were mostly of from 400 to 800 acres. The farm labourers, or 'hinds' as they were called, were engaged by the year, and lived round the farmstead in cottages provided by the landlord. The larger farms had from eight to twelve cottages. The labour of the farm was reckoned according to the number of teams of horses required. To each team went a man and two women or boys ; and besides these there were the necessary shepherds. The hind had to provide the women, who were said in consequence to work to bondage and called 'bondagers.' If the hinds' families did not furnish enough women, sometimes a cottage was turned into a 'bondage house,' where an elderly woman kept house for a few bondagers. Somehow the cottages in the farmstead must supply the labour needed. This led to a great deal of shifting amongst the agricultural population. If a daughter married, or another grew old enough to work, the family might become unsuitable for a particular farm. The knowledge, moreover, that each engagement was for a year, made even a small cause for discontent sufficient to dissolve it. The hirings took place in March at Alnwick ; the farmer who engaged a hind had to send carts to fetch his furniture and family, so that in the early spring the lanes were alive with whole families on pilgrimage.

These constant changes made it difficult to gain much influence over the hinds, and gave them a sense of irresponsibility. They felt that they belonged to no particular place, and so were little affected or helped by public opinion. But families who had left one farm in the parish reappeared at another, or turned up again after years of more distant wandering, and though certainly the most difficult parishioners to deal with, many became real friends. The married women did not work in the fields. Before our day, wages had been largely paid in kind, but then most payments were in money.

The full hind's wages were equivalent to about twenty-five shillings a week, and whether well or ill he was paid regularly all the year round. The girls and boys made from eight to ten shillings a week, and more in harvest time; they were not paid when weather or health made it impossible for them to work. The neighbourhood of the pit villages kept the wages up. All the earnings of husband and children were taken to the mother, who gave back to each what she thought fit as pocket-money. The girls shared in the roughest farm work, carting manure and hoeing turnips in gangs; they might sometimes be seen ploughing, though this was rare. They wore thick short petticoats, and huge straw bonnets with curtains behind over the neck, and large 'uglies' to shade their faces. A great lady of the neighbourhood had introduced uglies among them at the time when they were fashionable, and they proved such an admirable protection from sun and wind and storm that they have been in use ever since. It was a surprise to overtake one of these sturdy rough figures with the huge bonnet which seemed to promise at least a middle-aged woman, and, as she turned her head, to discover the bright face and fresh complexion of a young girl. No one who saw the bondagers in their Sunday best, would have guessed that they had been busy during the week with the roughest labour, exposed to all weathers.

The cottages in the North were very poor according to South Country ideas. The majority in the parish of Embleton consisted of only one room, but the huge box beds, which were the rule, might be said to form separate sleeping cupboards. They could be shut in front with wooden shutters, and it was a cause of matrimonial dispute, whether the shutters should be open or closed at night. The furniture was in most cases good and substantial, and the appearance of the rooms clean and comfortable. Even where there were more rooms, the family often still preferred to live and sleep in one room. What the housewife cared most about was to have a 'back-end,' as she called it, some sort of washhouse or back kitchen for her dirty work. If she had that, one living and sleeping room was quite sufficient for her needs. Creighton was much struck with what he called the disregard of the comfort of a house, which he found universal in the Northumbrian labourer. He considered it 'largely due to the fact that he was not taught the money value of a house. As a hind he lived rent free, so he never learnt to consider house rent as a part of his necessary expenditure, and felt no call to take care of his house. These facts influenced the other inhabitants. One man earning some thirty shillings a week removed from a three-roomed to a one-roomed cottage, because he preferred to economise in house rent.'

On the farms the landlords had begun to build cottages of a better type, with two or even four rooms and good out-houses, but the old people at least still liked to live and sleep in the kitchen in their box beds.[1] Washing and baking were done at home. Good housewives considered baker's bread extravagant, saying with truth that it did not go as far as home-made bread. They were admirable bakers, and it was a pleasure to be in a cottage when the fragrant loaves were drawn out of the oven. But the neighbourhood of shops and modern fashions were fast destroying the old simple habits of the people. In former days, the keep of a cow had been part of the payment of a hind, and porridge, barley bread, and milk had been the chief part of the people's diet. In our day it was very difficult to get milk, porridge was almost unknown, and fine white flour had taken the place of barley and oatmeal. The children were mainly brought up on tea without milk, and red herrings or bacon, and the doctors considered that the fine physique of the people was likely to deteriorate. Creighton did what he could to improve the supply of milk, and let his fields to a woman in the village on condition that she kept cows and sold milk. But it was difficult to persuade the mothers that milk was worth the money it cost.

The dialect of the people was very soft and pleasing, with a sort of plaintive cadence, and characterised by the Northumbrian burr, the inability to roll the *r*, which was pronounced somehow deep back in the throat. They never dropped their

---

[1] Experience of the habits of the people showed us how much greater was the influence of a high standard on morals, than any increased housing accommodation. In Craster, with a great majority of one-roomed houses, illegitimate births were unknown ; among the agricultural labourers, with their improved cottages, they were very frequent. Little sense of shame attached to them. There was plenty to feed an extra mouth, plenty of work to look forward to, and the mother of the family, who stayed at home all day, could easily look after her daughter's babies.

h's, and used many quaint and charming expressions. ' My comely jewel' and 'canny hinny' were common terms of endearment. The old people were not always easy to understand—almost each class had its own vocabulary, and the dialect of the fisherfolk was very different from that of the hinds—but the elementary schoolmaster was fast destroying all the more marked peculiarities of speech.

In character, too, there were considerable differences between the various classes of the people. The fisherfolk no doubt had the most heart and the most imagination, and the hinds were the most unapproachable. They all prided themselves on their so-called independence. There was no perfunctory touching of hats to a superior ; I doubt whether any superiors were recognised. At first I thought the people unfriendly when they did not greet me on the road ; but I was told that they expected me to greet first, and then I always met with a kindly response and the invariable remark about the weather. But we felt doubts about the nature and meaning of the Northumbrian independence. A Northumbrian does not like to be beholden to anyone, but he will take all that he can get. He is very anxious not to commit himself, and very sensitive to public opinion. Ask a man to do something you know he is longing to do, and the only answer you will get is, ' Well, I will see if I can make it convenient.' All are ready to give as the prevailing motive for action ' the fear of reflections.' Their strongest expression of satisfaction would be, ' Well, I canna say we have anything to complain of.' I think that caution was really their chief characteristic. But what made them interesting was that they were people of real character. They were difficult to move, hard to win, stubborn in their prejudices ; but when once they gave their confidence or their affection, they gave it entirely, and for life. It was worth while to produce an impression upon them, for once produced nothing removed it. Strong themselves, they knew how to value strength in others. Weakness and silliness they despised. They were hardheaded, and could appreciate the intellectual force of others. But a weak amiable man, however well-meaning, however really virtuous, could do nothing with them. There was much drinking among them, though it was comparatively rare for a man to spend so much on drink as to make his home desolate, and there was little drinking among the women. To get drunk occasionally was considered no disgrace, even by quite respectable men. But, on the whole, things were improving. In former days the farmers had been heavy drinkers, now as a rule they were sober in their habits. Still, it was the ordinary thing to say of persons who were disapproved of for any reason whatever, that they drank. At first we were surprised at the number of servant maids we came across who had been obliged to leave their situations because their mistresses drank ; but we discovered that this was considered a convenient way of accounting for the loss of a situation, and that the fact that it was not true was immaterial.

Of graver vice there was enough to convince us that London slums alone are not responsible for turning men and women into beasts. The fact that Embleton had no squire made it a place where people could collect who were not tolerated in the villages around, and it had a bad reputation in the neighbourhood. Yet there were characters there as saintly as could have been found under the most favoured circumstances, lives the beauty of whose example can never be forgotten.

It was face to face with a parish so difficult that Creighton found himself, straight from a purely academic life, with no parochial experience, and little knowledge of the life of the working classes. In some ways his lack of clerical training was almost an advantage. It was a parish that could not have been worked on ordinary lines. In such a scattered district, to apply the ordinary parochial machinery would have been impossible, and to attempt much parochial organisation would have led to waste of time and energy, and resulted only in failure and disappointment.

The task that Creighton set himself first of all was to understand his surroundings. He started with no pre-conceived notions, with no definite plans. Though he always maintained that Cumbrians and Northumbrians were very different, yet as a Northerner he was by nature in sympathy with the Northern character, and knew that it was not easy to deal with. One thing he definitely impressed upon himself and me, that we must do our best and look for no results. He never complained of want of recognition or gratitude, and if, by some chance, he became aware of any effect produced by his words or actions, it came to him as an unlooked-for gratification.

We began our new life at Easter, 1875. The vicarage had needed complete redecoration, and was now very pretty and comfortable, and he had a convenient study with ample room for his books. He had at first hoped to get an old school friend as curate; but when this failed, Mr. Arthur Acland asked whether he would let him act as curate for a few months, as his health required a complete change from Oxford. His offer was gladly accepted; and when it was discovered that Embleton possessed no house where Mr. and Mrs. Acland could live, it was arranged that they should live with us at the vicarage, and they and their children stayed with us till September. Mr. Acland was in Deacon's Orders when he came, but was ordained Priest at Trinity, by the Bishop of Durham.[1] Their time with us, though they were both in delicate health, was a great pleasure and help in many ways.

After Mr. Acland left, Creighton engaged as curate Mr. C. E. Green, who was ordained Deacon at Christmas, 1875, and remained at Embleton for the whole time of Creighton's incumbency.[2] His simple, kindly nature helped him from the first to get on admirably with the people. Writing of the nine years he spent as Creighton's curate, Mr. Green says:

'I cannot imagine relations happier than those which existed between us during the whole of that time. . . . As a man to work under, he was invariably most kind and considerate; always taking more than his share of parish work, and always making me feel that I was associated with him in it on perfectly equal terms; I mean to say that there was no idea of the "senior and junior officer" about it. I do not think he ever did anything in the parish without telling me about it and asking my opinion on it. The points which struck me most about him as a parish priest were his kindness

---

[1] Mr. Acland afterwards laid aside his Orders, entered Parliament, and became Vice-President of the Committee of Council on Education under Mr. Gladstone.

[2] When Creighton left Embleton, Mr. Green, who had refused previous offers of promotion, was presented by Earl Grey with the living of Howick. He is now Vicar of Chulmleigh, Devon.

EMBLETON CHURCH.

and sympathy at all times with his parishioners, his judgment and tact in dealing with difficult questions, and his constant and unfailing wish, and his many efforts, to benefit and do good to, in a really practical way, the whole of his parishioners and the neighbourhood in which he lived.'

Church feeling cannot be said to have existed to any large extent in the parish of Embleton; and Creighton did not attempt to stimulate its growth too rapidly. After he left, he regretted often that he had not instituted daily services, but when he was there, he was too much impressed by the knowledge of how hopeless it would be to get anyone to come to them, and said that he would wait to start them till his own family was old enough to form a congregation.[1] He found only a monthly Communion, and at once started a weekly one, and was insistent in his sacramental teaching. There was no question of a surpliced choir, for the boys' voices were harsh and unpleasant, and we had a mixed choir of men and girls, in which both vicar and curate took much interest. He instituted the chanting of the Psalms, and at very rare intervals gratified the choir and vexed himself by allowing an anthem. Sir George Grove thus describes a service at Embleton. 'The service to-day was one of the nicest I ever took part in. There was Communion to about twelve people, so simple and quiet that it was most impressive.' As Craster was three miles off, the old people could not come to the parish church, and a service was held there in the afternoon, and once a month in the morning. Soon after he came, the Craster family built a little chapel that added much to the convenience of these services. He also held at different times a mission service at Newton on Sunday afternoons or evenings. Sunday was a busy day. Both

[1] His riper opinion as to the value of daily services is expressed in his Peterborough Charge: ' I know all that can be said by one who prefers to say them [the daily offices] privately, because he is hopeless of being joined by any of his parishioners in church. But the fact remains that you are directed to say them in church unless you are reasonably let or hindered; and the absence of others is certainly no hindrance to you. . . . You will best enforce your lessons by your example. The sound of the bell, especially when the listener knows that it is being rung by your own hands, if it does not operate as a summons, is yet a reminder, and brings a message of consolation and encouragement. It is well that you should pray with your people: it is well that they should know that you also pray for them.'—*The Church and the Nation*, p. 113.

vicar and curate had to teach at the Sunday school in the morning, as teachers were scarce. This Creighton found one of his hardest duties, as he had never been accustomed to it; he said that it took more out of him than anything else. Then came morning service, followed often by baptisms. After a hasty lunch, one of the clergy would start for Newton and the other for Craster, going in time to look in at the Sunday school before service. Creighton always walked, unless the fact that there were baptisms to be performed made it impossible for him to get to Craster in time. They were both back for Evensong at Embleton. On one Sunday in the month there was a children's service at Embleton in the afternoon. The Sunday duty was divided with absolute fairness between vicar and curate, and they preached alternately morning and evening at Embleton.

Mr. Green always dined and had tea at the vicarage on Sunday, but it was at once decided that after Evensong, vicar and curate should separate. Creighton feared that if they met in the evening after the labours of Sunday, they would inevitably ' talk shop,' and he wished for the few hours that remained to forget his cares and responsibilities. He said that the work of Sunday left him with an irresistible desire to talk nonsense and eat jam. Many visitors at Embleton will recall the fun and laughter of the Sunday evening suppers, when some perhaps would at first be amazed to see the man who had just been preaching to them with such deep earnestness, rolling on the floor with his children or telling one ridiculous story after another. Afterwards he would read poetry, chiefly Browning, to us, or often, if he found anyone who did not know them, some of his favourites among Morris's early poems, such as ' The Haystack in the Floods.' His taste was very catholic; he would ask for anything out of the bookcase, saying it did not matter what it was, and he did not murmur if a young man handed him a volume of American drolleries.

Creighton from the first preached extempore at Embleton. His habit was to settle in his mind on Sunday or Monday the subject of his sermons for the following Sunday, and carry it about in thought with him through the week. He gave comparatively little time to definite preparation in his study, though his opinion was that preaching extempore took more out of him, and needed a greater total expenditure of thought and energy than to write sermons. He did not use many books to help him in his preparation; the Commentary he found most suggestive was Cornelius à Lapide, to which he often referred. He nearly always chose a subject arising out of the special teaching of the day, generally the Gospel when he preached in the morning. In the evenings, his sermons were often of an expository nature. He gave courses on the Psalms and on different Epistles. A very devout old woman, a constant attendant at church, was much disturbed at having the shortcomings of the Corinthian Christians made so very clear to her. 'Oh, them Corinthians,' she said, 'I've no patience with them.' He very frequently preached on Old Testament characters, showing his deep interest in human nature by his subtle analysis of the disposition and motives of Jacob, Balaam, the old Prophet, the type of those who sacrifice principle to expediency, and above all of David One Sunday, when Mr. and Mrs. T. H. Green were with us he preached on the Queen of Sheba, a sermon which they never forgot, and they said that the day when the Queen of Sheba lesson was read never failed to bring back Embleton to their minds. It was not always easy for Creighton to translate his thoughts into a form which his hearers could understand; but he was very sensitive to his audience, he felt at once whether they followed him or not, and struggled with his thought till he had expressed it in such a way that they could take hold of it. Even to those who heard him constantly his sermons, though naturally they differed much in merit, never failed in interest. They were always new, always varied, always suggestive. He thought little of eloquence, and never cultivated it, though the beauty of his ideas at times drove him to eloquence almost against his will. His voice was clear and full of charm with tones of the deepest tenderness. He could make himself heard without effort anywhere, in any building, however large, owing to the clearness of his enunciation and the calibre of his voice rather than its loudness; he never shouted. He did not shrink from plain speaking in the pulpit, and the Northumbrians, so afraid of 'reflections,' did not always like his straight words. If a definite sin were

M 2

plainly attacked, it was sometimes taken as an attack on a definite sinner, and the woman who knew that her husband had come home drunk the night before, felt it as a personal affront if the Vicar preached against drunkenness on the following morning.   Creighton's aim in preaching was not to please, but to teach, above all to make his hearers think.   He said that a sermon should be about a definite subject, and not, as was so often the case, merely leave the impression that it was better to be good than to be bad.   His curate says :

' His preaching was always practical and helpful ; he was anxious to make his sermons really of use to his people in their every-day lives.   Occasionally he might be a little over their heads, but I distinctly remember thinking that in every sermon he preached, there was something which the people might, and I know did, carry away with them.'

One of the chief farmers, his churchwarden, writes :

' His great knowledge of and sympathy with human nature, our failures and attempted good points, was such that everyone was impressed.   The strong moral sense brought to bear had a most wonderful power in making people try to realise their position and discover if they were fulfilling a part worthy of that position for good or evil.'

An old pupil says :

' His sermons in Embleton church were models of what country discourses should be.   They were entirely simple, and no one could fail to understand their general tenour and teaching, but the thoughtful listener would see the deeper undercurrent, and could never think that the sermon did not give him ample food for consideration.'

He often quoted poetry, though seldom more than once in a sermon, generally a few lines of Browning or Tennyson or a verse of a hymn.   His preaching was much appreciated, and people came from other parishes to hear him.   Mr. Albert Grey (now Earl Grey) often walked over from Howick with Mr. Streatfeild, then Rector of Howick, for the Sunday evening service.   What attracted people most was the reality of the sermons.   He was not saying things because they ought to be said, or because they were what people expected him to say, but he was giving the fruit of his own keen observation of life and character, of his own spiritual experience, of his own fervent desire to lift himself and his hearers into a larger world, to a knowledge of God's purpose.

His first desire was to get to know his people, and for them to get to know and trust him. For this constant visiting was the only possible way, and in such a scattered parish to visit adequately was hard work. The usual plan was that vicar, curate, and I would start out together early in the afternoon for some part of the parish. On reaching Craster or Newton, or one of the big farms, we separated for visiting, and met again at a stated time to walk home. The conversational merits of vicar and curate were once judged as follows by a good woman : 'Mr. Creighton, he's a very good crack; but Mr. Green, he's a fair old wife's crack.' Sometimes the visits would end with tea at the farmhouse, and almost any cottager whom we found at tea was glad to offer us a cup. On first going to the North, in most of the farmhouses, and in the cottages of the better-to-do people, we were offered wine or spirits, and we were told that it would hurt their feelings if it were refused. But Creighton felt that it was better to show from the first that he, at any rate, did not consider drinking between meals desirable. It was rather terrible to see the farmer's wife get up and leave the room, and then hear the corks being drawn next door, and see the wine come in on a tray only to be refused. Yet it was impossible to refuse beforehand what had never been offered. But he knew how to refuse kindly, and to gratify the hospitable instincts of his hostess by asking for a cup of tea instead, and the habits of the vicar were soon known throughout the parish. In bad weather, if possible, the visiting was confined to the village of Embleton, but no weather hindered the vicar from going where he was needed. His walking habits stood him in good stead, and he took his long tramps over the parish in biting winds, or driving rain and sleet, plunging through the deep mud of the almost impassable lanes in winter, and enjoying to the full every change of light on fields or sea. He used to go about in winter in a cloak made after the pattern of those worn by the Venetian gondoliers, which he found most convenient, as he could easily throw it open when he entered a hot cottage, and toss it across his chest again on going out.

In the cottages he quickly made himself at home with the people. His method may be described in his own words, taken from a letter to a friend :

' Remember that in dealing with ordinary folk you do not gain their confidence at once. You must begin anyhow, gradually you can advance to more serious things *à propos* of passing events. If you speak out naturally what is in you, you do a great deal of good by showing them a higher standard of life and duty.'

At first he excited considerable wrath among the old women by discontinuing the existing habit of doling out to them in half-crowns the Communion alms ; but this soon blew over. Long years after, an old woman described him to the present vicar as 'more charitable' than his successor, who gave away plenty of half-crowns, but always to the same people. ' Now, I like Mr. Creighton,' she concluded ; ' he gave to nobody.' They found in the vicar a sympathetic listener to their long yarns about their ailments. ' Mr. Creighton he says,' remarked an old woman to me, ' it's my digester that is out of order, but I say it's my whole cistern.' He used to prescribe for them, and though his drugs were very simple, a bottle mixed and brought by the vicar was thought of sovereign efficacy. The larger the bottle and the nastier the taste, the better. He was especially careful in watching over the girls' health, for even in that wonderful air they tended to become anæmic and hysterical. He would go again and again to make sure that a girl took her tonic regularly. He himself escorted a consumptive girl to Miss Fox's Home at Falmouth. He acted as legal adviser, made wills for the people, and settled their disputes. Of course he prayed and read with the old and sick. One young woman recalls how he used to visit her brother, who was often ill, and how the invalid ' loved to have him sit and talk to him, and then his goodness in bringing all sorts of nice things in his pockets, port wine, jellies, medicines as well.' On occasions he would turn nurse and spend hours by the bedside of a sick person, or he would try patiently for a whole evening to control a woman in *delirium tremens* to whom he had been called from his dinner, or he would go daily to calm an hysterical girl who terrified the village by her shrieks. Above all, he cared for the children, and so readily made his way to the mothers' hearts. And it was no affected interest, it was real love for children and joy in intercourse with them. One of his old parishioners writes :

' My earliest recollection of the Bishop was of him when he used to meet us running about the village, picking us up and carrying us shoulder high, swinging us round, and then when you looked round he was gone. In the summer time he used to fetch us into his garden and tell us to come and pick some fruit for ourselves, and give us sweet little bunches of flowers, and altogether acted as though we were his own children.'

There was one family who were left early without parents. The boys and the elder girl were hired to work on a farm, and the younger girl when she was only ten years old had to keep the house. He made a point, though she lived some way off, of going to see her very often. He taught her to look upon him as a friend to whom she could tell anything, and encouraged her in every way to make the best of her life. She says :

' He always seemed to take such an interest in what we were doing. It didn't matter what it was, cleaning up, sewing, or baking. He used to ask all sorts of questions; really I have never seen a clergyman since who took half the interest that he did. I could tell him all my troubles. . . . Sometimes he used to say I did better and managed to keep the home always so clean and tidy, a deal more so than many grown-up women. He used to tell me I was a wonderful little woman. I many times wonder now how he could sit in some of the houses, as they were anything but clean. He would lend us books to read at home. Then the great trouble was to me when he was called away to Cambridge. I thought I should never hear or see him again, but he promised that he would write to me once a month, and that I had to write back and tell him all about myself. I did write pretty regularly for a time, then I began to put off writing for sometimes a few months together, but from seven years old I have kept in touch with him up to his last illness; for all his extra work he never seemed to think it a trouble to answer a letter of mine.'

This girl married and went to live in Yorkshire, where Creighton managed to see her twice by stopping between trains, and he never lost his interest in her.

There were four schools in the parish, and these he visited frequently. His experience of them did not make him much enamoured with our system of elementary education. He would have liked occasionally to teach the children himself, but he found that his methods of instruction were quite unfit to assist them to face the inspector. Speaking at a meeting of the College of Preceptors in 1899, he recalled these days.

'I can only tell you,' he said, 'that my own attempts at teaching young children when I had a country parish were disastrous. I was not alone in that, because both my wife and curate fared the same ; we all regarded ourselves as intelligent persons, and we took great pains in teaching the children. But when they came before the inspector, they failed in the subjects which we had taught. That raised the question, who was to blame for such a result? Was it the teachers, the children, or the inspector? I was so conceited that I thought the fault was the inspector's. It was quite natural. It was his business to examine in a kind of knowledge which I was not trying to give.'

Creighton never forgot how one afternoon, when visiting a school attended almost exclusively by the children of farm labourers, he found the master instructing them in the names of the capes of China in preparation for the visit of the inspector. He found it best to confine his efforts at instruction to religious teaching, but he always did what he could to help any of his parishioners, or indeed anyone he came across, who wished to continue their education. He taught the pupil teachers regularly, and lent books to any who would read.

Classes or gatherings of any sort in the evenings were difficult to manage in such a scattered parish. At one time he had a Shakespeare reading class for some of the young people ; and he gave lectures sometimes in the evenings in the schoolroom. On these occasions he often took a play of Shakespeare and explained it, reading the most striking scenes. At one of these lectures on 'Macbeth,' the school was filled with an audience so attentive that they even forgot to cough ; but it was almost too much for an old woman who was one of his most devout admirers. 'Oh, it was too terrible,' she said sadly the next day ; 'generally when I go home, I try to remember the vicar's sermons, but this time I tried to forget as quick as possible.'

He valued anything that could bring new ideas or new interests into the life of the village, where scandal and back-biting, often indulged in because there was nothing else to think about, seemed to do as much harm even as graver vices. On discovering how fond the young people were of dancing, and with what decorum they behaved at dances, he took to giving his choir a ball at the vicarage as their Christmas treat. They danced in the drawing-room and supped in the dining-room, and the vicar and the curate danced with them the whole evening. The programme consisted of a succession of different country dances, each danced with the greatest care and precision, and no dancer was allowed to pause from the beginning to the end of the dance. As the vicar had to dance with each of the twenty-five ladies for fear of hurting the feelings of anyone by neglect, and also to carve a huge round of beef at supper, he considered the choir dance the most severe physical exertion of the year.

Of course there were village concerts and penny readings, and whenever possible a neighbour or friend was secured to give a lecture. A small cottage at the vicarage gate, belonging to the vicar, was given up to be a reading room for the men and entrusted to their own management.

Creighton was glad to welcome deputations from the two great missionary societies, not only because of his strong interest in missions, but because he felt the educational value of missionary meetings in enlarging the mental horizon of his people.

The only Nonconformist place of worship in the parish, except the little Methodist chapel at Craster, was a Presbyterian chapel in Embleton, the minister of which had a manse in the village. Creighton was on friendly terms with all Non-conformists, but he used to say that it was hardly fair to regard the Presbyterians in Northumberland as Noncon-formists, since for the most part they were merely descendants of Scottish peasants who had wandered across the border. It was among the farm servants that the Presbyterians were mostly to be found, and their children often joined the Church quite naturally, and without any objection from the parents, who were content so long as they 'went some-where.' I remember a woman complaining to me once because her children went to church, but giving as her sole reason for objecting that 'when they had paid for a seat in chapel, it looked so bad for it to be left empty.'

Creighton was on excellent terms with the two ministers who successively occupied the manse in his day. The first was a man of the old school, who might be seen digging his garden or driving his cow to pasture, but kept a small school for the children of some of the farmers and better-to-do people in the neighbourhood. He also gave us an excellent lecture on Burns one evening in the village school, and brought up and started well in the world a large family on very small means. His successor, Mr. Spence, was a bachelor, a retired scholarly man, to whom Creighton was glad to be able to lend books. When he came to the village, Creighton, anxious to show friendliness, was present by invitation at the inaugural service in the chapel, where according to Presbyterian custom Mr. Spence was ordained to his new ministry, and also at the lunch given to him afterwards by his congregation. There, in obedience to request, he spoke a few words of welcome to the new-comer, and expressed the hope that they would work together in every way they could ; 'a hope,' writes Mr. Spence, 'which I am glad to say was realised. I am sure there never was even the shadow of a misunderstanding between us.' His conduct in this matter gave a good deal of offence to the neighbouring clergy, though I think they soon got over it. They did not perhaps understand the way in which he regarded Presbyterians, nor perceive that his view of toleration did not spring from any indifference or any desire to minimise differences, but from his reverence for the opinions of others and his belief in the paramount importance of liberty.[1] He tried to carry into action the Apostle's command to honour all men, and I think his people understood his action.

Mr. Spence, writing of his recollections of him, says :

'What impressed me was the esteem in which he was held by the people. It was evident that he had won their hearts to a degree which is not often the good fortune of a clergyman. They liked him and trusted him. They felt that he was deeply interested in their welfare. Many have told me

[1] Cf. Creighton's *Hulsean Lectures on Persecution and Tolerance.*

how they went to him with their troubles, and always found him sympathetic. . . . We sometimes had talks about our work in the parish, and when he told me his experience I always found it helpful.'

There were some local customs which Creighton felt it his duty to put down at once, even at the risk of unpopularity. He never offered spirits or beer to those who came to the vicarage on business. Soon after his arrival, a party of fishermen came over from Craster to arrange about the wedding of one of their number. They had fortified themselves on the way to face the ordeal, and were very cheerful and friendly. The business over, they sat on and talked, evidently expecting something. At last in despair they rose, and one said, 'A dry visit this.' 'Yes, very dry,' answered the vicar quietly, and they trooped sadly out.

A habit prevailed at weddings of placing a form across the church door for the wedding party to jump over when they came out, a jump which was said to take them over all their future troubles. A crowd of men assembled to help the happy couple and their friends to jump, with an accompaniment of much unseemly noise and joking. Creighton, at the second wedding which he celebrated in the parish, ordered the removal of the form from the church door. He said they could have it in the road outside if they liked, but at least they should leave the churchyard decorously. There was some desire among the rougher quarrymen to make a disturbance, but it soon quieted down. The jumping in the road was not found to be very amusing, and was, I believe, entirely discontinued.

An unpleasant custom prevailed on one of the days of the village feast, of getting hold of some tramp or wandering labourer, and dubbing him the mayor of the village. He was first made thoroughly drunk, and then put on a trolley and pushed round the village by a crowd of men and boys, who demanded, and generally received, money for drink at all the houses. The first year they even rolled him down to the vicarage. The vicar happened to be away that day ; but he determined to put an end to the performance another year, and told the policeman that if either the 'mayor' or those who pushed him about got drunk over the performance, he was to summon them for being drunk and disorderly. I believe they used still to drag the man about, but there was an end of the public exhibition of riotous drunkenness.

The village feast was not altogether edifying, as it was apt to lead to a good deal of drinking. It was held in connexion with the festival of the church, which was dedicated to the Holy Trinity. The girls and children wore their new summer frocks; everyone had their friends to visit them, and wonderful feast cakes, dark brown, and kept moist by a judicious use of vinegar, were baked in every cottage. On the Monday following, sports were held on the links by the sea. Creighton tried to emphasise the religious side of the festival, and lead the people, through it, to take an interest and pride in their church. He wanted them to feel the church as their home, and always kept it open, in hopes that some might use it for private prayer.

One of his most successful ventures in the village was a penny bank in connexion with the school. The Northumbrian is always suspicious. Creighton wrote in 1893 to an old parishioner who was leaving the North:

'You will find out now that there is a difference between North and South. The people in the South are more friendly and more open: they have not so much stuff in them as the northern folk; but they are nicer at first sight, and are not so suspicious. When first I went to Embleton, I felt everybody to be so cold, as if they were watching me, and looking out for fault to find. But when they do get to like one, they stick to it.'

So at first there were some who were suspicious about the penny bank, and thought it must have some ulterior purpose; but they soon learnt to appreciate and use it. He started a branch of the Church of England Temperance Society, and in his last year, we began a very successful Band of Hope. This was seriously endangered by a local custom. A certain Sunday in Lent, for some unknown reason, is called Carlin Sunday, and on that day the women provide 'carlins,' dried peas fried in rum and butter, for the children. The publicans much disliked the Band of Hope, and trusted that Carlin Sunday would lead the children to break their pledge. But the vicar decided that as carlins were not drink they might be allowed, and many of the mothers helped the temperance cause by preparing the carlins without spirits.

Northumberland contains but few country places in proportion to its size; and as the sea bounded us on one side, the number of our neighbours was very small. We had three squires resident in the parish, Sir George Grey at Fallodon, Mr. Craster at Craster Tower, and Mr. Foster at Newton, the house where Creighton found refuge on first coming into the parish in a snowstorm. When we first went to Embleton, Sir George Grey was away. His only son, Equerry to the Prince of Wales, had died at Sandringham of congestion of the lungs in the preceding November, just at the time when his father was lying dangerously ill of typhoid fever at Fallodon. Sir George, on his recovery, went away for change of air, but soon after we were settled at Embleton he returned to face his desolated life at Fallodon. His son's widow and her children made their home with him, and Sir George, with true Christian resignation, set himself to conquer his own sorrow, and live for others. He had been Home Secretary till 1865, and had remained in Parliament till 1874, but he had now absolutely left political life. Creighton's short biography of him describes the rare beauty of his old age, which none who saw could ever forget. We considered it one of the greatest privileges of our life to be allowed for seven years to live on terms of close intimacy with him. The day after he returned he drove down to call upon us, and to urge us to come to Fallodon as soon as possible.

On our first visit he at once made us feel at home, and himself came to show us the short way back through his grounds, and to make us admire the beautiful silver firs which stood round the pond at the bottom of his lawn. The friendship between him and Creighton grew rapidly. Sir George, with his white beard and venerable appearance, and the long experience of life and affairs behind him, remained to the last young in mind and heart. He entered to the full not only into the games and amusements of his grandchildren, but, what is far rarer, he took the keenest delight in the exchange of ideas with a younger man trained under quite different conditions from his own, and of an exceptionally active and independent turn of mind. Creighton could talk to him as freely as to a man of his own standing, and be sure of an interested and sympathetic listener. Sir George might not agree, but he was never shocked. The two men appreciated one another thoroughly. Creighton's visits did much to cheer and brighten Sir George, and help him in his struggle against the depressing effects of sorrow, and Creighton not only found constant pleasure in the intercourse with Sir George, but learnt much from his wide experience, from his political sanity, from his unfailing sobriety of judgment. Sir George took keen interest in the affairs of the parish. He knew all the people on his estate, and visited them in their cottages. On the whole he preferred talking about local affairs, about people, and, above all, about books, to discussing political questions. Sometimes, not often, he would talk about his political experiences. He was always ready to discuss books, and liked to hear of anything new that we were reading, that he might read it too. He even read French novels under our direction, rather to the horror of Lady Grey, who used in her emphatic way to express her anxiety as to what mischief Sir George and Mr. Creighton together might not be guilty of. But Lady Grey also thoroughly appreciated her vicar, even though he sometimes puzzled her. She consulted him about all her people, in whom she, too, took the deepest interest. One direction she gave us at the first amused us by its shrewdness : ' If you hear anything about my household when you are going about the place, don't tell me ; I don't want to know.' Visiting in that part of the parish always ended up with tea at Fallodon, and Lady Grey would exclaim as we entered the room, ' Another teapot for Mr. Creighton ; I know he always likes three cups.' Whenever he had anyone of interest with him, Sir George invited us to meet them, and in that way Creighton met Lord Northbrook, Lord Loch, and many others. In Sir George's grandchildren, Creighton, with his love for children, took from the first an affectionate interest. The present Sir Edward Grey was then at a private school, but as time went on Creighton saw more and more of him, and the friendship begun at Embleton only grew closer as the years passed.

Another neighbour just outside the parish was Lord Grey at Howick, Sir George's cousin. He was growing old and deaf, and after Lady Grey's death in 1879 he led a very secluded life; but Creighton had many interesting talks with him, and formed a close friendship with his nephew and heir, Mr. Albert Grey. The only other near neighbour was Mr. Bosanquet at Rock Hall, who had been the first secretary of the Charity Organisation Society in London, and on succeeding to his father's estate took an active part in all diocesan and county affairs, and so was much thrown together with Creighton.

There were of course a certain number of clergy within reach of a drive, of whom we saw a good deal. We dined frequently at Fallodon, and occasionally at Howick or else-where. We kept only an open pony carriage, which Creighton used to drive himself when we dined out. Many a wild drive we had in rain or snow and nearly always wind, having to pass over level crossings on the North-Eastern, waiting with an impatient pony while the great Scotch expresses dashed by. Creighton smoked cigarettes as he drove home, lighting them with extreme difficulty under the shelter of his cloak. Whenever it was at all fine he much enjoyed the drives and the intimate communion with nature which the lonely darkness of the country roads allowed, as we watched the stars and the revolving lights of the Farne Island light-houses.

He formed friendly relations with all the chief farmers in the district. Mr. George Robertson, who had a large farm close to the vicarage, was his churchwarden and a great help to him. He was a man of exceptional character, for whom Creighton felt strong respect and affection, and he was glad to see as much of him as possible. Mr. Robertson says of him :

'He did more for me than ever I could possibly thank him for; he always seemed to know how I felt, and helped me to see my way, without having to repeat any of the hackneyed phrases generally used by clergymen with the stilted stateliness of manner that is so irritating to people who have nerves.'

Creighton got to know by degrees many of the chief people in Newcastle and in the more distant parts of the county, most intimately the Peases and Hodgkins, who were prepared by their close connexion with his Falmouth friends to welcome him with cordiality, Sir Charles Trevelyan at Wallington, whom he often visited, and Mr. Widdrington at Newton Hall, whose daughter married Sir Edward Grey.

The Northumbrian county was full of inexhaustible interest to him, both on account of its beauty and of its historic associations. His own parish contained the lonely ruin of Dunstanborough Castle, and a walk there was always a delight, whether on a radiant summer afternoon, when he would join the Grey children and his own in boiling a big kettle for tea within the castle precincts—it was always his part to build the fire—or on a wild stormy day, when the waves dashed mountain high over the rocks. He explored the county far and wide. His favourite recreation was to go off for a day's ramble, helping himself by the train to get to some unexplored region, and he loved to show the many friends who visited him, the beauties which he had discovered.

A frequent companion on his walks was Mr. Topley, a member of the Geological Survey, at that time resident in Alnwick. His knowledge and his intelligent appreciation of nature made him a delightful companion, and Creighton enjoyed learning from him something about the interesting geological formations in the county. On these walks a sandwich in his pocket did for lunch ; and if no inn was handy, he would turn into a cottage and ask the good woman to make him tea, which she always gladly did. There was a little inn at Bamborough which he often visited. He admired a wooden tray on which his tea was brought him, and wanted to buy it of the landlady, but she could not decide to part with it. Some years afterwards she died, and left directions with her son that he was to give Mr. Creighton the tray, which he did.

He was always a great trespasser, and no one interfered with him. Northumberland was quite undisturbed by tourists, and as a rule on a long day's walk it was rare to meet a human being.

But few letters remain written during the early years at Embleton.

To his sister, from Windsor Castle, where he visited
Prince Leopold just before going to Embleton

'Windsor Castle : March 10, 1875.

'My dear Polly,—Will you please tell the governor that
I am very much obliged for the kind offer he has made me to
lend me money if I want it at first ? . . . But I will try as long
as I can to get on without borrowing : at present I can survive ;
I am afraid, however, it won't be for long. I shall have a
good many things to get at first, and my chief deficiency will
be in ready money just then. We will see how things go :
I will ask for money when I want it.

'I got your letter just before starting for Windsor. What
a splendid place it is, to be sure. . . . The whole Castle is of
course full of things to see : it is rather like living in a vast
museum. I simply keep on losing myself hopelessly among
the pathless windings of the place. My bedroom is about
ten minutes' walk from the Prince's room, and a servant has
to conduct me that I lose not myself. The Prince is wonderfully well ; in some points better than before his fever. . . .
We wandered yesterday through the gardens, the Prince in a
pony chaise led by a groom, and the rest of us walking with
him. I saw the Royal Dairy, which is all covered, floor and
walls with lovely tiles : the milk stands on slabs in the middle
and against the walls, and above the slabs all round the walls
are hung on shelves beautiful old china dishes. Also we
visited the Prince Consort's Mausoleum at Frogmore, which
is all decorated inside with marbles and mosaics, and in the
centre is the tomb with a colossal recumbent figure of the
Prince. Then I was turned loose into the Library, and saw
simply the most splendid collection of drawings of Leonardo
da Vinci that exists in the world. So you see I am making
the most of it. . . .'

To C. T. Cruttwell   'Embleton : May 15, 1875.

'Dear Cruttwell,— . . . I am deeply grateful for letters
with Oxford news : those which I get occasionally indulge
too much in the "allusive" style. . . . I cannot think
that the University will gain much by my sermons. I feel
that I am neither controversial nor speculative. All I can do
is to apply common sense to matters whence by consent
of all parties it is at present banished. . . . My life here is
tolerably busy : all my afternoons from two till seven I spend
in rambling among my parishioners, and innumerable small
duties always come upon one. I manage to get about four
hours' reading in the day, not more. The country is quite
beautiful just now ; and the sea coast around us is delightful.

. . . Diocesan and all other politics I entirely eschew. Those
who want my opinions must find them in my life and works.
Greater sanity will, I trust, come over both by greater quiet.
I like my life here very much, and am far from regretting that
I left Oxford. . . . The time of your Ordination draws near :
may you be happy. . . . If you do anything awful at your
meeting, tell me, as Merton's " policy " will always interest me.'

'Embleton : January 27, 1876.

'Dear Cruttwell,— . . . I am here very busy ; small books
and editorial labours weigh upon me, added to which I have
just taken a pupil for the Indian Examination. . . . He is
such a nice fellow that I quite enjoy having a little teaching
now and then. I am also struggling to pay off the bills which
fitting up a large country house involves, and which are grievous.

'Missions are a mistake from our point of view. They
tend to keep up the popular belief in emotional states of
mind being of any serious value. It seems to me that man
wants as the basis of his personal religion a rational conviction
of the need of a spiritual side to his life. Missions obscure
this truth : they appeal to men's terrors or superstitions, and
they create something which is evanescent in most cases, and
in the few cases in which any permanent results are left, they
are *not the highest results of which the man is capable.* Is my
view just ?

'My wife sends her kind regards. May Merton flourish.'

To the Bishop of Colombo   'Embleton : February 21, 1876.

'My dear Cop.,—Bishop as you are, I can't call you
anything else in writing, so don't expect it. I hope you are
thriving, and found the prospect more pleasing and the men
less vile than the current idea about Ceylon represents. How
busy you must be, and in what a whirl of things you must be
plunged in trying to find out all that has to be found out.
Why, even I in my very scanty parish found a great labour
in finding out people's names, and where they lived, and all
the countless things necessary to know before one can move
freely in a new sphere. . . . How much more to you. We are
thriving. I have set up a curate, a jewel of a curate. . . . Also
I have set up a pupil reading for the Indian, who is a most
delightful youth, and is a pleasant addition to our scanty
society in the winter. Why say more about myself ? . . .
May you flourish, Cop., and abound. You have plenty of work
before you : may God give you strength and wisdom to do it,
in which wish my wife most entirely joins.

'Yours ever affectionately,

'M. Creighton.'

CHAPTER VII

LIFE AT EMBLETON

THE first summer was chiefly spent in getting to know the people, and in entertaining the friends who came to see our new home. The house was large enough to hold a good many guests, and though the distance from London was great, and our manner of life very simple, we found that friends were glad to come and see us, and enjoy our wild country and our beautiful shore. Creighton's ordinary habit was to spend his morning in his study : he never secluded himself, and could always work amid interruptions, and visitors went in and out of the study and used it as a smoking room. To his great satisfaction, there was but one post, which came in at 10.30 and went out at 2.30; so letter writing could not drag on through the day. He only wrote such letters as were absolutely necessary, and kept up no regular correspondence with any of his friends. ' I don't want to inflict upon you a correspondence,' he wrote to a friend, ' for that is one of the poorest gifts to bestow on anyone.' The afternoons were spent in the parish ; if he had friends with him, he made them walk with him to the houses he was going to visit, and often took them in to see his people. In the evening if there were visitors he sometimes played whist ; when alone he worked till eleven o'clock. He never sat up late ; during the twenty-nine years of our married life I never once knew him sit up to finish a piece of work.

New duties fell upon him quickly : he was elected guardian of the poor, and a member of the sanitary authority for the Alnwick Union, and attended his first meeting of the Board on April 24. Henceforward it was his regular habit to go into Alnwick, a distance of some seven miles, every Saturday, either driving himself in his pony carriage or accompanying Mr. Robertson in his gig. He valued much the experience gained as a guardian, and said that it taught him a great deal about human character, and helped him to learn how to manage men. He always lunched after the Board meeting with an old lady named Mrs. Thorpe, the widow of an Alnwick solicitor, to whom he became much attached. She was a cultivated woman, and owned an interesting collection of watercolour paintings by William Turner.

Among our visitors that first summer were the Andrew Langs, Mr. Copleston, who had just been appointed Bishop of Colombo, the H. J. Hoods, and Edward Talbots. Creighton was appointed this year Select Preacher to the University at Oxford. In the summer he examined for both the School and the University at Durham. He was glad to increase his income by examination work, as the expense of moving and putting the house in order had been heavy, and the cost of living in the country and keeping up a large house and garden was considerable. He several times examined for the Indian Civil Service as well as at various schools. He also took a pupil in the beginning of 1876; he did this very reluctantly, but he grew so attached to his first pupil, Mr. Trevor Berrington, that he found his presence only a pleasure. In 1876, he took a second pupil, Mr. Alfred Pease, elder son of Mr. (afterwards Sir Joseph) Pease, and thus began an intimate friendship with that branch of the Pease family. The eldest son of Mr. Stopford Brooke came to read with him in 1877, and during the next two or three years he generally had one and sometimes two pupils. He was very particular as to the men he took. ' I am deluged with applications,' he wrote, ' and generally refuse them all.' His treatment of his pupils was most unconventional. They sat and worked in his study while he wrote; at times he would break off in his writing, and spend an hour, not so much in definite teaching, as in discussing the point which the pupil had been reading. His object was to make those whom he taught think for themselves, to guide them and arouse their curiosity, to fertilise what was in their mind rather than to find out how much they knew. Sometimes the historical discussion would take place pacing up and down the terrace in the garden, and he would talk about the period of history his pupil was reading just as he might have talked about it to a friend in society.

'His method,' writes an old pupil, 'would, I should say, have been hopeless with a really stupid man, and it would not have driven an idle one, but it was very stimulating to anyone who was capable of being interested in his subject, and made a clever mind leap forward. It seems to me that he didn't like or encourage controversial argument in conversation, he never wanted to destroy what anyone else said ; he would, no doubt, get rid of what he thought mistaken or wrong, but what he cared to do was to fix on something with which he agreed, and then to give it life and permanence in the mind of the person who said it, by developing a point of view in which the thing originally said found a place and formed a part. I think he followed the same method in teaching ; he tried to get hold first of something which reading had started in the mind.'

He always treated his pupils as friends and equals, and much enjoyed their society. He never stood on his dignity ; they might chaff or tease him as they liked, but he always commanded their respect, they could never take liberties with him.

'It certainly was very flattering,' writes one of them, 'to be taken out and talked to frankly by a man of his age and position, especially as he did not do it as if it were for one's improvement, as was the case with Jowett. Creighton, on the contrary, just talked apparently for the sake of talking.'

Most of his pupils became friends, and he did not willingly lose sight of any of them.

'Embleton : August 21, 1876.

'Dear Pease,— . . . It is very good of you to say you enjoyed your time with us. Short as it was, I hope it was long enough to make us friends. You will not forget my desire to be of any use to you I can in your life at Cambridge.'

'Embleton : December 29, 1876.

'Dear Alfred,— . . . I was very glad to hear that you got through your Little Go all right. It is a great blessing to get anything of that sort off one's mind. I think you will find the History Tripos more amusing than Law. The Law requires more abstract thought, and would not, I think, interest you so much as History. Moreover, it does not open out any field of reading afterwards, which History does. You will find it a great thing in after life to have got some definite interest in the way of books. It is always hard to read a book unless one cares in some way about the subject. History gives one the key to many books, and prevents one from feeling them hopelessly dry. I was amazed, by the way, at Mr. Hodgkin's knowledge. I met him at Pendower.[1] He has all the tastes of a thorough-going historical student. Hence I say, on the whole, stick to History.'

In August 1875 Creighton finished the little book on the Age of Elizabeth which he was writing for Messrs. Longman. He now undertook to edit for Messrs. Longman a series of Epochs of English History.

Extracts from letters to Mr. C. J. Longman

'June 22, 1875.

'My notion of an Elementary Historical Series would be something of this kind. The books to be of eighty pages. . . . My idea would be to keep closely to the task of tracing the internal development of England, keeping clear the broad lines of constitutional progress and the increase of wealth and commerce, and avoiding as much as possible foreign affairs. . . . They should all be written in the simplest possible way for the use of beginners, and should avoid all unnecessary names and details which did not bear on the subject.'

'July 26.

'I must say at once that I should not be inclined to part with the copyright of such a book as I proposed. . . . In educational works especially, where the temptation is so great to write in a perfunctory manner, I think it is almost essential to the success of a series that the authors should have a direct interest in them.'

'March 15, 1876.

'I hope I am not too sanguine in anticipating that the Epochs of English History will be used in all kinds of schools. In the lower forms of the public schools I should think it very likely they would be found useful. In the Grammar Schools they certainly would, also in Middle Class Schools, and in the larger School Board Schools and National Schools. Also I think they would be of great service in Girls' Schools, which seem to me to be just now an element in the demand for school books, which is daily becoming more important, and I have kept my eye on them in this series.'

'March 21, 1876.

'The great danger to which all elementary series of educational books is exposed is, that they turn out to be

[1] The name of Mr. J. W. Pease's house in Newcastle. Mr. J. W. Pease and Mr. Hodgkin had both married Miss Foxes.

extremely useful and very interesting to *grown-up people.* Everything that I have yet seen intended for beginners has slipped away from its purpose. I feel my duty as editor to be a stern regard for the young readers. We must be neither literary, pictorial, nor accurate at their expense.'

'Creighton took a great deal of trouble to secure competent writers for the Epochs. It must be remembered that series of this kind were then comparatively new, and communications with authors and publishers had to enter into many details and took up much time and thought. But the prospectus of the series with the names of the eight parts and of their authors was issued in November 1875, and the publication began early in 1876. For the first of the series he secured the present Regius Professor of Modern History at Oxford, Mr. York Powell, 'a very competent though untried man.'

To Mr. C. J. Longman   'November 1875.

'I think the series will begin well with his [Powell's] book. . . . It is written in a charmingly simple, almost Biblical style.'

'January 1876.

'I think Powell's book is very good. It is really too good for its purpose, which is always what happens. It is most difficult to get good men to confine themselves within narrow limits. But Powell's book makes the whole history live.'

To Oscar Browning (author of the last of the series)

'Embleton : April 24, 1878.

'I conceive my great function as editor is to look out for the interests of the youthful reader and to advocate simplicity of language where possible. I hope you will forgive me if I seem sometimes needlessly minute in verbal criticism. But the continuity of the series may sometimes demand changes, the use of which is not obvious at first sight. I am responsible for the political phraseology throughout, and don't want each writer to use different words and phrases for the same things.'

'April 29, 1878.

'I have suggested a few alterations. . . . I have put myself in the place of the unlearned, and have demanded that everything should be made clear from that point of view.'

Writing many years afterwards, Mr. York Powell says of his work as editor : ' I owe him the great kindness of giving me my first opportunity of writing on History, and I know how extraordinarily kind and helpful he could be in giving most useful and necessary criticism, by which I have greatly profited, for it was a fine lesson for me to have my prentice work gone over by his advice and corrections.'

In February 1878 Creighton was able to write :

' Our series is now almost finished. . . . I trust that on the whole the series is fairly well established. The difficulty in all series is to keep them sufficiently elementary. This one, both in size and cost of the volumes, has strayed beyond what I intended originally. Still, I hope your firm is tolerably satisfied with its success.'

At the same time he proceeded with the short series of Historical Biographies for Messrs. Rivington. In these he hoped to gather round the lives of a few men who lived in stirring times the most distinctive features and the facts of the social life of their period, and by forming a few clear ideas in the pupil's mind to stimulate further reading. ' Something at least will be gained if the pupil realises that men in past times lived and moved in the same sort of way as they do at present.' His own contribution, ' The Life of Simon de Montfort,' appeared in 1876. After that, for a time, he rested from writing school books, and was able to devote himself to his own studies. He had possessed himself of a copy of Muratori, which greatly facilitated his work. He read few newspapers and no magazines, and belonged to no circulating library. He was at this time much interested in George Sand, and wrote to Mr. Longman :

'August 14, 1876.

' There is another point on which I will venture to trouble you. I believe Mr. Reeve is the editor of " The Edinburgh Review." I have not the pleasure of his acquaintance, and therefore hesitate about addressing myself to him directly. But I am stirred with a desire to write an article on " George Sand," an author whose writings I have long been greatly interested in—more than those of any other writer of literature in this generation. It is, of course, very probable that the subject may not seem to him suitable ; . . . but my interest in George Sand leads me to trouble you in the matter.'

'September 7, 1876.

'Thank you very much for the trouble you have taken about Mr. Reeve. I am afraid that George Sand is considered too burning a subject for immediate treatment.'

The winter of 1875–1876 was spent in steady work at Embleton, with the exception of a flying visit to Oxford in December, to preach before the University in his turn as Select Preacher. He took as his subject Christian Liberty, and contrasted the mental freedom which is given by culture and the spiritual freedom which is given by religion, saying that the object of the University was to bring these two into close union. The sermon seems to suggest some consciousness that through his new experiences he was winning for himself greater freedom. 'Freedom must above all things be accompanied by humility, by a constant teachableness of mind. It must be a means of increasing, not of destroying, the power of sympathy with others.' 'The sense of power which comes from self-development can only be fruitful for good if it be directed by the profound sense of responsibility, which the perpetual consciousness of life as lived in God's sight alone can give.' He considered the chief fruit of culture to be that it should lead to the knowledge of man, the knowledge which must guide those efforts for the service of man which the realisation of responsibility in the sight of God would prompt. Culture, therefore, was a necessary accompaniment of freedom.[1] This seems to be the sermon of which Canon Scott Holland said :

'It told something of the secret of his spiritual choice. For half an hour or so he elaborated the idea of art as the interpretation of life and conduct, with a skill and beauty which revealed how masterful had been its fascination for him, and then by a swift turn he rounded on his own picture —he displayed its moral insufficiency. It was a courageous act, in those far days, of self-revelation.'[2]

In July 1876 our eldest son was born, and the villagers greeted his father with, 'So you've gotten a little priestie.' They used to speak of the Vicar as the Church Priest, and of the Presbyterian Minister as the Chapel Priest. Mr. and

---

[1] This sermon is published in *University and other Sermons.*
[2] Memorial sermon preached in St. Paul's Cathedral, January 20, 1901.

Mrs. T. H. Green were god-parents to our son, who was called Cuthbert, after the Northumbrian saint. We always asked that there should be no christening presents, but Mr. Green would not be content until he had sent his godson a Bible.

In the early winter of 1876–1877 we spent some time at Oxford, where Creighton was examining in the Law and Modern History Schools, and much enjoyed being with our old friends. He went on afterwards to visit Prince Leopold at Boyton Manor, and then returned to spend the winter in quiet work with books and pupils and parish. His projected great work was beginning to take shape. He had meant to devote a long time to preliminary study and research, but a chance occurrence drove him to begin writing at once. In old days at Oxford he had occasionally met Prebendary Wilkinson, a member of Merton College, who had spent a long life in studying the history of European Universities. When he died he left behind him a mass of material, but nothing ready for publication. His widow was anxious to know whether some use could not be made of his papers, and wrote to consult Creighton, who suggested that she should send him them to look through. The greater part he found to consist merely of detached notes, that could be of use only to the man who had made them. The only paper that was at all in a condition to publish was a lecture on Wyclif, given in Oxford some years before, which both Dr. Stubbs and Creighton had thought very valuable. This Creighton now arranged for publication as an article in the 'Church Quarterly,' and, thinking that Mrs. Wilkinson would like to keep her husband's manuscript as it was, he copied it entirely afresh, so that the article might not be mutilated by his corrections and additions.

But he was really depressed to discover, that all that could be turned to any account out of the lifework of an industrious and conscientious student was this one article. Looking through the mass of unordered material, he resolved that he would not wait to amass notes before he began to write, but that in his case study and writing should go side by side. It was the sight of Mr. Wilkinson's papers that drove him to begin his book.

In May 1877, he was made Chairman of the School Attendance Committee formed in Alnwick under the Act of 1876 for enforcing the compulsory attendance of children at school. He attended the Northern District Poor Law Conference at Gilsland in the following August, and read a paper on 'The Duties of Guardians with regard to Education.' He urged that the Act should be worked in such a way that 'the old principle that rates are not for charitable but for necessary purposes should be rigidly asserted.' He considered that 'henceforth guardians are bound to see that pauper children set an example of regularity of attendance at school;' and said that 'the first object of the Act was to create a feeling of increased responsibility in parents by the sense of a constant watchful supervision over the regularity and efficiency of the education of their children.' The Act must therefore be worked in such a way as to educate the parent; the legal powers which it gave should only be used in the last resort; with tact and good humour the School Attendance Committees should use every possible means to create a public opinion which should make it easy to carry out the law, and to persuade rather than compel the parent to conform to it.' He was thanked by the Conference for his paper, and as the subject was new and experience still scanty, he was asked to speak again on the subject at the Conference in the following year. He gave zealous attention during the year to his duties as Chairman of the School Attendance Committee, and in his paper at the Conference in 1878 was able to say that experience had justified the conclusions which he had stated the year before, and that he believed that the working of the Act had created 'a more universal interest in the subject of education, and that the organised expression of public opinion had tended to impress on the minds of the parents generally a sense of their increased responsibility.' What he now felt to be necessary for the satisfactory working of the Act was to procure the adoption of bye-laws [1] in every parish, and he demanded increased facilities for so doing. As things were, 'it was possible for a child to attend school with an ingenious irregularity which

It will be remembered that the Education Act of 1876 made education compulsory only in those districts which adopted bye-laws.

put education entirely out of the question, yet which did not constitute habitual neglect.'

The desire for further knowledge of Italy, so necessary for his studies, made us plan a winter journey to Rome. We left England on December 27, and took with us his sister, a son and daughter of Mr. (afterwards Sir Joseph) Pease and an old Oxford pupil, Mr. Hamlyn. We went by Genoa, Pisa, Siena, and Orvieto to Rome. It was his first visit to Rome, and I think that then as always he was a little overwhelmed by it. He used to say that there was too much to see, that it was too much like a vast museum, that it produced such a combination of impressions as to be confusing ; it was impossible to know to which to attend, how to reconcile the claims of antiquity, of Imperial, early Christian, and Papal Rome. He always enjoyed the smaller Italian cities infinitely more. While we were in Rome, the King, Vittorio Emmanuele, died, and as a consequence all the galleries and museums were closed. We went off to Naples for a week, and returned to Rome when it was quiet again, and after a few days' further stay, travelled back to England by Florence, Padua, and Venice. The journey was marked with misfortune. In Rome he heard of his father's death, but too late for it to be possible for him to get back for the funeral. His sister returned at once to her aunt, but he thought it best not to break up his party, and to carry out our original plans. Some form of malarial poison, moreover, must have attacked us in Rome, for both Miss Creighton and Miss Pease were seriously ill on their return, and I began to be ill with violent fever on the way home. His strength and calmness gave me courage to make the effort to continue the journey, and I succeeded in reaching my old home at Sydenham in the first days of February. During the dangerous illness which followed, the doctors considered that one of the causes which helped to save my life was his genius as a nurse. He never failed to soothe and calm me. On February 18 our second son was born, and, contrary to all expectations, not only did the child live, but I made a speedy recovery. My husband was able to leave me and go back to his work early in March. I followed him before the end of the month, and our child was baptised at Embleton, and called Walter in remembrance of the founder of Merton College.

The constant calls made upon Creighton for work of every sort could not fail to give him sometimes a sense of strain which he deplored.   He writes on March 7, 1878 : ' I really must make a stand against my habit of being worried and fussed.   It is quite absurd ; when I am quite alone I feel just as much driven as if I had any quantity of pupils and children and wives.'   But he always found it difficult to refuse to do anything he was asked, and five days afterwards wrote to me that he was thinking of agreeing to a request to write a small book on Italian literature,   This fell through, but in June he undertook a new school book for Longman.

To Mr. C. J. Longman   'June 14, 1878.
    ' I think, as you say, that the Epochs would be rendered more useful by a general introduction.   I also think that I might see my way to undertaking such a volume.   I would not write it as an abridgment of the Epochs, but as an independent work, at the same time avowedly as an introduction to the Epochs. . . . I would propose for an introductory volume, one which did not deal much in facts, but which aimed at a clear impression of the march of English History.'

'July 19, 1878.
    ' I am not at all anxious to undertake this book : in fact, nothing but a sense of loyalty to the series as at present begun, made me think of doing it at all.   I had resolved to turn my back on English History henceforth, and please myself without thought of gain.'

'August 8, 1878.
    ' I feel that it is the sort of thing that must be written right off if it is to be of any good.   If I can succeed in doing it simply, clearly, and without undue details, I think it ought to succeed well ; but it is difficult, I know.'

'September 21, 1878.
    ' The work is harder than I expected.   The real truth is, that English History has not been sufficiently worked at in detail to admit of its salient points being seized with precision. Any other history admits of greater definiteness, and falls into more strongly marked epochs of development.'

'November 14, 1878.
    ' I hope in a week's time to send you the manuscript of my " Shilling History."   If it is at all adequate to the labours it has cost me, it ought to fulfil its function.   I have been working at nothing else for the last four months, as I was anxious to have it out as soon as possible.'

'January 3, 1879.

'I have kept the proofs longer than I intended, for I was anxious to make the book as good as possible. For this purpose I asked both Mr. Bright and Mr. Rowley to read over my proofs, and I have made use of all the suggestions of both of them. I am glad to say also that both of them think well of it. I have taken all the pains I can to make the book a good one for teaching purposes. I should like it to be known in girls' schools if possible. Books soon penetrate into the better schools, but no one who has not had experience has any idea of the heathen darkness which prevails in most girls' schools and among most governesses on the subject of school books.'

While writing the ' Shilling History ' he was at the same time arranging for the issue of the Epochs in one volume, which entailed a good deal of editing and correspondence with the different authors. But after this he definitely gave up writing school books and devoted himself to his big book.

To Mr. C. J. Longman   'February 27, 1877.

'You are very good in expressing your hope that our connexion may not cease. I am at present busy on what I intend to make the work of my life—a History of the Papacy during the fourteenth, fifteenth, and sixteenth centuries. I had spoken about it some time ago to the late Mr. William Longman, who had expressed a readiness to have the book when it was ready ; but as I have no hope of having the first instalment ready for two years at least, we did not go further than merely discuss it.'

'January 28, 1879.

'I have already mentioned to you that I am busy upon a book, " The Popes of the Reformation." . . . I feel that I should like to have an understanding, at all events a general one, about it. The object of my book is the History of the Papacy and of the Reformation in Europe from the year 1378 to the end of the Council of Trent. My book would be in no sense polemical nor ecclesiastical—it aims at dealing with the large political aspect of the time, and would embrace the history of Italy, its art and literature, at the time when these flourished most, as well as a survey of the whole of European history. The book would fill a void between Milman's " Latin Christianity " (which becomes very scrappy towards its close) and Ranke's "Popes," and my object is to get together the picturesqueness of Milman with the broad political views of Ranke.

'At present I have nearly finished one volume . . . in which I have an introductory sketch of the Papal History, and proceed in detail from 1378 to 1416, so that, compared to modern historians generally, I may claim to aim at compression. The book, as I at present contemplate it, would extend to about five of such volumes.'

To Mr. Oscar Browning   'Embleton: February 18, 1879.

'I can assure you from experience that life is not complete unless one has a "great work" on the stocks; I think one's happiness is increased if the work is so great that one has no hopes of ever finishing it. I have been for some time engaged on such a one: it is to be called, "The Popes of the Reformation," and I have advanced in three years from the outburst of the schism to the Council of Constance, in which I am now plunged.'

Creighton's interest in education made him willing to examine such schools in the North as asked him. He went several times to Middlesbrough to examine the new High School for girls there, and also to Leeds, Shields, and elsewhere. He often lectured in Newcastle at the Literary and Philosophical Institute, generally choosing some subject in connexion with his studies in Italian History, and he did much to encourage the University Extension movement both in Newcastle and elsewhere. Dr. Hodgkin remembers with regret how impossible it was to get him properly reported.

'Either because of the rapidity of his utterance, or because the thoughts were too subtle for the ordinary pressman's brain, it happened over and over again that a speech carefully thought out, and which it was most important that the public should see, was hardly reported at all.'

He gave his best not only in Newcastle, but in humble village schools, where he was often asked to lecture, and never failed to delight even the most rustic audience. His Shakespeare readings were specially appreciated, and often asked for in private houses. His love for children led him to penetrate into the schoolrooms of his friends and give history lessons of a very informal kind, which were a source of unfailing delight. It was a special joy to the children in the schoolrooms at Fallodon, Hutton Hall,[1] and Pendower[2] to see their governesses turned into pupils, and to hear their teaching criticised. For the elder girls he prescribed courses of reading, and made them write papers for him ; he even succeeded in getting several of them to read Stubbs's 'Constitutional History.'

To Miss Ella Pease   'September 30, 1878.

'Have you got home, and have you brought back Stubbs with you? I do hope I am not boring you by my proposal, or by my book which I have prescribed ; please tell me at once if you think me a nuisance, and forgive me for having tried to be one.

'I hope you understood my meaning ; it is that any reading worth mentioning must be hard work, and the subject must be stiff. I have chosen for you the hardest subject and the stiffest book that I know of in connexion with English History. Do not object to its being dull at first, but go at it steadily. . . . Remember that if our plan goes on, you are *never*, NEVER either to talk or think about giving me trouble, but are to believe that the more thoroughly I do what I take in hand the better I am pleased. . . .'

'June 23, 1879.

'Try and write with a little more attention to style, i.e. see that your sentences fit into one another, that each sentence fully and clearly expresses its idea, that the grammatical structure of the sentence agrees with the former sentence. . . .'

He goes on to explain the Home Study Society, and to suggest that a branch of it might be started in Newcastle.

'There is no doubt that the ignorance and want of culture in Northumberland and Durham is most deplorable. I was more than usually depressed yesterday by the account I received of the general impressions about Newcastle of an educated man who had lived there for a year. His attitude was one of hopeless amazement that there could be such a state of society as he saw about him—the ignorance and want of refinement of the Newcastle ladies especially overcame him. You say I always abuse Newcastle—at least I should like to see it do something to help itself.'

---

[1] Sir Joseph Pease's house in Yorkshire.
[2] Mr. J. W. Pease's house in Newcastle.

'August 7, 1879.

'You say that you have taken up enough of my time, and now that Stubbs is done you think you had better cease. You see I am in a false position. I certainly don't want to bore you. I don't want you to go on doing things to please me; but also I don't want you to think that writing to you and looking over papers is any serious draft upon my time, or otherwise than a pleasure to me. You must of course judge; but my experience of life convinces me that the best thing to do is to take people at their word, and if they have been fools enough to say what they don't mean, to let them suffer for it. Never try to be more considerate to people than they are to themselves. If you don't want to do anything more of this sort with me, by all means let us cease; everybody does best in going their own way. If you say what you say from a kind attempt to be considerate for me, I can only say that I entirely resent being taken care of, and refuse to be protected against myself by other people's good nature. So you must simply say what you wish.'

'September 22, 1879.

'You don't care much, I see, about Church History, but it is a most important part of all history. Popular Protestantism has so grotesquely misrepresented facts about the Reformation, that now one of the great means used by the Roman Catholics to make converts is to prove to any who will listen to them the falsity of their opinions about the facts of the past.'

It was not only his history lessons in the schoolroom which were appreciated by his friends' children. Probably no one was ever a better hand at a romp than he was. He would toss the children about like balls, and allow them to ill-treat him in any way they liked. Nervous parents were terrified at these games, and would watch with trembling anxiety as they implored for caution to absolutely deaf ears. But although to the onlooker he appeared the wildest and most careless of the lot, he always knew what he was doing, and no accidents resulted from his romps. He was also an adept at telling nonsense stories; sometimes on a walk with the children hanging round him, each struggling to get as close as possible, and their elders also trying to keep near enough to listen; or lying full length on the hearthrug before the fire with all the children sitting upon him, making what he called a 'regular pie.' He seemed to enjoy his own inventions fully as much as his hearers, as he spun them out of his brain without a moment's pause. The heroes of his stories would reappear again and again during successive years under the wonderful names which he had given them, Tuttery Buttery, Timothy Toozelwits, Kezia Hubbock, who was pursued by all the boys crying, ' Kissie, kissie !' the Nurse with the Cast-iron Inside, &c. &c.

Miss Violet Hodgkin writes of her early remembrances of him :

'" Mr. Creighton" and "Timothy Toozelwits" are still inextricably tangled together in my mind.

'A tall dignified gentleman with gold spectacles and a long beard used to come and sit in the library, talking learned talk to father and being gravely kind to us children. Then suddenly he would disappear behind a table or a sofa or an armchair, you never could tell when or where. Out on the other side would come Timothy Toozelwits, the fascination and terror of our hearts, a black and white figure on all fours, who tried to catch us with his long white arms, while he gnashed his teeth and his eyes gleamed in their gilt rims. "Timothy's" spectacles were quite different from " Mr. Creighton's," and yet they had an uncomfortable knack of looking very much the same. I was always afraid that if I had met him when he was a Bishop (I never did), and if he had worn them still, they would have made me begin in the old way, "Please, dear Mr. Creighton, *will* you do Timothy Toozelwits ?"

'" Mr. Creighton" and " Embleton " were next-door neighbours to "Zeus" and " Olympus " in my mind in those days ; I never knew where " Embleton " was—only heard of it as a place where clever people were asked to pay visits and where very clever children lived. We never knew exactly when he would come to see father, but whenever he did come there was joy.

'I remember one evening particularly ; I had been doing lessons with the Peases, and came home full of a battle between Greeks and Trojans in which all the schoolroom party was to assist on the following day. A battle song was necessary. Would father write one for us Trojans ? I came in at dessert to ask him. Joy ! There was Mr. Creighton sitting by his side. The rest of the evening remains as a dream of bliss, as I and my pencil and my large diary were passed from one of their knees to the other, as between us we wrote this poem, to be chanted over many a glorious Trojan victory thereafter :

> O you Greeks, you wretched Greeks,
> How we do hate your doings !
> You came so far from home to spoil
> Our happy Trojan wooings.
> Their homes you burn, and stalk with stern
> Black faces o'er their ruins.
>
> 'Twas not a deed to stir your pride
> Nor magnify your force,
> For you yourselves must basely hide
> Within a wooden horse.
> Achilles sulks—Ulysses skulks,
> And so you win of course.

I remember still the flourish with which he evolved "skulks" as a rhyme for "sulks."

'Years after, it was a shock to hear as we drove through a dreary little village, "This is Embleton," but when we reached Craster, in one of the fishermen's cottages there, his photograph was the first thing that caught my eye, in the place of honour, resplendent in a red plush frame, and the people seemed as eager to talk of him and hear about him as if he had only left them yesterday."

Old Lady Grey used to be half shocked at the wild games, and think that her grandchildren were wanting in proper respect for their vicar ; when they called out with entreaties to grandmama to come and look at some delightful antic, she would answer, 'No, my dears, I am afraid I should think of it when I see Mr. Creighton in the pulpit.' Sir George, on the other hand, enjoyed the games and nonsense quite as much as the children. I think Lady Grey sometimes feared that he was being led astray by the vicar into too great frivolity.

It was in 1878 that Creighton met Dr. Hodgkin for the first time at dinner at J. W. Pease's house in Newcastle. Dr. Hodgkin, a banker in Newcastle, and one of the most prominent members of the Society of Friends, was then writing his history of ' Italy and her Invaders.'

' We talked history hard all the evening,' writes Dr. Hodgkin, 'and I felt at once that I was in contact with one of the ablest and best stored minds that I had ever known. He gave me all sorts of tips, but more than all he raised my standard of the way in which history ought to be written. I think I had been a little dazzled by Michelet, and thought that the main point was to make history picturesque, if necessary by a little use of one's imagination. He said—and the saying has been a watchword to me ever since—" I always like to keep very close to my authorities." '

After this the two students met often.

' I always like to think of him,' continues Dr. Hodgkin, ' standing at his desk in his library at Embleton with a volume of his green parchment-bound Muratori before him, writing his History of the Popes; or else rolling and smoking one of his multitudinous cigarettes by the library fire when the household had gone to bed, and talking the while; or else taking a long walk and showing me (who had come into Northumberland near twenty years before him) some of the historic sites of our great county, talking all the while as only he could talk, history, literature, politics, spicy bits of that " merely personal talk" which Wordsworth professed to despise. One thing greatly struck me in his walks about Embleton : the very friendly, familiar footing on which he evidently stood with all his parishioners. Never a walk hardly without turning into some cottage—" Well, Mary, how are you to-day? And how's the old man? "—and all with such charming freshness and naturalness; not a touch of condescension, or, what is harder to avoid, shyness and *mauvaise honte.*'

A pupil also recalls these walks :

' What remains freshest in the memory of his pupils are the walks in the country. For all our preference for games to sober walks, we were not so blind as not to appreciate a Northumbrian walk with such a guide. Dunstanborough, Bamborough, Alnwick, and Chillingham were castles which I visited in his company, and every one of them was a ground for historical, architectural, and artistic discussions. Nothing could come under his eyes without his wishing to know the meaning and causes of what he saw. He was not a geologist, but he had learnt to know what the rocks around him were, and what they had taught geologists. He knew and could name the plants and flowers we saw. Sometimes our expeditions were of set purpose to visit an object of interest. Sometimes we merely accompanied him when he went to visit a sick person or hold a service in one of his outlying villages. The talk would pass from the heavens and the earth to the parishioner last visited, with some instance of a quaint phrase used, and back again to mediæval history.'

Dr. Hodgkin first introduced him to the Roman wall, the

wonder and interest of which at once captured his historic imagination, and he frequently revisited it.

'Embleton : September 2, 1879.

'My dear Hodgkin,—I don't think that I properly conveyed to you my thanks for the delightful and to me most interesting expedition which we made last week. . . . I most highly appreciated your kindness and valued its result.

'I got the wallet book on my way through Newcastle, and have been studying it. I think more and more of the enormous importance of the Roman wall as an historical monument. I feel as if I shall often go there again, and I also feel that having been there once under your able guidance I shall be better able to appreciate it on future visits.'

In February 1879, during one of the wildest storms which we experienced at Embleton, an Italian barque, the 'Padre Stefano,' was driven on to the Newton rocks. The coastguard, T. O. Williams, who has since received six medals besides other testimonials for saving life, says that on that day : 'Mr. Creighton walked over two miles through a blinding snow-storm, on one of the wildest and coldest days that I can remember, to give what assistance might be in his power. A boat with four of the crew was capsized in endeavouring to make the land. Three of these men were drowned ; the fourth I was happily able to rescue, although in an unconscious state, by running into the surf. With this man, who was taken to the village inn, Mr. Creighton remained until consciousness was restored, doing his utmost for him while all the men of the village were with me assisting in the rescue of the remainder of the crew. "How kind he was!" the landlady said when telling me afterwards about the vicar's goodness. He was present at other wrecks with the kindly anxiety which was part of his nature, but this was an exceptional occasion. Newton is the most north-easterly point of England, and Mr. Creighton faced the storm where there was not the least shelter, and in weather so severe that the rescuing party were so benumbed and exhausted that they had to be sent home. I would add that not many hours afterwards Mr. Creighton returned, and with Mrs. Creighton called at my house with the kindest inquiries after all of us, who had been waist high in the water for five hours.'

Creighton was full of admiration for the capacity and

courage shown by Williams, who, he said, was like 'a seal in the water.' The Italian sailors had to stay some time in the little inn at Newton, pending the inquiries of the Board of Trade, and Creighton walked over almost daily to cheer them by talking Italian with them, though they were a somewhat sulky, grumbling set of men.

In 1879 we were able to make another trip to Italy. We decided to go this year in the early spring after Easter. It was a time when it was comparatively easy for the vicar to be away, and even the most ardent lover of Northumberland cannot urge that it is pleasant in the spring, so that whenever possible we took our holiday then. As he hoped now to visit more remote places in Italy, Creighton was anxious to improve his Italian conversational powers. We therefore arranged that a young lady who had been brought up in Italy should spend some weeks with us, to talk Italian. He made rapid progress and gained considerable fluency in speaking Italian, which added greatly to his enjoyment of travel, as it enabled him to make acquaintance with Italians of all classes wherever he went.

We left Embleton at the end of April, and stayed at Cambridge on our way south, as he had been appointed Examiner for the Lightfoot Scholarship. This was his first official connexion with the University of Cambridge. His sister accompanied us, and we went by Avignon, Nîmes, and Arles to Nice, and then along the Riviera into Italy. He was disappointed with the ancient palace of the Popes at Avignon, transformed into a very dirty barrack. But he delighted in Nîmes and Arles, and still more in the Pont du Gard. We went afterwards to many towns in Northern Italy, where Pavia and Mantua especially interested him, and then to the Lake of Garda, and drove from Riva to Trent to visit the scene of the Council, and thence to Innsbruck, Munich, and Constance. He was at that time absorbed in the study of the Council of Constance, and traced with much interest the sad fortunes of Hus in the pleasant little Swiss town. Though the choice of the places he visited was regulated by his studies, and he seemed to imbibe history on the spot, he always made these journeys a complete holiday. He might put a serious book into his bag, but he never took it out ; he never wrote a letter, and resented that I insisted upon giving addresses at which I could get news of our children. 'They will get on just as well without your personal supervision,' he would say. He always read French novels in the train and at the hotels in the evening. During these years he was steadily reading through the novels of Balzac, for whom he had a great admiration. He was also fond of Cherbuliez, and thoroughly enjoyed Gaboriau and Boisgobey. On this particular journey, which was marked with much bad weather, he spent three days of persistent rain at Venice partly looking up some references in the Library, but otherwise entirely and happily absorbed in Gaboriau's ' M. Le Coq.'

We got back to Embleton in June, and he was at once busied with examining several schools in the North. He also lectured in Alnwick to a Young Men's Improvement Association, taking for his subject, ' Culture and its Dangers.' He was thinking much at this time about the condition of mind produced by a smattering of education, which puffed up without really cultivating those who received it. In this lecture he spoke of culture as the practical fruit of education, to which education must lead if it is to be of any use. He defined culture as making the best of our-selves, the assertion of our mastery over our own lives ; and said that culture required that a man should know the position he occupied ; that it was the essence of half-culture or unculture to claim the right to give an opinion on every possible subject ; that the first beginning of culture was humility. Half-culture he called the besetting failing of the day, leading men to think that they were capable of creating the world afresh from their own brain ; to take their opinions from the newspapers ; to believe that the world could be put right by Acts of Parliament. He ended by saying that one of the great problems of the day was how to escape from the evil results of this half-culture, so that men might gain the mastery over their own lives ; and this they could only do by knowing more about the things which they had to do, and studying what was before them and around them.

He frequently lectured in Alnwick, and among the subjects of his lectures were : ' Tragedy as handled by Shakespeare,' ' Italian City Life,' ' Books, and how to use them,' ' Elizabethan

Literature,' 'Pictorial Art,' 'Ceramic Art.' His object in all these lectures was to get his hearers to realise how large was the world in which they lived, how manifold its interests, and so to rouse them to fresh effort.

Contact with the narrow lives of the people who lived in remote country places gave him a new sense of the value of knowledge. Preaching at Embleton about this time on Solomon's desire for an understanding heart, he spoke of how knowledge and discernment helped a man to face the ordinary difficulties of the ordinary life, and maintained that the smaller the sphere the more necessary it was to try and get knowledge, because the rub of life taught those in large spheres, but in smaller spheres sympathy with great minds of other times was needed, if we would keep ourselves above the personalities of daily life.

In the summer and autumn of 1879 we had, among other visitors, the Andrew Langs, the Hugh Bells, the present Provost of Oriel, Mr. J. R. Thursfield, the T. H. Greens, Professor Sayce, Mr. R. L. Nettleship, the Humphry Wards, Mr. G. Howard (now Earl of Carlisle), with Signor Costa. Much though Creighton enjoyed the society of his friends, he was always quite ready to settle down to the quiet winter, with its short days and opportunities of steady, undisturbed work. He was at home all this winter except for absences to lecture and preach in Durham, Newcastle, and the neighbourhood. Our third daughter was born on January 1, 1880, and she too was named after one of those who had aided Dante in his pilgrimage, Mary.

In the beginning of 1880 a general election was known to be at hand. Mr. Albert Grey was to stand for South Northumberland, and Creighton accompanied him on several occasions to political meetings, and spoke for him in the mining districts of the southern part of the county; but he did not think it right to take an active part in the election in his own immediate neighbourhood. In February, before the actual election, he was persuaded to attend a political dinner and speak at a Liberal demonstration in Alnwick. It was long since there had been a Liberal meeting in Alnwick, and he felt how useful to the people would be an intelligent opposition to the predominant influence to which they were subjected.   But he spoke himself with much reluctance, saying that he could not imagine what he was wanted for.   In April, at Mr. George Howard's request, he spoke at a great Liberal meeting in Carlisle.

'Though he always had a strong admiration for Disraeli's gifts, he was at this time very suspicious of his imperialistic policy.   Speaking at Carlisle, he said that the new liberal government for which they looked would have to ' change the whole tendency of the way in which things had been managed in England during the last six years, the imperialism which had been forced upon us, the wrong way of looking at matters, the endeavour to draw England into the corporation of European diplomacy which boasted that it managed the opinion of Europe. . . . The people of England did not wish to enter into that diplomatic game. . . . This election showed a distinct uprising of the great profound common sense of the provinces against the centralising of the London clubs. . . . For the last few years we had seen the " sober-suited freedom " of England strangely bedizened in the garments of Oriental magnificence ; we had seen an imperial diadem placed upon her spotless brow, and we had put into her mouth the strange phrase " Imperium et Libertas." It would be no light task to restore again her spotless and sober suit, and again put freedom on her old pedestal, so that all things might go on as quietly and as sensibly as before, so that we might go back from assertions of our ascendency to the duties which we met with at home.'

His speech received immense applause, and created real excitement.   The citizens of Carlisle were delighted with their fellow Cumbrian, and many desires were expressed that the speech should be printed as a pamphlet.

When it was decided to run a Liberal candidate for North Northumberland, Creighton was asked to nominate him ; but this he did not consider his business.   He attempted in no way to influence the opinions of his own people, and beyond lending his pony carriage to fetch voters to the poll, and voting himself, he took no part in the election.   Curiously enough, it was the only time in his life when he was able to vote at a parliamentary election, and he used to say that on the solitary occasion when he exercised his privilege as an elector, he did so mistakenly, because he voted for his party without consideration of the qualifications of the particular candidate. He was quite satisfied at the defeat of the Liberals in this case, but he was pleased with the result of the contest, for it certainly woke up the people to take more interest in affairs. One old fisherman took him severely to task for being a Liberal.

In 1884 once more he took part in a political meeting in Alnwick, in order to help Sir Edward Grey, who made his first political appearance on that occasion. The meeting was a Franchise demonstration, held after the House of Lords had thrown out the Franchise Bill. Sir Edward Grey, who had never spoken in public before, was asked to take the chair.

To Sir Edward Grey   'Embleton : July 29, 1884.

'Dear Edward,—I am very glad that you are coming on Saturday. It is quite the right thing to do. Use every opportunity that may offer itself of making yourself a political personage, with a distinct line. Though I did not want to do anything myself, when I was shown your letter I said that I would go to the meeting. Frankly, it is rather hard work to keep Liberalism respectable in these parts, and I have been more political than I could have wished, from a feeling that it was my duty to do what I could to keep Liberal politics respectable and serious.

'I should say that a speech of a quarter of an hour was about the right thing. If you aim at a quarter of an hour you will perhaps hit twenty minutes, which will do very well. It does not much matter what you say ; you are sure to say what is all right and proper. . . . Have before yourself some point which you are going to lead up to and with which you are going to finish, and have the strength of mind to sit down when you have reached it, and have fired the shot which you meant to be your last.

'There is a great temptation not to have an ending definitely prepared. This leads a speaker to wander about aimlessly at last, and repeat himself and flounder about and do away with the effect of the first part of his speech. He is like a bore who has come to see you, and does not know how or when to say "good-bye."

'—— has spoilt all the speeches I ever heard him make

by that fault. He had prepared one or two good ideas, which were well worth saying. Encouraged by their good reception, he went on saying them over again, and watering them down, till at last he left off, because the audience was obviously bored, and he left off lamely. Avoid that mistake above all things. Remember that it is better people should say, " I am sorry it is over," than " I am glad that it is over." Therefore, I say, prepare a definite statement carefully which you are going to lead up to. You may trust your inspiration of the moment how you get there. But when you have got there, say it clearly and sit down. I shall hope to see you on Friday.'

Sir Edward went over what he thought of saying at this meeting to Creighton in the library at Fallodon. Ridiculous stories were circulated about this. In 1885, when Sir Edward was asked to become a candidate for the Berwick division, there was much competition as to who should stand, and three other possible Liberal candidates were put forward. It was agreed that they should all address meetings separately, and that a *plébiscite* should decide which should be selected. Sir Edward, who was ultimately the successful candidate, spoke at Alnwick, and rumours were circulated by his opponents that he had rehearsed the speech at Cambridge with Creighton, who had really composed it. This not only was without foundation, but, as subsequent correspondence will show, Creighton did not approve of the sentiments he uttered.

On April 17, 1880, Creighton was elected chairman of the Alnwick Board of Guardians and Sanitary Authority. This gave him an opportunity of showing his capacity for managing a meeting. He was an admirable chairman, quick to see a point, full of tact in guiding men. Mr. C. Bosanquet says : ' He was always on the look-out for a principle. I sometimes thought him a little too ready to accept a suggestion if it seemed to embody a principle.' He did his utmost to check the giving of outdoor relief, but he found it difficult to influence the mass of the guardians. It was a very large union, and most of the guardians attended very irregularly ; they would only attend if anything of interest in their neighbourhood was coming up, or there was some job to be done which affected them. Creighton used to say, that on looking round at the members present, he was sometimes surprised to notice all the farmers from some particular district. But the cause of their attendance was soon discovered. Some one from that district applied for outdoor relief, and the case was decided not on its merits, but by the votes of the acquaintances of the applicant.

Creighton set himself to reform the arrangements of the infirmary, and had also much trouble with the workhouse, where squabbles and jealousies were rife. He described some of his difficulties in a speech at the Northern Poor Law Conference in 1881 :

'In small workhouses, where there is not enough to do, and where the salary paid is not sufficient to secure the services of a superior person, the officials spend their time in quarrelling because they have nothing else to do ; and when this quarrelling has once begun, it is almost impossible to get over it by any system or arrangement that either local ingenuity or conciliatory tact can introduce. . . . In small workhouses, besides, there is the danger of too great interference on the part of guardians. . . . The small workhouse, some of the inmates of which may have been known in their earlier years to many of the guardians, tends to be regarded as a charitable institution into which people can drop, and the visiting committee becomes a body of philanthropists visiting poor pensioners in an almshouse. In such cases the visiting committee, however judicious the members may be, becomes another hindrance in the way of effective management by too readily listening to trivial complaints. Of course, real complaints of inmates should be readily considered, but the inmates should not feel that complaints will be welcomed about any trumpery matter. So long as a small workhouse goes on tolerably well, so long as there is a good conservative treatment, to which everybody has been accustomed for a long time, all will appear right, but the moment there begins to be any approach to energy, or new procedure on the part of any official, difficulties will arise.'

As chairman of the Sanitary Authority, he tried to start various schemes for the good of the neighbourhood. Some who then thought him cranky about sanitation, have since come to see that he was only ahead of his times. Many of the villages were badly supplied with water ; his own village of Embleton had only a pump in the centre, supplied by a well. This well received drainage from the village, which was mostly on a higher level than the pump. He advocated bringing water from the moors to supply all the villages along the coast line, but had to give this up in favour of a smaller scheme; now it seems probable that it will be necessary before long to resort to the larger scheme. There was considerable opposition, open and underhand, to his plans for improved drainage and water supply on account of the consequent high rates, but he succeeded in effecting many improvements.

He joined with the vicar of Alnwick in starting a Provident Dispensary for Alnwick and the neighbourhood, which went on well for some years, but the difficulties attendant on working it in such a scattered district, have since made most of the best doctors and their patients leave it.

During his first years at Embleton, Creighton hardly came into contact with his Bishop. We once spent a couple of days at Bishop Auckland, and Bishop Baring came once to Embleton to confirm. His plan, in his old age at any rate, was to drive straight to a church to confirm, and go away directly afterwards, sleeping at an hotel when he could not get home, for he had a profound distrust of the beds provided by his clergy. When Bishop Lightfoot succeeded to the diocese in 1879, new activity began at once to show itself in diocesan affairs. In his last years, on the death of a Rural Dean, Bishop Baring had allowed the office to lapse. Bishop Lightfoot now proceeded to fill up the vacant Deaneries, and asked Creighton to accept the office of Rural Dean of Alnwick. On his agreeing, the Bishop wrote :

'November 27, 1879.

'Your response to my request gave me much pleasure. What I desire above all things is that the clergy may be drawn together, and feel that they have a common bond of union. From all that I have heard, I do not suppose that there is anyone more competent to promote this brotherly feeling among the clergy in your Rural Deanery than yourself.'

The definite appointment did not take place till some time later, and Creighton held his first ruridecanal chapter at Embleton in April 1880. His plan was to hold in each year one gathering of a somewhat social character at Embleton, and to have the other meetings at Alnwick. His chapters and other meetings were well attended and enjoyed by the clergy. As a chairman he impressed men as singularly fair. He knew how to introduce with a few lucid words the subject to be discussed, how to keep others to the point, and, finally, by a clear summing up at the end to show the drift of the discussion. He explained in a letter to Mr. Albert Grey what he was trying to do at these meetings.

'May 14, 1880.

'At present I am trying to make my position as Rural Dean a means of promoting clerical co-operation and free discussion on all points. So far I have succeeded beyond my expectations. But I made a rule for myself at the beginning that I would not declare myself needlessly on any point, but would aim at a position as moderator. Situated as I am, I can do more good that way than as an agitator.'

It was at some clerical meeting about this time that he read a paper on 'Clerical Inaccuracies,' afterwards published in the 'Clergyman's Magazine.' He urged the clergy to regard the performance of Divine service as a work of art, in which no detail, however small, must be allowed to mar the harmony of the whole.

'The more intent a worshipper is upon his devotions, the more fatal is a trifling diversion. . . . Everything connected with the service should be carefully settled beforehand ; . . . the congregation ought not to see the process going on during the service. . . . The mechanism of the choir should not be a cause of distraction. . . . The service should begin decisively ; . . . the opening note should ring out sharp and clear as the keynote to all that follows. This is frequently neglected. The clergyman has not cleared his throat, the congregation are not quite prepared. . . . It is worth while to stand up for a brief space before beginning, to have one's throat cleared, to fill one's lungs, to make the very first word penetrate through the church, to read the sentence in such a way as to rivet attention, and then to settle down more quietly to the sober and practical tone of the Exhortation.

'A point on which there is much divergence of use . . . is giving out the Lessons. . . . I have frequently heard the amazing statement, "Here beginneth the second chapter of Genesis at the fourth verse." Now, all chapters begin at the first verse, and no amount of emphasis laid on the word *here* can make such an announcement sound otherwise than an Irish bull. . . . The titles of the books of the Bible ought to be taken from the Authorised Version carefully ; . . . any arbitrary changes are for the worse, . . . they generally contain inaccuracies, . . . they certainly tend to divert an educated mind from attending to the Lesson.   When I hear any change in the title of a book I begin to think at once, " What *does* the man mean by that ? " and the Lesson is often at an end before I have given myself the answer that it was probably simply heedlessness, and that certainly it was not worth thinking about. . . . I suppose that it is hopeless now to attempt to stem the degradation of language by which " offertory " has come to mean *money* instead of a portion of the Divine service. . . . The offertory is the service performed while the offerings of the congregation are collected. Is it too late for us to do something to preserve the phraseology of the Church from destruction ?   Could we give out notice saying that the alms or offerings of the congregation would be given to such an object, instead of saying that the offertory would be given ? . . . Let me add one word about clerical reading.   A golden rule to be generally observed by readers is, " Never emphasise a personal pronoun." . . . In the case of church services it hopelessly misses the mark. The reader is treating his hearers as though they were heathens ; he is perpetually asserting the personality of the Christian Deity as in opposition to some other deity whom his hearers persist in preferring. . . . Let me give an illustration.   How often do we hear reading with the following emphasis, " Come unto *Me*, all ye that are weary and heavy laden, and *I* will give you rest " !   Is not this very bald ? Does it not confuse the meaning ?   None of the hearers wish to seek any other saviour ; but they need to have set before them more fully, more intelligibly, the greatness, the sufficiency of the one Saviour.   We are agreed about the Person ; we need to have brought before us the fullness of His invitation.   Ought not the text to be read, " *Come* unto Me, all ye that are weary and heavy laden, and I will give you *rest* " ? . . . We cannot consider too carefully any suggestions which may enable us to perform more adequately the services of the Church.   Their meaning, their capabilities, their expressiveness, deserve our fullest consideration.'

In the autumn of 1880, Bishop Lightfoot held his first Diocesan Conference, the first that had ever been held in Durham, and in his opening address spoke of the foundation

of the See of Newcastle as a measure of immediate and pressing importance. The Conference was in every way a great
success ; the diocese showed its readiness to be inspired by the
large aims of its Bishop, and to work with enthusiasm under
his guidance. Creighton as one of his Rural Deans gave
earnest attention to assist the effort for the endowment of the
new See. It was owing to a chance remark of his that
Mr. J. W. Pease made his munificent gift to the See of
Benwell Tower, the present episcopal residence. The property adjoined Mr. Pease's own place, Pendower, in Newcastle ; on its coming into the market he had bought it, so that
it might not be cut up for building. He remarked to Creighton one day that he had not yet settled what to do with it.
' Why not give it to the See as a house for the Bishops of
Newcastle ? ' was the rejoinder. Mr. Pease was a member of
the Society of Friends, but in no narrow spirit he desired
above all things the highest good of the town in which he
lived and worked. In the words of Dr. Lightfoot, ' The
princely gift of Benwell Tower gave us a large margin,
scattered all misgivings, and rescued us from further delay.'
For three years Creighton worked under Dr. Lightfoot as his
Bishop. He was much impressed by his character and power.
Preaching in Worcester Cathedral many years afterwards,
at the time of Bishop Lightfoot's death, he said of him :
' When he spoke men listened with marvellous attention,
because they knew that what he had to say was the utterance
of a sober, well-balanced mind, entirely free from all littleness,
from all prejudice, trained and disciplined by the long pursuit of knowledge, speaking weightily because speaking
accurately, looking at the great issues before him, not
troubled with the little considerations which blur and dis-
figure the judgment of common men.'

He spoke of the way in which Dr. Lightfoot undertook
the division of his diocese. ' He won his way against all
opposition by making it clearly understood what he meant to
do, and that he meant to do it because he was profoundly
convinced of its necessity. He convinced men by stating in
a simple quiet way what was his own ideal of a Bishop's
work, and pointing out how impossible it was for him, in
spite of robust health and comparative youth, to fulfil that

ideal in the large district committed to his care. This was
his one argument, which he always used quite simply till
what was at first spoken of as an impossibility, or as a thing
far off, was, by his untiring energy and simple-hearted per-
sistency, achieved in two years.'

Creighton shared as far as he could in the work of raising
money for the new See, and took great pains to interest rich
men in Northumberland in the scheme. His life grew increasingly busy. In 1880 I wrote to one of my sisters : ' I think
Max [my name for him] has almost more to do than anyone
ought to have, particularly a man who wishes to write a big
book ; however, he is happy and likes it.' It was no sinecure
being Rural Dean, and the increasing number of meetings
was a great burden. A meeting in Newcastle meant the
waste of a day, for it took two hours to get there, and there
were very few trains. During these years he left off having
pupils with him for any length of time, and preferred having
several together for a short time in the summer, men already
at the Universities, who were reading for honours. In 1878
he had among others Lord Lymington (now Earl of Portsmouth), the Hon. Fitzroy Stewart, and the Hon. Hugo
Charteris (now Lord Elcho). In 1880 he had seven different
pupils, amongst them Hugo Charteris for the second time,
Sir George Sitwell, and Mr. Carmichael (now Sir Thomas
Gibson Carmichael). In 1881 Sir George Grey asked him
to allow his grandson to read with him, and he answered :

' My dear Sir George,—I have been thinking over the
plan that Edward should read with me. I cannot help thinking
that if he did so, it would be a help to him if he also stayed
here. Besides the supervision of work, there is need for a
general atmosphere of work, and that I think I can provide.
I find that the best thing I can do for anyone is to show him
how to work, and I have been pleased with the testimony of
pupils, not only that they did work here, but that they actually
began to enjoy the process. I only throw this out as a suggestion, on which you will decide. I was afraid that coming down
here daily might only be an additional distraction to Edward's
time ; and I feel that nothing can take the place of the hard
persistent reading which everybody has to do for themselves.'

Edward Grey in consequence spent some weeks at the

vicarage.   The same year the Hon. Schomberg McDonnell
read with Creighton.

In 1880 we did not go out of England, but took our holiday
in visiting friends in Oxford and London.   In the spring of
1881 we went to Italy, going first along the Eastern Riviera
to Spezia, and then by Lucca and Pistoja to Florence, from
which we visited Vallombrosa and San Gemignano, and
next to Siena, Monte Oliveto, and Monte Pulciano.   I do not
know how it may be now, but in those days Monte Pulciano
was very primitive.   We had received the usual warning
that we should find people extortionate, and have to do a
great deal of bargaining, but, as almost invariably in Italy,
we were delighted with the way in which we were treated.
We stayed two days at the little inn, where we found the
school inspector of the district, with whom we discussed
education, and our bill for lodging and food and an unlimited
supply of the admirable wine of the country was seventeen
francs.   We drove from there to Pienza on the track of Pope
Pius II., whose birthplace it is.   The Pope gave the little
town his own name, and adorned it with many mighty buildings, which now stand desolate and almost in ruins.   We
had heard of some frescoes by Sodoma at the convent of
S. Anna in Creta, and after a drive of eighteen miles to
Pienza drove five miles farther to see them.   Great was our
despair on being told, that the farmer who occupied the dis-
used monastery was away, and had the key of the room with
the pictures in his pocket.   My husband was looking about,
when he pushed open a door and exclaimed, ' Here they are ! '
and was greeted with the astonished remark, ' Oh, is that
what you want ? '   There on the walls of the old refectory,
now used as a sort of store-room, were some of the most
beautiful works of Sodoma, the finest being a fresco over the
high table representing the feeding of the five thousand.
These frescoes have been carefully photographed by Signor
Lombardi of Siena, and I can only hope that they are now better
cared for than they were in 1881.   On this journey we also
visited among other places Terni, Spoleto, and Monte Falco,
and then drove right through Umbria, staying at Gubbio and
Urbino, to Rimini.   From there we made our way to Orta,
whence we walked to Varallo, where we were captivated by

the beauty and interest of the representations of our Lord's life in the chapels on the Sacro Monte. These had a great fascination for Creighton, and he was glad to revisit them some years later. As a rule he did not much care to go back to places where he had once been. There was so much he wished to see, he wanted to visit every little town in Italy, for wherever he went he found unexpected treasures. On this journey, he first experienced the joy of driving across country, where there were no railways. A light one-horse carriage could convey us, and he was skilled in finding out the route he wished to go, picking up a suitable carriage, and making his bargain with the driver. We also walked a great deal, spending the whole day out and walking from fifteen to twenty miles. He never took a guide, but always made out the way himself, trusting to chance to find some place where we could turn in and get something to eat. In this way, walking and driving through the country in regions where the tourist never went, he got to know a great deal of the people and of their manner of life. In the little country inns at night after dinner, he would sit and smoke in the café and talk to the people of the place, who collected with interest round the stranger, and were invariably friendly and talkative. A journey of this sort was a most complete refreshment ; he left all thoughts of work and worries behind, and lived absolutely in the moment. Eye and mind alike were fed almost without effort. He was not an anxious, painstaking tourist, determined to leave nothing unseen, and to improve his mind at every opportunity. Rather he seemed to give himself to the impressions of the moment, and leave his whole nature open to what Italy had to offer him. 'Is not Italy delightful?' he wrote to a friend in 1887 ; 'one takes in new ideas through one's pores, it seems to me, without any conscious effort.' Each place that he saw suggested others that he wished to visit, and as he returned from one journey, he would study his guide-books and begin to plan the next.

He was fond of giving this particular journey as an instance of the uselessness of attaching any weight to forebodings. Our last two journeys had ended in sadness because we had heard by telegram in the first case of the death of his father, and in the second of the aunt who brought him up. These memories affected us both, and we started on this journey with a sense of impending misfortune. We did not communicate our fears to one another till after our return home from one of the most delightful and unclouded holidays we ever had.

In October 1881 the Newcastle Church Congress was held. Creighton was on the Subjects Committee, and took considerable part in the preparations, but, as is usual with members of the Subjects Committee, he read no paper himself. It was the first Church Congress at which he was present, but he took no part in any of the discussions. He was never anxious to put himself forward, and though in subsequent years he frequently read papers at Church Congresses, he did not once send up his name to join in the discussion. I asked him, years afterwards, whether he could imagine himself being moved under any circumstances to do so, and he said he thought not. He had no desire to keep himself before the public eye. He was much amused when, on leaving Oxford, a dignitary there exhorted him not to let himself be lost in the country, and advised him to keep himself before the public by writing to the ' Guardian,' the very last thing he was ever likely to wish to do. Mr. C. Bosanquet says :

' When Dr. Creighton was at Embleton, most of us did not see that he was a man of as much power as he afterwards showed himself to be, and he made no claim to deference ; but looking back now, I see that he was the same man he afterwards proved himself, strong in many directions, and doing work which has had lasting results. I seem to see also that in diocesan work especially, he habitually kept himself in the background, even when acting as mainspring, and put others forward.'

In the Newcastle Church Congress of 1881 the predominating figure was of course Bishop Lightfoot. It was wonderful to see his power over the Congress. There were some very disturbed debates ; the clergy, as so often, showing themselves to be a particularly noisy and self-assertive audience, but at the most troubled moment it was sufficient for Bishop Lightfoot to rise in his seat and raise his hand, and all was hushed ; a spirit of moderation and calm seemed to come out of him and compel a reasonable temper. The Bishop had hoped to be able to announce to the Congress the completion of the Newcastle Bishopric endowment fund, but he was disappointed, and an appeal was made to the members of the Congress to aid in making up the sum still needed.

A winter of hard work at Embleton followed the Church Congress. After Easter we went to Italy, travelling straight to Rome. There we spent ten days, during which my husband devoted himself mainly to papal Rome and to a careful study of the buildings erected by the different Popes of his period, and of the changes they had made in the city. He sought out their tombs and those of their contemporaries in many obscure churches, and we walked about a great deal in the more remote parts of the city. Then we went to explore the country round Rome. He was much interested by a visit to Subiaco, and by all the memories of St. Benedict awakened by the wonderful shrine that seems to grow out of the rocky mountain.

Thence we drove to Olevano and then went to see the Cyclopean walls of Cori and Norba. He always had a special feeling for the builder's art, not only when exhibited in some triumph of architecture, but also when, as in these stupendous monuments, it told of the power of those who made them to defy even time itself. Cori is a most primitive little town, and we were objects of great interest to the inhabitants. We started for the long walk to Norba and Ninfa without a guide, but somehow we got there, though we lost ourselves several times by the way. It was a moment of triumph when he discerned the great line of Norba's wall crowning the hill in the grandeur of its absolute loneliness and desolation. Then, after a thorough examination of the ruin and a long enjoyment of the wondrous view, came the plunge down the almost precipitous mountain side to the mysterious ruins of Ninfa, the city deserted in the tenth century on account of the malaria. There stand the walls of the houses, the crumbling campaniles, the shells of the ruined basilicas covered with wild flowers and creeping plants, and through them rushes a swift river sprung from the foot of the mountain. Except a stray shepherd on the mountain side, we met no one all that long day. As we started on our return, a sirocco sprang up and blew its parching breath in our faces all the ten miles back to Cori. There was not a house on the way, not a drop of water to be found, one orange shared between us seemed only to increase the raging thirst. Everyone in Cori when we got back was interested in our walk, and crowded round him in the café afterwards to hear our adventures.

Next we stayed at Albano, and in long walks explored the lovely region round, from Monte Cavo to Rocca di Papa, Azeglio, Frascati, &c. He felt in a new way the charm of Rome as from every halting-place on the hills, we saw its long line of walls, and the great dome of St. Peter's, bathed in some fresh wonder of light and colour, rise out of the mysterious Campagna, which reflects the moods of the sky like the sea itself.

On our way back to England we stopped at Chiusi, where he first felt the fascination of an Etruscan tomb, perhaps the most impressive of all the Etruscan tombs as one enters it from a vineyard on the hillside, through the doors formed of single slabs of stone, which swing back on their stone sockets as easily as when first placed in position, more than two thousand years ago. At Arezzo we stayed to enjoy a favourite painter, Piero della Francesca, and drove from there to see his great fresco of the Resurrection at Borgo S. Sepolcro. Then, after a few days among the pictures and churches of Florence and Milan, we stopped at Lugano for two more long days' walking on the mountains, and he was back at work by the end of May. He brought home a store of new impressions. 'I should much like to tell you about it,' he wrote to Dr. Hodgkin ; 'I cannot tell you how much the Latin, Sabine, and Volscian hills interested me.' He liked to live through his travels again in talking them over with his friends, and showing them the photographs which he gathered wherever he went.

He was interested at this time in the rising school of Italian fiction. On our first Italian journeys we had rarely been able to discover any Italian novels, but this time he was much attracted by Verga's books and in a less degree by Basili's. On subsequent journeys he always read a great many Italian novels : Verga remained the author whom he admired most.

LETTERS 1878–1882

To Mr. A. E. Pease on his engagement

'Embleton: August 19, 1878.

'. . . You know that I am but a bad hand at gushing ; but I wanted to say once for all that you have my permanent affection and esteem. It is not worth much, I confess ; but you may always feel that it is there, and may be called for at any period you like.

'Let me make one more moral remark. The beginning of life to each individual is to live for something else than oneself ; and the only use of knowledge is to enable one to extend that " something else " as widely as possible.

'I am very quotational : let me send you another, on the ideal of marriage :

> To live, and see her learn and learn by her,
> Out of the low obscure and petty world—
> Or only see one purpose and one will
> Evolve themselves i' the world, change wrong to right :
> To have to do with nothing but the true,
> The good, the eternal—and these not alone
> In the main current of the general life,
> But small experiences of every day,
> Concerns of the particular hearth and home.

'Remember me most kindly to Miss Fowler.
'Ever yours most affectionately,
'M. Creighton.'

'Embleton Vicarage . October 7, 1879.

'Dear Alfred,—. . . I have long been wanting to write to you, and to say that you don't know how much I was delighted with having you here, or how genuinely much I care about you. It is not perhaps worth telling you. You will have, you have, heaps of friends who are much better than me ; but you won't have one who will be more constant and on whom you can count more surely should you ever need him. Well, that's enough about that, and I won't ever bore you again by telling you anything about it.'

'Embleton : July 12, 1880.

'My dear Alfred,—I had had no news of your accident, which is sad, but you seem to have realised the use of a little leisure time in enabling one to read something which otherwise one would never have read. Don't you find the great difference between reading about a person and reading his own words ? Great is the power of a man's words to reproduce himself and his time. I don't know anything of Berkeley ; but then my knowledge of that period altogether is not great.

'Laud is an interesting character, excellent but narrow, with every private virtue and deep religious feeling, but unsympathetic towards others and believing too much in outward organisation—a sort of *ecclesiastical policeman* at best. Men differ more in real sympathy for their fellows, and so in real insight into what is the right thing to do, than either in goodness or wisdom. Gladstone—what a mess he is making through his own arrogance and want of sympathy with the House! Why are all Liberals like that now ? They are sympathetic with the masses, but not with their own equals. One sees the same in a small scale—philanthropic persons, who can raise the enthusiasm of the poor around them, are cold and arrogant to their equals in private life. Men most charming in a drawing-room, full of tact and wisdom, are tyrants to their tenants or their workmen. What small creatures we are! To gain one set of qualities we sacrifice another, and so mar our attainment. The present Ministry is certainly an awful warning. There they are with the best intentions redressing grievances that don't matter, helping farmers who don't want their help, allowing small-pox to spread for forty shillings, and anything anybody suggests, and ruining their party in the process. We shall soon have a Conservative reaction that will last our lifetime and will be richly merited.

'Thanks for the tract, which interested me much. I had always wondered what the Quakers had to say. A case can, of course, be made out always about anything ; and I always feel that one set of arguments is as good as another. The real question is *the nature of evidence*. Once abolish tradition, and I am free to confess that one thing is as good as another. How does one know that there was such a man as Julius Cæsar ? A little ingenuity could prove his books to be forgeries and himself a myth. I really only believe it because it is the traditional belief of mankind since his day to this. About any historic event, or the origin of any institution, I could produce an equal nebulousness as does the tract *if* I assumed that everything that everybody before me had said was necessarily mistaken because it had been said or believed. I mean to say that the primary position assumed in that tract, that everybody was deluded till the year 1680 or something of that sort, that the words on which they relied were capable of other meanings, that they had stupidly gone on doing something on the supposition that Christ meant it, when He didn't, I could never be prepared to allow—it would reduce all human knowledge to arbitrariness.

'Hegel said with profound truth, " Every man is right in what he affirms, wrong in what he denies." All beliefs that are negations, contradictions, protests, are to me naught. Every rite, ceremony, or belief that at any time has made the path of life easier to anyone, demands my reverence. That I cannot join it, is to me a source of sorrow. Without outward helps to spiritualise life, I am afraid that I for one am too feeble to get on. The writer of the tract says that the frame of mind of the recipient of the Lord's Supper is the important thing, not the reception. But without the opportunity of the reception, is one sure of getting the frame of mind ? I don't want to argue ; but I thought you might be interested to know how the tract struck my mind.'

'Embleton : July 16, 1880.

'. . . Why do you accuse me of seeking " subjects for dissection and study " ? I believe there is a popular prejudice against the study of mankind. But please don't give way to it. It *is* worth while to know more of men than the outside of their waistcoats. Everybody has an opinion of some sort about everybody else. It is as well to have a careful one as a heedless one. I find that B.'s [1] classification of mankind at present is into " rather nice " and " rather nasty." Many people rest content with that stage, which does not go far. I always think of Tennyson's description of heaven as happy, " Where we know as we are known." Nothing gives one higher or nobler feelings than to *know*, and nothing is so worth knowing as another's heart. I am always willing to take any trouble for the knowledge.'

'Embleton : July 26, 1880.

'Dear Alfred,—I don't think you have quite understood what I meant. I quite think that everyone should follow his own liking, but I agree with you in grieving over sectarianism, which is covered by my formula, " Everyone is right in what he affirms, wrong in what he denies." So far as anything involves a protest against somebody else, it becomes of the earth, earthy. So far as they did that, all the Reformation doctrines seem to me to be weak.

'I was not criticising Quakerism as a whole—far be it from me—but only one argument of the tract that you kindly lent me, which touched upon *historic fact*. Of course, the question of the Lord's Supper involves two things : (1) That Jesus instituted it, and that His Apostles understood Him so to do

---

[1] His eldest daughter, aged seven years and a half.

as a rite of general and universal observance; (2) What He meant by so doing, and how we are to regard it. I think that a quite different kind of evidence applies to these two questions. It is obvious that about (2) people will always differ. But your tract attacked question (1), which is a very different matter. As regards the opinion of the Apostles about Jesus' intention, I hold that the uninterrupted custom of Christendom is a testimony not to be explained away by any criticism of the possible meaning of Scripture applied 1680 years after the event. It seems to me that it would be absurd, if Julius Cæsar had made a law which was observed to this day, to say that he had not meant it to be a law, and that everyone had misunderstood it till I arose to put things straight. I might say, " Cæsar's law is now useless; let us observe the spirit, not the letter. It was made for babes—we are men." But I should lamentably weaken my case if I said, " This law is a mess which muddling people made, who misunderstood the whole thing."

'You say that my acceptance of tradition as the only evidence to *matters of fact* ought to lead me to Romanism. I know that is the constant repartee, and that in matters theological, if you want to have a sane mind and a sober judgment, you are hit on one side, " Why, you ought to be an atheist;" on the other, " Why, you ought to be a papist." But because Rome applies tradition to fix the meaning of doctrines, and also claims a right to develop tradition under papal guidance, I do not see that that justifies us in destroying the historical basis of Christianity. The current arguments against the Resurrection are exactly the same as your Quaker friend uses against the Lord's Supper. " It is only slightly mentioned in Scripture—the language is vague—the Apostles misunderstood Jesus; they turned the symbol of the risen life into an actual fact." This is precisely parallel to the arguments of the tract about the Lord's Supper.

' Please remember my remarks were merely those of dispassionate criticism on the steps by which the result was obtained, not on the result itself. On that I say nothing as a matter of argument. But I don't like the process of explaining away historical facts. Say boldly, " These things are not binding," but don't say, " They never occurred." Do you see my point? The Romans admit a development of doctrine, and thereby do not sacrifice historical Christianity to their ecclesiastical system. Why not others following a different line? But now-a-days everybody not only wishes to think as he pleases, but to make out that what he thinks is entirely in accordance with the first Christian century, and in the process the Bible and Christian antiquity get turned into myths. Where would we be if all constitutional questions were settled by reference to the laws of Ine and the witena-gemot of five hundred? Let us keep our history at all events clear.

'This may go on for ever. . . . Carmichael is most excellent. His knowledge is very large on practical matters, on politics, on natural history, on all sorts of things, and he knows the end of his tether, knows what he knows, and what he is capable of judging about. I should say he had a future decidedly. . . .'

'1880?

'Dear Alfred,—Knowledge about the history of this century is quite necessary for anyone who looks to politics. Foreign politics must for some time be prominent, and the woeful ignorance on the facts which prevails among public men is really distressing. . . . The ignorance of the British public about any other history than its own is so great that no one ever writes in English about anything except England.'

To —— 'October 7, 1879.

You don't know how often I have longed to ask you to stay to Communion at Embleton. . . . You know that I am not exactly a formalist, and you know also that I don't like talking about religious matters (which is perhaps weakness on my part), but I do consider that the whole circumstances attaching to the original institution of that rite make it the most powerful bond of religious life. It is a perfect pain to me when those whom I love are strangers to me in that point.'

To an old pupil 'Embleton Vicarage: July 27, 1881.

'Alas! people differ in this world; less, however, it seems to me, than they think. Carlyle well says of a talk between himself and Sterling, "So we walked and talked, *except in opinion not differing.*" The moment one looks at differences in the light of God, it seems to me that they become too despicable, and a source of real pain. That they should exist in all matters of human organisation, that is natural, inevitable : it is a law of human progress that advance should be made through antagonisms, and that from the crash of opposing forces, man's earthly dwelling should be bettered and beautified. Let this be so : it is a limitation of human affairs; but need it be also a limitation of the soul? Is not that one form of selling one's birthright here? To me it always seems that the best attitude towards all men is to go forth and say,

" What message can this man bring to me? Surely he too
comes from God, our Father, and may bring me some
message from Him." Perhaps you will now see why I like
the young and the old : because in my feebleness I can hear
their message better.

' Do not think that in our intercourse the teaching was on
my side only. Nothing is done in this world save on the
basis of exchange. I learned also much from you ; and if
the truth were told, my sympathies are least perfect with
those of your way of thinking because the chances of life
have given me least opportunity of seeing them. Therefore let
me see you some more : let me know from time to time how
you fare, and believe that my interest in you is sincerely felt.'

To Miss Ella Pease   ' February 10, 1881.

' I think I shall have to stir you up on another point,
viz. letter writing. You have not yet begun to cultivate it as
a *fine art*. Yet such it is. . . . To be a good letter writer
one must of course be egotistical. Letters are not history,
nor are they essays, but they are jottings of small things as
they strike *oneself* : records of one's own impressions : and
they owe all their interest to the belief that the person to
whom they are addressed is interested, not in things in
general, but in *oneself*. . . . In talking or letter writing all
depends on giving oneself rein : if one stops to be judicious
or wise or discreet, one simply becomes dull. If I can't trust
the person I am talking to with all I think, I am simply bored
by the conversation, and would much rather read a book.
My enemies would say, I was too confidential : be it so : I
am content.'

To J. R. Thursfield   ' Embleton Vicarage : February 17, 1881.

' Dear Dick,—I write to set your mind at ease. I did not
write the article on Fyffe in the " Athenæum ; " I have not
seen it. I never wrote an ill-natured article about anybody
in my life ; and I never review the book of anyone I know
unless I am conscientiously prepared to praise it on the
whole. I have sent many books back to editors, saying that
I know the writers, and think their books rubbish, and don't
think that I am the right man to say so.

' I have just written to Pease at Newcastle to suggest that
he should get on foot a great national meeting to make
Cowen dictator for five years in England, and Parnell for the
same time in Ireland. They seem to know all about everything so much better than anybody else, that it is a pity their
fine talents should be wasted. . . .'

To Mr. Albert Grey (now Earl Grey)

'Embleton Vicarage : May 14, 1880.

'Dear Grey,—Thank you for sending me the Report of the Church Reform Union, which I have read carefully and meditated upon. I cordially agree with most of it, and would like it all to be largely discussed ; but it seems to me that it will take a long time before any part of it becomes immediately practical. The question arises, who ought to take the lead in educating public opinion, the clergy or the laity ? I think the laity. I think the questions are all questions for the laity, and not for the clergy. The matter stands thus. The relations of a branch of the public service towards the public need readjustment. I think that the attitude of the members of that branch of the service ought to be one of readiness to hear and meet the popular demands, but I think they ought not to take the initiative. None of the grievances are grievances that weigh heavily on me ; but I am quite ready to help to remedy them if they are declared to be grievances by the laity, and I should think their statement that these grievances existed was a reasonable one.

'The position of a working clergyman who wished to help you, would be stronger if he gave you an independent support. On any of those points if they were practically brought forward, clerical opinion would have to be formed. I might do something to help to form it, if I had not declared myself beforehand ; if I were to do so, I should be useless. . . . So you will forgive, me if I do not at present join the Union. If I were a London clergyman with any influence over a mass of laity, it would be different. The great proportion of the objects of the Union do not much affect our country life or ideas.'

To the Bishop of Colombo (Dr. Copleston)

'Embleton Vicarage : June 16, 1881.

'My dear Copleston,—I was delighted to get your letter. I thought that an insignificant person like myself had sunk from episcopal remembrance, and was most delighted that it was not so. You will naturally say, " Why, then, did you not answer sooner ? " Alas ! your letter reached Embleton just after my departure for a six weeks' holiday in Italy, during which communication with me was suspended. We have just returned home. Though I have not heard from you, I have heard of you occasionally from Talbot. I never read the newspapers concerning you, for I knew beforehand that you were right. Why, therefore, should I read those who gainsaid it ?

' It is very nice to me to find that you have not forgotten me, also to my wife, for you must know that you are one of her idols, and we often talk of you. But it is hard to envisage you at Ceylon; to us you remain the pre-colonial Copleston. Do you mind?

' The course of things goes on peaceably with us, though very busily. I seem to live in a whirl and am always full of business. A parish supplies much to do and think of : my interest in drains and paupers has now made me the chief person in our local self-governing bodies of Guardians and Sanitary Boards and Education Boards. As Rural Dean I have much to do and find the older clergy very difficult to stir up. Under Bishop Baring we never had any common life : he distrusted his clergy and thought that when two or three were gathered together they were sure to make fools of themselves. Probably he was right, but he did not draw the obvious moral that they must go on doing it till they learned not to do it. Under him we had no rural dean at all; he thought us too abominable. Consequently the old folks have all learned to look upon themselves as such. Besides these avocations I spend such leisure as I have in reading and writing (sums I have omitted, they were never my strong point). I have been busy ever since I came here on a general history of the Papacy and the Reformation, considering that the British public are profoundly uninformed on that point and have no real notion what the Reformation was. Perhaps they don't want to know : however, it amuses me, and that is the main point.

' I spent two days at Oxford on my way home : Brodrick was most beaming : he is a good old soul and will be a useful sort of man in Oxford. Talbot also flourished and diffused mild wisdom on every side : his only fault is that he carries fairness of mind almost to a vice : no one *can* be so fair as he talks. Freeling was as excellent and as inarticulate as ever. Mrs. Talbot looks younger and more charming than ever. Of Merton otherwise I saw little : the generation that knows not Joseph has speedily arisen. . . . Saintsbury, as you know, is the literary dictator of minor poets and novelists : they bend before him and he scourges them at his will. . . . These scraps of information are somewhat disjointed, but I have to give a *résumé* of all things to one whom I have not seen so long. . . .

' Things in general are not good : England is not healthy : she is going through a process of economical readjustment of which no one can see the end : it may result in the development of new forces, or it may be the beginning of a quiet decay—not decay exactly, but subsidence. All this sorely exercises the mind of the spectator and fills him with wonder. Trade and agriculture cannot any longer go on the old lines : will they find new lines or will they collapse? Already I see the doctrine of protection taking a strong hold of the mind of separate classes. I believe that separate interests will coalesce against the public good and against the voice of wisdom. This, by bringing in a fallacious solution, will sus-pend the real settlement of the question and make a mess. No great mess—that would be better, as then something might be done to remedy it : but may we not live to see the relations of the world strangely changed? I am be-coming old and pessimistic : I must end. My wife sends her very kindest love. Do write again when you have time.

'Your ever affectionate

'M. CREIGHTON.'

CHAPTER VIII

LAST YEARS AT EMBLETON : 1882–1884

IN September 1881 Creighton was able to write to Mr. Longman : ' The first two volumes of my book, " The Papacy of the Reformation Epoch," are almost ready.' Life in the country had given him some of the increased leisure which he wanted, but it was inevitable that duties should grow around a man of such varied activities and powers. He had the tastes and instincts of a student, and would have been absolutely happy in a student's life. But though he never put himself forward, when asked to do something his inclination always was to agree ; he could not learn to say no. One of his pupils remembers asking him in 1881 if he would like to be a Bishop, and his answer : ' No, I should not ; but if I were offered a Bishopric, I have no doubt I should take it, as I always do what I am asked.' His practical capacity made him do anything he undertook so well that he was invariably asked to do more, and in consequence the life of a student and a recluse was impossible for him. But amid all distractions he worked on steadily at his book. He would sit in his study surrounded by his big folios, in the summer time with pupils at work in the same room. One of them remembers how he would every now and then burst out with a vivid description of some incident he had come across, or would take down a volume from the bookshelves and read aloud a racy letter of Æneas Sylvius Piccolomini, or a sonnet of Lorenzo the Magnificent, translating them into vigorous English as he went. He never objected to interruptions. His pupils might ask him questions, or his children come in for a Greek or Latin lesson, or a parishioner ask for an interview, and he would lay down his pen to attend to whatever was wanted from him, and then return to his work apparently without an effort. But though he submitted to interruptions and professed not to mind them, he valued the hours when he could work without distraction, long winter evenings when he was alone with me, and knew that he need not fear an interruption of any kind. He suffered most from the longer interruptions caused by his sometimes having to lay aside the book altogether for a time to turn to other work, so that he feared it must bear traces of 'having been written in detachments.'

He was obliged to make up for his distance from great libraries by occasional visits of a few days to the British Museum, the Record Office, or the Bodleian, and at times he procured transcripts of manuscripts from Venice or the Vatican. The London Library was of great use in supplying him with books, but most of the German and Italian books which he needed, he had to buy. After a long morning's work, as we walked about the parish in the afternoon, he would talk to me about what he had been doing in the morning, and discuss the characters of those about whom he was writing. During the winter of 1881–1882 and the following spring, the book was going through the press, and we were much absorbed in the interest of proof-correcting. It was his habit to take great care with his manuscript, so as not to have to make any serious alterations in the press. In matters of detail he was not a good proof-corrector, being apt to overlook small points. He was most grateful for the extreme carefulness of his 'unknown friend,' Messrs. Longman's reader. ' How hard it is to be accurate, or even consistent !' he wrote to Dr. Hodgkin.

The two volumes appeared in October 1882, and were from the first well received by those able to judge. The object of his book, as he states in the Preface, was, 'to bring together materials for a judgment of the change which came over Europe in the sixteenth century, to which the name of " The Reformation" is loosely given.' He did not wish to pass judgment ; he contented himself 'with watching events, and noting the gradual development of affairs.' He called his book, ' A History of the Papacy during the Reformation ;' [1]

---

[1] When it became clear that he would not be able to finish the book as he had planned it, the title was changed in the last edition to *A History of the Papacy from the Great Schism to the Sack of Rome.*

but he went back first to the gradual formation of the opinions which after long simmering below the surface culminated in the Reformation. He aimed at bringing before his readers those facts which conduced to form 'the political experience of those who moulded the immediate future.' With this object, 'much that was interesting was omitted, much that was dull was told at length; both omissions and details were intentional.' He did not wish to prove anything, to maintain any theories, to make any brilliant generalisations, his aim was simply and straightforwardly to tell what actually happened, to get at the truth. All critics alike agreed in recognising his absolute impartiality, some blamed him in consequence for being colourless. He was criticised both for not praising enough and for not blaming enough. But he would not own to any desire to whitewash. 'I don't think I try to whitewash John XXIII.,' he wrote, 'I only remove some of the black.' He distinctly did not aim at picturesqueness, and always said himself that his book was very dull, and warned his friends not to read it. Probably most readers would agree with the judgment of the writer in the 'Quarterly Review :' 'Cold and dry as much of the "History of the Papacy " is, it is never dull ; for the working of a keen intellect on a problem of great intricacy makes itself apparent on every page.'

He allowed himself no heroes, he never let himself go, he indulged in no bursts of eloquence, in no fine writing. Next to the clear grasp of the unity of a great subject, and the constant sense that he gives of his mastery over his material, probably what is most striking in the book is the manner in which he sums up the career of the leading personages with whom he deals, criticises their character, and indicates the effect which they produced. These character sketches are examples of rare insight and sobriety of judgment, the fruit of long and thoughtful study of men, in life as well as in books.

The book was very favourably noticed in the leading literary journals of both Europe and America. The man for whose opinion Creighton himself chiefly cared was Lord Acton, whom he considered the only person in England whose reading and learning entitled him really to judge of the merits

of his book. Lord Acton naturally differed in many respects
from Creighton's point of view ; but in his review of the book
in the ' Academy ' he said :

' The history of increasing depravity and declining faith,
of reforms earnestly demanded, feebly attempted, and deferred
too long, is told by Mr. Creighton with a fullness and
accuracy unusual in works which are the occupation of a
lifetime, and prodigious in volumes which are but the prelude
to an introduction, and have been composed in the intervals
of severer duty. He speaks with regret of his imperfect
command of books, but it is right to expose the guile that
lurks in this apology. The Northumbrian vicarage, in which
Bulæus and Traversari are as familiar as Burnet, must be a
rare and enviable spot. . . . Every particular is taken so
rigorously from the originals that he remains independent of
the moderns who have trodden his path.'

To Lord Acton   ' Embleton Vicarage : December 9, 1882.

' My Lord,—Will you permit me, though personally a
stranger to you, to express my gratitude for your review of my
book in " The Academy " ? I specially asked the editor to get
you to review it, as I wanted to be told my shortcomings by
the one Englishman whom I considered capable of doing so. I
am only afraid that you have estimated my knowledge too
highly, and have credited me with a motive where I erred
through mere ignorance. It is very hard for a Protestant
writer, with the best intentions, to be accurate in his reading
and interpretation of mediæval theology. He is misled by
words which have a technical meaning, and frequently makes
mistakes. I am only glad that you have not discovered more
serious misconceptions in my work.

' May I explain that I have erred through clumsiness of
expression about Transubstantiation (vol. i. p. 110 [1]) ? Where
I write, " He rebelled against the idolatry of the mass," &c., I
was abridging Wyclif's position : I meant " he rebelled against
what he thought was the idolatry," not " against what I think
is the idolatry." My note was meant to show that there was
a side of the popular conception which an orthodox theologian
of the time might have thought needed correction. I have
read many of the Italian *novelle*, and much that is unedifying, for the purpose of obtaining some conception of the
history of popular morals.

' I wish I was able to go more deeply into the development of ideas, theological and otherwise. There is no more

---

[1] In the last edition, vol. i. p. 124.

Q 2

difficult question to determine than the power of ideas in practical politics ; but for a working method, which I am obliged to construct for myself, I am driven only to recognise ideas when they show themselves as motive powers.   It was with great regret that I passed over St. Vincent Ferrier.

'I do not aspire to write a history of the Reformation, but merely of the Papacy as a factor in European affairs. The need for compression is the difficulty which I find at every step.

'Might I so far trespass on your kindness as to ask you at any time to put upon a post card the title of any book which you think I might be likely to overlook, and which might help me in my future work ?

'With many apologies for troubling you with this letter,
'I am, my Lord,
'Yours very truly,
'M. CREIGHTON.'

Lord Acton to M. Creighton

'Cannes : December 14, 1882.

'My dear Sir,—I did not write to thank you for the gift of your two volumes, supposing them to come from the "Academy."   When I knew my mistake I was already deep in the review, and uncertain whether the expression of difference of opinion might not appear presumptuous.   For I think we are at variance on one fundamental point—the principle on which you judge and acquit the Conciliar party, and I could not help regretting that the Introduction had run to a length detrimental to the essential topic.   So that I am much more grateful to you for the gift and for your letter than you could be for the critique.   As you consider it my proper function to pick holes, I wish I could justify the imputation.   Your book has passed into the hands of a literary friend ; but I remember one or two things, which will show you how little the most captious of cavillers could find to say. . . .'

He proceeds to point out some errors in matters of detail.

'I mentioned Ferrier not to set up a claim for him, but to bring in under cover my view, more uncharitable than yours, of the demoralisation of that age. . . . As I know well that you did not mean to write a history of dogmas, I have not perhaps made out clearly my meaning about ideas.   Looked at from outside, as Ranke or Macaulay look at things, I am not sure that the Papacy was weaker in 1514, after the stultification of Councils and the new combinations connected with the Medici and with the foreigners, after the establishment of the State and the development of absolutism based on Pelagianism, than in 1378. The change for the worse was very great if one looks to the progress of certain ideas, to what was going on underground. To justify so long an Introduction the outer change is not enough, and one wants to hear you about the other. You will not escape theological exposition when you come to the explosion at Wittenberg, the negotiations of Augsburg, the debates of Trent, about which there may not be much to say that is new. But there are two questions : What made Luther? and What made him so strong? which occur in the introductory period, and have never been properly answered. Here I think you could give much light which, from your sovereign impartiality, would be particularly valuable.

'There are not many families, with education going on in them, to whom you are a stranger. My son has his own reasons for being grateful to you. I shall be very glad if I may consider the stage of unacquaintance as gone by.

'I remain very sincerely yours,
'ACTON.'

M. Creighton to Mr. T. Hodgkin   'Embleton : December 19, 1882.

'Dear Hodgkin,—I feel moved to write to you about my reviews. As to the "Athenæum," I think the editor might have sent my book to some one who knew something about anything. I never read so ignorant a review of any book. To his literary judgment I humbly bow ; but his frank acknowledgment that he knows nothing about the subject is almost pathetic. I am quite sorry that the poor man should have had to cut the pages of so dull a book before he earned a guinea : it was hardly earned. Lord Acton has done me real service, but he has estimated far too highly my learning, which is as nought compared to his. His minute criticism in details rejoices me to find that I have omitted nothing important, and have made no positive errors. The things which he points out are trivial, and arise from a necessary difference of point of view. I have written to him, and had a letter from him since which has enabled me to see the difference of our positions more clearly : his review was enigmatical even to me in its general lines, and I am still rather doubtful whether I quite understand him. The difference between a Catholic and a Protestant is enormous when they try to understand each other. It is like a Jew and a Christian talking of the Messiah. His fault with me is that I have considered the reforming Councils genuine in their desire for reform. He thinks that wickedness was everywhere prevalent, and that

the world had hopelessly invaded the Church. He thinks
that Gerson and the rest were mere self-seekers, that they put
Hus to death through a desire to do something contrary to
the law of the Church, that they fought entirely with carnal
weapons, and were on a hopelessly wrong track. A Protestant
cannot recognise the law of the Church represented in the
Pope as an infallible rule, beyond criticism and incapable of
amendment. I have treated the Conciliar action as an open
question, genuine in its desire for reform, but going astray
through want of governance. Lord Acton thinks that I
ought to have decided this matter by reference to previous
canonists and to the general wickedness of the world. I am
afraid that I do not attach much importance to canonists,
and that I think the world has been generally wicked.

'Moreover, Lord Acton thinks that all my period had
nothing to do with the Reformation. From his point of view
I quite agree. But the ordinary Protestant speaks of Wyclif
as the "Daystar of the Reformation," and of Hus as a fore-
runner of Luther. I shall be attacked by Protestants for
doing scant justice to those admirable persons. But I think
I shall have shown before I am done that they contributed
nothing to the Lutheran movement, and that its causes are to
be sought elsewhere.

'As I go on with my book, volume iii. will do justice enough
to prevalent immorality, and volume iv. to the causes of Luther,
if I can discover them. Lord Acton writes—and I quite agree
with him—that there are two questions which have never been
answered, "What made Luther? and what made him so
strong?" I did not expect to do more in my first volumes
than clear away Protestant misconceptions about the steady
growth of what they call an "Evangelical spirit." To the
mind brought up on D'Aubigné I thought that my book was
likely to be a severe shock. I asked it to come away from
the search into casual expressions by isolated sectaries, into
the current of European affairs, where they might see how
little these counted for. Lord Acton in his letter is good
enough to speak of my "sovereign impartiality" as likely to
throw a light on the causes of Luther. You and I have both
found the disadvantages of publishing by instalments. We
are expected to do all at once. . . .

'May we soon meet.'

To Mr. A. E. Pease   'Embleton: November 6, 1882.

'My dear Alfred,— . . . You will put your friendship to
a severe test if you read my book. It is very dull: it makes
no attempt to gild the pill. The casual reader will complain

that it is unreadable. I am afraid that I regard history as a branch of science, not of novel writing. There is no reason why anyone should want to know about the past; but if he does, he can have such knowledge as exists, not fancy pictures. Such being my views, I have written accordingly. I have managed to be more dull than I could have thought possible. You, however, will perhaps agree with me, and will not mind the details, which I did not find it right to omit. : . . I should be interested to know your opinion of my book when you have read it through. Tell me any points where I am needlessly tedious or obscure. All suggestions are valuable for my own guidance for the future, and for a new edition if I ever reach one.'

To Mr. T. Hodgkin   'Embleton: October 25, 1882.

'Dear Hodgkin,—Your remarks are very kind. All that I aimed at was to write a " historical history." I don't think it is any good trying to popularise history except by writing it as clearly as possible and by avoiding all needless tediousness. When events are tedious, you must be tedious; when they are exciting, you must let yourself rise with them. I see no reason why anyone should want to know about the period I am studying; but if they do, they must know the whole truth as far as it can be known. My Protestantism will be more obvious in succeeding volumes. My arraignment against the Papacy is that it rendered a violent reformation necessary, because it refused to make a mild and wise one. My first two volumes go to show that a reformation was universally demanded, that its necessity was allowed, that defective organisation rendered it impossible by an ecclesiastical parliament, that men stayed their hands from revolution to give the Papacy a chance. My third volume will show the Papacy plunging into a career of secularity in Italian politics, and increasing instead of amending its aggressions; my fourth volume will show the inevitable revolution; my fifth the reaction of that revolution on the papal system, and the internal reform which converted the Mediæval Church into the Ultramontane system which we now are familiar with. This is my entire scheme. The present volumes are intended to show the political experience of reform which the German reformers had to warn them when they began their efforts. By all means review me if you will in the "Spectator." As you have taken me into your confidence I must let you into mine, and tell you that I was the writer of the review of your book in the "Times," the sole contribution I have ever made to that periodical.

'The newest part of my book is the attempt to show the political reasons for the failure of the reformers at Constance, the Bohemian question, and the character of Pius II.'

Extracts from Letters about the 'History of the Papacy'

From Dr. Bryce   'October 30, 1882.

'My dear Creighton,—I have just seen your book, and congratulate you most heartily on getting it out, and Oxford on so fine a piece of fruit from her School of Modern History. One was getting a little disappointed that more had not been produced by our historical men : this of yours goes very far to change that feeling into one of pleasure and hope. You seem to me to have done your work with admirable thoroughness ; and so far as a hasty glance enables one to form any opinion, with admirable judgment and penetration also.'

From Mr. George Howard (now Earl of Carlisle)

'Naworth Castle : November 20, 1882.

'My dear Creighton,—I have just finished your volume ii., and am bound by gratitude to tell you how delighted I have been in reading your book. . . . I do not feel that I am in a position to criticise to any purpose, but I think that the manner in which you have told the story of complicated and involved transactions, carried on by a mass of hitherto unknown characters, is " a real triumph of lucidity." As to the way in which the interest is kept up, I can only say that I, who am a rare and infrequent reader, was unable to put the book down after I had begun it. . . . I never should have believed that I could have taken an interest in the transactions of those pagans full of pride.'

From Mr. Horatio Brown   'Venice : April 2, 1883.

' . . . I cannot help writing to you to say how very much I am indebted to you not only for the great insight you have given me into the real movements of Papal History, but also for the brilliant and stirring account of that movement which you have set forth. I found the book so entertaining, so vivid in its portraiture of character, that I read a great deal of it aloud to my mother. . . . The way in which the importance of the Conciliar theory is brought out is a revelation to me ; and the way in which history falls into its place when threaded on this Conciliar idea, is a proof to me that that idea is really the central point in papal development. In fact, the whole of a formless period in the history of the Church has taken shape and been crystallised for me, thanks to your book. . . . And then beyond the mere sweep of the argument, there is such pleasure in your sketches of character.'

More acceptable even than the direct testimony of friends to the value of his book was the opinion of Dr. Stubbs, uttered to a common friend :

' I saw Canon Stubbs to-day, and he spoke of your book. He has been at work lately, which has made it necessary for him constantly to look up "what you have said" on the matter, and "the more he goes to your book the better he likes it." He is very much impressed by the amount of work you have given to it. He would like you to have made it more entertaining, but "it is a good book," he said twice. His tone was one of sincere and warm admiration of it.'

The reception of his book was very gratifying to Creighton.

To Mr. Longman   'February 9, 1883.

' I am more than satisfied with the way in which the book has been received by those competent to judge. You would see that I did not aim at immediate popularity, but I wanted to be thorough. I trust that you will find that the book has a steady sale, increasing as the next volumes come out. Of course I have not yet reached the point where the public interest is keenest.'

'March 24, 1884.

' I hear incidentally that my "Papacy" has attracted much attention at Rome, and that the Roman Catholics recognise its fairness. A long notice by a Catholic writer has been given in two numbers of the "Archivio Storico Italiano," which speaks of it more favourably than it deserves.'

In the summer of 1882 Sir George Grey's health began to fail. For nearly two months he was confined to bed, and suffered a great deal of pain. Creighton visited him constantly.

' He welcomed prayer, and spoke of himself with profound and touching humility. . . . He thought much and spoke often of his grandchildren, but refused to specu- late on their future. . . . The days passed slowly in incessant pain. He longed for death, and was distressed that he was not more patient. . . . His symptoms became more serious, and his strength failed. He was unable to speak, and could only press the hand of those who gathered at his bedside. But his ears were open to the voice of one who prayed, and the pressure of the hand was firmer when the words of God's comfort fell upon his heart.' [1]

To his sister, M. E. Creighton   'September 15, 1882.

'We are very grieved at the death of Sir George, more than I can say. He is an immense loss to us in every way. But it was most painful to me to see him day by day for the last month, suffering greatly as he did, and being fully conscious till the last two days. However, he is gone ; may we all go like him. His funeral is to-day. I shall be relieved when it is over. Poor dear Lady Grey is wonderfully brave ; I expect she will be at the funeral.'

Many gathered from all parts of England to do honour to the upright statesman and earnest Christian when he was laid to rest by the side of his son, in the little churchyard at Embleton on a grey September day. ' I never saw so many earnest faces wear such a serious look,' said one who was present to Creighton afterwards.

When, on the following Sunday, Creighton tried to speak in his sermon of the friend whom he, and indeed all those who listened to him, had lost, he broke down completely, and had to give up the attempt. Sir George had expressed to him his wish that no inscription, beyond the name and date, should be put over him ; that there should be no praise of him. But all who had known him wished that there should be some abiding memorial of the man whom they had loved and honoured. It was suggested that the windows of the chancel in Embleton Church should be filled with stained glass in his memory. Creighton asked the leading members of his family for their opinion about the proposal. Lord Grey answered :

'Howick, November 25, 1882.

'Memorials to men for their public services have of late years become so common, and have been given so indiscriminately, that I confess I now dislike them. But a memorial to a man as a mark of the respect and regard felt for him by his private friends and neighbours is quite a different matter, and I heartily approve of what you propose.'

[1] *Memoir of Sir G. Grey.* M. Creighton. (Longmans.)

The 540*l.* needed were subscribed quickly by Sir George's many friends, and after much consideration Creighton placed the design and execution of the windows in the hands of Mr. C. E. Kempe, who visited Embleton before making any suggestions as to how he would carry out the work. The result was a beautiful series of five windows symbolising 'the Holy Catholic Church and the Communion of Saints.' Among the figures chosen, especial prominence was given to the Saints of the Church in Northumbria. In December 1883 the windows were dedicated, and Creighton in his sermon was able to tell his people something of what these beautiful windows—a gift to them from many of the best and wisest in the land for the sake of one whom they held dear—should mean to them. He told them that their church had been made richer, because many of the highest minds in England had felt and said that their lives had been made richer and better to them by the memory of the lovely character of Sir George Grey. He spoke of the life which Sir George had lived among them ; how he went about with a kindly smile upon his face, and a word of cheerful greeting for all ; of how simple, how genial, how loving he was.

'He did not speak to you,' he said, 'as a great man, whose mind was above yours, whose thoughts were busy with great things, whose life was different from your own. He spoke to you as a friend. Your interests were his interests. Your welfare was his constant thought. . . . Nothing that concerned your well-being was too small for his careful consideration. . . . You do not know as well as I do how deeply he sympathised with your sorrows. He felt for others so keenly that their woes were a source of pain to him. . . . He remembered, after the lapse of years, the losses, the afflictions, the bereavements of those among whom he dwelt. . . . There were no opinions so different from his own that he would not listen to them with a kindly smile. He was no more genial, no more desirous of producing an effect in the society of the great world, or on the floor of the House of Commons, than he was in one of your cottages.' [1]

Creighton himself felt most deeply the words which he quoted in his sermon as spoken by another. ' No one could

---

[1] From the Memorial Sermon now published with the *Memoir of Sir George Grey.*

know him without being better for it.' He often spoke of how much he owed to those years of intimate friendship and constant intercourse with Sir George Grey. The loss of his society meant much to him, and he never ceased to take the warmest interest in his family.

When a wish was expressed by Sir George Grey's friends that there should be a memoir of him, Lady Grey asked Creighton to write it, and he at once accepted, though it was an interruption to his other work. It was not an easy task.

To Lady Grey   'January 17, 1883.

'I was very much touched with your letter this morning. You know that I consider the privilege of Sir George's friendship as one of the greatest blessings which I ever enjoyed. I do not expect that I shall ever look back on any period of my life with greater pleasure than that during which I enjoyed his intimacy. I know how much good it did me in every way. It is in many ways a painful task to write the life of one who has passed away. But "no man lives to himself or dies to himself," and to me it always seems a sacred duty to preserve the record of noble lives and precious memories. They are a deposit for the benefit of those who come after. The nature of my book will have to be determined by you and Lord Northbrook.'

'February 9, 1883.

'. . . It is difficult in a biography to exhibit side by side the course of a man's outward life and also of his inward life. The records of his inward life are secrets of his own heart which even himself could scarcely utter. The looker-on can see but the steady reflection of this inward life in the labours of the life in the world. But the assertion that the outer life of Sir George was the constant and unwavering expression of a strong and steadfast walk with God, is a point never to be forgotten about him. No desire for popularity, no immediate success, would have ever led him to deviate a hair's breadth from the path of duty.'

To L. C.   'Embleton : January 30, 1883.

'Yesterday was taken up with Fallodon, where I had a comic interview with Lady Grey. It seems that she only wants a brief memoir for private publication ; a memoir made out of no materials, as you said. In one way I am glad, as it will not take much time ; but she seems to have a horror of publicity.'

He spent many subsequent hours at Fallodon, during which Lady Grey would hunt through papers, full of indecision as to what she could bear to trust out of her own hands, and sometimes he would come away almost in despair at the small amount of material he had got. But he bore all with infinite patience, for he had a genuine affection for Lady Grey, and saw how much she was helped in her sorrow by her interest in every detail connected with the memoir. Lord Grey gave him important help in the political part, and wrote out a long memorandum about some Cabinet transactions which had not previously been made public. The memoir, when finished, gave complete satisfaction to Lady Grey. Lord Grey wrote: 'All Sir George Grey's relations and friends must be much gratified by the book ; the only thing that I regret is that it should not be published, instead of only given to so few.' And Lord Northbrook : ' I heartily congratulate you on the great ability of the sketch, and the way in which you have performed a most difficult task.' Everyone was anxious that the memoir should be published, but Lady Grey preferred to have it only privately printed and given to friends. It was hoped that perhaps at some future period it might be enlarged and given to the world.[1]

A number of circumstances combined at this time to make Creighton give special attention to the history of land tenure in Northumberland. His walks about the country, his investigations into the relative extent of townships and parishes, had long awakened his interest in the matter, when the publication of Mr. F. Seebohm's 'Village Communities' in 1882, challenged attention by the startling novelty of its theories.

'Embleton : January 4, 1883.

' Dear Hodgkin,—I have read Seebohm with the greatest interest. He has made many points clear. But I cannot agree with his conclusions. He has considered the economic as apart from the historical facts. He has contended for a uniformity of practice which it is difficult to accept on his

---

[1] Owing to his constantly increasing occupations, Creighton was never able to enlarge the memoir. At Sir Edward Grey's wish, it was published in 1901, after his death. The sonnet which appears at the beginning is one of the few of Creighton's poems which have ever been printed.

evidence. Beginning from the Manor of Hitchin, he has per-
sistently read into the past its phenomena of 1819. Moreover, he has aimed at proving an economic principle applicable
to modern questions, which is scarcely the attitude of mind
required by the complexity of the subject.

'He shows most ingeniously how the unit of cultivation
agreed with the unit of tenure. But this does not show which
was πρότερον φύσει. Bede's estimate of a holding as *terra
familiæ* seems to me to indicate a conception prior to that of
the land that can be ploughed by eight oxen. The fact that
eight oxen were generally found necessary for its cultivation
is interesting, and when the manorial system began from
grants of folkland to thegns and monasteries, it is quite conceivable that in many places the unit of cultivation was
supreme.

'I am afraid that I still believe in the free village community, and I think that there is ground for belief that it
survived in Northumberland up to the beginning of this
century; but I don't know that I can gather evidence
enough.

'Seebohm has certainly set me thinking. I wish he was
not quite so "slap-dash."'

About this time he was introduced to an old gentleman
living at Morpeth, Mr. Woodman, who had for years been the
solicitor of many of the chief Northumbrian gentry, and who, an
antiquary and student himself, had collected a great number
of documents relating to local history and custom. Feeling
that he was not likely, owing to his great age, to be able to
make any use of them himself, and delighted to find a man of
like interests, he handed over all his papers to Creighton to
make what use of them he could.

To Mrs. J. R. Green   'Embleton Vicarage: January 14, 1884.

'I have been finishing my Life of Sir George Grey. . . . I
am also investigating Northumbrian land tenure, with a view
of disproving Seebohm. These are wicked deviations from
the Popes, but I cannot exactly help them. They are forced
upon me, and it seems wrong to refuse to help on the truth
when one is called upon to do so. An old solicitor, aged
eighty-one, puts his papers of a lifetime into my hands. If I
don't use them, they will be lost. Though I can only use
them inadequately, yet I may kindle others to investigate
what will soon be past investigation. I feel that I must do it.
I am going to write a paper for the Archæological Society, which

meets at Newcastle this year, and I shall at least raise a discussion. I think that I am on the track of discovering survivals up to the beginning of the century in Northumberland of *free* village communities, scarcely touched by the manorial system. They survived in Northumberland owing to the need of border defence. Don't you think this is worth making out? . . . It seems to me that the great difficulty of life is to know what one ought to do. When a work is given me, I do it. But the difficulty is in finding out what is given.'

Some of the results of his researches were embodied in a paper which he read at the meeting of the Archæological Institute in Newcastle in August 1884, on the Northumbrian Border, which was published with considerable appendices in the ' Archæological Journal.'[1]

In this paper he urged that there should be a fuller recognition of the fact that English history is at the bottom a provincial history ; and stated his fear that under the influence of modern institutions, of the railway and the school inspector, the old provincial character of England was doomed to destruction. It was therefore necessary to gather together with care the remnants that remained. The facts about land tenure in Northumberland which he had been able to collect, led him to the belief that the Northumbrian townships were originally village communities holding land in common. He pointed out that the word ' farm ' had been used in Northumberland in a manner peculiar to that county, to signify an original unit of land tenure, meaning a fixed interest in undivided land, which varied largely in area according to circumstances.

He was much attracted by these studies, and began to project a Border History, which he hoped to write in the future, and for which he decided to collect materials. In 1890, as Bishop of Peterborough, he was glad to join the Committee which undertook the issue of a History of Northumberland.[2] The interest which he and others had shown in local history had prepared the way for a really monumental work.

---

[1] The article was published in *Macmillan's Magazine*, August 1884, and has since been reprinted in *Historical Essays and Reviews* (Longmans, 1902).

[2] This great work has continued to appear steadily ; it is to be completed in twelve volumes, of which six have now been published.

During these years Creighton, in common with most literary men, was much interested in Mr. G. M. Smith's great undertaking, the 'Dictionary of National Biography.' He wrote many articles for it, generally about comparatively obscure persons. He also wrote the article on Philip II. of Spain for the 'Encyclopædia Britannica.'

In 1883 he again examined for the Oxford History Schools.

To L. C.   'Oxford: June 1883.

'I find myself in the sad position of being the severest of the examiners, or rather I find Stubbs very woolly, and too lenient in my opinion. . . . To-day we go on with our *viva voce*. We shall be terribly bored before it is all over. So many days doing the same thing becomes very tedious. . . . It is very dull, awfully dull, and no one seems to be in Oxford save those who are busy examining.'

'June 20.

'Young —— has just returned for a holiday. How amusingly alike are all young men who have just started in life, so conceited and cocksure. I dare say we all are in our way, but ways change as life goes on.'

'June 23.

'I think I am getting more used to the Schools now. But examining renders it impossible to go and see people afterwards. One is so stifled, and wants a walk. My sole desire is to have a walk and be in peace.'

In July 1882 Dr. Wilberforce was consecrated Bishop of Newcastle at Durham. The formation of the new See naturally necessitated new work of many kinds, in which it was inevitable that Creighton should take a leading part. He was made Examining Chaplain, and appointed to an Honorary Canonry at the Cathedral of Newcastle. As there were no funds for resident Canons, the Honorary Canons formed the sole capitular body, and were called upon to take some part in the work of the Cathedral. Creighton, at the Bishop's request, gave courses of expository lectures there. He helped to arrange the issue of a Diocesan Calendar, and wrote a brief historical sketch of Northumberland for it. Some years afterwards he replied to some criticisms on the sketch made by a local antiquary.

To Rev. T. C. Dunn,

Editor of the 'Newcastle Diocesan Calendar.'

'Cambridge : October 22, 1889.

'The questions at issue between Mr. Bates and myself are not questions of fact, but only how much information you can condense into a page and a half.   In giving the main lines of the development of any institution in a short state-ment, it is difficult to introduce the modifications which are necessary for entire accuracy, and any brief account which aims at giving the main lines of a long process must expose itself to the charge of verbal inaccuracy, if subjected to verbal criticism.   It has always seemed to me that anything which is written straight off is difficult to amend verbally with the purpose of introducing modifications, because it has in its original form a certain proportion, which is lost if some points be amplified.   After all, the exact truth can only be suggested, not fully expressed, and the suggestion bewilders rather than enlightens. . . . With regard to "the mission sent from Rome," Southern England was converted by several mis-sions ; but the prevalent form of its Christianity was due to the mission of Augustine, and at the time of the Synod of Whitby there were only two alternatives.   Of course a great deal might be said about the conversion of South England, but to write *missions* instead of *mission* would only make a short statement more inaccurate than it is.

'The reason why Oswiu decided for Rome at the Synod of Whitby is a question of historical criticism.   Bede tells us Oswiu's speech at the opening of the Synod when he pro-posed the question, and said that all who served the same God should observe the same rule ; and therefore he sought the truest tradition.   His final remark about Peter as the door-keeper was merely a humorous application to a particular point of the principles which Wilfred laid down, and Colman could not deny.

'I admit that there is an attempt to give a bias to the early history of the English Church in an Anglican sense, and Mr. Bates seems to me to incline to that school.   I think that it is untenable in its main propositions, and that the attempts to minimise the connexion of the English Church with Rome do not lead to any good results.   Our position must be : the English Church had good reasons for its con-nexion with Rome, and had good reasons for breaking that connexion ; but we gain nothing by trying to prove either that the connexion never existed, or was slight or was fool-ishly established.

VOL. I.   R

'I am not obstinate in defence of what I have written. By all means discard it for something better. But Mr. Bates's amendments would not express my views.'

Creighton was Secretary of the Newcastle Diocesan Conference, which met for the first time in 1883.

To L. C.

'Benwell Tower, Newcastle : Tuesday night, September 26, 1883.

'You would see in the papers all about our Conference. It was rather dull, but not so dull as it might have been. I tried to make myself amiable, and I hope that I succeeded in some small degree.   Everybody seemed to expect me to do everything, and the whole management of the affair seems to have been left to me.   I even managed to be amiable to the Duke, and find his great-coat for him when he lost it in the Conference. . . . To-night we had a great crush of people in the evening, and nearly died of suffocation.   I had to take possession of the windows and make ventilation.   In fact, I have been trying to do all the duties of a domestic chaplain.'

He did not take much part in the discussions of the Conference, either in this or the following year.   In 1883 he only spoke once, in a discussion on the duty of the Church towards questions of Social Reform.   He urged that the primary duty of the clergy was to preach the Gospel, and that it was only as citizens, not as clergymen, that they should deal with questions needing legislative reform.   He considered that their part in philanthropy had been perhaps too prominent, and that they had taken upon themselves much that ought to be done by the laity ; but that they had not always done as much as they might to help the working classes in their schemes.   Their unique position between the different classes of society should enable them to know what the people wanted and to articulate for the people.   They should do their utmost to get the working man to trust them, and for that purpose should regard it as one of their duties to study economic and social questions, and try to look at them from the points of view of different classes.

At the Conference of 1884, in a discussion on the New Code, he advised managers to get a knowledge of the progress of individual children in their schools, by themselves holding an informal inspection once a year.   This was his own practice. He wished to find out for himself the condition of his school, and test the intelligence of the children by his own methods.

The Conference of 1883 appointed a committee to consider the organisation of the various Diocesan societies on a Church basis, and made Creighton secretary of this committee, for which he drew up a report which was presented to the next Conference. This report was adopted, and a representative Diocesan Society was formed, and incorporated under the Companies Act; the Bishop of Newcastle's Fund was merged in this Society, which has continued ever since to do most valuable work in the Diocese.

These frequent committees in Newcastle were felt by Creighton as an increasing burden, while his administrative capacity made the Bishop turn more and more to him for help in Diocesan affairs. The Bishop says of him : ' All went so smoothly and quietly. He was always there when wanted for anything. . . . His sympathies were always with the people.'

Early in 1884 Dr. Stubbs was appointed to the Bishopric of Chester, and the Regius Professorship at Oxford was left vacant. Creighton had felt for some time that the parting of the ways must come some day, and that he would have to choose between the life of an historical student and teacher, and the life of ecclesiastical and administrative activity into which he was being drawn almost against his will. When he heard that there was a wish in many quarters in Oxford that he should be the next Regius Professor, he wrote to one or two influential friends to express his desire for the post. It was, as he said afterwards, the only time in his life when he ever asked for anything. His friends were active in pressing his claims. The Duke of Albany wrote :

' Mr. Creighton I know very well indeed ; he is a most clear, unprejudiced, and enlightened man. I studied *much* with him at Oxford, and had a great respect for him. There *could not* be a better appointment. . . . At any rate I *do* hope he may get the Canonry at St. Paul's if he does not get the Professorship. He *well* deserves some promotion.'

This was one of the last matters in which the Duke interested himself before his death, and he was much disappointed that his wishes could not be carried out.

From Dr. Stubbs to M. Creighton

'Oxford : February 17, 1884.

'My dear Creighton,—Your kind letter, the kindest of the two hundred kind ones that I have received, has warmed my heart very thoroughly. I am very grateful for it. I feel not at all sure that my rashness has in it the element of faith, but I trust that it has; I am quite sure that anyone who knows what I am leaving will acquit me, on this point, of self-seeking. I wish, and so does my dear Dean (of course this is private), that you could have been my immediate successor here, supposing that you were willing to come; but although that, I suppose, cannot be, it is probably only delayed until a time when you will have done more of your practical work in Northumberland, and other claims have passed out of sight. My successor will be an older man than myself, and I heartily wish that he may have as peaceful a time as I have had.'

M. Creighton to L. C.   'Embleton : February 18.

'I am getting quite amused about the Professorship. I have had letters from —— and Stubbs saying practically that it will be Freeman or Gardiner, and that I must not expect it. No one seems to suggest that I should go to St. Paul's, which in many ways I would rather do. I don't see how Freeman and Gardiner could be passed over for a man twenty years younger. So I have dismissed that matter from my mind.'

Mr. Freeman was appointed to the Professorship, and Mr. Scott Holland to the Canonry at St. Paul's; but just at the same time Creighton was asked from Cambridge whether he would be a candidate for the new Dixie Professorship of Ecclesiastical History.

To O. Browning   'February 24, 1884.

'As regards your second question, I will only say that there is nothing which I should like better than a Professorship of Ecclesiastical History. But about the Dixie Professorship I know nothing. What is it worth? Who are the electors? Would they take an Oxford man?

'I would not under any circumstances do more than say that if they elected me I would come. But I do not know that the value of the Professorship would enable me to take it, anyhow. If it is not troubling you too much, please give me some more information.'

The Dixie Professorship was a new one, which had been established in consequence of the offer of Emmanuel College to provide the income for a Professorship of Ecclesiastical History, partly out of the Dixie Foundation, money coming from the bequest of Sir Thomas Dixie to the College in 1594, and partly by the stipend of a Fellowship which the Professor was to hold *ex officio*. Creighton signified his willingness to accept the Professorship if he were elected,[1] and heard in May 1884 that he had been chosen for the post.

From Mr. H. M. Gwatkin [2]   'Cambridge: May 18, 1884.

' My dear Professor Creighton,—Will you allow your rival of yesterday the consolation of giving you to-day an individual and hearty welcome to Cambridge? I envy you the splendid work before you; but it is your work now, not mine.

' For twelve years I have taught Ecclesiastical History, I may say almost alone in Cambridge. I have worked faithfully and to the utmost of my power hitherto, and I trust not without success; and now that my work is taken up by stronger hands than mine, I pray the Lord of all History, before whom we both are standing, to give you health and strength and abundant blessing to carry on far better than myself the high and arduous work entrusted to your charge.

' For myself, I am ready to work under you, and to support you loyally in all that falls to me to do. So far as I know my own heart, no jealousy of yesterday shall ever rise on my side to mar the harmony and friendship in which I ask and hope to live with the first Professor of Ecclesiastical History in Cambridge.

        ' I am yours faithfully,
            ' H. M. GWATKIN.'

M. Creighton to Mr. H. M. Gwatkin

        ' Embleton Vicarage: May 22, 1884.

' My dear Mr. Gwatkin,—Thank you very much for your exceedingly kind note. There are no congratulations which I value more highly than yours. I know so little of Cambridge that I did not know who were the other candidates for the Professorship, and I carefully avoided asking anyone anything. A wish was conveyed to me some little time ago that I should become a candidate. After some meditation

---

[1] The electors to the Dixie Professorship were the Vice-Chancellor, the Master of Emmanuel, Dr. Lightfoot, Dr. Hort, Prof. Seeley, Mr. G. Prothero, Dr. J. Bryce, Mr. S. R. Gardiner, Mr. H. Bradshaw, and Mr. B. E. Hammond.

[2] Now Dixie Professor of Ecclesiastical History at Cambridge.

I resolved. I felt that the electors were such as would choose according to the best of their knowledge, and I asked no further questions.

'Now that they have decided, I must do my best to justify their decision. You have worked at an earlier period; I have worked at a later. I cannot say at present what sort of work it would be best for me to shape out for myself; but I am exceedingly grateful to you for your kind promise of co-operation and support. I trust that we shall be in every way colleagues and friends. There is, in my opinion, no branch of study more important than that of Ecclesiastical History. In the face of questions which are pressing at the present, and which will be still more pressing in the future, it is most needful that there should be ready for a help in their solution a basis of sound knowledge, which at present is sorely wanting in England.

'If it is not asking too much, would you tell me what has been done in Cambridge, and how things stand? I hope to be in Cambridge in the middle of next month, when I shall hope to see you.'

To the Bishop of Newcastle (Dr. Wilberforce)

'Embleton Vicarage : May 22, 1884.

'My Lord,—Thank you very much for your kind expressions towards me. I sorrow much at the thought of leaving Northumberland, and very much at the thought of leaving you. I may now say without presumption, that I have learned much from you, and have looked with admiration on qualities in which I know myself to be deficient. You have shown me above all things how great a gift it is to speak out straightforwardly even where it may not be pleasing at the time, and how this may be done in such a manner as to leave nothing but a feeling of respect behind. I may add, because I think you would not be sorry to know it, that this is always the thing that strikes everyone. The general judgment is, "The Bishop knows his own mind, and we know what he means." I think this is a great testimony to the effect which your character is producing. But I have no right to write like this. I think that so many people have written to congratulate me and make remarks about myself, that I am following their bad example. Please forgive me.

'You have anticipated a request which I was about to make, that you would allow me, when I left Embleton, to continue to be your Examining Chaplain. In that capacity I might have a right to represent the Diocese in Cambridge, possibly with some good results.'

From Mr. Albert Grey (now Earl Grey)   'May 24, 1884.

'My dear Creighton,—The news has come upon me with all the stunning force of a blow. I always knew you were far too good for us, and that you would be called sooner or later to some busier sphere, but I always hoped that the time of the calling might be rather far than near. . . . I can assure you I do not like it a bit now that it is a reality. . . . What we shall sink into when you go, Heaven only knows ; the ripple which sprung from the vivifying of the waters at Embleton spread over a large surface ; we shall now stagnate into a pond, into the bottom of which I feel inclined to throw your successor because he is your successor. Tell Mrs. Creighton that there is weeping and lamentation here, and that we are not at the present moment in love with Dixie. I'm very glad, though, Cambridge has you, and not Oxford.

'Yours dejectedly,

'A. G.'

From Mrs. T. H. Ward   'May 28, 1884.

'. . . It will be a great change from Embleton to Cambridge, and from the Oxford to the Cambridge associations ; but I am sure it will be a change worth making, though for the last ten years you have had a humanising, educating life at Embleton, in the broadest sense, that anyone might envy. How few of us can ever come as close to the soil from which we all sprang as you have done in the North. You have seen the elemental human things nearer far than most men of letters have a chance of seeing them, and now you will carry with you all this fruitful experience to enrich the scholar's life that is to be. "Mieux vaut se perdre que de se sauver tout seul et c'est faire tort à son espèce que de vouloir avoir raison sans faire partager sa raison." There, it seems to me, is what you two have learnt at Embleton, and you must help those of us who love you, and have not had your training, to learn it too.'

M. Creighton to Rev. Robert Wilson

'Embleton Vicarage : May 19, 1884.

'My dear Wilson,—. . . A great change is to come over me. I have just been informed that I have been elected Professor of Ecclesiastical History at Cambridge. I go because I think I can be of more use there than here. Yet my sojourn in the wilderness has been most profitable for me, and I shall leave my few sheep with sincere regret.'

To Mrs. J. R. Thursfield   'Embleton Vicarage : May 22, 1884.

'Dear Emily,—Just a line to thank you for your congratulations, and to say that we shall certainly live at Cambridge. My conscience would not allow me to hold such a living as Embleton in plurality. It requires an active vicar. I am not sure that I have been active enough. I shall go to Cambridge a poorer man than I am here, which will be some consolation to me for leaving.'

To Mr. Oscar Browning   'Embleton: May 22, 1884.

'My dear Browning,—Thank you very much for your kind congratulations. It was you who suggested to me some time ago to become a candidate, or I should never have thought of it. I feel that it is very good of Cambridge to find a home for an alien, but I am quite ready to lend myself to the process of adoption.'

It was with no light heart that Creighton decided to give up his life at Embleton. We both felt that the ten years we had spent there must remain the happiest of our life. They had been full of work, of opportunities of gaining varied experience by coming in close contact with the realities of life. We had lived outside the rush of the world, and had been able to form our own intellectual atmosphere, to think out things by ourselves. We had seen our friends with a sense of leisure, which enabled us to get from them the best they could give. Our children had had for their early years an ideal country home, which gave them every opportunity for a free and healthy life. The strange charm of Northumberland had won us all, and henceforth no other part of the world could hold our affections in the same way.

But apart from other considerations, Creighton had always maintained that about ten years was as long as any clergyman should stay in the same place. He said that was long enough for him to give his message; if it was not understood in ten years, it would never be. Moreover, as he wrote to a friend, the questions which had constantly presented themselves to him during the last two years were :

'Is my line practical or speculative, or both ? How far can I combine the two ? How far am I justified in abandoning one for the other ? I have just devised a fresh departure by way of trying a better solution. My friends judge my wisdom differently, but few recognise the real issue. Bright of University saw it, and dissented the other day from my solution. He said : " It is a better thing to manage men than to write books. It is more amusing and more satisfying.

You should have gone on and become a Bishop, and made yourself a practical power." . . . The present day tends to be practical. It regards the application of existing ideas as more valuable than the search for new ones. Plenty of new ones are made by men who are fit for nothing else.'

When once he had made his decision to go, he dismissed the matter from consideration and gave way to no regrets. He decided not to settle at Cambridge till November, and meanwhile life went on as usual. In April he received his first academic distinction, when he was made LL.D. of Glasgow University. We spent some very pleasant days there with his former tutor, Professor Edward Caird, and were entertained with true Scottish hospitality. At the end of May he felt the need of a complete change, and we went to France for a fortnight, and wandered along the Loire, exploring its interesting castles. Then we went to Oxford, that he might examine in the History Schools. A first visit was also paid to Cambridge, when he was admitted to his Fellowship at Emmanuel, and was present at the festivities in connexion with the commemoration of the Tercentenary of the College. We were the guests of Dr. Hort, who was also a Fellow of Emmanuel. At the banquet at Emmanuel, Creighton met for the first time Mr. James Lowell, then American Minister in England, and Mr. Charles Eliot Norton, who had come from America to represent Harvard at the Tercentenary of the College from which its founder John Harvard came. He was disappointed not to be able at this time to make the acquaintance of Mr. H. M. Gwatkin, who had already left Cambridge for the vacation.

'5 Bradmore Road, Oxford : June 13, 1884.

'Dear Mr. Gwatkin,—Your letter must have reached my house just as I left it for a fortnight's ramble along the Loire. As I had been overwhelmed with letters and business for some time, I cut myself off from them during my absence, and have just received yours. I shall be in Cambridge next week, but I fear you will be gone. I am here examining for the next three weeks. Would it be possible for you to pay us a visit in Northumberland any time after July 10? We are on the sea, in a most healthful spot, and could talk over all things peaceably. I hope this may be possible. Meanwhile, thank you very much for your information. I will only say gene-

rally that I have not paid any special attention to Ecclesiastical History before 476, and do not want to commit myself
to that earlier period, which requires special training and
special study to do it real justice.   I am glad to hear that you
are interested in the Iconoclasts ; so am I.   I once designed
to devote myself to the history of the Eastern Church from
476 to 1000, but abandoned it for a later time.'

Mr. Gwatkin visited Embleton in August, and the foundations of a true friendship were laid, which led to a loyal and
sympathetic co-operation in work between the two historical
students.   Creighton felt almost like an interloper when he
realised what a fitting crown to Mr. Gwatkin's devoted work
in Cambridge the Professorship would have been, and he was
much touched by the generous welcome which Mr. Gwatkin
extended to him.   Mr. Gwatkin, on the other hand, then and
always asserted that the disappointment of his hopes was more
than compensated for by the gain of a fellow worker to
whom, in his own words to me on leaving us, he could ' offer
the loving homage of unreserved esteem and warm affection.'

Many friends came that summer to pay a last visit to
Embleton Vicarage ; among others, the J. R. Thursfields
and Andrew Langs, who had been with us every year since
we went North, Mr. John Morley, the T. H. Wards, and Mr.
Robert Wilson.   In October we went to Carlisle for the
Church Congress, where Creighton read a paper on ' The
Influence of the Reformation on England.'[1]   It was the first
of a number of papers read at successive Church Congresses,
which taken together show what was his view of the historical
position of the Church of England and of its relation to the
national life.   More and more as the years went on did the
thought take shape in his mind, that his message to the world
was to try and get people to understand the meaning of the
Church of England.   At that time this thought had not been
formulated ; indeed, I do not think he spoke to me on the
subject till some fifteen years later in the garden at Fulham.
But looking back, reading the utterances of those early days,
it is easy to see how his studies and experience alike combined
to form the views to which later on he was able in part at least
to give expression.

[1] Reprinted in *The Church and the Nation.* (Longmans.)

His epigrammatic style, his lucid exposition, and his clear enunciation made him at once a welcome speaker at the Church Congress. But meetings always bored him, and he attended as little of the Congress as he could, and took no active part beyond reading his own paper.

The autumn was spent in bidding farewell to his parish. He called personally at every house, and gave everyone a photograph of himself. He was much gratified by the opinion expressed on his work by a woman who was famous for her talking powers, ' Well, if you ain't done no good, you've done no harm,' which from the mouth of a Northumbrian was glowing praise. He felt the pain of parting from his people very deeply, and said that if Sir George Grey had been still living, he never could have made up his mind to go.

To the Bishop of Newcastle

'Embleton Vicarage : November 1, 1884.

' My Lord,—It is very good of you to express yourself so warmly about the trifling things that I have been enabled to do since the Diocese of Newcastle was founded. I was only too glad to devote to the service of the Church such spare time as I had. I felt that my parish was one which would have been very hard work for one, but was easy work for two. I thought it my duty to do some public work besides. Before you came, I was busy with poor law and sanitary work. When you came, I gave that up for Diocesan business. But though I found the Diocesan work more laborious and less interesting in its details, it has been made more pleasant to me by your constant kindness. Nor has my intercourse with you only been pleasant, but also profitable. I shall always be grateful for many things that you have taught me, and I shall rejoice to think that our friendly relationship will always last so long as we are both strengthened to continue our labours in the Master's service.'

'Embleton Vicarage: November 10, 1884.

' My Lord,—If you find a clergyman thinking of quitting your Diocese whom you do not want to lose, refer him to me, and I will do my best to dissuade him. Since the Conference I have spent a fortnight of perfect agony in saying good-bye. If I had known how terrible it was, I do not think that anything would have induced me to do it. I shall go away bleeding and lacerated all over ; it will be long before I can get any nerve again. These poor dear folk—they are ignorant, they are often brutal, they seem cold enough—but oh, it is dreadful leaving them. I have often felt, I am now quite sure—and it is worth while knowing—if ever you get hold of a Northumbrian, you get him for life; if ever you teach him anything, he will never forget it. A paralysed woman dragged herself two miles yesterday to come to the Holy Communion. Another said to me, "A look at your photograph will keep me from doing wrong." A good farmer burst into tears and blubbered like a child in trying to say good-bye. And what am I to deserve this? I tell you these things only to show you that these cold folk are warm-hearted at the bottom, a fact that those who labour among them need sometimes to be reminded of.'

To Mr. G. Robertson (his churchwarden)

'My dear Robertson,—I cannot tell you how much I feel parting from you, and how grateful I shall always be to you for the kindness and confidence you have shown towards me. It is a sad business to say good-bye at any time, but it is very hard to me.

'However, we shall meet again. I shall come and see you some day, and you will come and pay Cambridge a visit.'

It was known that he did not care for testimonials, so his feelings were respected, and he left without any public leave-taking, though he received presents from the clergy of his Rural Deanery, from the children of his school, and from his personal friends in the county, as memorials of their affection. He preached his farewell sermon in Embleton Church on November 9, on the text, 'Because I have you in my heart,' and took as his subject the position and duties of a parish priest in the Church of England. In this sermon he showed what had been the aim of his own parochial life, and at the same time tried to prepare his people to receive his successor with understanding sympathy. After speaking of the priest's duties in church, he went on :

'The first duty of a clergyman is to make clear to himself the relation in which his office places him as regards his people. . . . A clergyman has constantly to examine himself to see that his heart is right. He has constantly to overcome feelings of disappointment. . . . A priest is bound, as his first duty in dealing with others, to pierce through this mist whereby the world strives to hide the truth of God. . . . He must keep before his eyes the sacredness of every human soul, yes, even of those who are most plunged in wickedness and sin. He has to go on his course watching for opportunities of usefulness. . . . He has many disappointments. . . . The best means of helping him is to treat him as a friend. . . . Do not keep him at arm's length. Do not suspect his intentions. Conceive it to be at least possible that he is seeking only your good. . . . In the course of his work, a clergyman must often expect to be misunderstood, to be misrepresented, to have hard things said of him. . . . He should never forget that his object is not to make people satisfied with themselves, but dissatisfied—not to leave them as they were, but to exhort them to advance in the way of godliness. Too often people talk as if a clergyman's chief duty was to make himself pleasant, as if he were bound above all things to strive to be popular, and to avoid all questions which might draw upon him antagonism or gainsaying. A moment's reflection would show you that this cannot be so. His life and works may be attractive in the eyes of those who are themselves striving after God. They cannot fail to be taken as a reproach by those who persevere in the way of wickedness. To such— there is no escape from it—a clergyman who does his duty must always be an annoyance. . . . Few men dare to mock at godliness in itself, but it is an easy matter to mock at one whose duty it is to teach godliness. . . . It is said that a clergyman should confine himself to his pulpit and his congregation, and should not meddle with other things or other persons. . . . This cannot be accepted by a priest of the Church of England. He is set over a definite parish ; . . . it must be his duty to secure, as far as he can, that everything concerning the life of his people should be arranged so as to lead them unto God. . . . This must lead him into many matters, which admit of great difference of opinion. . . . A clergyman cannot always have the wisdom necessary for the task ; but he ought to have one quality which entitles him to be heard. He ought to be free from selfish interests. . . . The priest . . . must be concerned with everyone. . . . He must watch over the progress of each individual soul. He must try to build up each individual character. . . .

'" That we may present every man perfect in Christ Jesus," that has been the aim, most imperfectly pursued, that has been always present with me. I have not dealt with you only as a congregation—you have been individually before my thoughts. I have wished to be on the completest terms of intimacy that you would each admit. I have tried to turn from talk about trivial things to the more important questions concerning our life and character. I have met with more answers than I had any right to expect. I have met with

more kindness than I deserved. If I have taught you anything, you have taught me much in return. I go away from
my intercourse with you a wiser and, I trust, a better man.
For all your kindness to me and mine, I thank you from the
bottom of my heart. . . . If you think of me in time to come,
think of me as one who cared much for you. Believe that,
with many failings, I was still true to one great principle of
the pastor's life—" I had you in my heart." '

These words show something of the kind of work which
Creighton tried to do among his people. It is impossible
to sum up what were the results of ten years' ministry
in such a parish as Embleton. The only visible result
of Creighton's incumbency is the beautiful series of stained
glass windows erected through his agency to the memory
of Sir George Grey.[1] The influence that he had upon
individual lives and characters cannot be measured any more
than it can be known. He himself did not ask to know it,
he was content to give of his best to anyone who needed.

Among his neighbours, clerical and otherwise, he seems
to have produced the same sort of stimulating effect as he
produced wherever he went. He was at first regarded with a
little suspicion in some quarters on account of his Liberal
opinions, but this to a great extent disappeared when it was
seen how little of a partisan he was. The general impression
he produced is described by a clerical friend and neighbour.

' I well remember your coming to Embleton, and all the
new ideas and interests of which it was the start. Even your
arrangement of the house and the wall papers (at that time
unknown to us) warned us that we were to be roused from
our old habits and thoughts, and made to see things with new
eyes. I think we never got back into our old forms again
with quite the same self-complacency. Your new-fashioned
wall papers were only typical of all the freshness you brought
to bear on everything and every person around you. Whether
it was in general society or among your own farmers or the
villagers or your pupils, it was always the same genial *sursum
corda* which raised us to a higher level, and made us pleased
with ourselves and all around us. It was not that all society
pleased your husband equally, but he never, so far as I

---

[1] Since his death his friends have erected in his memory a village hall and
club-rooms, which as ' the Creighton Hall ' perpetuate his name in Embleton.

remember, allowed himself to look down on any individual or
set of persons as being unworthy of his courteous, painstaking
attention. He was far more ready to see a man's virtues and
powers than his faults and weaknesses, and far more ready to
forget his own immeasurable superiority and breadth of view
than to take note of others' inferiority and narrowness.

'His entirely new outlook on things in general, and most
noticeably on things ecclesiastical and questions theological,
and his clearly expressed but reverent views on many burning
clerical questions, of course created a certain amount of semi-
suspicious self-restraint in the brotherly greeting we clergy
gave him, and the unknown quantity of his political creed did
not tend to lessen this self-restraint. But we all realised that,
whatever he might think of us, he would never allow even a
gesture of impatience, still less a word of discourtesy, arrogance, or bitterness, to mar our intercourse. We realised also
that he was not a man easily affected by his surroundings,
going on his own way, diffusing much light and happiness, but
not expecting to gain much in return. We felt his gifts to
lie in an intense appreciation of the good and beautiful, and
in an unwearied labour to help on their cause, rather than in
the spirit of dogmatic teaching and ritual, narrow clericalism,
or tender spiritual sympathy which one or the other mark
most clerical lives. My happiest memories, both as to the
brilliant man and his influence and the pleasure of your home,
are connected with Sunday evenings there, when the sense of
delighted relaxation after the efforts of the day was allowed
to pervade everything, when he shone in his perfect light as
host and leader of talk and starter of wild picturesque
paradoxes.'

His supposed habit of talking paradoxes puzzled people
in Northumberland as elsewhere ; but the visitors at Embleton
Vicarage recall with delight their enjoyment of his talk.
A pupil writes : 'There was plenty of laughter at the meals we
had together, and the bumptiousness of some of us was never
resented, although it received its fair share of ridicule. The
Vicar was particularly fond of defending some glaring paradox,
and often dinner would be spent in an argument in which we
were right, and he was all the while getting the better of the
argument, until coffee came, when he would give up his
position with evident regret.'

'He would rag us unmercifully,' says another pupil, 'and
make fun of our views, chiefly, I think, to see whether we would

stand our ground, and whether it was a real belief or just a
shibboleth picked up from others.'

Dr. Hodgkin writes: 'Would that I could remember
some of the innumerable magnificent paradoxes which he used
to maintain so brilliantly at the head of his table or in his
armchair in the smoking-room! But I early noticed that the
paradox was for the many, the disclosure of his real mind for
the few. When one was talking with him by oneself all the
whimsical paradoxes vanished, he put his mind seriously
alongside of yours, and was willing to work patiently and
steadily for the discovery of the truth.'

It has always seemed to me that the point which his critics
miss is that the assertion of a paradox was one of his ways
of seeking the truth. He wished to get people to see what
the problem was, to arrest attention. Dr. Hodgkin recalls a
conversation at Embleton on Socialism, in which Creighton, in
opposition to all his guests, seemed to imply that Socialism
was the goal to which society must tend, and said : ' I do not
mean that a cut-and-dry system of Socialism will be accepted
by the State in the lifetime of any one of us ; but I do think
that legislation will more and more assume a socialistic bias,
and rightly so, and that the rights of the individual will be
less and less regarded when they evidently clash with the
welfare of the people as a whole.'

This statement was apparently in those days considered a
paradox, now it sounds more like a platitude ; but, Dr. Hodgkin adds : ' Whether it was paradox or sober earnest with
him, he convinced me, when I came to think over his arguments, and I have never since been able to think other
thoughts than his on this great question.'

Other statements of his, which were always in those days
sure to provoke an argument, were his preference of day to
boarding schools, his attacks on our public school system, his
assertion that he would be quite content to live on a fixed
income of a hundred a year. These arguments never became
dangerously serious, but were always illumined by humour,
and varied by anecdotes and much pure nonsense.

It was perhaps at Embleton that he was able to get the
most unbroken enjoyment out of family life. He allowed his
children to share his life in every possible way. He took

them with him on his walks, even allowed them to play in his study while he worked. He helped in their education by giving them Greek and Latin lessons. When I was away from home on visits to my parents, he took my place in every detail of their care, letting them do their lessons in his study and reading aloud to them in the evenings. He was always a very severe critic of his own children, and cherished no delusions as to their capacities. Though he was morally convinced of the supreme importance of character, and the comparative unimportance of intellectual gifts, it was, I believe, a real disappointment to him that none of his children showed anything exceptional in the way of intellectual powers, and did not have very distinguished school or college careers. He would always tell strangers that his children were quite stupid. His own intellectual gifts seemed to him so ordinary, that he rather appeared to believe that anyone who chose could do what he had done. At all times the standard which he applied to his own family was absolutely different from that which he applied to others; but this did not in the least interfere with the absolute freedom of intercourse and the devoted love which characterised his relations with them. His eldest child recalls as follows those early days.

' I believe the first thing I can remember was being played ball with by father and mother. It was an exciting and rather awful joy, and I can recall now that breathless moment when, released from one pair of arms, I was tossed through the air to be caught and kissed in safety at the other end. It was my joy when I got a little older to clamber up on to father's shoulders, and there stand proudly, with one foot on each, while he ran about the room skilfully dodging a hanging candelabrum. Many were the acrobatic feats we performed together, to the imminent peril of life and limb, onlookers used to think, but I didn't know what fear meant when I was with him.

' No children ever had a more delightful playmate than we had, and all our best games and romps are bound up in our minds with him. No paraphernalia were ever needed; we cast aside toys and bricks when he was there—he himself was all we wanted. One moment he would be an awful giant, who with mighty roaring would seize us by the legs or pinafores or anything else he could lay hands on. This was a thrilling but a noisy game.

'Then—this was what we loved—he would be a rocking-horse. This meant lying upon the floor with several of us seated upon him, and rocking violently up and down. It was exceedingly exhausting for the horse, I expect, but for the riders most exhilarating. Outsiders looking on at our games used to wonder sometimes why no one was killed, so wild and violent were the romps, so daring the gymnastic feats when we scrambled and clambered all over father, and fell in a heap of indistinguishable arms and legs and tangled heads, only to extricate ourselves again and start afresh. I cannot remember any sort of accident ever happening, beyond the occasional damaging of his spectacles in the fray. Sunday evenings in the drawing-room were always a great time for romps, and the wildest and most furious took place then. Perhaps he found them a rest and relaxation after his Sunday duties.

' On wet days, when we were obliged to stay in the nursery instead of going out to play in the garden, towards the end of the afternoon, just as we were getting rather bored with our games, and the day seemed very long, we were nearly certain to see the nursery door open gently and a face peep round the corner, and in he would come to be seized upon by us with screams of joy. Sometimes he would read to us, lying on the floor—always a favourite position of his—with us all huddled round him as close as we could manage to get. How real those stories became to us when he read them! One day, I remember, he had picked up a book and was reading to us a sweet, sad little tale. We were all so quiet that mother looked into the nursery, wondering what had happened, and she found us on the floor as usual, but father and all of us in tears over the touching story he had just finished.

' Occasionally on a wet day we had a hair-cutting afternoon, for he was hair-cutter to all of us children, and we thought it great fun to be perched on a high chair with a towel round us, and have our untidy mops snipt by him. Never failing was the joke, when we had each had our turn and the nursery floor was strewn with curls, that we must be sure and gather them all up carefully and take them to cook, so that he might have " hare soup " for dinner that evening. He did not need a book to amuse us, for what book ever written had in it such wonderful and delightful stories as he wove for our amusement? They would perhaps hardly be called stories. It was amazing nonsense, often in verse, in which strange weird creatures with still stranger names played a part. People

Photo. J. Marshall.

THE GARDEN, EMBLETON VICARAGE.

too, there were, boys and girls, unlike any who had ever lived, and quite unaccountable in their actions. These stories he would tell us generally out of doors, on walks or picnics, or seated among the sandhills by the sea.

' I think we regarded him in those early days chiefly as the most delightful of playfellows, some one who, in spite of being the wisest and best of all grown-up persons, could yet understand and care for the things of children, and without whom no games and fun would be quite perfect. He could be very stern and angry sometimes, though, when we were naughty. Then it was very terrifying, but it never lasted long.

' We knew that there were some things we must never do, or he would be angry, things fairly harmless in themselves we sometimes thought, but which he considered criminal, such as talking and making a noise on the stairs or in the passages, banging doors, aimlessly coming in and out of the room where he was sitting, being, as he called it, " disorderly and futile."

' At a very early age, six I think, he began to teach me Greek. On the whole I enjoyed my lessons enormously. I liked going to the smoky study, sitting on his knee or on a stool by his side, while between the puffs of his cigarette he would hear me my verbs and correct my feeble exercises. It was delightful when all went well, particularly when we gaily left grammar behind and after the very slightest grounding in that respect I plunged into Homer and Euripides. But I do not think he could ever have been a good teacher of children, he demanded so much, and perhaps was not sufficiently patient over their shortcomings. Many a time did my Greek lesson end in tears, when in my carelessness I forgot a word he had told me over and over again, above all when I made excuses. Then with a bang the book would be thrown across the room, and I would be told to go.'

Our sixth child was born in 1883, and received the name of a Northumbrian saint, Oswin. My husband was great at inventing nicknames for his children, but they never lasted, he varied them so often that sometimes there was a new one every day. He wished their life to be in every way as simple as possible. They were never allowed to behave as if the house belonged to them, or was regulated to suit their convenience. His strong respect for individual liberty led him never to interfere with what they chose to do, as long as it was not harmful to others ; any attempt to manage others, even his own children, to organise their lives for them, was utterly distasteful to him.　But he never let them forget that it was his house, and that his must be the ruling will.　In after days he used to say : ' I keep a hotel ; if you choose to live there, you must conform to my regulations.'　His rules and his commands were very few, but they had to be kept, and above all he hated an excuse.

There are no letters of his which give any idea of the course of his life at Embleton.　I can only give some short extracts from his letters to me during my occasional brief absences on visits to my parents.

'March 6, 1878.

' I become most wicked in my habits, as I sit up till twelve reading vaguely, and then am very late for breakfast.　I think seriously about myself, that I wish I was not such a feeble, fussy, fretful person, but could pull myself together and do things more quietly without having so much taken out of me.'

'February 1, 1883.

' The weather goes on being lovely, which is very nice of it. . . . Nothing exciting occurs to me. . . . Yesterday I went to Newton, taking the children, who gloried in the sea-shore.　The sun was like summer, and high tides had washed up many shells.　I find somebody ill in almost every house.'

'February 5, 1883.

' I was kept hard at work yesterday.　Confirmation class at ten ; then full service, as Green was at Craster.　Children's service and a baptism. . . . I brought Robertson and Green to supper. . . . I go to Newcastle on Wednesday, 14th, for a lecture.'

'February 5, 1884.

' I have just had a triumph over ——'s naughtiness at lessons.　I cured her by resoluteness, made her sit down till she was ready to begin with care, and then she submissively did her work.'

'February 6.

' The children are very good, and all seems peaceable.　I have absolutely nothing to tell you.　I began the " Ingoldsby Legends " last night.　They were a great success.　I wrote hard at Cesare Borgia, and am more and more interested.'

'February 8, 1884.

' Egypt is turning out as I expected. You can't do things half and half, but the British Constitution is a very poor machine for doing anything whole.'

'February 11.

' I had a dull day on Saturday in Alnwick. . . . I went to a meeting where we discussed the Kindergarten system. Trotter's mistress expounded it, with illustrations. The impression left on my mind was that its use entirely depended on the teacher : an intelligent teacher will teach intelligently, and you can't invent a system which will make an unintelligent teacher intelligent.'

'February 12.

' Yesterday I took a little walk with the children, pottered in the village . . . read "Ingoldsby" to the children, worked all my spare time at a murder attributed to Cesare Borgia, and wrote a long excursus upon it. These are the records of a quiet day.'

'February 13.

' Yesterday I was overwhelmed with excitements. I had two meetings, a Band of Hope and an Odd Fellows'. All the children turned up, about fifty, and we practised some songs, and I read them a story or two, and they all seemed very good and nice. Then I was initiated into all sorts of horrible rites as an Odd Fellow. . . . I see Stubbs is to be made a Bishop. Don't you think I ought to be Regius Professor ? I should like it, I must confess. . . . The only thing is that I think S. R. Gardiner deserves it more, certainly as a student, but I might be more useful to the place altogether.'

'February 14.

' I don't feel as if I had any news to tell you. . . . I do nothing save Popes and parish, only very little Popes.

' I am the more desirous to leave Embleton the more I think of it. I have long been dimly conscious that I was coming to a turning point ; I have gained in quietude all the strength and decision I shall ever have. A year or two more here would make me an interesting old fogey like ——. It is time that I either went more into the world or became an entire student.'

'February 19.

' I nearly toiled myself dead yesterday morning with letters to write, proofs of the Memoir to correct, and school accounts to make up. I did not succeed in doing any of them properly. Then I had to bustle to the train to lecture

at Amble. I stopped at Warkworth and called on the Dixons
on the way. Dixon is a good soul, shy and reserved, but a
well-read man all round. . . . I wonder whether it is *right* to
wish to go away. But I wish I did not feel that I was comparatively useless here.'

LETTERS, 1883–1884

'Embleton: February 8, 1883.

'Dear Hodgkin,—. . . How nice it is to find anyone who
is interested in one's own subject! I made the acquaintance of Garnett in the British Museum. He kindly sought
me out as I was reading, and placed himself at my disposal.
We have already had a long correspondence about recondite
books. You know whom I mean—the Director of the
Reading Room. He offered to do anything for me I wanted
at any time. How nice and kindly are real students! How
much otherwise, as a rule, is the man of letters!'

'Embleton: February 26, 1883.

'Dear Hodgkin,—. . . I incline to think with you that
the attribution of general causes to a particular person, as
the Lombards to Narses, is a disease of the human mind.
I am discovering, as I go on with Alexander VI., that his
unparalleled wickedness is similarly a result of the general
desire to find a scapegoat for the decay of Italy in the
sixteenth century. He was bad enough, but not exceptionally bad. The awakening conscience of Italy seized on him
as an example.

'Newcastle politics will now rest in peace. Morley is
a great improvement on Dilke; but I share your view that
Newcastle might have afforded to have a Christian for a
change.'

To Mr. Albert Grey   'Embleton Vicarage: May 25, 1883.

'. . . I was glad to see your name affixed to a circular
which I received this morning with Gladstone's speech on
the Affirmation Bill. At the same time I was very glad that
the Bill was thrown out, simply because I objected on
constitutional grounds to the House passing an Act to
deliver it from a dilemma which was the result of its own
unconstitutional proceedings. I do not want Bradlaugh to
be kept out of the House; but I cannot see why the House
refuses to allow him to take the oath. The Government
allowed the House, without any effective protest, to behave

with gross illegality, and then, with much emotion, asked the House to put itself right by altering its laws.

'I know all the arguments in favour of respecting everybody's conscience. They don't convince me. Society cannot be altogether abolished to suit people's consciences. A government that does not respect Mr. Healy's conscience need not be so chary about—I really don't know whose—not Bradlaugh's, for he does not object to take the oath. Why then, I ask, in the name of wonder—why make a change? Where is this respect for hypothetical consciences to stop? If a man behaved rudely to a lady, and said that his conscience prevented him from showing politeness to anyone whom he did not genuinely respect, you would kick him. Yet there is a great deal in his plea, and I don't see how society can defend the amount of hypocrisy which it rigidly demands.

'Not that I have any objection to the abolition of oaths altogether—in everything, on the ground that they are generally useless and tend to irreverence.

'But I am bored with people's consciences. Let them be requested to leave off growing conscientious scruples, and grow cauliflowers, or some other useful product.

'These remarks are futile, and only show that I have no head for serious politics. I know that in the House the Bradlaugh question is regarded by all serious persons as of infinitely more importance than the future of the British Empire; but I am not equal to such heights.'

'Embleton Vicarage : July 18, 1883.

'Dear Hodgkin,—Your letter fills me with amazement at your mental versatility. I always admire it, and I sorely wish that I was like you. When a subject gets hold of me I find it becomes exclusive. My mind seems to churn in a narrow circle when I am interested in anything. . . .

'I am sorry that you think me a waxing Conservative. I own that I am not pleased with the levity and thoughtlessness with which great questions are treated ; but my views have been reinforced by an article of Fawcett's in this month's "Macmillan," which please read. I remember that last time I talked with Albert Grey he said, "The man who thinks with you is Fawcett. He is the only member of the present Government who is prepared to oppose Socialism."'

To Mrs. J. R. Green   'Embleton Vicarage : December 31, 1883.

'Dear Mrs. Green,—I have been prevented from writing to you (1) because I did not want to write before I had read the "Conquest of England," wherein I was delayed; (2) when that was done, Christmas came upon me and overwhelmed me with its festivities. I don't think feasts of the Church are made more impressive by the mixture of mundane revelries.

'Now, to go back to the "Conquest of England." It greatly impressed me by the vividness of its realisation of things as a whole. The first chapter is admirable. The coming of the Vikings illuminated me by its picture of things in motion. The sketch of the growth of English towns was equally good. The difference between it and Freeman is enormous. Freeman tries to make you understand each detail by isolating it, and surrounding it with nineteenth-century settings. He iterates and reiterates, but you don't see it. His history is a series of tips. But in the "Making" and the "Conquest of England" the whole thing moves together. Still, lack of material leaves many problems unsolved. How did the English and Northmen settle down together? How did they affect one another in daily life? Nobody knows. The estimate of Godwin and Harold quite satisfies me. Freeman's worship of them is ridiculous. They were clearly ruffians. . . .

'Thanks for telling me Stubbs's remarks. I am much gratified by them. It was for such as him that I wrote, and I tried to make the book as thorough as I could. I have a student's love for a book which I never read, but to which I always refer with confidence. Do you know that there is no book on English History after the Conquest in which I can find definite knowledge save in Pauli's "Geschichte von England"? It is a sad confession, but long experience has taught me so. I aimed so to write that he who went to me would find enough to put him on the right track. All my friends agree that they wish I had been more entertaining. So do I, and I have seriously thought about it. I want your advice on the subject. I cannot say that it is not in me. I could be picturesque if I tried, I dare say; but I don't think that my subject admits of it. To be picturesque you must have a decided opinion; you must deal with a subject where your sympathies are on one side. Now I have deliberately chosen a subject in which every step leads me to controverted matter. I don't want to say that the Popes were a pack of scoundrels, or that they were the enemies of free-thought, or anything else. I don't think that we yet know what the Reformation really was. I am writing to try and help on the matter. If I let go my grip on the general aspect of things in Europe, and

descend to personalities, I am lost. I try to sympathise
with everybody, and see what was the upshot of his activity.
You can be very funny about modern politics if you resolve
them into modes of Bismarck's digestion or Gladstone's
success in felling trees. But these are backstairs politics,
and don't do much good. Moreover, my subject has not the
unity for pictorial treatment. I don't want to show how the
Popes lived in Rome, but how they affected Europe. Even
now, when I have Savonarola before me, I have to take his
halo off and look at him as an ally of France and a
disturber of Italian politics. A few good souls in Florence
put the halo on; but the mass of his contemporaries did not
see it. He is a grand subject for a biography, but he cannot
be made out an exciting figure in history. So, too, with the
rest of them. Alexander VI. was an unscrupulous politician,
but not a villain; and Cesare Borgia was neither better nor
worse than most other folk. All this is very dull to have to
record. I would gladly denounce the abominations if
I found them there. At present all that can be said of me
is, that I left a dull period of history as dull as I found it.
As I go on, it will be said that I have carried my own
dullness into what was interesting before. I suppose really
that living and reading alone has caused me to lose touch
of the popular taste, and I must stagger on in my benighted
condition. This is all about myself; but I want you to
lecture me on this point. I am sure I must be wrong somewhere.

'I have read " Altiora Peto." Why does Oliphant mock
at dynamite when his own views are social Nihilism? He
proposes to make a new environment as the Nihilists do,
only they take a more rapid and practical way. But a
novel without any character, except that of its author, is an
artistic failure.'

'Embleton : February 12, 1884.

'Dear Hodgkin,—I am glad that you are having some
time for quietness and work. I am glad that you are giving
some attention to St. Benedict. Have you looked at
Montalembert's "Monks of the West"? Perhaps he would
give you some help as regards the sentiment with which one
can approach these saints of old. I quite feel with you.
Read the records and weigh them; allow for mythology as
you may, there still remains something quite beyond the
common, a distinct atmosphere of holiness nowadays rarely
thought of, a possession of a distinct spiritual power.

'I have before advised you, I advise you again, to get
the five little volumes of Gregorovius's " Wanderjahre in

Italien." I think of him now in reference to Subiaco. I find Gregorovius excellent for recalling the sentiment of historical Italy. I constantly look him up to be revived on that subject. . . .

'About Seebohm. I think that he will captivate many, and will have a following. He simplifies legal theories; he answers George; his attitude suits the optimism of the present day. . . . I am busy with the Borgias; it is like spending one's day in a low police court.'

'Embleton Vicarage : January 14, 1884.

'My dear Mrs. Green,—I am very much obliged to you for your letter, which was helpful to me.

'I saw long ago, when I looked back upon my book, that it bore the traces of having been composed amid many distractions. I have not been careful enough to obliterate the joinings. In some points my views modified as I went on, and I have not sufficiently recast previous parts. From your testimony and that of others I see that I have to some extent succeeded in giving my book the interest which I think genuinely belongs to any period, the interest that comes from the movement of events. But the European background was hard to make clear, because it was so entirely indefinite. In the period of which I wrote, the nationalities of Europe were unconsciously forming themselves, and the catastrophe of the Council of Constance lay in the fact that national sentiment was too strong for a joint European action ; but Europe did not understand the fact.

'I have all my life laboured from a disadvantage of an Oxford training. In all my writing I am too reserved. I say to myself, "Everybody knows this ; it is not worth saying again." I struggle against the tendency, and try to remind myself that nobody knows anything. In preaching and in speaking I have learned that it is the commonplace, judiciously applied, which attracts attention. I have not yet learned to apply this to writing. Perhaps I may learn in time. But honestly I have not yet attained in my book to any conclusion which it is worth while urging on the *popular* as apart from the reflecting mind. My conclusion, so far, is that the Reformation was primarily a demand for a redress of the grievances inherent in the absolutism of the papal administration over the Church. There was no discontent with the doctrines. If the Papacy could have put its administration into better order there would have been no Reformation, but the new learning would have modified men's attitude towards dogma without causing a breach of the unity of the Church. It is useless to put this in a popular form at first. It may be done some day.

'I have been finishing my "Life of Sir George Grey." I will send you, in a day or two, a sermon which I have just published about the memorial to him. Sermons are dull literature, and I won't ask you to read it.'

'Embleton Vicarage : February 21, 1884.

'My dear Mrs. Green,—My letter-writing power seems to have been paralysed lately by Louise's absence . . . partly because solitude tends to develop abnormal activity, and my mind was entirely taken up by Cesare Borgia. Though I have not yet finished him, I have laid him aside with sorrow overwhelmed with a number of other things, to do which will swallow up a fortnight at least. So wags the world with its interruptions.

'The Reformation problem is beset by difficulties of every sort. Why did the Lollards and Hussites come to nothing ? I see no reason why, if Luther had not wrought a schism, the old system of the Church should not have been adapted to all the requirements of the religious sense of Christendom. I think we have accustomed our minds to look on the 'dissidency of dissent' as a necessity of things. I don't know why we should think so. It is a trick like anything else. I differ as much, if not more, from many Anglicans as I do from most Dissenters. I don't want to attack the Anglicans from whom I differ ; but the Church Association seems to like to attack people, and carry on its dissidence inside the Church. Lord Salisbury and Mr. Gladstone are not popularly supposed to agree, but they don't cause disruption of the State. There were very large differences of opinion in the mediæval Church : risings were rarely for opinions, but for very practical causes. If the Pope would have left off pillaging Germany, I believe that " justification by faith only " would have created only a languid interest. This is a very low view. I know that we ought to believe that mighty movements always swayed the hearts of men. So they have —when they made for their pecuniary interest. But I believe that ideas were always second thoughts in politics—they were the garb with which men covered the nudity of their practical desires. I mean that I can never ask myself first, " What mighty ideas swelled in the hearts of men ? " But, " What made men see a chance of saving sixpence, of gaining sixpence, or escaping from being robbed of sixpence ? " What man was clever enough to devise a formula round which men could rally for this purpose ?

'This crude philosophy of history is composed in the middle of a school examination, and must stop because the inspector is done, and clamours for lunch.'

To his Sister　　　　　　　　　　'Embleton : January 30, 1884.

'My dear Polly,—To show you that I may be trusted, I return Miss Blamire's Poems. They are very much worth reading, also the Memoir. She was a real poet, and I have been able to speak of her with high praise. She is a person of whom Cumberland ought to be proud, and she ought to be known more largely. The songs, " The Nabob," " The Siller Crown," " The Waefu' Heart," and " What ails this Heart o' Mine ? " are excellent. . . .

'I hope you were not quite blown away on Saturday night. The church suffered somewhat from the gale : one of the pinnacles was blown off, and only good luck saved it from going through the chancel roof. It lit on the coping-stone and slid down the slates, so that it only damaged them.'

'Embleton Vicarage : April 16, 1884.

'Dear Hodgkin,— . . . Mrs. Pease brought the Lord Mayor [1] to lunch last Saturday. He impressed me much when I got to talk with him. He plunged gaily into Popes, and the amount of genuine knowledge and real insight which he had was perfectly amazing to me. If he knows other subjects correspondingly, he is an extremely cultivated man.

To a young Friend A.B.
'Embleton Vicarage, Chathill : May 22, 1884.

'My dear ——,—I was delighted to get a letter from you ; but you need not feel guilty for your silence. In many people I should have felt hurt ; but it would never strike me to feel hurt by you, because I should always entirely trust you. I very often think of you, and always with pleasure. You are the subject of refreshing thoughts. Perhaps you will wonder why. I hope you may never have occasion to find out how full the world is of morbid people, and people who *will* make fools of themselves. Sometimes it seems to me as if the world was made up of moral invalids and moral lunatics ; and then it does me good to think of a strong, large-hearted, clear-sighted girl, who is neither affected nor moody nor distraught, but who looks at things frankly as they are, and sees the world as God saw it when it was "very good." . . . I hear of you sometimes through Miss ——, and all I hear is very nice. I wish I was going with you to the

[1] Sir Thomas Fowler.

Italian lakes. Bellagio and Lugano are the two nicest places. *Do* go to Orta if possible, and if you want a walk go some of you from Stresa over the hills. I hope you will like the Luini pictures in the church of Lugano. It is a place I love. If you go to Orta, do walk over the hills to Varallo, which has a " Monte Sacro" of the most lovely sort : it is a unique spot ; and there is a church full of pictures by Gaudenzio Ferrari, whom I love also. There, if I go on I shall write a guide-book. The only thing that bores me on the Lakes are the big hotels and the stupid people who crowd there. . . Now let me tell you something about myself. I have been made a Professor at Cambridge, and am going to leave Embleton some time this year. It is sorrowful in many ways. But I believe I shall see more of you all than if I had stayed. Somehow in the country one never sees one's neighbours whom one wants to see. When we are at Cambridge you will come and stay with us often, and I believe we shall then see you more than if we stayed here, which is one faint source of consolation.

'Don't read any more Tasso, you will die under it : Ariosto is much more amusing. There are two good Italian novelists who may be read, Verga and Barilli. I think Verga especially is really a great man, though sometimes tedious through his minuteness. I can't think how anybody can ever praise Tasso's " Gerusalemme." His prose writings, his other poems, and his letters are nice ; but his epic is most intolerable. Try Petrarch's sonnets instead. I have written so many answers to congratulations that I have become a writing machine. If my letter is very stupid, forgive me. . . .'

To a friend after a great bereavement

'Embleton Vicarage : May 6, 1884.

' I felt when you went away, that you had given me much to ponder over ; and I don't yet feel that I have pondered to much effect. You know the dreadfully practical and analytic turn of my mind, which could not work fast enough to say anything worth saying when you were here. I could only assure you mutely of my sympathy. Time after time the words recurred to my mind, " No man can deliver his brother ; so that he must let that alone for ever." All that we can do for one another is to try and get out that which is within. The reconciling words can only be spoken by oneself to oneself. I have been reading lately Delitzsch's Commentary on the Book of Job. What a splendid poem it is—so modern in sentiment, so intimate ; and Delitzsch's psychology is very delicate and profound. I can commend it to you. You will be deeply interested.

' It seems to me—forgive the impotence of the suggestion —that you need some working hypothesis of the meaning to you of the past, before you can construct a satisfactory view of the future. One's mental operations depend for their cogency upon the order of their problems. Let us class the problems roughly :

'(1) What am I ?
'(2) How have I become so ?
'(3) What am I to do henceforth ?

' I think one has to look to (2) for help in (3). A stage of development has come abruptly to an end. Can it be continued by other means, or must a new one be sought ? Is not that the hard cold way of putting your problem ? I feel as if it was dreadful even to attempt to express in the terms of cold reason such a problem. I feel as if you will resent it ; but bear with me for a moment. Feeling can only be felt, and sympathy can only be shown, by looks and manner. Reasoning about life must rest on the basis that life is a practical matter—that the soul's progress is a continued process of destruction and reconstruction. To some, disillusionment and change is gradual, and reconstruction has to go on perpetually little by little, with an uneasy consciousness of the fact. I am not sure that life as a whole is easier to them than to those who suffer under sudden demolitions ; it may not cause such pain, such necessity for sudden effort, but it is beset with greater dangers.

' Great as may be individual problems and difficulties, we must try to look on them in relation to the general life of man. Though to us they are individual, they are in their nature universal. Prostration and despair, slow recovery and growing strength, reluctant facing of the actual question and gradual reduction of it within possible limits, weary efforts towards a far-off end which at last grows more capable of realisation, all these are steps before the final triumph and the peace which follows victory.

' How dull, how obvious, how cold, how unhelpful, how brutal almost is all this ! I am ashamed to send it to you. But I will trust you to read my affection between the lines.'

To the same   ' Embleton Vicarage : May 22, 1884.

' We are still rather at cross purposes about life in general. My object in my last letter was to try and show that in matters of the soul, as in matters of the body, there are two processes : (1) to diagnose the disease ; (2) to work a cure.

I rather wanted to lead your mind from (1) to (2); but I admitted that it was much to ask, and that the process which I advocated must needs seem brutal, as all suggestions founded upon cold reasoning seem brutal to the emotions I suggested that you should keep before you, or try to put before yourself, the object of reconstructing your life. The past and the present alike get a new meaning to us as we look into the future. Our very emotions are quickened by prospect as much as by retrospect. I know that you will say, this advice is easy to give, but difficult to follow. I admit it, but I find that in all things mental the faintest recognition of a possibility, if set before oneself, tends to grow more and more.

'Your description of your ardent friend is interesting. I sympathise with you. Some people are quite intolerable to one by the way in which they insist that sympathy means looking at things as they do, without any feeling of real conviction. Now, to me sympathy means understanding other people, and acting in accordance with one's perception, though neither one's feelings nor reason may approve of their condition. An abandonment of one's personality to another makes sympathy a quite useless gift. Yet that is the sort of sympathy which people most demand. They come in a defiant way and say, "You shall feel with me : you shall tell me that my feelings are the best, the noblest, the rightest." I am afraid that I never look for more than a modified approval of my own doings. In proportion as a man is really worth consulting, he will show his appreciation of my difficulties, but will suggest, without expressing, a more excellent way in the future. But this again is cold and dull : I believe I am growing too improving.

'Yes, the Book of Job stirs one deeply. The dramatic skill with which it works out its problem is quite amazing, and the majesty of the picture is overpowering. The blundering friends who agonise the sufferer by commonplace moralities that suffering is the punishment of sin ; the noble impatience with which Job makes for them, and proudly confronts an angry God who has turned hostile to him ; the well-meant mediation of an impartial bystander, who suggests to Job that his impatience has shown that he needed chastening, and that God's justice is vindicated in the chastisement ; Job's silence before this, in which he feels some grain of truth ; all lead up to a great revelation of God's glory as the purpose of the world—a purpose in which each man bears his part in a mysterious way which God only can explain. Then finally the outward justification of the Almighty by the happy lot reserved to him who has borne the trial, through which a new

truth was given to the world, and man's spiritual being was per·
manently enriched.   It is all so ancient and yet so modern.
There are few mightier works in all literature.'

To the same   'Embleton Vicarage : July 31, 1884.

'I was not surprised by your letter.   A rumour had
reached my ears.   I had revolved the question in my mind,
and am therefore prepared to answer you at once.   The problem which is before you is one which is often brought before
many, and which it is very hard for any individual to decide
for himself, and about his answer outsiders will judge very
differently.   " Is my line practical or speculative, or both ?
How far can I combine the two ?   How far am I justified in
abandoning one for the other ? "
'But how does the matter stand with you ?   You have
not yet embarked definitely on literature, you are feeling your
way ; you have much to do to recover strength and spirits
and force, to restore yourself into unity with the ordinary
world of ordinary folk.   You know that nothing fruitful can
be done save in conscious harmony with a world that is real
to one's own mind.   You are struggling, partly consciously,
partly unconsciously, to form such a world for yourself.   Now,
without prejudice to the ultimate future, I think that for
the immediate present such work as —— would be very
useful to you.   Of course you would do it very well, and be
very interested in it.   The exercise of sympathy with other
minds which it would give you would be excellent for
you.   Everybody gains enormously in depth of thought by
actual contact with the problems of the lives of others.
Besides the knowledge which I have gained at Embleton of
the stern realities of the hard lives of common folk, I have
felt a need for refreshing myself by some knowledge of the
minds of the young.   I have grudged time given to pupils,
and have taken them sadly ; but I have always felt that they
did much for me intellectually.   They led me to see the
forms in which ideas came to others ; they taught me intellectual tolerance and breadth—lessons which I still only
imperfectly have learned.   I do not think that I am wrong if
I say that you have much to learn on these points.   Think
of —— ; how quick were his intellectual sympathies ; how
readily he entered into others' difficulties ; how he divined
the working of their minds.   The quality which was at the
root of his work was an intellectual large-heartedness,
unequalled by any other writer of the day. . . . I know that
my own literary defect is absence of these qualities.   I

regard it as a duty which lies at the bottom of all others to acquire them if I can. I think —— would do much to bring them home to you. The fact that it is not exactly what you proposed is an argument in its favour. I am always ready to submit to the consensus of others about what I am best fitted to do. The sum of the impressions which one produces on others shows what one really is : what one proposes to oneself shows what one would like to be. I think that I shall reach the second most surely by moving along the lines of the first. I believe that after a time at —— you would find yourself more ready for literary work. Then you would have to consider afresh whether you could do what you wanted to do there or not. No one knows till they have tried how a certain amount of practical, even of routine, work helps rather than hinders literary activity. It creates habits, it quickens the mind, it acts as a precipitate for thought. Ideas of study gained at night are suddenly brought into contact with some small detail in the morning. Often one smiles to find how a mighty theory crumbles at a touch. Often a fruitful conception is suggested by some trivial problem which one has to solve. I learned much history at a board of guardians.'

To Mr. J. W. Pease   'Cambridge : December 3, 1884.

'My dear Pease,—I was so much touched when you told me of the kind intentions of some of my Northumbrian friends that I could find nothing to say. My departure from Northumberland has filled me with humility when I see how much more highly people think of me than I deserve. I can never forget the kindness of many friends, whose friendship has taught me much, and whom I shall always value very highly. I feel as if no other place can be to me what Northumberland was, and I have no expectation that I shall ever again be as happy as I was at Embleton. I shall have other work to do, work which I thought it a duty to undertake, but I shall scarcely find again such warm friends or such cordial appreciation. To you and yours I can never sufficiently express my gratitude. . . . I quite appreciate the form which the kindness of my friends has taken. I will choose for myself, and tell you what I have chosen.' [1]

---

[1] This refers to a present of money given him by a number of his Northumbrian friends, with which he bought a chiming clock.

CHAPTER IX

LIFE AT CAMBRIDGE

WE settled at Cambridge in the end of November 1884. There was some difficulty in getting a suitable house, and we finally bought an ugly villa residence in Brooklands Avenue, the only house we could find large enough to contain us. Its advantage was that it was pleasantly situated among beautiful trees, and had about three-quarters of an acre of garden. It was not easy to get accustomed to the small rooms and the confined space after the large vicarage and gardens at Embleton, and it was a real deprivation to one of Creighton's hospitable instincts to have but little room for visitors ; but the house was made as pretty and comfortable as possible.

To Miss Dorothy Widdrington   'December 2, 1884.

'Yes, it was dreadful work leaving Embleton. I was surprised to find how much the people cared for me. I knew that I cared for them, but I felt as if I was useless to them, just as you say you do when you visit people ; but I found out that in the course of years I had been woven into their lives.

'We have been settling down with difficulty into a little poky house, which, however, looks habitable at last. For a fortnight we have been toiling in cold weather amid innumerable workmen, and now I find it hard to resume a regular life. People here are very friendly, and I have much to learn before I understand a new University ; but I am amazed at people's kindness. The most touching thing that has ever befallen me is the conduct of the Cambridge man who hoped to have been made Professor, when I was taken. He had for five years been preparing himself for it, and had written a book for the purpose. He is a simple student whose one aim in life it was, and who has no other prospect,

All this I did not know at the time; but he wrote to me immediately on my appointment, and I asked him to come and see me. He took to me, and has now formed a strong friendship for me. So far from bearing me a grudge, he says that my coming to Cambridge will be a greater boon to him than the Professorship. Where else are people so good and so unselfish? Still more wonderful, his wife agrees with him, and we are all fast friends.

'We are taking to dissipation, and spend our evenings in dinner parties. I have met some interesting people, especially Lord Justice Bowen and Sir Henry Maine, whose books about early society I dare say you never read. I also met Mrs. Benson, wife of the Archbishop of Canterbury, who, strange to say, is one of the wittiest and most amusing ladies I ever talked to. To-morrow I am going to London to meet at dinner Lord Acton, whom I have long been pining to see. He is a Roman Catholic, and is the most learned Englishman now alive, but he never writes anything. . . .'

Creighton went to Newcastle before Christmas to conduct the Ordination Retreat, and then came back to spend Christmas at home.

To Miss Dorothy Widdrington   'December 31, 1884.

'It seems very strange to have a Christmas without a church. But I listened on Christmas Day to one of the finest musical services in England at King's College Chapel. It is nearly perfect. Cambridge in vacation time is almost deserted, and festivities seem to have ended. I only dined out once for the last ten days. We have Miss Herbert staying with us and another young lady : I show them Cambridge. I go to the library : I get out books and read and write. My time passes quietly, and it is a great relief to me to feel that I can go on with my books and not feel that perhaps I ought to be doing something else, which always troubled me at Embleton. When I was at Newcastle the Bishop kept me hard at work. I preached seven sermons in three days. Don't you think the young men ordained must have had enough said to them in that time? I came back quite worn out.'

Creighton gave his first course of lectures as Dixie Professor in the Lent Term of 1885. It was characteristic that he treated his inaugural lecture simply as the first of the course, and made no attempt to call attention to it, nor did he publish it afterwards.[1] Writing to a friend, he says : ' I give my first lecture to-morrow, and don't know how people will take me at all. I still feel very fresh and green, and do not know what is expected of me.' The subject of his first course of lectures was ' The Struggle about Investitures.' He had already explained his views in a letter to Mr. Gwatkin.

' Embleton Vicarage : July 16, 1884.

' My dear Gwatkin,—Thank you very much for your letter, which explains your views fully. Let me explain mine, such as they are at present, though I feel they ought to be subject to modification when I am better informed.

' I do not wish *ever* to lecture directly on any period offered for examination. I should prefer to take a subject within some such period, a subject concerned with ecclesiastical history, and show its general bearing on the problems of the time. For instance, I should treat Investitures as a phase of the permanent problem of the relations of Church and State. I should deal chiefly with Hildebrand, Anselm, and the Concordat of Worms. I dare say that half my course would be devoted to England, where the condition of the Church under Rufus serves admirably to illustrate the abuses which supplied Hildebrand with his strength to protest. I dare say such a course is not needed and will meet with scanty attendance ; but I had rather have a class of two or three who were interested than a herd who were only anxious to get up enough for an examination and to be spared the trouble of reading themselves.

' I only contemplated *one* course on the Investitures, so as not to be lecturing on the period where you were. I apprehend that no one who came to the course which I have in my mind, would think himself exonerated from pursuing his period further. If I were very fortunate, I might have stirred some to want to know more about it ; but this is Utopian.

' My desire, however, is always to lecture in such a way that anybody may come if he likes, and will find a subject treated, not a period. If he is reading for an examination, it may make his own reading intelligent. If he only wants a little general knowledge, he may perhaps find it.

' Now do you think my course likely to interfere with yours ? If so, away with it, and suggest something else within the limits which I wish to observe. You see my

---

[1] It is now published in *Lectures and Addresses* (Longmans).

notion is that I want to teach Ecclesiastical History to any-body who wants to learn. I am willing to take a subject within a period prescribed for the History Tripos; but I don't want to commit myself simply to teach for that Tripos by taking a period as prescribed for examination, and above all things I don't want to derange your plans in any way.'

The moment in which Creighton began his Cambridge life was a critical one for historical study in the University. For some time a growing dissatisfaction with the regulations for the Historical Tripos had been felt by some of the leading teachers of history in the University. This Tripos had been established in 1873 under the auspices of J. R. Seeley, Regius Professor of History. It is probably true to say of both Seeley and his predecessor in the Chair, Charles Kingsley, that they were men of letters in the first place rather than historians. Seeley, in his inaugural lecture, had insisted on the principle that a knowledge of history, and especially of the most recent history, is indispensable to the politician. And with this view in his mind when the Historical Tripos was established, he infused into it a strong political element, and would have preferred to call it a Political Tripos. In 1884 letters were written to the 'Cambridge Review' by some examiners and teachers in history calling attention to the unsatisfactory character of the Tripos. It was said that its aim was prac-tical rather than scientific, that it was political and hardly more than incidentally historical, that it called few mental faculties into play, that it was no preparation for a teacher, that a student might get a first class without ever having consulted an original authority, or learnt anything of the methods of historical research. Mr. Gwatkin asked whether the only object of the Tripos need be political, 'the training of public servants for the service of the State;' whether 'there might not be room for history even as an alternative.'

Professor Seeley's answer to these criticisms was to attack the view that the nature of the historical studies in Cambridge depended on the Tripos. 'I myself,' he wrote, 'have always regarded the Tripos as a thing which does not concern me, and which might conceivably, though it has not done so, mar the effectiveness of my teaching.' Mr. G. W. Prothero's rejoinder was obvious, that, whatever a professor might do, college lecturers could not treat the Tripos as non-existent, and that it must therefore exercise an important influence on the teaching of history. He urged that the Tripos should be made either political or historical.

The indifference, if not opposition, to reform shown by Professor Seeley made the introduction of any change very difficult. He was at that time the only historical professor in the University. His brilliant gifts both as a thinker and a lecturer produced a profound impression upon those who attended his lectures. He was a most attractive teacher, who could not fail to interest and stimulate his hearers by the width and suggestiveness of his views and by his convincing generalisations. There could be no doubt about his own genuine love of learning, but his influence did not tend towards gathering a body of historical students round him or creating a scientific historical school such as had grown up round Dr. Stubbs at Oxford. This was not his aim. He wished to fit men to be statesmen and diplomatists.

It was natural that those teachers and students of history who desired reform should look with interest to the arrival of the first Dixie Professor. One of them writes :

'His inaugural lecture filled us with courage and energy. Here we at once perceived we had among us a man who was an historian to the backbone, one who regarded history as concerned with all human affairs, and who looked at all human affairs from an historical point of view ; one who realised, moreover, the difficulties and the responsibilities of those who search for truth in this wide field, and who had no *arrière-pensée* as to the possible "usefulness" of the subject.'

In his inaugural lecture Creighton dwelt on the special responsibility which he felt as the first occupant of his Chair, since he had no predecessor in whose steps he could aspire to follow or whose work he could propose to carry on. But when he turned to consider what traditions he could find in the University to guide him, he did not allude to the historical school but to the Cambridge school of theologians, 'strong in the use of the historical method. . . . They have gone far to dispel difficulties and settle problems by reducing them to definite proportions, by regarding them in strict reference to the circumstances which gave them birth. The traditions of theological learning have been thoroughly leavened by the historic spirit. . . . Theology has become historical, and does not demand that history should become theological.' He made clear his single-minded pursuit of truth. 'One point cannot be too clearly stated, though it is almost superfluous to state it, that science knows no difference of methods, and that Ecclesiastical History must be pursued in exactly the same way, and with exactly the same spirit, as any other branch of history. The aim of the investigators is simply the discovery of truth.' He defined his own conception of history. 'All differences of historical judgment resolve themselves into differences of the conception of progress. Historians mainly differ according as their conception of progress is historical or political. By a political conception I mean one which is directly derived from the political movements or political theories of the present day, which takes as its starting-point ideas which are now prevalent, or problems which are now pressing for solution. According to this view the student of history knows exactly what he wants to find in the past. He wishes to trace the development of the principles which he himself holds and which he believes to be destined to succeed. To him the past was a failure so far as it did not follow those principles. . . . He has no doubt that the perspective of the present is the true perspective, and draws the sketch according to its rules.

'The historical conception of progress is founded on historical experience of the evolution of human affairs. Its object is to understand the past as a whole, to note in every age the thing that was accomplished, the ideas which clothed themselves with power. It tries to estimate them in reference to the times in which they occurred. It knows no special sympathies, for it sees everywhere the working of great elemental forces which are common to human society at all times. It strives to weigh the problems of the past in their actual relations to their times, it tries to strip them of their accidental forms, and show their fundamental connexion not merely with present ideas, but with the process of man's development. . . . I will not defend but will only state my own preference for the historical rather than the political view

of progress. I turn to the past to learn its story without any
preconceived opinion about what that story may be. I do
not assume that one period or one line of study is more
instructive than another, but I am ready to recognise the
real identity of man's aspiration at all times. . . . Men's
minds were always active. Great struggles were always going
on. Great principles were always at stake. At some periods
it takes more care and patience to discern them than at
others.'

He did not wish to send men to study history in
order to find opinions. To him the important thing in all
methods of education was not the knowledge they supplied, but the temper they created. He goes on to say:
'A study which has for its subject-matter the experience
of the past, must beware of seeking too direct results. The
aim of all study is the education in method. It ought to
develop the power of observation rather than supply opinions.
It ought to fit the student to discern between what is
plausible and what is true. The aim of the study of
history should be the formation of a right judgment on the
great issues of human affairs. The work of the present is
carried on perforce amid the tumult of conflicting opinions.
When we stand aside and watch for a moment, it is almost
painful to observe on what a scanty fund of real knowledge
the strongest and most decided opinions are accepted and up-
held. The study of history can give no mathematical
certainty ; but it can create a sober temper, which is the
basis of all true wisdom. It can give a sense of the largeness
of problems, of their complexity, of the danger of over-haste,
of the limits of man's power over his surroundings. The
study of history rightly pursued ought to be the most useful
means of forming a capacity for dealing with affairs. It shows
us great ideas prevailing at all times ; it shows us repeated
failure to give these ideas effect; it shows the conditions
under which these ideas influenced political action : it shows
us seeming triumphs which ended in disaster : it enables us to
judge of the qualities which led to permanent achievements :
it points out the nature and limits of man's foresight. These
are the important lessons of history, and they are lessons
which may be learned from any period and from any field of

man's activity. For my own part, I think that they are best learned in periods which do not challenge direct comparison with the present. We are calmer and more impartial when the conditions of the problem are somewhat remote, when there is no danger of awakening our own feelings of partisanship.'

He went on to point out the special advantages of the study of Ecclesiastical History, and dwelt on its capacity to kindle an interest in local history, a point which he considered of great importance in inducing a man of leisure to pursue his studies in later life. ' My experience,' he said, ' has led me to the conclusion that the study of history in the Universities is useful to many different classes of minds. Some use it as a direct training for a political or administrative career, to others it gives an interest for serious reading in the intervals of a busy life, to others it has given a genuine interest in their own locality and has put them in the way of fruitful research. There is yet another class which it should be the special purpose of a University to create. I mean the class of students who devote themselves to the furtherance of knowledge.'

He concluded his lecture by a consideration of the position and work of a professor. ' It is his first duty to represent his subject, to urge its claims on attention, to do what he can to promote its study. . . . The objects which a professor might reasonably set before himself in his lectures are : first, to give a stimulus to those who are reading for examinations, so as to widen and deepen their views ; secondly, to give general instruction in such a way as to bring his subject into greater prominence and create more interest in it. . . . His ultimate object should be to catch a few who may become genuine students. . . . The highest result of a professor's labours would be the formation of a small class of those who were willing to prolong their university course, that they might study methods of research, that they might begin some work which would be capable of expansion into a worthy contribution to historical literature. There could be no part of his work more gratifying to himself than that of giving counsel and advice to such students in later years. . . . I need not say, that for this purpose a professor must be above all things a diligent student himself. Perhaps the most powerful influence that he can exert is the example of a life devoted to the pursuit of knowledge.'

Seeley and Creighton were alike powerful through the influence of such an example, but their views of history and of the place of history teaching in a university were widely different; yet, since each could see in the other a single-minded devotion to the pursuit of knowledge, the difference of their views led to no want of harmony in their intercourse. Seeley welcomed the new history professor with cordiality, and always consulted him on all points connected with their common work. Creighton valued greatly the friendship of his distinguished colleague and much enjoyed his intercourse with him.

It was in May 1885 that the Board of Historical Studies took up the question of recasting the Historical Tripos. Creighton was present at all the meetings, but, as a newcomer, and true to his habit of never thrusting himself forward, he did not take up any definite position as leader of the reforming party. Still the force of his opinions made itself felt ; he was always ready to talk over privately the questions under debate, and did much to strengthen the reformers by his advice and sympathy. In the discussions at the Board he acted chiefly as a moderator, as one who saw both sides, and tried to reconcile conflicting views and parties. Mr. G. W. Prothero says that it was largely due to his skill and influence that a satisfactory compromise was reached. Seeley also showed himself most open-minded in these discussions. The whole matter seemed to him very futile and tiresome ; he had no belief in examinations, and feared anything that might seem to increase their importance. Creighton was equally bored at such discussions, and shared Seeley's want of belief in examinations, but felt that as they had to exist it was well to make them as little harmful as possible.

In June the Board issued a report recommending the changes which had been agreed upon, and this report was adopted by the Senate in the following November. The general effect of these changes was : (1) a reduction in the number of subjects with the special view of testing more thoroughly a knowledge of original authorities and of the Constitutional History of England; and (2) the introduction of the principle of alternatives so as to enable students to give particular attention, according to their tastes, either to the theoretical or to the purely historical subjects included in the examination. These changes were fundamental and also durable, for when the Tripos was recast again in 1897 nothing was done to disturb the principles laid down in 1885.

It was also early in 1885 that the regulations for the Prince Consort and Thirlwall Historical Prizes were laid down by a syndicate of which Creighton was a member, and he was largely responsible for the permission given to students to choose, if they preferred it, their own subject for the dissertation to be sent in, rather than write on one of the set subjects. He describes some years later his satisfaction at the results of this scheme.

To Mr. R. L. Poole   'May 3, 1893.
'I can strongly recommend at Oxford a scheme which substitutes dissertations for prize essays. When I went to Cambridge, I tried to work out such a scheme; and its results exceeded my expectations.

'The principles of the plan there adopted were :

'(1) The question to be decided by the examiners was : Is this essay worth publishing?

'(2) The prize consisted in the publication of the essay by the University Press; a bronze medal was also given.

'(3) Subjects were suggested by the examiners as samples, but they were also suggested by candidates, so that practically a choice of subjects was allowed.

'I would point out one advantage of this system : it was open to students in all the various Triposes. Men interested in ancient history, in legal institutions, in ecclesiastical history for the Theological Tripos, all found a place as well as men from the History Tripos proper. It was thus a stimulus to post-graduate studies in a number of subjects, and was of weight in marking out men as suitable for fellowships. It also gave a man an opportunity to take up a line of research, just at the time when he was ripe for it. Success and criticism helped him greatly. In several cases a turn was given to a man's studies for life.'

Though, in his opinion, it was not the work of a professor definitely to lecture in preparation for examinations, Creighton was willing, after the new regulations came into force, to lecture on one of the special subjects for the Tripos. His coming to Cambridge strengthened the teaching staff so as to make these special subjects practical in a way impossible before. In the infancy of the School, there had not been sufficient trained teachers for a great variety of subjects, but his help made it just possible to provide the teaching requisite for a Tripos, for which the study of special periods in the original authorities was required. He was a regular attendant at the meetings of the Historical Board, and was particularly useful on committees appointed to select the special historical subjects and the authorities to be studied for them.[1]

The meetings of boards and syndicates were a source of weariness to him, but he did not succumb to their depressing effect, and he is said to have infected them with an atmosphere of cheerfulness. He ventured to indulge in an occasional joke, which in those days some of the older and more serious were inclined to consider a sign of frivolity; but most men were quick to see how shrewd and ready were his opinions even when coloured with what some took for frivolity, and how exceptionally prompt and acute was his knowledge of men.

One of the younger men who were associated with him regards him as pioneer of a change from the heavy and dull proceedings of University meetings to less formal ways, and says that he demonstrated by his practice that a light touch might co-exist with wisdom and weight in affairs.

He did not limit his lectures to the number required by statute, but was guided by his estimate of the needs of his subject. From the first he took a leading part in the teaching of the School. In his choice of subjects he aimed at 'kindling a greater interest in the nature and influence of the ecclesiastical organisation, when considered as a factor in European civilisation.' He desired to work rather from the historical than from the theological side, and to call attention to the importance of the ecclesiastical side of mediæval history, because, as he said, 'ecclesiastical history is concerned with the ideas round which mediæval civilisa-

[1] I am indebted to Dr. G. W. Prothero and Mr. J. R. Tanner for information about Dr. Creighton's work and influence on the Board of Historical Studies.

tion centred, and from which modern ideas took their rise. It is not too much to say that till the end of the seventeenth century, ecclesiastical history is the surest guide to the comprehension of European history as a whole.'

But he wished to approach his subject without prejudice.

'If ecclesiastical history,' he said, 'is to be studied historically, all preconceived opinions must be dismissed. The Church and the world must be studied together, in their mutual relations. All forms in which the ideas of Christianity clothed themselves must be regarded as equally important. . . . When I say that ecclesiastical history must be studied in the same way as secular history, I do not mean that the student must lay aside the belief in a Divine purpose accomplishing itself by human means. All history alike teaches that. For this very reason greater care is necessary to recover the truth. The more the study is approached with a spirit of reverence and seriousness, the less danger there ought to be of partial judgments and the blindness of partisanship. The more we appreciate the greatness of the issues, the more care ought we to take in considering them fully, in pausing before we condemn, in exercising sobriety. . . . Especially in ecclesiastical matters ought our moral standard to be lofty. All that we can do is to apply it impartially, and regulate our judgment fairly by a view of all the conditions of the time. Generally this method leaves us a sense of disappointment. Heroes are dwarfed, and great events seem robbed of their greatness. . . . But this is the first part of a process which will lead to the discovery of deeper truths. Better than hero worship is the discovery of great principles.'

In the May term of 1885 Creighton lectured on the History of the Crusades, and in the October term on the special period of the Ecclesiastical History of England appointed for the Tripos (1603-1640). In subsequent years he lectured on special periods of Ecclesiastical History, either English or general; but perhaps his most interesting courses were those on the Rise of the Mendicants, intended for advanced students, and those on the Age of Elizabeth, one of the special subjects appointed for the historical Tripos. He lectured, as a rule, twice a week, for the first few terms in the Divinity Schools, and afterwards in Emmanuel Hall. There was always a large attendance at his lectures, both of regular students for the Tripos and of the general public. Indeed, so popular did they become that it is said to have been a current joke, that if anyone happened to have a visitor upon his hands, 'he or she might be left in Creighton's lecture-room till called for.'

His method of lecturing was much the same as in his Oxford days. He spoke extempore from full notes, and would enter the lecture-room laden with ancient quartos or folios, with extracts from which he illustrated his lectures. As a rule his treatment of his subject was restrained and reserved. He did not often indulge his humour, nor let himself go in flights of eloquence. Once in beginning a lecture on the Renaissance, he said, ' It is almost impossible to talk about this subject without talking nonsense,' and then proceeded to show how well he knew how to avoid the snare. One of his pupils says : ' A curious quality of all his teaching was its vividness at the time, and the sharpness of the impression it made. I never seemed to get the same grip of any other part as I did of what I learned with him.'

The same pupil writes that he can best explain the peculiar character of his teaching by contrasting him with Seeley.

' Seeley kept before you the main lines of history, few but sharply defined ; the motives at the root of abiding national aims ; constant factors of influence ; the low beginnings, steady working out, and far-reaching effects of a policy or an idea. He suggested his conclusions rather than presented them. His argument placed you in such a position that you anticipated his conclusion. It was often so plain that you triumphantly felt that you had really thought so yourself all the time. . . . Now Creighton was the exact opposite of this. Historical characters in his hands never seemed to be in the grip of relentless circumstances, determining them to a course of action perfectly inevitable. He made you see them as men and women swayed not only by considerations of high policy, but by those commoner feelings and passions which influence the action of all human beings. He made you feel that you knew them ; you might like them, feel sorry for them, despise them, admire them, be puzzled by them, but you could not escape being interested by them. He understood men, even men from long past centuries, just as he understood the men whom he met. And himself understanding, he made you understand also. Again, where

Seeley made you fondly think that the insight was your own,
Creighton never did. There was no deception possible, the
cleverness was his. The value of his half humorous, half
serious judgments was very great. It was, so to speak, the
showman lifting the curtain with a smile and revealing the
works ; it was the conjuror pleasantly explaining how the
trick was done, and you felt you could do the trick yourself.
Of course you couldn't—you were not Creighton. But you
tried, and learned by your failure.'

He was always anxious to impress upon his hearers the
continuity of history, the truth that people in the past were
like people in the present, that nothing was inevitable ; in fact,
it has been said that ' the upshot of his teaching is that it is
all a matter of personality.' But he did not often draw
morals, he only suggested them, by making the people and
the events he described as real as the people and events of
the present day. He made his hearers see that at all times
men were essentially the same ; telling them for instance
that they ' must not think that it was so very nice in
the Mediæval Church, where there were no Dissenters ; for
if a lot of cats are tied together in one bag, they will bite
and scratch one another even more than if they are prowling
about in a room.'

Once, when speaking of the defects of the policy of Mary
Tudor, of her impatience, incapability of compromise, and
general want of balance, he said that these defects were the
result of her essentially feminine mind. One of the lady lecturers who was present felt herself bound to remonstrate with
him afterwards, because, as he was addressing a large mixed
audience, she considered that such general remarks about female
inferiority were not particularly good for the undergraduates.
I think he must have intended to show that in his search for
truth, he did not consider himself bound to respect the special
susceptibilities of any part of his audience, when in his
next lecture he insisted emphatically that the mistakes of
Cardinal Pole were due to his having an essentially clerical
mind.

His lectures on the Rise of the Mendicants were considered, by those able to appreciate them, as the most remarkable course he ever gave. They were intended for

advanced students, and contained long bibliographical lists, and much minute learning about the heresies and the charac-ter of the theological teaching which prevailed before the rise of the new orders. St. Francis held a special place in his heart. One who knew his work and teaching well says, 'He was no hero worshipper, unless his intense admira-tion for so unique and simple a character as St. Francis made him count him as such.' He said once of St. Francis, 'One man raises human nature to a level which it has never reached before. Then follow people who wear his clothes, and so you get hypocrisy.' While of St. Dominic he said, ' Dominic fades into that state of obscurity into which we are glad to see all statesmen ultimately settle down.'

Of all his lectures, those on England under Elizabeth were undoubtedly the most popular. They were repeated several times, but always with additional knowledge. It was a period in which he had long been specially interested, but he groaned over the way in which its glamour disappeared with increased knowledge. ' As for the Tudors,' he wrote, ' they are awful; I really do not think that anyone ought to read the history of the sixteenth century.' He found it difficult to untangle before a mixed audience the complicated web of motive and intrigue of an age which he felt to be more and more demoralised the better he understood it ; those whom Froude had called ' wanderers on the Spanish main,' or ' pioneers in the tangled path of discovery,' he saw to have been men who deserved no better name than buccaneer or pirate ; while with an increasing appreciation of the extraordinary ability of Elizabeth, he had a constantly diminishing opinion of her morals.

Creighton wished to get into close relations with the more serious of the historical students who attended his lectures, and to do something towards really training them in historic method ; with this object he started in the Lent Term of 1887 conversation classes both for the women students and for the undergraduates. From his first coming to Cambridge, he took much interest in the women students, and especially in Newnham College. He had already noticed with genuine appreciation the writings of Miss Alice Gardner, the historical lecturer at Newnham, and now encouraged her to come and consult him about any points connected with her own work or that of the students. His first conversation class, held at Newnham in 1885, was too large and did not answer his purposes. In 1887 he tried another experiment.

'Cambridge : January 10, 1887.

'Dear Miss Gardner,—I have a suggestion to make about a method for a conversation class. It is a system now largely adopted in Germany, and even in America. After specifying the nature of the subject and the books (which I shall do in my first lecture), let each member of your class have a subject to look up, and let her task be to give a *résumé* of the views on the books, and her opinion of what else is needed. For this purpose you may define the books to be such as are contained in your library. If a girl took six accounts, say, each of half a page, compared them, noted the points of difference, and saw why there were these different views, she would have done an exercise of ingenuity which did not tax her memory. I will talk to you about this more in detail. The Tudor period is bad partly because it is demoralising, partly because it is so large. There was a complete political, religious, social, and intellectual revolution, complicated by an admixture of foreign politics always influencing it. Each one of these divisions would be sufficient in itself : when they all come together they are awful in their unmanageableness.'

His constant effort was to make history and historical personages real. 'Which of the kings of England would you like best to take you down to dinner?' he asked his class one day. He tried hard to get the students to talk freely. After a couple of years' experience he writes to Miss Gardner again :

'I have been driven to make its object even more humble than it used to be. I tried at first to give them points to look up, and report the results of their researches. I found that this was too ambitious, and now I go through the set documents, calling attention to important points, and supplementing them by other authorities and giving them accounts of their writers ; going into details of subjects treated of in lecture, and trying above all things to get them to raise points for discussion. This is very rudimentary, and only serves to give an insight into the way that history may be studied ; but I have to be careful not to overburden them, and they are, as you know, tender plants.'

VOL. I.   U

One of those who attended his first conversation class writes :

' He always made us feel that his mind was absolutely at our disposal for the time being ; it was this that made him so ideal as a teacher. He did not try to instruct, but he helped us to draw what we could from his own stores of thought and knowledge. He used to give us a subject for study for each week, and he listened first to whatever facts we had gathered on the subject, and then showed us, or helped us to discover, what the true bearing of our facts was. The main lesson that I learned was the great value that history may have as a vehicle of education. I had certainly never realised its educational value before, but he made us see how it could train the mind to form judgments on the facts that had been gathered, and to discern the possibly immense importance of the apparently least important action. He made us feel that historical problems were after all problems of life, and that by learning how to deal with them by looking at them all round and not from one point of view only, by making sure of our facts and dealing fairly with them, we should learn also how to deal with the problems of life. He always made us feel that it was *we* who mattered. I remember his saying to me afterwards that he had always wanted to talk to us about ourselves, instead of about Elizabeth. As a matter of fact he did teach us about ourselves, by making us realise that the people of Elizabeth's day were of the same flesh and blood as ourselves. It always seemed to me that it was his wonderful intuitive sympathy with human nature that was his great power, whether in dealing with an historical problem or with a human being. We often branched off into ethical discussions. He put problems to us as to what action we would take under certain difficult circumstances, and showed us how the ordinary emotional standard was very often a false one. He was sometimes rather severe on the faults that women are prone to. I am sure those Tuesday afternoons were the great interest of the week to us, and the interest did not stop with ourselves, for the subjects and thoughts he had suggested were generally rather eagerly discussed by ourselves and our friends at Newnham afterwards, and everyone was keen to hear what he had said about them. He was always affectionately called " the Admirable " in our particular set. All that he said was so stimulating and suggestive, that it appealed especially at an age when one's great interest was in discussion and argument. I always feel that he was the only person who really taught me at Cambridge.

Other people helped us with our historical work, but he educated us as well. What surprises me so much now is the extent to which he did this in the comparatively short time we had with him—it was only, after all, one hour a week for two terms. I think it made in some ways the deepest impression of my life upon me.'

Another pupil was especially struck with his patience with mistakes, and with indifferent careless work; he was quick to discern how much real work his pupils had put into their essays.

Creighton's conversation classes for undergraduates were held in his own rooms at Emmanuel after dinner on Wednesday evenings. A conversation class was not a novelty in Cambridge. Seeley had held one for some years, but his idea of such a class was very different from Creighton's. Seeley's conversation class is thus described by Mr. J. R. Tanner: [1]

'The subject was political science studied by way of discussion, and discussion under the reverential conditions that prevailed resolved itself into question and answer—Socrates exposing the folly of the Athenians. It was mainly an exercise in the definition and scientific use of terms.'

The Professor would examine previous definitions of the term under discussion, and then 'proceed to the business of building up by a gradual process, and with the help of the class itself, a definition of his own. . . . The leisurely process had the highest educational value. It was an application to literature of the methods that are usually regarded as peculiar to science.'

Creighton in his conversation classes wanted both to make his pupils think and to train them in historical method and criticism. He believed, as he once wrote to a pupil, that 'one only begins to learn when one masters the authorities and makes up one's own opinion.' He exercised much less restraint over his own wit and love of paradox in these classes than in his lectures. His talk abounded in epigrams; he would sum up a man's character and motive in terse sentences, pointed at times with a sly allusion to modern events and modern politics. He tried to get his pupils to talk, and no

---

[1] *English Historical Review*, vol. x. p. 512.

doubt some of his more startling statements were made with the definite intention of provoking opposition.

' Sometimes,' writes a pupil, ' a dialectically minded youth, proud of his skill, would put on the gloves with his teacher. The Professor always listened ; and then came the fun.   He would question him with a certain tender irony ; then, with a mastery of facts and a dialectical skill which seemed almost superhuman, he would lay the hapless combatant out, and turn to his neighbour, almost saying, " Next, please." '

In spite of his desire to get the members of the class to talk, the impression left on them is that he did all the conversation, that they never wanted to interrupt.   One of them records :

' Master of fun as he was, he never used his power merely for paradox' sake.   These little epigrammatic phrases, which bring him back best to my mind, had always the truth in them, truth dry, or grotesque, or ironical, or topsy turvy in form, but always truth.   I find some of them in my old notebooks.

' " Not bustling politicians, nor sagacious diplomatists, nor people who talk—men of thought really influence things."

' " There is no abuse so obvious that some one will not be found to stand up for it."

' " Ideas are no use by themselves in politics—politics are a matter of organisation."

' After speaking of the hard life of students in the Middle Ages, " Nowadays we only pursue learning so far as it is compatible with our own comfort.".

' " People expect to get more out of it than there is in it, that is the reason of all failure in life."

' " Penance was the plank on which a shipwrecked man escaped."

' " Beliefs are not imposed on an unwilling people."

' " Teaching is created by popular wants."

' " There are two grand policies in the world—the Policy of Muddle and the Policy of Dawdle."

' " In the Middle Ages poverty was respected for itself : there was an aristocracy of poverty.   We are the poorer by its loss."

' After noticing the number of universities abroad in comparison with only two in England, " The English character loathes a multiplicity of ideas—so bewildering." '

Remarks like these always came out on the spur of the

moment. 'He would look up from his text and deliver them with that queer gleam in the corner of his eye that we all know.' At such classes he got to know his pupils personally. He was always quick to discern from whom he would be likely to get any response, and quick to notice any cool reception of his advances. But, to those who responded, he gave at once of his best in affection, sympathy, and interest : his relations with his own children always led him to treat other young people in a fatherly way ; that is, with a ready and easy show of affection, but with perfect equality in talk. He invited his pupils, men and women, to join him on walks.

'He was, of course, extremely easy to talk to,' says a pupil ; 'it is not always easy for an undergraduate or a young man to converse with a professor, but it was simple with him. He encouraged you to find the topic, anything on earth would do, and he always had something fresh to say on it.'

To those who asked him for advice as to their future reading or their choice of a career, he was invariably helpful. He had an unending store of subjects to suggest for research, and constantly spoke of books which needed to be written, and urged on those who had done brilliantly in their University career that this was not a reason for resting content, but a call to continuous and harder study. 'You must get an object, you must decide to write a book, for your own good, to pull yourself together,' he would say to them. Sometimes he would not rest content till the subject of the book was chosen. It did not matter if further study led to a change, if the book first planned was never carried out, so long as something else took its place. He never lost his interest in any one to whom he felt he could be of any use. 'I will not let you go,' he said to an old pupil about whose future he felt anxious. Later he wrote to the same pupil when he proposed doing University Extension work.

'Cambridge : June 21, 1889.

'I was very glad to get your letter. When I talked to you the other night I could not go beyond generalities, nor are my views of course unreasonable. I know that a man has to earn his livelihood, but I think that very often a young man beginning life does not sufficiently consider the aim of his career. It is no more necessary for a student to retire from the world than of old it was desirable for a monk. Literature and research can easily be made subsidiary to any course of life, but they drop out unless they are recognised. It is hardly worth while to take oneself as an example, but my book was mostly written in the intervals of my work as a country clergyman with a great deal to do. Further, S. R. Gardiner's books have been written in the intervals of maintaining himself and a family of seven children by teaching in London. But to do this an object is necessary and perseverance. Gardiner's first volumes brought him nothing, and did not sell. Only as he went steadily on did the importance of his writing become obvious.

' I only wanted to warn you that Extension lecturing might be a snare : (1) because it is no career ; (2) because a little knowledge goes a great way among ignorant people ; (3) because it tends to create glibness and facility in speaking which may be mistaken for more than it is worth, and leads young men to think that they are influencing the masses when they may be blind leaders of the blind. The difficulties of Extension lecturing are that you are bound to be amusing, and the temptation is to suit the prejudices of your audience. There are the same difficulties about coaching up here; it is easy to sink to the level of cooking up notebooks and dodging examiners. But salvation lies in the recognition of difficulties. . . .'

To the same, when beginning University Extension work

' Cambridge : October 14, 1890.

' I am glad to gather from your letter that you are tolerably well employed. Also that my warning about Extension lecturing has been verified to some degree by your experience. But do not imagine that the work is not worth doing : it has its use and produces its results, but its results are surest and best when one knows exactly the nature of one's occupation. If you plunge enthusiastically into the task of supplying the popular market, you lose a capacity for raising the popular standard. Give them what they want, but urge them to want something more. The object of teaching is to make all learners dissatisfied with their own attainments. If it does not produce that result, it is sophistry. To put it practically, it is possible to lecture so as to make people think what a clever fellow you are, and look on you as a kind of performing monkey ; or to make them think that you have told them all about it, and be content with that amount of knowledge ; or to stir them to learn for themselves.   Only the last is of any consequence.'

He was always on the look-out for work for his pupils, especially in editing manuscripts or looking up obscure historical points.   This was in his mind wherever he went, even in the busy years of episcopal life.   He would find manuscripts that needed editing, and spare no trouble in getting the owner's leave to publish, or in finding a journal where the paper could be printed.   But the object of all his care for his disciples was to get them to stand alone ; he insisted upon their carrying out their work in their own way, though he was always ready to criticise what they wrote, to enter into their difficulties, and use his influence on their behalf.

When a scheme for an Historical Essay Prize was started at Newnham, he interested himself much in the arrangements for it.   Miss Alice Gardner says :

' The preliminary work of choosing subjects for dissertations, specifying authorities, and settling regulations, was almost all his own.   He gave a great deal of time and thought to it, and seemed to take real pleasure in the scheme.   Moreover, year after year he read all the essays sent in, often very bulky, and awarded the prize.'

The subjects he set for historical essays were always fresh ; they pointed to the big historical quarries, which are too often neglected, and alike avoided fashionable problems and stale subjects.

Creighton rejoiced that the Dixie Professorship carried with it a Fellowship at Emmanuel, and so brought him into close relations with a college.   From the first he identified himself with the college life and interests, and was always proud to call himself an Emmanuel man.   He regularly attended the college meetings, held three or four times a term, but did not take much share in the details of business and administrative work, and occasionally felt some impatience at the amount of time devoted to them.   On matters of principle he would sometimes speak, always briefly and to the point.   His counsels were usually for moderation and compromise, but during his time no very burning questions were agitated. Once he stood alone in opposing a proposal to build a new Lecture Room from motives of economy, on a scale which he considered too mean to be consistent with the dignity of the College. His opposition was so resolute that in time he carried others with him, and saved the College from what all afterwards agreed would have been a great mistake. On another occasion he opposed on characteristic grounds, but without success, a proposal to found a Junior Students' Library for the use of undergraduates. He was jealous for the independence of the undergraduate, and thought it important that he should learn to think and act for himself, and take the trouble to economise and exercise his judgment in buying his own books, rather than have them provided for him. Though he was consulted by the Master and Fellows both then and after he left Cambridge on all important matters connected with the College, it was perhaps in its social life that he made his influence most felt. He always dined in College on Sundays, and often on other days. On Sunday the College generally assembled in force. Creighton used to bring with him any friends whom he happened to have staying with him. The large gathering in the Combination Room after dinner would be followed by a smaller gathering of smokers, generally in the rooms of Mr. Rose, the Senior Bursar. In both places Creighton was, in the words of a brother Fellow, 'a perpetual fountain of light and talk. Sometimes he would discuss questions of history, literature, and art, sometimes touch on his travels, more frequently he would talk of education and educational questions, but there was no trace of the pedant about him, and he invested everything he talked about with that peculiar attractiveness which comes from a living and overpowering interest in men and women and all that appertains to humanity. He often talked about people, but never spitefully. I never heard him say a really unkind thing about anybody. Looking back upon his life at Emmanuel, I should say that the motive, perhaps the unconscious motive, of most of his conversation was educational. He seemed to me to have a rooted distrust of that gravity and solemnity of aspect which passes for wisdom in certain circles, and showed us by his own example that it was possible to be learned and yet frivolous. Everything that he said tended to rouse us from acquiescence in the traditional, the commonplace, and the conventional. His whole life here was a sort of protest against the idea that solemnity means wisdom.'

It is clear that some were puzzled and perhaps shocked by the nature of this protest. Another of his brother Fellows writes : ' He blurted out the most outrageous paradoxes, and supported them with fantastic arguments, and defied all conventional views in a way of which no serious man would have approved. No wonder that a sober head of a college complained, " Professor Creighton is so frivolous." . . . Nowhere did he talk such nonsense as in our Combination Room on Sundays.'

Creighton was quite aware of the kind of effect he produced on some. ' People in Cambridge,' he wrote to a friend, ' are rather too serious for me : they don't often make jokes, they think it right to be very wise, and I never was wise, and I don't see any chance of becoming so in my old age.' And again, ' I still feel fearfully on my good behaviour in Cambridge. I think people look on me as a sort of strange beast. . . . I see that any approach to humour is like a slight magnetic shock to the company.' Those who saw him often soon realised how superficial his seeming frivolity was, even if it sometimes puzzled them. With Dr. Phear, the Master of Emmanuel, and Dr. Hort, its most distinguished Fellow, both men considerably older than himself and of very different temperaments, he was soon on terms of cordial friendship. ' Though Hort could not help smiling at Creighton's random words,' says a brother Fellow, ' and Creighton was at times impatient with Hort's cautious carefulness, it was very pretty to see the really friendly relations between these two, in spite of great differences of temperament and view.'

Speaking after Dr. Hort's death, Creighton said of him, ' No one impressed me more. There was no one to whom I personally owed a greater debt of gratitude than to him. He will live with me always as being one of the highest types of the academic character, as being a man of a kind whom the University ought to be especially proud to produce.'

With the Emmanuel undergraduates as a body, Creighton was not much brought into contact ; his personal relations

with undergraduates were confined to those who were reading
history, or who were the sons of friends.   He tried to see as
much of undergraduates as possible, but was inclined to think
that they were not so alert mentally or so ready to take trouble
to learn as they had been in his Oxford days.   He once
remarked to a Cambridge lecturer that it seemed to him that
the men simply stood passive as pitchers waiting till their
teachers poured knowledge into them.   The other agreed,
adding that it was even necessary first to take off the pitcher
lids.

Creighton regarded the absorbing hold that athletics had
on the time and interest of the men as responsible to a large
extent for their lack of general interest.   He had no objection
to athletics for those who took part in them, but he constantly
condemned the habit of spending hours in looking on at games,
reading newspaper accounts of them, and considering them as
the sole attractive subject of conversation.   He caused a good
deal of indignation by speaking on this subject in a sermon
in the College Chapel, when he called men to task for the
indolence which led them to crowd the football field day after
day, gaping in admiration at an exhibition of physical skill
and endurance on the part of others.   He said that in this way
they lost one of the chief educative influences of the University,
the walks and talks in which, first with one friend, then with
another, questions of conduct, philosophy, art, religion, were
discussed ; it was talks such as these that formed a man's
character and helped to determine his intellectual development

He often preached in the College Chapel.

' To my mind,' writes a brother Fellow, ' his sermons
were an important part of his work in Emmanuel.   They
always interested the men.   They were not, except on rare
occasions, elaborate efforts.   It was often said that he
must have chosen his text in the Avenue, and developed his
ideas as he walked down to College ; but there was always
something which tended to lift us out of the narrow, the dull,
the commonplace, and gave us a breath of that wider and
more invigorating atmosphere in which the student and the
thinker lives.   I remember in particular the effect which he
produced by apt quotations.   His sermons were seldom doc-
trinal, but all the more telling on that account.   They were
the sermons of a scholar and of a student of human nature,

rather than of a profound theologian. The subjects he most affected had usually an educational aspect. I have always thought that the effect caused by a Socratic discourse must have been just such as Creighton produced in his College sermons—stimulus and stir, discontentment with the obvious and the commonplace, not unmingled with a slight feeling of discomfort and distrust of the speaker himself. In particular, no man ever dwelt more on the inherent nobility of a life of study and research. His sermons always arrested attention and made men talk about them ; no one could call them dull.'

On more than one occasion Creighton preached at a Sunday evening service at Girton College which was organised by Mr. Cook, Fellow of King's College. He liked the service, and wished that something similar might be introduced at Newnham. This the authorities did not think necessary, as the situation of Newnham made it easy for such students as desired to attend churches in Cambridge. But he was anxious to do something for the religious teaching of the Newnham students. He consulted Miss Gladstone, then head of one of the Halls

'Worcester : September 15, 1885.

'My dear Miss Gladstone,—I did not expect to hear from you about my Newnham proposal. I was merely ready to do what you bade me do, if anything, when term began.

'I certainly intended, when I made my offer, that whatever I did should be of a kind that would injure no one's conscience. I purposed some course of instructions in the Scriptures, with applications to conduct. I should naturally begin and end each address with prayer, and I presume that a few collects from the Prayer Book would be unobjectionable. I should be glad if a hymn or two were sung. Now suppose I were to suggest that I should take as my subject St. Paul's Epistles to the Corinthians ; they are interesting ; they are full of historical instruction ; they raise questions which are suggestive of large principles of conduct at every turn. Suppose I first explained the meaning fully, giving differences of opinion as in duty bound, and then considered briefly the practical application—I suggest this method as likely to supply the needs of many. I think that very many girls are very ignorant of the meaning of the Epistles, but are interested when once started.

'By all means let it be for a term at first ; let the students at the end of the term express their opinions about its usefulness: let them submit any suggestions to me which they think necessary.

'Please assure Miss Clough that I will do nothing which in any way contravenes the character of Newnham as an undenominational establishment, and that after a term's experiment I shall not be at all hurt if she decides that my class had better be discontinued.'

Miss Gladstone writes:

'The audience was at first very large, but partly consisted of those who only meant to come occasionally, and others who came to see what it was like. A good number came throughout the first term, and the addresses were certainly much appreciated, so I asked him to continue next term. The second term the audience was smaller, so that I did not think we ought to ask him to continue to take so much trouble. It is a considerable effort to students to give time regularly for what is not their special work.'

In many ways Creighton showed a special interest in Newnham, and entered into close and helpful relations with the College and its authorities, so that, Miss Alice Gardner says, 'we felt as if we had more of a share of him than any but his own College, Emmanuel.' He had a great admiration for the Principal, Miss Clough, and after her death spoke with warmth of 'the rare beauty of her temper, and the grace of her character.'

Though we came as almost complete strangers to Cambridge, in such a sociable place it did not take long to get into friendly relations with the majority of the university people. Like everyone else we dined out a great deal, and gave many little dinners in return. My husband grumbled at the interruption to his work, but enjoyed the dinners when he was once there. We walked when the weather was not too wet, even when the distance was considerable; and during the walks home, which were enlivened in the spring by concerts of nightingales, he enjoyed talking over, always in a kindly, sympathetic way, the people we had met.

'The impression produced by Dr. Creighton on Cambridge society,' writes a friend, 'was that of stimulating power. This quality showed itself in many ways, sometimes by a conversation in which he would develop his views on some subject, or book, or person, or occasionally by a certain paradoxical treatment of the same topics, or perhaps by a somewhat Socratic questioning by which he endeavoured to ascertain, or rather to make the other persons ascertain, what they thought, and why they thought it. In his social relations with others there was constantly present this solvent power, by which assertions or beliefs were tested and traced to their source. Consequently he often puzzled those who were not conversant with his method, and who saw with perplexity all the ordinary views and statements questioned and apparently upset. When, however, he was treating any subject from his own point of view, he possessed the rare power of developing his own opinions without haranguing, so that people came away from listening to him both with new ideas imparted by him, and with their minds stimulated by the manner in which they had been imparted. He was never, under any circumstances, in the background ; tire or worry or uncongenial company never made him silent, though they may sometimes have increased his love for paradox, but they left his conversational powers and the influence of his personality untouched. If people knew they were to meet him, they might rejoice or they might be alarmed, but they could not be indifferent.'

Dr. Verrall writes :

'There was beyond doubt a very general and rapid conviction that the new Professor was a man to be counted with. If one had with him five minutes' talk upon any subject of public interest, one got something definite, not so much a formal doctrine or theory of the matter, as a view of the agents and interests actually at work in the particular case ; especially about the agents, the personal forces. He always seemed to me to be strangely and most effectively frank in the expression of his opinions about men, what they were likely to effect in a given direction, or as to the amount of power in them generally. He estimated, or at least that was my opinion, persons as instruments in a large work, whom it would be absurd to represent as having more force than they actually had. Cambridge society in general was always a little afraid of him. I myself was always disposed to mind what he said, and not be more foolish than I could help when he was present. If one made mistakes, he let one know quite clearly, and it did not hurt, because he gave the sense that one was being measured and weighed for practical purposes, with which a desire to " score " or to " hit " could not possibly be connected. I do think that he was severe, beneficently severe, and the severity seemed to be guided by a large purpose. He made people ask themselves how much work for public and social purposes really was got out of them, and not confuse the estimate, if they could help it, by irrelevant likings and dislikings. How he did this I cannot describe, but that he did it I cannot doubt. His manner was light, and seemed to remind the hearer that he was only receiving a personal opinion ; and the wording, though admirably exact, rather avoided than sought what is generally called " brilliance." But for this very reason perhaps, because *something* had evidently been studied, and that something was not the making of a point, one had a vivid sense of reality. This was at least an opinion, the real and considered judgment of one mind. Of course he could also play, and play amusingly, with ideas and language. He was very enjoyable in this vein, and sometimes perfectly enjoyable. But I thought it always a little dangerous, much as I relished it. When he did not mean to be serious, his fear of being misunderstood (so it seemed to me) made him tend to extreme audacity, as if to say, " Now, that you must see to be nonsense." The danger was that sometimes people did not see all the same ; and yet he did not, speaking generally, displease even those whom he evidently puzzled. I have never quite understood how this was. He was bracing ; to consider what he would say or think of a problem helped to keep me up to the mark. He was very good for us, as Cambridge men. To forget the end of study in the means, to lose sight of the large connexion of things, is, I suppose, the defect of our quality. His large outlook and practical measure was an excellent corrective. I go back to the soundness of his estimate of men, their force, the stuff in them, and their possible utility to the world. He spoke often about individuals and freely ; he tended to severity ; yet no one could conceivably charge him either with frivolity or with malice.'

Creighton was always interested in discussing the character and capacities of those whom he came across. His judicial estimate of the intellect and capability of his friends did not at all interfere with his affection for them. He was under no illusion as to the deficiencies and weaknesses even of those nearest and dearest to him. He had no desire to idealise his friends, he took them for what they were, it was they themselves that attracted and interested him ; but his love for them did not prevent his passing a severe judgment on them if he felt it called for. There was never any inquisitiveness or malice in his talk, it was not the small affairs and doings of people that interested him, but their characters, and, especially as he became more and more concerned with affairs, their capacities. He was unwilling to believe evil of anybody, and would not listen to malicious stories. I never knew him to express strong dislike except in the case of one lady, whom he had had to take in to dinner twice. He said that he could not stand her malicious tongue and uncharitable insinuations, and that if he were asked to take her in to dinner again, he should really have to refuse.

Creighton did not allow himself to be immersed in university business. The only two Syndicates on which he served were the Library and the Press, in the work of which he was naturally much interested. He spent the time not occupied with his professorial duties at work either in his own study or at the University Library. He enjoyed much the freedom allowed to students in the Cambridge Library, and made great friends with the three eminent men who successively filled the post of librarian during his day. He gladly seized every opportunity of helping any one whom he met in the Library. Miss Gardner writes : ' If a hesitating, puzzled student came his way in the University Library, which he seemed to haunt, a strong arm would lift out the books she wanted, place them where she could read them, perhaps turn over the pages to find what she wanted.'

In the afternoon, whenever he was free, he walked with me and his children. He liked to go out with as many of them as possible. True to his principles, he did not send his boys away to school young, and would gladly have sent them to a day school had the circumstances of our life allowed it. They were educated at home till they went to Marlborough at the age of twelve. So during our early years at Cambridge we had a lively party of six children at home, and Creighton enjoyed to the full not only the companionship of his own children, but that of their friends. All young people were dear to him. On Saturdays he often made expeditions into the surrounding country, and especially devoted himself to a study of the beautiful churches which adorn the eastern counties. He attended with much interest a course of lectures given by Professor Middleton on the development of

church architecture, and used to make notes and rough drawings of any striking points in the churches he visited.   Some
of his pupils or friends were generally his companions on
these walks, which were as a rule as yet beyond the walking
powers of his children.   Mr. Townsend Warner writes of them :

‘ They nearly always took the form of going to some small
place by rail and walking across country to another railway
station.   He used particularly to visit the church in each
village.   He was annoyed when it was locked, but used to
send me to the rectory for the key, because, as he explained,
“ If he sees *you*, he won’t come out ; if he does me, he will.”   I
learned from him the habit of always going first to the parish
church. “ Never say there is nothing to see in a place,” was one
of his maxims on these occasions ; and another, “ Always trespass until you are turned out.”   A third was “ to talk to the
natives.”   He used to hammer into me the necessity of learning foreign languages while travelling, by walking and talking
to everyone I met.   He did it himself, I know, with the
invariable preface of the offer of a cigarette.   There was a
Spartan simplicity about these excursions : lunch generally
eaten on the tramp : water from a pump, usually drunk out
of the brim of his soft clerical hat : a grand reconnoitring of a
suitable place for tea if there was time before the train went
home : what he liked was an old-fashioned inn, the less pretentious the better.’

Newnham and Girton pupils were also sometimes invited
to accompany him on these walks ; and he arranged several
summer excursions for large numbers of the women students
to places of interest.   He took them to Ely, to Audley End,
and to Hinchinbrooke.

‘ These were very delightful occasions.   He always seemed
at his happiest and his best in the open air, and his quick eye
and lucid utterance enabled his hearers to see the importance
of architectural and topographical points which the ordinary
tourist commonly fails to notice.’ [1]

‘ He had a remarkable power for quickly grasping the
topography of a place and holding it clearly in his mind.
In a church he would so quickly seize upon and point out
the more remarkable and unusual features, that you seemed
to learn more in half an hour with him than a very prolonged
search would be likely to give you without the help of such
quick and ready insight and observation.’ [2]

---

[1] Miss Alice Gardner.   [2] Rev. A. Rose.

CHAPTER X

THE WORCESTER CANONRY

THOUGH Creighton had never been an active party politician, he was much disturbed at the condition of political parties in the winter of 1884–85, when the capture of Khartoum and the distracted condition of Ireland produced such deep uneasiness, and men seemed to look in vain to Mr. Gladstone for wise and determined leadership. Sir Edward Grey had just decided to offer himself as Liberal candidate for the Berwick division.

'Cambridge: January 22, 1885.

'Dear Edward,— . . . I am glad to hear of your political intentions. It will be a great thing to fight Percy, and will cover you with glory.

'It is difficult to foresee the result of the enlargement of the constituency at first; but if you win against Percy, you will have won a big event and will be a marked person. Use your time in making up your mind about questions, so that you do not show yourself weak-kneed. There is a great temptation to candidates to say things they do not quite mean, and then disappoint their constituents by hedging. It is far the best to make up your mind what you are going to hold to definitely, on what points you are ready to be better informed, and what points you genuinely consider as immaterial and are prepared to do what is wanted. It is a good thing to have these three categories quite prepared.'

'Cambridge: February 14, 1885.

'Dear Edward,—Politics are in a perfectly deplorable condition—not so much for the difficulties which they present, but because they reveal such an entire want of statesmanship. The policy of dawdle, the policy of sentiment, the policy of good intentions without definite purpose, has long gone on. For my own part, I am rather glad that its results have been made apparent. Anything is good that compels us to make a decision and get out of the slipshod way in which we have been feebly drifting. But I doubt whether Gladstone has the wisdom and the courage to come to a clear decision on our national business as a whole. He is a good hand at mending details ; but he lives for the time entirely in the question of detail which most interests him. He does not take a clear view of national affairs all together, and only feels aggrieved when unexpected things turn up. . . . The course of the next election is difficult to foresee at present. The future will belong to the man who can put forward a strong and intelligible policy. I think the country will wake up to the need of that. Imperial policy will drive home affairs into a corner. What are your views about land ? It seems to me that the great principle is that landlords have public duties, and must act in accordance with public needs. Their rights must be limited by the public good. This is a moral principle of universal application : its details may be a matter of dispute.'

'Cambridge : March 18.

'You are beginning to experience that dubious pleasure of public life, perpetual misrepresentation. The more you do, the more enemies you raise. The more you say, the more chances you give them of setting you in a false light. It is the way of the world. One has to learn to grow case-hardened. Success in life is to the thick of skin.'

'Cambridge : June 3, 1885.

'Dear Edward,—I have read your address to the electors. . . . Old folks cannot judge of young folks ; but I did not approve of it, and if I were a voter for North Northumberland, I am not sure that I could vote for you on the strength of it. But then I have not seen the others, and probably I would not be able to vote at all. I find I am relapsing into an impracticable politician, whereat I grieve. The times are too fast for me, and politics are degenerating into a game of brag which has no interest for one who wishes our national welfare. A cricket match is better fun to look at than the debates in the House, and is more healthy for those engaged.

'I have just risen from reading Auberon Herbert's letter in the " Times." I find that I mostly agree with it. We live in a day of political phrases without meaning. Have you read Sir Henry Maine's article on " The Age of Progress " in the April " Quarterly " ? If not, do so ; Maine is as qualified as any living man to express political wisdom.

'The fault that I have to find is, that everybody is concerned with proposing legislative changes of no importance, and no one cares for capable administration and wise states-manship. These things made England, and they are becoming lost arts. If the coming democracy is going to turn Parliament into a large vestry, if reforms of the House of Lords, and Disestablishment of the Church, are to be the objects of legislative energy, the future can only be disastrous. England is in difficulties in every part of her Empire : she is isolated in Europe, she is neither liked nor trusted. The democracy must be told these things till it has grasped them. It will not save its Indian Empire by reforming the House of Lords. We shall have nothing but disaster in the future unless we learn wisdom.

'There, I have bored you enough. I am a befogged old fogey.'

'Cambridge : June 26, 1885.

' Politics grow worse and worse—really everything seems to be at stake, nothing more so than the future of Parliamentary Government as a whole. If England grows dissatisfied with it, it is in a bad way. It is growing increasingly difficult to see how government is to be carried on by means of a parliamentary system. That seems to me to be the great question of the future, and I incline to think that Home Rule for Ireland, Scotland, Wales, and England North and South, is a plan which will deal with Ireland, with County Government, and all kinds of other questions at once. Then an Imperial Council might include colonial representatives and get rid of Federation as well.

' I commend this to you as a plan to expose to your future constituents. They would think you were crazy.'

'Examination Schools, Oxford : July 1.

' My dear Edward,—I dare say by this time your candidature has been agreed upon. If so, go at it.

' It is quite true that politics is a practical pursuit. There are only some things possible to do. But none the less ought one to have a definite ideal, and definite opinions and definite knowledge.

' Physiology is a science. I hope that my doctor knows it, and all its cognate sciences. But I call in my doctor on general grounds—people speak well of him, he is a clever fellow, a nice fellow, has good manners, is cheerful, &c. &c. So stands a candidate to his constituency. He is chosen on general grounds ; but he is needed for a very important service. He is chosen by those who are incapable of grasping his real knowledge ; still that knowledge is required.

' But if my doctor came to me and said, " How do you feel

to-day ? " and I said, "Better," and he answered, " Then you are better," I should be surprised, and begin to distrust.   Suppose he said, " Tell me what medicine you would like to take, and I will write a prescription," I should know that he was an impostor.   Many doctors make large fortunes for a time on that stock in trade : ultimately they are found out.

'Almost all politicians have that stock in trade, and no more.   They say, " Tell us what you want, and we will do it." Of course, if the people want anything decidedly they are sure to have it, for the simple reason that they are strong enough to take it.   But the duty of a politician is to educate the people, not to obey them.   No man ought to go into politics without a clear conception that there is a sphere in which he can work, and there is a point where he is not going to advance.   All men must be prepared to make sacrifices for their country.   One of the greatest sacrifices is to be ready if need be to sacrifice prospects rather than lose one's self-respect—to abandon a possible career rather than listen to the *civium ardor prava jubentium.*

'Forgive my twaddle, and believe me
                    ' Your always affectionate
                              ' M. CREIGHTON.'

In the Easter Vacation we went for a short walking tour in Norfolk, putting up at small country inns, and spending the days in walking and inspecting every object of interest on our way.

To Dr. Hodgkin   'Cambridge : April 23, 1885.

' I was just meditating a letter to you when yours arrived. I had been having a week's ramble in Norfolk after my fashion, and was impressed by Roman remains at Burgh Castle near Yarmouth.   I think you once spoke about them, and said you had not seen them : perhaps you have paid them a visit since.   Their interest lay in the general view they gave of the Roman occupation.   The rivers Yare and Eure roll sluggishly to the sea through a district that in old days must have been a swamp always covered with water. Where the land begins to rise and was inhabitable the Romans built their fort at Burgh.   It is a mighty building of flint and Roman tiles : interesting as showing how the Romans used the material to hand, but made it stable by mixing their own.   The flint is secured at intervals by layers of tiles, and so has stood.   The monastic buildings and castles of the neighbourhood, built of flint faced with stones, are now shapeless masses of ruins. When the stone facings of the doors and windows were taken away the whole thing disappeared quickly. The Roman tiles have held their walls together. The station at Burgh was a hill rising straight from the swamp. The side towards the swamp was left unwalled ; it was protected by its position. The walls on the other three sides enclose a square. But the walls are strengthened as I never saw elsewhere, by huge circular bastions, at regular intervals, one at each corner, one in the middle of each side. They are solid, and seem built only for strength to the wall. There at Burgh the Romans were on the highest point in the neighbourhood, and could command sea and land alike. On the north, where the estuary ceased and dry land began to rise timidly, is a Roman camp at Caister, with earthworks. Between these two points has risen the modern Yarmouth on what was originally a sandbank, but has been gradually heightened. The whole place was very suggestive of the past.

' I have been writing like a guide-book, and perhaps telling you what you already know. . . .'

Creighton was Examiner in the Oxford History Schools, and this made the May Term very busy. It was in the press of examination work at Oxford that he received a letter from Mr. Gladstone, offering him a Canonry at Worcester.

To Mr. M. Gwatkin   ' University College, Oxford : June 12, 1885

' On Wednesday I received a letter which took me away by an early train on Thursday morning. . . . The letter was from Gladstone, offering me a Canonry at Worcester. I went to look, and have accepted. It does not, however, take me away from Cambridge in term time, but gives me a country residence in Vacation. . . . All things seem to come upon me at once, more than I desire or deserve. The result of my promotion will be for a year or two pecuniary ruin, but that must be faced.

' Where are you ? I wish I was with you. I go back home to-morrow, carrying vast masses of examination papers.'

At first Creighton hardly welcomed the idea of the Canonry. He did not yet feel settled at Cambridge, and the thought of another change and new responsibilities was rather overwhelming ; but a visit to Worcester made him look at things differently. He was delighted with the place and with the beautiful house attached to his canonry ; but he had a little anxiety lest residence in a cathedral body should involve him in squabbles and animosities such as sometimes prevail in those quarters. The only canon he found at home was old Canon Wood, who had been William IV.'s tutor, and had been appointed to his canonry before Creighton was born ; and in the course of his inquiries Creighton quite horrified the courtly old gentleman by saying that he had been offered a canonry, and wished before accepting it to know whether the members of the chapter quarrelled ; because if so, nothing could induce him to come. 'Quarrel !' was the answer ; 'what put such an idea into your head?' Creighton replied that, unfortunately, he was aware of some chapters where harmony did not prevail. The look on Canon Wood's face carried even more conviction than his words, and later experience most fully confirmed the truth of his assurance. Another doubt was whether the duties of a Canon would be compatible with the duties of a University Professor. Here the friendly help of Canon Melville made the way easy. He always arranged his own residence so as to be able to exchange with Creighton when necessary, and allow him to get in his three months' residence in vacation.

Creighton's first residence was fixed for the coming September. After he had finished his work as Examiner at Oxford, he stayed a short while in London in order to work at the British Museum, and then we paid a visit to Northumberland, while our Worcester house was being got ready. It stood at the entrance of the precincts, or College as it is called at Worcester, a red brick Queen Anne house, comfortable and spacious, with a small garden inclosed by the walls of the Cathedral and the graceful red sandstone arches of the ruined Guesten Hall of the Abbey. On September 2 Creighton could already write to a friend, 'I like Worcester, and I love the Cathedral.' It was an intense joy to him to live under the shadow of the Cathedral, and every day it grew dearer to him as his loving study discovered new beauties in it. Worcester Cathedral cannot claim to be one of the most beautiful among the great English cathedrals, but it is full of charm and of very special beauty in details. Moreover, not only is it very well adapted for use, but it is used in every possible way, and is a real centre for the religious life of the town. Creighton learnt to know every stone of the Cathedral, and, so far as it could be discovered, every detail of its history. He never tired of showing it to his friends, and each time the inspection lasted longer, for, as he constantly learned more about the Cathedral, he always had more to tell. He was ready at all times to take round parties of excursionists from the neighbouring towns, and other bodies of visitors, whether learned or ignorant. He loved every part of his connexion with the Cathedral, the daily services, the care of the fabric, the association with the staff and the choristers. The choristers lived in a house immediately opposite ours, to which no playground was attached. Dr. Butler, Creighton's predecessor, had allowed them the use of his tennis ground, a lawn lying immediately under his study windows. Creighton continued the permission, and there outside his study windows, the boys spent most of their play hours. He liked the sense of their neighbourhood, and used to say that it was pleasant to hear their voices as he worked, and that he never overheard a bad word of any kind.

The chapter received us in the kindest possible way. Lord Alwyne Compton was then Dean, and the other canons were, Wood, Melville, and Knox Little. Lord Alwyne Compton became Bishop of Ely in 1886, and was succeeded by Dr. Gott, and Mr. Wood died in the same year and was succeeded by Canon Claughton. The nature of the social life of the College showed how completely happy can be the relations of a cathedral body. There were many young people among us, and our doors always stood open to one another. We used to say that at night it was necessary to sort the children, to be sure that the right ones were in their own homes. When Canon Knox Little was in residence, he seldom failed to come over and smoke his last pipe with us, or to send for us to go and spend the warm summer nights on his charming terrace overhanging the Severn. Then questions of every kind, art, literature, religion, and politics were discussed to the accompaniment of much tobacco smoke and the two canons, so dissimilar in temperament and in many of their opinions, learnt from the first to love and respect one another.

Canon Melville, a much older man, of decidedly academic interests, welcomed Creighton from the first as a man with whom he had much in common. He was a splendid old man, more than six feet tall, with a fine keen face, and though he was growing very deaf, his bright eyes saw and noticed everything and forgot nothing. Many a morning after service might Creighton and he be seen pacing the College Green together, discussing educational or political questions, interspersed with many jokes and much laughter.

The only fault that Creighton found with a canon's life was its liability to constant interruptions. He said that the fact that everyone knew that he would be found at home after Matins, made those who had nothing else to do ready to drop in upon him for five minutes' talk. His study looked out on to the College Green, and his head could be seen through the window as he sat at his writing table. 'I shall have to put up a notice,' he said, 'that it is not fair to shoot a canon sitting.' Those who interrupted him always received such a pleasant greeting, that they never realised how much they were disturbing his work. The country round Worcester was delightful for walking. He always went out between lunch and Evensong at 4.15, and, till he had learnt the district, many were the desperate races he had to get back in time from a ramble which had unexpectedly led him too far.

The custom at Worcester was for the canons in residence to preach at the Sunday evening service in the nave of the Cathedral, and an immense crowd assembled to hear Creighton's first sermon on September 6. He preached on a favourite subject, David's heroism as a shepherd boy, the result of his belief that God was 'a living God.' He pointed out the unconsciousness of David's, as of all true heroism, and how it showed itself in entire simplicity of character and singleness of aim, the two qualities on which strength of character mainly rests.

His preaching was from the first much appreciated at Worcester. The cathedral staff was strong in preachers. Canon Knox Little no doubt was the most popular, but the congregations were always large, and it was said that even the factory girls had their favourite preacher among the canons. At any rate, as they differed in gifts and intellectual qualities, so each appealed to a certain extent to different minds. Creighton once said to Dr. Gott, 'You are the mystical one among us, Knox Little the eloquent, Melville the learned, and I am the practical.' A citizen, who always frequented the Cathedral, speaks thus of Creighton's preaching :

'The essential feature of his sermons was lucidity. Although dealing with the greatest mysteries of our Faith, his expositions were such as might be followed by any intelligent youth. No tricks of voice or manner were allowed to take the attention away from the subject-matter; the earnestness of the teacher swallowed up the elocutionist, but did not check real eloquence, if that word may be taken to mean the ready choice of the fittest word to express the desired idea. Indeed, the flow of admirably selected words might be taken as the second great characteristic of his preaching. Never at a loss, never needlessly repeating, always with some definite object in view, and without any apparent assistance from notes, Creighton drew his hearers along with him to his goal, and left the desired impression printed on their minds. He was not a preacher to please those who go to have their ears tickled. He never treated the pulpit as a place to enhance the popularity of the man; he scorned the extraneous aids by which poor matter may be made to pass muster for oratory.'

These Worcester sermons were entirely extempore, and no record of them remains beyond a few brief notes on half-sheets of paper. Probably they were the best he ever preached, with the exception of the carefully written sermons preached at different times before the Universities. He had time to prepare, he was living in a sympathetic atmosphere, and preaching in a building where everything combined to elevate thought. The sight of the vast congregation in itself was a stimulus. The Cathedral is perfect for sound, and Creighton made himself heard in every corner without difficulty; the special tones of his clear and musical voice seemed to be admirably in tune with the building. During each residence, he generally chose a special subject for his course of sermons. Perhaps the most remarkable course he ever preached was on the different revelations of God, in art, in nature, in history, and in man.

His ideas about the influence of a cathedral were expressed in a paper read at the Exeter Church Congress in 1894.

' I am afraid that there sometimes exists a kind of jealousy of the cathedral in the mind of the parish priest, who complains that popular services in the afternoon or evening have the effect of detaching congregations from their own parish church. Now, everyone will sympathise with a clergyman's desire to see his church filled with a regular and devout congregation ; but I think that this praiseworthy result must be attained by his own zeal and fervour rather than by the removal of competition. Granted that some prefer to go to the cathedral, there are others who go nowhere. What he loses at the top he can replace at the bottom. . . . Further, cathedrals have functions of their own just because they are not parochial. Many who are feeling their way from Nonconformity or from indifference, who wish vaguely to know what is to be said in favour of religion, or in favour of the Church, will go to a cathedral when they would feel that their presence in a parish church would be interpreted to mean more than they were prepared at the time to admit. It is the curious feature of cathedral congregations that they consist partly of cultivated and devout Church people, who are aided by the cumulative impressiveness of the place, and partly of the vaguely inquisitive.'

He insisted that there should be a distinctive difference between the cathedral and the parish church.

' The cathedral ought not, even in its popular services, to be merely a glorified parish church. It should seek to discover how it can best supplement parochial activity. . . . In many cases the cathedral and the parochial clergy might co-operate for special services. That every parish should have its own courses of addresses in Advent, Lent, and Holy Week seems to me to be needless. . . . Why should not a cathedral supply the needs of a given area, and the parochial clergy take counsel with the cathedral clergy about the arrangements ? Such services gain by a large congregation, and still more by the performance of really great music. The man who has not heard, say, Bach's Passion Music, or even Allegri's " Miserere," has still much to learn.'

These last words show how much he appreciated the great musical services held at special seasons in Worcester Cathedral. He did not try to interfere in details of cathedral management, but when possible he urged that the older English Church music should be more often given, and grieved at the preference shown for what he called the modern sentimentalists. He dwelt on the value of the example of the cathedral services to the Diocese as a whole.

'The ideal of Anglican worship—catholic, dignified, simple, free from sensuous excitement, appealing to the whole man, to the head as well as to the heart, quietly stimulating and invigorating, without calling for undue effort, fostering reflection and gradually heightening the spiritual consciousness; this is expressed and cherished in the historic services of the cathedral. They set forth in an artistic form the ideal of the English Church—the noblest because the largest, the simplest, the most refined, and the most spiritual ideal of worship that has been systematised by any branch of the Catholic Church.'

Worcester is no sleepy country town. It contains a great variety of manufactories, among which the china works and the various glove factories are best known; and it lies in the centre of a beautiful and well-inhabited district. With all the varied life around it the Cathedral stood in close connexion. The chapter and the city were on the best of terms, and in all matters of educational and philanthropic concern the help of the chapter was freely claimed and liberally given.

The first public meeting at Worcester in which Creighton took part was that in aid of the Worcester Diocesan Penitentiary Association on September 26. This was work in which so far he had been called to take little active share, but from this time onwards he took a deep interest in it. Speaking on this occasion, he said :

'We cannot have our moral sense stirred to pity, and then simply rest content with that pity, without evil results. Acts of Parliament cannot work a radical reformation; all they can do is to register a higher moral standard, but the mere registration effects no practical purpose.'

He dwelt upon the disadvantage of penitentiaries being allowed to depend too much on the earnings of the inmates.

'No institution of a reformatory description can be considered to be on a satisfactory basis unless it is free to consider what can best be done for the immediate interests of those whose recovery it aims at, and is not primarily obliged to choose work because it is remunerative.'

Speaking in the following year for the same object, he urged that the scope of the Association should be extended to include more preventive work, and that a Vigilance Committee should be started. He described a penitentiary as 'a mute protest, silent and humble, against the thoughtlessness, the frivolity, the want of self-restraint, the wickedness of mankind.'

In October, Creighton attended the Church Congress at Portsmouth, and read a paper on the Teaching Work of the Church. He pointed out how great were the opportunities for teaching possessed by the clergy, and pleaded that room should be found for a variety of subjects within the scope of their teaching, especially for Ecclesiastical History. He said :

'I have no particular dread of the tendencies of the present day as being more dangerous than the tendencies of any previous time ; but every time has its weaknesses and its dangers, though it is perhaps presumptuous to attempt to weigh those among which we live. The dangers of the present day do not so much spring from ignorance as from half knowledge. Every man thinks himself bound to have an opinion on every subject, and every man's opinion is weighty. . . . The dangers of half knowledge, of over haste and want of sober judgment, beset a clergyman as much as anyone else. The nature of his work and calling does not in itself raise him above the general whirl of the world around him. . . . Some course of study is needed as a mental discipline. If fewer schemes were started, and they were twice as wise, the world would be better off. The man who is too busy to find time to read anything not absolutely necessary, would discover that if he saved half an hour a day for study and reflection, with the purpose of self-discipline, his practical work would gain in efficiency, and his arrows, instead of being shot vaguely in the air, would hit some definite mark.'

He himself used every opportunity to teach. During his next residence, being asked to address the Young Men's Christian Association, he spoke to them about Anselm. As usual, he made his hearers feel the close connexion between the past and the present.

'There is no more common delusion than that we live in days such as have never been in the world before, but history teaches us that all days are pretty much the same; at all times there are great problems to be solved, great dangers which seem imminent, and great difficulties which require the united strength and firmness, and above all the wisdom and sobriety of thought, of all men.'

He naturally took special interest in the King's School, which was domiciled under the shadow of the Cathedral, and used the splendid old refectory of the Abbey as its big schoolroom. Its head master, the Rev. E. Bolland, had been his pupil at Merton College, and Creighton did all in his power to help him to make the school really effective. At the Christmas prize-giving he expressed strongly his views in favour of day schools.

'It is lucky for Worcester to have a school to which its children can go without interrupting home influences. Nothing would induce me to send a child to a boarding school if I could get a good education elsewhere. My ideal of a complete educational organisation would be, that within a radius of ten miles there should be a first-class school, to which people could send their children, so that they might return home every day.'

The time given to Worcester was not limited to the three months of compulsory residence. We always spent the vacations there, leaving Cambridge with our whole family and household as soon as term was over. Thus we had to change homes six times in every year; organisation and habit made the move rapid and simple, and by the evening of the day of transit, we were always completely settled down. But the double life was exacting in its claims; duties, interests, charities, social calls, were all doubled. Creighton wrote to a friend in November 1885:

'I enjoy my work at Worcester much. It is a lovely place and a lovely cathedral, with a great deal going on, and a good deal of intelligence. We are just starting Extension Lectures there, and have on hand a scheme of technical education. I am kept very busy here and there : in fact, I grow busier and busier, so that I scarcely know where to turn.'

It was sometimes tiring to come from the strain of a Cambridge term to pick up without any pause all the threads of the full Worcester life. Creighton, however, was thoroughly interested in both lives, and rejoiced that while Cambridge supplied a sphere for his more purely intellectual activities, at Worcester he was part of such an effective organisation for spiritual work as the Cathedral. But just as he was always ready to help in every possible way the work of the Church in Cambridge, so he was keen to stimulate the intellectual life of Worcester.

In July 1886, he began an evening course of lectures on Church History in the Chapter House, and so long as he remained Canon, he continued these lectures during his summer months of residence. They were from the first much appreciated, and were always well attended. He began with the History of the Cathedral, and in the last lecture he gave on September 30, 1890, had reached the period immediately before the Reformation. At the last lecture in 1886 a vote of thanks to him was seconded by a Nonconformist minister, a regular attendant at the lectures, who spoke of the high esteem in which he was held by those outside his communion. In these lectures he made no parade of learning, and interspersed the easy flow of his narrative with many spicy anecdotes, so as to keep alive the interest of his hearers. But anyone who knew could see to how much research even these popular lectures testified, for the kind of facts which he handled so familiarly could only be learnt by exploring original authorities. The continuity of history, its use in aiding the formation of a right judgment on present affairs, was constantly brought home to his hearers ; but he impressed upon them in the first lecture that he went to history simply to find the facts, and not to illustrate any theories or opinions which he might entertain, though he would sometimes point out where what had happened in the past threw light on the questions of the present.

Speaking of how the Church had aided the State in the

days of Stephen, when the country had got into a condition from which there seemed no escape, he said that such a contingency might arise again. This was one of the strongest reasons against disestablishment.

'It would destroy an organisation the importance of which only those could understand who had meditated on the general lines of English history, an organisation identical with the national life, representing the national life as it is and as it might be, and showing itself at a crisis a very great safeguard. The Church can do work which the State cannot do, and untie knots which the State cannot untie.'

In another lecture he instanced the enormous popularity of Thomas Becket immediately after his death as 'a fact worth considering in days when it was supposed that popular opinion was always right. Thomas was certainly not the wisest and most admirable of men, though the popular opinion of Europe voted so, and went on voting so for a couple of centuries; popular opinion was not only wrong in its estimate of the man, but was in absolute ignorance about his policy. . . . Thomas by his action broke up the reforming party which had been making for a revival of the Church of England on a definite spiritual basis. Like all short-sighted politicians, he won the point he aimed at, which was not worth fighting for, staked everything upon it, and the Church lost all along the line.'

He made his audience feel that the characters he handled were real human beings, speaking for instance of Edward I. as more often right than anyone he had met with in English history. Suggestive remarks abounded in the lectures. For example: 'As soon as Wiclif entered into the politics of the day, the value of his previous writings was blemished: he was an example of the evil arising from mixing up higher work with politics.'

Another time he said: 'The Franciscan movement, by elevating poverty into a merit, staved off revolution from Europe for a long time;' and again he spoke of 'that great revolution which we call the Reformation,' and of the moral of the period between 1300-1500 being 'the danger of putting off reformation, since reform deferred necessarily leads to revolution.'

LETTERS 1885–1886

To Mrs. J. R. Thursfield   'Cambridge: February 27, 1885.

'My dear Emily,—I was very sorry for the news of your letter this morning, though from Dick's account when I was with you I had small hopes of the ultimate future of your father's illness. I deeply feel for Mrs. Herbert and for all of you; it is heartrending work to watch the slow ebb of vigorous life, especially when the sufferer is unconscious. But I find myself, year by year, growing less and less sorrowful for those who pass away. My pity solely is for the blank they leave in the lives of others. I have no feeling of sadness for the life that ends, whenever and however it ends. More and more I feel that this world has no measure for the preciousness of an individual soul. All that a man is, he is to himself and God. His work is in himself; all else is accidental. Life seems to me to consist in *becoming* more than in *being*, and in *being* rather than *doing*. I should wish for my own part to pass away while I was still active, and to leave to others the memory of myself at my best, before bodily frailty had dimmed my mind or wasted my faculties. The slow decay of old age is the saddest sight there is. . . . I need not send you any messages of comfort. I know that you all will be strong and comfort one another.

'God bless you, and tell Mrs. Herbert that she and all of you will have my prayers.'

To the same   'Cambridge: March 12, 1885.

'My dear Emily,—I waited a day before writing to you, because I thought that you would get many letters of sympathy at once. I wanted to sympathise with the second thoughts, not with the first thoughts, of sorrow. At first the blow falls and we have to face it, everyone as best he may, and no one else knows the secret of another's strength. But it is soothing, after the first grief is past, to think that the memories which are awakened in one's own heart are shared by others. Men are gathered to their fathers, but their influence is even stronger when they are gone. I often meditate on the profound meaning of the words, " It is expedient for you that I go away." Even Jesus felt that His bodily presence obscured and made more difficult the meaning of His message. Not till all earthly memorial was departed, not till the soul received the Spirit of their Lord while the eye no longer saw the body, not till then was the message of the Life understood. So it is always. Clearer and more distinct grow the lineaments of a character when the outward form has departed. Louder speaks the voice which is heard only by the inward ear.

'I know how you are all recalling to one another and to yourselves the lessons of the vanished life. How cheerful he was, how diligent : how love for knowledge and love for man went hand in hand and grew together : how tenderness and sympathy grew with advancing years : how he loved you and laboured for you : how others respected him for his simple unaffected goodness. I knew him only little personally, but I knew him much through all of you. To me too he is a memory and a pattern, and I share with you in gathering up for my own profit the fruits of his well-spent life.'

To a young Friend, A. B.   'Cambridge : February 1, 1885.

'I have the greatest sympathy with all your difficulties and feelings. I think I understand them. I have long thought that no class is really more neglected than girls developing into womanhood. Their minds are active : they think, and they want to act. But what are they to do? Boys go away from home—have interests and careers of their own. It is regarded as natural that a girl should belong to her home, make herself generally agreeable, and wait to get married. I don't say that it should be otherwise, but I think that it ought to be generally known that her task is a very difficult one. It is very hard to live at home, however happy the home may be. It is hard to find any expression for the strong individual life which rises in the heart. It is hard to express oneself at home. One has grown up there naturally, life goes on from day to day ; . . . there are no crises, nothing to call for notice. It is hard to find a place for oneself, duties for oneself to do. Parents are very good, very thoughtful, very kind ; but one wants more than that. It is hard to pass from feeling towards them as parents, to feeling towards them as friends. How few parents really know their daughters, invite or receive their confidence. I simply notice the fact. I do not see any remedy except greater frankness. I do not know that when my time comes I shall succeed better than other people ; but I admit the problem. I think one great thing is to cultivate a capacity for natural and spontaneous affection. It is the only way of breaking down the barriers of habit. Sometimes one must run at people and insist on telling them one's inmost thoughts, whatever they may think of it. . . . But I wanted you to think about your parents and their views. What are your parents to do? They want to do for you all that they can. They want to give you a full opportunity of seeing what the world is. Are they wrong in that, even if you do not care about it? I do not think so. No parents like so to behave that their children in after life may say or think, " You kept me in ignorance : you kept me shut up : you did not show me the world. I made a wrong choice because I did not know the facts." Your parents wish you to see the world, and see what you think of it. What you do, what you make of your experience, that is left to yourself. Everybody has to judge for themselves. The greatest step one has to make in life is to realise one's own responsibility. One begins life by having everything done for one. Everything is arranged. One has to learn that one's soul is one's own, that one's life is in one's own hands. To settle the question one needs experience. Therefore I say be glad to get it, and look out for it wherever you go. The end of life is happiness, and happiness lies in the contentment of one's nature. One begins by wanting too much : one has to learn what one can get, and one has to settle how one can best get it. Here am I quite content to read books, to get knowledge where I can, to try and make it useful to others in any way I can. That is what I have learned on the subject. It is a very small line, but it satisfies me. Everybody has to learn what will satisfy them. But no amount of outward things will give satisfaction, no mere shows, no things that do not last. Look at all the people you come across : ask yourself what they are doing, what they are aiming at, how they are trying to satisfy themselves. Then say, " Will these things do for *me* ? " Don't do like other people if that won't satisfy you. Be true to yourself. I would not say this to everybody ; but you have a self which is precious.'

'Cambridge : April 3, 1885.

' You must remember that there is no greater failure than a manner which means nothing and is only on the outside. *You* can no more make a manner than you can fly. Manner is only the expression of character, and it owes its charm entirely to that fact. Now you have plenty of character of your own ; . . . but you have not been much encouraged to show it, and you do not think it worth while. The only thing that I can say is, that it is worth while showing it. Really the object of life, so far as society goes, is to *be* something and to make what one is effective. This requires practice : it requires sympathy with those one is speaking to : it needs curiosity to see what they are. The beginning of a conversation is like fishing, you make a few throws to see if you can hook a fish. When you have hooked him the sport begins. I mean you try to find out vaguely at first the character and interests of the person you are talking to. When you have found out something in common with yourself, you want to know all about it. So, beginning with general things, you find out a point of interest ; then by frankness on your part you encourage frankness on the other, and try to find something which carries the matter further on. But remember that the only two things engaged are your character and another character. Until these two are laid alongside one another, the conversation is a failure.'

'Cambridge : May 14, 1885.

' I am always giving you horribly wise advice. I think you will soon vote me an intolerable old bore. . . . The chief danger that I see in store for you is a tendency to grow cynical without knowing it. There is a certain amount of cynicism in all of us, but it has to be checked by other things. I suppose that cynicism is natural to one who observes the current of life without plunging into it. People seem to strive after such little things, to waste their energies over what profits not, to do little acts of meanness, to try and show themselves something that they are not. . . . You are yourself straightforward, and therefore see the weaknesses of others. It is well to do so, but there is need of something to make one's observation useful. What is needed is sympathy. We should all of us try to feel something of the Divine love towards man, in spite of his weaknesses. " Men my brothers " should be a thought constantly before us. I freely admit that what is called " society " is a sore trial to one's charity. The failings of the natural man are not so revolting as the meannesses of the cultivated and pretentious world. The empty head and the cold heart are unpleasant to see ; yet most heads are not entirely empty, and most hearts are not entirely cold. There is often a great deal of mute misery concealed under an affectation of frivolity. One can try to understand and help all sorts of people, and no one is quite hopeless. All answer in some degree to a call to them to bring out the best that is in them. You never know what you may do if to your observation you add a readiness of sympathy. Therefore I say, do not only look at people from the outside, but try to understand them from the inside.'

To the same on her engagement to be married

'The College, Worcester : September 2, 1885.

'. . . Yes, you have found out what I tried to lead you to discover, that the joy of life lies in self-knowledge, and that love is the one key to that knowledge. Only through and by love does one take possession of the world which is one's heritage. The love of parents, the love of friends, the love of married life, the love of God—all are but steps in one great process whereby one wins oneself. But the love of lovers is the central point in which this is clearly manifest. It comes suddenly, abruptly, it is overwhelming and complete : it has to pass on to something less dazzling but more permanent, less splendid but more useful—to the large-eyed steadfast love that will bear the wear and tear of common life. " They married and lived happily ever after " ends the ordinary novel. " Did they ? what extraordinary people ! " is the comment of common sense. Marriage is the beginning, not the end, of real life. The time of engagement is a merciful preparation in which knowledge grows by instinct—knowledge of self, knowledge of others, knowledge of the world, of life, of duty. Yet knowledge comes not with austere looks, needing no toil for its attainment, but comes in a golden haze of glory and flashes full into the soul.

'All that you say is true, true to the utmost. . . . One thing only let me say, the truth of which I have profoundly felt, and feel more and more day by day : the love which does not increase in both the love of God—that does not blend with our highest feelings of reverence and quicken them and sweep us upward, humbled yet satisfied with our humility— the love which does not do this falls short of that completeness which is the guarantee of its eternity.

'There, I am nothing if not instructive. Forgive me. You know as well as I do ; but my heart is very full whenever I think of you both, and I take an elder's privilege of looking onwards.'

To another young Friend, C. D.   'Cambridge : July 1, 1885.

'The great danger of the present day is the confusion of knowledge and feeling. It marks our politics, which are sentimental and not sensible ; it marks our views about everything. Let us feel by all means, feel deeply and strongly —then let us think wisely and act soberly. It is the habit to think that strong feeling covers everything else. Not so—it is a stimulus, and as such ought to do much for us ; but we must work it out in patient resolute action.'

'Worcester : September 2, 1885.

'. . . Let me at once say why I do not think that Ruskin's "Political Economy" is good food for you. I think that one of the nuisances of the present day is the attempted revival of the "prophet." Carlyle, Froude, Ruskin, all bore me in their prophetic capacity. It is a cheap line to denounce, it satisfies the sense that something ought to be done : I am weary of denunciation. We of this generation all go about the world each abusing everybody else, and each forgetting to amend himself. The world's evils are many and patent. We can all do much to cure them, "here a little and there a little," but do not let us expend our energy in meaningless abuse. Mankind will not be saved by that. I remember listening with sorrow to Ruskin describing a railway journey from Carnforth to Oxford. He ridiculed everyone whom he had seen, described his fellow passengers without a touch of sympathy, and ended by saying, "I saw over 700 people on the way, and not one face had a look of happiness." I looked at Ruskin's own face : that certainly had not. I should have liked to ask him what contribution he had tried to make to the happiness of those whom he met. Did he expend a smile, a kind word ? No ; I respect Ruskin's goodness, but his method is disastrous. The times do not want a Hebrew prophet denouncing woe : they want the spirit of loving sympathy. How large-hearted was Jesus, how sober-minded, how "sweetly reasonable" as M. Arnold puts it. Teacher for teacher, there is more in M. Arnold than in Ruskin. Both are one-sided, both omit much, but the spirit, the tone of M. Arnold is fruitful, while that of Ruskin (save in art) is not.

'But this is a matter of opinion. All things are good that teach us ; but we must recognise that our teaching is gradual, and that teaching is best for us which leads us to some definite object of pursuit. However, let me make one remark. It is not the task of a young girl to sound human misery and to put all things right. Too many girls nowadays think so, and act in a way disastrous to themselves. They ruin their nervous power early in life. . . . I know that it is almost impossible to induce a woman to recognise the limits of her physical powers. But please do not let your mind prey on your body just now. There is a future in which much may be done : resolve to spend the next three years quietly in study, in reflection, in gaining experience of life, in feeling your strength, in training your forces. . . . Do not feel any constraining necessity to do anything in particular just yet. Concentrate yourself upon a subject sometimes, then expand and dip into all sorts of other things. Decision will come with fullness. But take things easily for a time. Think that you have time on your side. All that you learn, all impressions you obtain, will be useful. Take them, and let them sort themselves for a time. Different minds move differently. . . . Let your chief pleasure be in curiosity : be ready to feel and learn. Do not trouble to sort and arrange your gleanings just yet.'

'Cambridge : November 1, 1885.

'I scarcely know what to say to you, because I do not want you to think that I am unsympathetic, but I think all the same that you are not quite going in the right way. You have a touch of the *maladie du siècle*, which I fear is not to be cured by advice. But I know that you will let me give you mine, the more so because it is not definite advice, but rather general considerations.

'I see how you are and what you feel : you want to have room to develop in, and quietness for the purpose. In this you are quite right. But you think that the requisite room has a local habitation if it could only be discovered ; and that quietness also is to be found somewhere or other. Let me use the language of Jesus : " If any man shall say to you, Lo, here is Christ, or lo, there, go not after him. The kingdom of God is within you." It is most profoundly true : all development is from within, and for the most part is independent of outward circumstances.

'One part of the training of life is to learn *how* to go one's own way quietly, wherever one is. Listen to people, but pay no heed to what does not approve itself to you (I include myself and my present letter). Perhaps you would say that you had that faculty. I know that you have, and you tend to fill up your time with dreaming, while you wait for the moving of the waters. You feel that this is rather unsatisfactory, and you wish to turn your dreamings to account by pursuing the lines to which they lead you. Now will that really help you ? I only ask, I do not answer the question. No one can do more for another than suggest the real issue. . . . My advice always has been, Get method : only through this comes practical strength. Get it by patient study of anything that requires accurate thinking and clear expression. It matters not what : learn to read and understand a Greek play if you will. I know that this prospect only fills you with shivering. You would like something more congenial, more in accordance with yourself. But *self* is a shifting quantity, and every step in development has to be by the loss (often with pain and grief) of a smaller self to gain a larger. Growth is a painful process at some stages, but it is pleasant in its results, and the stock of pleasure goes on increasing, and the pang becomes less every stage we consciously pass through.'

'Cambridge : November 6, 1885.

' Will you believe that my interest in you is for yourself alone, and that when I write, I write just such thoughts as are suggested to me by looking back on my own past and what I know of that of others ? I know how hard is the process of realising one's own responsibility, of undertaking the conscious duty of moulding one's own life and character. I know that each one has to judge and decide for himself, and that the words of others seem cold and far off, mere hollow echoes of the past. I know that the thoughts, the hopes, the fears, which beset you are beyond words. . . . In fear and trembling must each man work out his own salvation—not unaided, but in solitude. You have gone into an intellectual retreat ; I doubt not that it was well for you so to do. In quietness and confidence possess your strength.

' Therefore go on and prosper, and take my blessing on your efforts. I do not want to advise you or lecture you. I only want to tell you that I feel for you and with you. Ask me anything that I can tell you : forgive me when I answer wide of the mark : do not suspect me of misjudging you : regard me as often blundering and clumsy, but never unkind. Make such use of me as you will, and think that my only wish is to be of service, but I cannot [count] my usefulness as much, and I do not think that I know everything or can decide any question with certainty. I only hold to the seriousness of the issues of life, and the grave importance of the crisis, which all go through, in which character is made.'

'Worcester : January 15, 1886.

'. . . One of the great things to learn in life is one's own individuality, one's own separate responsibility. It is not a nice thing to learn. It is more pleasant to live among others, to think of oneself as part of a circle, acting upon and being acted upon by a definite number of permanent associates chosen by oneself. But life is not so. One stands alone, and one's acts must be thought of in reference to all the cold dull world around one.'

Cambridge : June 2, 1886.

' You utter the cry which goes up constantly from every believing soul. It seems to me that the great difference

between the Christian and the unbeliever is this : the unbeliever says that he cannot lay hold of God, and so believes
in himself only.   The Christian in proportion as he lays hold
of God cannot believe in himself.   Now the highest point of
the Christian character is that in which we attain forgetfulness
of self and act simply as God's creatures.   Such is the temper
seen in St. Paul and St. John very clearly.   But this self-
forgetfulness is the fruit of a long process of training in trust
in God.   To you and me the pain of life lies in the perpetual
contrast between the aspiration of our spirit and the poor
realisation of our actual life.   It is no wonder that people
have tried at many times to simplify the problem—that
they have sought a special form of life in which they might
be free from ordinary temptations, the monastery, the
brotherhood, the ascetic practice ; but all in vain, for the
difficulty lay not without, but within—not in the world,
but in their own heart.   The means of self-discipline lie
round every path ; the temptations to self-seeking beset
every career : no life is in itself more spiritual than any
other.   We have to transform our natural life, and one form
of it is the same as another.   "First that which is natural,
then that which is spiritual," such is the law.   I often think
that we fail because we do not sufficiently grasp how that
process is carried on.   Just now we are reminded clearly
enough.   The Holy Spirit is sent by our Ascended Lord to
carry into the lives of believers the principle of the life of
Christ.   "Send Thy Spirit to fashion my heart like Thine."
That is the essential part of prayer for ourselves, and in the
light of that our inner life becomes intelligible.   We are like
children : who can say how a child grows or learns ?   Yet
we see the result of growth and wisdom.   Day by day we teach,
and are disappointed at the stupidity and forgetfulness of
our pupils : yet they learn each according to the measure of
their capacity.   So is it with our spiritual lives : if we submit
ourselves to the Spirit's guidance, we grow and we learn : we
cannot take stock of it ; it is not well to do so ; but we waste
our energies if we sit down to complain.   Let us be more submissive, more earnest to learn, more ready to do, and the
light will grow clearer before us.   I do not like to think of
my life as my own choosing.   I do the things that come, and
try to learn their lessons.   I know my faults, my failings, my
weaknesses : they only teach me more the duty of submission : all I can do after a consciousness of wandering is to
return ashamed and seek for guidance afresh.'

To Dr. Hodgkin   'Cambridge : January 27, 1885.

'Dear Hodgkin,—The " Deutsche Rundschau " for February publishes in advance the chapter on Britain from Mommsen's forthcoming volume of his Roman History. It is a masterly condensation of all sound learning on the subject. It delights me to find that he has come to the conclusion, which I ventured to hint at in my paper to the Archæological Society, that the Roman wall was not strictly a frontier defence at all, but that the Roman border was all the land between the Forth and the Tyne. This view makes its building by Hadrian intelligible. The forts of Agricola were scattered over the north, and the work of Antoninus Pius, strengthened by Severus, made Agricola's northern rampart tenable. He has a note about the evidence. Pius is said to have made a *murus cespiticius*.[1] Severus is said by Victor to have made a wall 132 miles : 132 is a mistake of the manuscript for thirty-two miles, which agrees with the forty miles of Pius' work. I commend the article to you very much. . . .

' Yours ever,
' M. Creighton.'

To Miss Ella Pease   'January 23, 1886.

'I greatly doubt if before our own age we have any letters which were absolutely written without thought of publication. You mention Byron rightly as the first of a new kind of letters. I doubt whether in old times a collection could have been made without the knowledge of the writer : even Cicero must have known. There is a kind of mind which is common to literary men, and says, " The more that is known about me the better. Men misjudge my actions : they will think better of me if they see me as I really was : if they read my confessions." I doubt if collections were made in old times by gathering letters together from those who received them : they are collections of copies kept by the writer and meant to serve as a sort of diary. They must all be judged by a literary standard, and we must not flatter ourselves that we get more behind the scenes than we are meant to get. Moreover in times when letter writing was less common, it was more formal. . . . The commonness of letters is the best security for their frankness. I have so many letters to read of my own that I never want to read those addressed to others : therefore letters are written intimately as not likely to go beyond those to whom they are

---

[1] A wall made of turf.

addressed.   But a man in India writes home once a month
and knows that his letter will be passed round amongst his
family ; that is a very different affair and involves a conscious
literary effort.   *All* letters before the penny post were like
letters from the Colonies now.   Now we write for one person
only and go straight to the point : of old, letters were written
to an unknown and indeterminate audience, and therefore
were necessarily literary. . . . Have you ever looked at
Sydney Smith's letters?   They would make you roar. . . .
It seems to me, however, that Madame de Sévigné stands
far ahead of anyone else.'

To Mrs. J. R. Green   'The College, Worcester.
    'Dear Mrs. Green,—I send you some aphorisms which
may serve to indicate the outlines of a mental attitude, which
is so critical that it criticises even criticism itself, and tries to
see "our noisy lives as moments in the silence of the Eternal
Being."
                          'Yours affectionately,
                              'M. CREIGHTON.

    'Historical criticism is not a science : it is only an investi-
gation of the value of evidence.
    'It rests on presumptions which are derived from ex-
perience.   I am disposed to believe what is analogous to my
experience : my criticism is awakened by what is not
analogous.
    'The destructive criticism of the New Testament rests on
the presupposition that miracles do not happen.
    'As the writers of the New Testament record miracles, it is
necessary to explain how those records came into being.
    'A number of ingenious and plausible theories about their
date and authorship and gradual growth have consequently
been formed.
    'Their number and persistency seem to add to their force.
    'You say, "Why are they not refuted?"
    'The only possible refutation is to show that apart from
the presupposition on which they rest, their conclusions are
not capable of positive proof.
    'How are those who believe that Shakespeare wrote the
plays attributed to him to refute the ingenious theories of the
Baconians?   They simply answer that the presupposition of

the Baconians does not affect them sufficiently to make them abandon the historical tradition.

'The object of Christian belief is the Person of the Lord Jesus Christ.

'The record of that Person has been transmitted by human agency.

'God's revelation was the Person.

'Scripture is not the revelation, but only the record of the revelation.

'The nature of the record and the means of its formation is a worthy object of human research : much light has been thrown upon it by criticism.

'But the less we make of the record, the more marvellous becomes the Person recorded.

'The acceptance of evolution only explains, but does not overthrow, the Divine creation of the world to the religious mind.

'The establishment of an irrefutable explanation of the formation of the New Testament would not overthrow to a religious mind the doctrine of the Person of Christ.

'The miracles connected with that Person are analogous to the spiritual experience of the believing Christian.

'Therefore he is not moved by the presupposition that they are contrary to nature.

'The real question in dispute is the conception of *nature*.

'Biblical criticism will not solve that question'

To Dr. Hodgkin

About his edition of the Letters of Cassiodorus.

'Cambridge : June 10, 1886.

'Dear Hodgkin,—Thank you very much for "Cassiodorus," which I have just found time to look into. It is an excellent piece of work of a kind which is rare in England. I very much hope that your example may spread to others. I remember talking to dear Bradshaw about your plan some time before his death. He was much interested purely as a librarian, and said that all the collections of letters of medieval times needed such work before they were available. Really the only other attempt I know of the same kind is that of Voigt, who dealt with the letters of Æneas Sylvius, and whose labours were of incalculable use to me in writing my Popes.

'As editor of the " Hist. Rev." I see many signs of the interest which your book is creating. . . . So that you are the cause of energy in others. They all begin, " After reading Mr. Hodgkin's book I was struck, &c." This is the highest compliment you could receive. . . .

'I had Albert Grey on Saturday, who predicted then a majority of thirty.[1] I am very glad that we have reached a point when a decision must be made, but I cannot approve of the statesmanship which has inconsiderately caused the crisis. Nor do I see that the crisis will be ended except by great efforts on all sides. We must all try to be as sane as we can according to our lights.'

[1] This refers to the impending general election.

CHAPTER XI

THE 'ENGLISH HISTORICAL REVIEW'

EARLY in 1885 Creighton was invited to dine at Dr. James Bryce's house to discuss the possibility of starting an English Historical Review. Lord Acton, Dean Church, Dr. A. W. Ward, and Mr. York Powell were also present. This project had been debated for nearly twenty years. J. R. Green had agitated for it with Bryce and Freeman in 1867. Macmillan had been consulted as publisher, and Stubbs had been thought of as editor. Later on, it was suggested that Green himself should be editor, but difficulties always arose, and the Review was not started. Now Creighton was surprised to find a general wish expressed that, could such a Review be started, he should be editor. This was sure to entail much difficult and anxious work, but he felt that the Review would advance the study of history at home, and promote intercourse between English, American, and foreign students, and that if he was considered the right man to start it by those whose judgment he could trust, he must do his best. Messrs. Longman were suggested as publishers, and Creighton at once communicated with them on the subject.

To Mr. York Powell   'May 11, 1885.

'His [Mr. C. J. Longman's] answer is better than I expected. It is very much better that he should undertake it. If he cannot float it, no one can. . . . I will edit for nothing, to start the concern, for a year. . . . Of course we might get articles gratis at first, but no one should be asked to write without some remuneration being offered.'

Mr. R. L. Poole accepted the post of sub-editor, and the first necessary business of drawing up a prospectus and getting a representative list of supporters was rapidly proceeded with.

To R. L. Poole   'June 12, 1885.

'I have just this morning got Longman's authorisation to
say that the Review will be published by him. . . . I think
that now we had better get on as fast as possible.'

'June 20.

'Send out prospectus and ask for help widely. . . . Let
us now go on *fast*, as fast as possible. . . . Please keep a
note of all arrangements promised. Records in books are a
great saving of time and order.'

To C. J. Longman   'June 20, 1885.

'You will have received the prospectus of the "Historical
Review" by this post. . . . I think that if you make known
your wish, books will flow in. I only wanted to emphasise
the *foreign* books about which English students need information and which are hard to get. The next thing which
we propose to do is to get promises of help from all who are
likely to help.'

'August 5, 1885.

'I wished to report progress about the "Historical Review."
All that has been done is very favourable to its success.
Everybody who has been applied to is ready to help. I can
count upon a staff, more or less regular, which includes
practically everybody who is worth having. As helpers by
their counsel and warm co-operation, I have Dean Church,
Bryce, Seeley, Robertson Smith, S. R. Gardiner, R. Garnett,
A. W. Ward, Freeman, and Lord Acton. The last especially
is most helpful through his learning, which is probably greater
than that of any other Englishman now alive. . . . I have
been surprised to find how warmly the project is greeted. I
think I can promise you that the experiment will be tried
under circumstances and conditions as favourable as the
present state of historical research in England allows of.'

To Lord Acton   'Cambridge : July 28, 1885.

'My dear Lord Acton,—Your letter was a great relief to
me. The assurance of your hearty co-operation gives me
hope of the success of the Review which I had not felt before.
We must confess that we are not strong in historical method
in England. Our work has all the advantages and all the
disadvantages of amateur work. Most of the well-known
persons have already said all that they have to say. You are
one of the very few persons who can add any novelty. You

are the only person who has a knowledge of the general European literature of the subject. The impression left upon my mind by our conference at Bryce's was that you were the only person who had a clear notion of the scope and object of our undertaking and of the difficulties which an editor would have to face. I only warn you that you must not be too kind to me, or you will find me taking an unfair advantage of your kindness and troubling you by requests for advice.

'The subjects you propose—the Catholic negotiations before the Civil War, and the Conclave of 1550—are both excellent. I have no fear of the Conclave seeming polemical. Notes and quotations would certainly be necessary for an original article. We need not support everything by a reference after the elaborate German fashion, but quotations are always necessary for anything that is meant for scholars. . . .

'Correspondence in the case of such a review would tend to fall under two heads : (1) queries ; (2) corrections of articles or remonstrances from reviewed. I think, as things are at present in England, that queries probably deserve a place or would fulfil a useful purpose. Men might raise a question, or point out a difficulty, or make a suggestion, but this must be on strictly historical subjects, and I should like it to take the form of notes rather than of letters. The second head of remonstrances or controversy I should like to be sparing in admitting. Some points are cleared up by an argument carried on by advocates ; but I should use my discretion sparingly in allowing such points : they must be important, and must require special competence. Ordinary remonstrances are better met by a private correspondence carried on through the editor, and he might, if he thought fit, redact a memorandum at the end which he should submit to both parties before publishing. Does that seem to you right ?

'The last point that you raise is valuable. A conspectus of similar reviews, with some account of what they have done, would be most useful, but no one could do it except yourself. Would you do it . . . for our first number ? Would you add to it your advice about our future ? Again I apologise for asking. It would be the best possible introduction that we could have : do not dismiss the suggestion.'

To the same   'Fallodon : August 6, 1885.

'. . . Your advice is indeed most valuable, and my own deficiencies for the post of editor are many. I have lived long in the country away from books, and only able to pick up such as I actually needed. I have no thorough knowledge of history as a whole. I have always been busied with many things, and have had no opportunities of becoming a thorough student. I am at present more busy than ever. I only undertook the office of editor because I saw no one obvious who could or would give to it his whole time and attention. My only hope is to overcome some of the initial difficulties, and find as soon as possible some one to relieve me. Your ungrudging help is the greatest possible encouragement. Now I will not thank you any more, but will take your help with a constant gratitude.

'Your proposal of a letter to the editor setting forth briefly what other reviews there are, and what is their public, and what are your hopes about an English Review, seems to me to be an excellent form for an introduction to take. It was quite clear to me that an attempt to issue an editorial programme would be a mistake. We have not sufficient agreement about the method and scope of history. Freeman and Seeley may appear side by side, but I could not draw up a detailed prospectus in which they could both agree. The editor must keep open house, and let in all recognised historical students, and make as much room as possible. But a sketch of possibilities from a well-wisher outside would be acceptable to everyone, and would do much to make the lines clear for the future. Of course we are very insular ; that is a fact which strikes me in every English book ; a correlation of ourselves with other nations would be of the greatest value, and you would do it lightly and with brevity, which would mean much to those who chose to understand. Therefore I entirely favour your suggestion.

' . . . The student and the general reader are hard to combine. The student wants to know about foreign books, the general reader has no interest in them at all. Moreover, there is the publisher's question. English publishers demand notices of their books, advertisements depend upon that, and we have our publisher to consider. You must pardon me if you think sometimes that trifling English books exclude good German books. An editor must be also a man of business—more is the pity. I am also hampered at first by want of funds. If German publishers will not send their books, I cannot ask a man to get a book and review it for nothing. Publishers do not rise much to a prospectus ; they want to see a magazine in the flesh, or in the paper, before they believe in its reality. . . . I agree with you that our motto ought to be, " One man, one book to review " but at first this is difficult from the reasons

I have mentioned.   Church is too busy to write.   B. F. Dunelm says it is quite impossible, . . . so too Stubbs.   I will pester Stubbs some more, for I think he ought to write something, at all events just once.   Really busy men dislike putting pen to paper, and if they do so at all would rather write an article than a review. . . .   What I feel generally is that the success of the Review at first will depend on its articles.   If it succeeds at all, the organisation of the review and notes departments will have to be thoroughly looked to ; but I have no hope of getting that done before starting.   It will get gradually into shape, because I think that I have fairly good material in many departments.   But in most cases there is a preliminary languor to be overcome.   Nothing succeeds in England like success ; if the Review gets on its feet, the scholars will be glad to write in it.   At first we must trust to the energy of a few who are determined. . . . Your ideal list of contributors opens up a splendid prospect. Most of them have in some shape promised.   Many addresses are difficult to find.   The saddest thing is that almost everybody who undertakes to write to some whom he knows, fails to do so or forgets to forward the answer.

'I am going to venture to write to Döllinger : will you support me ?   I hear that he is very indignant with John Inglesant's Molinos : perhaps he would like to tell the true story.'

To Mr. R. L. Poole   'Worcester : September 1, 1885.

'About the list.   One question strikes me, Do we do well to omit Froude ?   I think not : let us be entirely catholic.   He need not be asked to contribute at once : he will not wish to do so, but he should be asked to support.   We ought not to leave any possibility of a faction against us.'

'September 8, 1885.

'I don't like asking Froude, but I feel that one ought not to let one's personal prejudices [1] stand in the way of catholicity. . . .   They are indeed misguided who fear lest the Review be too popular.   My fear is lest it die of dullness ; but oh how the dullards croak with dread lest the atmosphere in which they live should by any chance be rarified.   I wish I saw much chance that we would not be portentously dull.

'I think that a good many people at first will not want to be paid.   The more I meditate about payment, the less chance

---

[1] These 'personal prejudices' were solely on historical grounds.   Creighton had never met Froude.

VOL. I.   Z

do I ever see of reaching an adequate rate on commercial grounds.'

All through the first months of residence at Worcester, while he was learning his work there, he was occupied in elaborate and detailed arrangements for starting the 'Historical Review,' getting contributors, conciliating those who sent useless papers, making careful plans as to the bibliography and the order of the various matter contained in the Review. An idea of the work that he had to do, and of his plans and hopes for the Review, can best be given in his own words.

To Mr. C. J. Longman   ' September 1, 1885.

'It is a matter of great importance that we should get foreign books early and direct. The great fault of the existing historical journals in all languages is that they are so terribly long in noticing new books. The scientific criticism generally comes a year after the literary criticism. Now, I have exceptional means of getting early information about really valuable books through Lord Acton. He is a vast reader, he lives abroad, he is most ready to help me. . . . Knowing the book to be valuable, I could get a man to read it at once. The fresher the book the more readily would a specialist seize upon it.

' September 24.

'I quite agree with your proposed form of the "Historical Review." We do not wish to look ornamental or gaudy.'

' September 30.

'Would this do as a motto for the "Historical Review"?

'Not professing any art, the historian, as his matter leads him, deals with all arts ; which—because it carrieth the life of a lively example— it is wonderful what light it gives to the arts themselves, so as the great Civilians keep themselves with the discourses of Historians.—SIR PHILIP SIDNEY.'

To Mr. R. L. Poole   ' December 19, 1885.

'Bryce raises the question, "Ought we to have some introductory remarks?" If you think so, would you mind drafting something short, a page or two? I think perhaps it ought to be, but I hate doing it.'

' December 20.

'Trouble not yourself. Bryce has sent me a preface.'

December 23.

'Thanks for your suggestions. I think Bryce had incorporated most of them. I think also that in beginning we must not apologise. I never like deprecating; it goes without saying that we have done our best, and it equally goes without saying that that is not much to begin with. I have just received the proof of an excellent article by Lord Acton—the sort of thing that takes your breath away, a philosophical criticism of all German historians of this century, most brilliant.'

To Mr. C. J. Longman   'December 28.

'Will you think me exorbitant if I ask for another sheet for the first number of the " Historical Review"? . . . My contributors have been too good. Lord Acton, Freeman, and Seeley have all sent me articles of considerable length and importance. Acton has written a survey of German historians which will at once command attention all over the Continent, and will, I think, secure our reputation abroad as first-rate. The article on the Greville Memoirs will, unless I mistake, attract general attention in England, and is the best thing that has been said about Greville, besides giving much information. . . . I can only report generally that I have succeeded as regards the first number beyond my most sanguine expectations.'

'January 13, 1886.

'I thought you would be pleased with the first number; it is quite a remarkably strong number for any periodical to start with, as every one of the articles contains absolutely new material, and is a real addition to knowledge. They are also varied, so as to attract various classes of readers.'

'January 27, 1886.

'The press has done all it can for us, and I am glad to mark in the notices an appreciation of serious work, as apart from shoddy, which is higher than I should have expected. Lord Acton's candid criticism is that the first number takes its place in European literature between the "Revue Historique" and Sybel's "Zeitschrift." He is good enough to say that he sees no reason why by the end of the year it should not have distanced them both.'

Lord Acton wrote :

'I congratulate you very sincerely. The Review is solid, various, comprehensive, very instructive, and sufficiently entertaining. It is not insular; there is no preference for certain topics, and no secret leaning towards any opinions. At least half the great names are there, and I discern the makings of a sacred band of university workers.'

These satisfactory results had not been attained without much labour.

To Mr. R. L. Poole   'December 29, 1885.

'I wish this number were fairly off my hands; it consumes all my time.'
        'January 2, 1886.

'I have decided to go to London on Monday to see how I can make the best of the space' (for the Review).
        'January 12.

'The sooner we get on with material for our next number, the better. I cannot stand being harassed at the end as I was this time.'
        'January 18.

'I feel above criticism on the main points—paper, type, get-up are better than any existing journal. The contents are far beyond the average. We shall not always do so well. Now that you see it all, you will appreciate my labours. . . . At last I had to sit in Spottiswoode's and see what they could manage to set up.'

To his sister, Miss M. E. Creighton
        'Worcester: December 26, 1885.

'. . . . I have been so busy this Christmas time that I have heeded nothing. The first number of the "Historical Review" is on me, and I spend my time in proofs and letters. However, we made merry with a Christmas tree yesterday, and gathered a few children round us. It is very nice being here at Christmas and having a church with which one is connected. We had such a nice service last night; no sermon, but the first part of the "Messiah," with a large choir reinforced for the occasion. Of course we are all wondering who is to be our Dean, but Lord Salisbury seems to get on very slowly with his appointments.

'I think I shall produce a first-rate number of the Review. It is rather amusing being editor, but one has to offend a good many people. . . . The children are very much on the rampage; it is a mercy that Christmas comes only once a year. . . .'

The Review naturally added greatly to his work. In March 1886 he speaks of himself as 'in the midst of more toil and labour than I have ever had.' He had to read over large numbers of articles sent to him for possible insertion, as well as to try and secure contributors who would add to the reputation of the Review, to balance the different parts of the Review, to secure that the right books were reviewed by the right people at the right time, to see that no important foreign books were neglected, to make the bibliography really full and accurate ; these and many other points required constant attention, and he was fortunate in having the diligent assistance of Mr. R. L. Poole in his exacting task.   He exerted himself to get distinguished contributors, but he was equally eager to find new men and also women to write for him.   'I never dismiss young contributors without due consideration, and err on the side of leniency,' he wrote.

To Mr. C. J. Longman   'May 8, 1889.
   'Part of my policy is to be willing to give a start to a young man ; a work in which I have really done good service to many.   I have pointed out to many aspirants their shortcomings, have put them in the way of things that they knew not, and have caused them to rewrite their articles to good purpose. . . . I thought it might interest you to know that the "English Historical Review" is really worked to some extent as a training ground, and that it enables me to take the measure of a young man.'

   'I should like some ladies,' he said to Lord Acton at the first ; and besides asking women of literary experience to write for him, he gave reviews and notices to promising Newnham students, chiefly to Miss Mary Bateson.   He asked foreigners to write for him, and made special efforts to get American co-operation.   In Mr. Justin Winsor, the Librarian of Harvard College, he secured an American editor.   He also had much correspondence with Mr. H. W. Lea of Philadelphia, the learned author of the ' History of the Inquisition,' who helped him both with contributions and suggestions.

   In spite of all his work and devotion, the great difficulty remained that the Review did not pay.   Mr. Bryce urged that they should try to make it more popular.   ' Bryce's desire for popularity is very excellent,' wrote Creighton, ' and if I had 500l. capital it might be done a little.'   Mr Gladstone consented to write an article.

To Mr. C. J. Longman   'January 21, 1887.

' May I tell you privately that I have extorted a sort of promise from no less a person than W. E. G. to write something about the last instalment of the Greville Memoirs? Surely after this you will not despair of the Review.'

To the Right Hon. W. E. Gladstone   'January 19, 1887.

' When I spoke to you some time ago about the project of starting an "English Historical Review," you were good enough to express a kindly interest in the scheme. I now write to ask if it would be at all possible that you could lend us a helping hand by a small contribution. It seems to me that the publication of the third part of the Greville Memoirs might bring before your mind many points, which have now become matters of history, on which your personal knowledge could throw much valuable light. . . . Lord Acton warned me that the primary duty of an editor was to make himself a bore. If I am now acting up to his ideal, please attribute it to my official duty and not to my personal wish.'

To the same   'Cambridge: February 15, 1887.

'. . . I am greatly obliged for your remarks about the " Historical Review." I am not myself very sanguine about its prospects, and I only occupy the post of editor in obedience to a pressure, which I felt that I ought not to resist. My post is a purely honorary one, and my endeavour is to co-ordinate the work which is being done by a scattered body of those interested in historical studies from any side. I thought that the Review would do a great deal for improving English historical literature, and on that head I am more than satisfied. But I doubted if there was a sufficiently large public to take an interest in purely historical questions ; and I am not surprised to find that there is not a large enough body to make the Review remunerative, but enough to enable it to pay its actual expenses. . . . The combination of readableness and research is so difficult as to be almost impossible, and the ordinary monthly magazine can get the most readable historical articles by paying for them. I think your suggestion of trying always to have an article on quite modern history is the only way to make the Review of interest to the general public. But these articles are the most difficult to get. The student will not set to work till he has all the materials, and no one save politicians, diplomatists, or journalists can write about modern affairs. The first of these are too busy, the second too reserved, and the third use their knowledge from day to day for current purposes. It may interest you to know that in 1879, when foreign affairs were much before the public, I suggested to a publisher a series of books dealing quite shortly and clearly with the political history and constitution of the chief states of Europe from 1815. I designed them for popular instruction, thinking it of great importance that people in general should know what they were talking about, when they spoke of *France* or *Russia*. My plan was highly approved, but broke down because I could not get any one to write such volumes. Members of the diplomatic service declared that they were afraid. Politicians pleaded that they were too busy. Several journalists frankly said that they were too ignorant; accurate information would be most valuable for them, but they never had time to acquire it. The result of my inquiries was to convince me that our ignorance of the last sixty years was colossal.

' For this reason I venture to think that your kindness in making a few notes on recent affairs will be of very real use as an example, and I shall greatly rejoice if I can make the " Historical Review " a means of promoting political education about events which have the closest connexion with problems on which men are requested to form their own opinions.'

Mr. Gladstone's article appeared, but it made no appreciable difference in the sale; and while historical students and serious readers felt that the Review abundantly fulfilled its purpose, it seemed clear that no attempt to popularise it without entirely changing its character and making it useless to students would succeed. Messrs. Longman were very patient, but in 1889 said that they could not go on permanently at a loss.

To Mr. R. L. Poole   ' October 17, 1889.

' Perhaps the question of the " Historical Review " ought to be faced more definitely. Personally I think I am out of pocket by it; but I think it is useful, and do not mind giving my trouble. But I take it that the Review only just floats, as is the case with all special journals in England and everywhere else.'

To Mr. C. J. Longman   ' October 28, 1889.

' I have been considering the prospects of the Review. It seems to me under the circumstances that we must recognise the fact that at present the Review is chiefly the organ of historical students and has little attraction for the general public. So long as this is so, I think that the appearance of payment to contributors might be dropped. . . . I find no failure of material or of interest on the part of historical students. So long as this is the case, it is clear that the Review supplies a need, and I should not like to see it cease.'

By strict economy, and by giving up, as he suggested, all pretence of paying contributors, the Review was just made to pay its way. Creighton always said that historical students owed a great debt of gratitude to Messrs. Longman for the way in which they stood by it. He himself gave his services as editor during the whole time he filled that post. Dr. Garnett says : 'The position which it held under his direction was fully as much due to his editorial diligence and capacity as to the prestige imparted by his reputation.'

He had left Embleton with a considerable portion of the continuation of his History of the Papacy almost ready for publication, and he was working on at this during the first year of the ' Historical Review.'

To Mr. C. J. Longman   'January 1, 1884.

' As I am writing . . . I will ask you if you will publish as my next instalment *one* volume. I ask this, because my next volume will cover a purely Italian period, of special interest to some people, and I should like it to be read and considered apart from the Lutheran movement. It really deals with the Renaissance Popes, the Borgias and the rest, concerning whom there is no connected account in England at present. When that volume is over I pass into Germany and theology, into quite different ground. I think that volume iii. may serve as a useful make-weight in the middle. I think that two more volumes afterwards would have exhausted everyone's patience, and my book would be finished in five volumes.'

'January 3, 1884.

' My work is laborious and gets on slowly. I am not more than half through my next volume. It will not be ready for another year.'

'March 24, 1884.

' I hear incidentally that my Papacy has attracted much attention at Rome, and that the Roman Catholics recognise its fairness.'

'October 31, 1885.

' At present I am devoting all the time I can to the third volume of the Popes, which will shortly be ready. I am at present engaged in revising it. It will be more interesting generally than the first two volumes, as it will deal with the Popes of the Renaissance time. . . . It has been a work of exceeding labour, that is all I can say for it.'

'May 7, 1886.

' I shall have ready for delivery by the end of this month the MS. of volume iii. of my Papacy. I am a candid critic of my own work, and can only say that it is decidedly better than the first volumes, and will awaken much adverse criticism. No one in England except Lord Acton, A. W. Ward, and Stubbs could follow me before. Everybody thinks he has an opinion about the Renaissance.'

'June 11, 1886.

' I have sent off the MS. of my Popes. It has grown more than I could have wished ; but I had so many extracts of MSS. of importance that I put them in an appendix, which will be grateful to many of my readers. I think it would be better to make two moderate volumes rather than one fat one which is unpleasant to hold.'

In addition to his other labours, he undertook in 1885 to edit for Messrs. Longman a series of Epochs of Church History, of which fifteen volumes appeared in the course of the next few years. He was to have written one himself on the History of the Reformation in Germany; but this was put off because the series did not take as well as had been hoped, and later he had no time to write it. He himself was very satisfied with the majority of the volumes, and had no doubt of the ultimate success of the series.

To Mr. C. J. Longman   'September 29, 1887.

' I send you the MS. of Dr. Plummer's volume, " The Church of the Early Fathers." I think the volume is exceedingly well done, and has every prospect of becoming a handbook on this subject.'

'October 21, 1887.

' I have every reason to suppose that the sale of the series will be steady and will increase steadily. The subject of Church History is one of the most growing subjects in popular interest.'

He also at this time and in subsequent years was frequently consulted by Messrs. Longman on matters concerning
the publication of books offered to them, and often looked
through MSS. for them.

These were troubled years for England. Creighton, bred
and trained in Liberal principles, followed, like so many other
Liberals, with much anxiety the break-up of the party under
Mr. Gladstone's Home Rule schemes.

To Mr. Albert Grey 'Cambridge : November 1, 1885.

'I fear me that politics grow daily more and more distasteful to an increasing number of people, of which I am
sorry ; but we must not cease to be hopeful, and you at least
are not likely to despair of the republic. . . . I am convinced
that all moderate Liberals must stick to their colours, and save
Liberalism from the hands into which it seems likely to fall.
The more—— wants to kick us out, the less we must be
kicked out. . . . The election after this will find the moderates
much stronger if only they stem the tide now. In the
strength of this belief, I exhort the waverers not to quit the
Liberal side, but defections are very frequent among thoughtful men.'

To Dr. Hodgkin 'December 24, 1885.

'Politics, as you say, are disgusting. It requires all one's
courage to believe in anybody or anything concerning them.
In former days theologians would be busy at present discussing the important thesis, " Quæritur cur salvari possit qui
rebus publicis hoc tempore studeat." I am beginning to
have very serious doubts concerning the salvability of politicians—and, perhaps I should add, of plumbers.'

The elections of 1885 and 1886 had a special interest
for him because several of his pupils were entering public life.

To Sir Edward Grey 'October 14, 1885.

'1 follow your career with interest in the pages of the
"Alnwick Gazette." Your energy is indeed surprising, but
youth is nothing if it is not energetic.'

'November 30, 1885.

'Warmest congratulations on your success, which has
been most complete. . . . You have begun political life by a
signal success. I know you will show yourself worthy of it.
To me, who am growing old, politics look very different to

what they once did.   I see dangers and difficulties, which I
wish I could see my way through.   Of one thing only I am
sure, that the House of Commons needs men of high
character and firm principles, who will not be blown about by
every blast of popular doctrine, and will not strive to find
arguments to prove that wrong is right.   I rejoice in the
election of such as you and Alfred Pease.   Please remember
that just now the earth of politics seems to want some salt,
and take all the salt you can scrape together to the House
with you.   I am afraid that it will not be a very merry Parliament, and that it will not do much.   There will be little
chance for young members.   This is an increasing evil, and
in a balanced state of parties becomes more inevitable.'

'December 1, 1885.

'It was very good of you to write to me.   I received your
letter, and read it this morning with the greatest joy.   You
seem to have divined my thoughts, for I had been wondering
what effect your canvass and your speeches had produced upon
your mind.   I might have trusted your good sense to show
you the truth : forgive me that I even doubted.   What you
say is excellent, though I do not know that I have any right
to express my opinion upon the conduct of one so great as
the elected of the Berwick division.

'Please do not imagine that I have turned Conservative.
I have no vote (by the way, is it not a grievance that a man
should be disfranchised for changing his house ?), and therefore could afford to look on candidly.   Naturally the Church
question came foremost, and I used my influence to keep
Liberal Churchmen Liberal still.   My action was to insist that
Disestablishment should be removed from the candidate's
programme, as not being a practical question ; and that being
done, no questions should be asked about his principles or
opinions.   In Cambridge, for instance, the Liberal candidate
is a Quaker : I joined in demanding that he should declare
that during this Parliament he would vote for no bill or
resolution favouring Disestablishment.   He agreed as a fair-
minded man : then I was full on his side.   I know that if
Disestablishment becomes practical, I should have to vote
against him, unless my opinions change meanwhile.   Moreover I machinated that Liberals should put on record their
deliberate view on this subject.   In this I succeeded, and
I inclose you the result, which I think is Liberal enough in
spirit, and points out the nature of the arguments by which
the Church question must be tried.   I can quite sympathise
with your objection to squires and parsons politically : they

are not wise bodies of men, but a great many clergy are
Liberal still and intend to remain so. . . .

'This election really was not interesting. I do not know
plainly what are the issues submitted to the electors, nor
does anybody else. Ireland and Egypt are the two great
questions. Both parties have mismanaged Ireland : in Egypt
the Conservatives will do better. . . . Gladstone is showing
the worst signs of old age : he keeps his energy, but has lost
his clinch : he cannot distinguish, but thinks that one thing is
quite the same as another. On the other hand, I don't
know what Salisbury means. . . . My views seem to have
been reproduced by the constituencies. The result will be a
weak Government, which cannot do much and will behave
with moderation. Perhaps this is the best thing till people
have had time to look around.

'Meanwhile, we want principles. I am afraid that
Gladstone is responsible for having destroyed them. His
basis has been emotional, not intellectual. Nice as our
emotions are, they cannot be our only guides. They are
most useful when they express spontaneously the results of
thought, and when they recur to reflection for their renewal.
The English people want principles and they want guidance.
A man once wrote to me from Leeds saying that he was
engaged in addressing working men about things in general,
not politically. He is a strong Liberal, but holds an office
which prevents him from speaking as a partisan. He therefore told his men facts of history and records of his own
observations on social phenomena. They questioned him
each time closely, and at last their spokesman said, " Sir, we
are more obliged to you than we can say : we never knew
where to find the facts : we read Mr. Chamberlain, and do not
know how to judge." I was much impressed by this attitude,
and I believe it to be common. I am sure that the way to
be a statesman is not to go cap in hand to people and say,
" Tell me all you want, and I will do it." Rather a man must
take the responsibility of being a leader of the people. He
must tell them what is the nature of human society, what are
the limits in which it can be modified by any causes external
to the individuals who compose it, what is the nature of
international duty, and he must interpret to them their
present conditions in the light of principles founded on sound
knowledge. The old Radicals, Grote, Molesworth, Mill,
deserved their name, for they tried to go to the root of
matters. I see nothing in common between them and the
charlatanism of ——, who could not tell you what he thought
a State could do, or what were the limits of legislative action,

or what was the basis of individualism as against State direction. . . . Have you read Maine's "Popular Government"? If not, do so. It is very suggestive : do not dissent from his arguments till you have found an answer.'

The declaration spoken of at the beginning of this letter was drawn up by a small committee of Cambridge Liberals, who met at Dr. Hort's house. Canon Stanton, who was present, recalls that those who took most part in the discussion were : Dr. Hort, who presided ; Creighton, H. Bradshaw, and A. T. Lyttelton. The first draft of the paper was prepared by Dr. Hort, and it was then criticised and amended by the others. It is of course impossible to discover Creighton's share in this declaration, but some of its words seem to express with special clearness his firm convictions.

'Our plea is not against Nonconformists, but on behalf of the Church, and on behalf of the Church only as the primary spiritual organ of the nation. . . . The influence which connexion with the State exercises on the religion taught and practised by the Church . . . is a powerful antidote to the inclination to confine religion within the limits of individual emotion or belief, and keeps up a sense of the intimate relations between the Christian faith and character on the one hand and all human interests and social duties on the other. If it were removed, the ideals of religion prevalent in England would assuredly be lowered and impoverished, not in the Church only, but in other Communions likewise. There would, moreover, be great reason to fear lest by the natural operation of ineradicable causes a deep antagonism should arise between the Church and State, which would be equally calamitous to both, and would fill the whole land with discord. We cannot affect to overlook the wide currency of theories which aim at a complete separation of the religious and the secular spheres in public matters. Believing that the separation can never be really effected, and that much evil and misery must be caused by the attempt to bring it about, we recognise with thankfulness the growth of other strong currents of thought and feeling which flow in the opposite direction.' [1]

The declaration was signed by fifty-six Liberal members of the Senate of the University of Cambridge. The same com-

[1] This declaration is given in full in the Life of Dr. Hort by his son, Sir Arthur Hort.

mittee also prepared a brief memorial to the Archbishop and Bishops, asking that advantage might be taken of the revival of public interest in ecclesiastical questions for the authoritative consideration of temperate measures of Church Reform. The reforms asked for were first in connexion with patronage and discipline within the Church, but the chief need was stated to be a more complete development of the constitution and government of the Church, such as would admit laymen who were *bona fide* Churchmen to a real share in the control of Church affairs. This memorial was largely signed by members of the Senate of all parties.

To his sister, Miss M. E. Creighton

'The College, Worcester : July 7, 1886.

' I have been following the politics of Carlisle with amazement. Gladstone knew his man, and measured his words when he snuffed out Ferguson by his discreditable speech at the station. I am a decided Unionist, and should have voted for any Liberal or Conservative, who was on the Union side. But I had no vote, I am not yet on the register. I belong to that unhappy class of intelligent people which Herbert Gladstone tells us are always on the wrong side. I examined the young man at Oxford some time ago, and persuaded the other examiners to give him a First Class in History. So goes the world.

' The political prospect is gloomy. The country is shaken, and there is every chance of two more elections before the end of 1887. I do not see how things are to settle down again for some time. Gladstone won't get an effective majority, and there will be a general mess. I rather trust that some foreign complication may arise to turn us away from Ireland. The whole Irish question has been sprung so suddenly, and is still so vague, that Gladstone's precipitation fills me with amazement.'

To Mrs. J. R. Thursfield

'Worcester : July 17, 1886.

' Dear Emily,— . . . The general result of the elections is to convince me that the country requires an extension of the Home Rule plan. Let us really accept the verdict of the country and give Mr. Parnell to Ireland, *minus* Ulster, which would naturally be ruled by Lord Randolph Churchill. Scotland, *plus* Northumberland, Cumberland, and Durham, would go to Mr. Gladstone. I should be content to live in the insignificant portion which remained and would be glad to be governed by anybody, provided it was not one of the three afore mentioned.   I think I am kept busier here than at Cambridge.   Everybody else is ill or away, and I have the whole concern on my shoulders and cannot get away, even for a day.   Tell Dick to use his holiday in preparing speeches for the next election, when he really must stand.   I suppose it will be in about six months. . . .'

In June 1886 we made a fortnight's trip to Flanders, visiting Antwerp, Bruges, and Ghent, and staying some days at Dinan and other places on the Meuse.   It was not possible, owing to his many engagements, to take a long holiday abroad this year.   In July he was in residence in Worcester, and in the early part of August he first visited Mr. Freeman, and then joined me for a walking tour of a few days up the Wye.   Any spare days he could get at Worcester were always devoted to exploring the beautiful country in the neighbour-hood.   The rest of August was spent in visiting friends.

To Sir Edward Grey   'August 20, 1886.

'I was delighted to hear from you, and to find that you were not entirely doubled up by your labours.   Two elections in eight months is severe. . . . At present we are rambling for a fortnight, and are now staying with the Aclands.   I hope you like Arthur Acland; he is an admirable politician, it seems to me : he knows more than any other M.P. about the actual life and aspirations of the artisan class, and he estimates their ideas at their true importance : he is neither fanatical nor doctrinaire : he regards his elections as oppor-tunities for educating his constituents.   So far as I can make out, he has quietly used the last election as an opportunity for a course of lectures on Irish history and Irish social and economic conditions.   He regards the duty of a M.P. to be that of teaching and studying his people.   He takes an active part in all the societies of the artisans, and wins them by his capacity.   He has a very distinct line, which will not lead to great fame, but which seems to me to be most useful.   I have been much interested in talks with him, but he had to flee to a co-operative committee, so I ramble up Snow-don and elsewhere in his absence. . . . Politics are difficult, but they generally are so.   History shows me how much there is always of momentous importance, and how vaguely it is dealt with.   There have been very few great statesmen ever : things are generally left to drift and depend on the native force of the people.   If there is vigour, no amount of muddling can make an irretrievable mess.   Wisdom comes by experience : few questions have ever been settled delibe- rately : they settle themselves by the survival of the strongest. (We may postulate in nature the survival of the *fittest* ; but history only shows me the survival of the strongest : strength *may* turn into fitness, but it is not the same thing at first.) The Irish question seems to me simply a wrestle : which is stronger—the governing instincts of England, or the Irish discontent ?   We are going through a phase of experiment, and no sensible person can feel very strongly sure of his opinion on one side or the other.   The last election has given me a much greater confidence in the sense of the English people.   So far as I saw, the people admitted that it was a difficult question, and they have put off its solution in one way because they were not satisfied that way would work. If Randolph Churchill seriously meant his remarks about a reform of the administration, he has got hold of one of the great questions of the future.   I rather think the last election is the end of *sensational* politics, and means *attention to busi- ness*.   Whatever our difficulties may be, the last two elections show that the English people do not believe in nostrums ; neither " three acres and a cow " nor " Home rule " will in their opinion be specifics.

' But enough of politics.   We cannot forecast the future. It is enough to make our opinions to the best of our know- ledge, and hold them with that humility and openness to the teaching of events which mark true wisdom. . . . I have been coming to the conclusion that the idyllic rustic of social reformers is rather an unusual being.   I believe that moral progress is to be found in the industrial rather than in the rural classes.   The terrible isolation and stagnation of the country is very difficult to overcome.'

Early in 1886 a new labour came to him.   He received a request from Dr. Philpott, then Bishop of Worcester, to be his examining chaplain.   He did not know the Bishop at all, and was much surprised at this mark of confidence. The Bishop, after telling him that his existing chaplain wished to resign, wrote : ' My thoughts turn at once to you, and lead me to be bold enough to ask whether you would do me the great personal kindness, and give the diocese the great benefit of your services.'   Creighton used to wonder what could have led the Bishop to ask him.   He said that it could only be because he was a Cambridge professor that the Bishop, a thorough Cambridge man, was prepared to trust him. But he did not feel that he could undertake the work alone, and asked the Bishop to associate Canon Melville with him ; and in the following year, when Dr. Bigg (now Canon of Christ Church) came into the diocese, obtained that he also should be appointed an examining chaplain. He saw at once that the office would be no easy one.

To Dr. Wilberforce, then Bishop of Newcastle

'Worcester : April 8, 1886.

' My dear Bishop,—I am afraid that the melancholy time has come when I must ask you to release me even from the nominal title of examining chaplain. My reason is one which causes grief to the flesh : it is that the Bishop of Worcester has asked me to be his examining chaplain. I never was more surprised in my life, and I should have thought that I was a person whom he would have regarded with suspicion ; but it seems to me so important for the diocese that the office should be in the hands of some one who will try to make something of it, that I could not refuse, great as the burden will be. You know enough of the Bishop not to be surprised when I say, that the Ordinations here simply filled me with despair. They are of the oldest fashion. The examination is held in Worcester immediately before Ordination. The candidates live in hotels, and see the Bishop for a moment on Saturday afternoon in the most formal way, and are ordained the next day without a word of counsel. The Bishop has only *one* chaplain, who is now resigning after twenty-five years' service . . . and is reported to have only one set of papers. The whole thing is as unedifying as it could be.

'You will see that I could not refuse to undertake the work. It seemed to me that as a Canon I could enlist the Dean and others to help me in talking to the men. It will entail on me an amount of labour for which I can scarcely find time ; but the only way to improve the present system is through the Chapter. The Bishop always fought shy of them before, and I cannot imagine what has changed his views. I have barely seen him, certainly had no talk with him, and was quite astounded at the offer.

'My loss will not be of great moment to you, as my services have been scanty of late, and I will still do what

I can for the diocese of Newcastle at Cambridge. Can I still retain the honorary title of chaplain to yourself? If so, I should much like to keep it, as you will always be my Bishop in a sense in which no one else will ever be. . . .'

Creighton at once proceeded to reform the arrangements for the Ordination. The Dean and the Canons were most willing to help. It was arranged that the candidates should be lodged in the different houses in the College, and should meet in the Chapel at the Deanery for special services and addresses. Before long Creighton obtained the Bishop's consent to hold the examination some weeks before the Ordination. He was touched by the way in which the Bishop was willing to fall in with his suggestions, only begging that he should not be asked to allow the men to be ordained in surplices instead of black gowns. So this point was never pressed, and to the last black gowns were worn at Bishop Philpott's ordinations. There were three Ordinations a year, and they were a great addition to Creighton's work. He succeeded in raising considerably the standard of the examination. It had been one of the easiest examinations for orders; but the candidates soon discovered that it had now become a reality. He also tried to check the growing habit of the young clergy to wear moustaches, not invariably with success, even though he told the owner of an exuberant moustache, that an incumbent had implored him not to persuade curates to shave, because their moustaches were such excellent 'foolometers.' He was of opinion that a clergyman should either wear a full beard or shave entirely ; but it was not an opinion that he cared to enforce with authority, and later, as Bishop, he left the matter to the good sense of the candidates.

In addition to all his other work in the summer of 1886, he was seeing the two new volumes of his 'History of the Papacy' through the press. We had plenty of room in our Worcester house, and he always liked to have friends to visit us there, so that life in every sense was very full, and it is not surprising to find him saying that he was busier than he had ever been before, and had no time to take a holiday.

CHAPTER XII

JOURNEY TO AMERICA

In August 1886, just when Creighton was absorbed in all the new and varied work which had come to him, he received a request from Dr. Phear, Master of Emmanuel, to represent the College at the commemoration by Harvard University, Massachusetts, of the 250th anniversary of its foundation John Harvard, the founder, one of the early emigrants to New England, had been a member of Emmanuel, and now, in celebrating an anniversary which marked it as the oldest university in America, the College was eager as always to show how much it valued the tie binding it to the mother College in England. Dr. Phear writes : 'How happily and entirely Professor Creighton had become naturalised in his adopted College, appears in his selection to represent it at Harvard.'

At first it seemed impossible to him to leave his work to accept this commission.

To Dr. Phear, Master of Emmanuel College

'Worcester : August 15, 1886.

' My dear Master,—I am very much gratified that you and others should have thought me worthy of being selected for such a distinction as that of representing Emmanuel at Harvard. There is nothing which in the nature of things I should have liked better, and had the time been one in which I was not called on to have other duties, I would thankfully have accepted your kind proposal ; but I feel that I have been too short a time at work in Cambridge to deserve a holiday. A new professorship, I think you will agree with me, has to justify itself in the University ; and I am sure that you will not think me lacking in devotion to the College if I think that my first duties are to the University, which the

College wished to benefit. I cannot pretend to think that
my lectures are of much importance in themselves, but they
are announced as part of the university teaching, and I do
not know anyone else who can undertake them at a short
notice ; moreover, I have a small class of pupils, who seem to
like to come to me, and I want to be regarded as part of the
university system. If I say that I have succeeded beyond
my hopes in weaving in my subject to the university studies,
I say it only to explain my aim ; but I feel that if my end
is to be obtained and my plans are to prosper, I must for
some years stick to my post, however slight may be the
immediate results. The omission of a term's lectures (which
a journey to America would necessitate) would destroy the
continuity of my work, and would throw me back in my
general designs. I have to get to know individual undergraduates, and must always be found at my place. When
my subject has become established, and when my method
has become known and recognised, I can afford to think of
holidays, but just now I feel that I would be doing wrong in
absenting myself from term. I write to you very frankly,
for I do not at all like to refuse to do anything which you
ask me ; but I trust that I have made my motives intelligible, and I think you will be of opinion that there is something in them. . . . To-morrow I am going away to pay a
few visits, my only holiday this year.'

The College was so anxious that he should go, that the
Master wrote again to ask him to reconsider his decision, and
Mr. Rose came to Worcester to enforce the request.

To Dr. Phear, Master of Emmanuel College

'Worcester : August 31, 1886.

' My dear Master,—Thank you very much for your kind
consideration, which I greatly appreciate. I have had a talk
with Rose, and fully understand the position. Before I wrote
to Rose, I had reviewed the situation, and had given so much
weight to your repeated wish as to go further in examining
my motives than I had done at first. I came to the conclusion (1) that a journey to America was in one way a
service to the University in spreading academic comity ;
(2) that by a little arrangement I could give my lectures for
this term in the Lent Term, by doing double work ; (3) that
I should learn a great deal which might make me a wiser
man by going to America ; (4) that owing to accidental
circumstances it so happened that I could get introductions to

the chief men of letters in my subject in America ; (5) that as editor of the " Historical Review " it was well that I should be personally known to some American historians ; (6) that it might not be undesirable if the University had some one to whom American historians might come on their visits to England.

' If you had not repeated your request, I should have gone no further in my meditations ; but when I came to reflect, I thought the balance was after all in favour of my going. When I thought that, I began to devise means which would make it possible.

' Therefore I will go, and Mrs. Creighton will go with me. I will do my best as the representative of the College, and I feel very highly the honour which it has conferred upon me.

' I have told Rose all my views about smaller points. My university work may stand over for a term ; the rest I can provide for.

' With many thanks to you for your thoughtfulness and kindness in the matter, I am

'Yours very sincerely,
' M. CREIGHTON.'

To the same   ' September 21, 1886.

' Rose discussed with me the desirability of presenting a Latin letter, which was done at the Edinburgh Commemoration ; but I do not know that the Americans care for these old-fashioned ways. . . . I have no notion what our plans may be : I think that I shall judge for myself what I want to see. Perhaps, if times suit, I shall wander as far as Chicago, where the Church Convention is to sit. I should like to see how the synodal constitution works. But this is only a vague idea. . . . I am immersed in the proofs of two volumes of the Popes, which I want to get corrected before I sail, so that they may be ready for publication soon after my return.'

' Worcester : September 29, 1886.

' Dear Master,—Thank you for sending on Professor Norton's letter, than which nothing could be more kind. . . . I have already been told about him that he is the most Europeanised American in America, a man of cosmopolitan tastes and culture. . . . I am beginning to breathe more freely as the time is approaching. The struggle of trying to finish off all sorts of things which I had on hand has been very severe for these last three weeks. I have not had time to read anything, and feel as if my brain was barren.

'I am very grateful to you for all the trouble you have taken to make my arrangements as little irksome as possible. I only hope that I may be able to do justice to the great institution which I go to represent.'

We left Liverpool on October 2 in the 'Arizona.' The first part of the voyage was very stormy, and we were not good sailors. But we struggled on deck every day, and sat there, sometimes with chairs roped to prevent them slipping, in biting wind and often driving rain, till the last few days, when we got into calm waters and brilliant sunshine under the lee of Newfoundland.

To Dr. Phear

'New York : October 11, 1886.

'The voyage was made very pleasant by making the acquaintance of a gentleman who was, I soon found, a friend of my friend Bryce. He is by name Brace, a philanthropist and man of letters, whose last book, "Gesta Christi" (an essay on the results of Christianity in creating modern civilisation), I had read with great interest. He was returning from England with his wife and two daughters, and we spent all our days with them. They are charming people, and told us much about American ways and doings. Besides them there was an American judge, who was one of the best informed men I have ever come across ; so that our society was remarkably pleasant.'

Mr. Brace used to say that never under the most favourable circumstances did he hear Creighton talk more brilliantly than he did on the deck of the 'Arizona' when feeling cold and wet and seasick.

On landing at New York we were met by a representative of Harvard, Professor Ware, of Columbia College, New York.

To Dr. Phear   'New York : October 11, 1886.

'Professor Ware . . . placed himself unreservedly at our disposal during our stay, in spite of my remonstrances, and seems prepared to map out our duties and arrange our life for us. Really anything like the amiability of the American people I never saw ; I was much struck on board ship by their genuine desire to do everything they could. Everyone I spoke to placed himself at my disposal if I should happen to go his way. Professor Ware simply asked who I should like to see, and they should be produced.

'At present my plans are to stay here till Friday, partly for repose, partly because I want to see some of the American institutions. On Wednesday Mr. Brace is going to show me the principal charities of New York, a very important thing to see, I imagine.'

He was much interested by some of the institutions started by Mr. Brace, especially by a school for the children of poor Italian emigrants, where they learnt enough English to fit them to enter the State schools, and by his Lodging Houses for Newsboys. We walked about New York a great deal, and he delighted in the brilliancy of the atmosphere and the beautiful views over the harbour.

To Dr. Phear   'October 20, 1886.

' We spent three days in New York, a place of surpassing noise and bustle, like London and Liverpool rolled into one, without any very clear distinction between the business parts and the rest. . . . On Thursday, Godkin, the editor of the " Nation" newspaper, took us off to his house by the seaside : on Friday Mr. Brace took us to his house on the Hudson river, which is most beautiful. On Saturday we went farther along the Hudson to West Point, the Cadet College, where I learned all about the American army, and even was made to preach to the cadets. On Monday we went farther again up the Hudson, and were taken by a good lady a long drive in lovely country. There we managed to escape from friends, and went to the Catskill mountains, which are very striking. . . . America is very unlike England in every way, and I do not like to generalise on my impressions so soon ; so I shall reserve all attempts at sagacious remarks.'

From the Hudson we went to Niagara, which in every way surpassed our expectations. My husband was specially struck by the beauty of the great stretches of water above the falls. He had been prepared for grandeur, but not for such exquisite beauty. Next we went to Cincinnati to visit a brother of mine, and then to Haverford, a Quaker University near Philadelphia, where we stayed with Professor Thomas, whose acquaintance we had made at Cambridge. Creighton lectured to the students at Haverford, and also visited Bryn Mar, the new women's university, and spoke to the students there. At Philadelphia he had the pleasure of making the personal acquaintance of Mr. H. C. Lea, the learned historian, for whose work he had a great admiration, and with whom he had already corresponded. After this we went to Harvard for the commemoration festivities, where we stayed first with President Eliot and then with Professor Norton.

To Mr. Charles L. Brace   'Haverford College : October 27, 1886.

'I have been so busy travelling since I left you that this is the first time I have taken up a pen. I warned you that my energy was boundless in rambling, but all my energy goes in that operation and leaves me useless for anything else. . . . Cincinnati amused me much. My brother-in-law had made friends with the sort of people whom I should not otherwise have seen, Englishmen making their fortunes and that sort of person, who interested me greatly : also a Roman Catholic lawyer, who entertained us sumptuously and had invited his Archbishop, who unfortunately was too ill to come. I was made to preach again in Cincinnati, and I was very glad to have seen a place which had at least a slight flavour of the West. . . . I am staying with a good Quaker who was in England and used to come to my lectures at Cambridge. I am glad to see Friends in their great centre.

'I am learning so much and so fast that I shall blow up soon. If anyone asks you if it is worth while to pay a short visit to America, I think you may safely answer that it is worth while to come for a week. My ideas on social, political, and economic questions have been indefinitely expanded already. When I doubted about my journey, a friend who had been in America said : "I do not know that your journey will make you a better professor, but it will make you a better citizen, and I imagine that will react." Please do not imagine that I am so foolish as to form opinions, I am content to receive impressions.'

To Dr. Phear   'Shady Hill, Cambridge, Mass. : November 5, 1886.

'Dear Master,—Your letter and Rose's parcel safely arrived. I read the College letter with great interest and much admiration, as did also Professor Norton. I have seen Sandys's letter on behalf of the University, and prefer that of Emmanuel. Perhaps it may be patriotic prejudice, perhaps the prejudice of one who thinks that the model of modern Latin writing is to be found in something later than Cicero : anyhow Emmanuel has said more that was worth saying, and its utterances ring more sincerely. We are enjoying Cambridge very much : it is quite English in its ways.　Boston is like a miniature London : Cambridge, on a flat low-lying plain just rescued from the salt marshes by the mouth of the Charles river, recalls by its position its English eponym.　The professors are very like English professors, Norton most of all, who is quite delightful and a man of universal culture. President Eliot is a very strong man, of imperturbable serenity of mind, great practical sense and capacity, holding the balance impartially between the various studies of this place, and quietly getting his own way through a somewhat complicated and decidedly irritating constitution.　I will not write you a discourse on Harvard University.　Certainly the place is full of vigour, is trying important experiments in educational methods, and holds a very high place in popular esteem, calling out great munificence on the part of its old members.　The various festivities begin to-day : the amount of talk required in America seems quite appalling.　Orations and sermons are to abound.　I have made the acquaintance of most of the chief people here, and they are all kindly to the last degree.　Everybody wants to show me something or explain something, till my brain reels and I can scarce contain my knowledge.　The President has asked me to lecture on Wednesday to the students, and I felt bound to obey.　I shall talk to them about the origin of European universities, and end with Emmanuel and its connexion with the movement which produced John Harvard.　It seemed to me that in that way I should best be able to discharge my mission without undue obtrusiveness.'

'Boston : November 13, 1886.

'Now that I have escaped from Harvard and can look back upon my visit, I feel moved to tell you my general impression of my visit. . . . The occasion was one of much greater *national* importance than I had thought possible. The Americans are much more formal than we are, and attach great importance to little things : they are extremely sensitive and very critical, and are eager for recognition.　I was quite surprised at the warmth of their sentiment towards Emmanuel.　They entirely accept her as a fostering mother, and care more for Emmanuel than for the University of Cambridge.　Lowell in his oration singled out as the only person for special mention the representative of Emmanuel, and brought down the house, so that I had to rise and bow acknowledgments.　So it was throughout the social entertainments.　I never had such hard work in my life.　I was on duty all day trying to say the right thing to innumerable folk.

Everybody wishes to be introduced in this land and shake hands and say something. I tried to do my uttermost in the way of cordiality, as I soon found that cordiality and warmth are what the Americans value most. When we went away, old Mrs. Agassiz, the widow of the great naturalist, said to Mrs. Creighton, almost with tears in her eyes, " I do not think your husband realises how grateful we are to him for the warm message he has brought us from Emmanuel College." That I did all I ought to have done I cannot pretend, but I did my best as a representative of the College. . . . I really never found myself with such an important charge to perform, and I had to be as cordial as I could without being in any way presumptuous. Though they are proud of being allied to Emmanuel, it was very necessary to observe all modesty on our side in dwelling on the relationship. In my speech at the dinner I tried to be warm and brief, and was amused at the testimony of a young man, who turned to Norton by the door and said, " Why, he speaks as well as an American." . . . I tell you this, not to praise myself, but because you will be interested and gratified to know how I was received in the name of the College, and because I want to say that if I failed to do all I ought to have done, it was not from want of will, as I did my utmost to strengthen the bond between us and Harvard, and I never forgot my representative capacity. I very much wish that you had been here, for I think you would never have forgotten the testimony to the historical greatness of Emmanuel which was so freely and thankfully rendered on all sides. Of course I saw everybody and more than everybody, but I will not tell you about them now. . . . We are well, but it will require the repose of the Atlantic to recover from all my exertions.'

The three days in which Harvard celebrated the two hundred and fiftieth anniversary of its foundation were crowded with festivities of every kind. In all these a prominent place was given to Creighton as the representative of Emmanuel College. He had the opportunity of meeting the most distinguished men in the intellectual world of America, who had come to show honour to Harvard. Probably no other occasion could have provided such an opportunity, for the position held by Harvard as the oldest University in America is unique, and it may be said to be the heart of the literary commonwealth of a nation that owns more universities than there are days in the year. Creighton much appreciated the opportunity of gaining so large an insight into the university life of America ; he was welcomed on all sides with warm cordiality, and formed many ties which were strengthened by subsequent intercourse when his American friends visited him in England.   Professor Norton writes :

' He was a conspicuous figure during the celebrations of the week, and he made himself agreeable to every one whom he met by a certain ease and accessibility of manner, and by his ready adaptation of himself to novel circumstances, qualities not always characteristic of the college don.'

The public notice which he received was no doubt mainly due to his representative character.   Dr. Lowell, in his admirable Commemoration Address, which Creighton described as ' a mixture of wit and wisdom, alike dignified and graceful . . . full of the *mitis sapientia* of one who has read much and seen much,' after extending a general welcome to the guests, added these words :

' I should not represent you fitly if I gave no special greeting to the gentleman who brings the message of John Harvard's College, Emmanuel.   The welcome we give him could not be warmer than that which we offer to his colleagues, but we cannot help feeling that in pressing his hand our own instinctively closes a little more tightly, as with a sense of nearer kindred.'

After the Commemoration Addresses, honorary degrees were conferred, and Creighton together with the other delegates was made a D.C.L. of Harvard.

At the great banquet which followed, Creighton was struck by the simplicity of the meal—no wine was provided— and by the great number of the speeches, twenty-two in all. His own speech met with universal approval.   After a few words on the early history of Emmanuel, he said :

' The pathetic dignity of the act which you commemorate to-day, the resolution of the General Court to found a college, has been eloquently put before you.   Let me carry your thoughts a little farther, to the pathos of the life of him whom you have agreed to recognise as your founder. I would not for a moment be supposed to disparage research of any kind, and I fully recognise the industry and patriotism which has led one of your graduates to search the records of John Harvard's life; but I cannot help feeling a little glad that he has not discovered too much. To me the solitary figure of the unknown scholar, from whom you take your name, has a special significance through its very indistinctness. To some it is given to work out their ideas through a long course of intellectual production or of public service ; others can only express themselves in some one decisive act. We know enough of John Harvard's character to justify our admiration ; we know that he was devoted to the spread of learning and the promotion of the public welfare. His munificence was applied to further the object of popular aspiration. What the scanty revenues of the community could scarcely compass was accomplished by the example which his hopefulness set forth. He was at once a scholar, a statesman, and a philanthropist ; a man whom Emmanuel may be proud to have trained, and whom Harvard may be proud to recognise as her founder. It matters not that John Harvard cannot be shown to have been a man of social or of intellectual distinction. It may be that John Harvard's teachers shook their heads sadly over an awkward lad who sat silent in their lecture rooms ; but the names of John Harvard's teachers are, I fear, forgotten, while John Harvard's name lives and is venerated to-day, and judging from to-day's enthusiasm is likely to live through the long future of this great University. For John Harvard learnt a lesson beyond what his teachers could impart ; his fine sense caught the spirit of the institution which had inspired his intellectual life, and with the strength of that spirit he could inspire others.

'It is true that learning is cosmopolitan, and knows no distinction of place or clime ; but we who dwell by the banks of the sluggish Cam rejoice that we can see in John Harvard, ours and yours alike, a bodily symbol of the link that unites us with you who have called into being a new Cambridge where the Charles River broadens into the Atlantic. Our efforts as teachers can have no higher aim than to send forth into the world young men such as was John Harvard, " a godly gentleman and a great lover of learning." To both of us there are " new worlds to conquer not a few," new places which the light of knowledge may illumine. The good wishes which through me Emmanuel College tenders for the prosperity of this great University are warm and heartfelt ; and every Emmanuel man will feel himself strengthened for our common work when I tell him how cordial is the welcome which you have to-day given to the memory of his College.'

To Professor Thomas of Haverford

'Boston : November 19, 1886.

'Dear Mr. Thomas,—I am afraid that my labours at Cambridge have hopelessly prevented my correspondence. Indeed, I never was kept so hard at work in my life as I have been for the past week. I was driven to become a public character, to go from one reception to another, and from one ceremony to another, with a rapidity which quite bewildered me and which left me quite exhausted. When nothing else was demanded of me, I was taken away to Plymouth and Salem. From this whirl I have just escaped. . . . I was certainly very much struck with the vigorous life which is shown at Harvard. Eliot is a very capable man, who devotes himself to organisation, and discharges a difficult and thankless task with remarkable power. He greatly impressed me during my stay with him. My other host, Norton, is a most charming man, and so are his daughters. His culture and his literary knowledge are, I imagine, very rare in this country. At Cambridge I seem to have seen everybody and had long talks with them. I saw a good deal of Lowell, Child, Winsor, Emerton, and Agassiz, who particularly interested me. I had a talk with Wendell Holmes, Parkman, and all the Presidents of all the Universities who were there. Also Mr. Martin Curtis was a guest of Norton's, a truly delightful man. Everybody was most cordial to me, and I was rejoiced to find that Harvard cherished its connexion with Emmanuel College. Last night I was driven by the President to give a lecture to the undergraduates, and I talked to them about the growth of universities in Europe generally. The ceremony in the theatre was very impressive, and I was much interested to see the enthusiasm which gathered round President Cleveland. The dinner speeches afterwards lasted interminably : truly the Americans are an oratorical race, and no Englishman could venture to compete in tall talk. Lowell's address was exceedingly good : read it in its pamphlet form, which will soon be issued. . . . I often wished myself back to the quiet of Haverford in the midst of the turmoil. . . .'

He wrote an account of the Commemoration for the 'Times,'[1] in which he says :

'The chief impression left on the spectator was the homeliness, the simplicity, and the heartiness of the entire

[1] Published in *Historical Essays and Reviews*.

proceedings. There had been no thought of grandeur, no waste of time in elaborate preparations. The men of Harvard welcomed their guests and gave them of their best with abundant cordiality; but Harvard did not try to disguise its work-day look, and was content to appeal to those who knew and esteemed it for its work's sake.'

He was struck by the generous way in which the graduates of Harvard still aided the fortunes of their University, and contrasted it with the attitude of the graduates of the old Universities in England, who 'feel that their Universities are immemorial institutions which need little help from them.' The alumni of Harvard, on the other hand, felt that 'the College belonged to themselves, had been enriched by the munificence of many who were present, and looked to them all for the means of increasing her future usefulness.'

On leaving Harvard we spent a couple of days at Boston, and then visited President Gilman at Johns Hopkins University in Baltimore, where Creighton again lectured to the men. Our last days in America were spent at the house of the distinguished lawyer, Mr. Joseph Choate,[1] in New York, and we left for England at the end of November. Creighton went straight on landing to Cambridge before joining his children at Worcester, in order to report in person to the Master and Fellows of his College the results of his mission.

He was very grateful for having been induced to visit America. His own special travelling tastes and interests would never have led him thither, but once there he enjoyed it much and profited greatly by his new experiences. Perhaps the strongest impression he brought home with him was one of hopefulness. In America it seemed to him that the future of the Anglo-Saxon race was assured, and that if in the course of time the influence of England as a world power should diminish, yet many of the ideas which it was the work of England to express would still prevail through the influence of America.

The abundant life and vigour of the American Universities, and their willingness to try experiments, also delighted him. He felt that they were really trying to grapple with the

---

[1] Afterwards American Ambassador at the Court of St. James.

problems of education, and did not shrink from bold experiment.

In the course of the following term he gave a lecture to the Emmanuel men on his impressions of Harvard, thinking that an account of his mission was due to the junior as well as to the senior members of the College. He contrasted with much humour and insight the life of undergraduates at Harvard and in Cambridge, not always to the advantage of Cambridge. He is said to have given some offence by his remarks on the schoolboyishness and idleness of the Cambridge undergraduate. He had been struck at Harvard by the way in which a young man was made to realise his own responsibility in life, so that matters of discipline occupied but a small place, and the problems of a common life were left to the students to settle for themselves.

CHAPTER XIII

HISTORICAL WORK

JUST before starting for America, Creighton had corrected the proofs of two new volumes of the 'History of the Papacy,' which appeared early in February 1887. These volumes deal with the Popes of the Italian Renaissance, and are thus concerned with a period about which much had been written of late years by specialists of great merit. The result in Creighton's opinion had perhaps been 'to isolate unduly this period and exaggerate some of its characteristics.' His aim was 'to found a sober view of the time on a sober criticism of its authorities.' His subject led him to deal with some of the characters who have been painted in general estimation with the blackest possible hues. He did not attempt to whitewash the Borgias, but he did not see why they should be made the scapegoats of all the vices of the Renaissance. In his opinion it was not fair 'to isolate the Popes from their surroundings and hold them up to exceptional ignominy.' He considered that Alexander VI. represented the tendencies of his age, and that 'the exceptional infamy that attaches to him is largely due to the fact that he did not add hypocrisy to his other vices.' But in judging the Popes he considered it 'impossible to forget their high office and their lofty claims.'

'I have tried,' he says in his preface, 'to deal fairly with the moral delinquencies of the Popes, without, I trust, running the risk of lowering the standard of moral judgment; but it seems to me neither necessary to moralise at every turn in historical writing, nor becoming to adopt an attitude of lofty superiority over anyone who ever played a prominent part in European affairs, nor charitable to lavish undiscriminating censure on any man. All I can claim is, that I have not allowed my judgment to be warped by a desire to be picturesque or telling.'

One of the rare moral judgments in his book is his statement that 'the substitution of cleverness for principle was Italy's ruin.'

A striking testimony to the impartiality of his book was a criticism in the 'Dublin Review' by a Roman Cardinal Archbishop, who spoke of it as marked 'by research of original documents, by accuracy in dealing with ecclesiastical matters, and by a calm judicial discernment.'

These volumes show the same sobriety and restraint that characterised the earlier ones ; but probably the exceptional interest of their subject made them more quickly popular, as they provided an historical background for those who wished to study the Renaissance in detail either in books or in Italy herself. Creighton asked Lord Acton to notice this fresh instalment of his work for the 'Historical Review.' Lord Acton, when he sent the review, wrote :

'March 11, 1887.

'Let me add the condition that it shall not appear until seen and passed by Gwatkin or Hort, or if there be any other of equal counsel ; for you must understand that it is the work of an enemy. . . . I need not explain, what you partly know, the width of yawning difference between your view of history and mine. . . . As the Review is not a cathedra for a private philosophy of history, I have said no more than was necessary to mark our difference without enlargement. My fear is that I have not succeeded in doing this without appearing hostile and depreciatory, and that I may have insisted more on my objections than on our obvious points of contact.'

Creighton was somewhat surprised that Lord Acton should have undertaken to notice his book for the 'Historical Review' when he meant so definitely to attack it.

To Mr. R. L. Poole　　　　　　　　　　'March 29.

'I am rather perplexed about a matter in which it seems to me that the humour of the situation is great. I asked Lord Acton to review my Popes, and he graciously consented. Now he sends me a review which reads to me like the utterances of a man who is in a furious passion, but is incapable of clear expression. He differs *toto cælo* from my conception of the time, apparently on some concealed grounds of polemics esoteric to a Liberal Roman who fought against

Infallibility. That is all right if he would say so ; but he hints and sneers and divagates in a way which seems to me ill-natured.

'Now the absurdity rather lies in the choice of the "Historical Review" as a vehicle for making an onslaught on its editor. It seems to me so funny that I shall be sorely tempted to add a note to the review, "The Editor is not responsible for the opinions expressed in the above article." However, I have sent it to the press, and you will see it in a few days. . . . It is rather long . . . and has some interesting things, especially some from bits from manuscripts in his possession. Don't mention this to anyone at present, but meditate first on the general question, and then give me your opinion on the specific document when you see it. It may be that I am over-sensitive : it may be that Acton does not clearly see what he has done ; but the situation is such an odd one that I have no precedent. I think the public would be greatly amused at an editor inviting and publishing a savage onslaught on himself. And the proceeding seems so odd on Acton's part. It would have seemed to me obvious to say frankly that I did not agree with the point of view of a book, and would like to say so freely elsewhere. . . . I was very angry at first, but now I am amused. . . . I shall trust to your judgment in this matter.'

'April 5.

'When I see Acton in print he does not read so malicious as when I spelled through his manuscript ; but he is terribly obscure. I can only guess what he means in many passages, and to the ordinary reader he will be quite unintelligible. His view is that of one who fought against Infallibility, and he studied the conciliar movement from that point of view. He had better be printed as he stands, don't you think so ? '

Creighton at first wrote to Lord Acton simply acknowledging the receipt of the review.

'March 26, 1887.

'Thank you for your review.
' . . . I wish I could induce you some day to put forward your philosophy of history in a substantial form. I am often called upon to explain it, and can only dimly guess ; but many would like to know more of it.

'For myself I know my own limitations, and I also know that my view of history pleases nobody ; but I cannot help thinking that there must be something in it because it so much *dis*pleases opposite characters. In haste,
'Yours ever,
'M. CREIGHTON.'

A few days later he wrote again more fully, but his letter unfortunately has not been preserved. Lord Acton made many corrections in the review, and wrote that he had 'altered every passage which could be construed or misconstrued into hostility.' He explained his point of view at great length in a letter from which the following extracts are given to make Creighton's answer more clear.

'What is not at all a question of opportunity or degree is our difference about the Inquisition. . . . The point is not whether you like the Inquisition . . . but whether you can without reproach to historical accuracy speak of the later mediæval Papacy as having been tolerant and enlightened. . . . We are not speaking of the Papacy towards the end of the fifteenth or early sixteenth century, when for a couple of generations and down to 1542 there was a decided lull in the persecuting spirit. Nor are we speaking of the Spanish Inquisition. . . . I mean the Popes of the thirteenth and fourteenth centuries from Innocent III. down to the time of Hus. These men instituted a system of persecution . . . it is the most conspicuous fact in the history of the mediæval Papacy . . . that is the breaking point, the article of their system by which they stand or fall. . . . I do not complain that it does not influence your judgment; . . . but what amazes and disables me is that you speak of the Papacy not as exercising a just severity, but as not exercising any severity. . . . You ignore, you even deny, at least implicitly, the existence of the torture chamber and the stake. . . . The same thing is the case with Sixtus IV. and the Spanish Inquisition. . . . In what sense is the Pope not responsible for the Constitution by which he established the new Tribunal? . . . The person who authorises the act shares the guilt of the person who commits it. Now the Liberals think persecution a crime of a worse order than adultery, and the acts done by Ximenes considerably worse than the entertainment of Roman courtesans by Alexander VI. The responsibility exists whether the thing permitted be good or bad. If the thing be criminal, then the authority permitting it bears the guilt. Whether Sixtus is infamous or not depends on our view of persecution and absolutism. Whether he is responsible or not depends simply on the ordinary evidence of history. . . . Upon these two points we differ widely; still more widely with regard to the principle by which you undertake to judge men. You say that people in authority are not to be snubbed or sneered at from our pinnacle of conscious rectitude. I really don't know whether you exempt them because of their rank, or of their success and power, or of their date. . . . But if we might discuss this point until we found that we nearly agreed, and if we do agree thoroughly about the impropriety of Carlylese denunciations and Pharisaism in history, I cannot accept your canon that we are to judge Pope and King unlike other men, with a favoured presumption that they did no wrong. If there is any presumption, it is the other way, against holders of power, increasing as the power increases. Historic responsibility has to make up for the want of legal responsibility. Power tends to corrupt, and absolute power corrupts absolutely. Great men are almost always bad men, even when they exercise influence and not authority: still more when you superadd the tendency or the certainty of corruption by authority. . . . The inflexible integrity of the moral code is to me the secret of the authority, the dignity, the utility of history. If we may debase the currency for the sake of genius or success or reputation, we may debase it for the sake of a man's influence, of his religion, of his party, of the good cause which prospers by his credit and suffers by his disgrace. Then History ceases to be a science, an arbiter of controversy, a guide of the wanderer ; . . . it serves where it ought to reign, and it serves the worst cause better than the purest. . . . Of course I know that you do sometimes censure great men severely ; but the doctrine I am contesting appears in your preface. . . . I am sure you will take this long and contentious letter more as a testimony of hearty confidence and respect than of hostility, although as far as I grasp your method I do not agree with it. Mine seems to me plainer and safer, but it has never been enough to make me try to write a history, from mere want of knowledge. . . .

'I remain yours most sincerely,
'ACTON.'

To Lord Acton   'The College, Worcester: [April 9, 1887].

'My dear Lord Acton,—Your letter is an act of true friendliness, and I am very grateful to you for it—more grateful than I can say. It is a rare encouragement to me to have such a standard set up as you have put before me. Judged by it, I have nothing to say except to submit ; *efficaci do manus scientiæ.* Before such an ideal I can only confess that I am shallow and frivolous, limited alike in my views and in my knowledge. You conceive of History as an architectonic for the writing of which a man needs the severest and largest of training ; and it is impossible not to agree with you : so it ought to be. I can only admit that I fall far short of the equipment necessary for the task that I have undertaken. I was engaged in reading quietly for the purpose, and the beginning of writing lay in the remote distance in my mind, when I received a letter asking me to look through the papers of an old gentleman whom I slightly knew, who on his deathbed had made me his literary executor. I came across him in the Bodleian, where he came to read for a history of the rise of Universities. He died at the age of seventy-four, possessor of a vast amount of notes, out of which all that I could piece together was an article on Wyclif's Oxford life. This filled me with a horror of note-books, and urged me to begin definitely to write. I thought that I had best frankly do what I could ; anything would serve as a step for my successors. So I wrote. I entirely agree with your principles of historical judgments ; but apparently I admit casuistry to a larger extent than you approve. I remember that in 1880 I met John Bright at dinner : he was very cross, apparently a Cabinet meeting had disagreed with him. Among other things he said, " If the people knew what sort of men statesmen were, they would rise and hang the whole lot of them." Next day I met a young man who had been talking to Gladstone, who urged him to parliamentary life, saying, " Statesmanship is the noblest way to serve mankind." I am sufficient of a Hegelian to be able to combine both judgments ; but the results of my combination cannot be expressed in the terms of the logic of Aristotle. In studying history the question of the salvability of an archdeacon becomes indefinitely extended to all officials, kings and popes included. What I meant in my offending sentence in my preface was, that anyone engaged in great affairs occupied a representative position, which required special consideration. Selfishness, even wrong-doing, for an idea, an institution, the maintenance of an accepted view of the basis of society, does not cease to be wrong-doing ; but it is not quite the same as personal wrong-doing : it is more difficult to prove, and it does not equally shock the moral sense of others, or destroy the moral sense of the doer. The acts of men in power are determined by the effective force behind them of which they are the exponents : their morality is almost always lower than the morality of the mass of men ; but there is generally a point fixed below which they cannot sink with impunity. Homicide is always homicide ; but there is a difference between that of a murderer for his own gain, and that of a careless doctor called in to see a patient who would probably have died anyhow ; and the carelessness of the doctor is a difficult thing to prove.

'What is tolerance nowadays? Is it a moral virtue in the possessor, or is it a recognition of a necessity arising from an equilibrium of parties? It often seems to me that we speak as if it was the first, when actually it is the second. My Liberalism admits to every man the right to his own opinion, and imposes on me the duty of teaching him what is best ; but I am by no means sure that that is the genuine conviction of all my Liberal friends. French Liberalism does not convince me that it is universal. I am not quite sure how Frederic Harrison or Cotter Morison would deal with me were they in a majority. The possession of a clear and definite ideal of society seems to me dangerous to its possessors. The Mediæval Church had such an ideal : the result was the Inquisition, which was generally approved by the common consciousness. In the period at the end of the fifteenth century the Papacy seems to me to have wearied of the Inquisition, which was not much supported. The Popes were comparatively tolerant to Jews, Marrani, Turks : they did not attack the humanists : they did not furbish up the old weapons and apply them to new cases, except in the recognition of the Spanish Inquisition by Sixtus IV., about whom I have probably expressed myself loosely ; but I have not my volumes here, and I do not know exactly what I said. What I meant was, that to Sixtus IV. this recognition was a matter of official routine. To have refused it, he would have had to enunciate a new principle and make a new departure in ecclesiastical jurisdiction. I should have honoured him if he had done so ; but I do not think him exceptionally persecuting because he did not do so. He accepted what he found. My purpose was not to justify him, but to put him in rank with the rest. I think, however, that I was wrong, and that you are right : his responsibility was graver than I have admitted. I think he knew better.

'You judge the whole question of persecution more rigorously than I do. Society is an organism, and its laws are an expression of the conditions which it considers necessary for its own preservation. When men were hanged in England for sheep stealing, it was because people thought that sheep stealing was a crime, and ought to be severely put down. We still think it a crime, but we think it can be checked more effectually by less stringent punishments. Nowadays people are not agreed about what heresy is : they do not think it a menace to society, hence they do not ask for its punishment ; but the men who conscientiously thought heresy a crime may be accused of an intellectual mistake, not necessarily of a moral crime. The immediate results of the Reformation were not to favour free thought; and the error of Calvin, who knew that ecclesiastical unity was abolished, was a far greater one than that of Innocent III., who struggled to maintain it. I am hopelessly tempted to admit degrees of criminality, otherwise history becomes a dreary record of wickedness. I go so far with you that it supplies me with few heroes, and records few good actions; but the actors were men like myself, sorely tempted by the possession of power, trammelled by holding a representative position (none more trammelled than popes), and in the sixteenth century especially, looking at everything in a very abstract way. I suppose statesmen rarely regard questions in the concrete. I can rarely follow the actions of contemporary statesmen with much moral satisfaction. In the past I find myself regarding them with pity: who am I that I should condemn them? Surely they knew not what they did.

'This is no reason for not saying what they did; but what they did was not always what they tried to do, or thought that they were doing.

'Moral progress has indeed been slow; it still is powerless to affect international relations. If Bright's remedy were adopted, and every statesman in Europe were hanged, would that mend matters?

'In return for your wisdom I have written enough to show my foolishness. Your letter will give me much food for meditation, and may in time lead to an amendment of my ways. That you should have written, shows that you think me capable of doing better. I will only promise that if I can I will; but the labours of practical life multiply, and I have less time for work at my subject now than I had in the country. For the period coming on I ought to spend years in archives, which is impossible. . . . My jottings bear the traces of the incoherence of one who has preached five sermons this week and has two more to preach to-morrow. I have not had time to think over your letter; but I wanted to thank you. Perhaps the effort to rid myself of prejudice has left me cold and abstract in my mode of expression and thinking. If so, it is an error to be amended and corrected.

'Will you not some day write an article in the "Historical Review" on the Ethics of History? I have no objection to find my place among the shocking examples. Believe me that I am genuinely grateful to you.

'Yours most sincerely,
'M. CREIGHTON.'

To Mr. R. L. Poole   'April 12, 1887.

'I have had a long correspondence with Lord Acton, and now begin to understand him. He demands that history should be primarily a branch of the moral sciences, and should aim at proving the immutable righteousness of the ideas of modern Liberalism—tolerance and the supremacy of conscience. He has used me as a peg to indicate that belief. He is revising his original remarks, but I do not expect that much clearness will ensue, though it will be very interesting.

'My view of history is not to approach things with any preconceived ideas, but with the natural *pietas* and sympathy which I try to feel towards all men who do and try to do great things.

'*Mentem mortalia tangunt* is my motto. I try to put myself in their place : to see their limitations, and leave the course of events to pronounce the verdict upon system and men alike. No doubt Acton is more logical, but his view would reduce history to a dreary record of crimes to which I am unequal. Some day I will show you his letters, which are most interesting.' [1]

Mr. J. A. Symonds writing to a friend says : 'I see that you and I fully agree about Creighton. The book has been one of absorbing interest to me, not only in these last two volumes but in the first couple. I think it a really great book, which does honour to the school of English historians. The grasp of the whole field shown in his treatment, his power of turning from a Pope in Rome to the same Pope in Europe, is very remarkable.' [2]

---

[1] Those who are interested in these different methods of forming historical judgments will find Lord Acton's ideas more fully developed in his striking preface to L. A. Burd's edition of Machiavelli's *Principe*. Creighton did not materially change his method, but he was to some extent influenced by Lord Acton's views, and shows how carefully he weighed his words in his remarks about Lord Acton's Preface to Burd in the *Historical Review* in 1892. 'His pages . . . raise questions which every historian is bound to face. They exhort him to consider well his aim and object, and determine his relations to the moral law, which he professes to regard as supreme in his own nature, but shrinks from asserting as equally applicable to great characters in history, or to great social movements. They point to principles which are of the first importance in determining the future of historical science.' His own ideas on the subjects of dispute between him and Lord Acton are further illustrated in his Hulsean Lectures on 'Persecution and Toleration,' and in a lecture on Heroes published in the *Cornhill Magazine*, 1898, reprinted in *Lectures and Addresses*.

[2] *Life of J. A. Symonds*, by Horatio Brown, ii. 289.

To Mr. H. C. Lea   'Worcester: December 10, 1887.

'My dear Mr. Lea,—Your first volume gave me the keenest pleasure : it is a work which will take a permanent place in historical literature. Your work at the actual operation of ecclesiastical institutions is quite new in spirit. I mean that it brings before the reader the actual facts of daily life in their reference to the two important classes of those who paid, and those who were paid. It was of as much importance in the Middle Ages as it is now to which class the individual belonged. Your hold on the social and economic aspect of ecclesiastical institutions makes your book luminous at every turn. I shall look with great interest for the forthcoming volumes. I can to some degree appreciate the labour which your first volume has required, for I had occasion to look up the Cathari and Waldenses in the course of my lectures, and found the question very thorny. . . . I quite agree with your feeling that the sight of one's book bound is a source of woe. I never pick up one of my volumes without finding some mistake or misprint, or clumsiness, or ambiguity, or something that causes me a pang.'

'Cambridge : May 21, 1887.

'I feel with you the great difficulty of treating the Papacy fairly. One's objections are deeply seated : how far ought they to be perpetually repeated ? '

'Worcester: July 17, 1888.

'Dear Mr. Lea,—. . . The papers which you are good enough to promise concerning Parsons will be full of interest for English History. The exact facts of the Jesuit doings in England are only lately beginning to be looked into, mostly by the Jesuits themselves. I am afraid that the story in full tends to show that Elizabeth's advisers were not much more enlightened than Torquemada, and carried their political alarm into religious matters. The breach in England between the Jesuits and the secular priests is still very little recognised.

'I have been reading your book with increasing admiration for its thoroughness. You will not think me faithless to my promise when I tell you that after all I have abandoned it to Lord Acton for the " Historical Review." He had looked into the book, and was so much impressed by its importance that he expressed a desire to review it. His capacity for that task is unequalled by anyone in Europe ; indeed, it is his chief subject, for his view of the decline of the Papacy is that it became untrue to its chief duty when it became antagonistic to liberty ; and his objection to me is that I do not bring that fact sufficiently forward.   My answer, in my own mind, is, that I have not yet reached the point where according to my method those considerations come in, and I cannot criticise the Papacy of the fifteenth century from the point of view of the nineteenth century.   I apprehend that your book will just suit him, and probably he will have a few points of detail which may interest you.'

CHAPTER XIV

In June 1887 Creighton went up to London for the Jubilee.

To L. C.   'The Savile Club: June 21, 1887.

'The day has been a complete success to everybody concerned, it seems to me. I breakfasted at 8, started at 8.30,
found my door, and was ready before 9. There was no
particular crush or difficulty: the arrangements were excellent. Inside the Abbey it was quite cool, and there was no
crushing in the seats. I saw many people whom I knew.
. . . The Queen was a little late, not her fault, but the other
royalties. My gallery was just over the altar, and therefore
opposite the Queen. Anything more magnificent you cannot
imagine: it surpassed what I should have thought possible;
but I will keep my account till I come. The nicest thing was
the Queen receiving the homage of her children after the
service: they all came and kissed her hand, and she kissed
their cheek. I got back quite quietly to Harry's at 2, and
then walked hither past Buckingham Palace, where I saw the
royal carriages, and so got an idea of the outside procession.
Then I rambled through the Park and along Piccadilly to
study the crowd, which was an excellent crowd, most good-
humoured and thoroughly enjoying itself; the people looked
quite delighted. . . . I think the whole thing is really most impressive. Tell the children that I shall have tremendous
stories when I get back.'

Worcester celebrated the Jubilee by a Mayoral Banquet
on July 1, at which Creighton proposed the toast of the
Houses of Parliament, and concluded his speech by saying
that 'the House of Commons is dearer to us now than it has
been at any time, because it is entirely our own and reproduces
our own infirmity.'

In July, as I was unable to leave home, he went for a
short ramble in the North of France with Mr. Rose of

Emmanuel, and satisfied his love of architecture by the study of some of the finest cathedrals in the world, Ypres, Tournai, Noyon, Laon, &c.

To L. C.   'Noyon : July 8, 1887.

'We are getting on famously, and I feel that I have seen things innumerable. I can't say that the country is very lovely, but the towns are nice, and the churches are to me amazingly interesting.'

'Rheims : July 10.

'The Cathedral of Rheims I have only hurriedly glanced at. . . . The whole thing is of the very finest late Gothic work. . . . It shows me more than any other building why the Renaissance triumphed. The complexity of the French Gothic became so great that men turned with joy to the simplicity of the classical style. The same thing applies in England : the strength and simplicity of the classic style charmed men who were lost in the Perpendicular vaulting and its excessive ornamentation. It was a natural reaction.'

'Soissons : July 11.

'We had a good day at Rheims, which needed all our time. . . . The Cathedral is a marvel of Gothic architecture. I was immensely impressed by it : it took five good hours of patient study. . . . It far surpassed my expectations, being superior to Chartres and quite comparable to Orvieto. It pulls up French architecture in my mind to a very high place, in fact I think there is more to learn in France than in Italy from an architectural point of view. . . . It is becoming rather hard to keep all my churches distinct : they run into one another, but the general features of the group are very distinct and quite unlike anything we have in England.'

'Pierrefonds : July 12.

'I have certainly got out of this journey a notion of the charm of French scenery which I never had before. . . . I have just been playing with two little French children, whose father assures me that they are *vrais polissons*. I told him that I knew that, as I had six at home. . . . I have really enjoyed my ramble very much and have learned a great deal. That may be some consolation to you, but I do wish that you had been with me.'

On July 23 he distributed some prizes at Worcester in connexion with the University Extension Lectures, and spoke of the advantage it would be to the community if women would use their leisure to gain knowledge ; England would make a great step in advance when she had a thoroughly educated class of women to set a standard in social life.

He was in residence at Worcester during August and September, preaching in the Cathedral on Sunday evenings, and lecturing each week in the Chapter House on Church History. Whenever possible he liked to make himself useful in the diocese of Worcester generally, by going to preach in different parishes. He went often to Birmingham, where he was especially anxious to help on the work of Church extension. He felt deeply the need for the establishment of a bishopric in Birmingham, and did all in his power to promote the scheme. Later when he went to Peterborough he spoke of the valuable experience he had gained from going about the diocese of Worcester and seeing something of the work in many various parishes, an experience which helped him much as a Bishop.

On August 22, 1887, our fourth daughter was born. In choosing her name he carried on the Dante tradition, and called her Gemma after Dante's wife.

Early in September the Festival of the Three Choirs was held at Worcester. It was a source of great pleasure to Creighton, who interested himself in every detail of the arrangements, and delighted in the music. As was the custom at Worcester, we kept open house. President Eliot of Harvard and Mrs. Eliot stayed with us among others during the Festival, and we entertained about sixty people to lunch and tea every day.

On September 20, Creighton spoke at a meeting of the Worcestershire Union of Workmen's Clubs and Institutes. He told the working men that the great work of their Union must be 'to extend popular education,' and went on to say :

' In spite of all the talk about education, the mass of Englishmen do not believe in education ; they do not really like it. They like to talk about it, but they do not wish too much to be done. Some people speak as if we had established such a magnificent system of education with our Board Schools, that we need do nothing more but let them go on working. I do not think that Board Schools have got us very far yet. Instead of being at the end, we are only at the beginning of education. . . . Your Union can do no better work than to spread among the members of the clubs scattered throughout town and country a desire to educate themselves. . . . Unless freedom is founded upon virtue, it must rapidly cease to be freedom and degenerate into tyranny. Popular government is good, if the people want what is right and good in itself, if they have the capacity to choose between good and evil. . . . The whole object of education is to equip them for that purpose.

'Unless we take some steps to carry on the teaching of those who have left school, to teach them how to use the means with which they have been supplied, we have done no good at all. This is the great educational problem which has to be faced nowadays. . . . Times of ignorance have advantages of their own. People know they are ignorant, and are in consequence willing to be guided by others. Times of perfect knowledge, in which everybody is capable of forming an intelligent and wise opinion on the materials submitted to them—these also have their advantages ; but what we are now confronted with is a time of half knowledge, when everyone thinks he is called upon to form an opinion and that he is as capable of doing so as anyone else, and when he considers that it is not the wisdom of his opinion, but the loudness of voice and violence of character with which he enunciates it, which will carry the day. We need greater humility. A man should know what he knows and what he does not know. Politics have lately raised in my mind serious considerations. Has the extension of the franchise had the result, as was hoped and promised, of promoting the education of the people? . . . Have those who have spoken to the people since that extension spoken more freely, more frankly, more on the basis of principles, less about purely party matters, than before? I fear that never have political questions been discussed with less reference to principles than of late. . . . It must be by means of intellectual training that things will be improved. Men must learn to think for themselves, and so to form sound and deliberate opinions.'

The same thoughts were in his mind when a few days after, in the last of that year's series of lectures on Church History, he spoke of the enormous popularity enjoyed by Thomas Becket immediately after his death.

'These things are worth considering in days when it

is supposed that popular opinion is always right. Thomas was certainly not the wisest and most admirable of men, though the popular opinion of Europe voted him such, and went on so voting for a couple of centuries. Popular opinion was not only wrong about this man, but was in absolute ignorance about his policy. Thomas by his action broke up the reforming party which under the guidance of Archbishop Theobald had been making for a revival of the Church of England on a definite spiritual basis.

In October he read a paper at the Wolverhampton Church Congress on 'The Church and History.'[1]

In 1888 he was examiner for the Historical Tripos, and also adjudicator for the Prince Consort, the Norrisian, and the Thirlwall Historical prizes. This year saw the beginning of the agitation for conferring degrees upon women in Cambridge. Creighton's attitude on the subject was a disappointment to most of his Newnham friends, who had hoped that with his genuine interest in women's education he would certainly be in favour of granting them degrees. He considered the University to be a corporation founded for definite purposes, and that the admission of women to degrees would involve a fundamental change in the idea of the University, and would not really advance the cause of women's education. He was always anxious for educational experiments, and would have preferred to see women free to devise their own educational system, rather than be fettered with the limitations imposed on men in many cases by the traditions of the past. He did not take any active part in the struggle, and did not sign any of the various memorials presented to the Senate on the subject, but he was sympathetic with the suggestion that a new and independent authority should be formed to grant degrees to the women of both the Oxford and Cambridge Colleges; however, as this proposal did not commend itself to the women concerned, he thought it useless to press it.

In April 1888 his monograph on Cardinal Wolsey appeared in the series of Twelve English Statesmen published by Messrs. Macmillan. He had a great admiration for Wolsey's intellectual powers and force of character, and considered

---

[1] Reprinted in *The Church and the Nation.*

him a notable exception to the great majority of English statesmen, who are 'generally opportunists or choose to represent themselves as such.' He speaks of him ' as probably the greatest political genius whom England has ever produced ; ' as 'greater than his achievements, to be estimated by what he chose to do rather than by what he did.'

He next undertook to write on his native city of Carlisle for Professor Freeman's series of Historic Towns ; this book he wrote for the historical not for the antiquarian student. His object was to show how the life of the town developed amid the unrest produced by its position on the border. It was a subject to which his early memories attracted him. 'Much as I have learned from books,' he says in the preface, 'I feel that I have learned more from many wanderings on foot through the Border land.' His understanding of the character of the people of Carlisle, above all his sympathy with the fortunes of the fabric of its cathedral and his loving appreciation of its shattered beauty, show how permanent had been the influence of his early surroundings. The book was published in 1889.

In April of this year he had the pleasure of making the personal acquaintance of one of his historical correspondents, Count Ugo Balzani, of Rome. This acquaintance rapidly became a close friendship ; the two men had many tastes and sympathies in common, and the friendship extended to their families. After this not a year passed in which we did not spend some time with the Balzanis either in Italy or England. The delight and ease of this intercourse increased Creighton's attraction to the Italian character, which he considered, in spite of such marked superficial differences, more really sympathetic to the English than either the French or German. He said that he found it easy to understand the Italians, and that the common sense which was the foundation of their character harmonised with the English disposition.

In September 1889 we were able to go abroad together. We went this time to Dalmatia ; going down the coast from Trieste in one of the Austrian Lloyd steamers, and stopping at the most interesting towns. He had prepared himself for this journey by studying Mr. T. G. Jackson's admirable book on the architecture of that district.

MANDELL CREIGHTON AND HIS DAUGHTERS, 1888.

The strange beauty of the coast, the varied costumes of the people, and the exceeding attraction of the buildings, made it a most interesting journey. He felt that much was to be learnt from the study of the architecture which showed an unbroken tradition from the time of the Romans till the end of the sixteenth century, and made clear the steps by which classical architecture passed into Gothic.

We went as far as the enchanting Bocche di Cattaro, and from Cattaro ascended the Montenegrin mountain and visited Cettigne. We had only a day for this excursion, as we had to catch a returning steamer, and in order to accomplish it had to leave Cattaro at four in the morning. In the mysterious darkness we mounted the marvellous road which zigzags up the face of the almost perpendicular mountain that overhangs Cattaro.

The dawn broke in incomparable beauty as we reached the top of the ascent, and the blue waters of the Bocche lying far below looked as if we could have dropped a stone into them. Thence through a sea of tossing limestone peaks and stony valleys we drove to Cettigne, the desolate village which ranks as one of the capitals of Europe. The drive back down the mountain was made in glorious moonlight, and my husband never forgot the late supper at the little inn at Cattaro, where we were allowed to join some of the natives in eating what he considered the best dish he ever ate in his life, a great stew of quails and rice.

We lingered a few days at Venice on our way back, and then went into the mountains, first to join Mr. Horatio Brown at Possagno, and thence to Bassano, Marostica, Castelfranco, Conegliano, and Belluno, where we refreshed ourselves with some lovely mountain walks.

To Sir Edward Grey   'Cambridge : October 25, 1888.

'We kicked our heels in September and the beginning of October in a very interesting way, by visiting Dalmatia, Montenegro, and the Venetian territory. I quite lost my heart to the Slavonic peoples with their magnificent costumes, their primitive habits, and their simple ways. I went with an open mind into their complicated politics ; but Montenegro did not convince me that small independent states were desirable. Montenegro is a mere Russian dependency sub-

sidised by Russia and protected by Russia as a useful outpost.
Its capital was a gross parody of a village not much bigger
than Embleton, trying to look important.   On the other hand,
I was favourably impressed by Austria as a civilising and
governing power.   It seemed to be doing a very difficult
work with great skill and no unnecessary fuss.   They are
much better rulers than the North Germans.   I stopped in
Elsass a few days coming back, and was appalled at the
stories of the German tyranny, for it was nothing less.'

While we were away, our eldest son went to school for
the first time, at the age of twelve.   His father had given
much thought to the choice of a school, and had decided on
Marlborough, to which he sent all his three sons ; they went
there straight from home without going first to a prepara-
tory school.   He wrote the following letters to his son from
abroad.

'Conegliano: September 19, 1888.

'Dear Cuthbert,—By the time you get this you will be at
Marlborough, and will be settling down to your new life.
What that new life will be you alone can decide for yourself ;
but there are one or two things that I should like to say to
you, in the hope that they may help you.   First of all set
before yourself the fullness of your own responsibility : life at
home tended to hide it : if you did anything wrong some one
was sure to call your attention to it ; you trusted to them to
do so, and had a sort of outside conscience kept for you.
Well, you will have that no more : you will have to judge
yourself, and be responsible to yourself and look after yourself.   Try to do it well.   I do not intend to go on giving you
good advice ; for neither I nor mother can really help you
much ; we can only be of use to you if there is anything
definite you want to ask.   Moreover, I very much want you
to feel that I have no wish to exercise authority over you in
a needless way ; when once a boy leaves home he has to take
a father as a friend when he comes back, and that is what I
hope you will be able to do to me.   I have been the friend of
many young men, and I wonder whether I shall be the friend
of my own sons as they grow up.   I hope so.
'Well, of course you will have a temptation to be idle.
The only thing I can say is, that the future of your life is
before you, to make of it what you will.   All that I can do is
to give you a good start and a good chance ; and in sending

you to Marlborough I have tried to do the best I could. But you alone can settle what your own life is to be. It depends upon your industry, your intelligence, your capacity for taking pains. Now the reason why boys are taught Latin and Greek is because learning these languages is the best exercise in carefulness, attention, accuracy, quickness of perception, and suchlike qualities. Many boys will talk as if you might be ever so clever in other ways which were far better. Of course this is not so : if there are some things better to learn, they had better find out what they are and learn them. But some like to talk as if there was in some people a natural cleverness which makes them do things without trouble. I never saw it : I never knew anyone who did anything worth doing without taking a great deal of trouble. In fact, you may make up your mind that a thing is generally valuable exactly in proportion to the amount of trouble which it takes to get.

'You are started among a number of other boys of your own age. You will find them of all sorts, I have no doubt. Use your own judgment about your friends, your companions, your pursuits. Judge for yourself, and do not be content simply to go with the multitude. Be true to yourself. Be courageous. Act up to what you know to be right. Do not laugh feebly at what you know to be wrong. Never forget to say your prayers, and let nothing prevent you. I had far rather you turned out a good boy than a clever boy ; but the two generally go together. Remember that your mother and I trust you entirely, and hope all our lives to be proud of you. There, I have said more than I meant to say. May God bless you, and keep you under the shadow of His wings, and may you always rest in peace with a sense of His protection.

'Your loving father,
'M. CREIGHTON.'

'Venice : September 28, 1888.

'Dear Cuthbert,—I was glad to get your letter this morning, and to hear that you had got on pretty well so far in your new life. Of course it will be strange at first, and will have difficulties which you had not at home ; but you must learn to act for yourself. Make up your own mind and stick to it ; change your mind when you see a better way ; only change it because you see for yourself that another way is better, not because other people say so. Meanwhile everybody will after a little think better of you for having a mind of your own. I was very well satisfied with the place you

c c 2

have taken in the school. You have begun very well for your age; stick to it and do better. Perhaps you will find that you have to give most attention to Latin verses, and you may think them troublesome. But remember that they are meant to teach you good taste and elegance of expression. But we have to learn to be careful and accurate, and then to be elegant. We have to learn first, that is, to say what we mean to say, and then to say it well and pointedly. Latin prose teaches you to say what you have to say accurately, and Latin verse teaches you to say it well. I am rather glad that you are in Mr. Thomas's form : he is a good master of the old-fashioned kind, which is a very good kind. When I first went to school I had a master who gave the most terrible impositions for carelessness : he made us write out ten times every lesson in which we made careless mistakes. I think he was too severe, but we all liked and respected him, and it was very good for us in the long run.

' I advise you to make up your mind which of the boys you like, and make a few real friends rather than a number of companions. It is much worth while in the long run : school friendships often last all one's life, and it is a great training of character to choose friends.'

At the Conversazione of the Worcester Architectural and Archæological Society in December, Creighton gave a lecture on his impressions of Dalmatia ; this was a kind of lecture which henceforth he often repeated and which was most popular. Easy and conversational in style, he yet avoided merely personal anecdotes, but gave to others something of what his keen powers of observation had enabled him to extract from the countries he visited.

In 1889 he was able to get to Worcester early enough after the Lent Term to take his share of the special Lenten services, and he gave a series of addresses in the Cathedral on ' Teachers of Holiness,' taking as his examples St. Wulstan, St. Francis, and St. Thomas à Kempis. In addresses of this sort he knew very well how to combine historical and moral teaching, how both to instruct and to edify. Learning was never paraded, and his hearers hardly realised why it was that he seemed to give them so clear an insight into the past, and to make them see its connexion with the present. In the first address he spoke a few special words to the Ordination candidates who were then gathered at Worcester, and told them that

'The work of the clergy is to know what the world is, what men actually do and think, not to trace out for themselves a little circle of practical orthodoxy, and say, "There will I walk, this is my duty."'

It was about this time that he organised lectures for the clergy of the Diocese in the Chapter House, and persuaded a number of distinguished scholars, including Dr. Bigg (now Regius Professor of Ecclesiastical History at Oxford) and Dr. Gore (now Bishop of Worcester), to come to Worcester and give courses of lectures.

As treasurer of the Chapter he was responsible for the manner in which the money allowed for keeping the external fabric and the approaches to the Cathedral in order, should be spent. At the west end of the Cathedral, between it and the river, was a piece of broken ground railed in and covered with the ruins of some of the monastic buildings. He suggested that this should be put in order, turned into a garden, provided with seats, and opened to the citizens of Worcester for their use. The Chapter agreed; the alterations were completed, and the garden and walks were opened to the public on June 12, 1889, and added much not only to the enjoyment of the citizens and visitors, but to the beauty of the west view of the Cathedral.

Educational matters were much debated in Worcester during 1889. The city possessed two schools, the Grammar School and the Cathedral or King's School. Neither seemed to be doing all they might for the education of the city. The Charity Commissioners suggested a new scheme for the Grammar School, which would have turned it into a Commercial School, but this was refused by the City Council, who suggested instead that the two schools should be amalgamated, and that there should be one school with a classical and a modern side. Creighton was naturally interested in the controversy, both as a governor of the Cathedral School and because of his constant desire to help on education in Worcester. He did not put himself forward as an advocate on either side, but exerted himself to keep the real educational question to the front, to get people to state clearly what they wanted, to make them see how their proposals would work out, and disentangle the real issues from merely temporal and personal considerations. By his fairness and moderation he preserved the confidence of both sides, and helped to make it clear that the one anxiety of the Chapter was to promote the best educational interests of the city.

Speaking at the prize-giving of the Cathedral School on October 8, he said :

' Education in any place can only divide itself into three branches : (1) the education of those who must go to work at twelve or thirteen, which is provided by the Elementary Schools ; (2) the education of those who go to some commercial pursuit at fifteen or sixteen ; (3) the education of those who go into a profession or to the University at eighteen or nineteen. The question to be considered is, whether in Worcester the two should go on together at the same school. It is impossible that the education of boys who are to leave school at the age of sixteen should be carried on, on the same lines as that of boys who are only to leave at eighteen.'

The matter was not settled when he left for Cambridge, and he came back to be present at a Conference on the subject, held on October 25. There he was the spokesman of the Chapter, and stated that they as the Governing Body of the Cathedral School were prepared to consider any scheme which might be brought before them, but that they thought it best that they should not be represented on the committee appointed to consider the matter in detail, and wished to be left with perfect freedom to consider any scheme that might be proposed. The Head Master of the Cathedral School was therefore left alone to defend the existing organisation of his school.

Still, though determined not to appear as a partisan, Creighton desired that there should be no obscurity with regard to his views on the general education question. He therefore wrote a letter to the 'Worcester Herald' on November 7, in which he said that his interest in the question arose from his concern for the educational advantages of the city, which he did not think had been sufficiently considered He went on :

' The education in which I am interested is that which fits

a boy for life, which develops his intelligence, trains his judgment, and gives him inward resources which promote his happiness and make him master of himself. . . . The process of education is only begun at school, where the object is to give as thorough a training of the mind as the time of the pupil's stay will allow. All educational methods are adapted to this end, and the question which all educational reformers are trying to solve is, What are the subjects and what are the methods best fitted to develop the intelligence and discipline the mind of a boy who leaves school and goes to work at the age of thirteen, or sixteen, or eighteen, or twenty-one? . . . The question what is best to be done with the boys who leave school and go to work between fifteen and eighteen has not yet received adequate attention, and Lord Derby truly said that our middle classes were for their position the worst educated class in the community. . . . Common sense and experience alike show that institutions with different aims had better be kept apart—I say institutions with different aims, for my experience of education would lead me to arrange both the nature, the order, the number of subjects, and the importance attached to each quite differently from the beginning in the two kinds of schools.'

To the Rev. E. Bolland. Head Master of the Cathedral School, he wrote :

'Cambridge : November 11, 1889.

'. . . I am opposed to a Modern School altogether, though I agree with a Grammar School having one standard through-out, in which some boys are being prepared for the Univer-sities and others not ; and I can conceive a differentiation of some of their pursuits in accordance ; e.g. Greek might take the place of Natural Science and Modern History and such like things. But to get a good education you want a high standard. Modern Schools at —— &c. are *bad* schools for duffers and shirks, and it is notorious that a classical boy can beat the modern boys in their own subjects and do his Latin and Greek as well.

'There is no difficulty in making schools *on paper*; the question is, how will they work under our circumstances? I have written a letter to the " Herald " in which I have indicated the lines of my opposition. I thought it fair to do so lest I should seem to be wilfully obstructive. But the question lies with the Charity Commissioners. It is easier to persuade the Worcester public than to persuade them.'

Conducted in this spirit, the discussion did nothing

to embitter the happy relations which existed between the
Chapter and the City.   In the end, the Charity Commission
sent down a deputy Commissioner, who went carefully into
the matter and reported that no general desire for the amal-
gamation of the two schools existed; ultimately a new
scheme was provided for the Grammar School, which has
worked satisfactorily.

Experience of the way in which a cathedral town was
beset with beggars and impostors of every kind led Creighton
to desire to introduce the Charity Organisation Society into
Worcester.   After some deliberation a public meeting was
called to start a branch on January 10, 1890, at which
he produced the rules that had been drafted by a provisional committee for the Society.   He said that the Society
aimed to be

'not only negative but decidedly positive in character,
that one of its main objects was the definite and actual improvement of the poor. . . . It wished to be the servant of
other institutions, to work without pedantry, beginning in
humility, and with the desire to learn in what way it could be
most useful.'

He took personal interest in the working of the Society,
and whenever he was in Worcester attended the weekly
meetings of the committee.

After speaking about Charity Organisation on the afternoon of January 10, he spoke in the evening at the Conversazione of the Worcester Students' Association, and impressed
upon them the need of having a methodical line of study.
He said that the gain of knowledge was not comprised in the
facts obtained, but in the way in which the facts were ascertained.   Careful study in connexion with the lectures was
the best way of building up their minds and rendering
them capable to form a proper judgment in all things.

In the summer of 1889 we went for a short ramble in
Normandy and Brittany, taking for the first time our two
eldest daughters with us.   On our return to England we
visited some of our friends in the north.   It was one of
the rare occasions on which Creighton revisited his former
parish.   He felt it a difficult and not altogether desirable
thing to do, much though he loved the place.   The con-

gregation which gathered to hear him preach showed the affection with which he was still regarded. In the spring of 1890, when the time of the University vacation and the arrangements for his residence at Worcester would make it possible for him to get a five weeks' holiday, we hoped to make a journey to Spain. He prepared for it by studying Spanish during his spare minutes, and while in Spain we continued our studies, reading Spanish novels with the help of a dictionary during the long train journeys. He was much attracted by the beauty and dignity of the language, and even managed to get on fairly well with speaking it.

We visited Carcassonne on our way, and then went to Barcelona and Tarragona, where he delighted in the wonderful walls. Thence we went to Valencia, Seville, and Granada, and stayed there some days, revelling in its rare beauty. Next we went to Cordova and on to Madrid. There the picture gallery was a revelation. He was charmed by the early Spanish painters, whose works are seldom seen out of Spain, and for the first time learnt to know Velasquez in his full force, and to recognise him as the supreme painter. We visited Toledo from Madrid, and stayed at Avila and Burgos on our way home. Avila with its mediæval walls and superb Romanesque churches interested him as much as any of the places he saw. He enjoyed the bright invigorating air of Spain, which was often bitterly cold, and considered this one of the most health-giving holidays he ever had. His general impressions are recorded in a letter written in the following autumn.

To Count Ugo Balzani   'Worcester : September 4, 1890.

'Dear Balzani,—I was very glad to hear from you that you were enjoying idle days—idle, that is, from outward business, not from quiet reading and the real joys of life. I wish that I could say the same. Every year seems to bring more outward things to do, and gives me less time for quiet of any kind. Then occurs the question—which after all is more useful? But perhaps the question is not worth answering, and either may be equally useful or useless as the case may be.

' We had a hope at one time in April of paying you a visit in Paris, but it disappeared. When we returned from Spain we had to hasten home without staying in Paris at all, because labours had gathered round me which left me no time to loiter. I enjoyed Spain in many ways very much ; it was full of interest, but it has not the *charm* which is reserved for two countries above all others, England and Italy. Moreover, Spain leaves the curious impression of a country which never did anything original—now the Moors, now France, now Italy have influenced it : when one asks what there is which is purely Spanish, there is nothing save a few pictures of Velasquez, a few plays of Calderon, and a novel of Cervantes, all sprung from foreign impulses. In another point Spain is impressive : it bears the marks of one moment of importance —the Catholic Reaction—which is intelligible after a glance at any Spanish town.

'But I dare say you knew all this before. Since returning from Spain I had the business of term, then much to do here, where we have been all the summer, indulging only in an occasional ramble.

'Yes, I have received with joy the volumes of the " Istituto Storico Italiano ; " they are printed most charmingly and are a delight to read. . . .

'We are all well : Cuthbert is at home for holidays, and when he returns takes Walter back with him to school, thus the family diminishes and the expense increases. It is a stupid system. I am sure the Contessa will agree with me. Our love to her and to all yours.

'Yours ever,
'M. CREIGHTON.'

To C. D.

'I was not impressed by Roman services in a country where they are supposed to be best. The people are devout, but their devotion strikes a northern mind as being frivolous, and not influencing the depths of character.'

He never revisited Spain, though he often talked of it, and would have liked to see something of the northern parts, but the opportunity never came.

During these years he was working on steadily at his History of the Papacy, absorbed in the study of the German humanists, and the events which prepared the way for the Reformation.

To Miss Mary Bateson   'August 6, 1889.

'I am reduced almost to idiocy by attempting to understand the mediæval doctrine about *Indulgences*. Let me commend it you when you feel in a lazy mood ; it will turn your hair grey if anything will.'

He gave a great deal of thought and investigation to this question of *Indulgences*. He repeatedly said that no other point in history which he had studied seemed to him so obscure, or so difficult to explain in terms which would not lead to misconception. The way in which he approached this subject was typical of his whole method in dealing with historical questions. He would not dismiss a matter off hand, nor pass a ready judgment on it. He laboured not only to find out all he could about it, but to realise its real significance in the past. It was not enough for him to know how an institution struck him, he wanted to discover how men whom he recognised as having like passions with himself came to frame it, what it meant to them, and what they meant by it.

Neither at Worcester nor Cambridge could he find much time for his own work. This year the Festival of the Three Choirs was again held at Worcester, and made the summer a very busy one. In the October Term at Cambridge, at the request of Dr. Cunningham, Vicar of Great St. Mary's, he joined in giving a course of addresses at St. Mary's on the Protestant Sects. He lectured on the Congregationalists and the Baptists. In his first lecture he said :

'The object of these addresses is to try and understand the principles on which rest the differences which divide Christian bodies from one another. Our tendency when first we are brought face to face with such differences, is to approach them from the point of view of common sense, to consider them as contained in so many formulated statements which can be discussed on their own merits. But this attitude is soon found to be superficial. The causes of disagreement lie deeper than the surface. They are interwoven with every part of a man's view of life : they are a portion of his moral and intellectual heritage : they have been handed down to him from the past, and appeal to his emotions by the halo of noble tradition with which they are surrounded. English Nonconformity has great memories. All its various forms corresponded to some genuine need of the time in which it arose. Each embodies some great truth which was once overlooked or neglected.'

These words show the spirit in which he always approached

Nonconformity. The concluding words of his lecture show the nature of his own feelings as a member of the Church.

'We who rejoice that we are members of the Holy Catholic Church find in the records of our Lord's life clear witness that one great aim of His earthly ministry was the formation of a society and the education of its leaders. As a matter of fact He did not found a number of small congregations, but He selected Apostles and bade them preach the Gospel in all the world, and gave them the assurance of His abiding presence. . . . We know that Christ hears any prayer anywhere and anyhow offered to Him. . . . There is an invisible Church known only to its Lord, in which we humbly hope our membership will some day be made manifest. But that does not exclude a visible Church. . . . That visible Church is the eternal legacy of our Blessed Lord to the world. . . . The broad lines of its organisation were determined in the time of the Apostles. . . . This organisation we steadfastly maintain as being, next to God's written revelation, His greatest gift to struggling men. . . . We of the Church of England have increasing reason to rejoice that our country in its time of trial preserved the immemorial heritage of the Catholic Church. The days are past when it can be regarded as a matter of policy or convenient arrangement. It has become the object of our deepest reverence, of our most passionate regard. We can point, as to a witness of God's presence, to the marvellous recuperative power which it has shown and is showing; to its capacity to adapt itself to altered circumstances and conditions of life and thought. . . . In spite of all its faults, it is the historic Church which has influenced and is influencing the world by its testimony to the abiding presence of the Lord.' [1]

Early in December, Creighton received a letter from Lord Salisbury asking whether he would be disposed to exchange the Canonry of Worcester for the Canonry of Windsor, which was just vacant. His letter ended as follows:

'To the Queen the matter, of course, is of considerable interest; and the Canonries of Windsor are always filled up in deference to the Sovereign's personal wishes. She would be glad to be able to nominate you to this vacancy.'

Creighton did not welcome the thought of the change, but he did not see how he could refuse, and he hoped that Windsor might give him more leisure than Worcester.

---

[1] These lectures are published in *Lectures and Addresses.*

To Miss Ethel Brown   'December 12, 1890.

'Thank you for your congratulations.   I do not know that
I am much to be congratulated.   The life at Worcester was
much to my liking.   I do not know that Windsor will be so
much so.   The work will be less obvious and more subtle.
It will perhaps fit in better with my life as a Professor.
'However, I must make the best of it.   We are just going
to Worcester for the last time.'

To C. D.   'Worcester: January 7.

'People seem to think that we ought to be glad to go to
Windsor: at present we are only sorry to leave Worcester, and
the thoughts of what people call society have absolutely no
charms for me.   I find that I grow simpler as time goes on,
and the mere externals of life are indifferent to me.   I prefer
artisans to dukes; but I suppose dukes have souls to be helped,
though it is hard to realise.'

Christmas was a gay time at Worcester.   There were
many entertainments for the various members of the cathedral
staff, the choristers being specially fêted to make up for their
having to spend Christmas away from their homes.   We
always had a Christmas tree for them, followed by games
of all kinds, in which my husband shared; the boys were
absolutely at their ease with him, and he enjoyed playing
and talking with them.   In 1887 he wrote to a friend on
December 29:

'We have been busy with festivities to the cathedral
staff, entertaining choristers and such like.   The children are
very rampant, as they have had a festivity every night this
week. . . . We have had a very nice and happy Christmas.
I feel as if I was growing wiser and better—and there was
great need to do both.   Louise says the same, and we both
agreed that the children were much improved.   So we
generally congratulated ourselves and feel happy.'

The same simple festivities took place in 1890, and we
felt sadly that we were sharing in them for the last time.
Worcester had grown very dear to us; we had met with
great kindness there, and made many friends.   Creighton
undertook to come back to take the Three Hours Service on
Good Friday, as he was not required to go to Windsor at
once.

In 1891 Lent came early, so that the greater part of it fell within the University term. Creighton thought that special services and addresses ought to be provided for the undergraduates. In 1888 he had given a course of Lenten addresses in the chapel at Emmanuel, of which Mr. J. O. F. Murray writes : ' I remember the first very well. It was a very powerful and direct appeal to all that is most tender, most sacred in the hearts of young men, pleading with them not to let the religious side of their nature starve while the physical and intellectual asserted their rights.' This year he spoke to Dr. Cunningham on the subject, and said that he ought to do something of the sort at St. Mary's on a weekday evening. Dr. Cunningham objected that it was hopeless to fill so large a church as St. Mary's, but Creighton insisted that it was the right church for the purpose, and that it was incumbent on Dr. Cunningham to organise the services. Finally Dr. Cunningham agreed, on condition that Creighton would give the addresses, and to this he at once consented. Dr. Cunningham writes :

' He gave four addresses on the Sense of Wrong-doing, the Sense of Sin, the Joy of Pardon, the Forgiven Life. . . . There were exceedingly good congregations. Personally, and as one who knew him well in his lighter moods, I was deeply impressed by these devotional addresses.'

Before these addresses were delivered, a great change had come over Creighton's prospects. On February 12 he received a letter from Lord Salisbury saying that he had the Queen's permission to nominate him to the Diocese of Peterborough, vacant by Dr. Magee's translation to York. For some years he had been troubled by the constant talk of his friends and others that he was bound to be a bishop some day. He had absolutely no wish for the office. I remember on one occasion walking with him by the river at Worcester, when he spoke about the things which people said, and remarked, ' I should like to put a special petition in the Litany that I might be saved from becoming a bishop ; ' then he added, ' and the worst of it is, that I believe I should make quite a good bishop.'

I was in London with some of the children on the day when Lord Salisbury's letter came. When I returned late in the evening, I was surprised at his restless manner as he paced about the room while we had our supper. As soon as the children had gone to bed he said to me, ' Well, the blow has fallen.' I asked whether he felt clear that he was bound to accept. He answered that he was afraid so, that when a man had once entered a service, he must not shrink from the call to advance in it, however unwelcome it might be, but that on the morrow he meant to consult Bishop Philpott (his late Bishop at Worcester, now living in retirement at Cambridge) and Dr. Hort, as to whether they thought he could be possibly justified in refusing. He felt that Dr. Hort at least would estimate rightly the value of a scholar's life, and appreciate justly what giving it up would mean. When he did consult them next day, neither of them had any doubt that he must accept. He said to Bishop Philpott, ' You know what kind of a person I am, and how little fitted I am for the office, so I want you to advise me not to be a bishop.' Bishop Philpott looked at him for a moment and then said, ' No, you must go, you must do what you are told.' He added, ' But let me tell you that a bishop's life is a happy one. It is full of troubles, full of hard work, but it has got this advantage—it gives you endless opportunities of doing little acts of kindness and of saying little words of sympathy which go a great way from the fact of your position.' Creighton realised that he must make the sacrifice ; the struggle agitated him for one day and night, and then he wrote his answer to Lord Salisbury. After that the matter was done with. But it was a great renunciation.

I do not think anyone realised the sacrifice it was, for he did not speak of it and he did not show it. The brightness, the sense of power, the living energy which he carried into public life, would naturally lead to the belief that in it he found his chief joy. Only those who knew him best understood that it was the student's life which he really craved for. A couple of years later he wrote of himself :

' My life has been that of a man who tries to write a book, and is the object of a conspiracy to prevent him from doing so. It is quite true that no one cares to read my book, but that has never interfered with my pleasure in reading for it.'

In after years, it was pathetic to see the eager pleasure with which he corrected a chance proof, or hunted out the answer to some historical question sent him by a stray correspondent. But he never looked back, and there was no murmuring ; the single-minded directness with which he set his feet in the new way was even to me a source of enduring surprise.

As soon as the news was made public, congratulations poured in, and Creighton's time was almost entirely absorbed in answering them, which he did entirely with his own hand. I remember the astonished admiration expressed by that most courteous Chinese scholar, Sir Thomas Wade, who met him one day in the Avenue at one o'clock going out himself to post the seventy letters which he had written that morning. The following extracts from some of his answers to congratulations will show something of what he felt.

To Mr. J. R. Thursfield   'Cambridge : February 17, 1891.

' Dear Dick,—A bishopric is to me personally after the flesh a terrible nuisance. But how is a man to refuse the responsibilities of his branch of the service? I saw no way out. I am an object of compassion ; but I must not grumble, for that is foolish. Only, as hundreds of men are pining for such a post, and I was not, it seems mere contrariety.'

To Rev. E. Talbot (now Bishop of Rochester)
                                'Cambridge : February 17, 1891.

' Dear Talbot,—Thank you very much for your letter. It was a great wrench from my previous mode of life even to contemplate a bishopric. The natural self abhorred it ; and I had to pull myself together and submit—not through any sense that I was fitted, but because I felt that a tranquil conscience could no longer be mine if I ventured to take my life in my own hands and presumptuously say that I preferred the inward responsibility of the student to the graver responsibility of taking my part in the rough work of the world.

' Well, you went through some such thoughts yourself, and your example was one which strengthened me.

' You are quite right in your warnings, and I am grateful for them. I absolutely and entirely agree. But if I was to explain myself, I should say that I feel my function in life is changed. It is no longer to *teach*, but to *edify*. I have no longer to startle people out of self-complacency, but to be

kindly, sympathetic, humble, and helpful.   Yes, *servus
servorum Dei* — that much abused title needs to be revived
in its deepest sense.   How incompetent I am, I know.   I can
only commend myself most earnestly to your prayers.   Our
most affectionate thanks to Mrs. Talbot.

'Yours affectionately,
'M. CREIGHTON.'

To Mr. J. W. Pease   'February 17, 1891.

'Dear Pease,—My wandering career seems to have come
to an end.   My peace of mind is gone : my books will be
shut up : my mind will go to seed : I shall utter nothing but
platitudes for the rest of my life, and everybody will write
letters in the newspapers about my iniquities.   Well, we
must endure this and more for the chance of going about in
many a quiet country village, and saying now and then a
kindly and helpful word to some poor soul.   A good lady
said to me the other day, " After all, men are more interesting
than books."   Doubtless this is true, but you can choose your
own books, and you must take your men as you find them.
Well, I must make the best of it, and bare my back to the
burden.'

To Count Balzani   'Cambridge : March 12, 1891.

'Dear Count Ugo,—Your letter was very nice, as your
letters always are.   It is a great change in life to leave the
peaceful home of the Muses at Cambridge for the struggle of
active practical work. . . .

'I do not mean to abandon my *Popes* : they will still be a
recreation for my leisure ; and even a bishop must have some
leisure, I suppose. . . . Of course I am plunged in business,
and have to end all my affairs at Cambridge and Worcester,
and transfer myself to Peterborough and pick up threads of
various kinds of affairs.   I shall not get much holiday this
summer, but I must try and get some.   We had projected a
voyage to the Baltic.   You will find us in a quite other
house when next you come to England.   I hope it will not
be very long.   I already want to have a talk with you about
many things.   Writing is so poor a substitute for speech.'

To the Bishop of Colombo (Dr. Copleston)

'Worcester : March 24, 1891.

'. . . My Consecration is to be on St. Mark's Day, April 25.
No man could have less desire than I have for the office of a
bishop.   Nothing save the cowardliness of shrinking from

responsibility and the dread of selfishness led me to submit to a call from which the natural man entirely shrunk. I am struggling to be submissive and pull myself together. I often think of the quiet days you spent at **Embleton** before you sailed. As yet I have had no quiet ; and now am spending a busy week of preaching.'

To Professor Thomas of Haverford

'Worcester : March 30, 1891.

'Thank you very much for your kind words and good wishes. I by no means rejoice in my call to new work of an arduous kind, and was quite contented where I was. But it seemed to me wrong to refuse responsibility only because it was arduous ; but I still feel the wrench, and I feel that I have much to learn before I am fit for my new duties. The office of a bishop in England is very laborious. I am the chief officer over some 800 clergy, and have to wander over a large district, with a vast correspondence coming upon me daily. I suppose I must do my best. The one thing that I look forward to is that the system of the English Church brings a bishop into direct contact with all the young people in his diocese once at least in their lives. This I feel to be a great opportunity ; but indeed I shall have many more opportunities of usefulness than I can hope to discharge efficiently. I am at present having a few days' holiday before I take up my work.'

He was much gratified by the regret expressed in Cambridge at losing him, and the many kind things that were said. Among others Dr. Schechter, the Reader in Talmudic, wrote :

' It occurs so rarely that the Crown of Learning and the Crown of Priesthood adorn the same head, that even outsiders as we are must be rejoiced at seeing the author of the great History in one of the most sacred offices.'

The feeling among the historical teachers in Cambridge is shown by the following letters :

From Mr. G. W. Prothero

' Many of us must have felt that it was once to come, but I at least hoped we should be allowed to keep you here a little longer, that this backward school of History would be able to rely on you for a few years more. I cannot help feeling our loss, and the loss of the Historical School here more than anything else. You have done so much for us since you have been here, you would have done so much more, that we shall miss you terribly.'

From Miss Alice Gardner

'I cannot pretend to be so unselfish as to congratulate you. Though certainly it is not only on my own behalf, but on that of many friends, and of this University and of historical studies generally, that I feel grieved to think of what we are losing. . . . At the same time I feel thankful that you came here at a time when, as it seems to me, you were so much needed—though I cannot see that the need will not be felt again.'

To one historical friend who seriously remonstrated with him on his decision, and thought that his highest duty was to remain faithful to history, he explained his views as follows :

'Cambridge : February 21, 1891.

'I am somewhat bewildered at your views about me. It seems to me that you have made an ideal of what my life ought to be, and are very angry because it is not my own ideal. If you had told it me I might have understood it ; as it is, I do not. To me life has always been a simple matter, and has consisted in doing the duties which lay to my hand as well as I could. I never was so presumptuous as to suppose that I was pre-eminently fitted for some duties, and could therefore absolve myself from others. I have been a tutor, a parish priest, a professor, a canon—none of these things by my own choice, but through the choice of others whose business it was to fill up those posts. By no wish or seeking of mine I have been chosen to another post. I meditated long, but felt that it was the act of a self-indulgent coward to refuse work because it was hard, and responsibility because it was onerous.

'I do not know what your notion of a bishop's life may be, but mine is only to do and be what I have done and been before—to go about and try and help others, with kindliness and sympathy. The only ideal I have ever had of life is that : to cheer up young clergy is as good as to cheer on undergraduates : the daughters of poor clergy who cannot afford to come to Newnham may perhaps be as much worth a word of encouragement as those who can afford it. Why should I be degraded by talking in a kindly way to children who come to be confirmed, by trying to stir up people to work harder for the good of man, and by going about in the counties of Leicester and Northampton instead of living alternately at Cambridge and Windsor? You seem to apprehend some vital change in my nature in consequence. I do not understand.

'Yours always affectionately,

'M. CREIGHTON.'

To the same 'Cambridge: 1891.

'To me the one supreme object of human life is and always has been to grow nearer to God; and I regard my own individual life as simply an opportunity of offering my-self to Him. All knowledge has been to me merely a further revelation of Him, and my relations to my fellow creatures are dependent on His call.

'I am grieved, I always have been grieved, that one who has been endowed with so many natural gifts as you, should not see your way to any vital principle of life. I have, I trust, been always tolerant to you; but it seems that you can-not tolerate me. I have lived long enough to know that many to whom I am bound by deep sympathy do not agree with me about the fundamental basis of life. You still have to learn the lesson; but I always hope that the day will come when you will agree with me, because I know that I am right and I can afford to wait: so I shall always be

'Your loving friend,

'M. CREIGHTON.

At the end of the Lent Term, Creighton went to Worcester for the last time, and took all the Good Friday addresses at the Cathedral. This involved a short address at an early service, the addresses on the Last Words at the Three Hours Service, and a sermon at the evening service. Some of his hearers had wondered whether he would be at his best in such devotional addresses, but I believe there was a general impression that never had his teaching been so profound or so convincing.

On the evening of Easter Day he preached in the Cathedral to an immense congregation, and ended with these words:

'On such a day as this personal matters seem entirely out of place. Yet I cannot forget that this is the last time on which I shall speak from this pulpit as a Canon of this Church. It is to me a comforting thought that I take leave of you with the message of the new life and its boundless future ringing

in my ears. The word "farewell" is soon spoken, but it is
hard to speak. I can never forget all that I have learned
here, from this great Church, its memories, its beauty, its
reverent services; from the companionship of dear friends,
from the atmosphere of high endeavour and lofty purpose
which I will venture to say surrounds this Cathedral; not
least from the sympathy and kindliness which I have met
with from the people of Worcester, since the day when I
came a stranger among them. And to you to whom I have
been privileged to speak from time to time my warmest
thanks are due. A preacher in a cathedral pulpit has not the
bond of close personal intercourse which connects the parish
priest with his congregation ; yet a bond of spiritual sympathy
forms itself and is powerful. Something came to me from
you, and gave help to my thoughts and to my means of
expression. If I have said anything worth saying, anything
that was helpful, it was you who gave me the power to say it.
Some glance of an upturned face stirred my mind ; some few
words of comment on what I said supplied material for
thought, and set me to probe my own soul and search my
own experiences. I am conscious of a personal tie which
binds me to you all, a tie which it is sad to me to sever. The
memories of Worcester and its great Church have become
part of my being ; and in times of difficulty and discourage-
ment in the future, I shall look back on my years spent here
and shall take comfort. One remembrance on your part I
would venture to ask. I beg for your prayers, and specially
on St. Mark's Day, the day of my consecration as bishop,
that God would strengthen me by His grace for the work to
which He has called me. And now I say "farewell," and
from the bottom of my heart wish you all God speed. May
He of His mercy lead us all to drink of the waters of life
freely, that it may be to each of us a wellspring rising unto
life eternal.'

When in the following summer he was presented by his
friends in Worcester with a beautiful ebony and silver cross
for the altar of his chapel, he said that he hoped they would
not feel vexed if he told them that the result of his meditations
since he left them had been that the dearest thing to him in
Worcester was the Cathedral itself.

'Not, I am sure,' he continued, 'because I did not value
the strong bonds which here bound me to so many, but
because I felt that there was a magnificent grandeur about
that great memorial of the past, which carried the same

message through the ages, and which was instinct with beauty and with teaching in every part of it—that that building on which I had looked out from my windows, that building through which I had so often strayed and meditated, that building in whose services I had been privileged to take a part—that building had sunk into the very innermost part of my soul and had become a portion of my being and was united to all that was best and noblest in my aspirations. . . . I felt too how very much I had learned from the Chapter. . . . I found there a readiness and openness of mind, a sincere and absolute desire that good should be done by all possible means, a breadth of mind, a tolerance, a conciliatory disposition, an entire absence of petty jealousies and self-seeking, the noblest spirit, the most entire unselfishness pervading every relation into which I was brought with my friends the Dean and Chapter. . . . I never experienced such friendliness as I did in Worcester, such ready receptiveness of anything I had to say and do which approved itself to the minds of those to whom I spoke.'

LETTERS: 1887-1891

To C. D.   'Cambridge: February 1, 1887.

'Nor do I quite grasp what you mean about your reading. Methodical reading is of slow growth, and comes after one has got a general culture. Then it is useful in proportion to anyone's wish to learn, and this is a quality which it is hard to create. Most people are content with *notions*, and are rather cross if one tells them to " get *understanding*." Others, on the other hand, quite rejoice to labour at something for themselves. I have just had a class of young ladies, to one of whom I had given a subject to look up, " the life of the Lady Margaret, Countess of Richmond." She had gone of her own accord to the right thing : Bishop Fisher's funeral sermon, of which she had waded through a black-letter copy and seemed to be much pleased with what she had discovered. This is my way of teaching people the reign of Henry VII. I try and get them to take some trouble to find out things that are not quite obvious. It matters not what the subject is, the same plan seems to be applicable, and is the only one of any value.

'I had a talk with Mr. Gladstone this morning : he is very vigorous and very festive ; the only sign of old age is that he is growing rather deaf.'

To a young Friend on her engagement

'Cambridge : May 5, 1887.

' There is nothing that I can say that will not seem very dull. You will be busy in discovering a great deal about yourselves which you did not know before. For love is the supreme revealer, and therein testifies that it is the holiest and most Divine of all God's gifts to us. The months that are before you have a teaching peculiarly their own, which stands one in good stead in the future. The problem of life after all is to find one's ideal in the real and weld the two together, so that the consciousness of a larger meaning and a more enduring purpose streams through the small actions of life. It is one thing to feel, another thing to let one's feelings find expression in words, but greatest of all is to embody one's feelings in one's life and actions. Love is the great master.'

To C. D.   'Worcester : Easter Eve 1888.

' I can feel for you in having had to face the mystery of human suffering and human sorrow. It is easy to account for it and explain it, but no explanation of the reason satisfies the heart. Nothing but the grasp of the principle of the spiritual life can enable one to weave together the fragments of the world's experiences into a connected whole. One thing only strikes me : we see the outside of the lives of others, not the inside : we see the breakage, the fragments ; we cannot see the inward discipline, the process of restoration, the recovery. We can share more vividly in the sorrows of others than in their compensations. Thus modern philanthropy can sympathise with the misery of poverty, but has lost all sense of the intrinsic dignity of poverty ; this oversight leads it to sentimentalism. There is a grandeur which we do not know developed by the necessity of struggle. . . . Well, thoughts like these are fitting for Holy Week, and enable us to understand in some degree better as the years roll on and the experience of life gathers round us—to understand the Mystery of the Cross as the supreme truth which absorbs all else, and explains to the heart if not to the understanding the riddle of life. You and —— will be in my thoughts and in my commemoration to-morrow at the Easter Communion. I hope you will find room for me in your thoughts too.'

To Mr. W. S. Lilly   'Cambridge : March 4, 1888.

' I had just yesterday been reading your article with pleasure, and was on the point of writing to thank you when your letter arrived. I quite agree with your view of Spencer's inconsequence, and I think you are quite right in insisting that thinkers should face the result of their systems.

'The attempt to drape materialism in trappings to which it has no just claim is a modern delusion which is entirely disingenuous, and which entraps the unwary. I much prefer such a system as Karl Pearson enunciates in his "Ethics of Free Thought." There the modern scientific materialism is unashamed, and boldly claims to make its own ethical theory, so that it can be fairly appraised.'

To Sir Edward Grey   'November 21, 1888.

'I congratulate you heartily on your speech last night. It seems to me to be an excellent example of the way in which a young member can do something towards heightening the tone of politics by insisting that principle is higher than party. And the admirable way in which you did it enabled you to act without any strain upon the loyalty which party government renders necessary. There is an increasing number of thoughtful persons who mourn over the shock which public morality has received through an undue development of parliamentary tactics. They look vainly for consistency and adherence to principles. By such a body of men, who are likely in my opinion to be of increasing importance, such action as yours will be highly appreciated.'

To Miss Mary Bateson   'The College, Worcester : August 4, 1888.

'Dear Mary,— . . . Your mocking letter to Mrs. Creighton shows that you have not grasped my meaning.

'Let me give you a few aphorisms.

'Advice to those who are going to make political opinions, *Don't* : if you do, free yourself from prejudice and prepossessions before you begin : as this is difficult, it is easier to follow Mr. Pickwick's example and shout with the crowd.

'Politics is an art, not a science.

'It rests on principles, but it deals with facts.

'The utterances of politicians are like the advertisements of St. Jacob's Oil : to sell their wares they have to profess that they have discovered a panacea.

'The facts of social life are complicated, and are rarely covered by one formula.

'Words are not things.

'Party cries sometimes embody principles, but never show that the principles quoted cover the facts to which they are applied,

'Practical wisdom is concerned mainly with forethought. Society does not admit of indefinite experiments.

'Legislation can only embody the results of social development.

'Social development depends upon the virtue and wisdom of the individuals who compose society.

'No legislative result is worth attaining at the expense of virtue and wisdom.

'The Grace of God, which is the cause of human virtue, cannot operate by sin.

'That is sinful which is less good than the best we know.

'Politicians, by the very nature of their occupation, are rarely in the forefront of those who maintain virtue and wisdom.

'Politics is only one of the branches of human energy : he who enters upon it ought to weigh the dangers which it involves.

'Men serve their fellow men as they promote virtue and wisdom.

'Finally, there is no one among your acquaintance who less wishes you to accept any of his opinions as infallible than

'Yours affectionately,

'M. Creighton.'

To a young Friend, E. F.   'Cambridge : November 11, 1888.

'. . . The periods of Advent and Lent were in the Mediæval Church the two great times of teaching and preaching. Sermons were rare except at those times. . . . The period of Advent suggests *instruction*, while Lent tends more to *edification*. I mean the preparation for Christmas is more a preparation of the mind for grasping and understanding; that of Lent an abasement of the soul for the purpose of feeling and self-surrender. . . . In fact, Advent suggests for thought, " What has Christ done for the world ? " while Lent suggests, " What has Christ done for me, and how have I answered Him ? " '

To Miss Alice Gardner   'Worcester : January 2, 1889.

'Thank you for your notice, which is just what I wanted. You are quite right about the Americans, except Lea : he is a real scholar, and his work is thorough. His introduction of local colour is simply by the way; for he is engaged in following up his massive history of the Mediæval Inquisition by a history of the Spanish Inquisition, and has put together a bit of his material. If you don't know Lea's books, read them ; for no one knows more about the institutions of the Mediæval Church. But Schaff is a curious person : he is well enough versed in historical method ; but he tries to popularise Yankee bunkum, and he is a shocking example of the evil result of groundless optimism as a basis of historical philosophy.

' I think that Pole would be a good subject to anyone who had time to research in the Venetian and Roman archives; but I think he would need full treatment, and the attempt to deal with him ought to aim at completeness.'

To Miss Mary Bateson   'Worcester : July 26, 1889.

' We came back to England last Saturday. . . . We enjoyed Brittany and rambled much by the sea. The girls of course were delighted with strange experiences, and the Breton folk are wonderfully old world and far off from modern things. . . . The Brittany coast struck me as an excellent place for a cheap holiday.

' I am glad you enjoyed the " Doll's House." I thought better of it on reflection than I did when I heard it. In spite of obvious impossibilities, it is the work of a man of genius ; and I thought that the exhibition of man's selfishness, carried to a point of honour, is profoundly true.

' I am just engaging in a sentimental effort to prevent the boundaries of Worcester being so adjusted as to rob it of Daylesford, Warren Hastings's birthplace. Don't you think counties ought to cherish their worthies ? '

To Mr. W. S. Lilly about his 'Century of Revolution

'The College, Worcester : August 5, 1889.

' Dear Lilly,—I have been rambling for a short time in Brittany, and found your book when I came home. Thank you very much for sending me a copy. I have just finished reading and weighing it—last night I even went so far as to preach some of it. I entirely agree with all you say. The book seemed to me excellent : it put together all sorts of things which I had been thinking in an incoherent manner. . . . I quite agree with you about evolution. It is quite established by quiet acceptance : the thing is to see what it comes to, how much it explains and how much it does not. Has it ever struck you that evolution has been the working theory of historians long before Darwin examined it in reference to species ? Hegel's " Philosophie der Geschichte " contained its metaphysical basis, and Ranke's " Weltgeschichtliche Bewe-

gung" set forth the " survival of the fittest " in human affairs.
I hope your book will meet with the attention it deserves.'

To a Pupil

'Worcester : August 13, 1889.

'It is no bad thing really to be ordered to take a complete
rest. Really when one is ill one's business in life is to get
well, and it is most important to realise that and to proceed
to get *quite well.* Many people make the mistake of pro-
longing the period by mixing up work with convalescence in
a way which really does not help either. It is very desirable
to make a good start, and have one's head clear at the
beginning.

'However, this is perhaps cold comfort. But my practical
suggestion was going to be that you should come and spend
a few days with us here. . . .'

To a Pupil reading for the Lightfoot Scholarship

'Cambridge : March 9, 1890.

'I had long been wondering how you were getting on, and
why you did not tell me something about yourself. The
account is good so far ; but I am not surprised that you do
not feel as if you learned much. Reading for an examination
is not likely to give you that impression, it is only more books
and more things taken second-hand. One only begins to
learn when one masters the authorities and makes up one's
own opinions.'

To E. F.

'Cambridge : April 19, 1890.

'. . . The question of Confession, I need hardly tell you,
is one that is left by our Church to individual responsibility.
The more I see of the working of the Church of Rome, the
less I believe in its elaborate machinery. The Anglican
plan of laying down a minimum, and leaving room for more
as each individual thinks fit, is certainly more invigorating.
Moreover, in our Church, Confession can be approached in
any way, varying from the mere asking of advice, or submitting
questions on points of conscience, up to submission to a
regular system. Further, there is entire liberty in the choice
of a person ; and there is no obligation to continue the habit
if, in one's judgment, it is not suitable to one's needs.'

'Different minds and different natures develop in different
ways. Some regard life as a whole, others take it in detail.
Some develop harmoniously, others with difficulty in a one-
sided way. It is to these last that Confession is useful ; it
may encourage them by turning them to larger views of things,

and showing them that progress lies in some other field than that which they are too exclusively cultivating. A wise doctor will often see that the general health of a patient must be improved before drugs for his special ailment can be availing. The question is one to be settled by yourself, and I dare say has been settled already. I should have liked to have a talk with you about it; but tell me what you have resolved.'

To Mr. Robert Bridges   'Cambridge : April 29, 1890.

' . . . I read " Ulysses " with the greatest delight. Your boldness and versatility were alike conspicuous. The story itself seemed scarcely capable of dramatic treatment, but you have made it eminently dramatic. The characters are all clear and distinct, and there is plenty of relief in an action which threatened to be monotonous. In fact, the play is full of movement. Your boldness in the use of various styles of rhythm, and the varied treatment of the blank verses, gives material for more study than I have yet had time for. The worst of a holiday is the mass of arrears which follow upon it. In them I am still immersed.'

To Mr. W. S. Lilly about his 'On Right and Wrong'

'Langdale Lodge, Cambridge : May 9, 1890.

' Dear Lilly,—Thank you very much for your book, and still more for the dedication, in which you have spoken of me in terms far beyond my desert, while you have managed to say to me many things which were much worth saying. I like your revival of the ancient form of preface, which is a more artistic conception than that which has succeeded it. . . .

' It seems to me that in future times this age of ours, judged by its literature, will be called " the crazy age." Never was a time when ill-digested statements were so cast forth on all sides, when views were put forward without any thought of their relationship to any system either of thought or possible practice. If you can succeed in getting a few to think what is the result of their divagations and whereto they are tending, you will have done a good work.'

To Mr. Robert Bridges   'Worcester : July 2, 1890.

'The "Christian Captives" reached me just as I was leaving Cambridge, and had to go into my book box for the time being, while I went to London to explore records in the Record Office. When I got here it was exhumed, and has been subjected to the ordeal of reading aloud to my daughters, who have been thrilled   I really think that is a very good test of what is the primary object of a play : its dramatic qualities.   The family vote was that it was better than " Palicio." '

To Miss Mary Bateson   Worcester : July 11, 1890.

'. . . About that book—remember that it must be a good one.   Therefore do not be in a hurry.   Gather material as fast as you like, but do not be in haste to begin to write, and be ready to write it over again three times.   You have to learn to consume your own smoke and leave things tidy.   A book requires more thinking over than writing.   It makes a good deal of matter how you begin.   Get your plan quite clear.   Above all, pay heed to proportion.   Don't let one part of your subject run away with you.   Carefully form a style.   It is hard to make a book run smoothly without abrupt transitions.

'Many other maxims I could pour forth, but these are enough at present.'

To the Rev. A. S. Porter, who had considered some
     remarks in a lecture on the fifteenth century and its
     architecture as exaggerated
                                   'Worcester : September 26, 1890.

'My dear Porter,—The men of the fifteenth century were feeble because they had no ideas, no great men, no spiritual aspirations ; but they were carefully pursuing material pro-sperity.   The decay of villenage and the rise of tenant farmers, the increase of the wool trade and the gradual development of commerce, created a wealthy middle class.   All art depends mainly upon the existence of a public *who will give orders*, a practical detail which is generally forgotten.   It was not be-cause there was a multitude of eager and able architects that churches were built ; but because a number of wealthy wool merchants wished to commemorate their munificence, and had no better way of doing it than in pulling down the old parish church and building another.   We see what the fifteenth cen-tury built, not what it destroyed.   Yet we admire as rare gems the fine Norman, Early English, and Decorated churches, on a smaller scale, which still remain in the lucky villages which did not produce a wealthy man, who ground down the people during his life and then built a new church to serve as a chantry to himself.

'Opinions may differ as to the artistic value of the Perpendicular work. Whenever I study a cathedral which is of composite origin—e.g. our own—I am left with the feeling that the fifteenth century work is soulless and ideal-less compared to what went before it. It has the notion of size; it has the inheritance of a sense of proportion; but it has little individuality, no intimacy, no traces of originality in detail. It is cold and mechanical. As a proof of this, it can be reproduced now; whereas we cannot build a Norman or an Early English church, and our attempts at Decorated are elaborate failures. But we can build as good Perpendicular as the fifteenth century.'

To Mr. H. C. Lea   'Worcester: October 6, 1890.

'I am very much obliged to you for sending me your new book, which deals with a part of Ecclesiastical History which is generally overlooked. The development of the Spanish Church after the Visigothic times is left in obscurity till the days of Ximenez, and is illustrated only by the scanty light of St. Dominic. Your book is the only one in English which attempts to carry matters farther, and is an indispensable introduction to the study of the Inquisition. For indeed the question, how came the Spaniards to welcome the Inquisition? is one which requires a deeper answer than it has received. It always seems to me that general talk about " the tendencies of the popular mind " and " the previous facts of national history " is rather misleading. Things arise from specific causes, and one wants to see them.

'I have been very busy with the " Historical Review," for which Lord Acton at the last moment sent me a long article on Döllinger, which will interest you. It is of course allusive and overweighted with learning in a way which makes it unintelligible to the uninitiated; but it shows a marvellous knowledge of the results of historical investigation during the last fifty years.'

To Mr. J. N. Figgis   'October 14, 1890.

'As to myself, I have been busy with scanty energies at Worcester, very busy, and my work has not progressed very quickly. However, I am toiling on at Luther and Charles V. and Adrian VI. and such like troublesome persons I have just returned to Cambridge, and can discover no Cambridge news of any importance. . . . I hear that Westcott is quite pleased with episcopal functions, but has not opened a book since he left Cambridge. Such is the pressure of practical life : it is terrible to contemplate such a condition.'

To E. F.   'Cambridge : November 25, 1890.

'Is your brother to be confirmed as a member of the Church? Please tell him that *no one* believes in Transubstantiation. The Church of Rome is weighted with a doctrine which has lost all meaning, because it is connected with a system of philosophy which is no longer held : "substance" and "accidents" are now echoes of extinct metaphysics.

'But ask him to consider that there are only two alternatives : either there is a *real presence* of our Blessed Lord in the Sacrament, or there is a *real absence*. Ask him if it is not absolute "common sense" to a Christian to hold that the results of Christ's Incarnation are communicated to the individual soul. Tell him that the sacramental system is the only means of holding the nearness of Christ to the believer : tell him that it is a matter of fact that all bodies which reject or explain away the Sacraments drift into Unitarianism. They push our Lord farther and farther away, till He is lost to their eyes.

'Forgive these rambling remarks : they are the clearest way I can think of to help a good boy to understand things.'

To Mr. C. L. Brace of New York

         'Cambridge : January 25, 1890.

'Dear Mr. Brace,—Thank you very much for your book,[1] which I received to-day and have been reading with increasing interest. Your general view seems to me to be a necessary consequence of the doctrine of development applied to God's moral purpose in the education of the world. Revelation shows us a chosen people : reason shows us besides them chosen individuals whose influence worked in the same direction. Revelation tells us of the highest development of the religious consciousness, and shows us its progress.

'Besides that was going on a corresponding development of other levels of the religious consciousness Your attempt to co-ordinate these stages of development is a most useful undertaking. We ought to try and recognise relationships. The higher consciousness must appeal to the lower on the basis of sympathy, not of antagonism : it must absorb not crush. I am entirely in agreement with your aim, and I trust your book will attract the attention which it deserves.'

[1] *The Unknown God.*

To Miss Alice Barlow   'Cambridge: March 4, 1891.

'Dear Miss Barlow,—I am very glad that you asked me your question. May I put it this way? The contents of the Christian revelation is the Person of the Lord Jesus. Scripture is the *record* of that revelation. The Church is the *witness* of that revelation.

'In early times, amongst a rude and semi-barbarous people, the Church was greatly engaged in considering how she was to discharge her function as a witness. But this process was largely concerned with mechanism. Just as the State was striving at the same time to embody the idea of justice; the method was imperfect, but the idea existed nowhere else. Still, at the present day, the State embodies that idea imperfectly; but we do not doubt about the idea itself. So with the revelation of which the Church is the guardian. That revelation is immediate to each human soul; and the attempts to express it in the forms of outward organisation— their partial success, their conspicuous failures—only make the eternal meaning of the revelation itself clearer and more precious.'

END OF THE FIRST VOLUME.

PRINTED BY
SPOTTISWOODE AND CO. LTD., NEW-STREET SQUARE
LONDON

𝔄 Classified Catalogue

OF WORKS IN

GENERAL LITERATURE

PUBLISHED BY

LONGMANS, GREEN, & CO.

39 PATERNOSTER ROW, LONDON, E.C.

91 AND 93 FIFTH AVENUE, NEW YORK, AND 32 HORNBY ROAD, BOMBAY

CONTENTS.

INDEX OF AUTHORS AND EDITORS.

INDEX OF AUTHORS AND EDITORS—*continued.*

History, Politics, Polity, Political Memoirs, &c.

Acland and Ransome.—*A HANDBOOK IN OUTLINE OF THE POLITICAL HISTORY OF ENGLAND TO* 1896. Chronologically Arranged. By the Right Hon. A. H. DYKE ACLAND, and CYRIL RANSOME, M.A. Crown 8vo., 6s.

Airy.—*CHARLES II.* By OSMUND AIRY, LL.D., M.A. With Photogravure Portrait. Crown 8vo., 6s. 6d. net.

Allgood.—*CHINA WAR*, 1860: *LETTERS AND JOURNALS.* By Major-General G. ALLGOOD, C.B., formerly Lieut. G. ALLGOOD, 1st Division China Field Force. With Maps, Plans, and Illustrations. Demy 4to. 12s. 6d. net.

Annual Register (The). A Review of Public Events at Home and Abroad, for the year 1903. 8vo., 18s.
Volumes of the *ANNUAL REGISTER* for the years 1863-1902 can still be had. 18s. each.

Arnold.—*INTRODUCTORY LECTURES ON MODERN HISTORY.* By THOMAS ARNOLD, D.D., formerly Head Master of Rugby School. 8vo., 7s. 6d.

Ashley (W. J.).

ENGLISH ECONOMIC HISTORY AND THEORY. Crown 8vo., Part I., 5s. Part II., 10s. 6d.

SURVEYS, HISTORIC AND ECONOMIC. Crown 8vo., 9s. net.

Bagwell.—*IRELAND UNDER THE TUDORS.* By RICHARD BAGWELL, LL.D. (3 vols.) Vols. I. and II. From the first invasion of the Northmen to the year 1578. 8vo., 32s. Vol. III. 1578-1603. 8vo., 18s.

Belmore.—*THE HISTORY OF TWO ULSTER MANORS, AND OF THEIR OWNERS.* By the EARL OF BELMORE, P.C., G.C.M.G. (H.M.L., County Tyrone), formerly Governor of New South Wales. Re-issue, Revised and Enlarged. With Portrait. 8vo., 5s. net.

Besant.—*THE HISTORY OF LONDON.* By Sir WALTER BESANT. With 74 Illustrations. Crown 8vo., 1s. 9d. Or bound as a School Prize Book, gilt edges, 2s. 6d.

Bright.—*A HISTORY OF ENGLAND.* By the Rev. J. FRANCK BRIGHT, D.D.

Period I. *MEDIÆVAL MONARCHY*: A.D. 449-1485. Crown 8vo., 4s. 6d.

Period II. *PERSONAL MONARCHY.* 1485-1688. Crown 8vo., 5s.

Period III. *CONSTITUTIONAL MONARCHY.* 1689-1837. Crown 8vo., 7s. 6d.

Period IV. *THE GROWTH OF DEMOCRACY.* 1837-1880. Crown 8vo., 6s.

Period V. *IMPERIAL REACTION*: Victoria, 1880-1901. Crown 8vo., 4s. 6d.

Bruce.—*THE FORWARD POLICY AND ITS RESULTS*; or, Thirty-five Years' Work amongst the Tribes on our North-Western Frontier of India. By RICHARD ISAAC BRUCE, C.I.E. With 28 Illustrations and a Map. 8vo., 15s. net.

Buckle.—*HISTORY OF CIVILISATION IN ENGLAND.* By HENRY THOMAS BUCKLE.
Cabinet Edition. 3 vols. Crown 8vo., 24s.
'*Silver Library*' *Edition.* 3 vols. Crown 8vo., 10s. 6d.

Burke.—*A HISTORY OF SPAIN, FROM THE EARLIEST TIMES TO THE DEATH OF FERDINAND THE CATHOLIC.* By ULICK RALPH BURKE, M.A. Edited by MARTIN A. S. HUME. With 6 Maps. 2 vols. Crown 8vo., 16s. net.

Casserly.—*THE LAND OF THE BOXERS*; or, China under the Allies. By Captain GORDON CASSERLY. With 15 Illustrations and a Plan. 8vo., 10s. 6d. net.

Chesney.—*INDIAN POLITY:* a View of the System of Administration in India. By General Sir GEORGE CHESNEY, K.C.B. With Map showing all the Administrative Divisions of British India. 8vo., 21s.

Churchill (WINSTON SPENCER, M.P.).

THE RIVER WAR: an Historical Account of the Reconquest of the Soudan. Edited by Colonel F. RHODES, D.S.O. With Photogravure Portrait of Viscount Kitchener of Khartoum, and 22 Maps and Plans. 8vo., 10s. 6d. net.

History, Politics, Polity, Political Memoirs, &c.—*continued.*

Churchill (WINSTON SPENCER, M.P.)
—*continued.*

THE STORY OF THE MALAKAND FIELD FORCE, 1897. With 6 Maps and Plans. Crown 8vo., 3s. 6d.

LONDON TO LADYSMITH VIÂ PRETORIA. Crown 8vo., 6s.

IAN HAMILTON'S MARCH. With Portrait of Major-General Sir Ian Hamilton, and 10 Maps and Plans. Crown 8vo., 6s.

Corbett (JULIAN S.).

DRAKE AND THE TUDOR NAVY, with a History of the Rise of England as a Maritime Power. With Portraits, Illustrations and Maps. 2 vols. Crown 8vo., 16s.

THE SUCCESSORS OF DRAKE. With 4 Portraits (2 Photogravures) and 12 Maps and Plans. 8vo., 21s.

ENGLAND IN THE MEDITERRANEAN : a Study of the Rise and Influence of British Power within the Straits, 1603-1713. With 1 Map and 2 Illustrations. 2 vols. 8vo., 24s. net.

Creighton (MANDELL, late Lord Bishop of London).

A HISTORY OF THE PAPACY FROM THE GREAT SCHISM TO THE SACK OF ROME, 1378-1527. 6 vols. Cr. 8vo., 5s. net each.

QUEEN ELIZABETH. With Portrait. Crown 8vo., 5s. net.

HISTORICAL ESSAYS AND REVIEWS. Edited by LOUISE CREIGHTON. Crown 8vo., 5s. net.

HISTORICAL LECTURES AND ADDRESSES. Edited by LOUISE CREIGHTON. Crown 8vo., 5s. net.

Dale.—THE PRINCIPLES OF ENGLISH CONSTITUTIONAL HISTORY. By LUCY DALE, late Scholar of Somerville College, Oxford. Crown 8vo., 6s.

Falkiner (C. LITTON).

STUDIES IN IRISH HISTORY AND BIOGRAPHY, Mainly of the Eighteenth Century. 8vo., 12s. 6d. net.

Falkiner (C. LITTON)—*continued.*

ILLUSTRATIONS OF IRISH HISTORY AND TOPOGRAPHY, Mainly of the Seventeenth Century. With 3 Maps. 8vo., 18s. net.

Freeman.—THE HISTORICAL GEOGRAPHY OF EUROPE. By EDWARD A. FREEMAN, D.C.L., LL.D. Third Edition. Edited by J. B. BURY, M.A., D.Litt., LL.D., Regius Professor of Modern History in the University of Cambridge. 8vo., 12s. 6d.

ATLAS to the above. With 65 Maps in colour. 8vo., 6s. 6d.

Froude (JAMES A.).

THE HISTORY OF ENGLAND, from the Fall of Wolsey to the Defeat of the Spanish Armada. 12 vols. Crown 8vo., 3s. 6d. each.

THE DIVORCE OF CATHERINE OF ARAGON. Crown 8vo., 3s. 6d.

THE SPANISH STORY OF THE ARMADA, and other Essays. Cr. 8vo., 3s. 6d.

THE ENGLISH IN IRELAND IN THE EIGHTEENTH CENTURY. 3 vols. Cr. 8vo., 10s. 6d.

ENGLISH SEAMEN IN THE SIXTEENTH CENTURY.
Cabinet Edition. Crown 8vo., 6s.
Illustrated Edition. With 5 Photogravure Plates and 16 other Illustrations. Large Cr. 8vo., gilt top, 6s. net.
'Silver Library' Edition. Cr. 8vo., 3s. 6d.

THE COUNCIL OF TRENT. Crown 8vo., 3s. 6d.

SHORT STUDIES ON GREAT SUBJECTS.
Cabinet Edition. 4 vols. 24s.
'Silver Library' Edition. 4 vols. Crown 8vo., 3s. 6d. each.

CÆSAR : a Sketch. Cr. 8vo, 3s. 6d.

SELECTIONS FROM THE WRITINGS OF JAMES ANTHONY FROUDE. Edited by P. S. ALLEN, M.A. Crown 8vo., 3s. 6d.

Gardiner (SAMUEL RAWSON, D.C.L., LL.D.).

HISTORY OF ENGLAND, from the Accession of James I. to the Outbreak of the Civil War, 1603-1642. With 7 Maps. 10 vols. Crown 8vo., 5s. net each.

A HISTORY OF THE GREAT CIVIL WAR, 1642-1649. With 54 Maps and Plans. 4 vols. Cr. 8vo., 5s. net each.

History, Politics, Polity, Political Memoirs, &c.—*continued.*

Gardiner (SAMUEL RAWSON, D.C.L., LL.D.)—*continued.*

A HISTORY OF THE COMMONWEALTH AND THE PROTECTORATE. 1649-1656. 4 vols. Crown 8vo., 5s. net each.

THE STUDENT'S HISTORY OF ENGLAND. With 378 Illustrations. Crown 8vo., gilt top, 12s.
Also in Three Volumes, price 4s. each.

CROMWELL'S PLACE IN HISTORY. Founded on Six Lectures delivered in the University of Oxford. Cr. 8vo., 3s. 6d.

OLIVER CROMWELL. With Frontispiece. Crown 8vo., 5s. net.

German Emperor's (The) Speeches : being a Selection from the Speeches, Edicts, Letters and Telegrams of the Emperor William II. Translated by LOUIS ELKIND, M.D. 8vo., 12s. 6d. net.

German Empire (The) of To-day : Outlines of its Formation and Development. By 'VERITAS'. Crown 8vo., 6s. net.

Graham.—ROMAN AFRICA : an Outline of the History of the Roman Occupation of North Africa, based chiefly upon Inscriptions and Monumental Remains in that Country. By ALEXANDER GRAHAM, F.S.A., F.R.I.B.A. With 30 reproductions of Original Drawings by the Author, and 2 Maps. 8vo., 16s. net.

Greville.—A JOURNAL OF THE REIGNS OF KING GEORGE IV., KING WILLIAM IV., AND QUEEN VICTORIA. By CHARLES C. F. GREVILLE, formerly Clerk of the Council. 8 vols. Crown 8vo., 3s. 6d. each.

Gross.—THE SOURCES AND LITERATURE OF ENGLISH HISTORY, FROM THE EARLIEST TIMES TO ABOUT 1485. By CHARLES GROSS, Ph.D. 8vo., 18s. net.

Hamilton.—HISTORICAL RECORD OF THE 14TH (KING'S) HUSSARS, from A.D. 1715 to A.D. 1900. By Colonel HENRY BLACKBURNE HAMILTON, M.A., Christ Church, Oxford; late Commanding the Regiment. With 15 Coloured Plates, 35 Portraits, etc., in Photogravure, and 10 Maps and Plans. Crown 4to., gilt edges, 42s. net.

Hart.—ACTUAL GOVERNMENT, AS APPLIED UNDER AMERICAN CONDITIONS. By ALBERT BUSHNELL HART, LL.D., Professor of History in Harvard University. With 17 Maps and Diagrams. Crown 8vo., 7s. 6d. net.

HARVARD HISTORICAL STUDIES.

THE SUPPRESSION OF THE AFRICAN SLAVE TRADE TO THE UNITED STATES OF AMERICA, 1638-1870. By W. E. B. Du BOIS, Ph.D 8vo., 7s. 6d.

THE CONTEST OVER THE RATIFICATON OF THE FEDERAL CONSTITUTION IN MASSACHUSETTS. By S. B. HARDING, A.M. 8vo.,6s.

A CRITICAL STUDY OF NULLIFICATION IN SOUTH CAROLINA. By D. F. HOUSTON, A.M. 8vo., 6s.

NOMINATIONS FOR ELECTIVE OFFICE IN THE UNITED STATES. By FREDERICK W. DALLINGER, A.M. 8vo., 7s. 6d.

A BIBLIOGRAPHY OF BRITISH MUNICIPAL HISTORY, INCLUDING GILDS AND PARLIAMENTARY REPRESENTATION. By CHARLES GROSS, Ph.D. 8vo., 12s.

THE LIBERTY AND FREE SOIL PARTIES IN THE NORTH WEST. By THEODORE C. SMITH, Ph.D. 8vo, 7s. 6d.

THE PROVINCIAL GOVERNOR IN THE ENGLISH COLONIES OF NORTH AMERICA. By EVARTS BOUTELL GREENE. 8vo., 7s. 6d.

THE COUNTY PALATINE OF DURHAM: a Study in Constitutional History. By GAILLARD THOMAS LAPSLEY, Ph.D. 8vo., 10s. 6d.

THE ANGLICAN EPISCOPATE AND THE AMERICAN COLONIES. By ARTHUR LYON CROSS, Ph.D., Instructor in History in the University of Michigan. 8vo., 10s. 6d,

THE ADMINISTRATION OF THE AMERICAN REVOLUTIONARY ARMY. By LOUIS CLINTON HATCH, Ph.D. 8vo., 7s. 6d.

Hill.—THREE FRENCHMEN IN BENGAL; or, The Commercial Ruin of the French Settlements in 1757. By S. C. HILL, B.A., B.Sc., Officer in charge of the Records of the Government of India. With 4 Maps. 8vo., 7s. 6d. net.

Historic Towns.—Edited by E. A. FREEMAN, D.C.L., and Rev. WILLIAM HUNT, M.A. With Maps and Plans. Crown 8vo., 3s. 6d. each.

Bristol. By Rev. W. Hunt.	Oxford. By Rev. C. W. Boase.
Carlisle. By Mandell Creighton, D.D.	Winchester. By G. W. Kitchin, D.D.
Cinque Ports. By Montagu Burrows.	York. By Rev. James Raine.
Colchester. By Rev. E. L. Cutts.	New York. By Theodore Roosevelt.
Exeter. By E. A. Freeman.	
London. By Rev. W. J. Loftie.	Boston (U.S.) By Henry Cabot Lodge.

History, Politics, Polity, Political Memoirs, &c.—*continued*.

Hunter (Sir WILLIAM WILSON).

A HISTORY OF BRITISH INDIA.
Vol. I.—Introductory to the Overthrow
of the English in the Spice Archipelago,
1623. With 4 Maps. 8vo., 18s. Vol.
II.—To the Union of the Old and New
Companies under the Earl of Godolphin's
Award, 1708. 8vo., 16s.

THE INDIA OF THE QUEEN, and
other Essays. Edited by Lady HUNTER.
With an Introduction by FRANCIS HENRY
SKRINE, Indian Civil Service (Retired).
8vo., 9s. net.

Ingram.—*A CRITICAL EXAMINA-TION OF IRISH HISTORY.*. From the Eliza-
bethan Conquest to the Legislative Union
of 1800. By T. DUNBAR INGRAM, LL.D.
2 vols. 8vo., 6s. net.

Joyce (P. W.)

A SHORT HISTORY OF IRELAND,
from the Earliest Times to 1608. With
Maps. Crown 8vo., 10s. 6d.

*A SOCIAL HISTORY OF ANCIENT
IRELAND:* Treating of the Government,
Military System and Law; Religion,
Learning and Art; Trades, Industries
and Commerce; Manners, Customs and
Domestic Life of the Ancient Irish People.
With 361 Illustrations. 2 vols. 8vo.,
21s. net.

Kaye and Malleson.—*HISTORY OF
THE INDIAN MUTINY*, 1857-1858. By Sir
JOHN W. KAYE and Colonel G. B. MALLE-
SON. With Analytical Index and Maps and
Plans. 6 vols. Crown 8vo., 3s. 6d. each.

Lang (ANDREW).

THE MYSTERY OF MARY STUART.
With Photogravure Plate and 15 other
Illustrations. Crown 8vo., 6s. 6d. net.

*PRINCE CHARLES EDWARD STUART,
THE YOUNG CHEVALIER.* With Photogravure Frontispiece. Cr. 8vo., 7s. 6d. net.

*THE VALET'S TRAGEDY, AND OTHER
STUDIES IN SECRET HISTORY.* With
3 Illustrations. 8vo., 12s. 6d. net.

Lecky (WILLIAM EDWARD HARTPOLE)

*HISTORY OF ENGLAND IN THE EIGHT-
EENTH CENTURY.*

Library Edition. 8 vols. 8vo. Vols. I.
and II., 1700-1760, 36s.; Vols. III. and
IV., 1760-1784, 36s.; Vols. V. and VI.,
1784-1793, 36s.; Vols. VII. and VIII.,
1793-1800, 36s.

Cabinet Edition. ENGLAND. 7 vols. Crown
8vo., 5s. net each. IRELAND. 5 vols.
Crown 8vo., 5s. net each.

*LEADERS OF PUBLIC OPINION IN
IRELAND: FLOOD—GRATTAN—O'CON-
NELL.* 2 vols. 8vo., 25s. net.

*HISTORY OF EUROPEAN MORALS
FROM AUGUSTUS TO CHARLEMAGNE.* 2
vols. Crown 8vo., 10s. net.

A SURVEY OF ENGLISH ETHICS:
Being the First Chapter of the 'History
of European Morals'. Edited, with
Introduction and Notes, by W. A. HIRST.
Crown 8vo., 3s. 6d.

*HISTORY OF THE RISE AND INFLU-
ENCE OF THE SPIRIT OF RATIONALISM IN
EUROPE.* 2 vols. Crown 8vo., 10s. net.

DEMOCRACY AND LIBERTY.
Library Edition. 2 vols. 8vo., 36s.
Cabinet Edition. 2 vols. Cr. 8vo., 10s. net.

Lieven.—*LETTERS OF DOROTHEA,
PRINCESS LIEVEN, DURING HER RESIDENCE
IN LONDON*, 1812-1834. Edited by LIONEL
G. ROBINSON. With 2 Photogravure Por-
traits. 8vo., 14s. net.

Lowell.—*GOVERNMENTS AND PAR-
TIES IN CONTINENTAL EUROPE.* By A.
LAWRENCE LOWELL. 2 vols. 8vo., 21s.

Lumsden s Horse, Records of.—
Edited by H. H. S. PEARSE. With a Map,
and numerous Portraits and Illustrations in
the Text. 4to., 21s. net.

Lynch.—*THE WAR OF THE CIVILI-
SATIONS: BEING A RECORD OF 'A FOREIGN
DEVIL'S' EXPERIENCES WITH THE ALLIES
IN CHINA.* By GEORGE LYNCH, Special
Correspondent of the 'Sphere,' etc. With
Portrait and 21 Illustrations. Crown 8vo.,
6s. net.

History, Politics, Polity, Political Memoirs, &c.—*continued*.

Macaulay (Lord).

THE LIFE AND WORKS OF LORD MACAULAY.
'*Edinburgh*' *Edition.* 10 vols. 8vo.,6s.each.
Vols. I.-IV. HISTORY OF ENGLAND.
Vols. V.-VII. *ESSAYS, BIOGRAPHIES, INDIAN PENAL CODE, CONTRIBUTIONS TO KNIGHT'S '*QUARTERLY MAGAZINE'.
Vol. VIII. *SPEECHES, LAYS OF ANCIENT ROME, MISCELLANEOUS POEMS.*
Vols. IX. and X. *THE LIFE AND LETTERS OF LORD MACAULAY.* By Sir G. O. TREVELYAN, Bart.

Popular Edition. 5 vols. Cr.8vo,2s.6d.each.
ESSAYS WITH LAYS OF ANCIENT ROME, ETC. Crown 8vo., 2s. 6d.
HISTORY OF ENGLAND. 2 vols. Crown 8vo., 5s.
MISCELLANEOUS WRITINGS, SPEECHES AND POEMS. Crown 8vo., 2s. 6d.
THE LIFE AND LETTERS OF LORD MACAULAY. By Sir G. O. TREVELYAN, Bart. Crown 8vo., 2s. 6d.

THE WORKS.
'*Albany*' *Edition.* With 12 Portraits. 12 vols. Large Crown 8vo., 3s. 6d. each.
Vols. I.-VI. *HISTORY OF ENGLAND, FROM THE ACCESSION OF JAMES THE SECOND.*
Vols. VII.-X. *ESSAYS AND BIOGRAPHIES.*
Vols. XI.-XII. *SPEECHES, LAYS OF ANCIENT ROME, ETC., AND INDEX.*

Cabinet Edition. 16 vols. Post 8vo., £4 16s.

HISTORY OF ENGLAND FROM THE ACCESSION OF JAMES THE SECOND.
Popular Edition. 2 vols. Cr. 8vo., 5s.
Student's Edition. 2 vols. Cr. 8vo., 12s.
People's Edition. 4 vols. Cr. 8vo., 16s.
'*Albany*' *Edition.* With 6 Portraits. 6 vols. Large Crown 8vo., 3s. 6d. each.
Cabinet Edition. 8 vols. Post 8vo., 48s.
'*Edinburgh*' *Edition.* 4 vols. 8vo., 6s. each.
Library Edition. 5 vols. 8vo., £4.

CRITICAL AND HISTORICAL ESSAYS, WITH LAYS OF ANCIENT ROME, etc., in 1 volume.
Popular Edition. Crown 8vo., 2s. 6d.
'*Silver Library*' *Edition.* With Portrait and 4 Illustrations to the '*Lays*'. Cr. 8vo., 3s. 6d.

CRITICAL AND HISTORICAL ESSAYS.
Student's Edition. 1 vol. Cr. 8vo., 6s.
'*Trevelyan*' *Edition.* 2 vols. Cr. 8vo., 9s.
Cabinet Edition. 4 vols. Post 8vo., 24s.
'*Edinburgh*' *Edition.* 3 vols. 8vo., 6s. each.
Library Edition. 3 vols. 8vo., 36s.

Macaulay (Lord)—*continued*.

ESSAYS, which may be had separately, sewed, 6d. each; cloth, 1s. each.

Addison and Walpole.	Frederick the Great.
Croker's Boswell's Johnson.	Ranke and Gladstone.
Hallam's Constitutional History.	Lord Bacon.
	Lord Clive
Warren Hastings.	Lord Byron, and The
The Earl of Chatham (Two Essays).	Comic Dramatists of the Restoration.

MISCELLANEOUS WRITINGS, SPEECHES AND POEMS.
Popular Edition. Crown 8vo., 2s. 6d.
Cabinet Edition. 4 vols. Post 8vo., 24s.

SELECTIONS FROM THE WRITINGS OF LORD MACAULAY. Edited, with Occasional Notes, by the Right Hon. Sir G. O. TREVELYAN, Bart. Crown 8vo., 6s.

Mackinnon (JAMES, Ph.D.).

THE HISTORY OF EDWARD THE THIRD. 8vo., 18s.

THE GROWTH AND DECLINE OF THE FRENCH MONARCHY. 8vo., 21s. net.

Mallet.—*MALLET DU PAN AND THE FRENCH REVOLUTION.* By BERNARD MALLET. With Photogravure Portrait. 8vo., 12s. 6d. net.

May.—*THE CONSTITUTIONAL HISTORY OF ENGLAND* since the Accession of George III. 1760-1870. By Sir THOMAS ERSKINE MAY, K.C.B. (Lord Farnborough). 3 vols. Cr. 8vo., 18s.

Merivale (CHARLES, D.D.).

HISTORY OF THE ROMANS UNDER THE EMPIRE. 8 vols. Crown 8vo., 3s. 6d. each.

THE FALL OF THE ROMAN REPUBLIC: a Short History of the Last Century of the Commonwealth. 12mo., 7s. 6d.

GENERAL HISTORY OF ROME, from the Foundation of the City to the Fall of Augustulus, B.C. 753-A.D. 476. With 5 Maps. Crown 8vo., 7s. 6d.

Montague. — *THE ELEMENTS OF ENGLISH CONSTITUTIONAL HISTORY.* By F. C. MONTAGUE, M.A. Crown 8vo., 3s. 6d.

Moran.—*THE THEORY AND PRACTICE OF THE ENGLISH GOVERNMENT.* By THOMAS FRANCIS MORAN, Ph.D., Professor of History and Economics in Purdue University, U.S. Crown 8vo., 5s. net.

Pears.—*THE DESTRUCTION OF THE GREEK EMPIRE AND THE STORY OF THE CAPTURE OF CONSTANTINOPLE BY THE TURKS.* By EDWIN PEARS, LL.B. With 3 Maps and 4 Illustrations. 8vo., 18s. net.

History, Politics, Polity, Political Memoirs, &c.—*continued*.

Powell and Trevelyan. — *THE PEASANTS' RISING AND THE LOLLARDS :* a Collection of Unpublished Documents. Edited by EDGAR POWELL and G. M. TREVELYAN. 8vo., 6s. net.

Rankin (REGINALD).

THE MARQUIS D'ARGENSON ; AND RICHARD THE SECOND. 8vo., 10s. 6d. net.

A SUBALTERN'S LETTERS TO HIS WIFE. (The Boer War.) Crown 8vo., 3s. 6d.

Ransome.—*THE RISE OF CONSTITUTIONAL GOVERNMENT IN ENGLAND.* By CYRIL RANSOME, M.A. Crown 8vo., 6s.

Scherger.—*THE EVOLUTION OF MODERN LIBERTY.* By GEORGE L. SCHERGER, Ph.D. Crown 8vo., 5s. net.

Seebohm (FREDERIC, LL.D., F.S.A.).

THE ENGLISH VILLAGE COMMUNITY. With 13 Maps and Plates. 8vo., 16s.

TRIBAL CUSTOM IN ANGLO-SAXON LAW : being an Essay supplemental to (1) 'The English Village Community,' (2) 'The Tribal System in Wales'. 8vo., 16s.

Smith.—*CARTHAGE AND THE CARTHAGINIANS.* By R. BOSWORTH SMITH, M.A. With Maps, Plans, etc. Cr. 8vo., 3s. 6d.

Stephens. — *A HISTORY OF THE FRENCH REVOLUTION.* By H. MORSE STEPHENS. 8vo. Vols. I. and II. 18s. each.

Stubbs.—*HISTORY OF THE UNIVERSITY OF DUBLIN.* By J. W. STUBBS. 8vo., 12s. 6d.

Stubbs (WILLIAM D.D., formerly Bishop of Oxford).

HISTORICAL INTRODUCTIONS TO THE 'ROLLS SERIES'. 8vo., 12s. 6d. net.

LECTURES ON EUROPEAN HISTORY, 1519-1648. 8vo., 12s. 6d. net.

Sutherland.—*THE HISTORY OF AUSTRALIA AND NEW ZEALAND,* from 1606-1900. By ALEXANDER SUTHERLAND, M.A. and GEORGE SUTHERLAND, M.A. Crown 8vo., 2s. 6d.

Taylor.—*A STUDENT'S MANUAL OF THE HISTORY OF INDIA.* By Colonel MEADOWS TAYLOR, C.S.I. Cr. 8vo., 7s. 6d.

Thomson.—*CHINA AND THE POWERS :* a Narrative of the Outbreak of 1900. By H. C. THOMSON. With 2 Maps and 29 Illustrations. 8vo., 10s. 6d. net.

Todd. — *PARLIAMENTARY GOVERNMENT IN THE BRITISH COLONIES.* By ALPHEUS TODD, LL.D. 8vo., 30s. net.

Trevelyan.—*THE AMERICAN REVOLUTION.* By Sir G. O. TREVELYAN, Bart. Part I., 8vo., 13s. 6d. net. Part II., 2 vols. 8vo., 21s. net.

Trevelyan.—*ENGLAND IN THE AGE OF WYCLIFFE.* By GEORGE MACAULAY TREVELYAN. 8vo., 15s.

Wakeman and Hassall.—*ESSAYS INTRODUCTORY TO THE STUDY OF ENGLISH CONSTITUTIONAL HISTORY.* Edited by HENRY OFFLEY WAKEMAN, M.A., and ARTHUR HASSALL, M.A. Crown 8vo., 6s.

Walpole (Sir SPENCER, K.C.B.).

HISTORY OF ENGLAND FROM THE CONCLUSION OF THE GREAT WAR IN 1815 TO 1858. 6 vols. Crown 8vo., 6s. each.

THE HISTORY OF TWENTY-FIVE YEARS (1856-1881). Vols. I. and II., 1856-1870. 8vo., 24s. net.

Willoughby.—*POLITICAL THEORIES OF THE ANCIENT WORLD.* By WESTEL W. WILLOUGHBY, Ph.D. Cr. 8vo., 6s. net.

Willson.—*LEDGER AND SWORD ;* or, The Honourable Company of Merchants of England Trading to the East Indies (1599-1874). By BECKLES WILLSON. With numerous Portraits and Illustrations. 2 vols. 8vo., 21s. net.

Wylie (JAMES HAMILTON, M.A.).

HISTORY OF ENGLAND UNDER HENRY IV. 4 vols. Crown 8vo. Vol. I., 1399-1404, 10s. 6d. Vol. II., 1405-1406, 15s. (*out of print*). Vol. III., 1407-1411, 15s. Vol. IV., 1411-1413, 21s.

THE COUNCIL OF CONSTANCE TO THE DEATH OF JOHN HUS. Cr. 8vo., 6s. net.

Yardley.—*WITH THE INNISKILLING DRAGOONS :* the Record of a Cavalry Regiment during the Boer War, 1899-1902. By Lieut.-Colonel J. WATKINS YARDLEY. With Map and numerous Illustrations. 8vo., 16s. net.

Biography, Personal Memoirs, &c.

Anstruther Thomson. — *EIGHTY YEARS' REMINISCENCES.* By Colonel J. ANSTRUTHER THOMSON. With 29 Portraits and other Illustrations. 2 vols. 8vo., 21s. net.

Bacon. — *THE LETTERS AND LIFE OF FRANCIS BACON, INCLUDING ALL HIS OCCASIONAL WORKS.* Edited by JAMES SPEDDING. 7 vols. 8vo., £4 4s.

Bagehot. — *BIOGRAPHICAL STUDIES.* By WALTER BAGEHOT. Crown 8vo., 3s. 6d.

Bain. — *AUTOBIOGRAPHY.* By ALEXANDER BAIN, LL.D. With 4 Portraits. 8vo., 14s. net.

Bowen. — *EDWARD BOWEN: A MEMOIR.* By the Rev. the Hon. W. E. BOWEN. With Appendices, 3 Photogravure Portraits and 2 other Illustrations. 8vo., 12s. 6d. net.

Carlyle. — *THOMAS CARLYLE:* A History of his Life. By JAMES ANTHONY FROUDE.
1795-1835. 2 vols. Crown 8vo., 7s.
1834-1881. 2 vols. Crown 8vo., 7s.

Colville. — *DUCHESS SARAH:* being the Social History of the Times of Sarah Jennings, Duchess of Marlborough. Compiled and arranged by one of her descendants (Mrs. ARTHUR COLVILLE). With 10 Photogravure Plates and 2 other Illustrations. 8vo., 18s. net.

Creighton. — *LIFE AND LETTERS OF MANDELL CREIGHTON,* D.D. Oxon. and Camb., sometime Bishop of London. By HIS WIFE. With Portraits and other Illustrations. 2 vols. 8vo., 28s. net.

Crozier. — *MY INNER LIFE:* being a Chapter in Personal Evolution and Autobiography. By JOHN BEATTIE CROZIER, LL.D. 8vo., 14s.

Dante. — *THE LIFE AND WORKS OF DANTE ALLIGHIERI:* being an Introduction to the Study of the 'Divina Commedia'. By the Rev. J. F. HOGAN, D.D. With Portrait. 8vo., 12s. 6d.

Danton. — *LIFE OF DANTON.* By A. H. BEESLY. With Portraits. Cr. 8vo., 6s.

De Vere. — *AUBREY DE VERE:* a Memoir based on his unpublished Diaries and Correspondence. By WILFRID WARD. With 2 Portraits and 2 other Illustrations. 8v., 14s. net.

Erasmus.
LIFE AND LETTERS OF ERASMUS. By JAMES ANTHONY FROUDE. Crown 8vo., 3s. 6d.
THE EPISTLES OF ERASMUS, arranged in Order of Time. English Translations from the Early Correspondence, with a Commentary confirming the Chronological arrangement and supplying further Biographical matter. By FRANCIS MORGAN NICHOLS. 2 vols. 8vo., 18s. net each.

Faraday. — *FARADAY AS A DISCOVERER.* By JOHN TYNDALL. Crown 8vo., 3s. 6d.

Fénelon: his Friends and his Enemies, 1651-1715. By E. K. SANDERS. With Portrait. 8vo., 10s. 6d.

Fox. — *THE EARLY HISTORY OF CHARLES JAMES FOX.* By the Right Hon. Sir G. O. TREVELYAN, Bart. Cr. 8vo., 3s. 6d.

Froude. — *MY RELATIONS WITH CARLYLE.* By JAMES ANTHONY FROUDE. Together with a Letter from the late Sir JAMES STEPHEN, Bart., K.C.S.I., dated December, 1886. 8vo., 2s. net.

Grey. — *MEMOIR OF SIR GEORGE GREY, BART., G.C.B.,* 1799-1882. By MANDELL CREIGHTON, D.D., late Lord Bishop of London. With 3 Portraits. Crown 8vo., 6s. net.

Hamilton. — *LIFE OF SIR WILLIAM HAMILTON.* By R. P. GRAVES 8vo. 3 vols. 15s. each. ADDENDUM. 8vo., 6d. sewed.

Harrow School Register (The), 1801-1900. Edited by M. G. DAUGLISH. 8vo. 10s. net.

Havelock. — *MEMOIRS OF SIR HENRY HAVELOCK, K.C.B.* By JOHN CLARK MARSHMAN. Crown 8vo., 3s. 6d.

Haweis. — *MY MUSICAL LIFE.* By the Rev. H. R. HAWEIS. With Portrait of Richard Wagner and 3 Illustrations. Cr. 8vo., 6s. net.

Higgins. — *THE BERNARDS OF ABINGTON AND NETHER WINCHENDON:* A Family History. By Mrs. NAPIER HIGGINS. 2 Vols. 8vo., 21s. net.

Hiley. — *MEMORIES OF HALF A CENTURY.* By RICHARD W. HILEY, D.D., Vicar of Wighill, near Tadcaster, Yorks. 8vo., 15s.

Biography, Personal Memoirs, &c.—*continued.*

Jackson.—*STONEWALL JACKSON AND THE AMERICAN CIVIL WAR.* By Lieut.-Col. G. F. R. HENDERSON. With 2 Portraits and 33 Maps and Plans. 2 vols. Cr. 8vo., 16s. net.

Kielmansegge.—*DIARY OF A JOURNEY TO ENGLAND IN THE YEARS* 1761-1762. By Count FREDERICK KIELMANSEGGE. With 4 Illustrations. Crown 8vo. 5s. net.

Luther.—*LIFE OF LUTHER.* By JULIUS KÖSTLIN. With 62 Illustrations and 4 Facsimilies of MSS. Cr. 8vo., 3s. 6d.

Macaulay.—*THE LIFE AND LETTERS OF LORD MACAULAY.* By the Right Hon. Sir G. O. TREVELYAN, Bart.
> *Popular Edition.* 1 vol. Cr. 8vo., 2s. 6d.
> *Student's Edition* 1 vol. Cr. 8vo., 6s.
> *Cabinet Edition.* 2 vols. Post 8vo., 12s.
> *'Edinburgh' Edition.* 2 vols. 8vo., 6s. each.
> *Library Edition.* 2 vols. 8vo., 36s.

Marbot.—*THE MEMOIRS OF THE BARON DE MARBOT.* 2 vols. Cr. 8vo., 7s.

Max Müller (F.)
> *THE LIFE AND LETTERS OF THE RIGHT HON. FRIEDRICH MAX MÜLLER.* Edited by his Wife. With Photogravure Portraits and other Illustrations. 2 vols., 8vo., 32s. net.
> *MY AUTOBIOGRAPHY:* a Fragment. With 6 Portraits. 8vo., 12s. 6d.
> *AULD LANG SYNE.* Second Series. 8vo., 10s. 6d.
> *CHIPS FROM A GERMAN WORKSHOP.* Vol. II. Biographical Essays. Cr. 8vo., 5s.

Morris.—*THE LIFE OF WILLIAM MORRIS.* By J. W. MACKAIL. With 2 Portraits and 8 other Illustrations by E. H. NEW, etc. 2 vols. Large Crown 8vo., 10s. net.

On the Banks of the Seine. By A. M. F., Author of 'Foreign Courts and Foreign Homes'. Crown 8vo., 6s.

Paget.—*MEMOIRS AND LETTERS OF SIR JAMES PAGET.* Edited by STEPHEN PAGET, one of his sons. With Portrait. 8vo., 6s. net.

Râmakrishna : *HIS LIFE AND SAYINGS.* By the Right Hon. F. MAX MÜLLER. Crown 8vo., 5s.

Rochester, and other Literary Rakes of the Court of Charles II., with some Account of their Surroundings. By the Author of 'The Life of Sir Kenelm Digby,' The Life of a Prig,' etc. With 15 Portraits. 8vo., 16s.

Romanes.—*THE LIFE AND LETTERS OF GEORGE JOHN ROMANES, M.A., LL.D., F.R.S.* Written and Edited by his WIFE. With Portrait and 2 Illustrations. Cr. 8vo., 5s. net.

Russell.—*SWALLOWFIELD AND ITS OWNERS.* By CONSTANCE LADY RUSSELL, of Swallowfield Park. With 15 Photogravure Portraits and 36 other Illustrations. 4to., gilt edges, 42s. net.

Seebohm.—*THE OXFORD REFORMERS —JOHN COLET, ERASMUS, AND THOMAS MORE :* a History of their Fellow-Work. By FREDERIC SEEBOHM. 8vo., 14s.

Shakespeare. — *OUTLINES OF THE LIFE OF SHAKESPEARE.* By J. O. HALLIWELL-PHILLIPPS. With Illustrations and Facsimiles. 2 vols. Royal 8vo., 21s.

Tales of my Father.—By A. M. F. Crown 8vo., 6s.

Tallentyre.—*THE WOMEN OF THE SALONS,* and other French Portraits. By S. G. TALLENTYRE. With 11 Photogravure Portraits. 8vo., 10s. 6d. net.

Verney.—*MEMOIRS OF THE VERNEY FAMILY DURING THE SEVENTEENTH CENTURY.* Compiled from the Papers and Illustrated by the Portraits at Claydon House, Bucks. By FRANCES PARTHENOPE VERNEY and MARGARET M. VERNEY. Abridged and Cheaper Edition. With 24 Portraits. 2 vols. Crown 8vo., 12s. net.

Victoria, Queen, 1819-1901. By RICHARD R. HOLMES, M.V.O., F.S.A. With Photogravure Portrait. Crown 8vo., gilt top, 5s. net.

Wellington.—*LIFE OF THE DUKE OF WELLINGTON.* By the Rev. G. R. GLEIG, M.A. Crown 8vo., 3s. 6d.

Wilkins (W. H.).
> *A QUEEN OF TEARS :* Caroline Matilda, Queen of Denmark and Norway, and Princess of Great Britain and Ireland. With 2 Portraits and 47 other Illustrations. 2 vols. 8vo., 36s.
> *THE LOVE OF AN UNCROWNED QUEEN:* Sophie Dorothea, Consort of George I., and her Correspondence with Philip Christopher, Count Königsmarck. With 24 Portraits and other Illustrations. 8vo., 12s. 6d. net.
> *CAROLINE THE ILLUSTRIOUS,* Queen-Consort of George II., and sometime Queen-Regent : a Study of Her Life and Time. With 42 Portraits and other Illustrations. 8vo., 12s. 6d. net.

Travel and Adventure, the Colonies, &c.

Arnold.—*SEAS AND LANDS.* By Sir EDWIN ARNOLD. With 71 Illustrations. Crown 8vo., 3s. 6d.

Baker (Sir S. W.).

EIGHT YEARS IN CEYLON. With 6 Illustrations. Crown 8vo., 3s. 6d.

THE RIFLE AND THE HOUND IN CEYLON. With 6 Illusts. Cr. 8vo., 3s. 6d.

Ball (JOHN).

THE ALPINE GUIDE. Reconstructed and Revised on behalf of the Alpine Club, by W. A. B. COOLIDGE.
Vol. I., *THE WESTERN ALPS :* the Alpine Region, South of the Rhone Valley, from the Col de Tenda to the Simplon Pass. With 9 New and Revised Maps. Crown 8vo., 12s. net.

HINTS AND NOTES, PRACTICAL AND SCIENTIFIC, FOR TRAVELLERS IN THE ALPS : being a Revision of the General Introduction to the 'Alpine Guide'. Crown 8vo., 3s. net.

Bent.—*THE RUINED CITIES OF MASHONALAND :* being a Record of Excavation and Exploration in 1891. By J. THEODORE BENT. With 117 Illustrations. Crown 8vo., 3s. 6d.

Brassey (The Late Lady).

A VOYAGE IN THE 'SUNBEAM'; OUR HOME ON THE OCEAN FOR ELEVEN MONTHS.
Cabinet Edition. With Map and 66 Illustrations. Cr. 8vo., gilt edges, 7s. 6d.
'*Silver Library' Edition.* With 66 Illustrations. Crown 8vo., 3s. 6d.
Popular Edition. With 60 Illustrations. 4to., 6d. sewed, 1s. cloth.
School Edition. With 37 Illustrations. Fcp., 2s. cloth, or 3s. white parchment.

SUNSHINE AND STORM IN THE EAST.
Popular Edition. With 103 Illustrations. 4to., 6d. sewed, 1s. cloth.

IN THE TRADES, THE TROPICS, AND THE 'ROARING FORTIES'.
Cabinet Edition. With Map and 220 Illustrations. Cr. 8vo., gilt edges, 7s. 6d.

Cockerell.—*TRAVELS IN SOUTHERN EUROPE AND THE LEVANT,* 1810-1817. By C. R. COCKERELL, Architect, R.A. Edited by his Son, SAMUEL PEPYS COCKERELL. With Portrait. 8vo., 10s. 6d. net.

Fountain (PAUL).

THE GREAT DESERTS AND FORESTS OF NORTH AMERICA. With a Preface by W. H. HUDSON, Author of 'The Naturalist in La Plata,' etc. 8vo., 9s. 6d. net.

THE GREAT MOUNTAINS AND FORESTS OF SOUTH AMERICA. With Portrait and 7 Illustrations. 8vo., 10s. 6d. net.

THE GREAT NORTH-WEST AND THE GREAT LAKE REGION OF NORTH AMERICA. 8vo., 10s. 6d. net.

Froude (JAMES A.).

OCEANA : or England and her Colonies. With 9 Illustrations. Cr. 8vo., 3s. 6d.

THE ENGLISH IN THE WEST INDIES : or, the Bow of Ulysses. With 9 Illustrations. Crown 8vo., 2s. boards, 2s. 6d. cloth.

Grove.—*SEVENTY-ONE DAYS' CAMPING IN MOROCCO.* By Lady GROVE. With Photogravure Portrait and 32 Illustrations from Photographs. 8vo., 7s. 6d. net.

Haggard.—*A WINTER PILGRIMAGE :* Being an Account of Travels through Palestine, Italy and the Island of Cyprus, undertaken in the year 1900. By H. RIDER HAGGARD. With 31 Illustrations from Photographs. Crown 8vo., 6s. net.

Hardwick.—*AN IVORY TRADER IN NORTH KENIA :* the Record of an Expedition to the Country North of Mount Kenia in East Equatorial Africa, with an account of the Nomads of Galla-Land. By A. ARKELL-HARDWICK, F.R.G.S. With 23 Illustrations from Photographs, and a Map. 8vo., 12s. 6d. net.

Howitt.—*VISITS TO REMARKABLE PLACES.* Old Halls, Battle-Fields, Scenes, illustrative of Striking Passages in English History and Poetry. By WILLIAM HOWITT. With 80 Illustrations. Crown 8vo., 3s. 6d.

Knight (E. F.).

SOUTH AFRICA AFTER THE WAR. With 17 Illustrations. 8vo., 10s. 6d. net.

THE CRUISE OF THE 'ALERTE' : the Narrative of a Search for Treasure on the Desert Island of Trinidad. With 2 Maps and 23 Illustrations. Crown 8vo., 3s. 6d.

Travel and Adventure, the Colonies, &c.—*continued.*

Knight (E. F.)—*continued.*

WHERE THREE EMPIRES MEET : a Narrative of Recent Travel in Kashmir, Western Tibet, Baltistan, Ladak, Gilgit, and the adjoining Countries. With a Map and 54 Illustrations. Cr. 8vo., 3s. 6d.

THE 'FALCON' ON THE BALTIC : a Voyage from London to Copenhagen in a Three-Tonner. With 10 Full-page Illustrations. Crown 8vo., 3s. 6d.

Lees and Clutterbuck.—B.C. 1887 :
A RAMBLE IN BRITISH COLUMBIA. By J. A. LEES and W. J. CLUTTERBUCK. With Map and 75 Illustrations. Crown 8vo., 3s. 6d.

Lynch. — ARMENIA : Travels and Studies. By H. F. B. LYNCH. With 197 Illustrations (some in tints) reproduced from Photographs and Sketches by the Author, 16 Maps and Plans, a Bibliography, and a Map of Armenia and adjacent countries. 2 vols. Medium 8vo., gilt top, 42s. net.

Nansen.—THE FIRST CROSSING OF GREENLAND. By FRIDTJOF NANSEN. With 143 Illustrations and a Map. Crown 8vo., 3s. 6d.

Rice.—OCCASIONAL ESSAYS ON NATIVE SOUTH INDIAN LIFE. By STANLEY P. RICE, Indian Civil Service. 8vo., 10s. 6d.

Smith.—CLIMBING IN THE BRITISH ISLES. By W. P. HASKETT SMITH. With Illustrations and Numerous Plans.
Part I. ENGLAND. 16mo., 3s. net.
Part II. WALES AND IRELAND. 16mo., 3s. net.

Spender.—TWO WINTERS IN NORWAY: being an Account of Two Holidays spent on Snow-shoes and in Sleigh Driving, and including an Expedition to the Lapps. By A. EDMUND SPENDER. With 40 Illustrations from Photographs. 8vo., 10s. 6d. net.

Stephen. — THE PLAY-GROUND OF EUROPE (The Alps). By Sir LESLIE STEPHEN, K.C.B. With 4 Illustrations. Crown 8vo., 3s. 6d.

Stutfield and Collie.—CLIMBS AND EXPLORATION IN THE CANADIAN ROCKIES. By HUGH E. M. STUTFIELD and J. NORMAN COLLIE, F.R.S. With 2 Maps, 24 Full-page Illustrations, and 56 Half-page Illustrations. 8vo., 12s. 6d. net.

Sverdrup. — NEW LAND : Four Years in the Arctic Regions. By OTTO SVERDRUP. Translated from the Norwegian by ETHEL HARRIET HEARN. With 62 Plates, 162 Illustrations (4 Maps) in the Text, and 4 Folding-out Maps. 2 vols. 8vo., 36s. net.

Three in Norway. By Two of Them. With a Map and 59 Illustrations. Crown 8vo., 2s. boards, 2s. 6d. cloth.

Tyndall.—(JOHN).

THE GLACIERS OF THE ALPS. With 61 Illustrations. Crown 8vo., 6s. 6d. net.

HOURS OF EXERCISE IN THE ALPS. With 7 Illustrations. Cr. 8vo., 6s. 6d. net.

Sport and Pastime.

THE BADMINTON LIBRARY.

Edited by HIS GRACE THE (EIGHTH) DUKE OF BEAUFORT, K.G., and A. E. T. WATSON.

ARCHERY. By C. J. LONGMAN and Col. H. WALROND. With Contributions by Miss LEGH, Viscount DILLON, etc. With 2 Maps, 23 Plates and 172 Illustrations in the Text. Crown 8vo., cloth, 6s. net; half-bound, with gilt top, 9s. net.

ATHLETICS. By MONTAGUE SHEARMAN. With Chapters on Athletics at School by W. BEACHER THOMAS ; Athletic Sports in America by C. H. SHERRILL ; a Contribution on Paper-chasing by W. RYE, and an Introduction by Sir RICHARD WEBSTER (Lord ALVERSTONE). With 12 Plates and 37 Illustrations in the Text. Cr. 8vo., cloth, 6s. net; half-bound, with gilt top, 9s. net.

BIG GAME SHOOTING. By CLIVE PHILLIPPS-WOLLEY.

Vol. I. AFRICA AND AMERICA. With Contributions by Sir SAMUEL W. BAKER, W. C. OSWELL, F. C. SELOUS, etc. With 20 Plates and 57 Illustrations in the Text. Crown 8vo., cloth, 6s. net; half-bound, with gilt top, 9s. net.

Vol. II. EUROPE, ASIA, AND THE ARCTIC REGIONS. With Contributions by Lieut.-Colonel R. HEBER PERCY, Major ALGERNON C. HEBER PERCY, etc. With 17 Plates and 56 Illustrations in the Text. Crown 8vo., cloth 6s. net; half-bound, with gilt top, 9s. net.

Sport and Pastime—*continued*.

THE BADMINTON LIBRARY—*continued*.

Edited by HIS GRACE THE (EIGHTH) DUKE OF BEAUFORT, K.G.,
and A. E. T. WATSON.

BILLIARDS. By Major W. BROAD-FOOT, R.E. With Contributions by A. H. BOYD, SYDENHAM DIXON, W. J. FORD, etc. With 11 Plates, 19 Illustrations in the Text, and numerous Diagrams. Crown 8vo., cloth, 6s. net; half-bound, with gilt top, 9s. net.

COURSING AND FALCONRY. By HARDING COX, CHARLES RICHARDSON, and the Hon. GERALD LASCELLES. With 20 Plates and 55 Illustrations in the Text. Crown 8vo., cloth, 6s. net; half-bound, with gilt top, 9s. net.

CRICKET. By A. G. STEEL and the Hon. R. H. LYTTELTON. With Contributions by ANDREW LANG, W. G. GRACE, F. GALE, etc. With 13 Plates and 51 Illustrations in the Text. Crown 8vo., cloth, 6s. net; half-bound, with gilt top, 9s. net.

CYCLING. By the EARL OF ALBEMARLE and G. LACY HILLIER. With 19 Plates and 44 Illustrations in the Text. Crown 8vo., cloth, 6s. net; half-bound, with gilt top, 9s. net.

DANCING. By Mrs. LILLY GROVE. With Contributions by Miss MIDDLETON, The Hon. Mrs. ARMYTAGE, etc. With Musical Examples, and 38 Full-page Plates and 93 Illustrations in the Text. Crown 8vo., cloth, 6s. net; half-bound, with gilt top, 9s. net.

DRIVING. By His Grace the (Eighth) DUKE of BEAUFORT, K.G. With Contributions by A. E. T. WATSON the EARL OF ONSLOW, etc. With 12 Plates and 54 Illustrations in the Text. Crown 8vo., cloth, 6s. net; half-bound, with gilt top, 9s. net.

FENCING, BOXING, AND WRESTLING. By WALTER H. POLLOCK, F. C. GROVE, C. PREVOST, E. B. MITCHELL, and WALTER ARMSTRONG. With 18 Plates and 24 Illustrations in the Text. Crown 8vo., cloth, 6s. net; half-bound, with gilt top, 9s. net.

FISHING. By H. CHOLMONDELEY-PENNELL.

Vol. I. SALMON AND TROUT. With Contributions by H. R. FRANCIS, Major JOHN P. TRAHERNE, etc. With 9 Plates and numerous Illustrations of Tackle, etc. Crown 8vo., cloth, 6s. net; half-bound, with gilt top, 9s. net.

Vol. II. PIKE AND OTHER COARSE FISH. With Contributions by the MARQUIS OF EXETER, WILLIAM SENIOR, G. CHRISTOPHER DAVIS, etc. With 7 Plates and numerous Illustrations of Tackle, etc. Crown 8vo., cloth, 6s. net; half-bound, with gilt top, 9s. net.

FOOTBALL. HISTORY, by MONTAGUE SHEARMAN; THE ASSOCIATION GAME, by W. J. OAKLEY and G. O. SMITH; THE RUGBY UNION GAME, by FRANK MITCHELL. With other Contributions by R. E. MACNAGHTEN, M. C. KEMP, J. E. VINCENT, WALTER CAMP and A. SUTHERLAND. With 19 Plates and 35 Illustrations in the Text. Crown 8vo., cloth, 6s. net; half-bound, with gilt top, 9s. net.

GOLF. By HORACE G. HUTCHINSON. With Contributions by the Rt. Hon. A. J. BALFOUR, M.P., Sir WALTER SIMPSON, Bart., ANDREW LANG, etc. With 34 Plates and 56 Illustrations in the Text. Crown 8vo., cloth, 6s. net; half-bound, with gilt top, 9s. net.

HUNTING. By His Grace the (Eighth) DUKE of BEAUFORT, K.G., and MOWBRAY MORRIS. With Contributions by the EARL OF SUFFOLK AND BERKSHIRE, Rev. E. W. L. DAVIES, G. H. LONGMAN, etc. With 5 Plates and 54 Illustrations in the Text. Crown 8vo., cloth, 6s. net; half-bound, with gilt top, 9s. net.

MOTORS AND MOTOR-DRIVING. By Sir ALFRED C. HARMSWORTH, Bart., the MARQUIS DE CHASSELOUP-LAUBAT, the Hon. JOHN SCOTT-MONTAGU, R. J. MECREDY, the Hon. C. S. ROLLS, Sir DAVID SALOMONS, Bart., etc. With 14 Plates and 160 Illustrations in the Text. Crown 8vo., cloth, 9s. net; half-bound, 12s. net.

A Cloth Box for use when Motoring, 2s. net.

Sport and Pastime—*continued.*

THE BADMINTON LIBRARY—*continued.*

Edited by HIS GRACE THE (EIGHTH) DUKE OF BEAUFORT, K.G.,
and A. E. T. WATSON.

MOUNTAINEERING. By C. T. DENT. With Contributions by the Right Hon. J. BRYCE, M.P., Sir MARTIN CONWAY, D. W. FRESHFIELD, C. E. MATTHEWS, etc. With 13 Plates and 91 Illustrations in the Text. Crown 8vo., cloth, 6s. net; half-bound, with gilt top, 9s. net.

POETRY OF SPORT (THE).— Selected by HEDLEY PEEK. With a Chapter on Classical Allusions to Sport by ANDREW LANG, and a Special Preface to the BADMINTON LIBRARY by A. E. T. WATSON. With 32 Plates and 74 Illustrations in the Text. Crown 8vo., cloth, 6s. net; half-bound, with gilt top, 9s. net.

RACING AND STEEPLE-CHASING. By the EARL OF SUFFOLK AND BERKSHIRE, W. G. CRAVEN, the Hon. F. LAWLEY, ARTHUR COVENTRY, and A. E. T. WATSON. With Frontispiece and 56 Illustrations in the Text. Crown 8vo., cloth, 6s. net; half-bound, with gilt top, 9s. net.

RIDING AND POLO. By Captain ROBERT WEIR, J. MORAY BROWN, T. F. DALE, THE LATE DUKE OF BEAUFORT, THE EARL OF SUFFOLK AND BERKSHIRE, etc. With 18 Plates and 41 Illusts. in the Text. Crown 8vo., cloth, 6s. net; half-bound, with gilt top, 9s. net.

ROWING. By R. P. P. ROWE and C. M. PITMAN. With Chapters on Steering by C. P. SEROCOLD and F. C. BEGG; Metropolitan Rowing by S. LE BLANC SMITH; and on PUNTING by P. W. SQUIRE. With 75 Illustrations. Crown 8vo., cloth, 6s. net; half-bound, with gilt top, 9s. net.

SHOOTING.

Vol. I. FIELD AND COVERT. By LORD WALSINGHAM and Sir RALPH PAYNE-GALLWEY, Bart. With Contributions by the Hon. GERALD LASCELLES and A. J. STUART-WORTLEY. With 11 Plates and 95 Illustrations in the Text. Crown 8vo., cloth, 6s. net; half-bound, with gilt top, 9s. net.

Vol. II. MOOR AND MARSH. By LORD WALSINGHAM and Sir RALPH PAYNE-GALLWEY, Bart. With Contributions by LORD LOVAT and Lord CHARLES LENNOX KERR. With 8 Plates and 57 Illustrations in the Text. Crown 8vo., cloth, 6s. net; half-bound, with gilt top, 9s. net.

SEA FISHING. By JOHN BICKER-DYKE, Sir H. W. GORE-BOOTH, Sir ALFRED C. HARMSWORTH, Bart., and W. SENIOR. With 22 Full-page Plates and 175 Illusts. in the Text. Crown 8vo., cloth, 6s. net; half-bound, with gilt top, 9s. net.

SKATING, CURLING, TOBOGANING. By J. M. HEATHCOTE, C. G. TEBBUTT, T. MAXWELL WITHAM, Rev. JOHN KERR, ORMOND HAKE, HENRY A. BUCK, etc. With 12 Plates and 272 Illustrations in the Text. Crown 8vo., cloth, 6s. net; half-bound, with gilt top, 9s. net.

SWIMMING. By ARCHIBALD SINCLAIR and WILLIAM HENRY, Hon. Secs. of the Life-Saving Society. With 13 Plates and 112 Illustrations in the Text. Crown 8vo., cloth, 6s. net; half-bound, with gilt top, 9s. net.

TENNIS,   LAWN   TENNIS, RACKETS AND FIVES. By J. M. and C. G. HEATHCOTE, E. O. PLEYDELL-BOUVERIE, and A. C. AINGER. With Contributions by the Hon. A. LYTTELTON, W. C. MARSHALL, Miss L. DOD, etc. With 14 Plates and 65 Illustrations in the Text. Crown 8vo., cloth, 6s. net; half-bound, with gilt top, 9s. net.

YACHTING.

Vol. I. CRUISING, CONSTRUCTION OF YACHTS, YACHT RACING RULES, FITTING-OUT, etc. By Sir EDWARD SULLIVAN, Bart., THE EARL OF PEMBROKE, LORD BRASSEY, K.C.B., C. E. SETH-SMITH, C.B., G. L. WATSON, R. T. PRITCHETT, E. F. KNIGHT, etc. With 21 Plates and 93 Illustrations in the Text. Crown 8vo., cloth, 6s. net; half-bound, with gilt top, 9s. net.

Vol. II. YACHT CLUBS, YACHTING IN AMERICA AND THE COLONIES, YACHT RACING, etc. By R. T. PRITCHETT, THE MARQUIS OF DUFFERIN AND AVA, K.P., THE EARL OF ONSLOW, JAMES McFERRAN, etc. With 35 Plates and 160 Illustrations in the Text. Crown 8vo., cloth, 9s. net; half-bound, with gilt top, 9s. net.

Sport and Pastime—*continued.*

FUR, FEATHER, AND FIN SERIES.

Edited by A. E. T. Watson.

Crown 8vo., price 5s. each Volume, cloth.

** *The Volumes are also issued half-bound in Leather, with gilt top. Price 7s. 6d. net each.*

THE PARTRIDGE. Natural History, by the Rev. H. A. Macpherson; Shooting, by A. J. Stuart-Wortley; Cookery, by George Saintsbury. With 11 Illustrations and various Diagrams. Crown 8vo., 5s.

THE GROUSE. Natural History, by the Rev. H. A. Macpherson; Shooting, by A. J. Stuart-Wortley; Cookery, by George Saintsbury. With 13 Illustrations and various Diagrams. Crown 8vo., 5s.

THE PHEASANT. Natural History, by the Rev. H. A. Macpherson; Shooting, by A. J. Stuart-Wortley; Cookery, by Alexander Innes Shand. With 10 Illustrations and various Diagrams. Crown 8vo., 5s.

THE HARE. Natural History, by the Rev. H. A. Macpherson; Shooting, by the Hon. Gerald Lascelles; Coursing, by Charles Richardson; Hunting, by J. S. Gibbons and G. H. Longman; Cookery, by Col. Kenney Herbert. With 9 Illustrations. Crown 8vo., 5s.

THE RABBIT. By James Edmund Harting. Cookery, by Alexander Innes Shand. With 10 Illustrations. Cr. 8vo., 5s.

SNIPE AND WOODCOCK. By L. H. De Visme Shaw. With Chapters on Snipe and Woodcock in Ireland by Richard J. Ussher. Cookery, by Alexander Innes Shand. With 8 Illustrations. Cr. 8vo., 5s.

RED DEER.—Natural History, by the Rev. H. A. Macpherson; Deer Stalking, by Cameron of Lochiel; Stag Hunting, by Viscount Ebrington; Cookery, by Alexander Innes Shand. With 10 Illustrations. Crown 8vo., 5s.

THE SALMON. By the Hon. A. E. Gathorne-Hardy. With Chapters on the Law of Salmon Fishing by Claud Douglas Pennant; Cookery, by Alexander Innes Shand. With 8 Illustrations. Cr. 8vo., 5s.

THE TROUT. By the Marquess of Granby. With Chapters on the Breeding of Trout by Col. H. Custance; and Cookery, by Alexander Innes Shand. With 12 Illustrations. Crown 8vo., 5s.

PIKE AND PERCH. By William Senior ('Redspinner,' Editor of the 'Field'). With Chapters by John Bickerdyke and W. H. Pope; Cookery, by Alexander Innes Shand. With 12 Illustrations. Crown 8vo., 5s.

Anstruther Thomson. — *Eighty Years' Reminiscences.* By Colonel J. Anstruther Thomson. With 29 Portraits and other Illustrations. 2 vols. 8vo., 21s. net.

Bickerdyke.—*Days of My Life on Water, Fresh and Salt;* and other Papers. By John Bickerdyke. With Photo-etching Frontispiece and 8 Full-page Illustrations. Crown 8vo., 3s. 6d.

Ellis.—*Chess Sparks;* or, Short and Bright Games of Chess. Collected and Arranged by J. H. Ellis, M.A. 8vo., 4s. 6d.

Blackburne. — *Mr. Blackburne's Games at Chess.* Selected, Annotated and Arranged by Himself. Edited, with a Biographical Sketch and a brief History of Blindfold Chess, by P. Anderson Graham. With Portrait of Mr. Blackburne. 8vo., 7s. 6d. net.

Ford.—*The Theory and Practice of Archery.* By Horace Ford. New Edition, thoroughly Revised and Re-written by W. Butt, M.A. With a Preface by C. J. Longman, M.A. 8vo., 14s.

Francis.—*A Book on Angling:* or, Treatise on the Art of Fishing in every Branch; including full Illustrated List of Salmon Flies. By Francis Francis. With Portrait and Coloured Plates. Crown 8vo., 15s.

Fremantle. — *The Book of the Rifle.* By the Hon. T. F. Fremantle, V.D., Major, 1st Bucks V.R.C. With 54 Plates and 107 Diagrams in the Text. 8vo., 12s. 6d. net.

Gathorne-Hardy. — *Autumns in Argyleshire with Rod and Gun.* By the Hon. A. E. Gathorne-Hardy. With 8 Illustrations by Archibald Thorburn. 8vo., 6s. net.

Sport and Pastime—*continued.*

Graham.—*COUNTRY PASTIMES FOR BOYS.* By P. ANDERSON GRAHAM. With 252 Illustrations from Drawings and Photographs. Cr. 8vo., gilt edges, 3s. net.

Hutchinson.—*THE BOOK OF GOLF AND GOLFERS.* By HORACE G. HUTCHINSON. With 71 Portraits from Photographs. Large crown 8vo., gilt top, 7s. 6d. net.

Lang.—*ANGLING SKETCHES.* By ANDREW LANG. With 20 Illustrations. Crown 8vo., 3s. 6d.

Lillie.—*CROQUET UP TO DATE.* Containing the Ideas and Teachings of the Leading Players and Champions. By ARTHUR LILLIE. With 19 Illustrations (15 Portraits), and numerous Diagrams. 8vo., 10s. 6d. net.

Longman.—*CHESS OPENINGS.* By FREDERICK W. LONGMAN. Fcp. 8vo., 2s. 6d.

Mackenzie.—*NOTES FOR HUNTING MEN.* By Captain CORTLANDT GORDON MACKENZIE. Crown 8vo., 2s. 6d. net.

Madden.—*THE DIARY OF MASTER WILLIAM SILENCE:* a Study of Shakespeare and of Elizabethan Sport. By the Right Hon. D. H. MADDEN, Vice-Chancellor of the University of Dublin. 8vo., gilt top, 16s.

Maskelyne.—*SHARPS AND FLATS:* a Complete Revelation of the Secrets of Cheating at Games of Chance and Skill. By JOHN NEVIL MASKELYNE, of the Egyptian Hall. With 62 Illustrations. Crown 8vo., 6s.

Millais. — *THE WILD-FOWLER IN SCOTLAND.* By J. G. MILLAIS, F.Z.S. With a Frontispiece in Photogravure by Sir J. E. MILLAIS, Bart., P.R.A., 8 Photogravure Plates, 2 Coloured Plates and 50 Illustrations from the Author's Drawings and from Photographs. Royal 4to., gilt top, 30s. net.

Modern Bridge.—By 'Slam'. With a Reprint of the Laws of Bridge, as adopted by the Portland and Turf Clubs. 18mo., gilt edges, 3s. 6d. net.

Park.—*THE GAME OF GOLF.* By WILLIAM PARK, Jun., Champion Golfer, 1887-89. With 17 Plates and 26 Illustrations in the Text. Crown 8vo., 7s. 6d.

Payne-Gallwey (Sir RALPH, Bart.).

THE CROSS-BOW : Mediæval and Modern ; Military and Sporting ; its Construction, History and Management, with a Treatise on the Balista and Catapult of the Ancients. With 220 Illustrations. Royal 4to., £3 3s. net.

LETTERS TO YOUNG SHOOTERS (First Series). On the Choice and use of a Gun. With 41 Illustrations. Crown 8vo., 7s. 6d.

LETTERS TO YOUNG SHOOTERS (Second Series). On the Production, Preservation, and Killing of Game. With Directions in Shooting Wood-Pigeons and Breaking-in Retrievers. With Portrait and 103 Illustrations. Crown 8vo., 12s. 6d.

LETTERS TO YOUNG SHOOTERS. (Third Series.) Comprising a Short Natural History of the Wildfowl that are Rare or Common to the British Islands, with complete directions in Shooting Wildfowl on the Coast and Inland. With 200 Illustrations. Crown 8vo., 18s.

Proctor.—*HOW TO PLAY WHIST: WITH THE LAWS AND ETIQUETTE OF WHIST.* By RICHARD A. PROCTOR. Crown 8vo., gilt edges, 3s. net.

Ronalds.—*THE FLY-FISHER'S ENTOMOLOGY.* By ALFRED RONALDS. With 20 coloured Plates. 8vo., 14s.

Somerville.—*SLIPPER'S A B C OF FOX-HUNTING.* By E. Œ. SOMERVILLE, M.F.H., Joint Author of ' Some Experiences of an Irish R.M.,' etc. With Illustrations in Colour by the Author. 4to., boards, 10s. 6d. net.

Thomas-Stanford. — *A RIVER OF NORWAY:* being the Notes and Reflections of an Angler. By CHARLES THOMAS-STANFORD. With 10 Photogravure Plates, 1 Map and 1 Plan. 8vo., 9s. net.

Thompson, Cannan and Doneraile.—*COMBINED · HAND-IN-HAND FIGURE SKATING.* By NORCLIFFE G. THOMPSON, F. LAURA CANNAN and VISCOUNT DONERAILE, Members of the Skating Club. 16mo., 2s. 6d. net.

Mental, Moral, and Political Philosophy.

LOGIC, RHETORIC, PSYCHOLOGY, ETHICS, &C.

Abbott.—*THE ELEMENTS OF LOGIC.*
By T. K. ABBOTT, B.D. 12mo., 3s.

Aristotle.

THE ETHICS: Greek Text, Illustrated
with Essay and Notes. By Sir ALEXAN-
DER GRANT, Bart. 2 vols. 8vo., 32s.

*AN INTRODUCTION TO ARISTOTLE'S
ETHICS.* Books I.-IV. (Book X. c. vi.-ix.
in an Appendix). With a continuous
Analysis and Notes. By the Rev. E.
MOORE, D.D. Crown 8vo., 10s. 6d.

Bacon (FRANCIS).

COMPLETE WORKS. Edited by R. L.
ELLIS, JAMES SPEDDING and D. D.
HEATH. 7 vols. 8vo., £3 13s. 6d.

LETTERS AND LIFE, including all his
occasional Works. Edited by JAMES
SPEDDING. 7 vols. 8vo., £4 4s.

THE ESSAYS: with Annotations. By
RICHARD WHATELY, D.D. 8vo., 10s. 6d.

THE ESSAYS : with Notes. By F.
STORR and C. H. GIBSON. Cr. 8vo., 3s. 6d.

THE ESSAYS : with Introduction,
Notes, and Index. By E. A. ABBOTT, D.D.
2 Vols. Fcp. 8vo., 6s. The Text and Index
only, without Introduction and Notes, in
One Volume. Fcp. 8vo., 2s. 6d.

Bain (ALEXANDER).

MENTAL AND MORAL SCIENCE : a
Compendium of Psychology and Ethics.
Crown 8vo., 10s. 6d.
Or separately,
Part I. *PSYCHOLOGY AND HISTORY OF
PHILOSOPHY.* Crown 8vo., 6s. 6d.
Part II. *THEORY OF ETHICS AND ETHICAL
SYSTEMS.* Crown 8vo., 4s. 6d.

LOGIC. Part I. *DEDUCTION.* Cr. 8vo.,
4s. Part II. *INDUCTION.* Cr. 8vo., 6s. 6d.

THE SENSES AND THE INTELLECT.
8vo., 15s.

THE EMOTIONS AND THE WILL.
8vo., 15s.

PRACTICAL ESSAYS. Cr. 8vo., 2s.

Bain (ALEXANDER)—*continued.*

*DISSERTATIONS ON LEADING PHILO-
SOPHICAL TOPICS.* 8vo., 7s. 6d. net.

Brooks.—*THE ELEMENTS OF MIND :*
being an Examination into the Nature of
the First Division of the Elementary Sub-
stances of Life. By H. JAMYN BROOKS.
8vo., 10s. 6d. net.

Brough.—*THE STUDY OF MENTAL
SCIENCE :* Five Lectures on the Uses and
Characteristics of Logic and Psychology.
By J. BROUGH, LL.D. Crown 8vo, 2s. net.

Crozier (JOHN BEATTIE).

CIVILISATION AND PROGRESS : being
the Outlines of a New System of Political,
Religious and Social Philosophy. 8vo.,14s.

*HISTORY OF INTELLECTUAL DE-
VELOPMENT :* on the Lines of Modern
Evolution.

Vol. I. 8vo., 14s.

Vol. II. (*In preparation.*)

Vol. III. 8vo., 10s. 6d.

Fite.—*AN INTRODUCTORY STUDY OF
ETHICS.* By WARNER FITE. Cr. 8vo., 6s. 6d.

Green (THOMAS HILL).—THE WORKS
OF. Edited by R. L. NETTLESHIP.

Vols. I. and II. Philosophical Works. 8vo.
16s. each.

Vol. III. Miscellanies. With Index to the
three Volumes, and Memoir. 8vo., 21s.

*LECTURES ON THE PRINCIPLES OF
POLITICAL OBLIGATION.* With Preface
by BERNARD BOSANQUET. 8vo., 5s.

Gurnhill.—*THE MORALS OF SUICIDE.*
By the Rev. J. GURNHILL, B.A. Vol. I.,
Crown 8vo., 5s. net. Vol. II., Crown 8vo.,
5s. net.

Mental, Moral and Political Philosophy—*continued*.

LOGIC, RHETORIC, PSYCHOLOGY, ETHICS, &C.

Hodgson (SHADWORTH H.).

TIME AND SPACE: A Metaphysical Essay. 8vo., 16s.

THE THEORY OF PRACTICE: an Ethical Inquiry. 2 vols. 8vo., 24s.

THE PHILOSOPHY OF REFLECTION. 2 vols. 8vo., 21s.

THE METAPHYSIC OF EXPERIENCE. Book I. General Analysis of Experience; Book II. Positive Science; Book III. Ana ysis of Conscious Action; Book IV. The Real Universe. 4 vols. 8vo., 36s. net.

Hume.—*THE PHILOSOPHICAL WORKS OF DAVID HUME.* Edited by T. H. GREEN and T. H. GROSE. 4 vols. 8vo., 28s. Or separately, ESSAYS. 2 vols. 14s. TREATISE OF HUMAN NATURE. 2 vols. 14s.

James (WILLIAM, M.D., LL.D.).

THE WILL TO BELIEVE, and Other Essays in Popular Philosophy. Crown 8vo., 7s. 6d.

THE VARIETIES OF RELIGIOUS EXPERIENCE: a Study in Human Nature. Being the Gifford Lectures on Natural Religion delivered at Edinburgh in 1901-1902. 8vo., 12s. net.

TALKS TO TEACHERS ON PSYCHOLOGY, AND TO STUDENTS ON SOME OF LIFE'S IDEALS. Crown 8vo., 4s. 6d.

Justinian.—*THE INSTITUTES OF JUSTINIAN:* Latin Text, chiefly that of Huschke, with English Introduction, Translation, Notes, and Summary. By THOMAS C. SANDARS, M.A. 8vo., 18s.

Kant (IMMANUEL).

CRITIQUE OF PRACTICAL REASON, AND OTHER WORKS ON THE THEORY OF ETHICS. Translated by T. K. ABBOTT, B.D. With Memoir. 8vo., 12s. 6d.

FUNDAMENTAL PRINCIPLES OF THE METAPHYSIC OF ETHICS. Translated by T. K. ABBOTT, B.D. Crown 8vo, 3s.

INTRODUCTION TO LOGIC, AND HIS ESSAY ON THE MISTAKEN SUBTILTY OF THE FOUR FIGURES. Translated by T. K. ABBOTT. 8vo., 6s

Kelly.—*GOVERNMENT OR HUMAN EVOLUTION.* By EDMOND KELLY, M.A., F.G.S. Vol. I. Justice. Crown 8vo., 7s. 6d. net. Vol. II. Collectivism and Individualism. Crown 8vo., 10s. 6d. net.

Killick.—*HANDBOOK TO MILL'S SYSTEM OF LOGIC.* By Rev. A. H. KILLICK, M.A. Crown 8vo., 3s. 6d.

Ladd (GEORGE TRUMBULL).

PHILOSOPHY OF CONDUCT: a Treatise of the Facts, Principles and Ideals of Ethics. 8vo., 21s.

ELEMENTS OF PHYSIOLOGICAL PSYCHOLOGY. 8vo., 21s.

OUTLINES OF DESCRIPTIVE PSYCHOLOGY: a Text-Book of Mental Science for Colleges and Normal Schools. 8vo., 12s.

OUTLINES OF PHYSIOLOGICAL PSYCHOLOGY. 8vo., 12s.

PRIMER OF PSYCHOLOGY. Cr. 8vo., 5s. 6d.

Lecky(WILLIAM EDWARD HARTPOLE).

THE MAP OF LIFE: Conduct and Character. Crown 8vo., 5s. net.

HISTORY OF EUROPEAN MORALS FROM AUGUSTUS TO CHARLEMAGNE. 2 vols. Crown 8vo., 10s. net.

A SURVEY OF ENGLISH ETHICS: being the First Chapter of W. E. H. Lecky's ' History of European Morals '. Edited, with Introduction and Notes, by W. A. HIRST. Crown 8vo., 3s. 6d.

HISTORY OF THE RISE AND INFLUENCE OF THE SPIRIT OF RATIONALISM IN EUROPE. 2 vols. Cr. 8vo., 10s. net.

DEMOCRACY AND LIBERTY.
Library Edition. 2 vols. 8vo., 36s.
Cabinet Edition. 2 vols. Cr. 8vo., 10s. net.

Lutoslawski.—*THE ORIGIN AND GROWTH OF PLATO'S LOGIC.* With an Account of Plato's Style and of the Chronology of his Writings. By WINCENTY LUTOSLAWSKI. 8vo., 21s.

Max Müller (F.).

THE SIX SYSTEMS OF INDIAN PHILOSOPHY. Crown 8vo., 7s. 6d. net.

THREE LECTURES ON THE VEDANTA PHILOSOPHY. Crown 8vo., 5s.

Mill (JOHN STUART).

A SYSTEM OF LOGIC. Cr. 8vo., 3s. 6d.

ON LIBERTY. Crown 8vo., 1s. 4d.

CONSIDERATIONS ON REPRESENTATIVE GOVERNMENT. Crown 8vo., 2s.

UTILITARIANISM. 8vo., 2s. 6d.

EXAMINATION OF SIR WILLIAM HAMILTON'S PHILOSOPHY. 8vo., 16s.

NATURE, THE UTILITY OF RELIGION, AND THEISM. Three Essays. 8vo., 5s.

Mental, Moral, and Political Philosophy—*continued.*

LOGIC, RHETORIC, PSYCHOLOGY, ETHICS, &C.

Monck. — *An Introduction to Logic.* By William Henry S. Monck, M.A. Crown 8vo., 5s.

Myers.—*Human Personality and its Survival of Bodily Death.* By Frederic W. H. Myers. 2 vols. 8vo., 42s. net.

Pierce.—*Studies in Auditory and Visual Space Perception:* Essays on Experimental Psychology. By A. H. Pierce. Crown 8vo., 6s. 6d. net.

Richmond.—*The Mind of a Child.* By Ennis Richmond. Cr. 8vo., 3s. 6d. net.

Romanes.—*Mind and Motion and Monism.* By George John Romanes, Cr. 8vo., 4s. 6d.

Russell.—*The First Conditions of Human Prosperity.* By the Hon. R. Russell. Crown 8vo., 2s. 6d. net.

Sully (James).

An Essay on Laughter: its Forms, its Cause, its Development and its Value. 8vo., 12s. 6d. net.

The Human Mind: a Text-book of Psychology. 2 vols. 8vo., 21s.

Outlines of Psychology. Crown 8vo., 9s.

The Teacher's Handbook of Psychology. Crown 8vo., 6s. 6d.

Studies of Childhood. 8vo., 12s. 6d. net.

Children's Ways: being Selections from the Author's 'Studies of Childhood'. With 25 Illustrations. Crown 8vo., 4s. 6d.

Sutherland. — *The Origin and Growth of the Moral Instinct.* By Alexander Sutherland, M.A. 2 vols. 8vo., 28s.

Swinburne. — *Picture Logic:* an Attempt to Popularise the Science of Reasoning. By Alfred James Swinburne, M.A. With 23 Woodcuts. Cr. 8vo., 2s. 6d.

Thomas. — *Intuitive Suggestion.* By J. W. Thomas, Author of ' Spiritual Law in the Natural World,' etc. Crown 8vo., 3s. 6d. net.

Webb.—*The Veil of Isis:* a Series of Essays on Idealism. By Thomas E. Webb, LL.D., Q.C. 8vo., 10s. 6d.

Weber.—*History of Philosophy.* By Alfred Weber, Professor in the University of Strasburg. Translated by Frank Thilly, Ph.D. 8vo., 16s.

Whately (Archbishop).

Bacon's Essays. With Annotations. 8vo., 10s. 6d.

Elements of Logic. Cr. 8vo , 4s. 6d.

Elements of Rhetoric. Cr. 8vo., 4s. 6d.

Zeller (Dr. Edward).

The Stoics, Epicureans, and Sceptics. Translated by the Rev. O. J. Reichel, M.A. Crown 8vo., 15s.

Outlines of the History of Greek Philosophy. Translated by Sarah F. Alleyne and Evelyn Abbott, M.A., LL.D. Crown 8vo., 10s. 6d.

Plato and the Older Academy. Translated by Sarah F. Alleyne and Alfred Goodwin, B.A. Crown 8vo., 18s.

Socrates and the Socratic Schools. Translated by the Rev. O. J. Reichel, M.A. Crown 8vo., 10s. 6d.

Aristotle and the Earlier Peripatetics. Translated by B. F. C. Costelloe, M.A., and J. H. Muirhead. M.A. 2 vols. Crown 8vo., 24s.

STONYHURST PHILOSOPHICAL SERIES.

A Manual of Political Economy. By C. S. Devas, M.A. Crown 8vo., 7s. 6d.

First Principles of Knowledge. By John Rickaby, S.J. Crown 8vo., 5s.

General Metaphysics. By John Rickaby, S.J. Crown 8vo., 5s.

Logic. By Richard F. Clarke, S.J. Crown 8vo., 5s.

Moral Philosophy (Ethics and Natural Law). By Joseph Rickaby, S.J. Crown 8vo., 5s.

Natural Theology. By Bernard Boedder, S.J. Crown 8vo., 6s. 6d.

Psychology. By Michael Maher, S.J., D.Litt., M.A. (Lond.). Cr. 8vo., 6s. 6d.

History and Science of Language, &c.

Davidson.—*LEADING AND IMPORTANT ENGLISH WORDS:* Explained and Exemplified. By WILLIAM L. DAVIDSON, M.A. Fcp. 8vo., 3s. 6d.

Graham. — *ENGLISH SYNONYMS,* Classified and Explained: with Practical Exercises. By G. F. GRAHAM. Fcp. 8vo., 6s.

Max Müller (F.).
THE SCIENCE OF LANGUAGE. 2 vols. Crown 8vo., 10s.
BIOGRAPHIES OF WORDS, AND THE HOME OF THE ARYAS. Crown 8vo., 5s.

Max Müller (F.)—*continued.*
CHIPS FROM A GERMAN WORKSHOP. Vol. III. *ESSAYS ON LANGUAGE AND LITERATURE.* Crown 8vo., 5s.
LAST ESSAYS. First Series. Essays on Language, Folk-lore and other Subjects. Crown 8vo., 5s.

Roget.—*THESAURUS OF ENGLISH WORDS AND PHRASES.* Classified and Arranged so as to Facilitate the Expression of Ideas and assist in Literary Composition. By PETER MARK ROGET, M.D., F.R.S. With full Index. Crown 8vo., 9s. net.

Political Economy, Economics, &c.

Ashley (W. J.).
ENGLISH ECONOMIC HISTORY AND THEORY. Crown 8vo., Part I., 5s. Part II., 10s. 6d.
SURVEYS, HISTORIC AND ECONOMIC. Crown 8vo., 9s. net.
THE ADJUSTMENT OF WAGES: a Study on the Coal and Iron Industries of Great Britain and the United States. With 4 Maps. 8vo., 12s. 6d. net.
BRITISH INDUSTRIES: a Series of General Reviews for Business Men and Students. By various Authors. Edited by W. J. ASHLEY. Crown 8vo., 5s. 6d. net.

Bagehot.—*ECONOMIC STUDIES.* By WALTER BAGEHOT. Crown 8vo., 3s. 6d.

Barnett.—*PRACTICABLE SOCIALISM:* Essays on Social Reform. By SAMUEL A. and HENRIETTA BARNETT. Crown 8vo., 6s.

Brassey.—*FIFTY YEARS OF PROGRESS AND THE NEW FISCAL POLICY.* By Lord BRASSEY, K.C.B., D.C.L. 8vo., sewed, 2s. net; cloth, 2s. 6d. net.

Chapman.—*WORK AND WAGES:* in continuation of Lord Brassey's 'Work and Wages' and 'Foreign Work and English Wages'.
Vol. I. FOREIGN COMPETITION. By SYDNEY J. CHAPMAN, M.A., Professor of Political Economy and Dean of the Faculty of Commerce in the Victoria University of Manchester. With an Introduction by Lord BRASSEY, K.C.B., D.C.L., LL.D., Commander of the Legion of Honour. Medium 8vo., 7s. 6d. net.

Devas.—*A MANUAL OF POLITICAL ECONOMY.* By C. S. DEVAS, M.A. Cr. 8vo., 7s. 6d. (*Stonyhurst Philosophical Series.*)

Dewey.—*FINANCIAL HISTORY OF THE UNITED STATES.* By DAVIS RICH DEWEY. Crown 8vo., 7s. 6d. net.

Leslie.—*ESSAYS ON POLITICAL ECONOMY.* By T. E. CLIFFE LESLIE, Hon. LL.D., Dubl. 8vo., 10s. 6d.

Macleod (HENRY DUNNING).
BIMETALLISM. 8vo., 5s. net.
THE ELEMENTS OF BANKING. Cr. 8vo., 3s. 6d.
THE THEORY AND PRACTICE OF BANKING. Vol. I. 8vo., 12s. Vol. II. 14s.
THE THEORY OF CREDIT. 8vo. In 1 Vol., 30s. net; or separately, Vol. I., 10s. net. Vol. II., Part I., 10s. net. Vol II., Part II. 10s. net.
INDIAN CURRENCY. 8vo., 2s. 6d. net.

Mill.—*POLITICAL ECONOMY.* By JOHN STUART MILL. *Popular Edition.* Cr. 8vo.,3s.6d. *Library Edition.* 2 vols. 8vo.,30s.

Mulhall.—*INDUSTRIES AND WEALTH OF NATIONS.* By MICHAEL G. MULHALL, F.S.S. With 32 Diagrams. Cr. 8vo., 8s. 6d.

Symes. — *POLITICAL ECONOMY:* a Short Text-book of Political Economy. With Problems for Solution, Hints for Supplementary Reading, and a Supplementary Chapter on Socialism. By J. E. SYMES, M.A. Crown 8vo., 2s. 6d.

Toynbee.—*LECTURES ON THE INDUSTRIAL REVOLUTION OF THE 18TH CENTURY IN ENGLAND.* By ARNOLD TOYNBEE. 8vo., 10s. 6d.

Webb. — *LONDON EDUCATION.* By SIDNEY WEBB. Crown 8vo., 2s. 6d. net.

Webb (SIDNEY and BEATRICE).
THE HISTORY OF TRADE UNIONISM. With Map and Bibliography. 8vo., 7s. 6d. net.
INDUSTRIAL DEMOCRACY: a Study in Trade Unionism. 2 vols. 8vo., 12s. net.
PROBLEMS OF MODERN INDUSTRY. 8vo., 5s. net.
THE HISTORY OF LIQUOR LICENSING IN ENGLAND, PRINCIPALLY FROM 1700 TO 1830. Crown 8vo., 2s. 6d. net.

Evolution, Anthropology, &c.

Avebury.—*THE ORIGIN OF CIVILISATION*, and the Primitive Condition of Man. By the Right Hon. LORD AVEBURY. With 6 Plates and 20 Illustrations. 8vo., 18s.

Clodd (EDWARD).

THE STORY OF CREATION: a Plain Account of Evolution. With 77 Illustrations. Crown 8vo., 3s. 6d.

A PRIMER OF EVOLUTION: being a Popular Abridged Edition of 'The Story of Creation'. With Illustrations. Fcp. 8vo., 1s. 6d.

Doubts about Darwinism. By a SEMI-DARWINIAN. Crown 8vo., 3s. 6d.

Gerard.—*THE OLD RIDDLE AND THE NEWEST ANSWER.* By JOHN GERARD, S.J., F.L.S. Crw n 8vo., 5s. net.

Keller.—*QUERIES IN ETHNOGRAPHY.* By ALBERT GALLOWAY KELLER, Ph.D. Fcp. 8vo., 2s. net.

Lang and Atkinson. — *SOCIAL ORIGINS.* By ANDREW LANG, M.A., LL.D.; and *PRIMAL LAW.* By J. J. ATKINSON. 8vo., 10s. 6d. net.

Romanes (GEORGE JOHN).

ESSAYS. Ed. by C. LLOYD MORGAN. Crown 8vo., 5s. net.

AN EXAMINATION OF WEISMANNISM. Crown 8vo., 6s.

DARWIN, AND AFTER DARWIN: an Exposition of the Darwinian Theory, and a Discussion on Post-Darwinian Questions.

Part I. THE DARWINIAN THEORY. With Portrait of Darwin and 125 Illustrations. Crown 8vo., 10s. 6d.

Part II. POST-DARWINIAN QUESTIONS: Heredity and Utility. With Portrait of the Author and 5 Illustrations. Cr. 8vo., 10s. 6d.

Part III. Post-Darwinian Questions: Isolation and Physiological Selection. Crown 8vo., 5s.

The Science of Religion, &c.

Balfour. — *THE FOUNDATIONS OF BELIEF;* being Notes Introductory to the Study of Theology. By the Right Hon. ARTHUR JAMES BALFOUR. Cr. 8vo., 6s. net.

Baring-Gould.—*THE ORIGIN AND DEVELOPMENT OF RELIGIOUS BELIEF.* By the Rev. S. BARING-GOULD. 2 vols. Crown 8vo., 3s. 6d. each.

Campbell.—*RELIGION IN GREEK LITERATURE.* By the Rev. LEWIS CAMPBELL, M.A., LL.D. 8vo., 15s.

James.—*THE VARIETIES OF RELIGIOUS EXPERIENCE:* a Study in Human Nature. Being the Gifford Lectures on Natural Religion delivered at Edinburgh in 1901-1902. By WILLIAM JAMES, LL.D., etc. 8vo., 12s. net.

Lang (ANDREW).

MAGIC AND RELIGION. 8vo., 10s. 6d.

CUSTOM AND MYTH: Studies of Early Usage and Belief. With 15 Illustrations. Crown 8vo., 3s. 6d.

MYTH, RITUAL, AND RELIGION. 2 vols. Crown 8vo., 7s.

Lang (ANDREW)—*continued.*

MODERN MYTHOLOGY: a Reply to Professor Max Müller. 8vo., 9s.

THE MAKING OF RELIGION. Cr. 8vo., 5s. net.

Max Müller (The Right Hon. F.).

THE SILESIAN HORSEHERD ('*DAS PFERDEBÜRLA*'): Questions of the Hour answered by F. MAX MÜLLER. With a Preface by J. ESTLIN CARPENTER. Crown 8vo., 5s.

CHIPS FROM A GERMAN WORKSHOP. Vol. IV. Essays on Mythology and Folklore. Crown 8vo., 5s.

THE SIX SYSTEMS OF INDIAN PHILOSOPHY. Crown 8vo., 7s. 6d. net.

CONTRIBUTIONS TO THE SCIENCE OF MYTHOLOGY. 2 vols. 8vo., 32s.

THE ORIGIN AND GROWTH OF RELIGION, as illustrated by the Religions of India. The Hibbert Lectures, delivered at the Chapter House, Westminster Abbey, in 1878. Crown 8vo., 5s.

The Science of Religion, &c.—*continued.*

Max Müller (The Right Hon. F.)—
continued.

INTRODUCTION TO THE SCIENCE OF RELIGION: Four Lectures delivered at the Royal Institution. Crown 8vo., 5*s.*

NATURAL RELIGION. The Gifford Lectures, delivered before the University of Glasgow in 1888. Crown 8vo., 5*s.*

PHYSICAL RELIGION. The Gifford Lectures, delivered before the University of Glasgow in 1890. Crown 8vo., 5*s.*

ANTHROPOLOGICAL RELIGION. The Gifford Lectures, delivered before the University of Glasgow in 1891. Cr. 8vo., 5*s.*

THEOSOPHY, OR PSYCHOLOGICAL RELIGION. The Gifford Lectures, delivered before the University of Glasgow in 1892. Crown 8vo., 5*s.*

Max Müller (The Right Hon. F.)—
continued.

THREE LECTURES ON THE VEDÂNTA PHILOSOPHY, delivered at the Royal Institution in March, 1894. Cr. 8vo., 5*s.*

LAST ESSAYS. Second Series— Essays on the Science of Religion. Crown 8vo., 5*s.*

Oakesmith. — *THE RELIGION OF PLUTARCH:* a Pagan Creed of Apostolic Times. An Essay. By JOHN OAKESMITH, D.Litt., M.A. Crown 8vo., 5*s.* net.

Wood-Martin (W. G.).

TRACES OF THE ELDER FAITHS OF IRELAND: a Folk-lore Sketch. A Handbook of Irish Pre-Christian Traditions. With 192 Illustrations. 2 vols. 8vo., 30*s.* net.

PAGAN IRELAND: an Archæological Sketch. A Handbook of Irish Pre-Christian Antiquities. With 512 Illustrations. 8vo., 15*s.*

Classical Literature, Translations, &c.

Abbott.—*HELLENICA.* A Collection of Essays on Greek Poetry, Philosophy, History, and Religion. Edited by EVELYN ABBOTT, M.A., LL.D. Crown 8vo., 7*s.* 6*d.*

Æschylus.—*EUMENIDES OF ÆSCHYLUS.* With Metrical English Translation. By J. F. DAVIES. 8vo., 7*s.*

Aristophanes. — *THE ACHARNIANS OF ARISTOPHANES,* translated into English Verse. By R. Y. TYRRELL. Crown 8vo., 1*s.*

Becker (W. A.), Translated by the Rev. F. METCALFE, B.D.

GALLUS: or, Roman Scenes in the Time of Augustus. With Notes and Excursuses. With 26 Illustrations. Crown 8vo., 3*s.* 6*d.*

CHARICLES: or, Illustrations of the Private Life of the Ancient Greeks. With Notes and Excursuses. With 26 Illustrations. Crown 8vo., 3*s.* 6*d.*

Campbell.—*RELIGION IN GREEK LITERATURE.* By the Rev. LEWIS CAMPBELL, M.A., LL.D., Emeritus Professor of Greek, University of St. Andrews. 8vo., 15*s.*

Cicero.—*CICERO'S CORRESPONDENCE.* By R. Y. TYRRELL. Vols. I., II., III., 8vo., each 12*s.* Vol. IV., 15*s.* Vol. V., 14*s.* Vol. VI., 12*s.* Vol. VII. Index, 7*s.* 6*d.*

Harvard Studies in Classical Philology. Edited by a Committee of the Classical Instructors of Harvard University. Vols. XI., 1900; XII., 1901; XIII., 1902; XIV., 1903. 8vo., 6*s.* 6*d.* net each.

Homer.—*THE ODYSSEY OF HOMER.* Done into English Verse. By WILLIAM MORRIS. Crown 8vo., 5*s.* net.

Horace.—*THE WORKS OF HORACE,* RENDERED INTO ENGLISH PROSE. With Life, Introduction and Notes. By WILLIAM COUTTS, M.A. Crown 8vo., 5*s.* net.

Lang.—*HOMER AND THE EPIC.* By ANDREW LANG. Crown 8vo., 9*s.* net.

Lucian. — *TRANSLATIONS FROM LUCIAN.* By AUGUSTA M. CAMPBELL DAVIDSON, M.A. Edin. Crown 8vo., 5*s.* net.

Ogilvie.—*HORAE LATINAE:* Studies in Synonyms and Syntax. By the late ROBERT OGILVIE, M.A., LL.D., H.M. Chief Inspector of Schools for Scotland. Edited by ALEXANDER SOUTER, M.A. With a Memoir by JOSEPH OGILVIE, M.A., LL.D. 8vo., 12*s.* 6*d.* net.

Classical Literature, Translations, &c.—*continued.*

Rich.—*A DICTIONARY OF ROMAN AND GREEK ANTIQUITIES.* By A. RICH, B.A. With 2000 Woodcuts. Crown 8vo., 6s. net.

Sophocles.—Translated into English Verse. By ROBERT WHITELAW, M.A., Assistant Master in Rugby School. Cr. 8vo., 8s. 6d.

Theophrastus.—*THE CHARACTERS OF THEOPHRASTUS:* a Translation, with Introduction. By CHARLES E. BENNETT and WILLIAM A. HAMMOND, Professors in Cornell University. Fcp. 8vo., 2s. 6d. net.

Tyrrell. — *DUBLIN TRANSLATIONS INTO GREEK AND LATIN VERSE.* Edited by R. Y. TYRRELL. 8vo., 6s.

Virgil.

THE POEMS OF VIRGIL. Translated into English Prose by JOHN CONINGTON. Crown 8vo., 6s.

Virgil—*continued.*

THE ÆNEID OF VIRGIL. Translated into English Verse by JOHN CONINGTON. Crown 8vo., 6s.

THE ÆNEIDS OF VIRGIL. Done into English Verse. By WILLIAM MORRIS. Crown 8vo., 5s. net.

THE ÆNEID OF VIRGIL, freely translated into English Blank Verse. By W. J. THORNHILL. Crown 8vo., 6s. net.

THE ÆNEID OF VIRGIL. Translated into English Verse by JAMES RHOADES. Books I.-VI. Crown 8vo., 5s. Books VII.-XII. Crown 8vo., 5s.

THE ECLOGUES AND GEORGICS OF VIRGIL. Translated into English Prose by J. W. MACKAIL, Fellow of Balliol College, Oxford. 16mo., 5s.

Wilkins.—*THE GROWTH OF THE HOMERIC POEMS.* By G. WILKINS. 8vo., 6s.

Poetry and the Drama.

Arnold.—*THE LIGHT OF THE WORLD:* or, The Great Consummation. By Sir EDWIN ARNOLD. With 14 Illustrations after HOLMAN HUNT. Crown 8vo., 5s. net.

Bell (MRS. HUGH).

CHAMBER COMEDIES: a Collection of Plays and Monologues for the Drawing Room. Crown 8vo., 5s. net.

FAIRY TALE PLAYS, AND HOW TO ACT THEM. With 91 Diagrams and 52 Illustrations. Crown 8vo., 3s. net.

NURSERY COMEDIES: Twelve Tiny Plays for Children. Fcap. 8vo., 1s. 6d.

RUMPELSTILTZKIN: a Fairy Play in Five Scenes (Characters, 7 Male; 1 Female). From 'Fairy Tale Plays and How to Act Them'. With Illustrations, Diagrams and Music. Cr. 8vo., sewed, 6d.

Dante. — *THE DREAD INFERNO:* Notes for Beginners in the Study of Dante. By M. ALICE WYLD. With Frontispiece. Fcp. 8vo., 2s. 6d. net

Gore-Booth.—*UNSEEN KINGS, AND OTHER POEMS.* By EVA GORE-BOOTH. Crown 8vo., 2s. 6d. net.

Graves. — *CLYTÆMNESTRA: A TRAGEDY.* By ARNOLD F. GRAVES. With a Preface by ROBERT Y. TYRRELL, Litt.D. Crown 8vo., 5s. net.

Hither and Thither: Songs and Verses. By the Author of 'Times and Days,' etc. Fcp. 8vo., 5s.

Ingelow (JEAN).

POETICAL WORKS. Complete in One Volume. Crown 8vo., gilt top, 6s. net.

LYRICAL AND OTHER POEMS. Selected from the Writings of JEAN INGELOW. Fcp. 8vo., 2s. 6d. cloth plain, 3s. cloth gilt.

Poetry and the Drama—*continued.*

Kendall. — *POEMS OF HENRY CLARENCE KENDALL.* With Memoir by FREDERICK C. KENDALL. Crown 8vo., 6s.

Lang (ANDREW).

GRASS OF PARNASSUS. Fcp. 8vo., 2s. 6d. net.

THE BLUE POETRY BOOK. Edited by ANDREW LANG. With 100 Illustrations. Crown 8vo., gilt edges, 6s.

Lecky.—*POEMS.* By WILLIAM EDWARD HARTPOLE LECKY. Fcp. 8vo., 5s.

Lytton (The Earl of), (OWEN MEREDITH).

THE WANDERER. Cr. 8vo., 10s. 6d.

LUCILE. Crown 8vo., 10s. 6d.

SELECTED POEMS. Cr. 8vo., 10s. 6d.

Macaulay.—*LAYS OF ANCIENT ROME, WITH 'IVRY' AND 'THE ARMADA'.* By Lord MACAULAY.

Illustrated by G. SCHARF. Fcp. 4to., 10s. 6d.

———————————— Bijou Edition. 18mo., 2s. 6d. gilt top.

———————————— Popular Edition. Fcp. 4to., 6d. sewed, 1s. cloth.

Illustrated by J. R. WEGUELIN. Crown 8vo., 3s. net.

Annotated Edition. Fcp. 8vo., 1s. sewed, 1s. 6d. cloth.

MacDonald.—*A BOOK OF STRIFE, IN THE FORM OF THE DIARY OF AN OLD SOUL:* Poems. By GEORGE MACDONALD, LL.D. 18mo., 6s.

Morris (WILLIAM).

POETICAL WORKS—LIBRARY EDITION. Complete in 11 volumes. Crown 8vo., price 5s. net each.

THE EARTHLY PARADISE. 4 vols. Crown 8vo., 5s. net each.

THE LIFE AND DEATH OF JASON. Crown 8vo., 5s. net.

THE DEFENCE OF GUENEVERE, and other Poems. Crown 8vo., 5s. net.

THE STORY OF SIGURD THE VOLSUNG, AND THE FALL OF THE NIBLUNGS. Cr. 8vo., 5s. net.

Morris (WILLIAM)—*continued.*

POEMS BY THE WAY, AND LOVE IS ENOUGH. Crown 8vo., 5s. net.

THE ODYSSEY OF HOMER. Done into English Verse. Crown 8vo., 5s. net.

THE ÆNEIDS OF VIRGIL. Done into English Verse. Crown 8vo., 5s. net.

THE TALE OF BEOWULF, SOMETIME KING OF THE FOLK OF THE WEDERGEATS. Translated by WILLIAM MORRIS and A. J. WYATT. Crown 8vo., 5s. net.

Certain of the POETICAL WORKS may also be had in the following Editions :—

THE EARTHLY PARADISE.

Popular Edition. 5 vols. 12mo., 25s.; or 5s. each, sold separately.

The same in Ten Parts, 25s.; or 2s. 6d. each, sold separately.

Cheap Edition, in 1 vol. Crown 8vo., 6s. net.

POEMS BY THE WAY. Square crown 8vo., 6s.

THE DEFENCE OF GUENEVERE, and Other Poems. Cheaper Impression. Fcp. 8vo., 1s. 6d. net.

** For Mr. William Morris's other Works, see pp. 27, 28, 37 and 40.

Mors et Victoria. Cr. 8vo., 5s. net.

** This is a drama in three acts, the scene of which is laid in France shortly after the massacre of St. Bartholomew.

Morte Arthur: an Alliterative Poem of the Fourteenth Century. Edited from the Thornton MS., with Introduction, Notes and Glossary. By MARY MACLEOD BANKS. Fcp. 8vo., 3s. 6d.

Nesbit.—*LAYS AND LEGENDS.* By E. NESBIT (Mrs. HUBERT BLAND). First Series. Crown 8vo., 3s. 6d. Second Series. With Portrait. Crown 8vo., 5s.

Riley. — *OLD FASHIONED ROSES:* Poems. By JAMES WHITCOMB RILEY. 12mo., gilt top, 5s.

Romanes.—*A SELECTION FROM THE POEMS OF GEORGE JOHN ROMANES, M.A., LL.D., F.R.S.* With an Introduction by T. HERBERT WARREN, President of Magdalen College, Oxford. Crown 8vo., 4s. 6d.

Poetry and the Drama—*continued.*

Savage-Armstrong.—*BALLADS OF DOWN.* By G. F. SAVAGE-ARMSTRONG, M.A., D.Litt. Crown 8vo., 7s. 6d.

Shakespeare.

BOWDLER'S FAMILY SHAKESPEARE. With 36 Woodcuts. 1 vol. 8vo., 14s. Or in 6 vols. Fcp. 8vo., 21s.

THE SHAKESPEARE BIRTHDAY BOOK. By MARY F. DUNBAR. 32mo., 1s. 6d.

Stevenson.—*A CHILD'S GARDEN OF VERSES.* By ROBERT LOUIS STEVENSON. Fcp. 8vo., gilt top, 5s.

Trevelyan.—*CECILIA GONZAGA :* a Drama. By R. C. TREVELYAN. Fcp. 8vo., 2s. 6d. net.

Wagner.—*THE NIBELUNGEN RING.* Done into English Verse by REGINALD RANKIN, B.A., of the Inner Temple, Barrister-at-Law.
Vol. I. Rhine Gold, The Valkyrie. Fcp. 8vo., gilt top, 4s. 6d.
Vol. II. Siegfried, The Twilight of the Gods. Fcp. 8vo., gilt top, 4s. 6d.

Wyld. — *THE DREAD INFERNO ;* Notes for Beginners in the Study of Dante. By M. ALICE WYLD. With Frontispiece. Fcap. 8vo., 2s. 6d. net.

Fiction, Humour, &c.

Anstey (F.).
VOCES POPULI. (Reprinted from 'Punch'.)
First Series. With 20 Illustrations by J. BERNARD PARTRIDGE. Cr. 8vo., gilt top, 3s. net.
Second Series. With 25 Illustrations by J. BERNARD PARTRIDGE. Cr. 8vo., gilt top, 3s. net.
THE MAN FROM BLANKLEY'S, and other Sketches. (Reprinted from 'Punch'.) With 25 Illustrations by J. BERNARD PARTRIDGE. Cr. 8vo., gilt top, 3s. net.

Bailey (H. C.).
MY LADY OF ORANGE : a Romance of the Netherlands in the Days of Alva. With 8 Illustrations. Crown 8vo., 6s.
KARL OF ERBACH : a Tale of the Thirty Years' War. Crown 8vo., 6s.
THE MASTER OF GRAY : a Tale of the Days of Mary Queen of Scots. Crown 8vo., 6s.

Beaconsfield (The Earl of).
NOVELS AND TALES. Complete in 11 vols. Crown 8vo., 1s. 6d. each, or in sets, 11 vols., gilt top, 15s. net.

Vivian Grey.	Contarini Fleming ;
The Young Duke ;	The Rise of Iskander.
Count Alarcos: a	
Tragedy.	Sybil.
Alroy ; Ixion in	Henrietta Temple.
Heaven ; The In-	Venetia.
fernal Marriage ;	Coningsby.
Popanilla.	Lothair.
Tancred.	Endymion.

NOVELS AND TALES. THE HUGHENDEN EDITION. With 2 Portraits and 11 Vignettes. 11 vols. Crown 8vo., 42s.

Churchill.—*SAVROLA :* a Tale of the Revolution in Laurania. By WINSTON SPENCER CHURCHILL, M.P. Cr. 8vo., 6s.

Converse.—*LONG WILL :* a Tale of Wat Tyler and the Peasant Rising in the Reign of Richard II. By FLORENCE CONVERSE. With 6 Illustrations by GARTH JONES. Crown 8vo., 6s.

Dougall.—*BEGGARS ALL.* By L. DOUGALL. Crown 8vo., 3s. 6d.

Doyle (Sir A. CONAN).

MICAH CLARKE : A Tale of Monmouth's Rebellion. With 10 Illustrations. Cr. 8vo., 3s. 6d.

THE REFUGEES : A Tale of the Huguenots. With 25 Illustrations. Cr. 8vo., 3s. 6d.

THE STARK MUNRO LETTERS. Cr. 8vo., 3s. 6d.

THE CAPTAIN OF THE POLESTAR, and other Tales. Cr. 8vo., 3s. 6d.

Dunbar.—*THE SONS O' CORMAC, AN' TALES OF OTHER MEN'S SONS :* Irish Legends. By ALDIS DUNBAR. With 8 Illustrations by MYRA E. LUXMOORE. Crown 8vo., 6s.

Fiction, Humour, &c.—*continued.*

Farrar (F. W., late DEAN OF CANTERBURY).

DARKNESS AND DAWN: or, Scenes in the Days of Nero. An Historic Tale. Cr. 8vo., gilt top, 6s. net.

GATHERING CLOUDS : a Tale of the Days of St. Chrysostom. Cr. 8vo., gilt top, 6s. net.

Fowler (EDITH H.).

THE YOUNG PRETENDERS. A Story of Child Life. With 12 Illustrations by Sir PHILIP BURNE-JONES, Bart. Crown 8vo., 6s.

THE PROFESSOR'S CHILDREN. With 24 Illustrations by ETHEL KATE BURGESS. Crown 8vo., 6s.

Francis (M. E.) (Mrs. FRANCIS BLUNDELL).

CHRISTIAN THAL : a Story of Musical Life. Crown 8vo., 6s.

FIANDER'S WIDOW. Cr. 8vo., 6s.

YEOMAN FLEETWOOD. With Frontispiece. Crown 8vo., 3s. net.

PASTORALS OF DORSET. With 8 Illustrations. Crown 8vo., 6s.

THE MANOR FARM. With Frontispiece by CLAUD C. DU PRÉ COOPER. Crown 8vo., 6s.

LYCHGATE HALL : a Romance. Crown 8vo., 6s.

Froude.—*THE TWO CHIEFS OF DUNBOY:* an Irish Romance of the Last Century. By JAMES A. FROUDE. Cr. 8vo., 3s. 6d.

Haggard Side, The : being Essays in Fiction. By the Author of 'Times and Days,' 'Auto da Fé,' &c. Crown 8vo., 5s.

Haggard (H. RIDER).

ALLAN QUATERMAIN. With 31 Illustrations. Crown 8vo., 3s. 6d.
Popular Edition. 8vo., sewed, 6d. net.

ALLAN'S WIFE. With 34 Illustrations. Crown 8vo., 3s. 6d.

Haggard (H. RIDER)—*continued.*

BEATRICE. With Frontispiece and Vignette. Crown 8vo., 3s. 6d.

BLACK HEART AND WHITE HEART, AND OTHER STORIES. With 33 Illustrations. Crown 8vo., 3s. 6d.

CLEOPATRA. With 29 Illustrations. Crown 8vo., 3s. 6d.

COLONEL QUARITCH, V.C. With Frontispiece and Vignette. Cr. 8vo., 3s. 6d.

DAWN. With 16 Illustrations. Cr. 8vo., 3s. 6d.

DR. THERNE. Crown 8vo., 3s. 6d.

ERIC BRIGHTEYES. With 51 Illustrations. Crown 8vo., 3s. 6d.

HEART OF THE WORLD. With 15 Illustrations. Crown 8vo., 3s. 6d.

JOAN HASTE. With 20 Illustrations. Crown 8vo., 3s. 6d.

LYSBETH. With 26 Illustrations. Crown 8vo., 6s.

MAIWA'S REVENGE. Cr. 8vo., 1s. 6d.

MONTEZUMA'S DAUGHTER. With 24 Illustrations. Crown 8vo., 3s. 6d.

MR. MEESON'S WILL. With 16 Illustrations. Crown 8vo., 3s. 6d.

NADA THE LILY. With 23 Illustrations. Crown 8vo., 3s. 6d.

PEARL-MAIDEN : a Tale of the Fall of Jerusalem. With 16 Illustrations. Crown 8vo., 6s.

SHE. With 32 Illustrations. Crown 8vo., 3s. 6d.

STELLA FREGELIUS : A Tale of Three Destinies. Crown 8vo., 6s.

SWALLOW : a Tale of the Great Trek. With 8 Illustrations. Crown 8vo., 3s. 6d.

THE PEOPLE OF THE MIST. With 16 Illustrations. Crown 8vo., 3s. 6d.

THE WITCH'S HEAD. With 16 Illustrations. Crown 8vo., 3s. 6d.

Fiction, Humour, &c.—*continued.*

Haggard and Lang.—*THE WORLD'S DESIRE.* By H. RIDER HAGGARD and ANDREW LANG. With 27 Illustrations. Crown 8vo., 3s. 6d.

Harte.—*IN THE CARQUINEZ WOODS.* By BRET HARTE. Crown 8vo., 3s. 6d.

Hope.—*THE HEART OF PRINCESS OSRA.* By ANTHONY HOPE. With 9 Illustrations. Crown 8vo., 3s. 6d.

Howard.—*THE FAILURE OF SUCCESS.* By Lady MABEL HOWARD. Crown 8vo., 6s.

Jerome.—*SKETCHES IN LAVENDER: BLUE AND GREEN.* By JEROME K. JEROME, Author of 'Three Men in a Boat,' etc. Crown 8vo., 3s. 6d.

Joyce.—*OLD CELTIC ROMANCES.* Twelve of the most beautiful of the Ancient Irish Romantic Tales. Translated from the Gaelic. By P. W. JOYCE, LL.D. Crown 8vo., 3s. 6d.

Lang (ANDREW).

A MONK OF FIFE ; a Story of the Days of Joan of Arc. With 13 Illustrations by SELWYN IMAGE. Crown 8vo., 3s. 6d.

THE DISENTANGLERS. With 7 Full-page Illustrations by H. J. FORD. Crown 8vo., 6s.

Lyall (EDNA).

THE HINDERERS. Crown 8vo., 2s. 6d.

THE AUTOBIOGRAPHY OF A SLANDER. Fcp. 8vo., 1s. sewed.
Presentation Edition. With 20 Illustrations by LANCELOT SPEED. Crown 8vo., 2s. 6d. net.

DOREEN. The Story of a Singer. Crown 8vo., 6s.

WAYFARING MEN. Crown 8vo., 6s.

HOPE THE HERMIT : a Romance of Borrowdale. Crown 8vo., 6s.

Marchmont.—*IN THE NAME OF A WOMAN:* a Romance. By ARTHUR W. MARCHMONT. With 8 Illustrations. Crown 8vo., 6s.

Mason and Lang. —*PARSON KELLY.* By A. E. W. MASON and ANDREW LANG. Crown 8vo., 3s. 6d.

Max Müller. — *DEUTSCHE LIEBE* (*GERMAN LOVE*) : Fragments from the Papers of an Alien. Collected by F. MAX MÜLLER. Translated from the German by G. A. M. Crown 8vo., gilt top, 5s.

Melville (G. J. WHYTE).

The Gladiators.	Holmby House.
The Interpreter.	Kate Coventry.
Good for Nothing.	Digby Grand.
The Queen's Maries.	General Bounce.

Crown 8vo., 1s. 6d. each.

Morris (WILLIAM).

THE SUNDERING FLOOD. Cr. 8vo., 7s. 6d.

THE WATER OF THE WONDROUS ISLES. Crown 8vo., 7s. 6d.

THE WELL AT THE WORLD'S END. 2 vols. 8vo., 28s.

THE WOOD BEYOND THE WORLD. Crown 8vo., 6s. net.

THE STORY OF THE GLITTERING PLAIN, which has been also called The Land of the Living Men, or The Acre of the Undying. Square post 8vo., 5s. net.

Fiction, Humour, &c.—*continued.*

Morris (WILLIAM)—*continued.*

THE ROOTS OF THE MOUNTAINS, wherein is told somewhat of the Lives of the Men of Burgdale, their Friends, their Neighbours, their Foemen, and their Fellows-in-Arms. Written in Prose and Verse. Square crown 8vo., 8s.

A TALE OF THE HOUSE OF THE WOLFINGS, and all the Kindreds of the Mark. Written in Prose and Verse. Square crown 8vo., 6s.

A DREAM OF JOHN BALL, AND A KING'S LESSON. 16mo., 2s. net.

NEWS FROM NOWHERE; or, An Epoch of Rest. Being some Chapters from an Utopian Romance. Post 8vo., 1s. 6d.

THE STORY OF GRETTIR THE STRONG. Translated from the Icelandic by EIRÍKR MAGNÚSSON and WILLIAM MORRIS. Cr. 8vo., 5s. net.

THREE NORTHERN LOVE STORIES, AND OTHER TALES. Translated from the Icelandic by EIRÍKR MAGNÚSSON and WILLIAM MORRIS. Crown 8vo., 6s. net.

*** For Mr. William Morris's other Works, see pp. 24, 37 and 40.

Newman (Cardinal).

LOSS AND GAIN: The Story of a Convert. Crown 8vo., 3s. 6d.

CALLISTA: A Tale of the Third Century. Crown 8vo., 3s. 6d.

Norris. — NATURE'S COMEDIAN. By W. E. NORRIS. Crown 8vo., 6s.

Phillipps-Wolley.—SNAP: a Legend of the Lone Mountain. By C. PHILLIPPS-WOLLEY. With 13 Illustrations. Crown 8vo., 3s. 6d.

Sewell (ELIZABETH M.).

A Glimpse of the World.	Amy Herbert.
Laneton Parsonage.	Cleve Hall.
Margaret Percival.	Gertrude.
Katharine Ashton.	Home Life.
The Earl's Daughter.	After Life.
The Experience of Life.	Ursula. Ivors.

Cr. 8vo., cloth plain, 1s. 6d. each. Cloth extra, gilt edges, 2s. 6d. each.

Sheehan. — LUKE DELMEGE. By the Rev. P. A. SHEEHAN, D.D., Author of ' My New Curate '. Crown 8vo., 6s.

Somerville (E. Œ.) and Ross (MARTIN).

SOME EXPERIENCES OF AN IRISH R.M. With 31 Illustrations by E. Œ. SOMERVILLE. Crown 8vo., 6s.

ALL ON THE IRISH SHORE: Irish Sketches. With 10 Illustrations by E. Œ. SOMERVILLE. Crown 8vo., 6s.

THE REAL CHARLOTTE. Crown 8vo., 3s. 6d.

THE SILVER FOX. Cr. 8vo., 3s. 6d.

AN IRISH COUSIN. Crown 8vo., 6s.

Stevenson (ROBERT LOUIS).

THE STRANGE CASE OF DR. JEKYLL AND MR. HYDE. Fcp. 8vo., 1s. sewed. 1s. 6d. cloth.

THE STRANGE CASE OF DR. JEKYLL AND MR. HYDE; WITH OTHER FABLES. Crown 8vo., bound in buckram, with gilt top, 5s. net.

' Silver Library ' Edition. Crown 8vo., 3s. 6d.

MORE NEW ARABIAN NIGHTS—THE DYNAMITER. By ROBERT LOUIS STEVENSON and FANNY VAN DE GRIFT STEVENSON. Crown 8vo., 3s. 6d.

THE WRONG BOX. By ROBERT LOUIS STEVENSON and LLOYD OSBOURNE, Crown 8vo., 3s. 6d.

Fiction, Humour, &c.—*continued*.

Suttner.—*LAY DOWN YOUR ARMS* (*Die Waffen Nieder*) : The Autobiography of Martha von Tilling. By BERTHA VON SUTTNER. Translated by T. HOLMES. Cr. 8vo., 1s. 6d.

Trollope (ANTHONY).

THE WARDEN. Cr. 8vo., 1s. 6d.

BARCHESTER TOWERS. Cr. 8vo., 1s. 6d.

Vaughan.—*OLD HENDRIKS TALES.* By Captain ARTHUR O. VAUGHAN. With 12 Full-page Illustrations by J. A. SHEPHERD. Crown 8vo., 6s.

Walford (L. B.).

STAY-AT-HOMES. Crown 8vo., 6s.

CHARLOTTE. Crown 8vo., 6s.

ONE OF OURSELVES. Cr. 8vo., 6s.

THE INTRUDERS. Crown 8vo., 2s. 6d.

LEDDY MARGET. Crown 8vo., 2s. 6d.

IVA KILDARE : a Matrimonial Problem. Crown 8vo., 2s. 6d.

MR. SMITH : a Part of his Life. Crown 8vo., 2s. 6d.

THE BABY'S GRANDMOTHER. Cr. 8vo., 2s. 6d.

COUSINS. Crown 8vo., 2s. 6d.

TROUBLESOME DAUGHTERS. Cr. 8vo., 2s. 6d.

PAULINE. Crown 8vo., 2s. 6d.

DICK NETHERBY. Cr. 8vo., 2s. 6d.

THE HISTORY OF A WEEK. Cr. 8vo. 2s. 6d.

Walford (L. B.)—*continued.*

A STIFF-NECKED GENERATION. Cr. 8vo. 2s. 6d.

NAN, and other Stories. Cr. 8vo., 2s. 6d.

THE MISCHIEF OF MONICA. Cr. 8vo., 2s. 6d.

THE ONE GOOD GUEST. Cr. 8vo. 2s. 6d.

'*PLOUGHED,*' and other Stories. Crown 8vo., 2s. 6d.

THE MATCHMAKER. Cr. 8vo., 2s. 6d.

Ward.—*ONE POOR SCRUPLE.* By Mrs. WILFRID WARD. Crown 8vo., 6s.

Weyman (STANLEY).

THE ABBESS OF VLAYE. With Frontispiece. Crown 8vo., 6s.

THE HOUSE OF THE WOLF. With Frontispiece and Vignette. Crown 8vo., 3s. 6d.

A GENTLEMAN OF FRANCE. With Frontispiece and Vignette. Cr. 8vo., 6s.

THE RED COCKADE. With Frontispiece and Vignette. Crown 8vo., 6s.

SHREWSBURY. With 24 Illustrations by CLAUDE A. SHEPPERSON. Cr. 8vo., 6s.

SOPHIA. With Frontispiece. Crown 8vo., 6s.

THE LONG NIGHT : A Story of Geneva in 1602. Crown 8vo., 6s.

Yeats.—*THE CHEVALIER D'AURIAC.* By S. LEVETT YEATS. Crown 8vo., 3s. 6d.

Popular Science (Natural History, &c.).

Furneaux (W.).

THE OUTDOOR WORLD; or The Young Collector's Handbook. With 18 Plates (16 of which are coloured), and 549 Illustrations in the Text. Crown 8vo., gilt edges, 6s. net.

BUTTERFLIES AND MOTHS (British). With 12 coloured Plates and 241 Illustrations in the Text. Crown 8vo., gilt edges, 6s. net.

LIFE IN PONDS AND STREAMS. With 8 coloured Plates and 331 Illustrations in the Text. Crown 8vo., gilt edges, 6s. net.

THE SEA SHORE. With 8 Coloured Plates and 300 Illustrations in the Text. Crown 8vo., 6s. net.

Hartwig (GEORGE).

THE SEA AND ITS LIVING WONDERS. With 12 Plates and 303 Woodcuts. 8vo., gilt top, 7s. net.

THE TROPICAL WORLD. With 8 Plates and 172 Woodcuts. 8vo., gilt top, 7s. net.

THE POLAR WORLD. With 3 Maps, 8 Plates and 85 Woodcuts. 8vo., gilt top, 7s. net.

THE SUBTERRANEAN WORLD. With 3 Maps and 80 Woodcuts. 8vo., gilt top, 7s. net.

Helmholtz.—POPULAR LECTURES ON SCIENTIFIC SUBJECTS. By HERMANN VON HELMHOLTZ. With 68 Woodcuts. 2 vols. Cr. 8vo., 3s. 6d. each.

Hoffmann.—ALPINE FLORA: For Tourists and Amateur Botanists. With Text descriptive of the most widely distributed and attractive Alpine Plants. By JULIUS HOFFMANN. Translated by E. S. BARTON (Mrs. A. GEPP). With 40 Plates containing 250 Coloured Figures from Water-Colour Sketches by HERMANN FRIESE. 8vo., 7s. 6d. net.

Hudson (W. H.).

HAMPSHIRE DAYS. With 11 Plates and 36 Illustrations in the Text from Drawings by BRYAN HOOK, etc. 8vo., 10s. 6d. net.

BIRDS AND MAN. Large crown 8vo., 6s. net.

NATURE IN DOWNLAND. With 12 Plates and 14 Illustrations in the Text by A. D. McCORMICK. 8vo., 10s. 6d. net.

Hudson (W. H.).—continued.

BRITISH BIRDS. With a Chapter on Structure and Classification by FRANK E. BEDDARD, F.R.S. With 16 Plates (8 of which are Coloured), and over 100 Illustrations in the Text. Crown 8vo., gilt edges, 6s. net.

Millais (JOHN GUILLE).

THE NATURAL HISTORY OF THE BRITISH SURFACE-FEEDING DUCKS. With 6 Photogravures and 66 Plates (41 in Colours) from Drawings by the Author, ARCHIBALD THORBURN, and from Photographs. Royal 4to., £6 6s.

THE WILD-FOWLER IN SCOTLAND. With a Frontispiece in Photogravure after a Drawing by Sir J. E. MILLAIS, Bart., P.R.A. 8 Photogravure Plates, 2 Coloured Plates, and 50 Illustrations from the Author's Drawings and from Photographs. Royal 4to., gilt top, 30s. net.

THE MAMMALS OF GREAT BRITAIN AND IRELAND. 3 vols. 4to. (13 in. by 12 in.), cloth, gilt edges, 18 guineas net.
⁎ Subscriptions will only be received for the Set of Three Volumes.

Vol. I. With 18 Photogravures by the AUTHOR; 31 Coloured Plates by the AUTHOR, ARCHIBALD THORBURN and G. E. LODGE; and 63 Uncoloured Plates by the AUTHOR and from Photographs. (In October, 1904.) £6 6s. net. It is hoped that Vols. II. and III. will be issued at intervals of eight months each.
⁎ Only 1,025 copies printed for England and America. Prospectus sent on application.

Proctor (RICHARD A.).

LIGHT SCIENCE FOR LEISURE HOURS. Familiar Essays on Scientific Subjects. Crown 8vo., 3s. 6d.

ROUGH WAYS MADE SMOOTH. Familiar Essays on Scientific Subjects. Crown 8vo., 3s. 6d.

PLEASANT WAYS IN SCIENCE. Crown 8vo., 3s. 6d.

NATURE STUDIES. By R. A. PROCTOR, GRANT ALLEN, A. WILSON, T. FOSTER and E. CLODD. Cr. 8vo., 3s. 6d.

LEISURE READINGS. By R. A. PROCTOR, E. CLODD, A. WILSON, T. FOSTER and A. C. RANYARD. Cr. 8vo., 3s. 6d.
⁎ For Mr. Proctor's other books see pp. 16 and 35, and Messrs. Longmans & Co.'s Catalogue of Scientific Works.

Popular Science (Natural History, &c.)—*continued*.

Stanley.—*A FAMILIAR HISTORY OF BIRDS*. By E. STANLEY, D.D., formerly Bishop of Norwich. With 160 Illustrations. Cr. 8vo., 3s. 6d.

Wood (Rev. J. G.).

HOMES WITHOUT HANDS: A Description of the Habitations of Animals, classed according to their Principle of Construction. With 140 Illustrations. 8vo., gilt top, 7s. net.

INSECTS AT HOME : A Popular Account of British Insects, their Structure, Habits and Transformations. With 700 Illustrations. 8vo., gilt top, 7s. net.

Wood (Rev. J. G.)—*continued*.

INSECTS ABROAD : A Popular Account of Foreign Insects, their Structure, Habits and Transformations. With 600 Illustrations. 8vo., 7s. net.

OUT OF DOORS ; a Selection of Original Articles on Practical Natural History. With 11 Illustrations. Cr. 8vo., 3s. 6d.

PETLAND REVISITED. With 33 Illustrations. Cr. 8vo., 3s. 6d.

STRANGE DWELLINGS : a Description of the Habitations of Animals, abridged from ' Homes without Hands '. With 60 Illustrations. Cr. 8vo., 3s. 6d.

Works of Reference.

Annual Register (The). A Review of Public Events at Home and Abroad, for the year 1903. 8vo., 18s.

Volumes of the Annual Register for the years 1863-1902 can still be had. 18s. each.

Charities Register, The Annual *AND DIGEST :* being a Classified Register of Charities in or available in the Metropolis. 8vo., 5s. net.

Chisholm. — *HANDBOOK OF COMMERCIAL GEOGRAPHY*. By GEORGE G. CHISHOLM, M.A., B.Sc., Fellow of the Royal Geographical and Statistical Societies. With 19 Folding-out Maps and Numerous Maps in the Text. 8vo., 15s. net.

Gwilt.—*AN ENCYCLOPÆDIA OF ARCHITECTURE*. By JOSEPH GWILT, F.S.A. With 1700 Engravings. Revised (1888), with Alterations and Considerable Additions by WYATT PAPWORTH. 8vo., 21s. net.

Longmans' *GAZETTEER OF THE WORLD*. Edited by GEORGE G. CHISHOLM, M.A., B.Sc. Imperial 8vo., 18s. ne cloth ; 21s. half-morocco.

Maunder (SAMUEL).

BIOGRAPHICAL TREASURY. With Supplement brought down to 1889. By Rev. JAMES WOOD. Fcp. 8vo., 6s.

TREASURY OF KNOWLEDGE AND LIBRARY OF REFERENCE. Fcp. 8vo., 6s.

THE TREASURY OF BOTANY. Edited by J. LINDLEY, F.R.S., and T. MOORE, F.L.S. With 274 Woodcuts and 20 Steel Plates. 2 vols. Fcp. 8vo., 12s.

Rich.—*A DICTIONARY OF ROMAN AND GREEK ANTIQUITIES*. By A. RICH, B.A. With 2000 Woodcuts. Crown 8vo., 6s. net.

Roget. — *THESAURUS OF ENGLISH WORDS AND PHRASES*. Classified and Arranged so as to Facilitate the Expression of Ideas and assist in Literary Composition. By PETER MARK ROGET, M.D., F.R.S. Recomposed throughout, enlarged and improved, partly from the Author's Notes, and with a full Index, by the Author's Son, JOHN LEWIS ROGET. Crown 8vo., 9s. net.

Willich.--*POPULAR TABLES* for giving information for ascertaining the value of Lifehold, Leasehold, and Church Property, the Public Funds, etc. By CHARLES M. WILLICH. Edited by H. BENCE JONES. Crown 8vo., 10s. 6d.

Children's Books.

Alick's Adventures.— By G. R. With 8 Illustrations by JOHN HASSALL. Crown 8vo., 3s. 6d.

Bold Turpin : a Romance, as Sung by Sam Weller. With 16 Illustrations in Colour by L. D. L. Oblong 4to., boards, 6s.

Brown.—*THE BOOK OF SAINTS AND FRIENDLY BEASTS.* By ABBIE FARWELL BROWN. With 8 Illustrations by FANNY Y. CORY. Crown 8vo., 4s. 6d. net.

Crake (Rev. A. D.).

EDWY THE FAIR; or, The First Chronicle of Æscendune. Cr. 8vo., silver top, 2s. net.

ALFGAR THE DANE; or, The Second Chronicle of Æscendune. Cr. 8vo., silver top, 2s. net.

THE RIVAL HEIRS: being the Third and Last Chronicle of Æscendune. Cr. 8vo., silver top, 2s. net.

THE HOUSE OF WALDERNE. A Tale of the Cloister and the Forest in the Days of the Barons' Wars. Crown 8vo., silver top, 2s. net.

BRIAN FITZ-COUNT. A Story of Wallingford Castle and Dorchester Abbey. Cr. 8vo., silver top, 2s. net.

Dent.—*IN SEARCH OF HOME:* a Story of East-End Waifs and Strays. By PHYLLIS O. DENT. With a Frontispiece in Colour by HAMEL LISTER. Crown 8vo., 3s. 6d. net.

Henty (G. A.).—EDITED BY.

YULE LOGS: A Story-Book for Boys. By VARIOUS AUTHORS. With 61 Illustrations. Crown 8vo., gilt edges, 3s. net.

YULE TIDE YARNS: a Story-Book for Boys. By VARIOUS AUTHORS. With 45 Illustrations. Cr. 8vo., gilt edges, 3s. net.

Lang (ANDREW).—EDITED BY.

THE BLUE FAIRY BOOK. With 138 Illustrations. Crown 8vo., gilt edges, 6s.

THE RED FAIRY BOOK. With 100 Illustrations. Crown 8vo., gilt edges, 6s.

Lang (ANDREW) EDITED BY—*continued.*

THE GREEN FAIRY BOOK. With 99 Illustrations. Crown 8vo., gilt edges, 6s.

THE GREY FAIRY BOOK. With 65 Illustrations. Crown 8vo., gilt edges, 6s.

THE YELLOW FAIRY BOOK. With 104 Illustrations. Cr. 8vo., gilt edges, 6s.

THE PINK FAIRY BOOK. With 67 Illustrations. Crown 8vo., gilt edges, 6s.

THE VIOLET FAIRY BOOK. With 8 Coloured Plates and 54 other Illustrations. Crown 8vo., gilt edges, 6s.

THE CRIMSON FAIRY BOOK. With 8 Coloured Plates and 43 other Illustrations. Crown 8vo., gilt edges, 6s.

THE BROWN FAIRY BOOK. With 8 Coloured Plates and 42 other Illustrations. Crown 8vo., gilt edges, 6s.

THE BLUE POETRY BOOK. With 100 Illustrations. Crown 8vo., gilt edges, 6s.

THE TRUE STORY BOOK. With 66 Illustrations. Crown 8vo., gilt edges, 6s.

THE RED TRUE STORY BOOK. With 100 Illustrations. Cr. 8vo., gilt edges, 6s.

THE ANIMAL STORY BOOK. With 67 Illustrations. Cr. 8vo., gilt edges, 6s.

THE RED BOOK OF ANIMAL STORIES. With 65 Illustrations. Crown 8vo., gilt edges, 6s.

THE ARABIAN NIGHTS ENTERTAINMENTS. With 66 Illustrations. Cr. 8vo., gilt edges, 6s.

THE BOOK OF ROMANCE. With 8 Coloured Plates and 44 other Illustrations. Crown 8vo., gilt edges, 6s.

Lyall.—*THE BURGES LETTERS:* a Record of Child Life in the Sixties. By EDNA LYALL. With Coloured Frontispiece and 8 other Full-page Illustrations by WALTER S. STACEY. Crown 8vo., 2s. 6d.

Macdonald. — *BABIES' CLASSICS.* Chosen by LILIA SCOTT MACDONALD. With 67 Illustrations and 37 Initial Letters by ARTHUR HUGHES. Large Crown 4to., 4s. 6d. net.

** *This book is a collection of poems that may fairly be called 'Children's Classics'. They are selected from William Blake, Jane and Anne Taylor, Mary Howitt, Isaac Watts, Charles Kingsley, George Macdonald, etc.*

Children's Books—*continued.*

Meade (L. T.).

DADDY'S BOY. With 8 Illustrations. Crown 8vo., gilt edges, 3s. net.

DEB AND THE DUCHESS. With 7 Illustrations. Cr. 8vo., gilt edges, 3s. net.

THE BERESFORD PRIZE. With 7 Illustrations. Cr. 8vo., gilt edges, 3s. net.

THE HOUSE OF SURPRISES. With 6 Illustrations. Cr. 8vo., gilt edges, 3s. net.

Packard. — *THE YOUNG ICE WHALERS:* a Tale for Boys. By WINTHROP PACKARD. With 16 Illustrations. Crown 8vo., 6s.

Penrose. — *CHUBBY: A NUISANCE.* By Mrs. PENROSE. With 8 Illustrations by G. G. MANTON. Crown 8vo., 3s. 6d.

Praeger (ROSAMOND).

THE ADVENTURES OF THE THREE BOLD BABES: HECTOR, HONORIA AND ALISANDER. A Story in Pictures. With 24 Coloured Plates and 24 Outline Pictures. Oblong 4to., 3s. 6d.

THE FURTHER DOINGS OF THE THREE BOLD BABES. With 24 Coloured Pictures and 24 Outline Pictures. Oblong 4to., 3s. 6d.

Roberts. — *THE ADVENTURES OF CAPTAIN JOHN SMITH :* Captain of Two Hundred and Fifty Horse, and sometime President of Virginia. By E. P. ROBERTS. With 17 Illustrations and 3 Maps. Crown 8vo., 5s. net.

Stevenson.—*A CHILD'S GARDEN OF VERSES.* By ROBERT LOUIS STEVENSON. Fcp. 8vo., gilt top, 5s.

Upton (FLORENCE K. AND BERTHA).

THE ADVENTURES OF TWO DUTCH DOLLS AND A 'GOLLIWOGG'. With 31 Coloured Plates. Oblong 4to., 6s.

THE GOLLIWOGG'S BICYCLE CLUB. With 31 Coloured Plates. Oblong 4to., 6s.

THE GOLLIWOGG AT THE SEASIDE. With 31 Coloured Plates. Oblong 4to., 6s.

THE GOLLIWOGG IN WAR. With 31 Coloured Plates. Oblong 4to., 6s.

THE GOLLIWOGG'S POLAR ADVENTURES. With 31 Coloured Plates. Oblong 4to., 6s.

THE GOLLIWOGG'S AUTO-GO-CART. With 31 Coloured Plates. Oblong 4to., 6s.

THE GOLLIWOGG'S AIR-SHIP. With 30 Coloured Plates. Oblong 4to., 6s.

THE GOLLIWOGG'S CIRCUS. With 31 Coloured Plates. Oblong 4to., boards, 6s.

THE GOLLIWOGG IN HOLLAND. With 29 Coloured Plates. Oblong 4to., 6s.

THE VEGE-MEN'S REVENGE. With 31 Coloured Plates. Oblong 4to., 6s.

Vaughan.—*OLD HENDRIK'S TALES.* By Captain ARTHUR O. VAUGHAN. With 12 Full-page Illustrations by J. A. SHEPHERD. Crown 8vo., 6s.

*** *This is a volume of animal stories collected by Captain Vaughan from the Hottentots during the late Boer War.*

The Silver Library.

CROWN 8vo.   3s. 6d.   EACH VOLUME.

Arnold's (Sir Edwin) Seas and Lands. With 71 Illustrations. 3s. 6d.

Bagehot's (W.) Biographical Studies. 3s. 6d.

Bagehot's (W.) Economic Studies. 3s. 6d.

Bagehot's (W.) Literary Studies. With Portrait. 3 vols., 3s. 6d. each.

Baker's (Sir S. W.) Eight Years in Ceylon. With 6 Illustrations. 3s. 6d.

Baker's (Sir S. W.) Rifle and Hound in Ceylon. With 6 Illustrations. 3s. 6d.

Baring-Gould's (Rev. S.) Curious Myths of the Middle Ages. 3s. 6d.

Baring-Gould's (Rev. S.) Origin and Development of Religious Belief. 2 vols. 3s. 6d. each.

Becker's (W. A.) Gallus : or, Roman Scenes in the Time of Augustus. With 26 Illus. 3s. 6d.

Becker's (W. A.) Charicles: or, Illustrations of the Private Life of the Ancient Greeks. With 26 Illustrations. 3s. 6d.

Bent's (J. T.) The Ruined Cities of Mashonaland. With 117 Illustrations. 3s. 6d.

Brassey's (Lady) A Voyage in the 'Sunbeam'. With 66 Illustrations. 3s. 6d.

Buckle's (H. T.) History of Civilisation in England. 3 vols. 10s. 6d.

Churchill's (Winston S.) The Story of the Malakand Field Force, 1897. With 6 Maps and Plans. 3s. 6d.

Clodd's (E.) Story of Creation: a Plain Account of Evolution. With 77 Illustrations. 3s. 6d.

Conybeare (Rev. W. J.) and Howson's (Very Rev. J. S.) Life and Epistles of St. Paul. With 46 Illustrations. 3s. 6d.

Dougall's (L.) Beggars All : a Novel. 3s. 6d.

Doyle's (Sir A. Conan) Micah Clarke. A Tale of Monmouth's Rebellion. With 10 Illusts. 3s. 6d.

The Silver Library—*continued*.

Doyle's (Sir A. Conan) The Captain of the Polestar, and other Tales. 3s. 6d.

Doyle's (Sir A. Conan) The Refugees : A Tale of the Huguenots. With 25 Illustrations. 3s 6d.

Doyle's (Sir A. Conan) The Stark Munro Letters. 3s. 6d.

Froude's (J. A.) The History of England, from the Fall of Wolsey to the Defeat of the Spanish Armada. 12 vols. 3s. 6d. each.

Froude's (J. A.) The English in Ireland. 3 vols. 10s. 6d.

Froude's (J. A.) The Divorce of Catherine of Aragon. 3s. 6d.

Froude's (J. A.) The Spanish Story of the Armada, and other Essays. 3s. 6d.

Froude's (J. A.) English Seamen in the Sixteenth Century. 3s. 6d.

Froude's (J. A.) Short Studies on Great Subjects. 4 vols. 3s. 6d. each.

Froude's (J. A.) Oceana, or England and Her Colonies. With 9 Illustrations. 3s. 6d.

Froude's (J. A.) The Council of Trent. 3s. 6d.

Froude's (J. A.) The Life and Letters of Erasmus. 3s. 6d.

Froude's (J. A.) Thomas Carlyle : a History of his Life.
1795-1835. 2 vols. 7s.   1834-1881. 2 vols. 7s.

Froude's (J. A.) Cæsar : a Sketch. 3s. 6d.

Froude's (J. A.) The Two Chiefs of Dunboy : an Irish Romance of the Last Century. 3s. 6d.

Froude's (J. A.) Writings, Selections from. 3s. 6d.

Gleig's (Rev. G. R.) Life of the Duke of Wellington. With Portrait. 3s. 6d.

Greville's (C. C. F.) Journal of the Reigns of King George IV., King William IV., and Queen Victoria. 8 vols., 3s. 6d. each.

Haggard's (H. R.) She : A History of Adventure. With 32 Illustrations. 3s. 6d.

Haggard's (H. R.) Allan Quatermain. With 20 Illustrations. 3s. 6d.

Haggard's (H. R.) Colonel Quaritch, V.C. : a Tale of Country Life. With Frontispiece and Vignette. 3s. 6d.

Haggard's (H. R.) Cleopatra. With 29 Illustrations. 3s. 6d.

Haggard's (H. R.) Eric Brighteyes. With 51 Illustrations. 3s. 6d.

Haggard's (H. R.) Beatrice. With Frontispiece and Vignette. 3s. 6d.

Haggard's (H. R.) Black Heart and White Heart. With 33 Illustrations. 3s. 6d.

Haggard's (H. R.) Allan's Wife. With 34 Illustrations. 3s. 6d.

Haggard (H. R.) Heart of the World. With 15 Illustrations. 3s. 6d.

Haggard's (H. R.) Montezuma's Daughter. With 25 Illustrations. 3s. 6d.

Haggard's (H. R.) Swallow : a Tale of the Great Trek. With 8 Illustrations. 3s. 6d.

Haggard's (H. R.) The Witch's Head. With 16 Illustrations. 3s. 6d.

Haggard's (H. R.) Mr. Meeson's Will. With 16 Illustrations. 3s. 6d.

Haggard's (H. R.) Nada the Lily. With 23 Illustrations. 3s. 6d.

Haggard's (H. R.) Dawn. With 16 Illusts. 3s. 6d.

Haggard's (H. R.) The People of the Mist. With 16 Illustrations. 3s. 6d.

Haggard's (H. R.) Joan Haste. With 20 Illustrations. 3s. 6d.

Haggard (H. R.) and Lang's (A.) The World's Desire. With 27 Illustrations. 3s. 6d.

Harte's (Bret) In the Carquinez Woods and other Stories. 3s. 6d.

Helmholtz's (Hermann von) Popular Lectures on Scientific Subjects. With 68 Illustrations. 2 vols. 3s. 6d. each.

Hope's (Anthony) The Heart of Princess Osra. With 9 Illustrations. 3s. 6d.

Howitt's (W.) Visits to Remarkable Places. With 80 Illustrations. 3s. 6d.

Jefferies' (R.) The Story of My Heart : My Autobiography. With Portrait. 3s. 6d.

Jefferies' (R.) Field and Hedgerow. With Portrait. 3s. 6d.

Jefferies' (R.) Red Deer. With 17 Illusts. 3s. 6d.

Jefferies' (R.) Wood Magic : a Fable. With Frontispiece and Vignette by E. V. B. 3s. 6d.

Jefferies (R.) The Toilers of the Field. With Portrait from the Bust in Salisbury Cathedral. 3s. 6d.

Kaye (Sir J.) and Malleson's (Colonel) History of the Indian Mutiny of 1857-8. 6 vols. 3s. 6d. each.

Knight's (E. F.) The Cruise of the 'Alerte' : the Narrative of a Search for Treasure on the Desert Island of Trinidad. With 2 Maps and 23 Illustrations. 3s. 6d.

The Silver Library—*continued.*

Knight's (E. F.) Where Three Empires Meet: a Narrative of Recent Travel in Kashmir, Western Tibet, Baltistan, Gilgit. With a Map and 54 Illustrations. 3*s.* 6*d.*

Knight's (E. F.) The 'Falcon' on the Baltic: a Coasting Voyage from Hammersmith to Copenhagen in a Three-Ton Yacht. With Map and 11 Illustrations. 3*s.* 6*d.*

Köstlin's (J.) Life of Luther. With 62 Illustrations and 4 Facsimiles of MSS. 3*s.* 6*d.*

Lang's (A.) Angling Sketches. With 20 Illustrations. 3*s.* 6*d.*

Lang's (A.) Custom and Myth: Studies of Early Usage and Belief. 3*s.* 6*d.*

Lang's (A.) Cock Lane and Common-Sense. 3*s.* 6*d.*

Lang's (A.) The Book of Dreams and Ghosts, 3*s.* 6*d.*

Lang's (A.) A Monk of Fife: a Story of the Days of Joan of Arc. With 13 Illustrations. 3*s.* 6*d.*

Lang's (A.) Myth, Ritual, and Religion. 2 vols. 7*s.*

Lees (J. A.) and Clutterbuck's (W. J.) B.C. 1887, A Ramble in British Columbia. With Maps and 75 Illustrations. 3*s.* 6*d*

Levett-Yeats' (S.) The Chevalier D'Auriac. 3*s.* 6*d.*

Macaulay's (Lord) Complete Works. 'Albany' Edition. With 12 Portraits. 12 vols. 3*s.* 6*d.* each.

Macaulay's (Lord) Essays and Lays of Ancient Rome, etc. With Portrait and 4 Illustrations to the 'Lays'. 3*s.* 6*d.*

Macleod's (H. D.) Elements of Banking. 3*s.* 6*d.*

Marshman's (J. C.) Memoirs of Sir Henry Havelock. 3*s.* 6*d.*

Mason (A. E. W.) and Lang's (A.) Parson Kelly. 3*s.* 6*d.*

Merivale's (Dean) History of the Romans under the Empire. 8 vols. 3*s.* 6*d.* each.

Mill's (J. S.) Political Economy. 3*s.* 6*d.*

Mill's (J. S.) System of Logic. 3*s.* 6*d.*

Milner's (Geo.) Country Pleasures: the Chronicle of a Year chiefly in a Garden. 3*s.* 6*d.*

Nansen's (F.) The First Crossing of Greenland. With 142 Illustrations and a Map. 3*s.* 6*d.*

Phillipps-Wolley's (C.) Snap: a Legend of the Lone Mountain With 13 Illustrations. 3*s.* 6*d.*

Proctor's (R. A.) The Orbs Around Us. 3*s.* 6*d.*

Proctor's (R. A.) The Expanse of Heaven. 3*s.* 6*d.*

Proctor's (R. A.) Light Science for Leisure Hours. 3*s.* 6*d.*

Proctor's (R. A.) The Moon. 3*s.* 6*d.*

Proctor's (R. A.) Other Worlds than Ours. 3*s.* 6*d.*

Proctor's (R. A.) Our Place among Infinities: a Series of Essays contrasting our Little Abode in Space and Time with the Infinities around us. 3*s.* 6*d.*

Proctor's (R. A.) Other Suns than Ours. 3*s.* 6*d.*

Proctor's (R. A.) Rough Ways made Smooth. 3*s.* 6*d.*

Proctor's (R. A.) Pleasant Ways in Science. 3*s.* 6*d.*

Proctor's (R. A.) Myths and Marvels of Astronomy. 3*s.* 6*d.*

Proctor's (R. A.) Nature Studies. 3*s.* 6*d.*

Proctor's (R. A.) Leisure Readings. By R. A. PROCTOR, EDWARD CLODD, ANDREW WILSON, THOMAS FOSTER, and A. C. RANYARD. With Illustrations. 3*s.* 6*d.*

Rossetti's (Maria F.) A Shadow of Dante. 3*s.* 6*d.*

Smith's (R. Bosworth) Carthage and the Carthaginians. With Maps, Plans, etc. 3*s.* 6*d.*

Stanley's (Bishop) Familiar History of Birds. With 160 Illustrations. 3*s.* 6*d.*

Stephen's (Sir Leslie) The Playground of Europe (The Alps). With 4 Illustrations. 3*s.* 6*d.*

Stevenson's (R. L.) The Strange Case of Dr. Jekyll and Mr. Hyde; with other Fables. 3*s.* 6*d.*

Stevenson (R. L.) and Osbourne's (Ll.) The Wrong Box. 3*s.* 6*d.*

Stevenson (Robert Louis) and Stevenson's (Fanny van de Grift) More New Arabian Nights.—The Dynamiter. 3*s.* 6*d.*

Trevelyan's (Sir G. O.) The Early History of Charles James Fox. 3*s.* 6*d.*

Weyman's (Stanley J.) The House of the Wolf: a Romance. 3*s.* 6*d.*

Wood's (Rev. J. G.) Petland Revisited. With 33 Illustrations. 3*s.* 6*d.*

Wood's (Rev. J. G.) Strange Dwellings. With 60 Illustrations. 3*s.* 6*d.*

Wood's (Rev. J. G.) Out of Doors. With 11 Illustrations. 3*s.* 6*d.*

Cookery, Domestic Management, &c.

Acton. — *MODERN COOKERY.* By ELIZA ACTON. With 150 Woodcuts. Fcp. 8vo., 4s. 6d.

Angwin.—*SIMPLE HINTS ON CHOICE OF FOOD*, with Tested and Economical Recipes. For Schools, Homes, and Classes for Technical Instruction. By M. C. ANGWIN, Diplomate (First Class) of the National Union for the Technical Training of Women, etc. Crown 8vo., 1s.

Ashby.—*HEALTH IN THE NURSERY.* By HENRY ASHBY, M.D., F.R.C.P., Physician to the Manchester Children's Hospital. With 25 Illustrations. Crown 8vo., 3s. net.

Bull (THOMAS, M.D.).

HINTS TO MOTHERS ON THE MANAGEMENT OF THEIR HEALTH DURING THE PERIOD OF PREGNANCY. Fcp. 8vo., sewed, 1s. 6d.; cloth, gilt edges, 2s. net.

THE MATERNAL MANAGEMENT OF CHILDREN IN HEALTH AND DISEASE. Fcp. 8vo., sewed, 1s. 6d.; cloth, gilt edges, 2s. net.

De Salis (Mrs.).

À LA MODE COOKERY: Up-to-date Recipes. With 24 Plates (16 in Colour). Crown 8vo., 5s. net.

CAKES AND CONFECTIONS À LA MODE. Fcp. 8vo., 1s. 6d.

DOGS: A Manual for Amateurs. Fcp. 8vo., 1s. 6d.

DRESSED GAME AND POULTRY À LA MODE. Fcp. 8vo., 1s. 6d.

DRESSED VEGETABLES À LA MODE. Fcp. 8vo., 1s 6d.

De Salis (Mrs.)—*continued.*

DRINKS À LA MODE. Fcp. 8vo., 1s. 6d.

ENTRÉES À LA MODE. Fcp. 8vo., 1s. 6d.

FLORAL DECORATIONS. Fcp. 8vo., 1s. 6d.

GARDENING À LA MODE. Fcp. 8vo. Part I., Vegetables, 1s. 6d. Part II., Fruits, 1s. 6d.

NATIONAL VIANDS À LA MODE. Fcp. 8vo., 1s. 6d.

NEW-LAID EGGS. Fcp. 8vo., 1s. 6d.

OYSTERS À LA MODE. Fcp. 8vo., 1s. 6d.

PUDDINGS AND PASTRY À LA MODE. Fcp. 8vo., 1s. 6d.

SAVOURIES À LA MODE. Fcp. 8vo., 1s. 6d.

SOUPS AND DRESSED FISH À LA MODE. Fcp. 8vo., 1s. 6d.

SWEETS AND SUPPER DISHES À LA MODE. Fcp. 8vo., 1s. 6d.

TEMPTING DISHES FOR SMALL INCOMES. Fcp. 8vo., 1s. 6d.

WRINKLES AND NOTIONS FOR EVERY HOUSEHOLD. Crown 8vo., 1s. 6d.

Poole.—*COOKERY FOR THE DIABETIC.* By W. H. and Mrs. POOLE. With Preface by Dr. PAVY. Fcp. 8vo., 2s. 6d.

Rotheram. — *HOUSEHOLD COOKERY RECIPES.* By M. A. ROTHERAM, First Class Diplomée, National Training School of Cookery, London; Instructress to the Bedfordshire County Council. Crown 8vo., 2s.

The Fine Arts and Music.

Burne-Jones.—*THE BEGINNING OF THE WORLD:* Twenty-five Pictures by Sir EDWARD BURNE-JONES, Bart. Medium 4to., Boards, 7s. 6d. net.

Burns and Colenso.—*LIVING ANATOMY.* By CECIL L. BURNS, R.B.A., and ROBERT J. COLENSO, M.A., M.D. 40 Plates, 11¼ by 8¾ ins., each Plate containing Two Figures—(a) A Natural Male or Female Figure; (b) The same Figure Anatomatised. In a Portfolio, 7s. 6d. net.

Hamlin.—*A TEXT-BOOK OF THE HISTORY OF ARCHITECTURE.* By A. D. F. HAMLIN, A.M. With 229 Illustrations. Crown 8vo., 7s. 6d.

Haweis (Rev. H. R.).

MUSIC AND MORALS. With Portrait of the Author. Crown 8vo., 6s. net.

MY MUSICAL LIFE. With Portrait of Richard Wagner and 3 Illustrations. Crown 8vo., 6s. net.

The Fine Arts and Music—*continued.*

Huish, Head, and Longman.— *SAMPLERS AND TAPESTRY EMBROIDERIES.* By MARCUS B. HUISH, LL.B.; also 'The Stitchery of the Same,' by Mrs. HEAD; and 'Foreign Samplers,' by Mrs. C. J. LONGMAN. With 30 Reproductions in Colour, and 40 Illustrations in Monochrome. 4to., £2 2s. net.

Hullah.—*THE HISTORY OF MODERN MUSIC.* By JOHN HULLAH. 8vo., 8s. 6d.

Jameson (Mrs. ANNA).

SACRED AND LEGENDARY ART, containing Legends of the Angels and Archangels, the Evangelists, the Apostles, the Doctors of the Church, St. Mary Magdalene, the Patron Saints, the Martyrs, the Early Bishops, the Hermits, and the Warrior-Saints of Christendom, as represented in the Fine Arts. With 19 Etchings and 187 Woodcuts. 2 vols. 8vo., 20s. net.

LEGENDS OF THE MONASTIC ORDERS, as represented in the Fine Arts, comprising the Benedictines and Augustines, and Orders derived from their Rules, the Mendicant Orders, the Jesuits, and the Order of the Visitation of St. Mary. With 11 Etchings and 88 Woodcuts. 1 vol. 8vo., 10s. net.

LEGENDS OF THE MADONNA, OR BLESSED VIRGIN MARY. Devotional with and without the Infant Jesus, Historical from the Annunciation to the Assumption, as represented in Sacred and Legendary Christian Art. With 27 Etchings and 165 Woodcuts. 1 vol. 8vo., 10s. net.

THE HISTORY OF OUR LORD, as exemplified in Works of Art, with that of His Types, St. John the Baptist, and other persons of the Old and New Testament. Commenced by the late Mrs. JAMESON; continued and completed by LADY EASTLAKE. With 31 Etchings and 281 Woodcuts. 2 vols. 8vo., 20s. net.

Macfarren. — *LECTURES ON HARMONY.* By Sir GEORGE A. MACFARREN. 8vo., 12s.

Matthay.—*THE ACT OF TOUCH IN ALL ITS DIVERSITY.* An Analysis and Synthesis of Pianoforte Tone Production. By TOBIAS MATTHAY, Fellow and Professor of the Royal Academy of Music, London, etc. With 22 Illustrations. 8vo., 7s. 6d.

Morris (WILLIAM).

ARCHITECTURE, INDUSTRY AND WEALTH. Collected Papers. Crown 8vo., 6s. net.

HOPES AND FEARS FOR ART. Five Lectures delivered in Birmingham, London, etc., in 1878-1881. Cr 8vo., 4s. 6d.

AN ADDRESS DELIVERED AT THE DISTRIBUTION OF PRIZES TO STUDENTS OF THE BIRMINGHAM MUNICIPAL SCHOOL OF ART ON 21ST FEBRUARY, 1894. 8vo., 2s. 6d. net. (*Printed in* 'Golden' *Type.*)

SOME HINTS ON PATTERN-DESIGNING : a Lecture delivered at the Working Men's College, London, on 10th December, 1881. 8vo., 2s. 6d. net. (*Printed in* 'Golden' *Type.*)

ARTS AND ITS PRODUCERS (1888) *AND THE ARTS AND CRAFTS OF TO-DAY* (1889). 8vo., 2s. 6d. net. (*Printed in* 'Golden' *Type.*)

ARTS AND CRAFTS ESSAYS. By Members of the Arts and Crafts Exhibition Society. With a Preface by WILLIAM MORRIS. Crown 8vo., 2s. 6d. net.

** For Mr. William Morris's other Works, see pp. 24, 27, 28 and 40.

Scott.—*PORTRAITURES OF JULIUS CÆSAR :* a Monograph. By FRANK JESUP SCOTT. With 38 Plates and 49 Figures in the Text. Imperial 8vo., 21s. net.

Vanderpoel. — *COLOUR PROBLEMS :* a Practical Manual for the Lay Student of Colour. By EMILY NOYES VANDERPOEL. With 117 Plates in Colour. Sq. 8vo., 21s. net.

Van Dyke.—*A TEXT-BOOK ON THE HISTORY OF PAINTING.* By JOHN C. VAN DYKE. With 110 Illustrations. Cr. 8vo., 6s.

Wellington.—*A DESCRIPTIVE AND HISTORICAL CATALOGUE OF THE COLLECTIONS OF PICTURES AND SCULPTURE AT APSLEY HOUSE, LONDON.* By EVELYN, Duchess of Wellington. Illustrated by 52 Photo-Engravings, specially executed by BRAUN, CLÉMENT, & Co., of Paris. 2 vols., royal 4to., £6 6s. net.

Willard. — *HISTORY OF MODERN ITALIAN ART.* By ASHTON ROLLINS WILLARD. Part I. Sculpture. Part II. Painting. Part III. Architecture. With Photogravure Frontispiece and numerous full-page Illustrations. 8vo., 21s. net.

Wotton.—*THE ELEMENTS OF ARCHITECTURE.* Collected by HENRY WOTTON, Kt., from the best Authors and Examples. Royal 16mo., boards, 10s. 6d. net.

Miscellaneous and Critical Works.

Auto da Fé and other Essays: some being Essays in Fiction. By the Author of 'Essays in Paradox' and 'Exploded Ideas'. Crown 8vo., 5s.

Bagehot.—*LITERARY STUDIES.* By WALTER BAGEHOT. With Portrait. 3 vols. Crown 8vo., 3s. 6d. each.

Baring-Gould.—*CURIOUS MYTHS OF THE MIDDLE AGES.* By Rev. S. BARING-GOULD. Crown 8vo., 3s. 6d.

Baynes. — *SHAKESPEARE STUDIES,* and other Essays. By the late THOMAS SPENCER BAYNES, LL.B., LL.D. With a Biographical Preface by Professor LEWIS CAMPBELL. Crown 8vo., 7s. 6d.

Bonnell. — *CHARLOTTE BRONTË, GEORGE ELIOT, JANE AUSTEN:* Studies in their Works. By HENRY H. BONNELL. Crown 8vo., 7s. 6d. net.

Booth.—*THE DISCOVERY AND DE-CIPHERMENT OF THE TRILINGUAL CUNEI-FORM INSCRIPTIONS.* By ARTHUR JOHN BOOTH, M.A. With a Plan of Persepolis. 8vo. 14s. net.

Charities Register, The Annual, *AND DIGEST:* being a Classified Register of Charities in or available in the Metropolis. 8vo., 5s. net.

Christie.—*SELECTED ESSAYS.* By RICHARD COPLEY CHRISTIE, M.A., Oxon. Hon. LL.D., Vict. With 2 Portraits and 3 other Illustrations. 8vo., 12s. net.

Dickinson.—*KING ARTHUR IN CORN-WALL.* By W. HOWSHIP DICKINSON, M.D. With 5 Illustrations. Crown 8vo., 4s. 6d.

Essays in Paradox. By the Author of 'Exploded Ideas ' and 'Times and Days'. Crown 8vo., 5s.

Evans.—*THE ANCIENT STONE IM-PLEMENTS, WEAPONS AND ORNAMENTS OF GREAT BRITAIN.* By Sir JOHN EVANS, K.C.B. With 537 Illustrations. 8vo., 10s. 6d. net.

Fitzwygram. — *HORSES AND STABLES.* By Lieut.-General Sir F. FITZWYGRAM, Bart. With 56 pages of Illustrations. 8vo., 3s. net.

Frost. — *A MEDLEY BOOK.* By GEORGE FROST. Crown 8vo., 3s. 6d. net.

Gilkes.—*THE NEW REVOLUTION.* By A. H. GILKES, Master of Dulwich College. Fcp. 8vo., 1s. net.

Haggard (H. RIDER).

A FARMER'S YEAR: being his Commonplace Book for 1898. With 36 Illustrations. Crown 8vo., 7s. 6d. net.

RURAL ENGLAND. With 23 Agricultural Maps and 56 Illustrations from Photographs. 2 vols., 8vo., 36s. net.

Harvey-Brooks. — *MARRIAGE AND MARRIAGES:* Before and After, for Young and Old. By E. C. HARVEY-BROOKS Crown 8vo., 4s. net.

Hime.—*GUNPOWDER AND AMMUNI-TION:* their Origin and Progress. By Lieut.-Colonel HENRY W. L. HIME. 8vo., 9s. net.

Hodgson.—*OUTCAST ESSAYS AND VERSE TRANSLATIONS.* By SHADWORTH H. HODGSON. Crown 8vo., 8s. 6d.

Hoenig. — *INQUIRIES CONCERNING THE TACTICS OF THE FUTURE.* By FRITZ HOENIG. With 1 Sketch in the Text and 5 Maps. Translated by Captain H. M. BOWER. 8vo., 15s. net.

Hutchinson.—*DREAMS AND THEIR MEANINGS.* By HORACE G. HUTCHINSON. 8vo., gilt top, 9s. 6d. net.

Jefferies (RICHARD).

FIELD AND HEDGEROW: With Portrait. Crown 8vo., 3s. 6d.

THE STORY OF MY HEART: my Autobiography. Crown 8vo., 3s. 6d.

RED DEER. With 17 Illustrations. Crown 8vo., 3s. 6d.

THE TOILERS OF THE FIELD. Crown 8vo., 3s. 6d.

WOOD MAGIC: a Fable. Crown 8vo., 3s. 6d.

Jekyll (GERTRUDE).

HOME AND GARDEN: Notes and Thoughts, Practical and Critical, of a Worker in both. With 53 Illustrations from Photographs. 8vo., 10s. 6d. net.

WOOD AND GARDEN: Notes and Thoughts, Practical and Critical, of a Working Amateur. With 71 Photographs. 8vo., 10s. 6d. net.

OLD WEST SURREY: Some Recollections. With 330 Illustrations from Photographs by the Author. 8vo., 13s. net.

Miscellaneous and Critical Works—*continued*

Johnson (J. & J. H.).

THE PATENTEE'S MANUAL : a Treatise on the Law and Practice of Letters Patent. 8vo., 10s. 6d.

AN EPITOME OF THE LAW AND PRACTICE CONNECTED WITH PATENTS FOR INVENTIONS, with a reprint of the Patents Acts of 1883, 1885, 1886 and 1888. Crown 8vo., 2s. 6d.

Jordan.—*ASTRONOMICAL AND HISTORICAL CHRONOLOGY IN THE BATTLE OF THE CENTURIES.* By WILLIAM LEIGHTON JORDAN. Crown 8vo., 2s. net.

Joyce.—*THE ORIGIN AND HISTORY OF IRISH NAMES OF PLACES.* By P. W. JOYCE, LL.D. 2 vols. Crown 8vo., 5s. each.

Lang (ANDREW).

LETTERS TO DEAD AUTHORS. Fcp. 8vo., 2s. 6d. net.

BOOKS AND BOOKMEN. With 2 Coloured Plates and 17 Illustrations. Fcp. 8vo., 2s. 6d. net.

OLD FRIENDS. Fcp. 8vo., 2s. 6d. net.

LETTERS ON LITERATURE. Fcp. 8vo., 2s. 6d. net.

ESSAYS IN LITTLE. With Portrait of the Author. Crown 8vo., 2s. 6d.

COCK LANE AND COMMON-SENSE. Crown 8vo., 3s. 6d.

THE BOOK OF DREAMS AND GHOSTS. Crown 8vo., 3s. 6d.

Matthews.—*NOTES ON SPEECH-MAKING.* By BRANDER MATTHEWS. Fcp. 8vo., 1s. 6d. net.

Max Müller (The Right Hon. F.).

COLLECTED WORKS. 20 vols. Vols. I.-XIX. Crown 8vo., 5s. each. Vol. XX., 7s. 6d. net.

Vol. I. *NATURAL RELIGION:* the Gifford Lectures, 1888.

Vol. II. *PHYSICAL RELIGION:* the Gifford Lectures, 1890.

Vol. III. *ANTHROPOLOGICAL RELIGION:* the Gifford Lectures, 1891.

Vol. IV. *THEOSOPHY;* or, Psychological Religion : the Gifford Lectures, 1892.

Max Müller (The Right Hon. F.)—*continued.*

CHIPS FROM A GERMAN WORKSHOP.

Vol. V. Recent Essays and Addresses.

Vol. VI. Biographical Essays.

Vol. VII. Essays on Language and Literature.

Vol. VIII. Essays on Mythology and Folk-lore.

Vol. IX. *THE ORIGIN AND GROWTH OF RELIGION*, as Illustrated by the Religions of India : the Hibbert Lectures, 1878.

Vol. X. *BIOGRAPHIES OF WORDS, AND THE HOME OF THE ARYAS.*

Vols. XI., XII. *THE SCIENCE OF LANGUAGE;* Founded on Lectures delivered at the Royal Institution in 1861 and 1863. 2 vols. 10s.

Vol. XIII. *INDIA:* What can it Teach Us?

Vol. XIV. *INTRODUCTION TO THE SCIENCE OF RELIGION.* Four Lectures, 1870.

Vol. XV. *RÂMAKRISHNA:* his Life and Sayings.

Vol. XVI. *THREE LECTURES ON THE VEDÂNTA PHILOSOPHY*, 1894.

Vol. XVII. *LAST ESSAYS.* First Series. Essays on Language, Folk-lore, etc.

Vol. XVIII. *LAST ESSAYS.* Second Series. Essays on the Science of Religion.

Vol. XIX. *THE SILESIAN HORSEHERD* ('Das Pferdebürla') : Questions of the Hour answered by F. MAX MÜLLER. Translated by OSCAR A. FECHTER, Mayor of North Jakima, U.S.A. With a Preface by J. ESTLIN CARPENTER Crown 8vo., 5s.

** *This is a translation of a work which was published some years back in Germany, but which is now for the first time translated into English. It consists of a controversy on religion carried on between Professor Max Müller and an unknown correspondent in America.*

Vol. XX. *THE SIX SYSTEMS OF INDIAN PHILOSOPHY* Crown 8vo., 7s. 6d. net.

Miscellaneous and Critical Works—*continued*.

Milner.—*COUNTRY PLEASURES:* the Chronicle of a Year chiefly in a Garden. By GEORGE MILNER. Crown 8vo., 3s. 6d.

Morris.—*SIGNS OF CHANGE.* Seven Lectures delivered on various Occasions. By WILLIAM MORRIS. Post 8vo., 4s. 6d.

Parker and Unwin.—*THE ART OF BUILDING A HOME:* a Collection of Lectures and Illustrations. By BARRY PARKER and RAYMOND UNWIN. With 68 Full-page Plates. 8vo., 10s. 6d. net.

Poore (GEORGE VIVIAN, M.D.).

ESSAYS ON RURAL HYGIENE. With 13 Illustrations. Crown 8vo., 6s. 6d.

THE DWELLING HOUSE. With 36 Illustrations. Crown 8vo., 3s. 6d.

THE EARTH IN RELATION TO THE PRESERVATION AND DESTRUCTION OF CONTAGIA: being the Milroy Lectures delivered at the Royal College of Physicians in 1899, together with other Papers on Sanitation. With 13 Illustrations. Crown 8vo., 5s.

COLONIAL AND CAMP SANITATION. With 11 Illustrations. Cr. 8vo., 2s. net.

Rossetti.—*A SHADOW OF DANTE:* being an Essay towards studying Himself, his World and his Pilgrimage. By MARIA FRANCESCA ROSSETTI. Crown 8vo., 3s. 6d.

Russell.—*THE FIRST CONDITIONS OF HUMAN PROSPERITY.* By the Hon. R. RUSSELL. Crown 8vo., 2s. 6d. net.

Seria Ludo. By a DILETTANTE. Post 4to., 5s. net.
* Sketches and Verses, mainly reprinted from the St. James's Gazette.

Shadwell. — *DRINK: TEMPERANCE AND LEGISLATION.* By ARTHUR SHADWELL, M.A., M.D. Crown 8vo., 5s. net.

Soulsby (L. H. M.).

STRAY THOUGHTS ON READING. Fcp. 8vo., cloth, 2s. 6d. net.; limp leather, gilt edges, 3s. 6d. net.

Soulsby (LUCY H. M.)—*continued*.

STRAY THOUGHTS FOR GIRLS. Fcap. 8vo., cloth, 2s. 6d. net; limp leather, gilt edges, 3s. 6d. net.
* Copies of the Original Edition can still be had. 16mo., 1s. 6d. net.

STRAY THOUGHTS FOR MOTHERS AND TEACHERS. Fcp. 8vo., cloth, 2s. 6d. net; limp leather, gilt edges, 3s. 6d. net.

STRAY THOUGHTS ON CHARACTER. Fcp. 8vo., cloth, 2s. 6d. net; limp leather, gilt edges, 3s. 6d. net.

STRAY THOUGHTS FOR INVALIDS. 16mo., 2s. net.

Southey.—*THE CORRESPONDENCE OF ROBERT SOUTHEY WITH CAROLINE BOWLES.* Edited by EDWARD DOWDEN. 8vo., 14s.

Stevens.—*ON THE STOWAGE OF SHIPS AND THEIR CARGOES.* With Information regarding Freights, Charter-Parties, etc. By ROBERT WHITE STEVENS. 8vo., 21s.

Thuillier.—*THE PRINCIPLES OF LAND DEFENCE, AND THEIR APPLICATION TO THE CONDITIONS OF TO-DAY.* By Captain H. F. THUILLIER, R.E. With Maps and Plans. 8vo., 12s. 6d. net.

Turner and Sutherland.—*THE DEVELOPMENT OF AUSTRALIAN LITERATURE.* By HENRY GYLES TURNER and ALEXANDER SUTHERLAND. With Portraits and Illustrations. Crown 8vo., 5s.

Ward. — *PROBLEMS AND PERSONS.* By WILFRID WARD, Author of 'The Life and Times of Cardinal Wiseman,' &c. 8vo., 14s. net.
CONTENTS.—The Time-Spirit of the Nineteenth Century—The Rigidity of Rome—Unchanging Dogma and Changeful Man—Balfour's 'The Foundations of Belief'—Candour in Biography—Tennyson—Thomas Henry Huxley—Two Mottoes of Cardinal Newman—Newman and Renan—Some Aspects of the Life-work of Cardinal Wiseman—The Life of Mrs. Augustus Craven.

Weathers.—*A PRACTICAL GUIDE TO GARDEN PLANTS.* By JOHN WEATHERS, F.R.H.S. With 159 Diagrams. 8vo., 21s. net.